Oracle Database 10*g* Data Warehousing

Oracle Database 10g Data Warehousing

Lilian Hobbs
Susan Hillson
Shilpa Lawande
Pete Smith

ELSEVIER
DIGITAL
PRESS

Amsterdam · Boston · Heidelberg · London · New York · Oxford
Paris · San Diego · San Francisco · Singapore · Sydney · Tokyo

Elsevier Digital Press
30 Corporate Drive, Suite 400, Burlington, MA 01803, USA
Linacre House, Jordan Hill, Oxford OX2 8DP, UK

∞ Recognizing the importance of preserving what has been written, Elsevier prints its books on acid-free paper whenever possible.

Library of Congress Cataloging-in-Publication Data
Application submitted.

British Library Cataloguing-in-Publication Data
A catalogue record for this book is available from the British Library.

ISBN: 1-55558-322-9

For information on all Elsevier Digital Press publications
visit our Web site at www.books.elsevier.com

04 05 06 07 08 09   10 9 8 7 6 5 4 3 2 1

Printed in the United States of America

To Mum, Dad & Reggie, no longer with us, but always in my thoughts
—Lilian

For Aji and Ajoba, my grandparents
—Shilpa

To Family and Friends, Thanks!
—Pete

To Max, who can fix most anything
—Susan

Contents

15   OLAP   671

16   Oracle Data Mining   725

Foreword

It was almost five years ago when I wrote the Foreword to the first edition of this book and over that time we have seen many changes. The challenge now facing most organizations after the dot-com boom and economic slow-down is how to deliver more, using fewer resources, without increasing costs or affecting the bottom line.

Information today is a critical business asset, and the demands placed upon it are rapidly changing. Historically, information was only kept for short periods of time, but once the business benefits of retaining all this information were realized, the Data Warehouse was born. Now they play a very important part in the daily running of the business and assist during tactical decision-making.

The user community who now regularly access the Data Warehouse are demanding ever more complex analysis and reporting. Portals have revolutionized access to the Data Warehouse because they provide easy access, while allowing each user to create their own customised view and set of reports.

New regulations and guidelines are now placing even more demands on organizations as they try to understand how they can cost-effectively store data for extremely long periods of time, while adhering to the rules as to which data must be held and how changes, if allowed, may be applied to the data. Today, Oracle Data Warehouses frequently contain many terabytes of data, but the arrival of the petabyte warehouse is not far away.

With demands upon data constantly changing, organizations need to be able to easily change their configurations to support the extra demands placed on the system. Oracle Database 10*g* introduced grid computing, where pools of computing resources can be shared.

In the future, the data center will be part of the grid, but it will only take from the grid the resources it needs to satisfy current demand, leaving those resources available for other systems to use which may need extra processing to satisfy their increase in demand.

Whether you are designing a large or small data warehouse, or looking for tips on how to improve performance using Oracle Database 10g, this book will provide you with advice and examples you can follow. It also includes thorough coverage of the data warehouse features in Oracle Database 10g, and the tools in Oracle Application Server 10g.

Chuck Rozwat

Executive Vice President

Server Technologies

Oracle Corporation

Preface

There was a time when it was rare for a company to have a Data Warehouse, but now they are an essential source of information to ensure that businesses make the right decisions. Initially data warehouses could only be built and maintained by large corporations, but with the recent advances in database software and computer hardware, any organization can now build a data warehouse or a data mart.

This book introduces the reader to the subject of data warehousing and data marts, with respect to implementing them using Oracle Database 10*g*. It has been designed so that anyone new to this subject can gather a basic understanding of data warehousing and what is involved in designing, creating, implementing, and managing this solution using Oracle Database 10*g*.

The authors have endeavored to make the book easy to read and have provided lots of examples to illustrate how various features can be used. Each chapter focuses on a specific topic and by reading each chapter, you will learn the flow and all the basic steps required to build a data warehouse on Oracle Database 10*g*.

The structure of the chapters is as follows:

- *Chapter 1* provides an introduction to the subject of data warehousing, introducing terms and discussing the need for a data warehouse or data mart. It also provides an overview of the major new features in Oracle Database 10*g*.

- *Chapter 2* shows how to design a data warehouse and illustrates how to create dimensions and fact tables. The EasyDW Inc. example is introduced which is used throughout this book.

- *Chapter 3* describes the architecture of a warehouse environment and talks about the hardware components and the different configurations in which they may be deployed. New features such as Automatic Storage Management are discussed along with how they are used in the warehouse.

- *Chapter 4* describes the physical design of the database and how different techniques such as indexing and partitioning are used in a data warehouse database design.

- *Chapter 5* shows how to extract data from your source system, transform it, and then load it into the data warehouse.

- *Chapter 6* describes various techniques that you can use to improve performance when querying the data warehouse. Advice is given on how to make best use of features such as join techniques, parallelism of the underlying architecture, and the powerful Oracle Analytic Functions.

- *Chapter 7* introduces Summary Management, and shows how to create and refresh materialized views to manage summary data.

- *Chapter 8* illustrates the creation of dimensions, to represent the hierarchies and relationships in your data.

- *Chapter 9* shows how Query Rewrite transparently rewrites your queries to use materialized views, dramatically speeding up the performance of the warehouse queries.

- *Chapter 10* describes new ways to tune your database for optimal performance in Oracle Database 10*g*. It shows how the SQL Access advisor is used to create the best set of materialized views and indexes for the warehouse, how the SQL Tuning advisor can be used to tune a poorly performing SQL statement, and how memory can be best optimized.

- *Chapter 11* discusses the techniques you can use to manage your data warehouse, such as scheduling and managing partitions, and takes a more detailed look at the new infrastructure of the Oracle Database 10*g* and Enterprise Manager.

- *Chapter 12* describes how the important task of backup and recovery is performed in order to protect the data in your warehouse.

- *Chapter 13* looks at some of the Oracle tools you can use to build and report upon in your data warehouse. Specifically described are Oracle Warehouse Builder, Oracle Discoverer, and Oracle Reports.

- *Chapter 14* shows how the Web can play a key role with your data warehouse and how it can be used to benefit your business. The importance of Oracle Portal technology for the presentation on the Web is discussed.

- *Chapter 15* discusses using the Oracle OLAP option to perform multidimensional analysis, forecasting, and allocation.

- *Chapter 16* illustrates using the Oracle Data Mining option to gain better insight into your business by finding hidden trends and patterns in the data.

- *Chapter 17* discusses high availability options and solutions for data warehouses that can afford minimal downtime per year.

Acknowledgments

When one is writing a book, there are many people who are involved at various stages of the production cycle. The extremely important, but often silent, contributors are those people who give up their valuable spare time to review the book. The authors are extremely grateful to the following people who reviewed numerous chapters in this book.

Ramu Arunachalam, Siddarth Velur, Jaganath Rai are developers in the Oracle Warehouse Builder group, India Development Center, Oracle Corporation.

Hermann Baer is the Product Manager for Oracle's ETL capabilities in the database.

Tammy Bednar is the Product Manager for Oracle's backup and recovery products.

Randy Bello is a Principal Software Engineer in Oracle Server Technologies, New England Development center, and is one of the main architects of Query Rewrite with Materialized Views.

Paula Bingham is a Principal Software Engineer and the Project Leader of Oracle Change Data Capture.

Ian Carney is a Senior Principal Consultant within Oracle UK Consulting.

Larry Carpenter is a Principal Member of the Technical Staff in Oracle Server Technologies, and has extensive experience working with customers implementing Data Guard.

Xiaobin Chen is a Development Manager for Oracle Enterprise Manager.

Jean-Pierre Dijcks is the Product Manager for Oracle Warehouse Builder, Oracle Corporation.

Mike Durran is the Discoverer Product Manager, Oracle Corporation

John Haydu is the Product Manager for SQL Analytics in the Oracle database.

Ramkumar Krishnan, Mark Hornick, Margaret Taft, Xiafang Barr, Bob Haberstroh, Sunil Venkayala, are from the Oracle Data Mining group.

Paul Manning is the Senior Product Manager at Oracle for the Automatic Storage Management feature.

David Martland is a Technical Architect with the Britannia Building Society in the UK, who has many years experience using the Oracle database.

Priya Panchapagesan is a Principal Software Engineer in Oracle Server Technologies, New England Development Center, and is one of the main developers of Partition Change Tracking for Summary Management.

Ananth Raghavan is the Senior Development Manager for Partitioning Technology, Oracle Corporation.

Ashish Ray is the Senior Product Manager for Oracle Data Guard.

Mark Rittman is an Oracle Certified Professional and the Consulting Manager at SolStone Plus in the UK.

Marilyn Saunders is a Principal Software Engineer and leader of the QA team for Oracle Data Pump.

Michael D. Schmitz is the President of Business Knowledge Professionals Inc., in Bend, Oregon, and specializes in dimensional modeling and building warehouses in his consulting practice.

Kathy Taylor is a Principal Technical Writer in the OLAP Technologies group at Oracle Corporation.

Murali Thiyagarajan is a Principal Software Engineer in Oracle Server Technologies, New England Development Center, and has worked on several query rewrite algorithms.

Paul Tsien is a product manager specializing in High Availability, Oracle Corporation.

Andy Witkowski, is an Architect in Oracle Server Technologies, responsible for much of the ROLAP functionality in Oracle RDBMS, including SQL analytic and aggregation functions and SQL Model clause.

Min Xiao is a Senior Software Engineer in Oracle Server Technologies, New England Development center, and has worked extensively on Dimensions.

The previous editions of this book was also reviewed by Srinivas Bala, Jay Davison, Bud Endress, Jay Feenan, Abhinav Gupta, Ramkumar Krishnan, James Lear, Lory Molesky, Judy Muller, Dennis Murray, Simon Oxbury, Jack Raitto and Mike Rubino.

We also need to say a big thank you to:

Max Hillson whose e-commerce site coolstuffcheap.com, served as the inspiration for many of the shopping examples.

Chuck Rozwat, Executive Vice President of Oracle Server Technologies, Steve Hagan, Vice President of the Oracle New England Development Center, and Juan Loaiza, Vice President of Oracle High Availability for their encouragement and support while writing this book.

Finally this book is dedicated to all the software developers at Oracle from around the world who build the software which makes this book possible.

Our thanks also go Theron Shreve and Pam Chester at Reed Elsevier and Alan Rose and his team for actually producing this book.

Data Warehousing

1.1 An Introduction to Oracle Database 10*g*

1.1.1 The Economic Climate Influences Technology Spending

One of the challenges of the post-dot-com bubble era that many organizations are facing is being asked to deliver more with little or no budget increase in order to improve the bottom line. You may find yourself looking for new ways to reduce technology costs, while at the same time supporting new applications and improving productivity.

In addition, in the wake of the recent corporate accounting scandals, new regulations have been put into place to enhance corporate responsibility, improve financial disclosures, and combat corporate accounting fraud. The Sarbanes-Oxley Act mandates that companies improve the overall control of the management and reporting of corporate financial information, and places the responsibility for implementing these controls on the CEO and senior management. This in turn places new demands on the IT organization.

So, how are you able to cut costs, while at the same time improve the overall view of critical business information? How can you use your data to target opportunities, track performance, improve decision making, gain competitive edge, increase profits, and provide better financial reporting?

1.1.2 Consolidation

One answer may be through consolidation. Many companies are streamlining their operations by consolidating their hardware, their information, and their business practices and applications into a smaller number of centralized systems. Simplicity can then be achieved through one common infrastructure. The ability to pull together data from each part of the company provides a complete enterprise view. The data warehouse plays a critical role in this consolidation.

1.1.3   Consolidation of the Hardware

In the past, companies generally purchased dedicated systems for each major new application. These needed to be sized to meet peak demands, which meant that some resources sit idle the rest of the time. Wouldn't it be nice if those resources could be applied to another application that needed them?

Consolidation involves both the reuse of existing hardware, and new purchases. Today, many hardware vendors are selling cheaper, faster machines, including server blades and networking equipment. Cost savings can be achieved by switching from proprietary hardware and operating systems to less expensive commodity hardware using Intel processors running the Linux operating system. The cost advantage of a blade farm running Linux is significant compared with a symmetric multiprocessor (SMP) system running a proprietary operating system.

The cost of storage is also continuing to decline each year, and it is now possible to buy storage for considerably less money. Why spend a few million dollars for a system when you can get the same capabilities for several hundreds of thousands?

For a large company, consolidation may also involve combining many decentralized data centers into fewer data centers. As a result of hardware consolidation, there are fewer systems to manage—less software to install, patch, and secure, further reducing expenses.

1.1.4   Consolidation of Data into a Single Company View

As a result of systems being consolidated, the data can also be consolidated in one place, often into a data warehouse. Eliminating data redundancy improves the quality and availability of the information. Many companies have a large number of database instances, from Oracle and from other vendors. By consolidating these, savings can be gained from reducing the number of adminstrators needed to support the systems.

1.1.5   Consolidation of Applications

As the data is consolidated, self-service applications become possible, allowing users to update their own information. As more business applications are moved to the Web, portals give users access to central databases with a Web browser or cell phone eliminating the need to purchase and install special purpose desktop software.

Self-service applications are instrumental in reducing operating costs by eliminating many administrative processes, reducing personnel costs, and providing access on demand 24 hours a day. In addition to applications such as store fronts, many traditionally back-office applications can also be made self-service, including travel, payroll, and human resources.

1.1.6   The *g* in Oracle Database 10*g*—The Grid

Consolidation sets the stage for the implementation of grid computing. Oracle Grid Computing, is an integrated infrastructure made up of the Oracle Database 10*g*, Oracle Application Server 10*g*, and Oracle Enterprise Manager 10*g*. With grid computing, centralized pools of computing resources are created that can be shared by many applications.

The term grid computing originated from an analogy to the electric power grid. A variety of resources contribute power into a shared pool, which many consumers access as they need it. Grid computing is a way to *consolidate* hardware to improve utilization and efficiency of those resources. To the end user, resources are available when they are needed, without the need to know where the data resides or which computer processed any given request.

As with the Internet, the idea of grid computing began in the academic and research communities. One of the early implementations of a grid is the SETI@home project, which is the "Search for Extraterrestrial Intelligence" that originated in 1999 at the University of California at Berkeley. Radio signal fluctuations are collected from the Arecibo Radio Telescope in Puerto Rico; these, may indicate a sign of intelligent life from space. Every day more data was received than the computers at the university could process, so volunteers were asked to donate idle processing time on their home computers. More than 5 million people from 226 countries have downloaded the software that makes their computers available whenever they are idle. You may have already done something similar—scavenged spare resources at off-peak times and used them to augment processing for one or more of your applications.

While the idea of grid or utility computing is not new, it is made possible today in part by advances in both hardware and software. Blade farms or groups of fast computers form the basis of grid computing. Oracle Real Application Clusters (RAC) serve as the foundation for enterprise grids by enabling these low-cost hardware platforms to deliver the highest quality of service levels of availability and scalability. You can buy just enough hardware capacity for the system's initial needs, knowing you can plug in additonal low-cost servers to handle temporary or permanent traffic surges. When a new server is added to the cluster, it is automatically detected, and the workload is balanced to incorporate the new system. If one node in the cluster fails, the application can still function, with a surviving node taking over the failed node's workload.

Just as companies today have both an internal intranet and and external Internet, in the future companies may have both internal grids and external grids without having to purchase or own all the technology themselves. In the data center of the future, you will have the ability to buy as much computing power as you need, and just pay for what you use.

1.2   What Is a Data Warehouse?

So, after all that, just what is a data warehouse and how does it fit in? A data warehouse is a database containing data from multiple operational systems that has been *consolidated,* integrated, aggregated, and structured so that it can be used to support the analysis and decision-making process of a business.

1.2.1   Why Do You Need a Data Warehouse?

Is all the information needed to run your business available when it's needed, in the form in which it's needed, and in sufficient detail and with accuracy to base decisions upon? Or, do two users arrive at a meeting with reports that don't match? One thinks sales for March are $500 million, and another says they are $524 million. After much analysis, you determine that different data has been used to calculate the sales in each report, and you spend considerable time trying to figure out why and correcting the problem.

Does your company have multiple systems for the same function—the old inventory system and the new one you just spent millions of dollars building? Do you need to get data from both of these to combine for reporting purposes? How well is this working? Do users need to understand the differences between the two systems to query them on-line? This may be an area that you want to consolidate.

Do you have sufficient historical detail for analysis purposes? How many months of history are you able to keep on-line? Did you save the right level of detail? Did you even save all of the historical data? Are you able to analyze the sales for each product for each geographical region before and after a major reorganization of the sales force reporting structure? Data warehouses are built to help address these types of problems.

1.3   A Historical Perspective

In the 1970s the first commercial applications were built to computerize the day-to-day operations of a business. These systems were built on mainframe computers which were very expensive. Only large businesses could afford the hardware, the programmers to program them, and the operations staff to keep them running. These systems were focused on inserting new data and reading it sequentially using magnetic tapes.

With the invention of disk storage, the data could be accessed directly. This led to the first database management systems, which organized the data either hierarchically or in a network. These database systems were very complex. Programmers had to understand how the data was stored on the disk and navigate through the data to generate reports. Application programmers used COBOL to create custom reports. It took several days or even weeks to write the program for each new report. Reports were printed on computer paper and manually distributed to the users. There were never enough programmers, so there was always an application backlog. Once data could be accessed directly, the first on-line transaction processing (OLTP) systems were built.

In the late 1970s and early 1980s, minicomputers such as Digital's PDP-11 and VAX 11/780 brought the hardware costs down. Data was often stored in the complex CODAYSL database, which was extremely difficult to change and hard to understand and design. All that changed with the introduction of the relational database. In 1979, the Oracle database became the first commercially available relational system.

With the relational model, data is organized into tables with columns and rows. Rather than using pointers to maintain relationships among the data, a unique value, such as customer number or student id, is stored in multiple tables to identify the row. The relational model was much easier to understand, and SQL, the language used to access the database, did not require knowledge of how the underlying data was physically stored. It became much easier to build applications, which led to widespread use of database management systems. After the initial release of relational systems, many companies began developing products used to access relational databases, including adhoc query, reporting, and analysis tools.

With the introduction of the PC, computing moved from mainframes to client/server systems. Oracle applications were introduced in the late 1980s. Companies no longer had to build their own custom applications, but could now purchase software that provided basic functionality from vendors, including Oracle, PeopleSoft, and SAP.

As relational databases matured in the 1980s, OLTP systems were built using relational systems to automate the operational aspects of the business. These included systems such as order processing, order entry, inventory, general ledger, and accounting. OLTP systems automate processes and represent the state of a system at a current point in time. In an inventory application, there are transactions to insert new items into the inventory, delete items when sold, and update the quantity on hand, while always maintaining the balance on hand. A limited amount of history is retained. It is easy to determine how many of product 111-45-222 is on hand, for example, or on which date order number 45321 was shipped. During this time, the relational database vendors focused on improving performance for OLTP applications and competed with each other using industry standard TPC-C benchmarks.

1.3.1   The Rise of the Data Warehouse

Once the OLTP systems were built to efficiently collect data, the challenge became how to best interpret it. In the late 1980s and early 1990s, in an effort to take a broader view across the entire business, the first enterprise data warehouses (a term invented by Bill Inmon, the father of data warehousing) were built. Data was brought together from the many operational systems used to run the day-to-day business operations in order to provide a corporate-wide view.

Data warehouses were built to view the business over time and spot trends. Many decisions require being able to look beyond the details of today's operations and take a broader view of the business. Typical warehouse queries involve reporting on product sales over the last two years or looking at the impact of a major snowstorm on retail sales versus Internet sales. Queries involve looking at how values have changed over time and what else also changed, and possibly discovering connections.

In order to perform this type of analysis, data in the warehouse needs to be retained for long periods of time, often 5 to 10 years.

The Data Warehouse Is Used to Look beyond the Data to Find Information

In a data warehouse, the primary activity is querying, or reading, the data. The only update activity occurs when new data is loaded. Decision-support systems (DSS), including Oracle Discoverer, provide interactive querying, charting, graphs, and reporting capabilities. Oracle has specialized types of access structures, such as bitmapped indexes, bitmapped join indexes, and materialized views, to improve query performance.

OLAP software is used to analyze business data in a top-down hierarchical fashion. It assumes queries will be posed iteratively, where the results of asking one question lead to asking many more questions.

It's not enough to know just the profit made this year; analysts also need to know profit over time of each product for each geographic region. This is a three-dimensional query: the dimensions are products, time, and geographical region.

An analyst may need to compare this month's sales to the same month last year for each store versus the Internet site. He or she may drill down to a more detailed level in the hierarchy to get the sales for individual stores to determine which ones are most profitable and which may have lost money.

The Data Warehouse Requires a Different Database Design

Data warehouses are designed for quick retrieval, when the access path is not known in advance. Information is often derived from other data, by rolling up data into summaries, drilling down to get more detail, or looking for patterns and trends.

In an OLTP system, entity relationship diagramming techniques (E-R) are used to design the database schema. Each entity becomes a table, attributes become columns, and relationships are represented by joining the primary-key and foreign-key columns together at run time.

A normalized design provides optimal performance for OLTP systems; it supports high volumes of transactions that frequently update data. Normalization ensures that the tables are correctly formed by putting related data together in one table and eliminating redundancy. By having only one copy of the data, update anomalies are avoided consistency is maintained. After normalizing the data, some redundancy may be reintroduced on columns that are not updated to improve performance.

In order to optimize performance for a warehouse, where the primary activity is querying the data, a new data model was needed. Ralph Kimball, the primary industry spokesperson for dimensional modeling and author of *The Data Warehouse Toolkit*, introduced the star schema, a new way of designing the database to facilitate OLAP processing. In order to optimize performance for a warehouse, dimensional modeling techniques are used.

The dimensional approach to modeling organizes data into fact and dimension tables. It represents data in a way that is easily understood by users. Users often ask for reports of sales results on a quarterly basis, broken down by store and geographical region. The sales numbers are the facts. Store, region, and quarter are the dimensions the data is analyzed by and are used to organize the data. With dimensional modeling, denormalization and redundancy are introduced. In Chapter 2, we will see how to actually create a design for Easy Shopping Inc., the example which will be used throughout this book.

The logical design is converted to a physical representation that will best optimize performance and manageability. Tables, constraints, indexes, and partitions are defined.

Oracle has added several features to support dimensional designs. The optimizer can recognize a star schema. In addition to creating tables and columns, you can also define dimensions to help analyze your data in various ways.

1.3.2   Data Warehouses Evolved As Separate Systems

You may already be wondering why you can't use your operational production systems for your data warehouse. You already have databases that are accessible through your corporate network, so why can't you just use those to get the information you need to run your business more efficiently? Why do you need to copy data from one system to another to build a warehouse? Because operational systems may not contain historical data, the information may not be available to analyze. Also, the schema is not designed and the data is not structured for business intelligence queries.

In addition, queries in the warehouse typically access large amounts of data, which requires a great deal of memory, CPU, and I/O resources. Running decision-support queries that require a large amount of computing power to sort and summarize millions of rows will have an impact on the performance of your operational systems.

To make it even more difficult, often the many different operational systems are running on different hardware platforms, with different operating systems and database-management systems. Some applications may have been purchased and others built in-house. On some, the source code may no longer even be available to make changes to, and many of the systems could be several years old.

It was once believed that distributed databases were going to allow you to issue a query and that global query optimizers would locate the data transparently, returning it to users fast enough so they never realized it was located on a machine in a different geographical location. But systems of this type never materialized.

As a result, data needs to be moved from the operational systems into a separate data warehouse, where it is stored in a common format on a different machine for analysis.

The Data Warehouse Is Built from the Operational Systems

Building a warehouse involves extracting data from operational systems, sometimes combining it with additional information from third parties, transforming it into a uniform format, and loading it into the database.

Once data is entered in the warehouse, it almost never changes, since it records the facts of an event or state that existed at some moment in time, such as a particular sale of a product that happened on 23-Dec-1998. If there were another sale of a similar product on 24-Dec-1998, it would generally be recorded as a separate event.

Often, up to 80 percent of the work in building a data warehouse is devoted to the extraction/transformation/load (ETL) process: locating the data; writing programs to extract, filter, and cleanse it; transforming it to a common encoding scheme; and loading it into the data warehouse.

Operational data must be extracted from the source operational systems and copied to the staging area, a temporary location where the data is cleansed, transformed, and prepared for the warehouse. Sometimes you have direct access to the source systems; however, often access is severely restricted, and you can only get files of data that have been extracted for you. The operational systems frequently must be running on a 24×7×365 basis, and performance cannot be impacted in any way.

Data from multiple systems needs to be transformed into a common format for use in the warehouse. A knowledge of the meaning of the data in the operational system is required.

- Each operational system may refer to the same item by a different name or key. For example, a tool company in the United States might call product_id "1234" a "wrench," while a company in another country may call the same product "1234" a "spanner."

- Each system might use a different encoding scheme. The product_id may be represented as characters separated by dashes (xxx-xx-xxx) in one system and characters separated by spaces (xxx xx xxx) in another. The data must be transformed to a common encoding scheme in the warehouse.

- An attribute of a table may have different names. One system might refer to a column in the customer table as gender, represented by values "0" or "1." Another system may call it sex, represented as "M" or "F."

- Different systems may use different units of measure. The sales amount might be in dollars in the United States, and the euro in the European Union. The data must be transformed to a common measure in the warehouse.

In designing the transformation process, these different column names from the operational systems are mapped into the common name chosen in the warehouse and transformed into a common encoding scheme.

Once the data is transformed, it is ready to be loaded into the warehouse. Often, the transformation area is on a machine separate from the warehouse; thus, the data will need to be transported or moved to the machine where the warehouse is located.

If the transformed data is stored in a flat file, it may be transported using FTP and then loaded using the SQL*Loader utility or Oracle Data Pump.

If the data has been transformed in an Oracle database, transportable tablespaces may be used to move a tablespace from one database to another.

New data is generally added to the warehouse on a periodic basis. It may be loaded in batch in the evenings or at another time when the warehouse is not being used heavily by the analysts. Oracle Database 10*g* Asynchronous Change Data Capture provides a mechanism to load data in near real time, providing access to the most recent transactional changes.

In addition to the data you already own, you can purchase data from external data providers to add to your warehouse. For example, you can buy information about the weather, demographics, and socioeconomic data.

Examples of usage would be:

- Adding data that tracks regional weather events on a daily basis: This way, you can determine which products show an increase or decrease in sales when there is a snowstorm.

- Adding customer demographic data: Selective marketing can be performed, targeting those customers most likely to respond to a sales promotion.

- Knowing which types of customers buy which types of products: You can anticipate demand and increase profitability. Demographic data can be used to help choose a location to place a new retail store.

- Adding Dun and Bradstreet data: This contains information on companies and products.

Many tools are available in the marketplace to help automate parts of the ETL process. An overview of Oracle Warehouse Builder, which can be used to help automate the extraction, transformation, transport, and load aspects of the process, will be presented in Chapter 13.

1.3.3 The Data Mart

Building a warehouse can be very complex and often takes anywhere from 18 months to three years to deploy. Because a warehouse contains many subject areas and crosses multiple organizations, it can also be highly political. Many early data warehousing projects failed.

It was discovered that many of the same benefits of a warehouse could be scaled down to the department or line of business, solving a particular business problem. Data warehouses contain multiple subjects that provide a consolidated enterprise view across all lines of business. Data marts are subject-specific or application-specific data warehouses and contain data for only one line of business, such as sales or marketing. The major difference between a data mart and a data warehouse is the scope of the information they contain. Because the scope of a data mart is much smaller, the data is obtained from fewer sources, and the typical time to implement it is shorter.

Independent Data Marts Were Built

Data marts can be dependent or independent, based on the source of information. The source of information for a dependent data mart is an existing data warehouse. A data mart is considered independent when no enterprise data warehouse exists, and the data is extracted directly from the operational systems.

Because independent data marts can be constructed very quickly, they became quite popular in the mid to late 1990s, as each department in a company created its own data mart for its own needs. Unfortunately, after creating a few data marts, problems begin to arise. Each data mart is its own "island of information." It's obviously a problem when there are two reports with different answers to the same question.

One of the reasons independent data marts can be deployed so quickly is that they postpone some of the critical decisions that later become necessary as the number of marts grows. Only the data needed by an individual department needs to be identified and understood. A complete understanding of all the corporate data is not necessary. Creating independent data marts avoids political issues related to the creation of common naming and encoding standards.

Other problems arose from the fact that the individual data marts were often built independently of one another by different autonomous teams. These teams will often select different hardware, software, and tools to use.

Each independent data mart gets its data directly from the operational system. If a company had five different data marts, each needing customer information, there would be five separate programs running to extract data from the customer table in the operational system. You probably don't have enough spare cycles on your operational systems to run five extract programs today, and you certainly won't be able to run more extract programs in the future as you add more data marts.

Each does its own data cleansing and transformations, possibly each in a slightly different way. It is very easy for the data to become inconsistent. Redundant and inconsistent data leads to different answers, making it difficult to make decisions. Imagine trying to merge these different views at a later point into a common data warehouse.

Operational Data Stores Appeared To Consolidate Reporting of Recent Information

As discussed previously, there is a major distinction between the data in the operational systems and that in the warehouse. Operational data is about the current state of the company and is used to manage the daily operations. Data in the warehouse is informational, containing a historical record about the past.

If there is a need to provide information about the current state of the business to make tactical decisions to support day-to-day operations, an operational data store (ODS) can be built as part of the information management architecture.

An ODS contains subject-oriented, integrated data that has been validated and cleansed. It is used to support operational queries and reports. One example is a customer service organization's need to access current account balances and billing information.

The ODS may be updated in near real time, so that it reflects the current state in time. The ODS may serve as the source of data for the warehouse or data marts.

Incrementally Building The Data Warehouse With Dependent Data Marts

To solve these problems, and still provide a timely return on investment, rather than building a warehouse representing the entire corporation, people began building the warehouse a functional area at a time using a phased approach.

Figure 1.1 shows the most common architecture used today. Data is extracted from the OLTP systems and external sources, loaded into operational data stores and enterprise data warehouses, and loaded into dependent data marts.

Building a data warehouse is just like building software. You cannot do everything in one release, and you will never be able to anticipate all of the possible uses. Another problem with the "big bang" approach is that it is often the case that in the years ahead things change, user requirements are different, and the warehouse implementation is simply wrong. It is much better to develop an overall architecture, building a framework with components that allow the warehouse to be built in phases. Phased approaches provide constant feedback to the business. Limit the scope, and plan for enhancements every three to six months.

Figure 1.1   *Enterprise Data Warehouse with Dependent Data Marts*

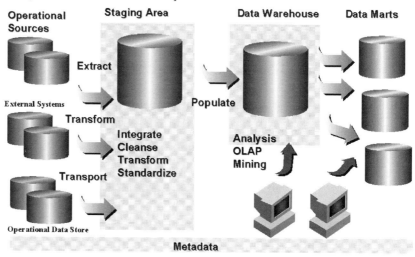

1.3.4   Reporting, Query, and Analysis Tools Became Browser Based

In 1995, Larry Ellison, the founder and CEO of Oracle, first introduced his vision of the network computer: a small, inexpensive device that makes it easy to run applications that access information via the Internet. Although the network computer never gained significant market share, the vision of internet-centric business computing accelerated the rapid price decline of PCs, meeting the demand for cheaper, simpler desktop computing.

The ability to publish reports on the Web can make information available to virtually anyone. It gives employees, partners, and customers real-time access to critical information. No longer do you have to be in the office to view a report. Just pop into the local Internet cafe or connect to the Internet from your hotel room. Placing information on the Web (either your company intranet or the World Wide Web) means that your office can truly be almost anywhere.

1.3.5   OLAP and Data Mining Functionality Are Embedded in the Oracle Database

OLAP was first defined by Dr. E. F. Codd, the father of relational databases. He stated that relational databases were not originally intended to provide data synthesis, analysis, and consolidation—functions being defined as multi-dimensional analysis. For many years separate analytical databases such as Oracle Express were necessary to provide the functionality not available in relational databases.

Oracle has added many features that facilitate OLAP queries, and it is now possible to use the Oracle server directly for OLAP. The SQL language has been extended to provide analytical functions, such as ranking, moving window aggregates, period-over-period comparisons, ratio to report, statistical functions, inverse percentiles, hypothetical rank and distributions, histograms, and first/last aggregates. Multiple levels of aggregation can be calculated using cube, rollup, and grouping sets. Most calculations are done directly within the server. These functions allow the OLAP queries to be expressed without complex self-joins and subqueries and allow the optimizer to choose a better execution plan.

Data mining functionality is provided with the Data Mining option of the Enterprise Edition for making classifications, predictions, and associations.

Data mining is part of the knowledge discovery process. By using statistical techniques, vast quantities of data can be transformed into useful information. Data is like the raw material extracted from traditional mines: when turned into information, it is like a precious metal.

Data mining extracts new information from data. It allows businesses to extract previously unknown pieces of information from their warehouses and use that information to make important business decisions.

The discovery process typically starts with no predetermined idea of what the search will find. Large amounts of data are read, looking for similarities that can be grouped together to detect patterns and trends.

OLAP and DSS tools look at predefined relationships associated with the structure of the data. These are represented by constraints and dimensions. Data mining detects relationships that are associated with the content of the data, and not yet defined, such as which products are most likely to be purchased together, known as market-basket analysis. When analyzing data over time, it can be used to detect unexpected patterns in behavior. The likelihood of an activity being performed some time after another activity can be determined. Common applications for data mining include customer retention, fraud detection, and customer purchase patterns. Data can be mined looking for new market opportunities.

OLAP tools allow you to answer questions such as: Did sales of lava lamps increase in November compared with last year? Data mining tools help to identify answers to questions such as: What factors determine the sales of lava lamps?

With OLAP tools, analysts start with a question or hypothesis and query the warehouse to prove or disprove their theory. With data mining tools, the work is shifted from the analyst to the computer. Data mining tools use a variety of techniques to solve a number of different problems, and can be used to answer questions such as: Which items is this person most likely to buy or like, with what likelihood? and Which other item will people who bought this item buy? This type of personalization can be seen at Amazon.com and is becoming common at many other Web sites.

1.4 Data Warehousing Features in the Oracle Database 10*g*

Many new features have been introduced into the Oracle Database 10g specifically aimed at improving performance and manageability of the data warehouse.

- ETL processing

    - Oracle Change Data Capture (CDC) simplifies the process of identifying the data that has changed since the last extraction. Changes can be identified either synchronously with respect to the transaction, by using a trigger-based mechanism, or asynchronously by mining the archived logs.
    - Heterogeneous Transportable Tablespaces provide an efficient mechanism for moving large amounts of data between Oracle databases on different hardware platforms.
    - External tables allow data to be transformed as it is, either being loaded or unloaded from the database.
    - Data Pump provides high-speed, bulk data and metadata movement between Oracle databases and is the replacement for the Export and Import utilities.

- Analytical Analysis. Business intelligence calculations can require extensive programming outside the SQL language. To eliminate this problem, many analytical calculations have been added to the Oracle database.

    - With the new SQL Model Clause, relational data can be viewed as a multidimensional array to which spreadsheet-like calculations can be applied for modeling applications such as budgeting and forecasting.

- Automatic Advisors

One of the most difficult parts of solving a problem is being able to reproduce it and capture what was happening on the system when the problem occurred. In Oracle Database 10*g*, performance statistics that represent the state of the system can be gathered periodically (once an hour by default) and stored in the database in the Automatic Workload Repository (AWR).

This data is then analyzed by the Automatic Database Diagnostic Monitor (ADDM) to detect and diagnose performance problems. It can detect excessive I/O, CPU bottlenecks, excessive parsing, concurrency issues, PGA, buffer-cache, or log buffer sizing issues.

Some problems can be fixed automatically. For example, Oracle Database 10*g* can automatically manage the shared memory area (SGA), eliminating the need for you to determine the optimal memory allocations for each of the components.

Recommendations may be provided to fix other problems. A suggestion may be to run one of the new advisors, such as the SQL Tuning Advisor to tune a poorly performing SQL statement, or the SQL Access Advisor to determine which indexes or materialized views should be built to improve the overall performance of the entire workload.

1.5 Building a Data Warehouse Poses Many Challenges

Data warehouses have become a mainstream part of the business operations, managed by IT departments with service-level agreements for availability and performance. Thus, data warehouse developers are faced with many challenges. They must ensure that performance is maintained as the warehouse grows in size, evolve the warehouse to meet new business requirements, manage it without bringing the system down, protect it from unplanned downtime, and do all this while at the same time reducing overall costs.

1.5.1 Managing the Warehouse

As large data warehouses are growing to many terabytes in size, with increasingly higher availability requirements, it is critical to maintain good performance for large numbers of geographically distributed users. On-line backup and recovery procedures must be established, and both the data content and the usage or activity in the warehouse must be managed.

The decision-support workload is highly variable. In an OLTP system, an application is tuned to process many identical update transactions as quickly as possible. In a data warehouse, performance must be tuned to process as many variable queries as possible.

Usage patterns provide the foundation for tuning the warehouse for better performance. Who is using which data? Which levels of summarization are people looking at? Which data is not being used? Is the data structured in the most efficient manner; is it indexed on the correct columns? Can the summary tables be used for most queries? If many queries join data from one table with another, it might be beneficial to denormalize the data, prejoining it. Workload information helps determine where indexes should be added, where tables should be combined, and where summaries should be created. The Oracle Database 10*g* new diagnostics engine mentioned previously can offer enormous help in detecting and diagnosing performance problems and also in recommending fixes.

Eventually, it may no longer be necessary or practical to keep all the detail data on-line for immediate access. The data may be purged without keeping a copy. Or it can be archived and moved to some low-cost medium such as tape or CD-ROM, where it can later be retrieved if necessary.

1.5.2   The Role of Metadata

Metadata is data that describes the other data and operations on that data. Metadata can be used for either technical or business purposes. As data flows from the operational systems into the warehouse, it is extracted, transformed, and summarized. Technical metadata is needed to describe this process and is essential for proper "drill down" to finer levels of detail.

Business metadata allows end users to determine which data is available in the warehouse or data mart and how it can be accessed. Metadata provides the integration and uniformity of data across the corporation. It is the place where the different departments describe their use of the term *product*.

Metadata is stored in a repository, which is typically a set of tables in an Oracle database. It can then be shared by any user or tool.

In 2000 the Object Management Group (OMG) published the "Common Warehouse Metamodel" (CWM) specification, which defines a metadata format for all data warehouse and business intelligence products. The specification was developed jointly by several companies including Oracle and IBM Corporation. Since the publication of the specification, many of the data warehousing products have evolved to adhere to the standard.

1.5.3 Increasing Data Volume

One of the biggest technology issues facing enterprises today is the explosion of data volumes. Data warehouses are "the" very large databases. In fact, at the time of writing this book in 2004, the world's largest commercial data warehouse, identified by the 2003 Winter Corporation Top Ten Survey, was built using Oracle, containing 30 terabytes of data. Many factors are contributing to this growth in data.

- With hardware improvements and storage costs continuing to decline each year, it is economically feasible to keep more and more detailed historical data. You may now be able to store a record of every product a customer bought in the supermarket, not just the fact that he or she bought five items for a total cost of $25.75.

- Businesses are storing more and more data for longer periods of time.

- Data is stored multiple times for different purposes. Indexes and materialized views are created to improve query performance, but these access structures require additional storage space, further increasing the size of the database.

- Unstructured data can be integrated with traditional business intelligence applications. Storing multimedia data increases the database size. To store one hour of video requires about 1GB of storage. To store one minute of audio requires a little less than 1MB. Images can range from 20KB to as much as 60MB depending on the type and quality of the image.

- Documents can be tagged with XML-based metadata and stored in the Oracle database.

However, a data warehouse should not be viewed as a repository for archived data; this is not its purpose.

1.5.4 Higher Availability

Ensuring the availability of the data warehouse is becoming more and more mission critical for many businesses. As data warehouses are becoming more operational in nature, feeding information back to the OLTP systems, in businesses that operate globally users need access to the data warehouse 24×7, often 365 days per year.

The Oracle database is designed to eliminate the need for planned downtime and withstand any failure: system failure, storage failure, site failure, or human error. If a server goes down, your applications keep running. Real Application Clusters (RAC) make applications scalable and highly available and, as discussed previously, are the foundation for the grid. A single database can be run on a group of servers clustered together. As additional servers are added to the cluster, applications can scale to support increased throughput, with no modification. The Oracle Application Servers can act in a load balanced, clustered "farm" capacity, and the entire configuration can be managed using Oracle Enterprise Manager Grid Control.

Data Guard can be used to maintain a standby database, which is a transactionally consistent copy of the data warehouse and can be used to ensure that operations continue with minimal interruption if there is a site disaster, human error, or data corruption. It can also be used to minimize downtime for planned maintenance, such as hardware upgrades, or rolling upgrades of Oracle software.

1.5.5　More Users/Better Performance

The ability to publish reports on the Web makes information available to many more people. As data warehouses and business intelligence tools make more and better data available, the number of end users continues to grow. The demand for better performance is more important than ever. In addition, the types of queries are increasing in complexity.

1.5.6　New Types Of Applications

Data warehouses are being used to support new types of e-business initiatives including customer relationship management (CRM) and supply chain management. CRM helps attract new customers and develop customer loyalty, important in the retention of existing customers. A data warehouse contains the information about a company's customers and is often the integration point for sales, marketing, and customer care applications.

1.6   The Future of Data Warehousing

Where are we going from here? While no one can predict the future, some trends seem to be underway.

1.6.1   Real-Time Data Warehouses

The data warehouse is evolving to support real-time analysis and decision making. Rather than updating the warehouse periodically in batch, when a transaction is committed on the OLTP system, it will become available in the data warehouse, providing the capability of real-time decision making.

This allows the warehouse to be used to support tactical as well as strategic decisions. It enables a credit card company to detect and stop fraud as it happens, a transportation company to reroute its vehicles quickly after an accident has taken place, and an on-line retailer to communicate special offers based on a customer's Web-surfing behavior.

Oracle Database 10*g* Asynchronous Change Data Capture provides a mechanism to load data in near real time, providing access to the most recent transactional changes. Once the data is in the warehouse, there is no need to move it to another engine, since OLAP and data mining capabilities are now native in the Oracle database.

1.6.2   The Disappearance of the Separate Data Warehouse

One day we may be using a single database for both OLTP and data warehousing. Oracle is building capabilities into the database that allow a blending of operational and analytical capabilities. With this approach it would no longer be necessary to have separate databases for the OLTP, ODS, data warehouse, and data marts. This would eliminate the need for huge volumes of data movement—the extraction, transformation, loading, and replication across these databases—and reduce the cost and complexity of integrating and managing multiple databases.

In Oracle Applications, both OLTP and decision support and reporting are being done in the same Oracle instance, using RAC. It is no longer necessary to have a separate relational, OLAP, data mining, or ETL engine. This greatly simplifies the operation and management of the data warehouse infrastructure.

Of course, there is still the need to integrate data from many sources—until all the data is stored within one Oracle database.

1.7   Summary

We've gone from the mainframe in the 1970s to the minicomputers in the 1980s to client/server in the 1990s. In the late 1990s and early 2000s Internet computing began to change the way we did everything, making it possible to deploy business intelligence applications to large, geographically distributed user populations both within the enterprise and outside of it to suppliers and customers.

After heavy technology investments in the late 1990s many companies have found they have underutilized assets and are looking at ways to reduce operating costs. Consolidation and grid computing, based on low-cost commodity hardware, can provide substantial savings.

In this chapter, we've taken a look at what gave rise to data warehouses and data marts, some of the highlights of Oracle Database 10*g*, some of the many challenges facing warehouse developers, and what we think the future holds. Now it's time to see how we can use all of this technology to build and access our data warehouse.

2

Designing a Warehouse

2.1 Designing a Warehouse

Readers of this chapter probably fall into one of three categories. They have either:

1. Never designed a database before

2. Designed a database for a transaction processing–type system

3. Built a data warehouse system

In the latter case, you could skip this chapter or use it as a refresher, especially if your last database used Oracle. Therefore, this chapter is aimed at readers who fall into categories one or two, which may surprise the person who has previously designed a non-data warehouse database. Why? Because the skills and techniques used to create a database for a data warehouse will be different from those required for a transaction processing–type (OLTP) system. Consequently, though you will have a head start because some of the techniques are the same, it is very important to say to yourself: I am designing a different type of database.

So what is different about designing a database in a data warehouse? In a transaction-processing system, the designer's goal is to make the transaction complete very, very quickly, and the designer also has the benefit of hopefully knowing how the business will interrogate and use the data. Typically, the data changed is just the specific individual records for the transaction, and reports only look at the current day, month, or week. Contrast that with a data warehouse, where, although queries must complete as quickly as possible, they could still take hours. In the data warehouse, a much larger volume of data, both current and historical, is typically scanned in order to fulfill the normal business intelligence types of queries.

Another major problem is determining what information should be held in the warehouse and at what level of granularity it should be retained. This book will not discuss the techniques that can be used to determine what should be included in the warehouse or how to go about collecting that data, because there are already many books available that discuss this topic extensively.

However, the importance of trying to determine what should be included in the data warehouse cannot be stressed enough. It is so important because it may not be until a year after the warehouse is in production use that you suddenly discover that the information is either not available or held at an inappropriate level, and this will limit or prohibit the types of queries that you can run on your warehouse

For example, a telephone company decides not to hold every call in its database, but instead holds a total of what the customer spent by day. Then someone in the company decides that he or she would like to offer customers a discount when certain numbers are called. Now, if the warehouse had contained every single telephone call made by its customers, the company would be able to find out exactly what this scheme would have cost if it had been implemented over the last 12 months. Instead, it has no data available and would either have to guess what the cost might be or postpone the planned new system until sufficient data is available to accurately determine the true cost to the company.

One of the difficult decisions for the designer is to determine at what level data will be stored in the warehouse. Often, storing every transaction, such as in our telephone example, may seem rather excessive, and, because it could easily mean the warehouse grows to many terabytes, there is a temptation to consolidate the data. Managing a terabyte warehouse requires careful and stringently controlled procedures that must be followed. The bigger the database becomes, the harder it is to manage and query it. However, with the easier availability of cheap storage devices, keeping vast quantities of data at the detailed level is becoming much more feasible and worthy of serious consideration.

Since aggregation is a major design decision, the designer would be wise to seek approval from the users of the warehouse before adopting such a strategy. It should also be clearly explained to these users the limitations that are likely to occur due to aggregating the data. With disks declining in price, hopefully most sites will store all of the data that they require.

2.1.1 Don't Use Entity Relationship (E-R) Modeling

The typical approach used to construct a transaction-processing system is to construct an entity-relationship (E-R) diagram of the business. It is then ultimately used as the basis for creating the physical database design, because many of the entities in our model become tables in the database. If you have never designed a data warehouse before but are experienced in designing transaction-processing systems, then you will probably think that a data warehouse is no different from any other database and that you can use the same approach.

Unfortunately, that is not the case, and warehouse designers will quickly discover that the entity-relationship model is not really suitable for designing a data warehouse. Leading authorities on the subject, such as Ralph Kimball, advocate using the dimensional model, and we have found this approach to be ideal for a data warehouse.

An entity-relationship diagram can show us, in considerable detail, the interaction between the numerous entities in our system, removing redundancy in the system whenever possible. The result is a very flat view of the enterprise, where hundreds of entities are described along with their relationships to other entities. While this approach is fine in the transaction-processing world, where we require this level of detail, it is far too complex for the data warehouse. If you ask a database administrator (DBA) if he or she has an entity-relationship diagram, the DBA will probably respond that he or she did once, when the system was first designed. But due to its size and the numerous changes that have occurred in the system during its lifetime, the entity-relationship diagram hasn't been updated, and it is now only partially accurate.

If we use a different approach for the data warehouse, one that results in a much simpler picture, then it should be very easy to keep it up-to-date and also to give it to end users, to help them understand the data warehouse. Another factor to consider is that entity-relationship diagrams tend to result in a normalized database design, whereas in a data warehouse, a denormalized design is often used.

2.1.2 Dimensional Modeling

An alternative to using the entity-relationship model is the **dimensional** model, which views and models the data from a different perspective. Instead of considering an entity, which represents a thing such as a product or a place and the relationships between those entities, a dimensional

Figure 2.1   *Dimensional Modeling*

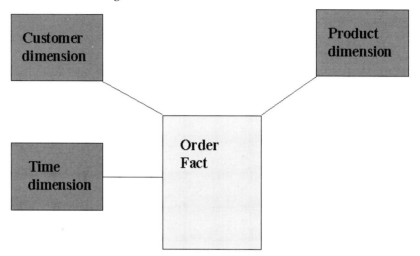

model describes data using **dimensions** and **facts**, which become actual tables in the database and which we will describe in more detail in the next two sections.

Dimensional models, as illustrated in Figure 2.1, despite sometimes looking quite simple, provide a very effective way of holding historical and current data in a form that makes it accessible to business users and that enables them to make the right business decisions. A dimensional data warehouse can be viewed as containing data that:

- Has been validated (i.e., no invalid product codes)
- Is historical (i.e., the last 36 months)
- Is integrated—therefore the same key is used by all systems
- Is easily accessible

2.1.3   Fact Table

The fact table, of which there could be more than one, contains factual information, and it is usually the largest table in the data warehouse and is often fast growing. The fact tables are typically where all of the detail data that you want to keep in the data warehouse is stored, such as all of the telephone calls made by a customer or the orders placed by your customer, as shown in Figure 2.1.

Therefore, if a customer made 20 telephone calls, then it is likely that 20 rows will be stored in the fact table for this customer. Consequently, the fact tables will be by far the largest tables in the database, possibly containing hundreds of millions of rows in a large data warehouse. If you are unsure as to whether data is factual, it is often numeric, and sometimes a value that can be computed, such as the value of an order or the number of items purchased.

The information contained in the fact table doesn't have to be at the finest level of detail; it could be summarized data, such as total telephone calls made by a customer today. The level at which data is held in the fact table is known as the *granularity* and is one of the important decisions the warehouse designer must make. In the example described here, the difference in the number of records stored over a 24-month period would be huge. Contrast the storage requirements between a record stored for every telephone call a customer made in a single day compared with a record for every telephone call a customer makes.

When designing a data warehouse, depending on your business, you may find that there are different types of fact tables, such as, transaction level, transaction item level, event based, status, or even summarized data.

2.1.4   Dimension Table

When designing using the dimensional model, there may only be one or a small number of fact tables, but there could be many dimension tables. The dimension table can be seen as a reference table to the fact table, where descriptions and more static information about a piece of data are held. For example, product is considered a dimension because, in this table, everything about the product is held, such as full product name, suppliers, and pallet size. In the fact table, there would be a column called "product_key," which is used to retrieve all of the product information from this dimension table.

If you are uncertain as to whether data is a dimension or a fact, ask these questions: Is the data relatively static? and Is the data describing something? Typically, dimensions such as a product_id do not change frequently, whereas a fact table would contain the details of the products you had sold. There is also usually at least an order of magnitude of difference between the number of rows in the fact table, compared with the much fewer rows in the dimension table. Also, the dimension tables tend to contain more textual fields, which describe the dimension object, whereas fact tables tend to contain more numeric measures.

For example, a fact table can contain millions of rows, whereas a dimension table could have only a few rows (e.g., the time dimension could have as few as 52 rows if data was stored weekly for one year). Or a region dimension could contain only 15 rows, if the country had only 15 regions. Dimensions don't have to be small in size, because you could sell 50,000 products or have a customer dimension with 5 million rows. All of these are examples of valid dimensions.

It is hard to say how many dimensions your design will require, but typically there will be less than 20 dimensions and at least 4. Therefore, our data warehouse will comprise only a few tables, but it will have huge storage demands because of the large number of rows in the fact table.

2.1.5   Warehouse Keys

Data in the warehouse will most likely come from a variety of sources, and a product code in one system may not be the same as in another system. Another problem is that when data is being stored over a period of time, keys used in the production system could be reused. Therefore, the designer should seriously consider implementing **surrogate keys**, so that they have total control over how data is identified within the data warehouse. The conversion of the production key to the data warehouse key will be handled during the ETL process and incurs negligible overhead during data loading; we will discuss this in Chapter 5. All keys are candidates for being transformed into surrogate keys, and that even includes the keys to our time dimension. Your surrogate keys do not have to be very sophisticated and could simply start at one and increase sequentially using Oracle sequences. There may also be data storage savings if surrogate keys are implemented.

However, we will retain the use of natural keys in the EASYDW schema, because it assists the clarity of the examples in the book if the more meaningful natural keys are used rather than the numerical surrogate keys.

2.1.6   Normalizing the Data Warehouse

When it comes to whether the data in the warehouse should be normalized, not everyone agrees on the same approach. Some experts believe that the warehouse should be normalized, while others think that using dimensional normal form is more appropriate.

Dimensional normal form is rather interesting, because it looks like a combination of normalization and denormalization. In Figure 2.2, we see the difference between the two approaches for the Store dimension.

Figure 2.2   *Normalized versus Dimensional Normal Form*

Normalized

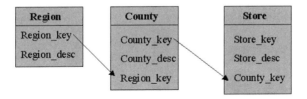

Dimensional Normal Form

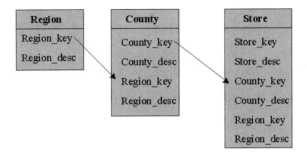

The normalized case, is also referred to as **snowflaking** and is where the dimension tables are designed so that repeating data is removed to their own tables, which are then linked via foreign keys. The dimension data is normalized in the same way that you would normalize the database design when performing entity-relationship modeling in an OLTP system. So a Store record doesn't contain the information about the county it is in but contains the key to the parent County record. Therefore, the information about a particular county will be recorded on only one County record. Although Oracle Database 10*g* will accept normalized dimensions, take care using this approach. One of the disadvantages is that it may impact performance, because more joins will be needed in queries, which will take time to execute. Snowflaking the dimension is a good example of a technique used in transaction-processing systems, which is not always appropriate in the data warehouse.

You will notice that the dimensional normal form version duplicates or triplicates the data or worse, depending on the levels in the dimension. The Store records contain the information for both the parent County and Region, so different Store records that are in the same county will duplicate the county and region information. While this may seem an unacceptable storage overhead, in reality, the number of rows in the dimensions is typically very small when compared with the size of the fact table. Therefore, you will probably be surprised to learn that storing this extra data may only cost you a few tens of megabytes. The advantage of this approach is that now only two levels of navigation in the model are required to access information, thus making it easier to construct queries that return data quickly.

2.1.7   Data Warehouse or Data Mart

An alternative to creating one large data warehouse is to create data marts, where a data mart contains a subset of the data in the warehouse. Data marts have the advantage of being focused into an area of the business, so they could contain regional or departmental data. However, care should be taken if the data mart approach is used, because instead of creating one data source, many data sources may be required. Multiple data marts may be easy to manage and ideal for reporting purposes, but trying to integrate that data might be extremely difficult. Thus, the end result could be data marts containing duplicated data that cannot communicate with each other. However, it is not uncommon for an organization to first create data marts and then use those as the basis for creating the enterprise data warehouse.

The other data mart approach is where the mart is created from the data warehouse by subdividing the warehouse data by specific criteria for a business requirement. For example, by geographical region so that the regional headquarters can have a smaller set of data that just relates to its business activities. The advantage of this approach is that all of the data is first integrated correctly within the warehouse prior to creating the data mart.

2.1.8   The Easy Shopping Inc. Example

Throughout this book, we will use an example based on a fictitious company called Easy Shopping. It is an organization that has no retail outlets and sells via its Internet site or via satellite or cable television. In Figure 2.3, we can see our dimensional model for Easy Shopping Inc.

In this example, we have a fact table called Purchases, where we record every item that our customers purchase. Four dimensions have been defined: customer, product, time, and details of our daily special offers. Although this may be a simple example for the purposes of this book, even the ones that you create will not be that much more complex than the one shown here. However, you will have more dimensions and many more columns in your fact table.

Figure 2.3   *Dimensional Model for Easy Shopping Inc.*

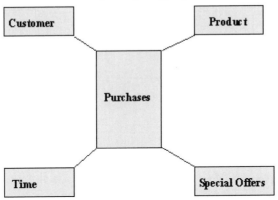

Warehouse schemas are sometimes called star schemas, and Figure 2.3 is an example of one. The center point is the fact table and the dimensions sit around the fact table as the points of our star. As per our entity-relationship diagram, once you have drawn the dimensional model, it can easily be translated into a physical database design since each box represents a table. Although in the text we refer to fact and dimension tables, inside the Oracle database they are all tables and are treated as such. However, before you jump in and create the physical database from this dimensional model, there are a few more decisions to make before the design is complete.

2.2   **Other Design Considerations**

When you are constructing a data warehouse, it is easy to become focused on ensuring that queries are processed quickly. However, blindly following this approach could easily result in a database that is difficult to manage or use.

2.2.1   **Design to Manage**

It's no good building a warehouse that answers all questions in under a minute if the data inside it is at risk because the database cannot easily be backed up. Therefore, always identify the crucial management tasks and determine if they can be performed easily using this design when designing a database. We will discuss in more detail the management tasks for a data warehouse in Chapter 11 and 12, but let us briefly review some of those tasks and see how they affect the design.

Some of the important management tasks include:

- Backup
- Loading new data
- Aggregating new data
- Data maintenance activities, such as indexing and archiving

All databases should be backed up regularly, and Oracle Database 10*g* has the RMAN utility, which allows on-line backups and incremental backups of the data that has changed. On the surface, backup may seem a trivial task, but backing up a terabyte warehouse takes time, even if it's an on-line backup. Therefore, the designer should carefully consider the tablespaces where the data is stored to make tablespace backups of read-only tablespaces, or use partitioning so that a full backup can be taken by running parallel backup tasks; you might even consider using Data Guard to protect the data warehouse against site disasters. In Chapter 12 and 17, we will discuss backup and recovery and Data Guard in more detail.

Full database backups are still likely to be a luxury in very large warehouses; therefore, you should design the warehouse to allow incremental backups to be taken that contain only the changes to the warehouse data. Oracle Database 10*g* includes new features with RMAN that enable incremental backups to be made (of the changed data), these can then be subsequently rolled into the main, full backup. This provides the advantage of being able to maintain full backups and perform full recovery by only taking incremental backups of the changed data. This will be discussed further in Chapter 12. Due to the huge volumes of data in the warehouse, any operation that can be performed in parallel will significantly reduce the time required to complete the task, especially if there are many parallel processes running concurrently. Most of the new data will have to be stored in the fact table; therefore, during the design phase, the designer should ascertain when and how much data is going to be loaded. Then calculate the anticipated load time, and if it cannot all be loaded in the available time, techniques such as partitioning the fact table so that the data could be loaded in parallel should be considered.

When the data warehouse is being tested by the design team, they should not concentrate only on performance testing but also on the impact of the data volumes, which will enable them to advise how long loads will take and discuss with the operations department how backups will be performed and how much time they'll need.

In Chapter 7, we will see how summary management, which was introduced in Oracle 8*i*, can be used to maintain aggregated data. One of the performance techniques widely used in the warehouse is to create summary tables of preaggregated data, known in Oracle Database 10*g* as a *materialized view*. Then a query is *transparently* redirected by the optimizer to read the materialized view instead of having to read all of the detail data. Hence, the performance improvements can be enormous, depending on the reduction in rows between the detail data and the materialized view.

Unfortunately, we get nothing in this world for free and materialized views have to be maintained. This can involve considerable time, depending on how many new records are added and whether the materialized view is created completely from the beginning or if it can be incrementally refreshed. If many materialized views are defined and they are all refreshed at the same time, consideration should be given to placing the materialized views in different tablespaces on different disks. Failure to do this will result in all I/O occurring on the same disk, thus slowing the refresh process considerably. This may be an even more important consideration if the refresh operations are to be performed in parallel.

2.2.2 Design for Performance

As we will see in Chapters 4, 6, and 7, there are various techniques that can be employed by the designer to improve query performance. Some will involve how queries are constructed, but many are actually in the database design. For example, all databases benefit from indexes, and a data warehouse is no exception. Therefore, do not forget to decide which type, where, and how much space is to be allocated for indexes. In a data warehouse, the designer does not have to worry about many users inserting new entries into the index and the associated problems that can result. Instead, the designer is now concerned with the time that is required to maintain or build an index. For instance, recreating an index on a fact table with 100 million rows will take more than a few minutes to complete!

Oracle Database 10*g* offers different types of indexes, and the designer should select the one that is most appropriate. Different types of queries in a data warehouse will use different access methods to the data that benefit from the different index types. For example, a star transformation uses a bit-mapped index.

Physical placement of the data is another important consideration, especially if it is used in conjunction with partitioning and parallel operations. If data is physically located on different disks, then queries or tasks can be performed that do not saturate the I/O limits on a specific disk drive. Oracle Database 10*g* introduces Automatic Storage Management, which is a powerful, new feature, where the database server takes the responsibility for managing disks, disk groups, striping, mirroring, and load balancing. This is described more fully in Chapter 3.

Significant performance gains can be obtained by using materialized views, which are described in Chapter 7. Since they have to be created and maintained, space must be reserved for this data, and the improvement in query response time must be balanced against the time required to maintain this data.

New data for a warehouse often arrives in batches. Hopefully, it will be loaded into the database when it is not in use, but this cannot be guaranteed. Therefore, if, during your investigations of the proposed system, you discover that data will be loaded into the warehouse while it is in use, review techniques, such as partitioning, that allow you to insert data into an area different from the one being used by the users.

Another consideration is whether the fact table is likely to be updated. With so many records in the fact table, there could be a significant impact on performance; therefore, procedures may have to be put into place to stop unauthorized updates to the fact table.

2.3   **Implementing the Design**

Once we are satisfied with the database design, it is time to physically create our database. Initially, you should create a small-scale version of the database and test design ideas here before building the full-size production system. There are various tools available to the designer to help create the warehouse; these will be discussed in other chapters.

Database designers often prefer to create a script file containing the SQL commands to create the database, and this is perfectly acceptable. An alternative approach is to use the Graphical User Interface (GUI) in Oracle Enterprise Manager, which will be discussed here.

Hint: If the SQL is complex, use these GUI tools to create the SQL, and then paste the SQL into your text file.

In this section, we will walk through the various stages required to create our data warehouse. First, we will see how to create the actual database, and then learn how to create the tablespaces and data files where the actual data is stored. That will be followed by illustrations of how to create the tables and a brief introduction on creating the indexes, partitions, and materialized views. We will end with a discussion of security of objects within the data warehouse.

2.3.1 Single Database or Many?

There was a time when the data warehouse was created in its own database. However, times are changing, and now some companies prefer to have a single database that contains all systems.

There are pros and cons with each approach, and whether you choose a single database or multiple databases will depend upon your business requirements. Creating a new database is not a difficult job, and the best approach is to use the GUI tool, Oracle Database Configuration Assistant. Once the database has been created, you can then add your own data files and tablespaces using Oracle Enterprise Manager or via SQL scripts.

A database can be created directly from SQL, but if this approach is used it should be performed with care, because you will need to run a number of script files that are required by Oracle Database 10*g*. If you use the GUI, this work is done automatically, and there are even some prepackaged databases that can be deployed.

2.3.2 Naming Conventions

Before anything is created in the database, the naming conventions used for all database objects, such as data files, tablespaces, and table and column names, should be reviewed. Depending on the tools available to your end users, they may actually see these table and column names. Therefore, if they do not have sensible names, these end users, who are generally not computer literate, could be very confused.

In our Easy Shopping Inc. example, there is a column in the fact table called time_key. Now, for people familiar with databases, it is obvious what that field contains, but to our end users of the warehouse, it means nothing. Therefore, in this instance, a better column name might be date_time_of_purchase. The warehouse designer should also remember that if end users will be using the warehouse, a more English-like column name should be used.

So far we have not discussed the topic of metadata, but in a data warehouse it is very important. There should be one definition of a data item, which in the ideal world would have only one set of values. For example, a region code is supposed to be a three alphanumeric code, and it is in all systems except one, where it is defined as a number. Therefore, as part of the **ETL** process (which is *extraction* from the source system, *transformation* of the data, and *load* into the warehouse) the data should be cleansed and made consistent.

These are some of the challenges for the team responsible for loading the data into the warehouse, discussed further in Chapter 5, and they will apply all the necessary conversions to the data to ensure that, when it is in the warehouse, all values are the same.

2.3.3 Database Configuration Assistant

Oracle Database 10*g* includes a number of GUI tools to assist with managing the database. A very useful one is the Oracle Database Configuration Assistant (DBCA), from which you can create, delete, and modify a database or manage the templates used to create a database. This tool runs standalone (look for DBCA in the ORACLE_HOME/bin directory), and it does not require Oracle Enterprise Manager to run. In Oracle Database 10*g* it comes with three pre-configured databases, and selecting one of these will significantly reduce the time it takes to create the database. The alternative is to create a new database from scratch, which is more time consuming because all of the scripts to create the database data dictionary must be executed.

The subsequent steps will vary, depending on whether a preconfigured or new database is built.

Using a Preconfigured Database

There are three types of preconfigured databases supplied with Oracle Database 10*g*:

- Data Warehouse
- General Purpose
- Transaction Processing

If you are uncertain as to which one is suitable for your environment, the physical attributes of the database and installed components can be seen by clicking on the *Show Details* button, which will show the template being used. (See Figure 2.4)

Figure 2.4 *Oracle Database Configuration Assistant—Database Templates*

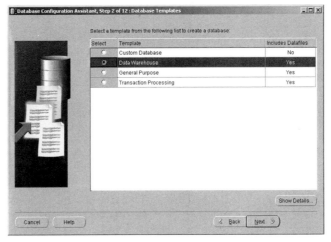

There are only a few screens requiring input when a preconfigured database is used. The next is that for naming the database, as shown in Figure 2.5, where we have called the database EASYDW.

Figure 2.5 *Oracle Database Configuration Assistant—Database Identification*

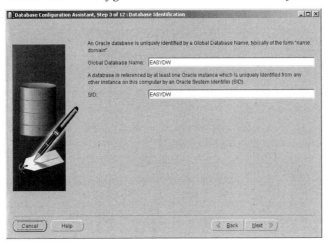

Oracle Database 10*g* introduces the whole concept of Database Grids and the centralized management of many databases. For the purpose of our database we are going to manage our warehouse database with the local database version of Enterprise Manager rather than the Grid Control version. (See Figure 2.6)

Figure 2.6   *Oracle Database Configuration Assistant—Management Options*

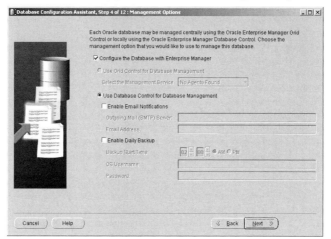

The next step, shown in Figure 2.7, is to enable the passwords for the critical Oracle accounts to be set. For simplicity in our warehouse, we will use the same password for all accounts: In a true production system you

Figure 2.7   *Oracle Database Configuration Assistant—Database Credentials*

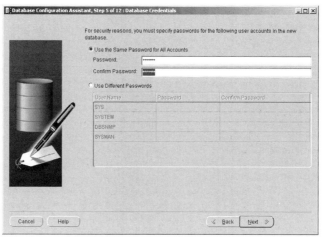

may well want to have different passwords to heighten the security on your system.

Now comes one of the new steps in Oracle Database 10*g* which gives us our first flavor of some of the new Oracle Database 10*g* features. In the next step, shown in Figure 2.8, we must decide how we want our database files stored on our disks.

Figure 2.8   *Oracle Database Configuration Assistant—Storage Options*

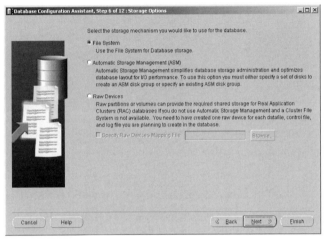

There are three options:

1. Using the File System (i.e., stored as normal files)

2. Using Automatic Storage Management (ASM). For this option you must identify a set of disks to Oracle, which it can use solely for its database files.

3. Using Raw Devices. A disk option, where disks are used without file systems, which is an option to enable Real Application Clusters (RAC) to be used.

For now, we will use option 1 to store the database files in the file system, but in Chapter 3 we will look more closely at both RAC and the new ASM option.

Because we have chosen option 1 to use the file system, the next screen, shown in Figure 2.9, provides us with some control over how and where the

Figure 2.9   *Oracle Database Configuration Assistant—Database File Locations*

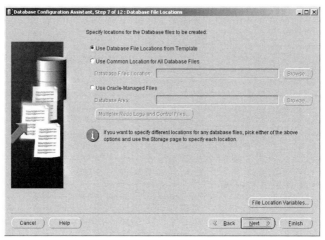

files are placed in the file system. If we had chosen either option 2 or 3, then we would get different screens at this stage.

Oracle Database 10*g* introduces new options for backup and recovery, including Flashbackup to disk in the Flash Recovery Area, where the disk usage is managed by Oracle. The next step, shown in Figure 2.10, enables the specification of the disk area for Flash Recovery and the amount of disk space to be allocated.

Figure 2.10   *Oracle Database Configuration Assistant—Recovery Configuration*

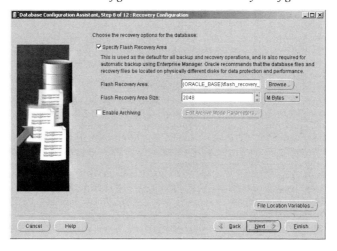

The ORACLE_BASE notation shown for specifying the Flash Recovery Area forms part of the directory structure of an Oracle installation. ORACLE_BASE denotes the directory of the root of the Oracle subdirectories, and ORACLE_HOME, which you will also see mentioned, denotes the directory that contains the software specific to this Oracle Database 10*g* installation—for example:

```
ORACLE_BASE = C:\oracle\product\10.1.0\
ORACLE_HOME = C:\oracle\product\10.1.0\Db_1\
```

You may also see ORACLE_HOME written as ORACLE_BASE\ Db_1\.

In Figure 2.10, the Flash Recovery Area is being placed in a subdirectory off ORACLE_BASE. The Flash Recovery area on disk should normally be distinct and separate from that used for the database files.

Along with these features there are some sample schemas that can be installed, where examples are provided to help illustrate the functionality available in these features. This is shown in the screen in Figure 2.11, where there is also the option for some custom scripts to be executed.

Figure 2.11   *Oracle Database Configuration Assistant—Database Content*

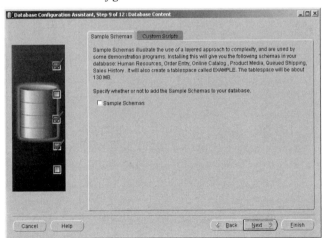

The next step is to define some of the parameters used to configure the database. Oracle Database 10*g* has a number of components that can be configured. In Figure 2.12, we see step 5 of 7 from the Database Configura-

Figure 2.12   *Oracle Database Configuration Assistant—Initialization Parameters*

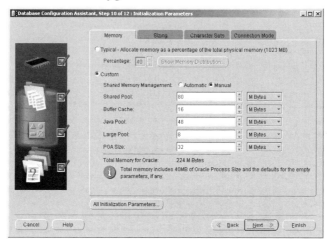

tion Assistant, where we can define the parameters for the respective areas by clicking on the appropriate tabs, which include:

- Memory
- Sizing, which enables the size of the database blocks to be specified and the number of processes that can connect to the database
- Character set of the database
- Connection mode for how client connections connect to the database
- Database initialization parameters

For the sizing, the option to specify the database block size defines the lowest level of granularity and control you have concerning the allocation of space in the warehouse. It is recommended that your data warehouse be created with a large block size, such as 16,384 bytes, which means that you can store more records of the same type together in a single block, thus helping to reduce our I/O demands.

The default parameters may be suitable for your environment. However, if you need to amend them, perhaps if the memory available to you is limited—for example, you may have two databases running on one server—then click on the *Custom* option and amend the memory being allocated.

You can see the effect of your changes instantly by monitoring the *Total Memory for Oracle* value.

Hint: If a parameter is set too low, you will be advised and given an opportunity to increase its value.

Clicking *Next* displays Figure 2.13 where one of the buttons is the *File Location Variables*. When the database is created, the location of all the files that comprise the database—that is, the data files, control files, initializa-

Figure 2.13   *Oracle Database Configuration Assistant—File Location Variables*

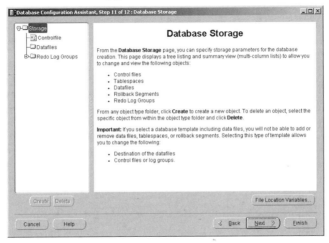

tion, redo log, and archiving files are located according to the values of these parameters that you can configure for each database, as illustrated in Figure 2.13. Also at this time you can define your own variables and use these in the definition of your database.

Finally, we get to the point where we can hit the *Finish* key for the database to be created. This screen also enables a template of your database creation script to be generated for future reference.

When using one of the preconfigured databases, you cannot control the size of the database, only the location of the files, which is the screen shown in Figure 2.13. By default all of the files are placed in one director; therefore, if you want them on different disks, now is the time to specify the new location.

Figure 2.14   *Oracle Database Configuration Assistant—Creation Options*

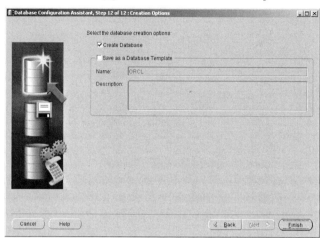

All the information needed to build the database has now been defined, and you can now create the database (see Figure 2.14) or save this definition as a template for use another time. You can monitor its progress as it is being built. Once the build has finished, it is now available for use.

2.3.4 **Which Schema?**

Now that we have a database, all objects defined in an Oracle database must reside inside a schema, a logical structure that describes a collection of objects. Therefore, before any tables are created, you should decide how many schemas you require. A data warehouse can contain anything from only a few tables for a simple warehouse up to many tens of tables for a complex, enterprise-wide warehouse, but it is still probably a good idea to keep them all in one schema to assist with their management.

However, you may prefer to create multiple schemas by subject area, but this approach will also increase the effort required to manage the database to make the information in the tables available, because there will be extra tasks to perform such as granting access to tables and defining synonyms.

Hint: It is very important to make this decision at the outset of the design, because the schema name plays an integral part in the naming convention used to retrieve information from the database.

A schema object is created every time a database user is defined. A user is created via the SQL CREATE USER statement or from within Oracle Enterprise Manager. To do this we must first logon to Enterprise Manager using a DBA account. We will discuss this more fully in Chapter 11, but for now, direct your browser to the following URL, which will display the Enterprise Manager login screen.

```
http://<hostname>:<port>/em
```

For example, if you have installed Oracle on a standalone server and opted for local management via Enterprise Manager as opposed to Grid Management, then Enterprise Manager is accessed via the previous URL. The normal port number on Windows is 5500, but this can vary depending on other installations that may have reserved that port. So if the database is on server "easydwsvr," then the URL will be:

```
http://easydwsvr:5500/em
```

Once you have logged in, you see the initial database summary home page shown in Figure 2.15.

Figure 2.15   *Oracle Enterprise Manager—Database Home*

Most of the browser screens for Enterprise Manager contain in excess of one typical screen's worth of information and are normally accessed by use of the scroll bar on the right-hand side. Our screen shots will generally only show the top section of the browser screen. At the top left there are a number of links for tabs for various other screens. Select *Administration* and you will see the screen shown in Figure 2.16. This may seem a little busy, but you will notice that there is a logical grouping into areas for different operations and each link takes you to a specific screen for the administration of that operation.

Figure 2.16   *Oracle Enterprise Manager—Administration Tab*

In the middle of the top row of groups entitled Security, select the *Users* link to get to the screen shown in Figure 2.17. This screen shows you all of the existing users in your database and enables you to select and modify these user accounts. We want to create a new user account. Click on the *Create* button on the right-hand side above the list of existing users to display the screen shown in Figure 2.18.

In our Easy Shopping example, we have decided to create a user called EASYDW. Here we can specify how the user will be authenticated, and we have selected the default mode of by password. This means a password must be specified and is used for all subsequent database access. Oracle permits

Figure 2.17 *Oracle Enterprise Manager—Users Screen*

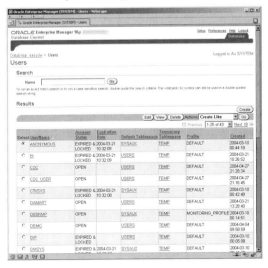

other options for authentication, which include *external* for authentication via the operating system or network service, or *global* if performed by an LDAP-type directory service. If, in the future, this password needs to be changed, then it can be done from within Oracle Enterprise Manager, using the screen shown in Figure 2.18 or via SQL.

Figure 2.18 *Oracle Enterprise Manager—Create User Screen*

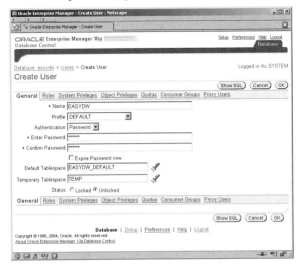

We must also select a default area where objects created by this user, such as tables and indexes, will reside. In a well-designed database, this is not an issue, because every object will explicitly state the tablespace in which it must be stored. There are a number of other options that can be specified for a user, such as privileges. It is important to set these; otherwise, you will not be able to retrieve data. As we progress through this book, you will be advised about which privileges are required when a topic is discussed—for example, Summary Management.

When the user is created, a schema is automatically created with that user name. However, you will not be able to see the schema name until the first object, such as a table, is defined for that user.

The schema name is very important, because it is used to fully qualify an object in the database. For example, we could have a table called TIME in the EASYDW schema and also in our ORDERS schema. To advise the optimizer which table you wish to retrieve data from, you specify the table name as :

```
schema name.table name
```

Therefore, to retrieve all the records in our time dimension, the fully qualified table name would be:

```
SELECT * FROM easydw.time;
```

You can create as many users of the database as you require, but it is recommended that only one of them be used for the purpose of creating objects, such as tables and indexes. Therefore, when the DBA connects as user EASYDW, all the tables and indexes created will reside here. In section 2.3.11, we will discuss enabling privileges for a user.

2.3.5 Data Files and Tablespaces

Once the database has been created, you can now add your own data files and tablespaces. By default, you will find a number of data files; on a Windows (e.g., NT, 2000, or XP) system, they will be located in:

```
<ORACLE_HOME>\Oradata\<database name>\
```

and will comprise three control files, two system spaces (system and sysaux), the undo, the example, and the user areas. In Oracle Database 10*g*, the SYSAUX tablespace is new and is an additional collective tablespace used by some Oracle components and products that require their own schema and therefore have their own database objects. It should ease administration by having the objects reside in the same tablespace. This is SYSAUX.

The tablespace is the logical name that is used within the database schema to specify where objects must reside; a tablespace has one or more data files associated with it, where objects are actually stored. Part of the tablespace definition is physical location and size of these data files; therefore, an object placed in a tablespace is actually stored in these files.

In our Easy Shopping Inc. example, we have decided to implement the following tablespaces:

- Dimensions—for all dimension data
- Default area, which users are assigned by default
- Summary—for the materialized views we will create
- One tablespace for each month of the year, named Purchases_<month>_<year>, for example, PURCHASES_JAN_2003
- Indx tablespace—for indexes
- Temp area—for temporary space

In this example, we will create only one data file per tablespace, but, of course, you can create more if required. Also, the files shown here will be very small, and in the real world, they could be extremely large.

These tablespaces and their associated data files can be created either directly from SQL or by using Enterprise Manager, illustrated as in Figure 2.19.

One of the advantages of using Enterprise Manager to manage your database is that it means that you no longer have to keep querying the metadata in the data dictionary tables and views to find out the state and information on objects in your database. This information is already available via the graphical interface in Enterprise Manager.

In Figure 2.16, we saw the EASYDW database Administration screen. We now select *Tablespaces* from the *Storage* group and we can see a list of tablespaces, their size, current state, and space used. This is shown in Figure 2.19.

Creating a tablespace using Oracle Enterprise Manager is very easy. From the Tablespaces screen click the *Create* button to navigate to the Cre-

Figure 2.19 *Oracle Enterprise Manager Console—Tablespaces*

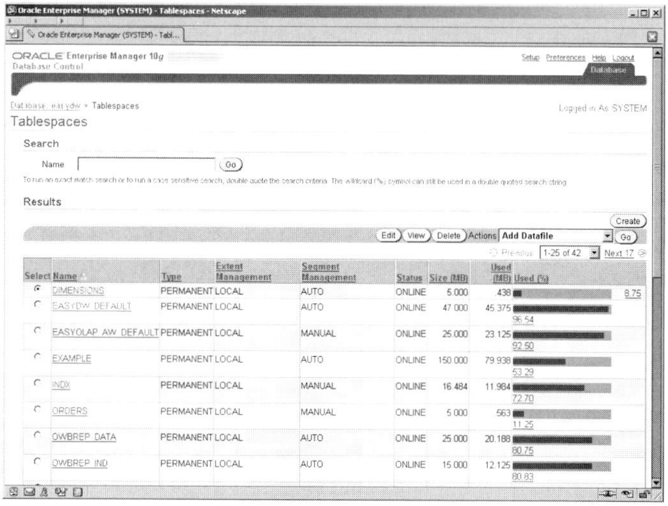

ate Tablespace screen shown in Figure 2.20 to create our Dimension tablespace where the parameters for our tablespace can be specified.

Figure 2.20 *Oracle Enterprise Manager Console—Create Tablespace*

The first step is to enter the name of the tablespace. It is wise to choose sensible names, because you will be using these constantly throughout the schema, and it helps if they mean something to you. For example, the tablespace called DIMENSIONS will be used to hold the dimension tables, whereas the purchases made in January are held in a tablespace called PURCHASES_JAN2003. Another favorite approach is to suffix all data tablespaces with a D and indexes with an X to identify the type of data that is held in that tablespace.

Provide the new tablespace name in the top *Name* field and accept the defaults in the other fields. The *Locally Managed* tablespaces and *Dictionary Managed* options control how the space within the tablespace is managed, either by using the database data dictionary or by storing the information locally within the tablespace itself. It is becoming standard practice to use locally managed tablespaces, because this removes the overhead of accessing the data dictionary, which contains the metadata about all of the objects in the database. Locally managed tablespaces are more efficient than dictionary managed ones and hence should be preferred.

We also want our tablespace to be Permanent for our data (rather than for temporary sort usage or for transaction undo information) and we also want to be able to update, insert, and delete the objects in our tablespace. Select *Add* in the *Datafiles* section to display the screen in Figure 2.21, which enables us to add the actual files to the tablespace where our data will reside.

Figure 2.21   *Oracle Enterprise Manager Console—Add Datafile*

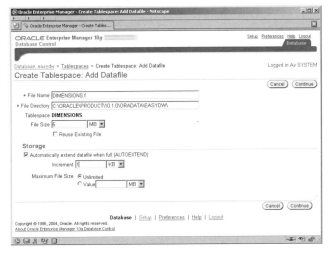

Complete the datafile information, which just consists of specifying the "dimensions.f" file name and a size of 5M. At this point you can also set the file to automatic allocation. Some designers do not like files that automatically extend; however, many do, because it means that a task will not fail simply because there is no space left in the database. Instead, the datafile will automatically extend itself, and you have control over how large those extents are. Of course, when the disk is full, autoextend will fail regardless. Selecting the *Continue* button returns you to the screen shown in Figure 2.22.

Figure 2.22   *Oracle Enterprise Manager Console—Tablespace With Datafile*

If you prefer to create your tablespace directly from SQL, then you can use either the SQL*Plus tool or the new browser-based i*SQLPlus tool (accessed from the browser at url http://<server>:5560/isqlplus). If you are uncertain of the SQL required to perform a task, you can click on the *Show SQL* button in most of the Enterprise Manager screens and a new screen containing the SQL will be displayed, as shown in Figure 2.23, for our tablespace creation example.

Figure 2.23 *Oracle Enterprise Manager Console–Dimension Tablespace SQL*

2.3.6 **Creating the Fact and Dimension Tables**

Now that we have a database, and the tablespaces and users are defined, we are ready to create the fact and dimension tables. The fact and dimension tables are created as if they were any ordinary tables inside the database. Therefore, all the options that one would specify on a table, such as the initial and subsequent extent size, may be specified. Although we call them "fact" and "dimension" tables, they are no different from any other table in the database.

When defining the fact table, carefully select the column data types, because selecting one that occupies too much space—when your fact table contains hundreds of millions of rows—will result in a considerable waste of disk space and also potentially result in performance problems if many disk blocks must be accessed to satisfy a command.

Tables are created using the SQL CREATE TABLE command, but we will now see how to create tables quickly using Enterprise Manager. For the moment, a dimension table is defined as if it were any other table in the database. In Chapter 8, we will see how to define an actual dimension object, which will be based on the table that we create here. In fact, the dimension table created at this stage is a prerequisite for creating a dimension object.

When Oracle Enterprise Manager Console is started, go to the *Administration* screen and in the *Schema* group select the *Tables* option, then the *Tables* screen shown in Figure 2.24 is displayed.

Figure 2.24   *Oracle Enterprise Manager Console—Tables*

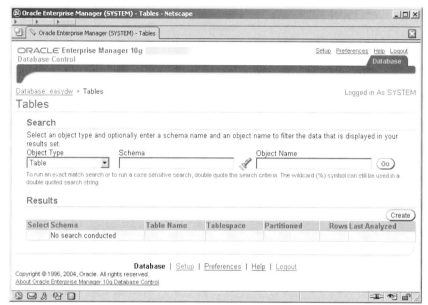

Select the *Create* button on the right-hand side, and on the new Table Organization screen (not shown) accept the default *Standard, Heap Organized* option and select *Continue* to get to the actual *Create Table* screen shown in Figure 2.25. We will discuss an alternative organization, index-organized tables, in Chapter 4.

In the screen in Figure 2.25, you specify the name of the table, TIME, the schema in which it will reside, and the tablespace for this table. This is a really nice screen for quickly creating the table. All you have to do is enter the column name in the Column list in the lower half of the screen, and select the data type and its size. If you run out of lines for defining your columns, select the *Add 5 Table Columns* button and five new column lines will be created for you.

Define each column using this approach, and don't click on the *OK* button until you have defined all of the columns in the table.

Figure 2.25   *Oracle Enterprise Manager Console—Create Table*

Once all of the columns in the table have been defined, clicking on the *Constraints* tab in the top left of this screen will allow you to create the constraints for this table.

Hint: If you do click on the OK button by mistake, you can always add the additional table parameters, such as constraints, by reopening the *Tables* page and selecting the table from the list and click the *Edit* button, where you will be back in the main *Edit Table* screen again.

2.3.7 Constraints

The job of the constraint is to ensure that all data conforms to its rules, such as a value corresponds to a specified range of values via a CHECK constraint. If a primary key is defined, then this guarantees that the value in the primary-key columns in the table is unique. A foreign key will ensure that all values correspond to one of the primary keys in another table.

Mention constraints to designers, and they will probably tell you that they do not want them in the database, because they are an overhead, especially when new data is being loaded. It is highly recommended that you implement at least primary- and foreign-key constraints, especially if you wish to use the Summary Management feature that is described in Chapter 7. One of the interesting aspects of Summary Management is the ability for the database to transparently rewrite a query to use a materialized view. If you have defined constraints in your database, then it will be possible to do some complex forms of query rewrite.

In a data warehouse, there is often concern that, because the data can come from many sources, it may not be as "clean" as normal data, and, therefore, constraints may fail. Although this is a valid concern, clean data should always be stored in the warehouse to ensure that accurate results are returned.

Another argument put forward for not implementing constraints is that validating every record when it is first inserted into the database imposes a considerable burden on the load operation. Therefore, it takes considerably longer than via a standard load, and if the loading window is very small, then one way to reduce the time is not to have constraints.

In Oracle, many of these concerns can be overcome thanks to some options on the constraint:

- ENABLE NOVALIDATE
- DISABLE NOVALIDATE

If you are still concerned about the overhead of having constraints and worried that your data isn't clean enough to get past the constraint checks, you can use the ENABLE NOVALIDATE clause, which turns on a constraint and applies it against all new inserts and updates, but it doesn't check existing records. It is enabled immediately, but you should be aware that incorrect results could be returned if existing rows in the table have violated the constraint.

By using the ENABLE NOVALIDATE clause, as illustrated in the following code segment, we can turn on the constraint SYS_C001136 without having to validate all of the data.

```
ALTER TABLE todays_special_offers
  ENABLE NOVALIDATE CONSTRAINT SYS_C001136;
```

Therefore, if we know or want to assume that the data is clean, we can just turn on the constraint immediately without incurring any overhead. Using this approach, the database doesn't spend time validating the constraint against all the rows in the table, but it does mean that the designer had better be certain that the data is clean.

Hint: Use sensible constraint names, such as customer_pkey, which will mean so much more than SYS_C001136.

Likewise, before data is loaded, the constraints can be quickly disabled using the DISABLE clause, as shown in the following code segment:

```
ALTER TABLE todays_special_offers
    DISABLE CONSTRAINT SYS_C001136;
```

The ETL stage, when we load our warehouse, can also be used to programmatically validate the constraint candidates—for example, using PL/SQL, resulting in the constraints being implemented as "disabled novalidate." This means that the data is already checked and the constraint is not enabled for new inserts or updates and does not validate the data already in the table.

Oracle Database 10*g* Enterprise Manager now supports the ability to specify the ENABLE/DISABLE and VALIDATE/NOVALIDATE clauses.

There is an additional clause called RELY, which is used by the summary management feature. This clause tells the optimizer that you can rely on the accuracy of the constraint. An example of using the RELY clause is shown in the following code on a constraint in the TODAYS_SPECIAL_OFFER table. Chapter 9 will discuss how RELY constraints are used by summary management.

```
ALTER TABLE purchases  MODIFY CONSTRAINT special_offer RELY;
```

You can check the constraints that have been defined in your database from the Tables screen. Select the table from the Tables screen list and then the *Edit* button to navigate to the Edit Table screen; then click on the *Constraint* tab to get the screen shown in Figure 2.26.

Figure 2.26   *Oracle Enterprise Manager Console—Constraints*

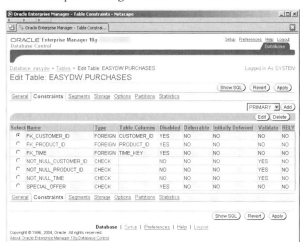

In Figure 2.27, we see how to create a primary key. Not every table in our data warehouse, such as the fact table, will have a primary key, but some of the columns may require that they are not null.

Figure 2.27   *Oracle Enterprise Manager Console—Add Primary Constraint*

For the *Constraints* screen while editing the TIME table, ensure that "PRIMARY" is displayed in the pick list box on the right-hand side and select the *Add* button.

Enter the name to use as the constraint name. Again, a good naming convention for constraint names is invaluable. We suggest using the following suffixes or prefixes to indicate the constraint type:

- PK for primary key
- UK for a unique constraint
- FK for a foreign-key constraint
- CK for a check constraint

Enter PK_TIME in the *Name* field, then select the column that forms the primary key from the *Available Columns* list, and select *Move* to move it into the *Selected Columns* box. If more than one column forms the primary key on your tables, then this operation is repeated for each of the required columns.

Select the attributes that you want the new primary-key constraint to have (enable/disable, validate/novalidate, etc.) and select *Add* to create the constraint on the database.

From the same *Constraints* tab on the *Edit Table* screen, check, unique, or foreign-key constraints can be similarly defined. A check constraint enables you to specify a condition that must be true for the columns for every row in the table. In our example in Figure 2.28, we have specified that the column DAY_NUMBER may take only the values between 1 and 366. Therefore, before a value is stored in this database, a check is automatically made by the database server that the column takes one of these values.

An alternative to using the GUI to obtain information from Oracle Database 10*g* is to query the many system data dictionary tables and views that are available; these provide a wealth of information about the state of your database and objects. In the following code, we can see the information held about constraints in the view USER_CONSTRAINTS.

Figure 2.28   *Oracle Enterprise Manager—Check Constraints*

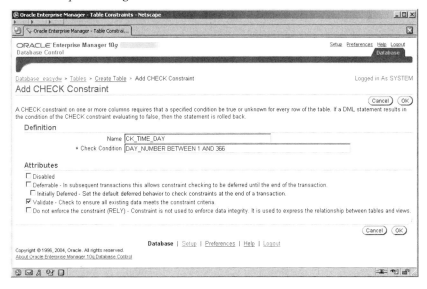

```
SQL> DESCRIBE user_constraints
 Name                                    Null?      Type
 ----------------------------------- --------  ------------
 OWNER                                NOT NULL VARCHAR2(30)
 CONSTRAINT_NAME                      NOT NULL VARCHAR2(30)
 CONSTRAINT_TYPE                               VARCHAR2(1)
 TABLE_NAME                           NOT NULL VARCHAR2(30)
 SEARCH_CONDITION                              LONG
 R_OWNER                                       VARCHAR2(30)
 R_CONSTRAINT_NAME                             VARCHAR2(30)
 DELETE_RULE                                   VARCHAR2(9)
 STATUS                                        VARCHAR2(8)
 DEFERRABLE                                    VARCHAR2(14)
 DEFERRED                                      VARCHAR2(9)
 VALIDATED                                     VARCHAR2(13)
 GENERATED                                     VARCHAR2(14)
 BAD                                           VARCHAR2(3)
 RELY                                          VARCHAR2(4)
 LAST_CHANGE                                   DATE
 INDEX_OWNER                                   VARCHAR2(30)
 INDEX_NAME                                    VARCHAR2(30)
 INVALID                                       VARCHAR2(7)
 VIEW_RELATED                                  VARCHAR2(14)
```

Every constraint that you define for this schema will be recorded in this data dictionary view. All of these views provided by Oracle will be prefixed either ALL_, USER_, or DBA_. Those prefixed DBA can only be accessed by user accounts with the DBA role assigned to them, those prefixed USER show information about your own accounts objects, and those prefixed ALL show information about other users' objects to which you have been granted privileges.

For example, to see on which constraints you have used the RELY clause, use the following query:

```
SQL> SELECT constraint_name, table_name, rely FROM all_constraints
     WHERE OWNER = 'EASYDW';


CONSTRAINT_NAME                TABLE_NAME                   RELY
----------------------------   -------------------------    ----
COST_PRICE_NOT_NULL            PRODUCT
FK_CUSTOMER_ID                 PURCHASES
FK_PRODUCT_ID                  PURCHASES
FK_TIME                        PURCHASES
NOT_NULL_CUSTOMER_ID           PURCHASES
NOT_NULL_PRODUCT_ID            PURCHASES
NOT_NULL_TIME                  PURCHASES
PK_CUSTOMER                    CUSTOMER
PK_PRODUCT                     PRODUCT
PK_SPECIALS                    TODAYS_SPECIAL_OFFERS
PK_TIME                        TIME
PUBLIC_HOLIDAY                 TIME
SELL_PRICE_NOT_NULL            PRODUCT
SHIPPING_CHARGE_NOT_NULL       PRODUCT
SPECIAL_OFFER                  PURCHASES                    RELY
```

Here we can see that the constraint SPECIAL_OFFER has the RELY clause enabled, whereas constraint SHIPPING_CHARGE_NOT_NULL does not. In Figure 2.29, we can see the constraints that have been defined on the table TIME.

The main Constraint tab for a table will also show you the full status of the constraints on your table. This information can also be determined by querying one of the constraint system tables, such as ALL_CONSTRAINTS. For example, to see which constraints have been enabled using the NOVALI-DATE clause, use the following query:

Figure 2.29   *Oracle Enterprise Manager—Viewing Constraints*

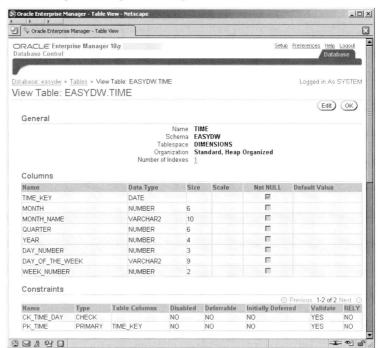

```
SQL> SELECT constraint_name, validated FROM all_constraints
  WHERE OWNER = 'EASYDW';


CONSTRAINT_NAME                    VALIDATED
------------------------------     -------------
PK_CUSTOMER                        VALIDATED
COST_PRICE_NOT_NULL                VALIDATED
SELL_PRICE_NOT_NULL                VALIDATED
SHIPPING_CHARGE_NOT_NULL           VALIDATED
```

The definition of the table is almost complete. We have defined the columns and the constraints that are required, and we could press the *Finish* button, but there are two more categories of information that the table wizard requests, storage and partitioning, which will be described later.

If you are happy with the table definition that you have entered (and you can check the SQL that will be applied by using the *Show SQL* button: see Figure 2.30), then press the *Apply* button; otherwise, select the correct tab and amend the entry accordingly.

Figure 2.30   *Table—Show SQL*

Hint: In order to create an object (e.g., table or index) in a tablespace, the user must have a quota in that tablespace. Go to the *Users* screen and edit the EASYDW user and select the *Quotas* tab: from here you can assign the space quota EASYDW has on a tablespace.

When you click on the *OK* button on the *Create Table* screen, the table is created, and you are now ready to create the next table. Hopefully, you will agree that this is a very easy way to create a table, and, since a data warehouse probably only has a few tables, you may prefer to use this friendly approach as opposed to writing SQL commands, where you will probably make many syntax errors that you will have to correct.

2.3.8   Indexes

A data warehouse is likely to contain a number of indexes, and, just like any other database, the designer must choose the indexes that are most suitable. Oracle offers several different types of indexes, but the ones that will be of interest to the data warehouse designer are:

- B*tree index

- Bitmapped index

- Bitmapped join index

Indexes should be selected carefully, and the various options and reasoning behind certain choices will be described in detail in Chapter 4. Please consult this chapter, because there you will learn whether to select a global or local index and how to partition it, if required.

To set the scene for this section, a bitmapped index is ideally suited to the data warehouse environment when you want to index a column that takes only a few values. For example, suppose we wanted to index the column PUBLIC_HOLIDAY, which has only two values: Y or N. A bitmapped index will store this information in an extremely compact manner, and this also has additional benefits for the way that the Oracle optimizer accesses the data for typical warehouse queries.

Although indexes easily can be dropped and created, due to the time required to create them, especially on a fact table with millions of rows, careful planning at the outset of the project will ensure that you won't have to spend a lot of time creating the index. An index can be created by using either the SQL CREATE INDEX command or Oracle Enterprise Manager.

Figure 2.31 shows the *Indexes* screen, which can be accessed from the *Schema* section on the main EM *Administration* screen. Completing the *Schema* and *Object Name* fields and selecting *Go* displays the indexes for that object.

Figure 2.31   *Oracle Enterprise Manager—Indexes*

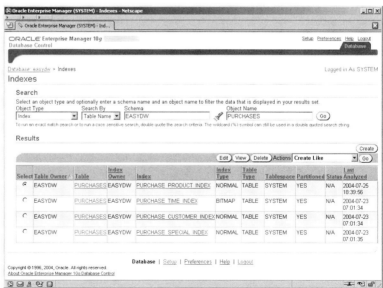

2.3.9 Partitioning

Partitioning data is a design technique that is very important in the warehouse, because it provides a means of managing large amounts of data and controlling its placement on the disks. Rather than place all of the data from a table in one tablespace, partitioning enables us to place the data in many tablespaces. Partitioning enables easier management of our tables and also enables the optimizer to use better techniques to access the data by only accessing the relevant partitions; this results in better performance. To determine how the data in a table is split into the different partitions (and therefore in which tablespace the data is stored), a partition key is selected, such as time_key, as illustrated in Figure 2.32.

Figure 2.32   *Partitioning—Range Partitioning by Month*

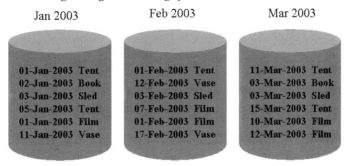

In this example, we are partitioning by month, so January's data goes in one partition, February's in another, and so forth. You must select the partition key carefully, although a common one is by time. Therefore, you could partition data by month, and then each month would reside in its own tablespace. This helps result in a more manageable partition, and it also has the advantage that if you ever had to archive the data, it would be as simple as dropping a partition. Of course, don't forget to back up the partition before you drop it! Dropping a partition is a very quick process and doesn't invalidate any of the data that is already in the fact table.

Oracle Database 10*g* provides several different types of partitioning techniques, and, after reading the partitioning section in Chapter 4, you can select the one that is most appropriate for your data warehouse. We will defer walking through the table partition screens of Enterprise Manager until Chapter 4, where the subject is dealt with in more detail.

2.3.10　Materialized Views

We have already seen that a data warehouse or data mart can hold a huge number of records in the fact table. Even if we had the fastest machine in the world and could cache some of the data warehouse in memory, the time required to respond to queries could be days—and it would certainly be minutes or hours.

To overcome this problem, warehouse designers use the technique of creating summaries, a summary being a preaggregated table of results, which Oracle calls a materialized view (MV). For example, suppose you always query on the number of purchases of today's special offer by day. Rather than compute those results every time, a materialized view is created that contains the required information. Then, whenever you make this query, instead of querying the fact table, you query the materialized view.

Although it partially defeats the object of a warehouse when you make unknown queries to the database, it is fair to say that quite a few queries upon the warehouse are well known. If we can improve the response time on those queries, then our users will be very grateful.

Oracle Database 10g includes a specific summary management component, which will enable you to create materialized views rather than ordinary tables, and then the optimizer will transparently rewrite your query to use the materialized view. This feature is described in detail in Chapter 9. At this stage of the design, if you can identify any queries that would lend themselves to being created as materialized views, they should be recorded now for subsequent creation. Some examples of the materialized views that we might create for our Easy Shopping Inc. examples are:

- Sum of sales by product by day

- Count of products sold by day

- Sum of sales by week

- Profit by product by day

If you don't know what materialized views you will need, then you can use the SQL Access Advisor, which has a number of methods to assess and create potential MVs: This is explained further in Chapter 10. Because some materialized views can be large, the number that you expect to create will impact how many tablespaces and data files should be defined for this data warehouse. For example, large materialized views may be partitioned in the same manner as we have partitioned tables, and the ease of management of these partitions is facilitated by using more than one tablespace in the same way as it does for partitioned tables.

Hint: It's not necessary to create a materialized view for every possible combination; this will all be explained in Chapters 7 to 10.

2.3.11   Security

One should not forget that some data in the warehouse could be very sensitive, and, therefore, for a variety of reasons, you may not want all of your staff to have access to it. Oracle Database 10*g* provides various types of security, which prevents users from changing the objects inside the database and accessing data.

Object Privileges

Privileges can be granted on objects in our schema to permit the type of access that other users have on these objects. For example, reading the data in a table, updating the data, or deleting the data is provided by three different privileges granted to a user on the table. Different object privileges can be placed on a variety of objects, including the following:

- Tables
- Views
- Sequences
- Synonyms
- PL/SQL modules
- Types
- Queues

You will most likely place security on tables and views, by stating whether a user can select, insert, and update the data, along with a number of other options. If you decide to create a number of users, then always ensure that sufficient privileges have been allocated so that everyone can read the data. This can be achieved by using either the SQL command,

GRANT SELECT ON for a table, or the GRANT SELECT ANY TABLE, or these privileges can be allocated directly to the user name using Oracle Enterprise Manager, within the Security section.

In Figure 2.33, we are giving a user of our warehouse, user EASY-DWUSER, the rights to ALTER, INSERT, SELECT, and UPDATE the TIME table in the EASYDW schema. This screen is accessed from the *Tables* screen by selecting the EASYDW table TIME, selecting *Grant Privileges* in the pick list box on the right, and selecting the *Go* button. Simply repeat this process for each user and the tables that he or she is allowed to access.

Figure 2.33   *Oracle Enterprise Manager—Object Security*

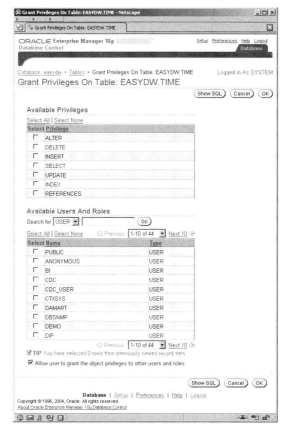

Role

Alternatively, you could create a role. Then you assign all of the privileges to the role, and the role is assigned to the user. This is the preferred approach, because it provides easier management and control of the privileges—especially if you create many users, because then you can create roles for the different job levels, and each user is granted one of those roles instead of assigning the privileges individually. Using the role approach, you reduce the likelihood of users accidentally being given access to data that they shouldn't have. It is also quicker if many users have to be defined. You can either use existing roles or create your own role using the SQL CREATE ROLE statement.

System Privileges

Most of the time will be spent granting object privileges to users and maybe creating roles. However, some users will require system privileges. A system privilege is one that gives you the right to perform high-level tasks, such as creating or dropping a table. Since you will not want to grant this right to many users, you shouldn't have to spend too much time giving system privileges.

The method used to define a system privilege is to select the target user from the list on the *Users* screen, select the *Edit* button, and then select the *System Privileges* tab on the *Edit User* screen. In a data warehouse, there are some specific system privileges that you may want to grant to specific users, such as CREATE DIMENSION and CREATE MATERIALIZED VIEW. In this instance, you would only be granting this privilege to users who would create dimensions and materialized views.

2.3.12 Using the Parallel Option

Our database is almost complete, but there is one other important feature available in Oracle Database 10*g* that should be mentioned, and that is the parallel clause. A number of the statements shown here can be executed in parallel, and the use of this technique is very important in a data warehouse, because it can significantly improve statement execution time. Parallel operations are available on table scans, sorts, joins, aggregates, and some table and index operations.

If you are using a symmetric multiprocessor system, then serious consideration should be given to using the PARALLEL clause. When specified, a statement, if eligible for parallel processing, will be decomposed into a number of parallel threads, and Oracle Database 10*g* will perform the job using parallel tasks and coordinate their running and the results. Therefore, all the user has to do is include the clause, and Oracle Database 10*g* does the rest.

The PARALLEL clause will expect you to specify the number of parallel processes to use. Choose this value carefully. Some testing may be required to determine the optimum value. For example, the following clause could be added to the CREATE TABLE statement for our purchases fact table:

```
PARALLEL (DEGREE 2)
```

This would mean that any operations on this table should be done using two server processes if they can be executed in parallel.

Data may also be loaded in parallel. The SQL*Loader facility, which we will discuss later, allows you to request parallel operations. Obviously, this can significantly improve the time required to store data; however, you should be aware of the possible fragmentation of your data that could occur. Therefore, it is suggested that, when data is being loaded in parallel, you specify the number of parallel operations to be equivalent to the number of datafiles available for that tablespace. Therefore, referring to our Easy Shopping Inc. example, if we decided to specify a value of:

```
PARALLEL (DEGREE 3)
```

on our purchases table, there should be three datafiles defined for every tablespace.

More importantly, Oracle Database 10*g* also has the facility to automatically control the degree of parallelism based on other criteria, such as number of users and other queries currently executing in the database. In this case, a degree does not have to be specified and only the keyword PARALLEL is used to activate parallelism for the particular object.

2.4   **Testing the Design**

None of us would write an application and send it live without testing it first. But it is amazing how many database designs are constructed and then unleashed on unsuspecting users. Your data warehouse is no different, especially since the business is relying on it for important information. Therefore, it is very important that all aspects of the design and processes are thoroughly tested prior to production release.

It is suggested that you initially load a small percentage of the data into the warehouse, and then test the following areas:

- Time required to load the data

- Data cleansing and transformation

- Query response times

- Summary data needs

- Time required for management tasks

If you are building a terabyte-size warehouse, then it is recommended that you repeat this process again with even more data in the warehouse, just in case there are any unexpected problems dealing with this volume of data.

Problems identified during testing are much easier to fix than trying to resolve them once the warehouse has gone live. A phased implementation to the user base is another way to test the warehouse if you don't want to wait until all of the testing is complete.

One very important point to remember is that, due to the size of the data warehouse, it will not only take much longer to load the data, but it is also unlikely that queries will complete quickly. Therefore, the entire testing process will take much longer than, say, a traditional OLTP database.

2.5   The Schema for Easy Shopping Inc.

We have seen in this chapter how to create our database using the GUI tools, but many readers may prefer to create the database directly from SQL. The SQL to achieve this is shown in Appendix A.

Our database is now complete. We have a basic framework, and now we will learn in the next chapter how to enhance our basic database design to include and use the sophisticated features that are available in Oracle Database 10*g*.

3

Architecture of a Data Warehouse

3.1 Introduction

Data warehouses have evolved because, in order for businesses to remain competitive in the marketplace, they need access to a wealth of information to help them make the right business decisions. To assist with those decisions, data may go back for many years and could entail keeping the details of every item that a business ever sold. Performance optimizations for update-centric OLTP systems are well understood; however, data warehouses, being query-centric, have vastly different requirements, and a single business intelligence query may need to retrieve and aggregate many records from the warehouse.

In order to understand how the database can efficiently access this large amount of data, we need to look at a more fundamental aspect of the warehouse implementation and that is the technical architecture and physical hardware. Good performance in a data warehouse, and the ability to retrieve and process the data quickly, is dependent on a sound physical database design, which must be supported by a solid foundation of server and infrastructure hardware. This hardware platform, in combination with specific features and techniques within the Oracle Database 10*g* database, can be used to significantly improve query performance in a data warehouse. This chapter introduces concepts about the technical architecture of a data warehouse and discusses the significant changes that Oracle has implemented with 10*g* and how they can be beneficially deployed in the data warehouse. In Chapter 4, we will look more at physical database design techniques, such as partitioning, and how they can use the strengths of the underlying architecture.

An important component of a data warehouse architecture is its ability to scale. A data warehouse will grow with an increase of users and reporting requirements and as more data is loaded to address new business areas. The architecture must be able to handle this growth to process the new data without any detrimental impact to the query response to our increasing user community. To grow our architecture normally means that we will need to add more processors to handle the increased processing requirements, more memory to accommodate the extra processes, and more disks to handle the larger data volumes.

There are various approaches that can be used to scale a system. Many servers scale simply by allowing more processors and memory to be added, though, ultimately, there is a physical limit as to what can actually be added into the server box. An alternative method of scaling is clustering, where multiple, possibly smaller, servers operate together in a coordinated fashion to service the increased demands. Oracle provides the Real Application Cluster (RAC) technology for clustering the database i.e., to have more than one set of database processes executing on separate servers but operating together as a whole and with an effective pooling of the separate server resources. Oracle Database 10*g* includes significant enhancements to the RAC technology and uses the RAC resources in an optimal fashion.

We will discuss RAC in more detail later in this chapter and show how RAC helps the scalability and robustness of our data warehouse environment. Next, we will look at the primary hardware components of our architecture.

3.2   Hardware Configurations for a Warehouse

Correct utilization of the available hardware is paramount to being able to run resource intensive queries found in a typical production data warehouse. As in the building industry, a solid foundation is critical.

3.2.1   Server Architectures

The Single-Processor, Single-Disk Architecture

In its simplest hardware deployment, the database can be implemented on a single-processor server, as shown in Figure 3.1. This configuration may be very viable for some small data warehouses or data marts and can provide valuable benefits and should not be dismissed. However, this configuration is obviously not going to run a large data warehouse and support the demands of a large user population requiring a quick response time to their queries.

This architecture has a number of inherent problems, not least of which is the risk to the data with this deployment, because it is dependent upon a

Figure 3.1 *A Single-Processor Server*

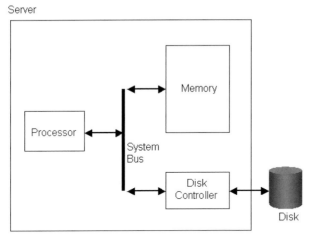

single disk with no built-in redundancy. In addition, because there is only one CPU, there is no facility for true parallelism in the warehouse, where more than one process is actually executing concurrently. There is a single CPU running a single process at a time, pulling data from one disk through one I/O channel from disk to server. Adding more disks does not necessarily enable any improvement if the queries that are running at peak times are already saturating that I/O channel. Therefore, we need to see how we can improve the delivery of the data from the disks.

The Multidisk Architecture

Although the single-disk architecture will suffice for a very small data warehouse, it is obviously totally unsuitable for a typical data warehouse with very large volumes of data. Now we need to look at a configuration that uses multiple disks and that uses a bigger capacity I/O channel between our disks and our server in order to transfer more data. An example of this is shown in Figure 3.2, where multiple separate controllers are used to interface with our multiple disks. The advantage of this approach is that more disks can be used to provide the data to answer the users' queries and can provide a bigger I/O channel, which enables more data to be communicated between the disks and the server at the same time. There are a number of technologies that can connect multiple disks to our server, from SCSI and Ethernet to Fibre Channel, and there are different architectures, such as *storage area networks* and *network attached storage*, for utilizing this connectivity. We will look at these in more detail later in this chapter.

Figure 3.2   *A Single-Processor, Multidisk Architecture*

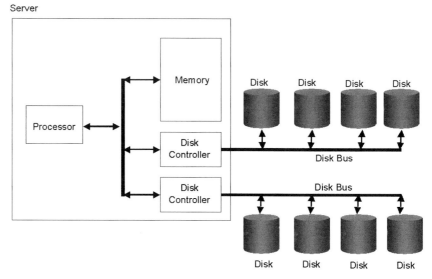

We also need to consider carefully how we use our multiple disks. For example, where do we put the data files for each of our tablespaces? Traditionally, the DBA, who has a number of separate disks, will try to split the tablespaces onto different disks so that the I/O requirements don't interfere with each other. A typical approach used by many DBAs is to place index tablespaces and data tablespaces on separate disks. In this way the I/O load is spread over multiple disks, improving performance.

However, even with careful placement of tablespaces on disks to avoid heavy loaded disks, we can still get hot spots, where certain disks are always heavily in demand and other disks are rarely used; what we really want is to smooth the I/O out across all of the disks. The sheer size of a typical data warehouse will necessitate a large number of disks, resulting in this type of manual placement quickly becoming an impractical and demanding chore that is prone to errors.

A solution to these problems is to use some form of RAID. This will transparently split our data files across multiple disks, improve response times, and also provide a higher level of protection against disk failure. In Oracle Database 10*g*, an important feature called Automatic Storage Management (ASM) is introduced and can be thought of as RAID within the database. We will look at RAID and ASM in more detail later in this chapter.

The Multiprocessor Server Architecture

Simply adding more disks is not sufficient for our large data warehouse if we only have a single processor handling all of the user workload. We may have multiple user queries being executed at the same time, but this parallelism is actually an illusion if we have only a single processor, because the processor can only really execute one process at a time. It provides the illusion of parallelism by swapping between, and executing small increments of, the processes in very quick succession. Adding more processors to the server enables Oracle to actually run more of the operations truly in parallel. This can be executing Oracle specific processes, running multiple separate users' queries or even just a single query that the database has transparently split among multiple processing threads operating on different parts of the warehouse data. Adding more disks and improving the I/O channels between the disks and server improves the ability of these multiple processing threads to concurrently access more data.

The server architecture, which uses multiple CPUs that are able to address a common memory structure, is called a **symmetrical multiprocessor (SMP)** architecture. The operating system runs across all CPUs concurrently and schedules and load balances its separate processes on all of its CPUs. A normal dual processor PC is an example of an SMP architecture server. Figure 3.3 shows a four-processor SMP system, where each processor accesses the same system memory via the system bus.

Figure 3.3   *A Multiprocessor, Multidisk Architecture*

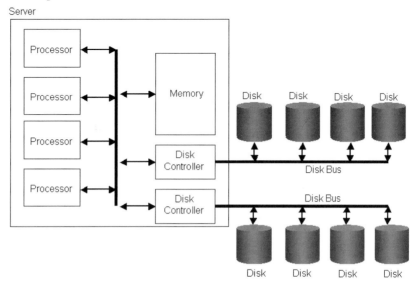

Let's look at an example of why multiple processors are required. The Oracle database can run a query by transparently splitting it into a number of cooperating parallel processes, where each operate on a different portion of the warehouse data. Executing these processes in parallel needs multiple processors if any speedup is to be achieved. Adding more disks and improving the I/O channels between the disks and server further improves the ability of these multiple processing threads to concurrently access more data. In addition, this parallelism in the database can be better utilized by physical database structures such as table partitions. However, the improved *ability* to use parallelism can only be realized if it is supported by the underlying hardware: multiple processors for the processing capability and handling the multiple process threads, more memory to support the multiple parallel processes, and multiple disks to maximize the available I/O and deliver the data in parallel to those parallel processes.

All of our server architectures so far have been SMP architectures that are limited in their ability to scale by the internal system bus, which must handle all of the data traffic and which also limits the number of processors because of the contention and demand that they place upon it. It is unusual to see SMP servers having greater than 16 to 32 processors without necessitating a more sophisticated, and therefore more expensive, internal system bus design.

Clustered Servers

Another architecture to consider is **clustering**, which involves multiple independent servers that work together to perform a common set of functions and may appear to client users and applications as a single server. The servers are physically connected by a network. We can identify two groups:

- Those that have disks shared and accessible to all servers

- Those that are "shared nothing" and do not have disks shared between the servers

In Figure 3.4, we have shown a simple two-node cluster that is accessing a common disk bus. We have shown our cluster nodes as having only two processors, but, of course, there is nothing preventing them from having more, as previously discussed. There are a number of technologies to share and connect external disks to our servers, and we will look at some of these in more detail later in this chapter.

Figure 3.4 *A Two-Node Cluster Using Shared External Disks*

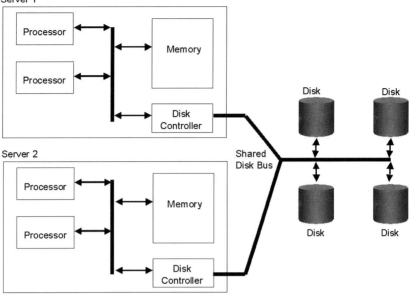

Clustering provides the benefits of:

- Improved scalability. Within limits, new nodes can be added to scale the architecture.

- Improved availability. If one node fails, then the other nodes are available to take over.

Massively Parallel Processor Architectures

Another alternative architecture is the **massively parallel processor** (**MPP**) architecture, where separate nodes or servers, each consisting of their own CPUs, memory, and which may or may not have their own disk, are connected to each other by a high-speed interconnect. Each node runs its own operating system, and the application typically coordinates its processing across the nodes in an MPP architecture utilizing the inter-node connectivity. Figure 3.5 shows just seven nodes in an MPP architecture using a single common interconnect, but large systems can have hundreds of nodes, which can be interconnected in a variety of different topologies.

Figure 3.5   *A Massively Parallel Architecture*

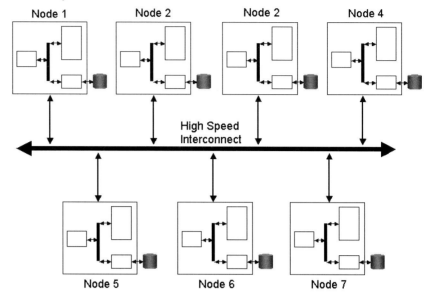

3.2.2 **The Oracle Database Architecture**

Before we proceed, now is the time to explain some of the various components of the Oracle database architecture.

The Oracle Instance and Database

An Oracle **database** is the set of database files that comprise the data warehouse, including the data files, control files, and redo log files. An Oracle **instance**, as shown in Figure 3.6, consists of the memory area (known as the **System Global Area** or **SGA**) and background processes—for example, SMON, PMON, and ARCH. The background processes access data files and manage user sessions. Background processes are shared by all database users.

The background processes each perform a specific set of tasks for the database. For example:

- SMON is the System Monitor and, among other things, performs instance recovery, cleans up the database transactions, and tidies up space utilization.

- PMON is the Process Monitor and cleans up failed user processes and their resources.

- DBW*n* are the Database Writer processes, and they write the changed data blocks from the SGA cache to the data files. There can actually be more than one of these background processes.

- LGWR is the Log Writer Process and is responsible for writing to, and managing, the redo logs.

- ARC*n* are the Archiver processes, which copy completed redo log files to a separate disk location.

- CKPT is the Checkpoint Process. When a special database event called a *checkpoint* occurs, this process synchronizes all of the headers of the data files with the new checkpoint information.

This is only a partial list. There are quite a number of Oracle processes, and each has its own area of responsibility and interacts with its own part of the Oracle database. For example, only the DBW*n* processes are responsible for writing out to the data files. A diagram of a single instance on a server and an overview of the background processes is shown in Figure 3.6.

Figure 3.6   *The Oracle SGA and Background Processes*

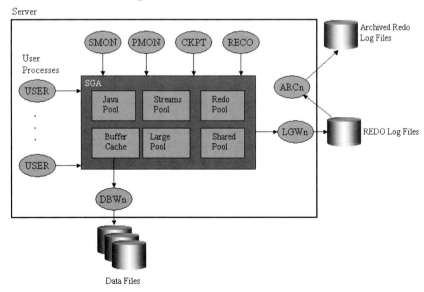

When an Oracle instance is started, the database initialization parameter file is read and the SGA memory area is allocated from the server's main memory and configured, the background processes are started, and the database files are opened. The SGA is where all the important information in the database is held when the instance is running. It contains the buffer and dictionary caches used internally by Oracle and the redo logs. However, it contains more than just data; it also contains the memory regions for the shared pool for SQL and PL/SQL and the Java pool for Java objects.

The Scalable Database: Oracle Database 10g RAC

When one database and instance are running on a single server, even on a very powerful multiprocessor server with a lot of memory, performance is still inherently limited by the server itself and by the number of processors and memory that it can contain. In order to scale our database beyond one server, we need to be able to cluster the database using Oracle Database 10*g* RAC.

Clustering the Oracle database requires more than one Oracle instance to access the same database data files and therefore uses the shared disk type of server cluster we identified previously. A clustered Oracle database offers a number of benefits:

- More CPU and memory resources are available for running the queries.

- The architecture is more robust: if one server falls over, then the others are available to continue to provide some system availability, albeit a reduced one.

The simplest example of this is shown in Figure 3.7, with two servers, each with their own CPUs, running their own database instance but both instances accessing *the same* database files stored on disks shared between the servers.

RAC was introduced in Oracle 9*i* as a replacement technology for Oracle Parallel Server. A key component of the Oracle RAC architecture is Cache Fusion. This uses a dedicated, high-speed interconnect to coordinate nodes in a RAC cluster and to keep data in each node's memory synchronized. Cache Fusion effectively enables the individual caches from the separate instances to act as a single cache.

Cache Fusion significantly improves the ability for clustered database instances to scale. Prior to Cache Fusion, one of the major problems

Figure 3.7 *Overview of a two-node Oracle RAC Architecture*

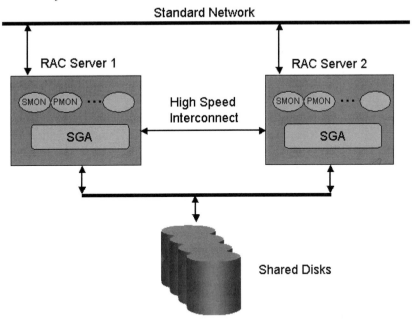

involved with more than one Oracle instance accessing the same database files concerned the interinstance communication, such as for passing Oracle data blocks between nodes. For example, if the same disk block were being accessed and updated by two separate database instances on different servers at the same time, then, in order for the second instance to access the block, it had to be transferred, via disk, from the first instance. Block pinging (as this was known) could occur repeatedly, since blocks were frequently written to disk in order to transfer them between instances and disk accesses are relatively slow in a database. To solve this without Cache Fusion necessitated clever partitioning of the data, often by splitting the user community between the two instances by the data that they were accessing. Partitioning in this fashion was not often a realistic possibility, was time consuming, and required skilled planning.

Cache Fusion, with its dedicated high-speed communication link, improves the communication between the instances. A number of technologies can be used for the interconnect. For example, the simplest, but still effective, one is a high-speed gigabit, or 10G Ethernet. If Ethernet is used then the Cache Fusion network should be dedicated to just the interconnect traffic and kept separate from the Ethernet network used for the normal LAN network to connect the users to the servers. There are also other new technologies, such as Infiniband, that offer a low latency and high speed interconnectivity. This improved, faster communication of the blocks between the instances in a RAC cluster removes the need for the slower block communication via the disks and therefore almost always removes the need for the careful partitioning of the data. This enables real applications, i.e., normal third-party applications and not just highly tuned and balanced ones, to be deployed on RAC and to fully use the benefit of the scalable architecture.

To scale the RAC architecture involves the addition of a new server and Oracle RAC instance into an existing cluster. This makes available a new set of CPU and memory resources to be utilized by the cluster. As new nodes are added, then the RAC cluster exhibits very good scalability and queries are transparently run across all of the nodes in the cluster to utilize any free resource on other nodes.

An additional benefit to our warehouse architecture from Oracle RAC is in the improved reliability of the whole environment. With RAC, instead of a single instance on a single server accessing our database, we have multiple instances on multiple servers. So, if one server fails, we still have the other servers in the RAC cluster that are able to pick up and continue the failed database sessions. For a production system that cannot afford downtime due to server failures, this is a very attractive and important feature.

Oracle Database 10g Grid

With Oracle Database 10*g*, Oracle has based its Database Grid upon the RAC architecture concept and has rearchitected many of its components as a consequence.

Declining hardware costs, leading to the increased availability of powerful, lower-cost servers, coupled with the easier availability and access within the Enterprise architecture to shared storage, make the appearance and use of interacting servers and clusters cheaper and therefore more likely. This means that isolated servers, with their isolated pools of storage and with their own application systems, can be consolidated into a lower-cost cluster offering better performance and reliability. This has evolved into the grid concept in Oracle Database 10*g*.

But plugging many servers and shared storage together to create a large cluster does not automatically provide you with the computing power that you need or use the computing resources to their best effect. The ability to harness and manage the power of this grid of multiple servers and storage comes from the sophistication of the management software to specifically address the issues that this type of environment presents. Oracle Database 10*g*

Grid is a new, integrated software infrastructure that enables the improved management and use of resources provided by a grid of servers and storage.

Previously, we have been administering our database using Enterprise Manager Database Control, but the new Oracle Enterprise Manager Grid Control administers and manages multiple database components in the grid as well as Oracle Application Server 10*g* components. The 10*g* Grid management by Enterprise Manager provides new features, such as:

- A unified management environment. A single environment to manage database servers as well as Oracle Database 10*g* AS application servers, to manage groups of the servers as easily as you could manage a single server and to manage storage across the grid.

- Improved management of the grid by simplifying and improving the management of the individual database nodes in the grid. Oracle Database 10*g* includes a whole new framework for monitoring, advising, and managing the administration of the separate databases.

- Software provisioning to automate the installation and configuration of the Oracle software across the multiple nodes in the grid, and also to automate the application of patches and upgrades.

- Dynamic Provisioning, which enables the balancing of the computing demands in one part of the grid with the availability of resources in another part by the use of **policies** to control and balance the allocation of resources.

- Integrated software. The new Oracle Database 10*g* clusterware, which enables the services and communication between servers in a cluster, is provided for all operating system platforms and eliminates the need to purchase and integrate with third-party clusterware. Having one software version from one vendor simplifies the environment and reduces the possibility of cluster failure.

We will examine Enterprise Manager in more detail in Chapter 11.

3.3 **Hardware Components**

Now that we have a better understanding of the different types of architectures that we need to build our data warehouse, let's take a step back and consider what our warehouse is trying to do:

- Support multiple users
- Execute large queries, in parallel and possibly split each query into smaller parallel threads automatically by the database
- Access very large volumes of data
- Load large quantities of data from operational systems

Therefore, the next step is to determine the requirements for the following three important components of our architecture:

- Memory
- Processing power (i.e., CPUs)
- Storage

We will now have a look at these components in more detail.

3.3.1   Memory

Our database will be servicing queries from users, running reports, and executing batch jobs to refresh the warehouse. Each of these queries may be split into multiple parallel processes by the database, and each of these processes will require a certain amount of memory. The main area here is the memory required for:

- The SGA, for storing all of the cache of the database data blocks and other memory structures
- The Program Global Area (PGA), which is a private memory space used by Oracle code for each user's server process for example, for sorts and hash operations

On top of the memory that Oracle needs, we must also ensure that there is sufficient memory for the operating system and for any other applications that must also execute on our warehouse server.

Oracle Database 10*g* has the new Automatic Shared Memory Management for dynamically tuning the memory used by the SGA and PGA (and which we will look at in more detail in Chapter 10). Memory requirements

can grow quickly and become large. Imagine 50 users running parallel queries. Each parallel process may require around 10Mb of memory. If each
query were split into four parallel threads, then the server would require
2Gb of memory to support these 50 users.

3.3.2   Processors

We have looked at the different server architectures that enable us to have
different numbers, and configurations, of processors, but what about the
processors themselves? It is not necessarily the case that we must have the
newest, fastest processors. Significant warehouse performance can be
obtained from using servers with processors that are not the fastest ones
available, particularly if we also deploy them in a clustered architecture
using RAC, which minimizes the contention and use of the internal system
bus on a single server.

An equally important criteria for a processor is the amount of memory
that it can address. Thirty-two-bit processors can address up to 4G of memory, but 64-bit processors can address significantly more. Even though it is
unlikely to ever need the maximum addressable space, many databases can
benefit from the increased memory capacity provided by 64-bit addressing.

3.3.3   Storage Configurations for a Warehouse

Now that we have seen the various architectures that are available to us to
implement our data warehouse, the next step is to decide upon the storage
requirements for our data warehouse.

The I/O Subsystem

One of the main objectives with our I/O subsystem is to keep the processors in our server constantly supplied with data when processing queries.
With data warehouses, this is much more relevant than with OLTP systems, because in a warehouse the queries are typically spanning a much
larger set of the data, whereas in an OLTP the data access is generally
more specific record oriented. This means that both the disk subsystem
and the I/O subsystem must have sufficient bandwidth to transport the
data to the warehouse quickly enough to support the processing needs.
This requirement is made more severe in a parallel environment, where
multiple processes are accessing data at the same time.

The other factor that must be considered for the I/O subsystem is the
latency of the technology used to connect the disks to the server. Latency is

the time it takes a packet of information to travel from the disks to the server. Latency and bandwidth together define the speed and capacity of the interconnectivity. In addition to this, there is the latency of the disk itself which is the time the disk takes to position the disk head over the required data block on disk before the data can actually be read.

When considering the number of disks for a warehouse, you must take into account both the capacity and the maximum transfer rate. If we were to base our disks for our warehouse purely on the disk capacity and go for a small number of large disks, then we are inherently limiting the ability of the disks to provide the data. Small numbers of disks may have sufficient storage capacity but are unlikely to have sufficient I/O capacity to meet our needs. For example, if we chose four disks, each with a 320Mbps transfer rate, then the maximum data that can be transferred even if everything is working ideally (which is probably not the case), is (4 * 320)Mbps. Alternatively, if we select a larger number of smaller sized disks, then we have more disks—each able to run up to their own maximum data transfer limit to provide the data to the servers.

Following this simple rule, we should, therefore, be looking at using a larger number of smaller disks that can deliver the data that we want "in parallel." *However*, the I/O subsystem should not be considered solely on the basis of the ability of the disks to provide data: the capability of the communication channel (the *data bus* and *controllers*) between the disks and the servers and the I/O channels at the server end are equally as important. One rule of thumb often seen is that there should be at least two disks per processor. Considering that the size of a warehouse will typically be very large, we will probably be using many times that multiplier.

The capability to use disks in this fashion in parallel comes from the ability to stripe our data across many disks and for that we need to have a brief look at RAID to understand how to use RAID and striping in our data warehouse.

Striping and RAID

Striping, or RAID, is the ability to spread the I/O requests across multiple disks in parallel. RAID is an acronym, which stands for *Redundant Arrays of Inexpensive Disks*, and the basic concept of RAID is to combine small, inexpensive disks to yield improved performance and reliability and have them appear to the server as a single, larger disk. We touched upon this problem earlier in the chapter when we looked at adding more disks into our warehouse architecture and where RAID provides a solution for better throughput and reliability by using multiple disks.

RAID can be described as levels, which progress from 0 to 10. As you progress through the levels, you get different performance and reliability. For example, rather than storing all of the data on one file on a single disk, the data is striped across multiple disks, which yields better performance during reading, because all of the disks potentially get read in parallel rather than just one.

Striping is the process where the disks are split into separate sections and the sections are utilized round-robin style on each disk. So, for example, if your stripe size is 1M, then the first 1M of your file is written to disk 1, the second 1M stripe is written to disk 2, and so on. This splitting of the data into stripes that are written to different disks is done either at the byte level or the block level and is performed automatically and completely transparently to the applications, whether it is a file for a word processor or a sophisticated database. Striping has the effect of reducing the contention for disk areas and improving I/O throughput to the server. Figure 3.8 shows a four disk RAID, where the stripe width is four and stripe size is the size of the individual amounts of data written to each disk.

Figure 3.8 *Four-way RAID Showing Stripe Size and Width*

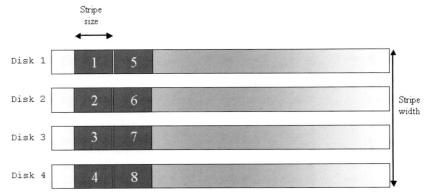

The process of mirroring the data across multiple disks involves duplicating the information that we write to one disk by writing a complete copy to a second disk so we always have a copy of our data.

The RAID levels are:

- **RAID 0:** striping (i.e., striping our files so that each successive stripe occurs on a different disk in a group of disks)

- **RAID 1:** disk mirroring. Where an exact copy of each disk is automatically maintained. If one disk fails, then the data is available on the other disk until a new disk can be inserted and the copy made while the system is on-line. The cost of this is that it doubles the number of disks that are required.

- **RAID 3:** striping with parity at the byte level. Uses an additional *parity* disk with other data, where parity data is simply a calculated numerical value from using the data on the actual data disks, so that if any one of the data disks fail, then the remaining data in conjunction with the parity data can rebuild the lost data. The parity information is on a separate, dedicated disk, for example, five data disks and one parity disk.

- **RAID 4:** block data striping with parity. Same as RAID 3 but working at the block and not byte level.

- **RAID 5:** block striping rotated parity. Both the parity and the data are striped across the disks. This removes the need for a dedicated parity disk, because the parity information is rotated across all disks. Read performance is better, but write performance can be poor. At least three disks are needed for a RAID 5 array.

- **RAID 10:** (also known as 0+1): mirrored stripe sets providing better security from the mirroring and better performance from the striping.

RAID can be implemented either in hardware, via a RAID controller for the disks, or in software, via a tool called a *logical volume manager* (LVM). An LVM is a piece of software that could be provided either as part of the operating system, from a third-party vendor (e.g., Veritas), or from the disk storage vendor (e.g., from EMC). The LVM combines areas on separate disks and makes them appear as a single unit to the operating system, and in the process it provides software striping and mirroring. Performing RAID in hardware may be easier, but there may be the disadvantage that it can be more difficult to change at a later stage—for example, if more disks are to be added; performing RAID in software can take advantage of a number of powerful volume managers available. Regardless of the mechanism, the I/O request from the server is transparently split by the controller or LVM into separate I/Os for the individual disks.

From a performance perspective, the DBA and systems administrator must carefully consider not just the type of RAID that they wish to employ and on which disks, but they must also consider items such as the RAID stripe size (i.e., the byte size of each stripe on the disks) and the number of disks in the stripe set.

A high-level perspective of the operations needed to use a volume manager to prepare the disks for Oracle can be seen in the following text. Different hardware vendors will have their own volume managers and there are third-party ones, and in addition, different operating systems may have a slightly different approach, so the steps listed here are intended to be very generic. The DBA and the system administrator must:

- Create or initialize the physical volumes. Define the disk as a *physical volume* and write certain configuration information to it.

- Create the physical volume groups. This is the process where the physical volumes are collected together to create the physical volume group. A physical volume can only belong to one volume group, but a volume group may contain many physical volumes. During this step the physical volume is partitioned into units of space called *physical extents*: These are the smallest units of storage used on the disk, and an extent is a contiguous section of the disk.

- Create logical volumes in the volume groups. This is the step when striping and mirroring are implemented.

- Create the file systems on the logical volumes. The file system is the structure on the disk necessary for storing and accessing the data. Without the file system it is not possible to create directories and files. For example, the file systems can be FAT32 or NTFS, which will be familiar to Windows users, or Linux Ext2, Linux Ext 3, and Linux Swap, which will be familiar to Linux users.

- Mount the file systems. Make the file systems known and usable to the operating system.

- Then, finally, use the file systems for the database files (i.e., create the database tablespaces using files on these file systems).

Stripe and Mirror Everything

After much research on the storage configurations that are optimal to the Oracle database for both OLTP and warehouse configurations, Oracle recommends using the SAME (Stripe And Mirror Everything) method. This method involves all of the disks being mirrored and striped using a 1M stripe width and with all of the database files being placed on these disks.

- By striping all database files across all disks using a 1M stripe size, the use of the bandwidth across all of the disks is maximized and the occurrence of disk hotspots and bottlenecks is reduced. The stripe size of 1M has been carefully analyzed as a balance point between the access time for the disks to get to the data location on disk compared with the transfer time for the data (i.e., 1M in this case).

- By mirroring, we increase the availability of the database by reducing the risk due to data loss from disk failure.

Equally important, SAME is a very simple storage configuration concept to grasp and is independent of any third-party's storage product; it provides significant benefits to our warehouse database.

Shared Storage

Our choice of architecture selected for the data warehouse will influence the type of storage that is needed. If we are using RAC, then we need to be able to access the disks from more than one server. We can use technologies such as SCSI, a bus technology that can connect up to 16 external devices (i.e., disks in the case of our warehouse) with our warehouse server. SCSI comes in many forms and can offer transfer speeds up to 160 MBps (megabytes/second); shared SCSI enables the bus to be shared between two servers. We will now have a brief look at two alternative solutions, *Storage Area Networks (SAN)* and *Network Attached Storage (NAS)*, which offer better capacity, scalability, and robustness.

A *Storage Area Network*, or *SAN*, can be viewed as a dedicated high performance network to connect servers and storage. An example of this is a disk array accessed using a technology such as Fibre Channel to link the disk array to the different servers (though other connection media, such as optical fiber, can also be used).

Fibre Channel is a technology for transmitting data at a rate of Gbps (giga-bits per second) between the devices in our warehouse architecture (i.e., between servers and between servers and disks). In addition, Fibre Channel technology allows a physical separation in terms of kilometers, so this also enables a large physical separation of the hardware components for our warehouse, if required. It may help to think of the Fibre Channel (or other technology) as a specialist data bus between the servers and the shared disk storage devices. High-availability systems will use multiple Fibre Channel routes from the servers to the disks and use hubs and switches to minimize the chance of system failure if any part of the SAN fails.

An alternative shared storage technology is *Network Attached Storage*, or *NAS*, which can be viewed as a set of disks running from its own special server platform and accessed via a normal network to which it has been assigned its own network IP address. For our warehouse architecture we may prefer to keep the normal company LAN network traffic separate from the warehouse server to NAS traffic and therefore use a separate LAN network between our database servers and our NAS.

It can be seen that the SAN concept encapsulates NAS. The Ethernet-connected disk devices in a NAS architecture are just a very specific example of storage available on a dedicated network (which SAN is). NAS performance, however, will be limited by the capacity of the network to move the data between the NAS storage devices and the servers: typically this limitation will be readily overcome by the network communication technology used in a SAN. In addition, new protocols, such as i-SCSI, are much more performant than old-style NFS.

The use of SAN and NAS in the Oracle warehouse architecture separates the disk storage system from the servers. This also means that these technologies are not just for the single-server environment. NAS and SAN storage are attached to a network that can have multiple database servers attached to it; therefore, it provides the required shared storage for Oracle RAC.

An example RAC architecture with shared NAS storage is shown in Figure 3.9. Taking our simple RAC architecture one stage further, for the example, we'll base the interconnects on Ethernet, add in the shared storage using NAS, and include two separate connections between the servers and the NAS storage, so if one fails, then the other is still present to enable the RAC to operate. Of course, the same redundancy could be introduced for the network providing the connection for the RAC Cache Fusion interconnect as well. The reason that three separate networks are used (i.e., the normal network to connect to the users, the RAC interconnect, and the NAS storage) is to ensure that the three different types of network traffic do not interfere with each other and degrade the overall system performance. Of course, our example is very simplified to demonstrate the point, and typical large warehouse production systems can be significantly more complex.

In this section, we have discussed the various hardware components of our architecture and how our storage can be configured and deployed. In the next section, we will see how a new storage feature in Oracle Database 10*g* can build upon the strengths of the RAID striping and mirroring.

Figure 3.9   *Overview of RAC and NAS Shared Storage*

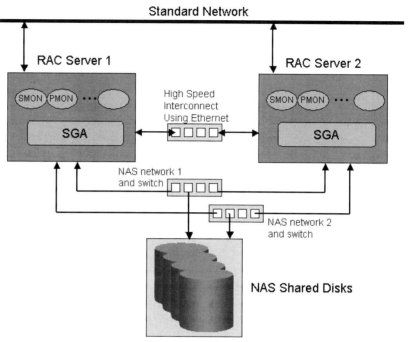

3.4   **Automatic Storage Management**

Automatic Storage Management (ASM) is new in Oracle Database 10*g* and provides the control and management of disks in conjunction with a purpose-built file system for the database files. Essentially, you provide the disks to Oracle and specify the degree of protection with mirroring that you require (unmirrored, mirrored once, or mirrored twice) and ASM manages the rest. ASM will also perform the striping by controlling the layout of the blocks across the disks, and it will effectively balance the load for you automatically. Furthermore, when new disks are added, removed, or simply fail, Oracle ASM will automatically redistribute the blocks and the load so that the database is open and available all the time. On top of this striped and mirrored set of disks, a file system for the Oracle files is implemented.

Prior to Oracle Database 10*g*, if you wanted to spread your I/O across multiple disks the DBA would work closely with the system administrator to make careful configuration of the underlying disks, for example, to provide the required RAID level that we have just discussed. While doing this, the administrator must plan and track the volume sizes, the striping sizes, and the extent sizes. There are a large number of steps in this process, the complexity of which can increase with the number of disks being used, the number and size of the logical volumes, and resultant file systems to be placed on these volumes. Generally, the bigger the database (and warehouses can get very, very large) the more disks and mount points required and, consequently, the greater the complexity.

This administration can quickly become a headache and a chore. What is worse is that if the database subsequently needs to be expanded at some point in the future, then the administrator will need to add more disks, and hence physical volumes, into an existing volume group. This process of rebuilding the underlying volumes may even necessitate our warehouse database being off-line, and the contents of certain areas of the database may need to be exported and reimported, which is a very undesirable situation.

The purpose of this task to implement RAID, is to stripe and mirror the underlying disks to get the higher throughput and availability. It is easy to see that it can be a complex and labor-intensive task and, even with a knowledgeable and experienced administrator, it can still be prone to errors because of its manual nature.

Now, it would be unfair to paint an overly negative picture, because there are powerful logical volume managers and other tools available to help the administrator with these tasks. There are also tools available to assist in tracking where the database objects in our warehouse actually reside (on which physical disks—Oracle File Mapper in 9*i* assists with this, for example) and for adding new disks into the physical volumes. The good news is that ASM in Oracle Database 10*g*, fundamentally, does the work of an LVM and all of these tasks for you, and, even better, ASM is a standard part of the Oracle Database 10*g* server and not a separately installed option. Using ASM allows all of your disk infrastructure, configuration, and definition to be handled by software from one vendor, Oracle, without introducing another layer of software from a third party. You provide the disks to the database and ASM, and the database will stripe and mirror the disks to provide the level of redundancy and protection that you require.

3.4.1 ASM Overview

There are two main concepts in understanding ASM:

- The *disk group*
- The *ASM instance*

The *disk group* can be viewed as the basic unit of control of the disks within ASM and is the logical collection of disks that you want to be managed by Oracle. Disk groups are either created via a new SQL statement (which we will look at shortly) or from Enterprise Manager and are then used as the repository for Oracle database files. One thing to bear in mind is that all of the disks in a disk group should have the same characteristics in terms of size and performance (i.e., you want to group together the same type of disks with the same performance characteristics). When you create files on an ASM disk group, these are known as ASM files and the names are automatically generated by Oracle (though you can retain some control of the format of the names).

In order to use ASM, a special form of an Oracle instance, called an *ASM instance*, must be up and running. The ASM instance is responsible for:

- Discovering and acquiring the ASM disks at startup

- Managing the disk groups

- Automatically providing the I/O balancing

- Protecting the data within the disk group

An ASM instance is much smaller than a normal database instance and it does not have a data dictionary: it has the very focused task of finding the disks at startup, managing the disks, and presenting the disk groups to the main database instances (i.e., our actual warehouse instance). You can have multiple normal instances on a server, but a server will only contain one ASM instance.

One important step that must be performed when the disk group is created is to specify which of the following three redundancy methods is to be used:

- **External Redundancy**—where Oracle will not mirror at all and mirroring is done externally and separately on the disk storage

- **Normal Redundancy** (i.e., mirror once)

- **High Redundancy** (i.e., mirror twice)

In order to use either of the redundancy options, more than one *failure group* must be specified. A failure group is some extra information that indicates to Oracle how the disks may fail collectively due to a fault. For example, consider Figure 3.3, which uses two disk controllers to access a set of disks; a failure group would be those disks that are accessed through the same I/O disk controller. The definition of failure groups enables Oracle to know how to store the redundant data required to protect the database data, or, in other words, the safe alternative disks to use for redundancy (i.e., mirroring), because they are in a separate failure group. Therefore, for the normal redundancy option, there must be at least two failure groups, and for the high redundancy option, there must be at least three failure groups.

3.4.2 Administering ASM

Now, we will show how to administer ASM either using the GUI interface or from within SQL*Plus.

Setting up ASM

In Oracle Database 10*g*, ASM is an attractive alternative to using the previously described Logical Volume Manager (LVM), so let's see how easy ASM is to use to manage our disks. The first step is to ensure that the disks that you want to use are made known to Oracle as candidate ASM disks, and this is done by using the ASM Tool to *stamp* an ASM header on the disks. On Windows systems you will find this in the bin directory as *asmtool.exe* (the command-line version) or as *asmtoolg.exe* (the graphical version); on UNIX based systems you will find *oracleasm* in the */etc/init.d* directory. Our examples are based on the Windows graphical version.

Hint: If you are creating an ASM-based database as part of the initial Oracle installation, you must still remember to use the ASM tool to stamp the disks; otherwise, they will not be visible to the installation program.

The ASM Tool marks the disks with a header, which identifies the disks as ASM disks: to do this the disks need to be configured with a single disk partition and without a file system. Figure 3.10 shows the initial ASM Tool screen, where we will begin by adding the header to our ASM disks.

Clicking the *Next* button displays a list of the disks with their different partitions, and what ASM Tool considers as potential candidates is shown in Figure 3.11.

Figure 3.10   *The ASM Tool*

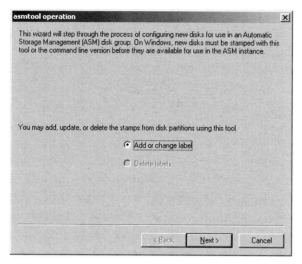

In Figure 3.11, we have four disks available, shown as Harddisk0 to Harddisk3, and ASM Tool has identified disks 2 and 3 (the last two in the list) which are actually two small SCSI disks and are the ones we want to use for ASM. Note that ASM Tool identifies and displays the file system on the partition, but it has marked three of them as candidates. Actually, on our system, this is a dual operating system machine and these partitions are Linux partitions, not ones we want to use for ASM. Generally, you must

Figure 3.11   *ASM Tool Disk Selection*

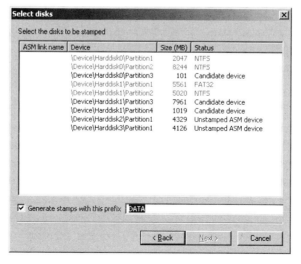

provide whole disks and not partitions of part of the disks to ASM, so you should not get this situation. In particular, any production system will probably not be a dual boot system. However, this example is used to make the point that you do need to be very aware of your disk and partition layout when you are using ASM.

Perform a multiple selection of both disks, click *Next* and you will see the screen in Figure 3.12, which shows the ASM stamp that will be applied to the disks. Note that the prefix stamp, DATA in our case, from the field in Figure 3.11, is incorporated into the ASM link name.

Figure 3.12   *ASM Tool: Stamp Disks Confirmation Screen*

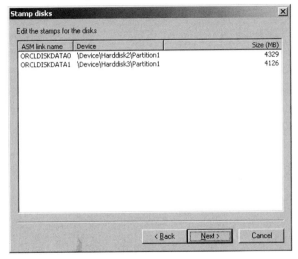

Configuring ASM during Installation

If we were creating the database as an ASM database using DBCA or the Universal Installer (during Oracle installation), then we could take a different choice for the storage option of the file system selection that we made in Chapter 2 (Figure 2.8). Now, we will choose ASM, as shown in Figure 3.13.

With ASM selected clicking the *Next* button displays the Backup choice screen as before, but after that we get a different screen, as is shown in Figure 3.14, which enables us to select the ASM disks that we stamped with the ASM Tool earlier. Because we are performing an actual installation at this point, we will need to have previously invoked ASM Tool directly from our installation disk and stamped our disks so that they are recognized as ASM disks. For Windows installations, ASMTool can be found on the installation disk in the ASM Tool subdirectory.

Figure 3.13　*Database Creation: ASM Storage Option*

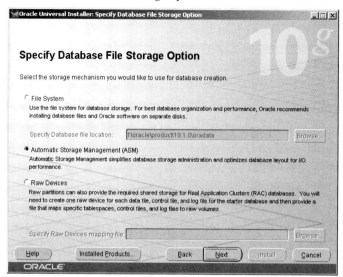

Here we have selected the *External* redundancy option, so no mirroring will be performed and we can see and check the tick boxes for both of the

Figure 3.14　*Configure Automatic Storage Management*

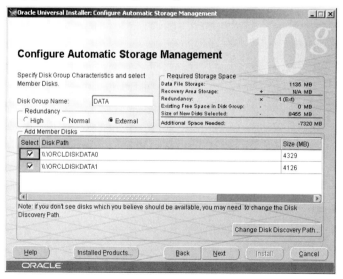

disks that we previously stamped and that we want to be members of our new ASM disk group. The disk group that we are creating is named DATA, which we will also refer to later when we manage the disk group via SQL and create tablespaces in it.

When we click *Next* and continue with the installation and database creation, these two ASM disks will now be used to hold our database files.

Managing ASM from the Command Line

The ASM disks and disk groups can also be created, deleted, and managed manually and to do this we need to be logged on to the ASM instance and not the normal warehouse instance. We will work through a simple example, but if you try to run these commands on a normal warehouse instance database, you will get Oracle error ORA-15000, saying, effectively, that it is the wrong command for the instance type. This is because there is a new database initialization parameter introduced with ASM called **instance_type**, which takes the value **RDBMS** for a database instance and the value **ASM** for an ASM instance. In our previous example, where we created a database using an ASM disk group, the ASM instance was created automatically for us as part of the database creation.

Before any ASM management tasks can be performed, you must first logon to the ASM instance. To logon to the ASM instance from the Windows operating system command line you, will need to reset your Oracle SID environment variable to that for the ASM instance. By default, this takes the value +ASM.

Hint: Note the + in front of ASM. If you omit this, you will not be able to logon, because your SID will not be set correctly.

A disk group is created as follows:

```
C:\> SET ORACLE_SID=+ASM
C:\> sqlplus /nolog
SQL*Plus: Release 10.1.0.2.0 — Production on Thu May 27 19:51:13
2004

Copywright (c) 1982, 2004, Oracle. All rights reserved.

SQL> connect sys/password as sysdba

SQL> ALTER SYSTEM SET asm_diskstring = '\\.\*:' ;

SQL> CREATE DISKGROUP data
        NORMAL REDUNDANCY DISK '\\.\H:', '\\.\I:' ;
```

Here, the disk group is being created with the name DATA with a normal redundancy, i.e. a single copy of the data will be maintained. The disk group is formed from the two disks which are visible on our Windows system as H and I.

The new ASM_DISKSTRING parameter controls and limits the disks that Oracle discovers at the ASM instance startup; it is normally placed in the ASM instance initialization parameter file. To illustrate its use, we have specifically set this parameter using a wildcard. The format of this string, as shown, is specific to the Windows platform and will be different for UNIX and other platforms. So the \\. indicates the current server and the *: indicates any disk on the server

If we want to add a new disk into our disk group, then we issue the following statement, which adds disks J and K into the precreated disk group DATA.

```
SQL> ALTER DISKGROUP data ADD DISK '\\.\J:', '\\.\K:' ;
```

Then Oracle will automatically distribute our blocks and rebalance the load from the initial set of two disks, which we specified earlier when the database was created, to include the new disks. All the time, the database is kept open to the users.

Creating tablespaces is now simplified, because we just need to refer to the ASM disk group. For example, to create a tablespace on our new DATA disk group we issue the following. The + used in +DATA for the datafile name indicates that it is a disk group data file.

```
SQL> CREATE TABLESPACE easydw_asmtest DATAFILE '+DATA' SIZE 5M;
```

Furthermore, using ASM for your database doesn't force the database to only use ASM. Oracle Database 10*g* enables a database to use both the standard file system method and the new ASM method at the same time. For example, previously we created our database as ASM during installation, but if we had created our database using the file system and subsequently decided that we wanted to start using ASM, then we would need to create the ASM instance manually. On Windows this is done using the ORADIM utility, which also creates the Windows service, and there are some new ORADIM parameters in Oracle Database 10*g* for ASM for specifying the ASM SID name and the ASM service name.

```
oradim -NEW -ASMSID +ASM -SYSPWD change_on_install
-PFILE c:\oracle\product\10.1.0\admin\+ASM\pfile\init+ASM.ora
```

The init.ora file for the ASM instance is much simpler, and, if the defaults for the parameters are used, it can be reduced to only the following parameters:

```
INSTANCE_TYPE = ASM
DB_UNIQUE_NAME = +ASM
ASM_DISKSTRING = '\\.\*:'
COMPATIBLE = 10.1.0.2.0
ASM_POWER_LIMIT = 1
USER_DUMP_DEST = 'c:\oracle\product\10.1.0\admin\+ASM\udump'
BACKGROUND_DUMP_DEST = 'c:\oracle\product\10.1.0\admin\+ASM\bdump'
CORE_DUMP_DEST = 'c:\oracle\product\10.1.0\admin\+ASM\cdump'
```

Once the ASM instance is created, it is accessed and used in exactly the same way described previously and an ASM-based tablespace can be created alongside our file system tablespaces without any problems.

ASM is an important new feature, which is easy to administer once you understand its deployment and operation. Two other areas indicate other aspects of the administration to investigate for understanding ASM further:

- The ASM instance initialization parameters. There are a very small number of parameters that control how ASM operates. For example, ASM_POWER_LIMIT is used prioritize the disk rebalancing operation: The higher the number assigned to this parameter, the higher the rebalancing priority (though a high priority can have a detrimental effect on other system operations due to the impact on processor and I/O resource).

- Special views, which are part of the V$ set, in the data dictionary for monitoring ASM operations and viewing the status of the disks and disk groups. For example, VASM_DISK, VASM_DISKGROUP, and V$ASM_OPERATION.

We think that you will agree that ASM is very easy to administer from the command line, but, as we shall now show, it is even easier by using Enterprise Manager.

Managing ASM from Enterprise Manager Grid Control

Now that we have a good understanding of how ASM operates and how it is controlled from the command line, we will have a look at how ASM is administered and controlled from Enterprise Manager.

To administer ASM, either Enterprise Manager Database Control version or Grid Control version can be used. We are going to use Grid Control for our ASM examples in this chapter, and in Chapter 11 we will discuss more about how EM Grid Control is deployed, started, and used. To complete this section on ASM we want to show how Enterprise Manager also supports ASM and the screens that complement what we have discussed so far.

From within EM Grid Control, you are able to drill down to view information on individual servers and then drill further to the Oracle software that is executing on the server. From the *Hosts Target* page within EM Grid Control, clicking the link that identifies an ASM instance will drill you down to the Home page (not shown) for that ASM instance, which displays the general status and alerts for the instance. From this page we can follow the *Configuration* link to display the screen shown in Figure 3.15, where you can see the parameters for the instance, some of which we have talked about earlier, and which can easily be set from this screen.

Figure 3.15   *EM Grid Control ASM Instance Configuration*

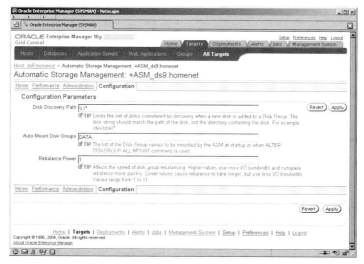

If the *Administration* link is followed, then we will see the screen shown in Figure 3.16, where the disk groups handled by this ASM instance are shown. Here we can see our DATA disk group, and we have expanded the pick list on the right to show the operations that can be performed on it. Mounting and dismounting a disk group makes it available or unavailable to the database instances running on that server.

Figure 3.16 *EM Grid Control ASM Instance Administration*

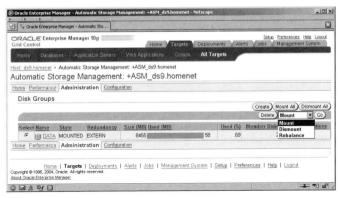

The third option involves the distribution of the file blocks across the disks in the group. When a disk is added or removed from the group, either intentionally or due to disk failure, ASM automatically redistributes, or rebalances, the file blocks. This *Rebalance* option enables you to manually perform a rebalance operation, though, because it is generally done automatically, you should rarely need to do this yourself.

By drilling down on the DATA disk group we see the screen in Figure 3.17.

Figure 3.17 *EM Grid Control ASM Disk Group Members*

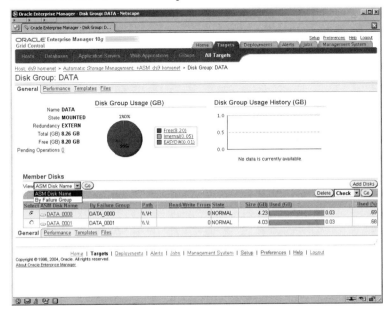

This screen shows more information about the individual disks that make up the disk group, their path on the server, status, and their capacity and free space. It is a nice and comprehensive way to show you information at a glance about your disk group members.

The final screen in our quick tour of ASM via Enterprise Manager is that shown in Figure 3.18, which shows the hierarchical contents of the disk group. Here you can expand the hierarchy to see the databases using the disk group, their folders, and the files that they have created. This screen also shows that the ASM is as much about implementing a file system on the disk groups as it is about the mirroring and striping of the underlying disks.

Figure 3.18 *EM Grid Control ASM Disk Group Files*

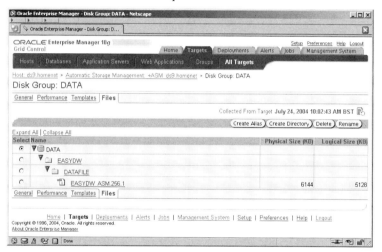

You can see that Enterprise Manager supports the easy configuration of the ASM parameters, and its clear, logical screens allow you to traverse and examine the ASM information with ease. You can drill up and down the hierarchies of ASM information from the instance, to the disk group, to the disks, and to the actual database files in the file system on the disk group in order to fully appreciate the structure of your storage.

In this section, we have only touched upon ASM to demonstrate its power and ease of use. The important question is how is it used to help us in our data warehouse, and this is what we are going to look at in the next section.

3.4.3 Using ASM in the Warehouse

Now that we understand what ASM is, how does ASM help us in our data warehouse physical architecture? Well, we can define different groups for the different major areas of our warehouse:

- Staging
- Warehouse data
- Warehouse indexes
- Summary data and indexes
- Flash recovery disk area (for backup and recovery files, which must be distinct from the disk areas for the database data, control, or on-line redo log files)
- Temporary tablespace (for sorting)
- UNDO
- Redo logs and archived redo logs

One of the challenges in the data warehouse is determining what the appropriate solution is for each of these areas. For example, staging is where data is loaded from disk files and cleansed and transformed prior to loading into the warehouse tables. Within staging we may not necessarily require mirroring, because if a disk fails then the data on it can always be recovered from the source data files and reloaded. However, for the warehouse data, we will want it to be mirrored (and striped) in order to protect the data that we have expended a lot of time and resources on getting into the warehouse. In addition, following the guidelines for having disks with the same characteristics in the same disk group and not mixing and matching, it may be preferable to have the faster disks for the high I/O files (e.g., TEMP or UNDO); other disks for the warehouse, index, or summary disk groups; and the slower disks in the flash recovery disk group.

However, recall our earlier discussion on RAID and the existing Oracle recommendation for the SAME method, which stands for Stripe And Mirror Everything. In many ways ASM is an extension to the SAME concept in that it is a transparent division of our Oracle data into 1M blocks, which are automatically distributed and balanced across all disks in the group. The reasoning behind SAME holds true for ASM, and we should be defining one disk group into which we place all of our disks; this disk group contains all of our database files. You may ask, in that case, why we need multiple disk groups if we are only going to use one. Recall that an ASM instance on a server manages the disk and disk groups for all database instances on that server, and using multiple disk groups can help to segregate and manage those disks that are specific to each of our database instances.

An exception to the rule about striping and mirroring everything in one disk group would be the placement of the flash recovery area. The flash recovery area can reside on ASM disk groups (as an alternative to the normal file system), and, in order to protect our warehouse, these must be on a disk group separate those used by the warehouse. This is an additional and sensible precaution to avoid any possibility of disk failure losing the main warehouse data and the backup files. This is discussed further in Chapter 12.

An important consideration when using ASM is that the ASM file system only manages Oracle database files. If your data warehouse receives files from external sources, such as a flat file from another database or application that is not integrated with the warehouse, these will need to be managed via another solution, such as traditionally by the operating system.

Finally, note that the use of ASM to protect your disks via mirroring does not remove the need for a carefully designed backup strategy and plan. An individual disk may fail and be recoverable because of mirroring, but if a disaster befell the entire data center—for example, fire or flood—then you will need to have a proper backup and recovery strategy in place in order to restore your warehouse onto another server environment.

3.5   File Management in Oracle

With ASM, Oracle manages the disks, but to complete the process of aiding our DBA to manage the many different types of files typically found in a data warehouse, we also need a better way to manage the files themselves.

3.5.1   Oracle Managed Files

With Oracle Managed Files (OMF), the database server takes on the management of the individual datafiles comprise the database; this removes a considerable burden from the DBA. This is particularly true in a very large, complex warehouse environment, which may have many hundreds of files. In reality, OMF is not a true architectural consideration but a managerial feature to aid the DBA; however, in many ways the path to ASM started with OMF, so we are going to discuss OMF briefly in this chapter.

To use OMF there are a small number of initialization parameters that specify the default location of the files that you want Oracle to manage.

Initilization Parameter	Brief Description
DB_CREATE_FILE_DEST	The default file location for database datafiles
DB_CREATE_ONLINE_LOG_DEST_n	The default file location for database redo logs and control files.
DB_RECOVERY_FILE_DEST	The default file location for database RMAN backups

If you perform a database operation that creates a file—for example, creating a tablespace—but do not specify a file name and location, then Oracle will use the parameter relevant to the operation and create the file. It is now an Oracle Managed File.

For example, try a simple test: Identify where your database files are currently residing and add a subdirectory "omf_test." Then from SQL*Plus alter the value of the DB_CREATE_FILE_DEST to use that subdirectory:

```
ALTER SESSION SET db_create_file_dest
            = 'f:\oracle\product\10.1.0\oradata\easydw\test';
```

Now create a test tablespace:

```
CREATE TABLESPACE omf_test DATAFILE SIZE 1m;
```

Within your new TEST directory, you should now have the subdirectory "EASYDW/datafile" (where EASYDW will be the unique name of your database) and within this directory a new datafile—for example, o1_mf_omf_test_05r8ggy9_.dbf. The string "05r8ggy9" is, in fact, a unique eight-character string generated by Oracle; it ensures that no two files will have the same name.

If, at some point in the future, this datafile has to be removed from the database, then when the tablespace is removed from the database the datafiles are removed from the server as well. To demonstrate this, now drop the tablespace from within SQL*Plus and this new datafile is automatically removed by the database server.

```
DROP TABLESPACE omf_test;
```

Other database operations (such as "ALTER DATABASE ADD LOG-FILE") will use the other OMF initialization parameters in a similar manner.

OMF is a very useful and powerful aid to the DBA. At the very least, this automatic removal prevents unneeded, old files from proliferating on your file system: it definitely helps to ensure that any manual removal, that would otherwise be necessary, doesn't inadvertently remove a wrong file that is still actually being used by the database! As a bonus, Oracle will also tidy up any partially created files, which may result from an operation that errored; so with OMF you should never be in doubt as to the validity and use of the Oracle datafiles found on your file system.

3.5.2   Bigfiles and Big Databases

Some data warehouses use terabytes of storage, and this means that the database will consist of some very large datafiles. On many systems the sizes of these files can be limited, and that results in a larger number of smaller files, which consequently necessitate careful management. However, on operating systems that support large files, Oracle is able to offer the facility to use them in the database and replace the many files with a significantly smaller number of much larger files.

Bigfile tablespaces are exactly that: tablespaces with a single, very large datafile. A bigfile tablespace using 8K-sized blocks can have up to a 32 terabyte datafile; if 32K block sizes are used, then this increases to a datafile size of 128 terabytes. Since the database can have up to 65,536 datafiles then the database size supported by Oracle Database 10*g* is extremely large at 8 exabytes. Bigfile tablespaces are intended to be used with locally managed tablespaces (which track space usage information in the tablespace rather than in the Data Dictionary) and with ASM (to handle the underlying mirroring and striping). Large files must obviously be supported on your underlying operating system for bigfiles to be used.

A bigfile tablespace is created simply by including the keyword bigfile in the create tablespace command:

```
CREATE BIGFILE TABLESPACE data_ts SIZE 20G;
```

Bigfile tablespaces can be resized and set to autoextend, as per normal, but now this is done by controlling the tablespace and not the datafile—for example:

```
ALTER TABLESPACE data_ts AUTOEXTEND ON;
```

3.6   Summary

In this chapter, we have looked at the range of architectures available for our data warehouse and provided information to help you decide which is the one that is most appropriate for your business. At the hardware level, you should now have an appreciation of the storage issues and options available both inside and outside of the data warehouse. Within the database, you should now also be familiar with Oracle features to aid in the administration and use of these storage options.

A well-designed warehouse, making proper use of these features, can deliver excellent query performance for large amounts of data. In the next chapter, we will discuss the physical database design of the various schema objects and how these make use of the underlying technical architecture.

4

Physical Design of the Data Warehouse

4.1 Introduction

In the previous chapters, we discussed the high-level architecture of a data warehouse and logical design concepts such as dimensional modeling. We also gave an overview of creating the database and all the different structures you will encounter in designing your database. Due to the large volumes of data handled by a data warehouse, it is important to have a physical design that supports both efficient data access and efficient data storage. In this chapter, we will discuss various techniques for physical design, such as partitioning and indexing, to improve the data access performance in a data warehouse. We will also discuss data compression, which can help reduce the storage requirements in a data warehouse.

4.2 Data Partitioning

We will begin this chapter by discussing data partitioning, a technique you are very likely to use in your data warehouse, especially as the size of the data grows, because it simplifies data maintenance and can improve query performance.

Whenever any task seems daunting, breaking it up into smaller pieces often makes it easier to accomplish. Imagine packing up your house and getting ready to move: dividing it up room by room would make it easier. If each member of the family packs a room at the same time, you could get the entire house packed faster. This is the idea behind partitioning: It is a "divide and conquer approach." Database objects, such as tables, indexes and materialized views can be divided into smaller, more manageable partitions.

A significant benefit of partitioning the data is that it makes it possible for data maintenance operations to be performed at the partition level.

Many maintenance operations, such as loading data, building indexes, gathering optimizer statistics, purging data, and backup and recovery can be done at the granularity of a partition rather than involving the entire table or index.

Another benefit of partitioning a table is that it can improve performance of queries against that table. If a table is partitioned, the query optimizer can determine if a certain query can be answered by reading only specific partitions. Thus, an expensive full table scan can be avoided. This feature is known as **Partition Elimination** or **Dynamic Partition Pruning**. For example, if a sales fact table were partitioned by month, and a query asked for sales from December 1998, the optimizer would know which partition the data was stored in and would just read data from that partition. All other partitions would be eliminated from its search. Partition pruning in conjunction with other query execution techniques, such as partition-wise join and parallel execution, discussed in Chapter 6, can dramatically improve response time of queries in a data warehouse.

Finally, partitioning can also improve the availability of the data warehouse. For example, by placing each partition on its own disk, if one disk fails and is no longer accessible, only the data in that partition is unavailable and not the entire table. In this situation, Oracle can still process queries that continue to access just the available disks; only those queries that access the failed disk will give an error. Similarly, while maintenance operations are being performed on one partition, users can continue to access data from the other partitions in the table.

4.2.1 How to Partition Data?

Partitioning should be considered for large tables, over 2GB in size. Partitioning is also useful for tables that have mostly read-only historical data. A common example is a fact table containing a year's worth of data, where only the last partition has data that can change and the other partitions are read-only.

A table can be partitioned using a column called the **partition key**, whose value determines the partition into which a row of data will be placed. In general, any column of numeric, character, or date data type can be used as a partition key; however, you cannot partition a table by a LONG or LOB column.

All partitions of a table or index have the same logical attributes, such as columns and constraints, but can have different physical attributes, such as the tablespace they are stored in.

Oracle Database 10g provides several methods to partition your tables:

- By ranges of data values (range partitioning)
- By via a hash function (hash partitioning)
- By specifying discrete values for each partition (list partitioning)
- By using a combination of these methods (composite partitioning)

We will now discuss each of these in detail.

4.2.2   Range Partitioning

One of the most frequently used partitioning methods is range partitioning, where data is partitioned into nonoverlapping ranges of data. In range partitioning, each partition is defined by specifying the upper bound on the values that the partition-key column can contain. As each row gets inserted into the table, it is placed into the appropriate partition based on the value of the partition key column. Range partitioning is especially suitable when the partition-key is continuous, such as time. It allows the optimizer to perform partition pruning for queries asking for a specific value or a range of partition-key values.

Figure 4.1 shows a table partitioned by range, using the TIME_KEY as the partition key. Each partition has data for one month and is stored in its own tablespace.

Figure 4.1   *Range Partitioning by MONTH*

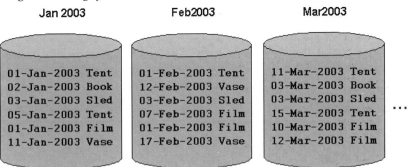

The SQL that would create this partitioned table is shown in the following code. The VALUES LESS THAN clause specifies the upper bound on the partition-key values in that partition. The lower bound is specified by the VALUES LESS THAN clause of the previous partition, if any. In our example, the purchases_feb_2003 partition has data values with time_key >= '01-FEB-2003' and < '01-MAR-2003'.

```
CREATE TABLE easydw.purchases
(product_id              varchar2(8),
 time_key                date,
 customer_id             varchar2(10),
 purchase_date           date,
 purchase_time           number(4,0),
 purchase_price          number(6,2),
 shipping_charge         number(5,2),
 today_special_offer     varchar2(1))
PARTITION by RANGE (time_key)
 (partition purchases_jan2003
     values less than (TO_DATE('01-FEB-2003', 'DD-MON-YYYY'))
     tablespace purchases_jan2003,
  partition purchases_feb2003
     values less than (TO_DATE('01-MAR-2003', 'DD-MON-YYYY'))
     tablespace purchases_feb2003,
  partition purchases_mar2003
     values less than (TO_DATE('01-APR-2003', 'DD-MON-YYYY'))
     tablespace purchases_mar2003,
  partition purchase_catchall
     values less than (MAXVALUE)
     tablespace purchases_maxvalue);
```

Notice that the last partition in the PURCHASES table has a special bound called MAXVALUE. This is an optional catchall partition, which collects all rows that do not correspond to any defined partition ranges.

4.2.3 Hash Partitioning

With range partitioning, it is possible to end up with a situation where the data is not evenly divided among the partitions. Some partitions may be very large and others small. For example, if the data was partitioned by month and some months experience peak sales (e.g., December due to Christmas), then this would result in partitions that are very different in size. When the data is skewed in this way, "hot spots" form where there is contention for resources in one area.

Hash partitioning reduces this type of data skew by applying a hashing function to the partitioning key. The resulting output value is used to determine which partition to store the row in. So instead of partitioning by MONTH, if we hash partition the PURCHASES table by PRODUCT_ID, all rows for a month would get scattered across several partitions, as shown in Figure 4.2, resulting in more evenly sized partitions.

Figure 4.2   *Hash Partitioning by Product*

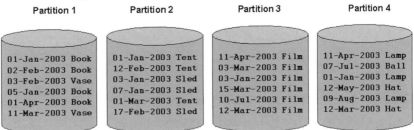

Notice that all products with the same PRODUCT_ID fall into the same partition however, the user has no control or knowledge of which products go into which partitions. You can only specify *how many* partitions you would like.

Hint: To avoid data skew it is recommended that the number of hash partitions be a power of 2.

In the following code, we illustrate the SQL required to create a hash-partitioned table with four partitions using the PRODUCT_ID column as the partitioning key.

```
CREATE TABLE easydw.purchases
 (product_id          varchar2(8),
  time_key            date,
  customer_id         varchar2(10),
  purchase_date       date,
  purchase_time       number(4,0),
  purchase_price      number(6,2),
  shipping_charge     number(5,2),
  today_special_offer varchar2(1))
PARTITION BY HASH(product_id)
PARTITIONS 4;
```

With hash partitioning, the optimizer can perform partition pruning if the query is asking for a specific value or values of the partition key. For example, if we had a query based on a specific product, such as "How many tents did we sell each month?" the optimizer could determine which partition to look in to find "Tents." However, if we had a query that asked for a range of product ids, we would need to search all partitions.

Because hash partitioning reduces contention on the table, you may find hash partitioning used in OLTP systems. However, recall that there is no logical correlation between the partition and the values stored in it. In a data warehouse maintenance operations often require knowledge of the data values, such as deleting or archiving old data from the table. Hence, in a data warehouse, hash partitioning is seldom used alone but instead is used in conjunction with range partitioning. This technique is known as Composite Partitioning and is discussed in section 4.2.5.

4.2.4   List Partitioning

In some cases, it may not be convenient to organize data into ranges of values. The data may not have a natural partitioning key such as time. For business reasons, values that are far apart may need to be grouped together. For instance, if we have sales data for the states of the United States, it is not very easy to put data for all states in a given region, such as the Northeast, into the same partition using range or hash partitioning. The partitioning technique to solve this problem is List Partitioning, which allows data to be distributed according to discrete column values. Figure 4.3 shows an example of a list-partitioned table by discrete values of states.

Figure 4.3   *List Partitioning by State*

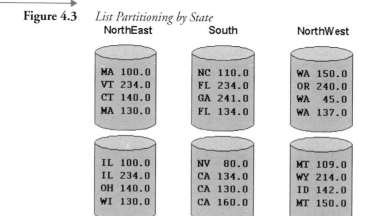

The following SQL statement uses list partitioning to organize the sales data by region. The last partition, which uses the keyword DEFAULT, is a catchall partition that captures the rows that do not map to any other partition.

```
CREATE TABLE easydw.regional_sales
(state                   varchar2(2),
 store_number            number,
 dept_number             number,
 dept_name               varchar2(10),
 sales_amount            number (6,2)
)
PARTITION BY LIST(state)
(
  PARTITION northeast    VALUES ('NH', 'VT', 'MA', 'RI', 'CT'),
  PARTITION southeast    VALUES ('NC', 'GA', 'FL'),
  PARTITION northwest    VALUES ('WA', 'OR'),
  PARTITION midwest      VALUES ('IL', 'WI', 'OH'),
  PARTITION west         VALUES ('CA', 'NV', 'AZ'),
  PARTITION otherstates VALUES (DEFAULT));
```

List partitioning allows the query optimizer to perform partition pruning on queries that ask for specific values of the partitioning key. For instance, a query requesting data for Massachusetts (MA) or New Hampshire (NH) only needs to access the Northeast partition.

4.2.5 Composite Partitioning

Oracle provides a two-level partitioning scheme known as composite partitioning to combine the benefits of two partitioning methods. In composite partitioning, data is divided into partitions using one partitioning scheme and then each of those partitions is further subdivided into subpartitions using another scheme. Currently, Oracle supports the following two types of composite partitioning schemes:

- Range-Hash

- Range-List

Range-Hash Partitioning

We mentioned earlier that hash partitioning does not allow a user control over the distribution of data. On the other hand, range partitioning suffers from the potential problem of data skew. Range-Hash composite partitioning combines the benefits of both range and hash partitioning. The data is first partitioned by range and then further subdivided into subpartitions by using a hash function. When partitioning by date, the last partition is often a "hot spot." Subpartitioning can eliminate such hot spots by placing each subpartition on different tablespaces and on different physical devices if required, thereby reducing the I/O contention.

In Figure 4.4, the data is first partitioned by the month and then further partitioned by the product. Each partition has four subpartitions.

Figure 4.4   *Range-Hash Composite Partitioning*

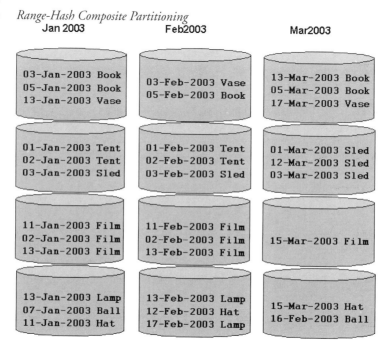

The SQL to create a composite partitioned table is shown in the following code. The STORE IN clause allows you to name the tablespace where each subpartition will reside. Each subpartition has been stored in its own tablespace.

```
CREATE TABLE easydw.purchases
  (product_id              varchar2(8),
   time_key                date,
   customer_id             varchar2(10),
   purchase_date           date,
   purchase_time           number(4,0),
   purchase_price          number(6,2),
   shipping_charge         number(5,2),
```

```
        today_special_offer            varchar2(1))
PARTITION by RANGE (time_key)
SUBPARTITION BY HASH(product_id)
SUBPARTITIONS 4
   (partition purchases_jan2003
     values less than (TO_DATE('01-FEB-2003', 'DD-MON-YYYY'))
        STORE IN (purchases_jan2003_1,
                   purchases_jan2003_2,
                   purchases_jan2003_3,
                   purchases_jan2003_4),
    partition purchases_feb2003
     values less than (TO_DATE('01-MAR-2003', 'DD-MON-YYYY'))
        STORE IN (purchases_feb2003_1,
                   purchases_feb2003_2,
                   purchases_feb2003_3,
                   purchases_feb2003_4),
    partition purchases_mar2003
     values less than (TO_DATE('01-APR-2003', 'DD-MON-YYYY'))
        STORE IN (purchases_mar2003_1,
                   purchases_mar2003_2,
                   purchases_mar2003_3,
                   purchases_mar2003_4));
```

To avoid data skew it is recommended that the number of hash subpartitions be a power of 2.

Range-List Partitioning

The Range-List composite partitioning method first range-partitions a table by a continuous key, such as time_key, and then subpartitions each partition with discrete values, such as states. In the following example, we have a SALES table range partitioned by MONTH and further list-partitioned by STATE. A query that asks for sales for dates for the month of January for the states in the Northeast region of the United States can be evaluated efficiently if the sales table is partitioned using Range-List partitioning.

```
CREATE TABLE sales
(state                  varchar2(2),
 store_number           number,
 dept_number            number,
 dept_name              varchar2(10),
 sales_amount           number (6,2),
 sale_date              date,
 item_number            number (10)
)
PARTITION BY RANGE (sale_date)
SUBPARTITION BY LIST(state)
SUBPARTITION TEMPLATE
```

```
(
SUBPARTITION "NorthEast"
   VALUES ('NH', 'VT', 'MA', 'RI', 'CT')
   TABLESPACE sales_ne,
SUBPARTITION "SouthEast"
   VALUES ('NC', 'GA', 'FL')
   TABLESPACE sales_se,
SUBPARTITION "NorthWest"
   VALUES ('WA', 'OR')
   TABLESPACE sales_nw,
SUBPARTITION "MidWest"
   VALUES ('IL', 'WI', 'OH')
   TABLESPACE sales_mw,
SUBPARTITION "West"
   VALUES ('CA', 'NV', 'AZ')
   TABLESPACE sales_w)
(PARTITION sales_jan_2003
   VALUES LESS THAN (TO_DATE('01-FEB-2003', 'DD-MON-YYYY')),
 PARTITION sales_feb_2003
   VALUES LESS THAN (TO_DATE('01-MAR-2003', 'DD-MON-YYYY')),
 PARTITION sales_mar_2003
   VALUES LESS THAN (TO_DATE('01-APR-2003', 'DD-MON-YYYY')));
```

In this example, we show the use of the SUBPARTITION TEMPLATE clause. The specification of Range-List partitioning can get quite verbose, since you have to specify the detailed subpartition clause for each range partition. It is common to have the same list subpartitioning within each of your range partitions. In such cases, the SUBPARTITION TEMPLATE makes it convenient to specify the same subpartition information for all range partitions in the table. Oracle will generate the subpartition name using a combination of the partition name and the name specified in the template. It then generates the subpartitions according to the definition in the template.

Hint: The SUBPARTITION TEMPLATE clause can also be used when defining Range-Hash partitioning.

The partition and subpartition information for a table can be obtained from the USER_TAB_PARTITIONS and USER_TAB_SUBPARTITIONS dictionary views. For our example, the partition and subpartition names are as follows:

```
SELECT partition_name, subpartition_name
FROM user_tab_subpartitions
WHERE table_name = 'SALES';
```

```
PARTITION_NAME                      SUBPARTITION_NAME
----------------------------------  ------------------------------
SALES_JAN_2003                      SALES_JAN_2003_NorthEast
SALES_JAN_2003                      SALES_JAN_2003_SouthEast
SALES_JAN_2003                      SALES_JAN_2003_NorthWest
SALES_JAN_2003                      SALES_JAN_2003_MidWest
SALES_JAN_2003                      SALES_JAN_2003_West
SALES_FEB_2003                      SALES_FEB_2003_NorthEast
SALES_FEB_2003                      SALES_FEB_2003_SouthEast
SALES_FEB_2003                      SALES_FEB_2003_NorthWest
SALES_FEB_2003                      SALES_FEB_2003_MidWest
SALES_FEB_2003                      SALES_FEB_2003_West
...
```

You can choose not to use the SUBPARTITION TEMPLATE but instead explicitly specify the list subpartition values and names for each range partition.

4.2.6 Multicolumn Partition Keys

A partition key used for range or hash partitioning can have multiple (up to 16) columns. Multicolumn partitioning should be used when the partitioning key is composed of several columns and subsequent columns define a finer granularity than the preceding ones. We will illustrate this with an example using range partitioning.

The following SQL creates a table with range partitioning using a multicolumn partitioning key, TIME_KEY, PRODUCT_ID.

```
CREATE TABLE easydw.purchases
(product_id                 varchar2(8),
 time_key                   date,
 customer_id                varchar2(10),
 purchase_date              date,
 purchase_time              number(4,0),
 purchase_price             number(6,2),
 shipping_charge            number(5,2),
 today_special_offer        varchar2(1))
PARTITION by RANGE (time_key, product_id)
 (
  partition purchases_jan2003_100
    values less than (TO_DATE('31-JAN-2003','DD-MON-YYYY'), 100)
    tablespace purchases_jan2003_100,
  partition purchases_jan2003_200
    values less than (TO_DATE('31-JAN-2003','DD-MON-YYYY'), 200)
    tablespace purchases_jan2003_200 ,
```

```
partition purchases_feb2003_all
  values less than (TO_DATE('28-FEB-2003','DD-MON-YYYY'), 100)
  tablespace purchases_feb2003,
partition purchases_mar2003_all
  values less than (TO_DATE('31-MAR-2003','DD-MON-YYYY'), 100)
  tablespace purchases_mar2003
);
```

To understand how data gets mapped to partitions, let us now insert some data values into this table and see which partitions they go into.

```
insert into purchases (product_id, time_key)
     values (1, TO_DATE('15-JAN-2003', 'DD-MON-YYYY'));

insert into purchases (product_id, time_key)
     values (150, TO_DATE('15-JAN-2003', 'DD-MON-YYYY'));

insert into purchases (product_id, time_key)
     values (101, TO_DATE('31-JAN-2003', 'DD-MON-YYYY'));
```

The first row obviously goes into the first partition. Intuitively, you would expect that the second row with TIME_KEY = 15-JAN-2003 and PRODUCT_ID = 150 would go into the second partition. However, this is not the case. Let us issue the following query, which shows all the rows that belong to the first partition. (Note the special PARTITION syntax, which allows you to query data from a specific partition by specifying the partition name.)

```
SELECT product_id, time_key
FROM purchases partition(purchases_jan2003_100);

PRODUCT_ID  TIME_KEY
----------  -----------
1           15-JAN-2003
150         15-JAN-2003
```

What we find is that the row is actually in the first partition! The reason for this is that the condition checked for the first partition is in fact the following:

```
  (TIME_KEY < '31-JAN-2003')
OR (TIME_KEY = '31-JAN-2003' AND PRODUCT_ID < 100).
```

In other words, the condition on the second column is checked only if the value of the first column is *equal to* the partition bound. Therefore, in our example, the row with TIME_KEY = '15-JAN-2003' actually falls into the first partition. On the other hand, the third row, which has TIME_KEY = '31-JAN-2003' and PRODUCT_ID = 101, does not satisfy the condition for the first partition. It will go into the second partition, as shown by the following query:

```
SELECT product_id, time_key
FROM purchases partition(purchases_jan2003_200);

PRODUCT_ID   TIME_KEY
----------   -----------
101          31-JAN-2003
```

This is because the condition for the second partition is:

```
(time_key = '31-JAN-2003' and product_id < 200)
```

Multikey range partitioning can be useful if you have one TIME_KEY value with lots of PRODUCT_ID values (e.g. lot of purchases may be made on Christmas eve). In this case, you can use the second column to distribute the data for the specific TIME_KEY value into multiple partitions.

Range partitioning with a multicolumn partition key must not be confused with Range-Range composite partitioning. As of the time of writing, Oracle does not support Range-Range composite partitioning. If it were supported, the row with TIME_KEY = 15-JAN-2003 and PRODUCT_ID = 150 would have mapped to the second partition in the previous example.

Now that we know all the partitioning methods, let us briefly review how you would go about choosing the partitioning method.

4.2.7 Choosing the Partitioning Method

Range partitioning should be used when your table has a continuous key, such as time. List partitioning is ideal for tables where you would like to place specific discrete values in one partition. Hash partitioning distributes data uniformly among all partitions and may be used alone or in combination with Range partitioning to avoid hot spots in the table. Finally, Range-List partitioning can be used when the table stores data along multiple dimensions, one continuous—for example, time—and the other discrete—for example, product or geography.

It is important to partition the data by a column that is not likely to change. Consider if partitioning were done by PRODUCT_ID and the business frequently changed the encoding scheme for its products. Every time this change occurred, data would need to be moved to a different partition, which can be a time-consuming operation.

In a data warehouse, it is a very common practice to partition by time. For example, in EASYDW, we have range partitioned the PURCHASES table by time_key, with each partition containing one month's worth of data. Partitioning by time allows us to perform a maintenance operation called a **rolling window** operation. This is a technique whereby the partitioned table has a fixed number of partitions, each residing in its own tablespace; as one set of partitioned data is aged out of the warehouse, this frees a tablespace, which can be used to house the forthcoming partition of data just being added. For example, assuming the PURCHASES table contained one year's worth of data, at the end of April 2004 we could add a new partition with that month's data and delete the data for April 2003. Chapter 11 will discuss this technique for data maintenance in more detail.

Next, we will look at Oracle Enterprise Manager, which provides simple wizards to create partitioned tables.

4.2.8   **Partitioning Using Oracle Enterprise Manager**

In Chapter 2, we discussed the basic user interface to create a table, which is available from the *Administration* page of Oracle Enterprise Manager. The create table interface has several tabs, which allow you to define the column names, storage options, and constraints, which we have already discussed in Chapter 2. In this section, we will take a look at the *Partitions* tab, shown in Figure 4.5.

Figure 4.5   *Create Table: Partitions*

When you first get to this page, you will see a *Create* button, which, when clicked, will take you to the *Create Partitions* screen shown in Figure 4.6. Here you can choose the partitioning method: Range, Hash, List, Range-Hash, or Range-List. In our example, we have chosen range partitioning.

Figure 4.6   *Choosing the Partitioning Method*

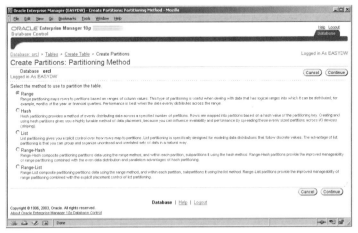

The next step is to choose the partitioning column (or possibly multiple columns for range partitioning). You will be shown a list of all the table columns and a box for each, under the heading *Order*. For those columns that you want to include in the partitioning key, you must enter their desired position in the box. For instance, if we wanted to partition by PRODUCT_ID, TIME_KEY, we would put a 1 in the Order box for PRODUCT_ID and 2 for TIME_KEY. In Figure 4.7, we have chosen to partition by TIME_KEY.

Figure 4.7   *Specifying the Partitioning Key*

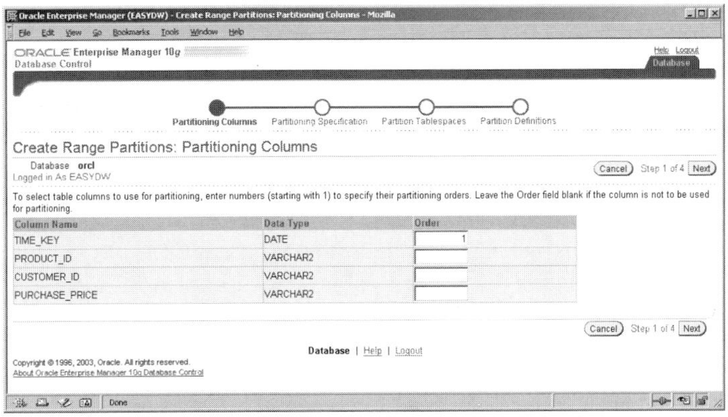

For range partitioning using a single column partition key of date or numeric type, this wizard provides a way to automatically generate the partition bounds. You need only to specify the desired number of partitions, the minimum value of the column, and the desired range of values in each partition. For instance, in Figure 4.8, we have specified that we would like five partitions with the earliest TIME_KEY value being 1/1/2003 and each partition containing one month of data. Later, you will be given a chance to edit the partition bounds and tablespaces; however, this is a very convenient starting point.

Figure 4.8   *Automatically Generating Range Partition Bounds*

The next screen (not shown here) asks you to pick tablespaces for the partitions. You can either specify a common tablespace for all partitions or a list of tablespaces, which will be used in a round-robin fashion for the partitions.

The final screen, shown in Figure 4.9, shows the automatically generated partitions. Now you can edit partition names, bounds, and tablespaces. You can also insert additional partitions or delete partitions.

Further, for each partition, you can click the *Advanced Options* button, which will bring you to the screen shown in Figure 4.10. Here you can specify all the storage parameters and also indicate whether you would like to turn on data segment compression, which we discussed previously. You can also specify whether you would like to use the NOLOGGING option, which will turn off redo logging during maintenance operations on that

Figure 4.9 *Editing Partition Definitions*

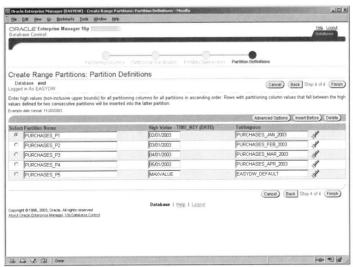

partition; this can significantly improve performance. However, with the NOLOGGING option you can no longer recover the data after a database crash, so you must ensure that you have adequate backups of the data.

Figure 4.10 *Specifying Advanced Storage Options for a Partition*

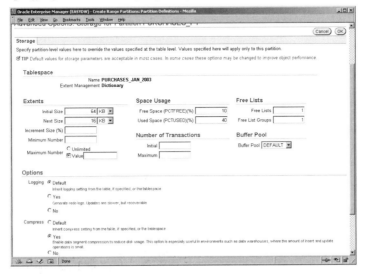

If you chose any other partitioning method, the overall flow would be very similar to what we have seen, except that you will not be able to generate partitioning bounds automatically. You must enter the bounds manually in the final screen. For instance, Figure 4.11 shows a table using list partitioning.

Figure 4.11 *List Partitioning*

4.2.9 **Partition Maintenance Operations**

We mentioned earlier that partitioning simplifies data management in a data warehouse. This is because you can manipulate partitions in various ways to add, delete and reorganize data within the table more quickly than performing individual INSERT or DELETE statements. Some of the operations you can perform with partitions are as follows:

- ADD PARTITION to add a new empty partition to a table
- DROP PARTITION to drop an entire partition for range or list partitioning
- TRUNCATE PARTITION to quickly remove the contents of the partition without dropping it
- MOVE PARTITION to change the tablespace or other physical attributes of a partition
- SPLIT PARTITION to split one partition into two at a specified boundary

- MERGE PARTITION to merge two partitions into one

- EXCHANGE PARTITION to interchange the contents of a partition with those of a table

- COALESCE PARTITION to reduce the number of hash partitions

For composite partitions, similar operations are available at the subpartition level also. These operations are available using the ALTER TABLE SQL command. For example, to add a new partition to the PURCHASES table, you would issue the following SQL:

```
ALTER TABLE purchases ADD PARTITION purchases_jan2005
values less than (TO_DATE('01-JAN-2005', 'DD-MON-YYYY'));
```

Using combinations of partition maintenance operations, you can speed up loading new data and archiving old data in a data warehouse. We will discuss various techniques using partition maintenance operations in Chapter 11.

In this section, we have seen how use of partitioning provides great benefits in a warehouse by improving query performance, manageability, and availability of the data. Next we will discuss techniques for indexing a data warehouse and how partitioning can be applied to indexes.

4.3 Indexing

Indexing has always been a very important technique for efficient query processing in database systems. Unlike OLTP systems, which have mostly update activity, data warehouses tend to read large amounts of data to answer queries. Hence, it is important to understand the indexing needs of a warehouse.

Deciding which indexes to create is an important part of the physical design of a database. Indexes should be built on columns that are often part of the selection criteria of a query. Columns that are frequently referenced in the SQL WHERE clause are good candidates for indexing. Most decision support queries require specific rows from a dimension table, and so it is important to have good indexing on the dimension tables.

For example, suppose we want to know how many customers we have in the Northeast region, as shown in the following query. An index built on the column REGION could be used to locate just those rows in the Northeast rather than reading every row in the table.

```
SELECT count(*) FROM customer WHERE region = 'Northeast';
```

An index is generally built on one or more columns of a table. These columns are known as the **index keys**. For each key value, the index contains a pointer to the location of the rows with that key value. Whenever data in the table changes, the index is automatically updated to reflect the changed data.

Oracle offers three types of indexes that are relevant to data warehousing:

- B*tree index
- Bitmap index
- Bitmap join index

4.3.1 B*tree Indexes

B*tree indexes are hierarchical structures that allow a quick search for a row in a table having a particular value of the index keys. A B*tree index stores pointers to rows of the table using **rowids**, which uniquely identify the physical location of rows on disk. There are two varieties of B*tree indexes:

- Unique
- Nonunique

A **unique** index ensures that each row has a distinct value for its key—no duplicates are allowed. A unique index is automatically created when a PRIMARY KEY or UNIQUE constraint is enabled on a table. The following SQL statement creates a unique index on the TIME_KEY column of table TIME:

```
CREATE UNIQUE INDEX TIME_UK ON TIME(time_key);
```

B*tree indexes can also be nonunique. Nonunique indexes improve query performance when a small number of rows are associated with each column value. In the SQL statement for creating an index, if you do not specify the UNIQUE keyword, the index is considered nonunique.

When multiple columns are used together in the WHERE clause, you can build an index on that group of columns. Indexes made up of multiple columns are called composite, multikey, or concatenated indexes. For example, city and state are both needed to differentiate Portland, Maine, from Portland, Oregon. The column that is used most frequently by itself should be specified as the first column in the index. In the example, state should be the leading column, since we can anticipate queries on state alone or city and state used together.

Whenever a row is inserted, deleted, or when the key columns are updated, the index is automatically updated to reflect the change. A B*tree index is designed such that the time required to search any particular value in the index is nearly constant. This design is called a **balanced** index. As new index nodes are created, the B*tree is automatically rebalanced. Index maintenance therefore adds overhead to the DML statement.

A B*tree index is most useful when the index key has many distinct values, each leading to a few rows in the table. For instance, a primary key implies each value of the key corresponds to one row in a table. However, if the index key column has only a few distinct values, then each value would lead to retrieval of large numbers of rows in the table. This provides little, if any, performance benefit. For instance, consider the query: How many women who live in California buy tents? There are only two possible values for the column GENDER. Since not all records with the same gender value may be stored together, finding all the rows corresponding to women may result in a random scan of nearly all data blocks in the table. In this case, a full table scan may be more efficient. Also, for large tables, space requirements for B*tree indexes could become prohibitive.

Bitmapped indexes are designed to solve these problems and hence are more commonly used in a warehouse.

4.3.2 Bitmapped Indexes

Bitmapped indexes are designed to answer queries involving columns with few distinct values but potentially large numbers of rows for each value. The number of distinct values of a column is known as its **cardinality**. Unlike B*tree indexes, which store pointers to rows of the tables using rowids, a bitmapped index stores a bitmap for each distinct value of a column.

The bitmap for each distinct value has as many bits as the number of rows in the table. The bit is set if the corresponding row has that value. Figure 4.12 shows a bitmapped index for the GENDER column (cardinality = 2, distinct values—M and F). Two bitmaps are created one for the value M and one for the value F. In the bitmap for M, all rows with male customers would have their bit set to 1 and all female customers would have their bit set to 0.

Figure 4.12   *Gender Bitmapped Index*

Row	Gender	Male Bitmap	Female Bitmap
1	M	1	0
2	F	0	1
3	M	1	0
4	M	1	0
5	M	1	0
6	F	0	1
7	M	1	0
8	M	1	0
9	F	0	1
10	M	1	0

Bitmapped indexes on two columns of a table can be combined efficiently using the AND and OR Boolean operators. This allows them to be used for queries involving multiple conditions on bitmapped columns of a table. This gives the benefit that you can answer a wide variety of queries with just a few single-column bitmapped indexes.

For instance, suppose we had a CUSTOMER table that contained the customer name, gender, and occupation (teacher, engineer, self-employed, housewife, doctor, etc.). We are looking at a new promotion targeted toward self-employed women and would like to find out the cities to target. This can be expressed as a query:

```
SELECT customer_id, city
FROM customer
WHERE gender = 'F' AND occupation = 'Self-Employed';
```

Figure 4.13 shows the bitmap for the occupation column.

The gender bitmap defined in Figure 4.12 and the occupation bitmap defined in Figure 4.13 can be combined, as shown in Figure 4.14, to quickly determine the rows in the customer table that satisfy this query.

The SQL statement used to create the bitmapped index on the CUSTOMER.GENDER column is as follows:

Figure 4.13   *Occupation Bitmapped Index*

Row	Occupation	Teacher	Engineer	Self-Employed	Housewife
1	Teacher	1	0	0	0
2	Engineer	0	1	0	0
3	Teacher	1	0	0	0
4	Teacher	1	0	0	0
5	Engineer	0	1	0	0
6	Self-Employed	0	0	1	0
7	Self-Employed	0	0	1	0
8	Housewife	0	0	0	1
9	Engineer	0	1	0	0
10	Housewife	0	0	0	1

```
CREATE BITMAP INDEX easydw.customer_gender_index
ON customer(gender) tablespace indx;
```

Bitmapped indexes are automatically compressed and therefore require much less space than a corresponding B*tree index. The space savings can be significant if the number of distinct values of the bitmap is small compared with the number of rows in the table.

Figure 4.14   *Using a Bitmapped Index: How Many Customers Are Self-Employed Women?*

Row	Female	Self-Employed	Result	
1	0	0	0	
2	1	0	0	
3	0	0	0	
4	0	0	0	
5	0	0	0	
6	1	1	1	(Self-Employed Woman)
7	0	1	0	
8	0	0	0	
9	1	0	0	
10	0	0	0	

The main disadvantage of bitmapped indexes is that they are expensive to maintain when the data in the table changes. This is because the bitmaps must be uncompressed, recompressed, and possibly rebuilt. Bitmapped index maintenance is optimized for the common case of loading new data into a warehouse via bulk insert. In this case, existing bitmaps do not need change and are simply extended to include the new rows. In Oracle

Database 10g, enhancements have been done to improve the performance and space utilization of bitmapped indexes even when DML other than bulk loads is done to the tables.

Another difference between B*tree and bitmapped indexes is that if a B*tree index updates a row, it only locks that particular row; however, with bitmapped indexes, a large part of the bitmap may need to be locked. Thus, bitmapped indexes reduce the concurrency in the system, and so bitmapped indexes are not suited for systems with lots of concurrent update activity. High update activity is generally not a characteristic of data warehouses and hence bitmapped indexes are very common there.

4.3.3 Bitmapped Join Indexes

A bitmapped join index is a bitmapped index that is created as the result of a join between a fact table and one or more dimension tables. To illustrate the concept of bitmapped join indexes, consider the following query, that asks the question: How much did women spend in our store?

```
SELECT sum(p.purchase_price)
FROM purchases p, customer c
WHERE p.customer_id = c.customer_id
     AND c.gender = 'F';
```

We could create a bitmapped index on the CUSTOMER.GENDER column, as discussed in the previous section, to find those customers who are women quickly. However, we would still need to compute the join between PURCHASES and CUSTOMERS to find the total purchases made by women.

Instead, if we take the answer to the join and then create a bitmap to identify rows corresponding to purchases made by men and women, we get a bitmapped join index. Figure 4.15 shows the answer to the join between PURCHASES and CUSTOMER table (only first 10 rows are shown).

The bitmapped join index has two bitmaps one for the value male and another for the value female, as shown in Figure 4.16. Each row in the bitmap corresponds to a single row in the PURCHASES table. Thus, we can immediately identify the rows for purchases made by women from the bitmap for value female.

The bitmapped join index on PURCHASES, joined with CUSTOMER, is created using the following SQL statement. The joining tables and their join conditions are specified using the FROM and WHERE

Figure 4.15   *Join on Purchases and Customer Tables*

Row	Customer_id	Gender	Purchase_price
1	AB123456	F	28.01
2	AB123457	F	28.01
3	AB123457	F	28.01
4	AB123457	F	28.01
5	AB123456	F	67.23
6	AB123457	F	67.23
7	AB123458	M	67.23
8	AB123459	M	67.23
9	AB123460	F	67.23
10	AB123461	M	50.71

...

clauses, similar to those in a SELECT statement. The table on which the index is built is specified by the ON clause, as with any other index.

```
CREATE BITMAP INDEX easydw.purchase_cust_index
ON
purchases (customer.gender)
FROM purchases, customer
WHERE purchases.customer_id = customer.customer_id;
```

We can immediately note some differences between a bitmapped index and a bitmapped join index. While a bitmapped index is created on col-

Figure 4.16   *Bitmap Join Index on Purchases and Customer on Customer.gender Column*

Row	Gender	Male Bitmap	Female Bitmap
1	F	0	1
2	F	0	1
3	F	0	1
4	F	0	1
5	F	0	1
6	F	0	1
7	M	1	0
8	M	1	0
9	F	0	1
10	M	1	0

...

umns of a single table, a bitmapped join index is built on the fact table (PURCHASES), but the index columns are from dimension tables (CUSTOMER).

As with a bitmapped index, columns included in a bitmapped join index must be low-cardinality columns. For a bitmapped join index to make sense, the result of the join should have the same number of rows as the fact table on which it is created (in our example, the PURCHASES table). To ensure this, a unique constraint must be present on the dimension table column that joins it to the fact table (in our example, the CUSTOMER.CUSTOMER_ID column).

Bitmapped join indexes put some restrictions on concurrent DML activity on the tables involved in the index, but, again, this is not a major issue for data warehouse applications.

4.3.4 Function-based Indexes

One of the common problems with indexes is that if the query involves a function on the indexed column, then the optimizer will not use the index. To solve this problem, B*tree and bitmapped indexes can be created to include expressions and functions involving table columns, instead of simple such as columns as the index key. Such indexes are known as **function-based** indexes. Function-based indexes are useful when your queries contain a predicate with a function, such as TO_UPPER() or TO_NUMBER(), or an expression such as PURCHASE_PRICE+SHIPPING_CHARGE. To be able to index a function, the function must be deterministic or, in other words, must return the same result every time it is called with the same arguments. For example, the built-in SQL function SYSDATE, which returns the current date, cannot be used, because it gives a different value every time it is invoked.

The following example shows a function-based index on the column PRODUCT_ID and the column CATEGORY, with the UPPER function applied to it to capitalize its contents.

```
CREATE INDEX  prod_category_idx
ON product (product_id, UPPER(category));
```

The function that we use in our index can also be a user-defined PL/SQL function, provided that it has been tagged as DETERMINISTIC, as shown in the following example:

```
CREATE OR REPLACE FUNCTION TAX_RATE(state IN varchar2,
                                    country IN varchar2)
RETURN NUMBER DETERMINISTIC IS
BEGIN
  ...
END;
/
```

This function, TAX_RATE, can now be used in an index, as shown in the following example:

```
CREATE INDEX  customer_tax_idx
ON customer (TAX_RATE(state, country));
```

When creating a bitmapped index with a function, just as with columns, you must ensure that the function has low cardinality or, in other words, a few possible output values; otherwise, a bitmapped index is not very useful. At the time of writing, bitmapped join indexes did not allow functions.

In the next section, we discuss how partitioning can be applied to indexes.

4.3.5 Partitioned Indexes

As with tables, B*tree and bitmapped indexes can also be partitioned. Oracle allows a lot of flexibility in how you can partition B*tree indexes. A B*tree index can be partitioned even if the underlying table is not. Conversely, you can define a nonpartitioned B*tree index on a partitioned table, or partition the index differently than the table. On the other hand, a bitmapped index must be partitioned in the same way as the underlying table.

Partitioned indexes can be of two types:

- Global, where the index partitioning is possibly different from the underlying table

- Local, where the index partitioning must be the same as the underlying table

Global Indexes

A global index cannot be partitioned at all, or, if it is partitioned, it can have a completely partition key different from the table. In a partitioned global index, the keys in an index partition need not correspond to any specific table partition or subpartition. Global indexes can be partitioned using range or hash partitioning methods. However, a partitioned global index must have the partitioning key of the index as the leading column of the index key.

Hint: Any index that is not partitioned is automatically considered a global index.

Figure 4.17 shows a global index, PURCHASE_PRODUCT_INDEX, on the PURCHASES table. Here, the PURCHASES table is partitioned by TIME_KEY, but the index is partitioned by PRODUCT_ID. The leading column of the index is also PRODUCT_ID.

Figure 4.17   *Global Index on Product, Partitioned by product_id*

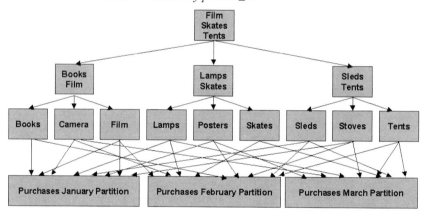

The SQL used to create this index is as follows:

```
CREATE INDEX easydw.purchase_product_index on purchases
 (product_id)
 GLOBAL
 partition by range (product_id)
 (partition sp1000 values less than ('SP1000') ,
  partition sp2000 values less than ('SP2000') ,
  partition other  values less than (maxvalue) );
```

Figure 4.17 shows why global indexes may not be very efficient for query processing. Since there is no correlation between the table and index partitions, accessing a specific value in a table may involve access to several or all of the index partitions. On the other hand, if you would like a unique index, which does not include the partitioning key of the table, you will have no choice but to use a global index.

Another reason why global indexes can be expensive is that when the data in an underlying table partition is moved or removed using a partition maintenance operation (see section 4.2.9), all partitions of a global index are affected, and the index must be completely rebuilt. The shortcomings of a global index are addressed by local indexes.

Local Indexes

Local indexes are the preferred indexes to use when a table is partitioned. A local index inherits its partitioning criteria from the underlying table. It has the same number of partitions, subpartitions, and partition bounds as the table. Because the index is partitioned identically to the table, when a partition maintenance operation is done on the table, the identical operation is also done on the index. Thus, when partitions are added, dropped, split, or merged in the underlying table, the corresponding index partitions are automatically modified by Oracle as part of the same statement. This makes maintenance of the local index extremely efficient, since the entire index does not need to be rebuilt, unlike a global index.

You can define a local index on a table using any of the available methods: range, hash, list, or composite partitioned.

Hint: You cannot define a partitioned bitmapped index unless the underlying table is partitioned. Further, the bitmapped index must be a local index (i.e., must be partitioned identically to the underlying table).

There are two types of local partitioned indexes:

- Prefixed
- Nonprefixed

Prefixed Local Indexes

If the partitioning key of the index appears as a leading column of the index keys, it is called a prefixed index. For example, suppose the PURCHASES table is partitioned by the TIME_KEY and the index columns are (TIME_KEY, CUSTOMER_ID). The partitioning key, TIME_KEY, is a prefix of the index key and hence this is a prefixed index. Figure 4.18 illustrates a prefixed local index.

Figure 4.18   *Prefixed Local Index on time_key*

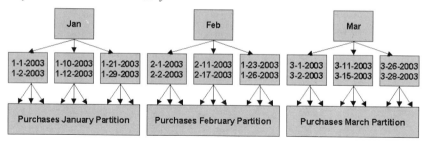

   Here is the SQL required to create this index: Note that the LOCAL keyword must be specified; otherwise, the index will be considered a global index. The local index follows the same partitioning scheme as the table, but you can name the partitions and also the tablespace where each partition resides.

```
CREATE   INDEX easydw.purchase_time_index
 ON purchases (time_key, customer_id)
local
 (partition indexJan2003 tablespace purchases_jan2003_idx,
  partition indexFeb2003 tablespace purchases_feb2003_idx,
  partition indexMar2003 tablespace purchases_mar2003_idx );
```

   With this index, if we wanted to know the purchases made by a certain customer in January, we need only to search the index partition indexJan2003.

Nonprefixed Local Indexes

Local indexes that do not include the partitioning key as the leading column of the index key are known as nonprefixed local indexes. Such indexes are useful when we would like to partition by one column for ease of maintenance but index on other columns for data retrieval. For instance, we may want our indexes and tables to be partitioned by TIME_KEY, so that it is easy to add a new month's data and rebuild the index partition for that month. However, to get good performance for queries for sales by PRODUCT_ID, we need an index on PRODUCT_ID.

   Figure 4.19 shows a local nonprefixed index on the PRODUCT_ID column of the PURCHASES table. The partitioning scheme is the same as that of the PURCHASES table (i.e., on the TIME_KEY column) however,

Figure 4.19 *Nonprefixed Local Index on Product, Partitioned by Month*

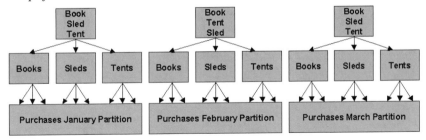

there is a separate search tree on the PRODUCT_ID column, corresponding to each table partition.

The following example shows the SQL to create this local index:

```
CREATE BITMAP INDEX easydw.purchase_product_index
ON purchases   (product_id)
LOCAL
 (partition indexJan2003 tablespace purchases_jan2003_idx,
  partition indexFeb2003 tablespace purchases_feb2003_idx,
  partition indexMar2003 tablespace purchases_mar2003_idx);
```

Note the difference between the local nonprefixed index on PRODUCT_ID, shown in Figure 4.19, and the global index on PRODUCT_ID, shown in Figure 4.17. In the local nonprefixed index, there is a separate search tree for each table partition, and so, when searching for sales of some product—say Tents the optimizer is not able to perform partition elimination and must search for the data for all months. On the other hand, in the global index, there is one common search tree for all the table partitions. Thus, in this case, a global index can in fact provide better performance, because multiple index search trees do not need to be probed. However, when searching for Tents sold in January, the optimizer can indeed eliminate the February and March partitions of the index and so the local index will perform better.

4.3.6 **Which Indexes to Create?**

An index improves performance of a query but is associated with two types of costs: First, it takes up disk space, and, second, it takes time to maintain when the underlying data changes.

Space requirements for indexes in a warehouse are often significantly larger than the space needed to store the data, especially for the fact table and particularly if the indexes are B*trees. Hence, you may want to keep indexing on the fact table to a minimum. Typically, you may have one or two concatenated B*tree indexes on the fact table; however, most of your indexes should be bitmapped indexes. Bitmapped indexes on the foreign-key columns on the fact table are often useful for star query transformation, as discussed later in Chapter 6. Bitmapped indexes also take up much less space than B*tree indexes and so should be preferred. On the other hand, dimension tables are much smaller compared with the fact table and could be indexed much more extensively. Any column of the dimension table that is frequently used in selections or is a level in a dimension object (to be described in Chapter 8) is a good candidate for indexing.

Typical warehouses have low update activity, other than when the warehouse data is refreshed, and usually you would have control over when and how the refresh is performed. Hence, a warehouse can have many more indexes than an OLTP system; however, you must ensure that they fit within the maintenance window you have for your data warehouse. When loading new data, it is often faster to drop indexes and rebuild them completely after the load is complete.

The maintenance window will also dictate whether you use partitioned indexes, which can be faster and easier to maintain.

Deciding between Local and Global Indexes

Local prefixed indexes are the most efficient type of indexes for query performance, since the optimizer can make best use of partition elimination to avoid looking at unnecessary partitions. Local indexes support efficient index maintenance.

Use global indexes when local indexes cannot meet your requirements. One such situation is if you need to create a unique index that does not include the partitioning key of the table. Unique local indexes must include the partitioning key of the table, and so in this case you have to use a global index. Global indexes can also provide better performance than local non-prefixed indexes for some queries, because multiple index search trees do not have to be searched.

Need Help Deciding Which Indexes to Create?

Determining the optimum set of indexes needed in your data warehouse is not an easy task, and you may need to adjust the indexes regularly to meet your application's needs. To help with this, Oracle Database 10g has a new tool called the **SQL Access Advisor**, which will recommend the best set of B*tree and bitmap indexes and materialized views (to be discussed in Chapter 7) to create for your application workload. Materialized views and indexes can go hand in hand in improving performance of queries. Depending on the query, the best choice may be a materialized view or an index, or a combination of both. Because indexes and materialized views both occupy storage and need to be maintained, it is important to strike the right balance between the two types of structures. Otherwise, you may end up with redundant structures, which can be a drain on precious storage and maintenance resources. The SQL Access Advisor is discussed in detail in Chapter 10.

4.3.7 Using Oracle Enterprise Manager to Create Indexes

The wizard to create indexes can also be found in the *Administration* section of Oracle Enterprise Manager. Figure 4.20 shows the first screen of the wizard, where you can create either a bitmapped or B*tree index. Once you have entered the table name, you can click the adjoining *Populate Columns* button to display a list of available columns. You can then indicate the columns you would like to include in the index by specifying their ordinal position in the index key. For example, in Figure 4.20 we are creating an index on (PRODUCT_ID, TIME_KEY) of the PURCHASES table. It is not possible to create a function-based index through this wizard at this time.

Figure 4.20   *Creating an Index*

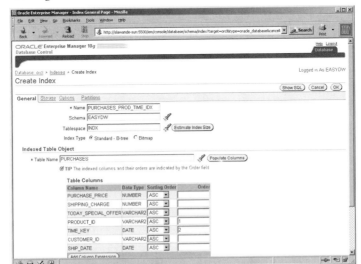

Notice that in Figure 4.20 near the *Tablespace* box there is a button *Estimate Index Size*. If you click this button, Oracle will estimate the storage the index would occupy once created. For this computation to be done, you must have at least specified the index columns. However, if you have specified storage options, such as the tablespace name and the PCTFREE value, you will get a more accurate figure.

If you click on the *Options* tab in Figure 4.20, you will be able to set various index options, as shown in Figure 4.21. These options include whether to build the index in parallel, with the specified degree of parallelism and whether to do index key compression. You can indicate if the data for the index is already sorted, which will speed up creation of the index.

Figure 4.21   *Setting Index Options*

If you are creating a partitioned index, you can define the index partitions by clicking on the *Partitions* tab. You will get the screen shown in Figure 4.22, with the *Enable Partitioning* box unchecked. Once you check this box, you will be able to choose the partitioning method: Local, Global Range, or Global Hash. If you choose local, recall that the partition bounds are identical to that on the underlying table. You can, therefore, either use default partition names and tablespaces (which are same as for the table) or choose *Override Partition Defaults* to edit them, as shown in Figure 4.22.

If you choose global partitioning, you will get the screen shown in Figure 4.23. You must first choose the partitioning key and specify the number of

Figure 4.22 *Partitioning an Index*

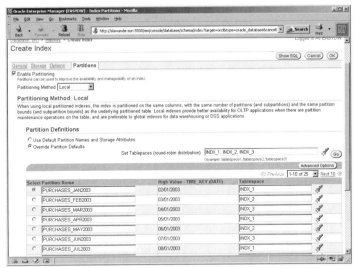

partitions. Once you have done this, click the *Add* button to get a list of partitions with default names. You can then specify the partition bounds (for range partitioning) and edit the partition names and the tablespaces to use.

Figure 4.23 *Global Partitioning*

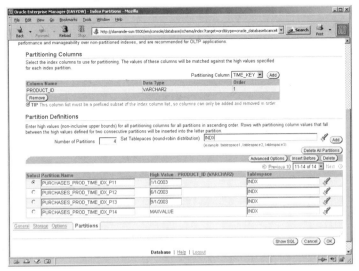

Once you have chosen all the options, you can click *OK* to create the index. The *Show SQL* button can be used to see the SQL statement for the index.

4.4   Index-Organized Tables

An index-organized table (IOT) is an alternative way to store data. An IOT requires that the table have a primary key. In a normal table, known as a **heap-organized** table, the data is stored without maintaining any specific order among rows. If you create a primary-key B*tree index on this table, the index will store the index key columns and store rowids to point to the table rows. Thus, the indexed columns are redundantly stored in both the table and the index. On the other hand, in an **index-organized** table, the table columns that form the primary key are directly stored in a B*tree index structure (i.e., there is no separate table as such). Due to the index, an index-organized table stores data ordered according to the primary key. Because the primary-key columns are not stored redundantly, an index-organized table can save storage space.

Figure 4.24 shows a conceptual picture of a heap-organized table with a primary key and the equivalent index-organized table. In the heap-organized table, the index leaf blocks store rowids, which point to the table rows. In the index-organized table, the index leaf blocks store the table columns, category, and description.

Figure 4.24   *Heap-Organized versus Index-Organized Table*

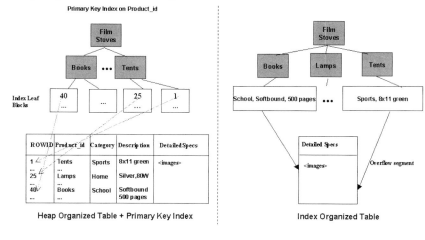

To keep the index to a reasonable size, only columns that are likely to be used for querying should be kept in the index. Columns that are not often used for querying are stored separately in an area known as an **overflow segment**. Access to columns in the overflow segment will be slower. In Figure 4.24, the detailed specs column has been placed in an overflow segment.

4.4.1 Creating an IOT

To create an IOT, you must specify the ORGANIZATION INDEX clause in the create table statement. When creating the index, you can specify the columns to include in the index using the INCLUDING clause. All other columns will be stored in the overflow segment. The following example shows the SQL to create an index-organized table:

```
CREATE TABLE       prodcat
(product_id        number,
 category          varchar2(10),
 description       CLOB,
 detailed_specs    BLOB,
 constraint pk_prodcat PRIMARY KEY(product_id)
)
ORGANIZATION INDEX
INCLUDING category
PCTTHRESHOLD 30
TABLESPACE prodcat_idx
STORAGE (INITIAL 8k NEXT 8k PCTINCREASE 10)
OVERFLOW
STORAGE
(INITIAL 16k NEXT 16k PCTINCREASE 10);
```

The INCLUDING clause indicates that all columns after CATE-GORY—namely, DESCRIPTION and DETAILED_SPECS—should be placed in the overflow segment. Notice that there are two separate storage clauses: one for the index segment and one for the overflow segment. You can also specify a threshold value, known as PCTTHRESHOLD, which indicates the maximum percentage of an index block to use to store non-primary-key index columns. For each row, all columns that fit within the threshold will get stored in the index segment, and the remaining will go into the overflow segment. In this example, the PCTTHRESHOLD value has been set to 30 percent.

Note that if the PCTTHRESHOLD value is not large enough to hold the primary key, or if you have not specified an overflow segment and it is needed, you will get an error.

If you use Oracle Enterprise Manager to create your tables, one of the very first choices you will need to make is whether you would like to create a heap- or index-organized table, as shown in Figure 4.25.

Figure 4.25   *Choosing Table Organization—Heap versus Index*

4.4.2   **Partitioning and Indexing an IOT**

With Oracle 9*i* and 10*g*, IOTs have been significantly enhanced and now support nearly all features that normal tables do. For example, you can partition an IOT with range, hash, and list partitioning. However, at this time, composite partitioning for an IOT is not supported. You can create B*tree and bitmapped indexes on an IOT. These indexes are known as **secondary** indexes and can be partitioned or nonpartitioned.

To create a bitmapped index on an IOT, the IOT must have a mapping table that maps logical rowids to physical ones. You can add a mapping table clause to the CREATE TABLE or add one later, as shown in the following examples:

```
-- create mapping table
ALTER TABLE prodcat MOVE MAPPING TABLE;

-- change mapping table storage options
ALTER TABLE prodcat MAPPING TABLE allocate extent (size 16k);
```

4.4.3 Using an IOT in a Data Warehouse

In a data warehouse, an IOT can be useful when you have dimension tables or lookup tables, such as product catalogs, where a small number of columns form a primary key and are used for querying, whereas other columns, such as product specifications or photos, are not frequently used and occupy, significant amount of space. To keep the index small, these non-key columns should be stored in the overflow segment of the index.

IOT organization for the fact table is not very common, because the fact table typically does not have a primary key. Another reason is that a fact table usually has several non-primary-key measure columns, which are frequently accessed, and therefore the space advantages of an IOT may not be realized. There are also a couple of other key differences between regular tables and IOTs, which make them somewhat unsuitable as fact tables. The primary key constraint on an IOT cannot be deferred or disabled. Checking validity of a constraint is a time-consuming operation, and, hence, when loading new data into the data warehouse, it is common practice to defer or disable all constraints and enable them only after the load is complete. This cannot be done if the fact table is an IOT, which can make the load process more expensive. Also, IOTs do not have physical rowids, which are necessary to use some refresh features of materialized views (see Chapter 7).

4.5   Data Compression

With the vast amount of data that has to be stored in the data warehouse, considerable demands can be placed on storage. Therefore, you should use data compression techniques whenever possible to reduce your storage requirements. Oracle performs data compression in a variety of ways to reduce the storage occupied by indexes and tables. The benefits of compression are greatest when the data has many repeated values (such as tables with foreign keys) and if data values are not updated frequently.

4.5.1   Table Compression

Oracle 9*i*, Release 2, introduced a technique for table compression known as **data segment compression**. In the Oracle database, data is stored in segments, each of which ultimately consists of data blocks: A data block can be thought of as the smallest unit of storage in the database, by default, 8K in size. Data segment compression compresses a table by identifying repeated values of data within each data block and places them in a lookup table at the beginning of the block. The data rows then point to the value in the lookup table. This can significantly reduce storage used when the data contains large repeating values, especially strings. It is especially useful for materialized views with aggregation, since the data values for the grouping columns are often repeated. Data segment compression can be done for a table or a partition of a table.

When a query is issued against a table compressed in this manner, Oracle will automatically uncompress the rows to return the result. Even though this may appear to be an additional overhead, it is not very significant and will be far outweighed by the I/O savings due to the reduced table size.

Table compression should be considered only if the table rows are not very likely to change. If new rows are added to a compressed table using a conventional INSERT statement, the new data is not compressed efficiently. Similarly, DELETE and UPDATE statements cannot maintain compression efficiently. However, if data is added using DIRECT PATH insert (using SQL Loader or an INSERT /*+APPEND */ statement), the new data is inserted into new blocks, which can be compressed. Hence, segment compression is well suited for data warehousing environments that do batch loads of data or for partitions that are mostly read-only.

To enable data segment compression you must specify the COMPRESS keyword when creating a tablespace, a table, or individual partitions of a range- or list-partitioned table. Note that data segment compression is not available for hash-partitioned tables, and, therefore, if reducing storage is your primary concern, you should consider an alternative scheme for partitioning. Data segment compression is also not available for index-organized tables.

The following example shows a range-partitioned table, PURCHASES, whose first three partitions are compressed. We have left the last one uncompressed, because more data may be added to this partition.

```
CREATE TABLE easydw.purchases
(product_id            varchar2(8),
 time_key              date,
 customer_id           varchar2(10),
 purchase_date         date,
 purchase_time         number(4,0),
 purchase_price        number(6,2),
 shipping_charge       number(5,2),
 today_special_offer   varchar2(1))
PARTITION by RANGE (time_key)
(
  partition purchases_jan2003
    values less than (TO_DATE('01-FEB-2003', 'DD-MON-YYYY'))
```

```
      tablespace purchases_jan2003 COMPRESS,
  partition purchases_feb2003
    values less than (TO_DATE('01-MAR-2003', 'DD-MON-YYYY'))
    tablespace purchases_feb2003 COMPRESS,
  partition purchases_mar2003
    values less than (TO_DATE('01-APR-2003', 'DD-MON-YYYY'))
    tablespace purchases_mar2003 COMPRESS,
  partition purchases_catchall
    values less than (MAXVALUE)
    tablespace purchases_maxvalue NOCOMPRESS );
```

If you are adding a partition with segment compression for the first time to a previously uncompressed partitioned table, you need to rebuild any bitmapped indexes on that table.

Hint: To achieve better compression when adding data into a new partition, sort the data first so that repeating values appear in the same block as much as possible.

You may want to merge and compress partitions corresponding to older data, since they are not likely to change very much. This allows you to keep more data on-line. For instance, at the end of each month, you could compress the last month's partition if it is unlikely to receive further updates. To change the compress attribute of a table you need to issue an ALTER TABLE MOVE command. For example, to compress the PURCHASE_CATCHALL partition of the PURCHASES table, you would issue:

```
ALTER TABLE purchases MOVE PARTITION purchases_catchall COMPRESS;
```

4.5.2   Index Compression

For B*tree indexes, Oracle performs key compression by storing only once the common prefix of index key values in an index block. Index key compression must be enabled using the COMPRESS keyword on the CREATE INDEX statement. Key compression is also possible for the index underlying an index-organized table.

For bitmapped indexes, the bitmap for each data value is automatically compressed by Oracle. For columns whose cardinality is much less than the number of rows in the table, the bitmaps tend to be dense (having a lot of 1s) and can be compressed greatly. Thus, a bitmapped index can occupy much less space than the corresponding B*tree index.

4.6   Summary

In this chapter, we have discussed various considerations and techniques for physical design of a data warehouse. We saw how data partitioning can be used to improve manageability, performance, and availability of a data warehouse. We explored various index types that are suitable for a data warehouse and how they can be partitioned. One factor that will significantly influence your physical design choices is how data will be loaded into the warehouse. In the next chapter, we will look in depth at this very important aspect of a data warehouse.

Loading Data into the Warehouse

5.1   The ETL Process

Populating a data warehouse involves all of the tasks related to getting the data from the source operational systems, cleansing and transforming the data to the right format and level of detail, loading it into the target data warehouse, and preparing it for analysis purposes.

Figure 5.1 shows the steps making up the extraction, transformation, and load (ETL) process. Data is extracted from the source operational systems and transported to the staging area. The staging area is a temporary holding place used to prepare the data. The staging area may be a set of flat files, temporary staging tables in the Oracle warehouse, or both. The data is integrated with other data, cleansed, and transformed into a common rep-

Figure 5.1   *The ETL Process*

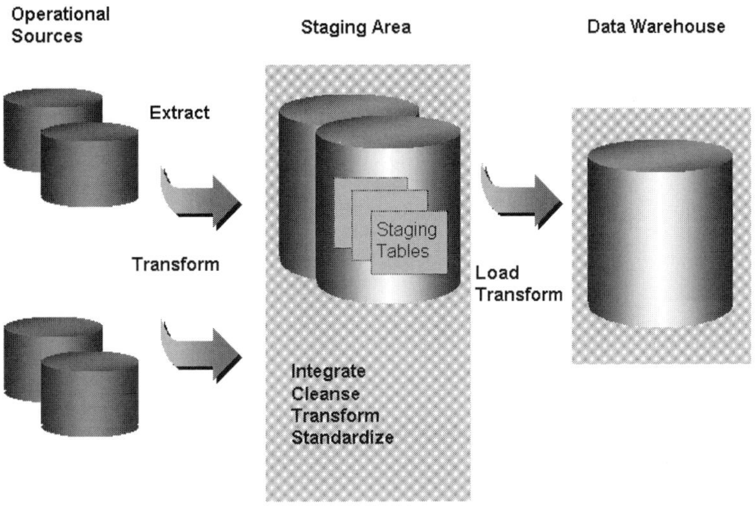

resentation. It is then loaded into the target data warehouse tables. Sometimes this process is also referred to as ETT—extraction, transportation, and transformation.

During the initial population of the data warehouse, historical data is loaded that could have accumulated over several years of business operation. The data in the operational systems may often be in multiple formats. If, for instance, the point-of-sales operational system was replaced two years ago, the current two years of history will be in one format, while data older than two years will be in another format.

After the initial historical load, new transaction and event data needs to be loaded on a periodic basis. This is typically done on a regular time schedule, such as at the end of the day, week, or month. During the load, and while the indexes and materialized views are being refreshed, the data is generally unavailable to warehouse users for querying. The period of time allowed for inserting the new data is called the **batch window**. The batch window is a continuously shrinking amount of time as more businesses are on-line for longer periods of time. Currently, with the ability to refresh the warehouse in real time, or near real time, batch windows are becoming a higher priority and requirement as businesses want and need to react to changes in a more immediate fashion. Higher availability can be achieved by partitioning the fact table. While data is loaded into a new partition, or being updated in an existing partition, the rest of the partitions are still available for use.

A large portion of the work in building a data warehouse will be devoted to the ETL process. Finding the data from the operational systems, creating extraction processes to get it out, transporting, filtering, cleansing, transforming, integrating data from multiple sources, and loading it into the warehouse can take a considerable amount of time.

If you are not already familiar with the company's data, part of the difficulty in developing the ETL process is gaining an understanding of the data. One object can have different names in different systems. Even worse, two different things could have the same name. It can be a challenge to discover all of this, particularly in a company where the systems are not well documented. Each column in the target data warehouse must be mapped to the corresponding column in the source system. Some of the data will be mapped directly; other data will need to be derived and transformed into a different format.

Once the data is loaded into the warehouse, further processing to integrate it with existing data, update indexes, gather statistics, and refresh materialized views needs to take place prior to it being "published" as ready for users to access. Once the data is published, it should not be updated again until the next batch window, to ensure users do not receive different answers to the same query asked at a different time.

5.2 Extracting Data from the Operational Systems

Once you have identified the data you need in the warehouse for analysis purposes, you need to locate the operational systems within the company that contain that data. The data needed for the warehouse is extracted from the source operational systems and written to the staging area, where it will later be transformed. To minimize the performance impact on the source database, data is generally extracted without applying any transformations to it.

Often the owners of the operational systems will not allow the warehouse developers direct access to those systems but will provide periodic extracts. These extracts are generally in the form of flat, sequential operating system files, which will make up the staging area.

In order to extract the fields and records needed for the warehouse, specialized application programs may need to be developed. If the data is stored in a legacy system, then these programs may require special logic—for example, if written in COBOL—in order to handle things such as repeating fields in the "COBOL occurs" clause. The data warehouse designers need to work closely with the application developers for the OLTP systems that are building the extract scripts to provide the necessary columns and formats of the data.

As part of designing the ETL process, you need to determine how frequently data should be extracted from the operational systems. It may be at the end of some time period or business event, such as at the end of the day or week or upon closing of the fiscal quarter. It should be clearly defined what is meant by the "end of the day" or the "last day of the week," particularly if you have a system used across different time zones. The extraction may be done at different times for different systems and staged to be loaded into the warehouse during an upcoming batch window. Another aspect of the warehouse design process involves deciding which level of aggregation is needed to answer the business queries. This also has an impact on which and how much data is extracted and transported across the network.

Some operational systems may be in relational databases, such as Oracle 8*i*, 9*i*, or 10*g*; Oracle Rdb; DB2/MVS; Microsoft SQL Server; Sybase; or

Informix. Others may be in a legacy database format, such as IMS or Oracle DBMS. Others may be in VSAM, RMS indexed files, or some other structured file system.

If extracting and transporting the data from the source systems must be done by writing the data to flat files, then there is also the issue of defining:

1.   The file naming specification.

2.   Which files constitute the batch—for example, if more than one source table is being read from each source system, then data in each table will probably be written to its own flat file. All of the data extracted at the same time from the source system should normally be batched together and transferred and loaded into the data warehouse as a logical unit of work.

3.   The method for transporting the files between the source system and the warehouse—for example, is the data pushed from the source system or pulled by the warehouse system? If FTP is being used, then typically it may require a new operating system account on the warehouse server if the source system is pushing the data, but this new account will normally only be able to write to a very restricted directory area that the warehouse load processes can then read from.

Let's consider the file naming convention, and, in particular, the situation if multiple different source systems provide their data using flat files. With this situation, it is quite typical for the file naming convention to incorporate the following:

1.   The source system name

2.   The date of extraction

3.   A file batch number—particularly if there can be more than one data extraction in a business day

4.   The source table name

5.   A single character indicator to show whether this is an original extraction or a repeat—for example, if some corruption occurred and the data had to be reextracted and resent

Alternatively, if you are able to access the source systems directly without recourse to using flat files, you can retrieve the data by using a variety of techniques, depending on the type of system it is. For small quantities of data, a gateway such as ODBC can be used. For larger amounts of data, a custom program directly connecting to the source database in the database's native Application Programming Interface (API) can be written. Many ETL tools simplify the extraction process by providing connectivity to the source.

5.2.1 Identifying Data That Has Changed

After the initial load of the warehouse, as the source data changes, the data in the warehouse must be updated or refreshed to reflect those changes on a regular basis. A mechanism needs to be put into place to monitor and capture changes of interest from the operational systems. Rather than rebuilding the entire warehouse periodically, it is preferable to apply only the changes. By isolating changes as part of the extraction process, less data needs to be moved across the network and loaded into the data warehouse.

Changed data includes both new data that has been added to the operational system as well as updates and deletes to existing data. For example, in the EASYDW warehouse, we are interested in all new orders as well as updates to existing product information and customers. If we are no longer selling a product, the product is deleted from the order-entry system, but we still want to retain the history in the warehouse. This is why **surrogate keys** are recommended for use in the data warehouse. If the product_key is reused in the production system, it does not affect the data warehouse records.

In the data warehouse, it is not uncommon to change the dimension tables, because a column such as a product description may change. Part of the warehouse design involves deciding how changes to the dimensions will be reflected. If you need to keep one version of the old product description, you could have an additional column in the table to store both the current description and the previous description. If you need to keep all the old product descriptions, you would have to create a new row for each change, assigning different key values. In general, you should try to avoid updates to the fact table.

There are various ways to identify the new or changed data. One technique to determine the changes is to include a time stamp to record when each row in the operational system was changed. The data extraction program then selects the source data based on the time stamp of the transaction and extracts all rows that have been updated since the time of the last extraction. For example, when moving orders from the order processing system into the EASYDW warehouse, this technique can be used by selecting rows based on the PURCHASE_DATE column, as illustrated later in this chapter.

However, this technique does have some potential disadvantages:

1.   If multiple updates have occurred to a record since the date and time of the last extraction, then only the current version of the record is read and not all of the interim versions. Typically, this may not have a significant impact on the warehouse unless it is necessary for analysis purposes to track all changes.

2.   The query to select the changed data based on the time stamp can have an impact on the source system.

3.   If records are deleted in the source system, then this mechanism is unsuitable because you cannot select a record that is no longer present. Converting the delete into a "logical delete" by setting a flag is normally not practical and involves considerable application change. This is where the next technique using triggers can help.

If the source is a relational database, triggers can be used to identify the changed rows. Triggers are stored procedures that can be invoked before or after an event, such as when an insert, update, or delete occurs on each record. The trigger can be used to save the changed records into a separate table from where the extract process can later retrieve the changed rows. One advantage of triggers is that the same transaction is used for writing the changed record to another table as is used to alter the source record itself. If this transaction aborts and rolls back for any reason, then our change record is also rolled back. However, be very careful of triggers in high-volume applications, as they can add significant overhead to the operational system.

Sometimes it may not be possible to change the schema to add a timestamp or trigger. The system may already be heavily loaded, and you do not want to degrade the performance in any way. Or the source may be a legacy system, which does not have triggers. Therefore, you may need to use a file comparison to identify changes. This involves keeping before and after images of the extract files to find the changes. For example, you may need to compare the recent extract with the current product or customer list to identify the changes.

Changes to the metadata, or data definitions, must also be identified. Changes to the structure of the operational system, such as adding or dropping a column, impact the extraction and load programs, which may need to be modified to account for the change.

5.2.2　Oracle Change Data Capture

Oracle Database 10*g* uses a feature called **Change Data Capture**, often referred to as CDC, to facilitate identifying changes when the source system is also an Oracle 9*i* or 10*g* database. CDC was introduced in Oracle 9*i* with just the synchronous form, where generation of the change records is tied to the original transaction. In Oracle Database 10*g* the new asynchronous form is introduced; this disassociates the generation of the change records from the original transaction and reduces the impact on the source system for collecting the change data. In this section, we will look at both forms and work through examples of each mechanism.

With CDC, the results of all INSERT, UPDATE, and DELETE operations can be saved in tables called **change tables**. The data extraction programs can then select the data from the change tables. CDC uses a publish-subscribe interface to capture and distribute the change data, as illustrated in Figure 5.2. The publisher, usually a DBA, determines which user tables in the operational system are used to load the warehouse and sets up the system to capture and publish the change data. A change table is created for each source table with data that needs to be moved to the warehouse.

Figure 5.2　*Change Data Capture Publish/Subscribe Architecture*

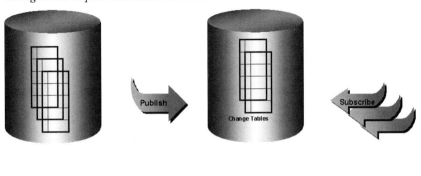

The extract programs then **subscribe** to the source tables; therefore, there can be any number of subscribers. Each subscriber is given his or her own view of the change table. This isolates the subscribers from each other while they are simultaneously accessing the same change tables. The subscribers use SQL to select the change data from their **subscriber views**. They see just the columns that they are interested in and only the rows that they have not yet processed. If the updates of a set of tables are dependent on each other, the change tables can be grouped into a **change set**. If, for example, you had an order header and an order detail table, these two tables would be grouped together in the same change set to maintain transactional consistency. In order to create a change table, you must first, therefore, create the parent change set. A **change source** is a logical representation of the source database that contains one or more change sets.

In Oracle 9*i* only synchronous data capture existed, where changes on the operational system are captured in real time as part of the source transaction. The change data is generated as DML operations are performed on the source tables. When a new row is inserted into the user table, it is also stored in the change table. When a row is updated in a user table, the updated columns are stored in the change table. The old values, new values, or both can be written to the change table. When a row is deleted from a user table, the deleted row is also stored in the change table. The change data records are only visible in the change table when the source transaction is committed.

Synchronous CDC is based on triggers, which fire for each row as the different DML statements are executed. This simplifies the data extraction process; however, it adds an overhead to the transaction performing the DML. In Asynchronous Change Data Capture, which is introduced in Oracle Database 10*g*, the capture of the changes is not dependent upon the DML transaction on the source system. With asynchronous CDC, the changes are extracted from the source system's redo logs, which removes the impact on the actual database transaction. The Oracle redo logs are special files used by the database that record all of the changes to the database as they occur. There are two forms of redo logs:

- On-line redo logs
- Archive redo logs

The on-line redo logs are groups of redo logs that are written to in a round-robin fashion as transactions occur on the database. When a redo log fills up, the database swaps to the next one, and if archiving of the logs is turned on (which is practically a certainty on any production database), then the database writes the completed redo log file to a specified destination where it can subsequently be safely stored. This is the archived redo log. Asynchronous CDC reads redo logs to extract the change data for the tables that we are interested in and therefore it is a noninvasive technique, which does not need to alter the source schema to add triggers to tables. The action of reading the logs in this fashion is often called mining the logs. In addition, the mining of the log files for the change data is disassociated from the source transaction itself, which reduces, but doesn't remove, the impact on the source system.

Asynchronous CDC needs an additional level of redo logging to be enabled on the source system, which adds its own level of impact on the source database, but this is much less than that of synchronous CDC.

Asynchronous CDC can be used in two ways:

1.   HOTLOG, where the changes are extracted from the on-line redo logs on the source database and then moved (by Oracle Streams processes) into local CDC tables also in the source database. The changed data in the CDC tables will still need to be transported to our warehouse database.

2.   AUTOLOG, where the changed data is captured from the redo logs as they are moved between databases by the Log Transport Services. The changes are then extracted from these logs and made available in change tables on this other database. If this other database is our data warehouse database, then, by using AUTOLOG, we have removed the transportation step to make our changed data available in the staging area of the warehouse.

Log Transport Services are a standard part of the operation of the database—for example, they are used by Oracle Data Guard for moving the log files to other servers in order to maintain standby databases and as such do not add any additional impact to the source database operation.

The time between the change being committed by the transaction and it being detected by CDC and moved into the change table is called the **latency of change**. This is smaller with the HOTLOG method than with the AUTOLOG method. This is because HOTLOG is reading the on-line redo logs and publishing to tables on the same source system, compared with AUTO LOG, where the logs must first be switched and then transported between databases—in which case the frequency of transporting the logs is the determining factor. For HOTLOG, mining the redo logs occurs on a transaction-by-transaction basis when the source transaction commits.

Publishing Change Data

In the EASYDW warehouse, we are interested in all new orders from the order-entry system. The DBA creates the change tables, using the DBMS_CDC_PUBLISH.CREATE_CHANGE_TABLE procedure, and specifies a list of columns that should be included. A change table contains changes from only one source table.

In many of the examples in this chapter, we will use a schema named OLTP, which represents a part of the operational database. In the following example, the DBA uses the CREATE_CHANGE_TABLE procedure to capture the changes to the columns from the ORDERS table in the OLTP schema.

The next two sections provide an example of the two different methods for setting up synchronous and asynchronous CDC and, following that, the common mechanism for subscribing to the change data. To do this we are going to use three new schemas:

- OLTP for the owner of our warehouse source tables
- OLTPPUB for the publisher of the change data that has occurred on our OLTP tables
- OLTPSUBSCR for the subscriber to the change data

Our source table for both methods is ORDERS, and the other two differences between the methods to note are:

- For synchronous, the change set is EASYDW_SCS and the change table is ORDERS_SYNCH_CT
- For asynchronous, the change set is EASYDW_ACS and the change table is ORDERS_ASYNCH_CT

In the subscriber section, we will highlight what needs to change in order to subscribe to the change data created by these two methods.

From a DBA account, create the new accounts and create a source table in the OLTP account:

```
CREATE USER oltp IDENTIFIED BY oltp
  DEFAULT TABLESPACE users
  TEMPORARY TABLESPACE temp
  QUOTA UNLIMITED ON users;
GRANT connect, resource TO oltp ;

CREATE USER oltpsubscr IDENTIFIED BY oltpsubscr
  DEFAULT TABLESPACE users
  TEMPORARY TABLESPACE temp
  QUOTA UNLIMITED ON users;
GRANT connect, resource TO oltpsubscr ;

CREATE USER oltppub IDENTIFIED BY oltppub
  QUOTA UNLIMITED ON SYSTEM
  QUOTA UNLIMITED ON SYSAUX;

GRANT CREATE SESSION TO oltppub;
GRANT CREATE TABLE TO oltppub;
GRANT CREATE TABLESPACE TO oltppub;
GRANT UNLIMITED TABLESPACE TO oltppub;
GRANT SELECT_CATALOG_ROLE TO oltppub;
GRANT EXECUTE_CATALOG_ROLE TO oltppub;
GRANT CREATE SEQUENCE TO oltppub;
GRANT CONNECT, RESOURCE, DBA TO oltppub;

CREATE TABLE oltp.orders
(order_id              varchar2(8)   NOT NULL,
 product_id            varchar2(8)   NOT NULL,
 customer_id           varchar2(10)  NOT NULL,
 purchase_date         date          NOT NULL,
 purchase_time         number(4,0)   NOT NULL,
 purchase_price        number(6,2)   NOT NULL,
 shipping_charge       number(5,2)   NOT NULL,
 today_special_offer   varchar2(1)   NOT NULL,
 sales_person_id       varchar2(20)  NOT NULL,
 payment_method        varchar2(10)  NOT NULL
)
TABLESPACE users ;
```

Synchronous CDC

For synchronous CDC, creation of the change set must use the predefined change source, SYNC_SOURCE, which represents the source database. The following PL/SQL block performs both of these steps:

```
BEGIN
  DBMS_CDC_PUBLISH.CREATE_CHANGE_SET
    (change_set_name =>'EASYDW_SCS',
     description => 'Synchronous Change set for EasyDW',
     change_source_name => 'SYNC_SOURCE'
    );
  DBMS_CDC_PUBLISH.CREATE_CHANGE_TABLE
    (
      owner => 'oltppub',
      change_table_name => 'ORDERS_SYNCH_CT',
      change_set_name => 'EASYDW_SCS',
      source_schema => 'oltp',
      source_table => 'ORDERS',
      column_type_list =>
        'order_id varchar2(8),product_id varchar2(8),'
       ||'customer_id varchar2(10), purchase_date date,'
       ||'purchase_time number(4,0),purchase_price number(6,2),'
       ||'shipping_charge number(5,2), '
       ||'today_special_offer varchar2(1),'
       ||'sales_person varchar2(20), '
       ||'payment_method varchar2(10)',
      capture_values => 'both',
      rs_id => 'y',
      row_id => 'n',
      user_id => 'n',
      timestamp => 'n',
      object_id => 'n',
      source_colmap => 'y',
      target_colmap => 'y',
      options_string => 'TABLESPACE USERS'
    );
END;
/
```

This script creates the change set EASYDW_SCS for changes to the table ORDERS owned by account OLTP to publish the changes into the change table ORDERS_SYNCH_CT owned by OLTPPUB. We must now grant select privilege on the change table to the subscriber account, OLTP-SUBSCR, so that it can see the contents of the table.

```
GRANT SELECT ON ORDERS_SYNCH_CT TO OLTPSUBSCR ;
```

When creating the change table, you must specify the column list, which indicates the columns you are interested in capturing. In addition, there are a number of other parameters that allow you to specify:

- Whether you want the change table to contain the old values for the row, the new values, or both

- Whether you want a row sequence number, which provides the sequence of operations within a transaction

- The rowid of the changed row

- The user who changed the row

- The time stamp of the change

- The object id of the change record

- A source column map, which indicates the source columns that have been modified

- A target column map to track which columns in the change table have been modified

- An options column to append to a CREATE TABLE DDL statement

An application can check either the source column map or the target column map to determine which columns have been modified.

A sample of the output will be seen later in the chapter. To see a list of change tables that have been published, query the CHANGE_TABLES dictionary table.

```
SQL> SELECT CHANGE_TABLE_NAME FROM CHANGE_TABLES;

CHANGE_TABLE_NAME
------------------
ORDERS_SYNCH_CT
```

The DBA then grants SELECT privileges on the change table to the subscribers.

Asynchronous CDC

For the asynchronous CDC example, we will use the HOTLOG method, where the change data is mined from the on-line redo logs of the source system.

First, make sure that your source database is in ARCHIVELOG mode, where the log files are being archived to a separate destination area on your file system. It would be very unusual for a source production system not to be already operating in archive log mode, because this is fundamental to any recovery of the database in the event of failure. To put the database in ARCHIVELOG mode, you will need to shut down the database and restart it, as summarized in the following code segment. These commands are executed from SQL*Plus using a sysdba account—for example, SYS:

```
shutdown immediate
startup mount
alter database archivelog ;
alter database open ;
```

Hint: Simply changing the ARCHIVELOG mode like this may be fine on a sandpit, test, or play system, but this operation can invalidate your backups—so on any production or similarly important system, you will want to redo your backups.

The next step requires altering the database in order to create the additional logging information into the log files.

```
ALTER DATABASE FORCE LOGGING;
ALTER DATABASE ADD SUPPLEMENTAL LOG DATA;
ALTER TABLE oltp.orders
    ADD SUPPLEMENTAL LOG GROUP log_group_orders
        (order_id,product_id,customer_id,
         purchase_date,purchase_time,purchase_price,
         shipping_charge,today_special_offer) ALWAYS;
```

The FORCE LOGGING clause to the alter database statement specifies that the database will always generate redo logs, even when database operations have been used with the NOLOGGING clause. This ensures that asynchronous CDC always has the necessary redo log data to mine for the changes. The SUPPLEMENTAL LOG DATA clause is adding minimal supplemental logging, but this does not add a significant overhead to the database performance and performing this enables the use of the Oracle log mining features. This statement is creating an unconditional log group for the data changes for those source table columns to be captured in a change table. Without the unconditional log group, CDC records unchanged column values in UPDATE operations as NULL, making it ambiguous whether the NULL means the value was unchanged or changed to be NULL. With the unconditional log group, CDC records the actual value in UPDATE operations for unchanged column values, so that a NULL always means the value was changed to NULL.

Asynchronous CDC utilizes Oracle Streams for the propagation of our change data within the database and to use Streams we must be granted certain privileges. These privileges enable the user to use Streams and the underlying Oracle Advanced Queue objects, such as queues, propagations, and rules. Execute the following command from your SYSDBA (e.g., SYS) account:

```
EXECUTE DBMS_STREAMS_AUTH.GRANT_ADMIN_PRIVILEGE
                     (GRANTEE=>'oltppub');
```

Each source table must be instantiated with Oracle Streams in order that Streams can capture certain information that it requires in order to record the source table data changes. This is achieved from a DBA account by calling the PREPARE_TABLE_INSTANTIATION procedure as shown here:

```
EXECUTE DBMS_CAPTURE_ADM.PREPARE_TABLE_INSTANTIATION
                     (TABLE_NAME=>'oltp.orders');
```

Now we must create our change set, which we are going to call EASYDW_ACS, using the predefined change source HOTLOG_SOURCE, which represents the current redo log files of the source database. If we were performing an AUTOLOG type of asynchronous CDC, then there would be no predefined change source to be used in this step. Instead, the DBA on the target staging database must define and create the change source using the CREATE_AUTOLOG_CHANGE_SOURCE procedure in the DBMS_CDC_PACKAGE. The call to this procedure uses:

1.   The global name of the source database

2.   The SCN number of the data dictionary build, which is determined by a call to DBMS_CAPTURE_ADM.BUILD() on the source database

In order to interpret the redo logs—for example, in order to know which internal reference number identifies what table—the log mining functionality needs a version of the source system data dictionary. This SCN number identifies a source system redo log, which contains the Log-Miner dictionary and therefore the correct definition of the tables.

Execute the following from the OLTPPUB publisher account. This command creates the change set and its associated Oracle Streams processes but does not start them.

```
BEGIN
  DBMS_CDC_PUBLISH.CREATE_CHANGE_SET
    (
    change_set_name => 'EASYDW_ACS',
    description => 'Asynchronous Change set for purchases info',
    change_source_name => 'HOTLOG_SOURCE',
    stop_on_ddl => 'y');
END;
/
```

Now we can create the change table, ORDERS_CT, in the OLTPPUB publisher account, which will contain the changes that have been mined from the on-line redo log. Execute the following from the OLTPPUB account:

```
BEGIN
 DBMS_CDC_PUBLISH.CREATE_CHANGE_TABLE
    (
    owner => 'oltppub',
    change_table_name => 'ORDERS_ASYNCH_CT',
    change_set_name => 'EASYDW_ACS',
    source_schema => 'OLTP',
    source_table => 'ORDERS',
    column_type_list =>
      'order_id varchar2(8),product_id varchar2(8),'
    ||'customer_id varchar2(10), purchase_date date,'
    ||'purchase_time number(4,0),purchase_price number(6,2),'
    ||'shipping_charge number(5,2),today_special_offer varchar2(1),'
    ||'sales_person varchar2(20), payment_method varchar2(10)',
    capture_values => 'both',
    rs_id => 'y',
    row_id => 'n',
    user_id => 'n',
    timestamp => 'n',
    object_id => 'n',
    source_colmap => 'n',
    target_colmap => 'y',
    options_string => 'TABLESPACE USERS');
END;
/

GRANT SELECT ON ORDERS_ASYNCH_CT TO OLTPSUBSCR ;
```

Finally, we will enable our change set EASYDW_ACS, which starts the underlying Oracle Streams processes for moving our change data:

```
BEGIN
  DBMS_CDC_PUBLISH.ALTER_CHANGE_SET
    (
     change_set_name => 'EASYDW_ACS',
     enable_capture => 'y'
    );
END;
/
```

To verify that everything is working, perform this simple test. Insert and commit a record into your OLTP.ORDERS source table. After a few minutes you will be able to see the change record in the publisher table OLTP-PUB.ORDERS_CT. We have now created the facility using database asynchronous CDC mechanisms to capture changes on our ORDERS table without needing to invasively alter the source schema to create triggers or amend any application.

Subscribing to Change Data

The extraction programs create subscriptions to access the change tables. A subscription can contain data from one or more change tables in the same change set.

The ALL_SOURCE_TABLES dictionary view lists the source tables that have already been published by the DBA. In this example, changes for the ORDERS table in the OLTP schema have been published.

```
SQL> SELECT * FROM ALL_SOURCE_TABLES;

SOURCE_SCHEMA_NAME                    SOURCE_TABLE_NAME
------------------------------------  ------------------
OLTP                                  ORDERS
```

Creating a Subscription

There are several steps to creating a subscription.

1. Create a subscription.

2. List all the tables and columns the extract program wants to subscribe to.

3. Activate the subscription.

The first step is to create a subscription. The following is performed from the subscriber account OLTPSUBSCR. Note that for our example, we are going to access the change data created by the asynchronous CDC method via the EASYDW_ACS change set. If we wanted to access the synchronous change data, then we would simply have to use the change set that we created for synchronous CDC, i.e., EASYDW_SCS.

```
SQL> BEGIN
DBMS_CDC_SUBSCRIBE.CREATE_SUBSCRIPTION
    (SUBSCRIPTION_NAME => 'ORDERS_SUB',
     CHANGE_SET_NAME => 'EASYDW_ACS',
     DESCRIPTION => 'Changes to orders table');
END;
/
```

Next, specify the source tables and columns of interest using the SUBSCRIBE procedure. A subscription can contain one or more tables from the same change set. The SUBSCRIBE procedure lists the schema, table, and columns of change data that the extract program will use to load the warehouse. In this example, the subscribe procedure is used to get changes from all the columns in the ORDERS table in the OLTP schema. The subscribe procedure is executed once for each table in the subscription, and in this example we were only interested in changes from one table. However, you could repeat this procedure to subscribe to changes to other tables in the change set.

Instead of accessing the change tables directly, the subscriber creates a subscriber view for each source table of interest. This is also done in the call to the SUBSCRIBE procedure.

```
SQL> BEGIN
DBMS_CDC_SUBSCRIBE.SUBSCRIBE
  (SUBSCRIPTION_NAME => 'ORDERS_SUB',
   SOURCE_SCHEMA => 'oltp',
   SOURCE_TABLE => 'orders',
   COLUMN_LIST => 'order_id,product_id,'
                 ||'customer_id, purchase_date,'
                 ||'purchase_time,purchase_price,'
                 ||'shipping_charge, today_special_offer,'
                 ||'sales_person, payment_method',
   SUBSCRIBER_VIEW => 'ORDERS_VIEW'
  );
END;
/
```

After subscribing to all the change tables, the subscription is activated using the ACTIVATE_SUBSCRIPTION procedure. Activating a subscription is done to indicate that all tables have been added, and the subscription is now complete.

```
SQL> EXECUTE DBMS_CDC_SUBSCRIBE.ACTIVATE_SUBSCRIPTION
  (SUBSCRIPTION_NAME => 'ORDERS_SUB');
```

Once a subscription has been activated, as new data gets added to the source tables it is made available for processing via the change tables.

Processing the Change Data

To illustrate how change data is processed, let us assume two rows are inserted into the ORDERS table. As data is inserted into the ORDERS table, the changes are also stored in the change table, ORDERS_ASYNCH_CT.

```
SQL> INSERT INTO oltp.orders
            (order_id,product_id,customer_id,
             purchase_date,
             purchase_time, purchase_price,shipping_charge,
             today_special_offer,
             sales_person_id,payment_method)
     VALUES ('123','SP1031', 'AB123495',
             to_date('01-JAN-2004', 'dd-mon-yyyy'),
             1031,156.45,6.95,'N','SMITH','VISA');

1 row created.

SQL> INSERT INTO oltp.orders
            (order_id,product_id,customer_id,
             purchase_date,
             purchase_time,purchase_price,shipping_charge,
             today_special_offer,
             sales_person_id,payment_method)
     VALUES ('123','SP1031','AB123495',
             to_date('01-FEB-2004', 'dd-mon-yyyy'),
             1031,156.45,6.95,'N','SMITH','VISA');

1 row created.

SQL> commit;
```

In order to process the change data, a program loops through the steps described in the following text and illustrated in Figure 5.3. A change table is dynamic; new change data is appended to the change table at the same time the extraction programs are reading from it. In order to present a consistent view of the contents of the change table, change data is viewed for a *window* of source database transactions. Prior to accessing the data, the window is extended. In Figure 5.3, rows 1–8 are available in the first window. While the program was processing these rows, rows 9–13 were added to the change table. Purging the first window and extending the window again can access rows 9–13.

Figure 5.3   *Querying Change Data*

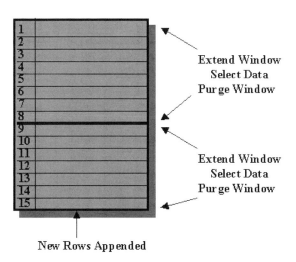

Rather than accessing the change table directly, the program selects the data from the change table using the subscriber view specified earlier in the SUBSCRIBE procedure.

Step 1: Extend the window

Change data is only available for a window of time: from the time the EXTEND_WINDOW procedure is invoked until the PURGE_WINDOW procedure is invoked. To see new data added to the change table, the window must be extended using the EXTEND_WINDOW procedure.

```
SQL> BEGIN
  DBMS_CDC_SUBSCRIBE.EXTEND_WINDOW
     (SUBSCRIPTION_NAME => 'ORDERS_SUB');
END;
/
```

Step 2: Select Data from the Subscriber View

In this example, the contents of the subscriber view will be examined.

```
SQL> describe ORDERS_VIEW
 Name                        Null?    Type
 ----------------------- -------- ----------------
 OPERATION$                          CHAR(2)
 CSCN$                               NUMBER
 COMMIT_TIMESTAMP$                   DATE
 RSID$                               NUMBER
 SOURCE_COLMAP$                      RAW(128)
 TARGET_COLMAP$                      RAW(128)
 CUSTOMER_ID                         VARCHAR2(10)
 ORDER_ID                            VARCHAR2(8)
 PAYMENT_METHOD                      VARCHAR2(10)
 PRODUCT_ID                          VARCHAR2(8)
 PURCHASE_DATE                       DATE
 PURCHASE_PRICE                      NUMBER(6,2)
 PURCHASE_TIME                       NUMBER(4)
 SALES_PERSON                        VARCHAR2(20)
 SHIPPING_CHARGE                     NUMBER(5,2)
 TODAY_SPECIAL_OFFER                 VARCHAR2(1)
```

The first column of the output shows the operation: I for insert. Next, the commit scn and commit time are listed. The new data is listed for each row, and the row source id, indicated by RSID$, shows the order of the statements in the transaction.

```
SQL> SELECT OPERATION$, CSCN$, COMMIT_TIMESTAMP$, RSID$,
            CUSTOMER_ID, ORDER_ID, PAYMENT_METHOD,
            PRODUCT_ID, PURCHASE_DATE, PURCHASE_PRICE,
            PURCHASE_TIME, SALES_PERSON, SHIPPING_CHARGE,
            TODAY_SPECIAL_OFFER
      FROM ORDERS_VIEW;

OP      CSCN$ COMMIT_TIMESTAMP      RSID$ CUSTOMER_ID
-- ---------- ---------------- ---------- -----------
ORDER_ID PAYMENT_METHOD PRODUCT_ID PURCHASE_DATE PURCHASE_PRICE PURCHASE_TIME
-------- -------------- ---------- ------------- -------------- -------------
SALES_PERSON         SHIPPING_CHARGE TODAY_SPECIAL_OFFER
-------------------- --------------- -------------------
I     6848693 05-JUN-04            10001 AB123495
123      VISA            SP1031     01-JAN-04       156.45          1031
                          6.95 N


I     6848693 05-JUN-04            10002 AB123495
123      VISA            SP1031     01-FEB-04       156.45          1031
                          6.95 N
```

Step 3: Purge the Window

The window is purged when the data is no longer needed, using the PURGE_WINDOW procedure. When all subscribers have purged their windows, the data in those windows is automatically deleted.

```
SQL> EXECUTE DBMS_CDC_SUBSCRIBE.PURGE_WINDOW
        (SUBSCRIPTION_NAME => 'ORDERS_SUB');
```

Ending the Subscription

When an extract program is no longer needed, you can end the subscription, using the DROP_SUBSCRIPTION procedure.

```
SQL> EXECUTE DBMS_CDC_SUBSCRIBE.DROP_SUBSCRIPTION
    (SUBSCRIPTION_NAME => 'ORDERS_SUB');
```

Transporting the Changes to the Staging Area

For synchronous and HOTLOG asynchronous CDC, now that the changes have been captured from the operational system, they need to be transported to the staging area on the warehouse database. The extract program could write them to a data file outside the database, use FTP to copy it, and SQL*Loader or external tables to load the change data into the staging area. Alternatively, the changes could be written to a table and moved to the staging area using transportable tablespaces. Both these techniques are discussed later in this chapter. Of course, if we were using the AUTOLOG form of asynchronous CDC, then we will have already moved our changes to the warehouse database and into the staging area as part of the CDC operation.

5.3   Transforming the Data into a Common Representation

Once the data has been extracted from the operational systems, it is ready to be cleansed and transformed into a common representation. Differences between naming conventions, storage formats, data types, and encoding schemes must all be resolved. Duplicates are removed, relationships are validated, and unique key identifiers are added. In this section, various types of transformations will be introduced; later in the chapter, we'll see specific examples of transformations.

5.3.1   Integrating Data from Multiple Sources

Often the information needed to create a table in the warehouse comes from multiple source systems. If there is a field in common between the systems, the data can be joined via that column.

Integrating data from multiple sources can be very challenging. Different people may have designed the operational systems, at different times, and using different styles, standards, and methodologies. They may use different technology (e.g., hardware platforms, database management systems, and operating system software). If data is coming from an IBM mainframe, the data may need to be converted from EBCDIC to ASCII or from big endian to little endian or vice versa.

To compound the problem, there may not be a common identifier in the source systems. For example, when creating the customer dimension, there may not be a CUSTOMER_ID in each system. You may have to look at customer names and addresses to determine that it is the same customer. These may have different spacing, case, and punctuation. Oracle Warehouse Builder helps address the customer deduplication problem.

5.3.2   Cleansing Data

The majority of operational systems contain some dirty data, which means that there may be:

- Duplicate records
- Data missing
- Data containing invalid values
- Data pointing to primary keys that do not exist

Sometimes, business rules are enforced by the applications; other times, by integrity constraints within the database; and sometimes there may be no enforcement at all.

Data must be standardized. For example, any given street address, such as 1741 Coleman Ave., can be represented in many ways. The word "Avenue" may be stored as "Ave," "Ave.," "Avenue," or "AVE.". Search & Replace transforms allow you to search for any of these values and replace them with the standard value you've chosen for your warehouse.

You may want to check the validity of certain types of data. If a product is sold only in three colors, you can validate that the data conforms to a list of values, such as red, yellow, and green. This list may change over time to include new values, for example in February 2002; the product may also be available in blue. You may want to validate data against a larger list of values stored in a table, such as the states within the United States.

Some types of cleansing involve combining and separating character data. You may need to concatenate two string columns—for example, combining LAST_NAME, comma, and FIRST_NAME into the CUSTOMER_NAME column. Or you may need to use a substring operation to divide a string into separate parts, such as separating the area code from a phone number.

An important data integrity step involves enforcement of one-to-one and one-to-many relationships. Often these are checked as part of the transformation process rather than by using referential integrity constraints in the warehouse.

5.3.3   Deriving New Data

While loading the data, you may want to perform calculations or derive new data from the existing data. For example, you may want to keep a running total or count of records as they are moved from the source to the target database.

During the design process, the appropriate level of granularity for the warehouse is determined. It is often best to store data at various levels of granularity with different retention and archive periods. The most fine-grained transaction data will usually be retained for a much shorter period of time than data aggregated at a higher level. Transaction granular sales data is necessary to analyze which products are purchased together. Daily sales of a product by store are used to analyze regional trends and product performance.

Data may be aggregated as part of the transformation process. If you did not want to store the detailed transactions in your data warehouse, the data can be aggregated prior to moving it to the data warehouse.

5.3.4   Generating Warehouse Keys

Instead of using the keys that were used in the operational system, a common design technique is to make up a new key, called the surrogate or synthetic key, to use in the warehouse. The surrogate key is usually a generated sequence of integers.

Surrogate keys are used for a variety of reasons. The keys used in the operational system may be long character strings, with meaning embedded into the components of the key. Because surrogate keys are integers, the fact tables and B*tree indexes are smaller, with fewer levels, and take less space, improving query response time. Surrogate keys provide a degree of isolation from changes in the operational system.

If the operational system changes the product-code naming conventions, or format, all data in the warehouse does not have to be changed. When one company acquires another, you may need to load products from a newly acquired company into the warehouse. It is highly unlikely that both companies used the same product encoding schemes. If there is a chance that the two companies used the same product key for different products, then the product key in the warehouse may need to be extended to add the company id as well. The use of surrogate keys can greatly help integrate the data in these types of situations.

Both the surrogate keys and operational system keys are stored in the dimension table, as shown in Figure 5.4, where product code SR125 is known in the data warehouse as PRODUCT_ID 1. Therefore, we can see that in the fact table, the product key is stored as 1. However, users can

Figure 5.4   *The Use of Surrogate Keys in the Warehouse*

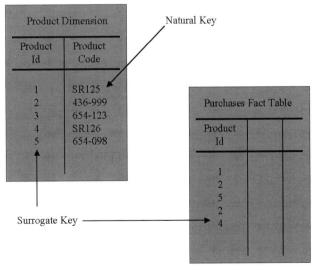

happily query using code SR125, completely unaware of the transformation being done within the data warehouse.

The surrogate key is used in the fact table as the column that joins the fact table to the dimension table. In this example, there are two different formats for product codes. Some are numeric, separated by a dash, "654-123". Others are a mix of alphanumeric and numeric characters, "SR125". As part of the ETL process, as each fact record is loaded, the surrogate key is looked up in the dimension tables and stored in the fact table.

5.3.5 Choosing the Optimal Place to Perform the Transformations

Transformations of the data may be done at any step in the ETL process. You need to decide the most efficient place to do each transformation: at the source, in the staging area, during the load operation, or in temporary tables once the data is loaded into the warehouse. Several powerful features are present in 9*i* and new in 10*g* to facilitate performing transformations.

- **Transformations can be done as part of the extraction process.** In general, it is best to do filtering types of transformations whenever possible at the source. This allows you to select only the records of interest for loading into the warehouse and consequently this also reduces the impact on the network or other mechanism used to transport the data into the warehouse. Ideally, you want to extract only the data that has been changed since your last extraction. While transformations could be done at the source operational system, an important consideration is to minimize the additional load the extraction process puts on the operational system.

- **Transformations can be done in a staging area prior to loading the data into the data warehouse.** When data needs to be integrated from multiple systems, it cannot be done as part of the extraction process. You can use flat files as your staging area, your Oracle database as your staging area, or a combination of both. If your incoming data is in a flat file, it is probably more efficient to finish your staging processes prior to loading the data into the Oracle warehouse. Transformations that require sorting, sequential processing and row-at-a-time operations can be done efficiently in the flat file staging area.

- **Transformations can be done during the load process.** Some important types of transformations can be done as the data is being loaded using SQL*Loader—for example, converting the "endian-ness" of the data, or, changing the case of a character column to uppercase. This is best done when a small number of rows need to be added—for example, when initially loading a dimension table. Oracle external tables facilitate more complex transformations of the data as part of the load process. Sections 5.4.1 and 5.4.3 discuss some examples of transformations while loading the data into the warehouse.

If your source is an Oracle 8*i*, 9*i*, or 10*g* database, transportable tablespaces make it easy to move data into the warehouse without first extracting the data into an external table. In this case, it makes sense to do the transformations in temporary staging tables once the data is in the warehouse. By doing transformations in Oracle, if the data can be processed in bulk using SQL set operations, they can be done in parallel.

- **Transformations can be done in the warehouse staging tables.** Conversion of the natural key to the surrogate key should be performed in the warehouse where the surrogate key is generated. But, in addition in Oracle Database 10*g*, a new SQL feature, called REGEXP, is introduced for processing character data using regular expressions. This new, powerful feature operates in addition to the simpler, existing text search and replace functions and operators and enables true regular expression matching, substitution, and manipulation to be performed on character data.

5.4   Loading the Warehouse

When loading the warehouse, the dimension tables are generally loaded first. The dimension tables contain the surrogate keys or other descriptive information needed by the fact tables. When loading the fact tables, information is looked up from the dimension tables and added to the columns in the fact table.

When loading the dimension table, you need both to add new rows and make changes to existing rows. For example, a customer dimension may contain tens of thousands of customers. Usually, only 10 percent or less of the customer information changes. You will be adding new customers and sometimes modifying the information about existing customers.

When adding new data to the dimension table, you need to determine if the record already exists. If it does not, you can add it to the table. If it does exist, there are various ways to handle the changes, based on whether you need to keep the old information in the warehouse for analysis purposes.

If a customer's address changes, there is generally no need to retain the old address, so the record can simply be updated. In a rapidly growing company the sales regions will change often. For example, "Canada" rolled up into the "rest of the world" until 1990, and then rolled up into the "Americas," after reorganization. If you needed to understand both the old geographical hierarchy as well as the new one, you can create a new dimension record containing all the old data plus the new hierarchy, giving the record a new surrogate key. Alternatively, you could create columns in the original record to hold both the previous and current values.

One dimension that will usually be present in any data warehouse is the time dimension, which contains one row for each unit of time that is of interest in the warehouse. In the EASYDW shopping example, purchases can be made on-line 365 days a year, so every day is of interest. For each given date, information about the day is stored, including the day of the week, the week number, the month, the quarter, the year, and if it is a holiday. The time dimension may be loaded on a yearly basis.

When loading the fact table, you typically append new information to the end of the existing fact table. You do not want to alter the existing rows, because you want to preserve that data. For example, the PURCHASES fact table contains three months of data. New data from the source order-entry system is appended to the purchases fact table monthly. Partitioning the data by month facilitates this type of operation.

In the next sections, we will take a look at different ways to load data, including:

- SQL*Loader—which inserts data into a new table or appends to an existing table when your data is in a flat file that is external to the database.

- Data Pump utilities for export and import.

- External Tables—inserts data into a new table or appends to an existing table when your data is in a flat file that is external to the database and you want to transform it while loading.

- Transportable Tablespaces—used to move the data from between two Oracle databases, such as the operational system and the warehouse, which may reside on different operating system platforms.

5.4.1   Using SQL*Loader to Load the Warehouse

One of the most popular tools for loading data is SQL*Loader, because it has been designed to load records as fast as possible. Its particular strength is that the format of the records that it can load are fully user definable, which can make it an ideal mechanism for loading data from non-Oracle source systems. For example, one possible format is to use comma-separated value (CSV) files. SQL*Loader can be used either from the operating system command line or via its wizard in Oracle Enterprise Manager (OEM), which we will discuss now.

Using Oracle Enterprise Manager Load Wizard

Figure 5.5 shows the Oracle Enterprise Manager *Maintenance* screen, from where you can launch the load wizard from the *Utilities* section. Click on the *Load Data from File* link. The wizard guides you through the process of loading data from an external file into the database according to a set of instructions in a control file and the subsequent submission of a batch job through Enterprise Manager to execute the load.

Figure 5.5   *Accessing SQL*Loader from Enterprise Manager*

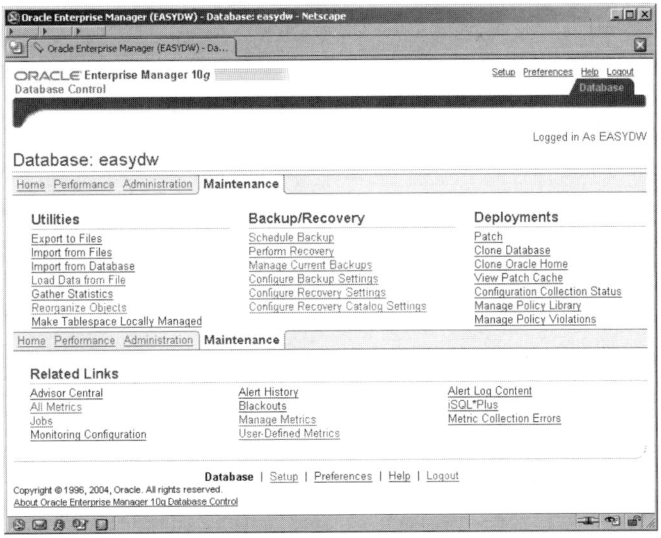

The Control File

The control file is a text file that describes the load operation. The role of the control file, which is illustrated in Figure 5.6, is to tell SQL*Loader which datafile to load, how to interpret the records and columns, and into which tables to insert the data. At this point you also need to specify a host server account, which Enterprise Manager can use to execute your SQL*Loader job.

Figure 5.6   *Identifying the Control File*

Hint: This is a server account and not the database account that you wish to use to access the tables that you're loading into.

The control file is written in SQL*Loader's data definition language. The following example shows the control file that would be used to add new product data into the product table in the EASYDW warehouse. The data is stored in the file product.dat. New rows will be appended to the existing table.

```
- Load product dimension
LOAD DATA
INFILE 'product.dat' append
INTO TABLE product
FIELDS TERMINATED BY ',' OPTIONALLY ENCLOSED BY "'"
(product_id,
 product_name,
 category,
```

```
cost_price,
sell_price,
weight,
shipping_charge,
manufacturer,
supplier)
```

5.4.2 The Data File

The following example shows a small sample of the datafile product.dat. Each field is separated by a comma and optionally enclosed in a single quote. Each field in the input file is mapped to the corresponding columns in the table. As the data is read, it is converted from the data type in the input file to the data type of the column in the database.

```
'SP1242', 'CD LX1','MUSC', 8.90, 15.67, 2.5, 2.95, 'RTG', 'CD Inc'
'SP1243', 'CD LX2','MUSC', 8.90, 15.67, 2.5, 2.95, 'RTG', 'CD Inc'
'SP1244', 'CD LX3','MUSC', 8.90, 15.67, 2.5, 2.95, 'RTG', 'CD Inc'
'SP1245', 'CD LX4','MUSC', 8.90, 15.67, 2.5, 2.95, 'RTG', 'CD Inc'
```

The datafile is an example of data stored in Stream format. A record separator, often a line feed or carriage return/line feed, terminates each record. A delimiter character, often a comma, separates each field. The fields may also be enclosed in single or double quotes.

In addition to the Stream format, SQL*Loader supports fixed-length and variable-length format files. In a fixed-length file, each record is the same length. Normally, each field in the record is also the same length. In the control file, the input record is described by specifying the starting position, length, and data type. In a variable-length file, each record may be a different length. The first field in each record is used to specify the length of that record.

In OEM, the screen shown in Figure 5.7 is where the datafile is specified, and here it is c:\easydw\load\products.dat. The alternative mechanism to specify the data file location is within the control file, as shown previously by the INFILE parameter.

Figure 5.7   *The Data File*

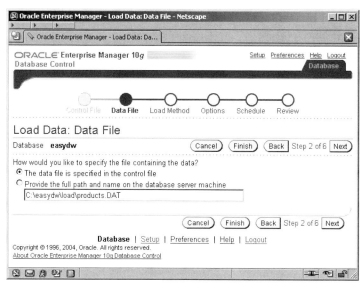

SQL*Loader Modes of Operation

Figure 5.8 shows SQL*Loader's three modes of operation:

- Conventional path
- Direct path
- Parallel direct path

Conventional path load should only be used to load small amounts of data, such as initially loading a small dimension table or when loading data with data types not supported by direct path load. The conventional path load issues SQL INSERT statements. As each row is inserted, the indexes are updated, triggers are fired, and constraints are evaluated. When loading large amounts of data in a small batch window, direct path load can be used to optimize performance.

Direct path load bypasses the SQL layer. It formats the data blocks directly and writes them to the database files. When running on a system with multiple processors, the load can be executed in parallel, which can result in significant performance gains.

Figure 5.8   *SQL*Loader Modes of Operation*

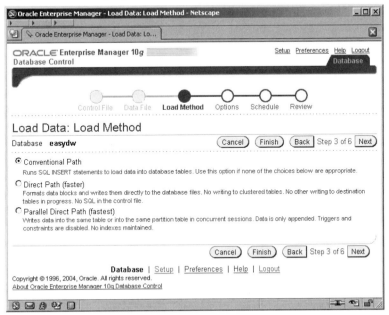

Data Load Options

In the next step in the wizard, you are presented with the screen shown in Figure 5.9, which contains various options to control the execution of your SQL*Loader operation.

A common method when extracting datafiles from the source system is to have the first record in the file contain the names of the fields of the subsequent data records. This mechanism helps to self-document the datafile, which can be particularly useful when resolving errors for files with large and complex record formats. However, we do not want to have to manually remove this record prior to loading files of this format every single time this datafile is received. The *Skip Initial Rows* option will instruct SQL*Loader to do this removal for us automatically.

You can create additional files during the load operation to aid in the diagnosis and correction of any errors that may occur during the load. A log file is created to record the status of the load operation. This should always be reviewed to ensure the load was successful. Copies of the records that could not be loaded into the database because of data integrity violations can be saved in a "bad" file. This file can later be reentered once the data integrity problems have been corrected. If you receive an extract file with

Figure 5.9   *SQL*Loader Advanced Options*

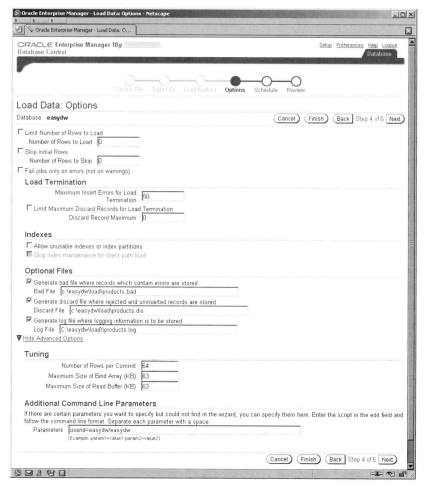

more records than you are interested in, you can load a subset of records from the file. The WHEN clause in the control file is used to select the records to load. Any records that are skipped are written to a discard file.

Select which optional files you would like created using the advanced option, as shown in Figure 5.9. In this example, we've selected a bad file, a discard file and a log file.

In order to specify the database account that SQL*Loader will log on with, you need to use the advanced options. Clicking on the *Show Advanced Options* link displays a hidden part of the page, where you can specify the account and password in the *Parameters*, field using the USERID parameter as shown.

Scheduling the Load Operation

Enterprise Manager's job scheduling system allows you to create and manage jobs, schedule the jobs to run, and monitor progress. You can run a job once or choose how frequently you would like the job to run. If you will run the job multiple times, you can save the job in Enterprise Manager's jobs library so that it can be rerun in the future. In Figure 5.10, the job will be scheduled to run immediately. Click on *Next* and you will see the

Figure 5.10   *Scheduling the Load*

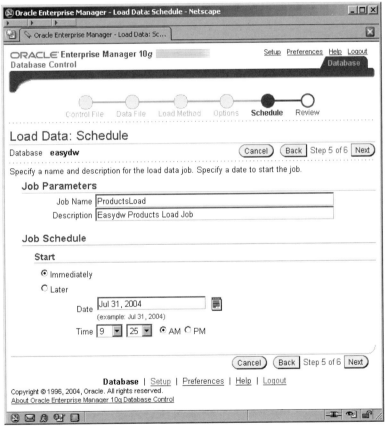

review screen (not shown) and clicking the *Submit Job* on this screen will actually submit your job for execution and display a status screen. At this point you will also have the option to monitor your job by clicking the *View Job* button which displays the screen shown in Figure 5.11 for monitoring your job.

Monitoring Progress of the Load Operation

You can also monitor the progress of a job while it is running by going to the bottom of the *Administration* screen and clicking on *Jobs* in the *Related Links* section. The *Job Activity* page shown in Figure 5.11 lists all jobs that are either running, are scheduled to run, or have completed.

Figure 5.11 *Monitoring Jobs in Enterprise Manager*

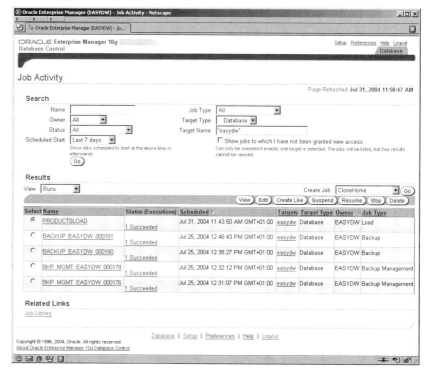

The *Results* section contains a list of jobs and their status. You can check to see if the job ran successfully after it has completed and look at the output to see any errors when a job has failed. By selecting the job and clicking on the *View* or *Edit* buttons you can view information about the job's state and progress, as shown in Figure 5.12.

Figure 5.12 *Monitoring Jobs in Enterprise Manager*

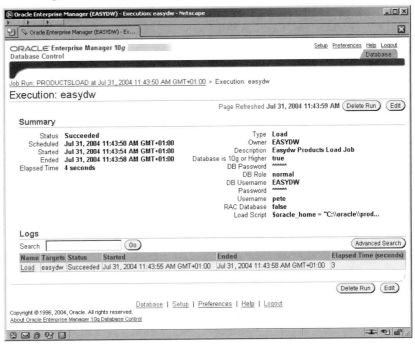

Inspecting the SQL*Loader Log

When SQL*Loader executes, it creates a log file, which can be inspected. The following example shows a log file from a sample load session that can be accessed by clicking on the Load name on the screen shown in Figure 5.12. The log file is also written to the file system (by default into the directory where the loader control file is held). Four rows were appended to the product table; one record was rejected due to invalid data. Copies of those bad records can be found in the file products.bad.

```
SQL*Loader: Release 10.1.0.2.0 - Production on Sat Jul 31 11:43:56 2004

Copyright (c) 1982, 2004, Oracle. All rights reserved.

Control File:   C:\easydw\load\products.ctl
Data File:      c:\easydw\load\products.dat
  Bad File:     C:\easydw\load\products.bad
  Discard File: none specified

 (Allow all discards)
```

```
Number to load: ALL
Number to skip: 0
Errors allowed: 50
Bind array:    64 rows, maximum of 64512 bytes
Continuation:   none specified
Path used:      Conventional

Table PRODUCT, loaded from every logical record.
Insert option in effect for this table: APPEND

Column Name                        Position   Len Term Encl Datatype
------------------------------     ---------- ----- ---- ---- --------
PRODUCT_ID                         FIRST      *   ,  O(') CHARACTER
PRODUCT_NAME                       NEXT       *   ,  O(') CHARACTER
CATEGORY                           NEXT       *   ,  O(') CHARACTER
COST_PRICE                         NEXT       *   ,  O(') CHARACTER
SELL_PRICE                         NEXT       *   ,  O(') CHARACTER
WEIGHT                             NEXT       *   ,  O(') CHARACTER
SHIPPING_CHARGE                    NEXT       *   ,  O(') CHARACTER
MANUFACTURER                       NEXT       *   ,  O(') CHARACTER
SUPPLIER                           NEXT       *   ,  O(') CHARACTER

value used for ROWS parameter changed from 64 to 27
Record 5: Rejected - Error on table PRODUCT, column PRODUCT_ID.
Column not found before end of logical record (use TRAILING
NULLCOLS)

Table PRODUCT:
  4 Rows successfully loaded.
  1 Row not loaded due to data errors.
  0 Rows not loaded because all WHEN clauses were failed.
  0 Rows not loaded because all fields were null.


Space allocated for bind array:   62694 bytes(27 rows)
Read   buffer bytes:   64512

Total logical records skipped:         0
Total logical records read:            5
Total logical records rejected:        1
Total logical records discarded:       0

Run began on Sat Jul 31 11:43:56 2004
Run ended on Sat Jul 31 11:43:56 2004

Elapsed time was:      00:00:00.66
CPU time was:          00:00:00.08
```

Optimizing SQL*Loader Performance

When loading large amounts of data in a small batch window, a variety of techniques can be used to optimize performance:

- Using direct path load. Formatting the data blocks directly and writing them to the database files eliminate much of the work needed to execute a SQL INSERT statement. Direct path load requires exclusive access to the table or partition being loaded. In addition, triggers are automatically disabled, and constraint evaluation is deferred until the load completes.

- Disabling integrity constraint evaluation prior to loading the data. When loading data with direct path, SQL*Loader automatically disables all CHECK and REFERENCES integrity constraints. When using parallel direct path load or loading into a single partition, other types of constraints must be disabled. You can manually disable evaluation of not null, unique, and primary-key constraints during the load process as well. When the load completes, you can have SQL*Loader reenable the constraints, or do it yourself manually.

- Loading the data in sorted order. Presorting data minimizes the amount of temporary storage needed during the load, enabling optimizations to minimize the processing during the merge phase to be applied. To tell SQL*Loader which indexes the data is sorted on, use the SORTED INDEXES statement in the control file.

- Deferring index maintenance. Indexes are maintained automatically whenever data is inserted or deleted, or the key column is updated. When loading large amounts of data with direct path load, it may be faster to defer index maintenance until after the data is loaded. You can either drop the indexes prior to the beginning of the load or skip index maintenance by setting SKIP_INDEX_MAINTENANCE=TRUE on the SQL*Loader command line. Index partitions that would have been updated are marked "index unusable," because the index segment is inconsistent with respect to the data it indexes. After the data is loaded, the indexes must be rebuilt separately.

- Disabling redo logging by using the UNRECOVERABLE option in the control file. By default, all changes made to the database are also written to the redo log so they can be used to recover the database after failures. Media recovery is the process of recovering after the loss of a database file, often due to a hardware failure such as a disk head crash. By disabling redo logging, the load is faster.

However, if the system fails in the middle of loading the data, you need to restart the load, since you cannot use the redo log for recovery. If you are using Oracle Data Guard to protect your data with a logical or physical standby database, you may not want to disable redo logging. Any data not logged cannot be automatically applied to the standby site.

After the data is loaded, using the UNRECOVERABLE option, it is important to do a backup to make sure you can recover the data in the future if the need arises.

- Loading the data into a single partition. While you are loading a partition of a partitioned or subpartitioned table, other users can continue to access the other partitions in the table. Loading the April transactions will not prevent users from querying the existing data for January through March. Thus, overall availability of the warehouse is increased.

- Loading the data in parallel. When a table is partitioned, it can be loaded into multiple partitions in parallel. You can also set up multiple, concurrent sessions to perform a load into the same table or into the same partition of a partitioned table.

- Increasing the STREAMSIZE parameter can lead to better direct path load times, since larger amounts of data will be passed in the data stream from the SQL*Loader client to the Oracle server.

- If the data being loaded contains many duplicate dates, using the DATE_CACHE parameter can lead to better performance of direct path load. Use the date cache statistics (entries, hits, and misses) contained in the SQL*Loader log file to tune the size of the cache for future similar loads.

SQL*Loader Direct Path Load of a Single Partition

Next, we will look at an example of loading data into a single partition. In the EASYDW warehouse, the fact table is partitioned by date. At the end of April, the April sales transactions are loaded into the EASYDW warehouse.

In the following example, we create a tablespace, add a partition to the purchases table, and then use SQL*Loader direct path load to insert the data into the January 2005 partition.

Step 1: Create a Tablespace

```
CREATE TABLESPACE purchases_jan2005
 DATAFILE
  'C:\ORACLE\PRODUCT\10.1.0\ORADATA\EASYDW\PURCHASESJAN2005.f'
 SIZE 5M
 REUSE AUTOEXTEND ON
 DEFAULT STORAGE
  (INITIAL 64K NEXT 64K PCTINCREASE 0 MAXEXTENTS UNLIMITED);
```

Step 2: Add a Partition

If our new partition is higher than the last partition in the table (i.e., based on the boundary clauses), then we can add a partition, as follows:

```
ALTER TABLE easydw.purchases
      ADD PARTITION purchases_jan2005
      VALUES LESS THAN (TO_DATE('01-02-2005', 'DD-MM-YYYY'))
      PCTFREE 0 PCTUSED 99
      STORAGE (INITIAL 64K NEXT 64K PCTINCREASE 0)
      TABLESPACE purchases_jan2005;
```

Step 3: Disable All Referential Integrity Constraints and Triggers

When using direct path load of a single partition, referential and check constraints on the table partition must be disabled, along with any triggers.

```
SQL> ALTER TABLE purchases DISABLE CONSTRAINT fk_time;
SQL> ALTER TABLE purchases DISABLE CONSTRAINT fk_product_id;
SQL> ALTER TABLE purchases DISABLE CONSTRAINT fk_customer_id;
```

The status column in the USER_CONSTRAINTS view can be used to determine if the constraint is currently enabled or disabled. Here we can see that the special_offer constraint is still enabled.

```
SQL> SELECT TABLE_NAME, CONSTRAINT_NAME, STATUS
     FROM USER_CONSTRAINTS
     WHERE TABLE_NAME = 'PURCHASES';
```

TABLE_NAME	CONSTRAINT_NAME	STATUS
PURCHASES	NOT_NULL_PRODUCT_ID	DISABLED
PURCHASES	NOT_NULL_TIME	DISABLED
PURCHASES	NOT_NULL_CUSTOMER_ID	DISABLED
PURCHASES	SPECIAL_OFFER	ENABLED
PURCHASES	FK_PRODUCT_ID	DISABLED
PURCHASES	FK_TIME	DISABLED
PURCHASES	FK_CUSTOMER_ID	DISABLED

```
7 rows selected.
```

The status column in the USER_TRIGGERS view can be used to determine if any triggers must be disabled. There are no triggers on the PURCHASES table.

```
SQL> SELECT TRIGGER_NAME, STATUS
     FROM ALL_TRIGGERS
     WHERE TABLE_NAME = 'PURCHASES';


no rows selected
```

Step 4: Load the Data

The following example shows the SQL*Loader control file to load new data into a single partition. Note that the partition clause is used.

```
OPTIONS (DIRECT=TRUE)
UNRECOVERABLE LOAD DATA
INFILE 'purchases.dat' BADFILE 'purchases.bad'
APPEND
INTO TABLE purchases
PARTITION (purchases_jan2005)
(product_id          position (1-6)    char,
 time_key            position (7-17)   date "DD-MON-YYYY",
 customer_id         position (18-25)  char,
 ship_date           position (26-36)  date "DD-MON-YYYY",
 purchase_price      position (37-43)  decimal external,
 shipping_charge     position (44-49)  integer external,
 today_special_offer position (50)     char)
```

The unrecoverable keyword is specified, disabling media recovery for the table being loaded by disabling the redo logging for this operation; this also necessitates that the DIRECT option be used as well. Database changes being made by other users will continue to be logged. After disabling media recovery, it is important to do a backup to make it possible to recover the data in the future if the need arises. If you attempted media recovery before the backup was taken, you would discover that the data blocks that were loaded have been marked as logically corrupt. To recover the data, if you haven't performed the backup following the load operation, you would have to drop the partition and reload the data.

Any data that cannot be loaded will be written to the file purchases.bad. Data will be loaded into the PURCHASES_JAN2005 partition. This example shows loading a fixed-length file named purchases.dat. Each field in the input record is described by specifying the starting position, its ending position, and its data type. Note: These are SQL*Loader data types representing the data formats in the file, not the data types in an Oracle table. When the data is loaded into the tables, each field is converted to the data type of the Oracle table column, if necessary.

The following example shows a sample of the purchases data file. The PRODUCT_ID starts in column 1 and is six bytes long. "Time_key" starts in column 7 and is 11 bytes long. The data mask "DD-MON-YYYY" is used to describe the input format of the date fields.

```
12345678901234567890123456789012345678901234567890
    |          |        |        |         |      |     |
SP100001-jan-2005AB12367501-jan-20050067.23004.50N
SP101001-jan-2005AB12367301-jan-20050047.89004.50N
```

The alternative method to invoke SQL*Loader direct path mode is from the command line using DIRECT=TRUE. In this example, skip_index_ maintenance is set to true, so the indexes will need to be rebuilt after the load.

```
sqlldr USERID=easydw/easydw CONTROL=purchases.ctl
LOG=purchases.log DIRECT=TRUE SKIP_INDEX_MAINTENANCE=TRUE
```

Step 5: Inspect the Log

The following example shows a portion of the SQL*Loader log file from the load operation. Rather than generating redo to allow recovery, invalidation redo was generated to let Oracle know this table cannot be recovered. The indexes were made unusable. The column starting position and length are described.

```
SQL*Loader: Release 10.1.0.2.0 - Production on Mon Jun 7 14:59:24 2004

Copyright (c) 1982, 2004, Oracle. All rights reserved.

Control File:   purchases.ctl
Data File:      purchases.dat
  Bad File:     purchases.bad
  Discard File: none specified

 (Allow all discards)

Number to load: ALL
Number to skip: 0
Errors allowed: 50
Continuation:   none specified
Path used:      Direct

Load is UNRECOVERABLE; invalidation redo is produced.
```

```
Table PURCHASES, partition PURCHASES_JAN2005, loaded from every logical record.
Insert option in effect for this partition: APPEND


   Column Name                  Position   Len  Term Encl Datatype
   --------------------------- ---------- ----- ---- ---- --------------------
   PRODUCT_ID                         1:6     6             CHARACTER
   TIME_KEY                          7:17    11             DATE DD-MON-YYYY
   CUSTOMER_ID                      18:25     8             CHARACTER
   SHIP_DATE                        26:36    11             DATE DD-MON-YYYY
   PURCHASE_PRICE                   37:43     7             CHARACTER
   SHIPPING_CHARGE                  44:49     6             CHARACTER
   TODAY_SPECIAL_OFFER                 50     1             CHARACTER


Record 3845: Discarded - all columns null.
The following index(es) on table PURCHASES were processed:
index EASYDW.PURCHASE_CUSTOMER_INDEX partition PURCHASES_JAN2005 was made unusable
due to:
SKIP_INDEX_MAINTENANCE option requested
index EASYDW.PURCHASE_PRODUCT_INDEX partition PURCHASES_JAN2005 was made unusable due
to:
SKIP_INDEX_MAINTENANCE option requested
index EASYDW.PURCHASE_SPECIAL_INDEX partition PURCHASES_JAN2005 was made unusable due
to:
SKIP_INDEX_MAINTENANCE option requested
index EASYDW.PURCHASE_TIME_INDEX partition PURCHASES_JAN2005 was made unusable due
to:
SKIP_INDEX_MAINTENANCE option requested
```

Step 6: Reenable All Constraints and Triggers, Rebuild Indexes

After loading the data into a single partition, all references to constraints and triggers must be reenabled. All local indexes for the partition can be maintained by SQL*Loader. Global indexes are not maintained on single partition or subpartition direct path loads and must be rebuilt. In the previous example, the indexes must be rebuilt since index maintenance was skipped.

These steps are discussed in more detail later in the chapter.

SQL*Loader Parallel Direct Path Load

When a table is partitioned, the direct path loader can be used to load multiple partitions in parallel. Each parallel direct path load process should be loaded into a partition of a table stored on a separate disk to minimize I/O contention.

Since data is extracted from multiple operational systems, you will often have several input files that need to be loaded into the warehouse. These files can be loaded in parallel, and the workload distributed among several concurrent SQL*Loader sessions.

Figure 5.13 shows an example of how parallel direct path load can be used to initially load the historical transactions into the purchases table. You need to invoke multiple SQL*Loader sessions. Each SQL*Loader session takes a different datafile as input. In this example, there are three data files, each containing the purchases for one month: January, February, and March. These will be loaded into the purchases table, which is also partitioned by month. Each datafile is loaded in parallel into its own partition.

Figure 5.13   *SQL*Loader Parallel Direct Path Load*

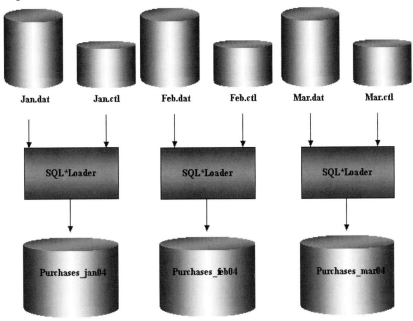

It is suggested that the following steps be followed to load data in parallel using SQL*Loader.

Step 1: Disable All Constraints and Triggers

Constraints cannot be evaluated, and triggers cannot be fired during a parallel direct path load. If you forget, SQL*Loader will issue an error.

Step 2: Drop all Indexes

Indexes cannot be maintained during a parallel direct path load. However, if we are loading only a few partitions out of many, then it is probably better to skip index maintenance and have them marked as unusable instead.

Step 3: Load the Data

By invoking multiple SQL*Loader sessions and setting direct and parallel to true, the processes will load concurrently. Depending on your operating system, you may need to put an "&" at the end of each line (i.e., to be able to invoke one sqlldr and immediately progress to invoking the second without waiting for number one to complete).

```
sqlldr userid=easydw/easydw CONTROL=jan.ctl DIRECT=TRUE PARALLEL=TRUE
sqlldr userid=easydw/easydw CONTROL=feb.ctl DIRECT=TRUE PARALLEL=TRUE
sqlldr userid=easydw/easydw CONTROL=mar.ctl DIRECT=TRUE PARALLEL=TRUE
```

Step 4: Inspect the Log

A portion of one of the log files follows. Note that the mode is direct with the parallel option.

```
SQL*Loader: Release 10.1.0.2.0 - Production on Sat Jun 5 18:30:43 2004

Copyright (c) 1982, 2004, Oracle. All rights reserved.

Control File:   c:\feb.ctl
Data File:      c:\feb.dat
  Bad File:     c:\feb.bad
  Discard File: none specified

 (Allow all discards)

Number to load: ALL
Number to skip: 0
Errors allowed: 50
Continuation:   none specified
Path used:      Direct - with parallel option.

Load is UNRECOVERABLE; invalidation redo is produced.

Table PURCHASES, partition PURCHASES_FEB2004, loaded from every logical record.
Insert option in effect for this partition: APPEND
```

Step 5: Reenable All Constraints and Triggers, Recreate All Indexes

After using parallel direct path load, reenable any constraints and triggers that were disabled for the load. Recreate any indexes that were dropped.

Transformations Using SQL*Loader

If you receive extract files that have data in them that you do not want to load into the warehouse, you can use SQL*Loader to filter the rows of interest. You select the records that meet the load criteria by specifying a WHEN clause to test an equality or inequality condition in the record. If a record does not satisfy the WHEN condition, it is written to the discard file. The discard file contains records that were filtered out of the load, because they did not match any record-selection criteria specified in the control file. Note that these records differ from rejected records written to the BAD file. Discarded records do not necessarily have any bad data. The WHEN clause can be used with either conventional or direct path load.

You can use SQL*Loader to perform simple types of transformations on character data. For example, portions of a string can be inserted using the substring function; two fields can be concatenated together using the CON-CAT operator. You can trim leading or trailing characters from a string using the trim operator. The control file in the following example illustrates both the use of the WHEN clause to discard any rows where the PRODUCT_ID is blank and how to uppercase the PRODUCT_ID column.

```
LOAD DATA
INFILE 'product.dat' append
INTO TABLE product WHEN product_id != BLANKS
FIELDS TERMINATED BY ',' OPTIONALLY ENCLOSED BY "'"
(product_id "upper(:product_id)",
 product_name,
 category,
 cost_price,
 sell_price,
 weight,
 shipping_charge,
 manufacturer,
 supplier)
```

The discard file is specified when invoking SQL*Loader from the command line, as shown here, or with the OEM Load wizard, as seen previously.

```
sqlldr userid=easydw/easydw CONTROL=product.ctl
LOG=product.log BAD=product.bad DISCARD=product.dis DIRECT=true
```

These types of transformations can be done with both direct path and conventional path modes; however, since they are applied to each record individually, they do have an impact on the load performance.

SQL*Loader Postload Operations

After the data is loaded, you may need to process exceptions, reenable constraints, and rebuild indexes.

Step 1: Inspect the Logs

Always look at the logs to ensure that the data was loaded successfully. Validate that the correct number of rows have been added.

Step 2: Process the Load Exceptions

Look in the .bad file to find out which rows were not loaded. Records that fail NOT NULL constraints are rejected and written to the SQL*Loader bad file.

Step 3: Reenable Data Integrity Constraints

Ensure, referential integrity is reenabled, if you have not already done so. Make sure that each foreign key in the fact table has a corresponding primary key in each dimension table. For the EASYDW warehouse, each row in the PURCHASES table needs to have a valid CUSTOMER_ID in the CUSTOMERS table and a valid PRODUCT_ID in the PRODUCTS table.

When using direct path load, CHECK and REFERENCES integrity constraints were disabled. When using parallel direct path load, all constraints were disabled.

Step 4: Handle Constraint Violations

To find the rows with bad data, you can create an exceptions table. Create the table named "exceptions" by running the script UTLEXCPT.SQL. When enabling the constraint, list the table name the exceptions should be written to.

```
SQL> ALTER TABLE purchases
        ENABLE CONSTRAINT fk_product_id
        EXCEPTIONS INTO exceptions;
```

In our example, two rows had bad PRODUCT_IDs. A sale was made for a product that does not exist in the product dimension.

```
SQL> SELECT * FROM EXCEPTIONS;

ROW_ID               OWNER       TABLE_NAME   CONSTRAINT
------------------   ----------  -----------  -------------
AAAOZAAAkAAAABBAAB EASYDW        PURCHASES    FK_PRODUCT_ID
AAAOZAAAkAAAABBAAA EASYDW        PURCHASES    FK_PRODUCT_ID
```

To find out which rows have violated referential integrity, select the rows from the purchases table where the rowid is in the exception table. In this example, there are two rows where there is no matching product in the products dimension.

```
SQL> SELECT * from purchases WHERE rowid in (select row_id from
exceptions);

PRODUCT TIME_KEY  CUSTOMER_ID SHIP_DATE PURCHASE SHIPPING TODAY_SPECIAL
   ID                                   PRICE    CHARGE            OFFER
-------  --------- ----------- --------- -------- -------- -------------
XY1001  01-JAN-05 AB123675     01-JAN-05   67.23     4.5 N
AB1234  01-JAN-05 AB123673     01-JAN-05   47.89     4.5 N
```

Hint: It is important to fix any referential integrity constraint problems, particularly if you are using summary management, which relies on the correctness of these relationships to perform query rewrite.

Step 5: Enabling Constraints without Validation

If integrity checking is maintained in an application, or the data has already been cleansed, and you know it will not violate any integrity constraints, enable the constraints with the NOVALIDATE clause. Include the RELY clause for query rewrite (which is discussed in Chapter 9). Since summary management and other tools depend on the relationships defined by referential integrity constraints, you should always define the constraints, even if they are not validated.

```
ALTER TABLE purchases ENABLE NOVALIDATE CONSTRAINT fk_product_id;
ALTER TABLE purchases MODIFY CONSTRAINT fk_product_id RELY;
```

Check for Unusable Indexes

Prior to publishing data in the warehouse, you should check to determine if any indexes are in an unusable state. An index becomes unusable when it no longer contains index entries to all the data. An index may be marked unusable for a variety of reasons.

- You requested that index maintenance be deferred, using the skip_index_maintenance parameter when invoking SQL*Loader.

- UNIQUE constraints were not disabled when using SQL*Loader direct path. At the end of the load, the constraints are verified when the indexes are rebuilt. If any duplicates are found, the index is not correct and will be left in an "Index Unusable" state.

The index must be dropped and recreated or rebuilt to make it usable again. If one partition is marked UNUSABLE, the other partitions of the index are still valid.

To check for unusable indexes query the table USER_INDEXES, as illustrated in the following code. Here we can see that the PRODUCT_PK_INDEX is unusable. If an index is partitioned, its status is N/A.

```
SQL> SELECT INDEX_NAME, STATUS FROM USER_INDEXES;

INDEX_NAME                          STATUS
------------------------------------------
CUSTOMER_PK_INDEX                   VALID
I_SNAP$_CUSTOMER_SUM                VALID
PRODUCT_PK_INDEX                    UNUSABLE
PURCHASE_CUSTOMER_INDEX             N/A
PURCHASE_PRODUCT_INDEX              N/A
PURCHASE_SPECIAL_INDEX              N/A
PURCHASE_TIME_INDEX                 N/A
TIME_PK_INDEX                       VALID
TSO_PK_INDEX                        VALID

9 rows selected.
```

Next, check to see if any index partitions are in an unusable state by checking the table USER_IND_PARTITIONS. In the following example, the PURCHASE_TIME_INDEX for the PURCHASES partitions for April, May, and June 2004 are unusable.

```
SQL> SELECT INDEX_NAME, PARTITION_NAME, STATUS FROM
     USER_IND_PARTITIONS WHERE STATUS != 'VALID';
```

```
INDEX_NAME                 PARTITION_NAME          STATUS
-------------------------  ---------------------   --------
PURCHASE_TIME_INDEX        PURCHASES_MAR2004       USABLE
PURCHASE_TIME_INDEX        PURCHASES_APR2004       UNUSABLE
PURCHASE_TIME_INDEX        PURCHASES_MAY2004       UNUSABLE
PURCHASE_TIME_INDEX        PURCHASES_JUN2004       UNUSABLE
```

Rebuild unusable indexes

If you have any indexes that are unusable, you must rebuild them prior to accessing the table or partition. In the following example, the PURCHASES_PRODUCT_INDEX for the newly added PURCHASES_APR2004 partition is rebuilt.

```
SQL> ALTER INDEX purchase_time_index
       REBUILD PARTITION purchases_apr2004;
```

5.4.3 Loading the Warehouse Using Data Pump

Data Pump is a new product in Oracle Database 10*g* that enables a very rapid movement of data and metadata. In any data warehouse environment there will be the problem of transporting data from the source database to the warehouse database. When your source system is also on an Oracle Database 10*g*, then it makes sense to use the fast database import and export utilities to transport your data rather than resorting to character-based operating system files. The performance increase afforded by Data Pump import and export enables the necessary rapid transfer of data from one database to another, which is very important when moving the large volumes found when sourcing data for a warehouse. Data Pump reads and writes dump files in its own binary file format; this is in contrast to SQL*Loader, which can use files of different formats as defined by the control file.

If you have used the existing import and export utilities, imp and exp, then the new Data Pump import and export will be very familiar to you. However, in addition to the improved engine for shifting the data, they also provide a lot more functionality and control.

Hint: The dump files created and used by imp and exp cannot be used by the new Data Pump import and export.

Data Pump Import/Export—impdp and expdp

The first, and most important, thing to note about Data Pump impdp and expdp is that they are client-side utilities, but the data movement is performed as a job running on the database that is accessing the dump file on the database host server directories. This detachment of the client utility from the server-side job means that more control, as well as independence, from the job is now available. For example, as a client-side tool, impdp and expdp no longer have to be dedicated to just one job on the server, but for long running jobs can, for example, detach from the job and re-attach, monitor and control a second job, or invoke a completely separate import/ export operation.

Let's have a brief look at the main new features of Data Pump impdp and expdp before working through an example of how they are used in our warehouse.

- Restartability. The new utilities may stop and start the database server-side job. The new commands are STOP_JOB and START_JOB.

- Attaching and detaching from a job. The client impdp and expdp can attach and detach from the database job, which provides a much needed improvement in the control over these potentially long-running operations.

- Performing a network import. A new parameter, NETWORK_LINK, when used on an import, instructs a local database to access a remote database, retrieve data from it, and insert it into the local database.

- Performing a network export. On export operations, NETWORK_ LINK allows data from a remote database to be written to dump files on the local database server.

- Mapping of datafile names. For import operations it is now possible to control the transformation of a datafile name on the source database to a different datafile name on the import database. Of particular importance, this feature can be used to change the file name formats used by different operating systems.

- Remapping of tablespaces during import.

- Filtering the objects that are exported and imported. Two new parameters are provided, called INCLUDE and EXCLUDE, which enable specification of the type of object and also control over the name of the objects.

- Filtering the data that is exported. By using the Data Pump QUERY parameter, a subset of the data can be exported via a WHERE clause.

- The ability to estimate the space an export job would use prior to performing the export.

- The ability to use multiple dump files.

- To control the degree of parallelism by use of the PARALLEL parameter. If multiple dump files are used, then it is normal for PARALLEL to be set to the number of the files.

Specifying the Location of the Datafile and Log Files for Data Pump Tools

Before using Data Pump, a directory object must be created in the database to specify the location of the dump files and log files. The dump and log files must be on the same machine as the database server, or must be accessible to the server (i.e., on a networked drive). This is different from SQL*Loader, where the SQL*Loader client sends the data to the database server. Directories are created in a single namespace and are not owned by an individual's schema. In the following example, the DBA creates directories for the data and log files.

```
CREATE OR REPLACE DIRECTORY data_file_dir AS 'C:\datafiles\';
CREATE OR REPLACE DIRECTORY log_file_dir AS 'C:\logfiles\';
```

Read and write access must be granted to the users that will be accessing the dump files in the directory. In the example below, the DBA grants read and write access to user easydw.

```
GRANT READ, WRITE ON DIRECTORY data_file_dir TO easydw;
GRANT READ, WRITE ON DIRECTORY log_file_dir TO easydw;
```

To find the directories defined in a database, check the DBA_DIRECTORIES view.

```
SELECT * FROM DBA_DIRECTORIES;

OWNER        DIRECTORY_NAME          DIRECTORY_PATH
-----------  ----------------------  ---------------
SYS          LOG_FILE_DIR            c:\logfiles\
SYS          DATA_FILE_DIR           c:\datafiles\
```

Moving Data between Databases

Suppose we want to export all of the OLTP ORDERS data for December 2004 from our OLTP database and move it to our warehouse database. Let us create a job to export the data using the new Data Pump export utility. We will use a parameter file called expdp_par.txt for this, which will contain all of the command-line arguments.

Hint: It is advisable to use a parameter file when the command contains keywords with values that contain spaces or quoted strings, such as QUERY and INCLUDE.

```
SCHEMAS=(OLTP)
INCLUDE=TABLE:"IN ('ORDERS')"
QUERY=OLTP.ORDERS:"WHERE purchase_date BETWEEN to_date('01-dec-
2004','dd-mon-yyyy') AND to_date('31-dec-2004','dd-mon-yyyy')"
DIRECTORY=data_file_dir
DUMPFILE=exp1.dmp
LOGFILE=log_file_dir:exporders2004.log
```

The QUERY clause allows us to specify a WHERE clause to filter the data. If the source table ORDERS were partitioned by date with a partition for each month, an alternative method to using the QUERY parameter would be to use the TABLES clause to specify the partition, as shown here.

```
TABLES=OLTP.ORDERS:DEC04 where DEC04 is the name of the partition.
```

Now we launch Data Pump export with the following command:

```
expdp oltp/oltp@easydw parfile=expdp_par.txt
```

The output at the start of the expdp execution is shown below:

```
Export: Release 10.1.0.2.0 - Production on Thursday, 08 July, 2004
21:11

Copyright (c) 2003, Oracle. All rights reserved.

Connected to: Oracle Database 10g Enterprise Edition Release
10.1.0.2.0 - Production
With the Partitioning, OLAP and Data Mining options
FLASHBACK automatically enabled to preserve database integrity.
Starting "OLTP"."SYS_EXPORT_SCHEMA_01":  oltp/********@easydw
parfile=expdp_par.txt
Estimate in progress using BLOCKS method...
Processing object type SCHEMA_EXPORT/TABLE/TABLE_DATA
Total estimation using BLOCKS method: 64 KB
```

```
Processing object type SCHEMA_EXPORT/TABLE/PROCACT_INSTANCE
Processing object type SCHEMA_EXPORT/TABLE/TABLE
Processing object type SCHEMA_EXPORT/TABLE/CONSTRAINT/CONSTRAINT
Processing object type SCHEMA_EXPORT/TABLE/STATISTICS/
TABLE_STATISTICS
```

Here we can see that the Data Pump export will automatically use the new Oracle Database 10*g* Flashback capability of the database to preserve the integrity of our exported data. Flashback is part of a much larger feature in Oracle Database 10*g* that enables earlier versions of the data to be retrieved by rewinding the view of the data to an earlier point in time. We will look at Flashback in more detail in Chapter 17 but for our export, Data Pump is using Flashback to maintain a consistent view of the data at the point where we issued the expdp command.

This should not be confused with the Data Pump export parameter called FLASHBACK_TIME that enables export of data that is consistent with an earlier point in time.

Another new item to note in the output from Data Pump export is that an estimate of the export file size is provided for each of the tables exported. There are two mechanisms that are used, BLOCKS and STATISTICS, which are specified by the ESTIMATE parameter. Associated with this, there is also the ability to cap the size of the generated dump file using the FILESIZE parameter.

Now that we have exported our data, we can move the dump file exp1.dmp between our source server and our warehouse server using any conventional means such as FTP.

On the warehouse server, we must now import the data using impdp. Let's look at some new options that are available to us. During the import we may want to put our source data in a different tablespace to keep it separated from the tablespaces that we are using for our warehouse tables. We do this using the REMAP_TABLESPACE parameter, which is used to specify the mapping between the tablespace on the source system (USERS) and the tablespace on the warehouse (STAGE).

Similarly, we want to change the ownership of the table from the OLTP account on the source system to the EASYDW account on the warehouse, and this mapping is specified using the REMAP_SCHEMA parameter.

```
impdp easydw/easydw@easydw DIRECTORY=data_file_dir
DUMPFILE=exp1.dmp
LOGFILE=log_file_dir:imporders2004.log
REMAP_TABLESPACE=users:stage REMAP_SCHEMA=oltp:easydw
```

In the same fashion that the control can be exercised over what is exported by Data Pump export, import also has the same facility to control the type of metadata this is imported. For example, by using the EXCLUDE=GRANT parameter and keyword during Data Pump import, it is possible to exclude object grants from being imported. In this way, Data Pump import will not try to regrant privileges that were only valid on the source database.

Improved Job Monitoring and Control

Let's look in more detail at the new improvements to monitoring and controlling our import and export jobs that the new impdp and expdp provide.

In Oracle Database 10*g*, impdp and expdp are client-side tools that communicate with a database server-side job that is actually doing the import and export. This provides the opportunity for the client to attach to the job that is running on the database, monitor its status, suspend it or alter some of its execution parameters, detach from it and reattach, and monitor and control another job. This provides a lot more flexibility over the preceding imp and exp utilities. Note that impdp and expdp can only be attached and control; one server-side job at a time; however, you can have multiple impdp/expdp clients running—each of which can be attached to the same or different server-side jobs.

When these tools are running in normal noninteractive mode, you can move into interactive mode by typing Control-C.

In interactive mode, the commands that we can issue are:

- ADD_FILE to add a new dump file for the export
- KILL_JOB to delete the job
- STOP_JOB, which will suspend the processing of our job and exit back to the operating system
- PARALLEL to alter the degree of parallelism

If we want to reconnect Data Pump export to a suspended job, then we can reinvoke expdp with the ATTACH command-line parameter. If we originally provided our export job with a job name (e.g., JOB_NAME=expfull), then we can specifically name the job that we want to attach to. If there is only one job executing for the database account, then Data Pump export will automatically attach to it.

An example of this activity is shown in the following code. We are running Data Pump export using the JOB_NAME=expfull parameter.

```
C:\> expdp easydw/easydw@easydw full=y directory=data_file_dir dumpfile=
full_dump.dat job_name=expfull

Export: Release 10.1.0.2.0 - Production on Saturday, 10 July, 2004 10:32

Copyright (c) 2003, Oracle. All rights reserved.

Connected to: Oracle Database 10g Enterprise Edition Release 10.1.0.2.0 - Production
With the Partitioning, OLAP and Data Mining options
FLASHBACK automatically enabled to preserve database integrity.
Starting "EASYDW"."EXPFULL":  easydw/********@easydw full=y directory=data_file_dir
dumpfile=full_dump.dat job_name=expfull
Estimate in progress using BLOCKS method...
                              ← Issue a Control-C here
Export> stop_job=immediate
Are you sure you wish to stop this job ([y]/n): y
                              ← Returned to the operating system


C:\easydw\dp>expdp easydw/easydw@easydw attach=expfull← Restart expdp and name
                                                 the job to attach to
Export: Release 10.1.0.2.0 - Production on Saturday, 10 July, 2004 10:32

Copyright (c) 2003, Oracle. All rights reserved.

Connected to: Oracle Database 10g Enterprise Edition Release 10.1.0.2.0 - Production
With the Partitioning, OLAP and Data Mining options

Job: EXPFULL                    ← Automatic report of the job status when we attach
  Owner: EASYDW
  Operation: EXPORT
  Creator Privs: FALSE
  GUID: F3A0628C541B4DD5B35F34C164A8408A
  Start Time: Saturday, 10 July, 2004 10:32
  Mode: FULL
  Instance: easydw
  Max Parallelism: 1
  EXPORT Job Parameters:
  Parameter Name      Parameter Value:
     CLIENT_COMMAND         easydw/********@easydw full=y directory=data_file_dir
  dumpfile=full_dump.dat job_name=expfull
     DATA_ACCESS_METHOD     AUTOMATIC
     ESTIMATE               BLOCKS
     INCLUDE_METADATA       1
     LOG_FILE_DIRECTORY     DATA_FILE_DIR
```

```
    LOG_FILE_NAME            export.log
    TABLE_CONSISTENCY        0
  State: IDLING
  Bytes Processed: 0
  Current Parallelism: 1
  Job Error Count: 0
  Dump File: c:\easydw\external\full_dump.dat
    bytes written: 4,096


Worker 1 Status:
  State: UNDEFINED


Export> continue_client       ← Restart the job and the logging.
                                Return to non-interactive mode
Job EXPFULL has been reopened at Saturday, 10 July, 2004 10:32
Restarting "EASYDW"."EXPFULL":  easydw/********@easydw full=y
directory=data_file_dir dumpfile=full_dump.dat job_name=expfull
Estimate in progress using BLOCKS method...
Processing object type DATABASE_EXPORT/SCHEMA/TABLE/TABLE_DATA
                               ← Issue a Control-C here
Export> stop_job=immediate
Are you sure you wish to stop this job ([y]/n): y
```

We have only touched upon some of the new, powerful features available with Data Pump import and export, but it should be apparent that the features provided are very important in a warehouse environment when dealing with large data volumes. There are three main areas that benefit our warehouse management from the new Data Pump import and export utilities:

1. The significantly improved speed and performance from the new Data Pump architecture used to move the data in and out of the database

2. The new parameters, which provide additional control of the import and export jobs

3. The new client architecture and commands, which provide better monitoring and management of the jobs

5.4.4   Loading the Warehouse Using External Tables

An **external table** is a table stored outside the database in a flat file. The data in an external table can be queried just like a table stored inside the database. You can select columns, rows, and join the data to other tables using SQL. The data in the external table can be accessed in parallel just like tables stored in the database.

External tables are read-only. No DML operations are allowed, and you cannot create indexes on an external table. If you need to update the data or access it more than once, you can load it into the database, where you can update it and add indexes to improve query performance. By loading the data into the database, you can manage it as part of the database. RMAN will not back up the data for any external tables that are defined in the database.

Since you can query the data in the external table you have just defined using SQL, you can also load the data using an INSERT SELECT statement. External tables provide an alternative to SQL*Loader to load data from flat files. They can be used to perform more complex transformations while the data is loaded and simplify many of the operational aspects while loading data in parallel and managing triggers, constraints, and indexes. However, in Oracle Database 10*g*, SQL*Loader direct path load may still be faster in many cases. There are many similarities between the two methods, and if you've used SQL*Loader, you will find it easy to learn to use external tables.

External tables require the same directory objects that we defined in earlier.

Creating an External Table

In order to create an external table you must specify the following:

- The **metadata**, which describes how the data looks to Oracle, including the external table name, the column names, and Oracle data types. These are the names you will use in the SQL statements to access the external table. The metadata is stored in the Oracle data dictionary. In the example in Figure 5.14, the external table name is NEW_PRODUCTS. The data is stored outside the database. This differs from the other regular tables in the database, where the data and metadata are both stored in the database.

- The **access parameters**, which describe how the data is stored in the external file (i.e., where it's located, its format, and how to identify the fields and records). The access driver uses the access parameters. An example of the access parameters is shown in the CREATE EXTERNAL TABLE statement.

Figure 5.14 *External Table*

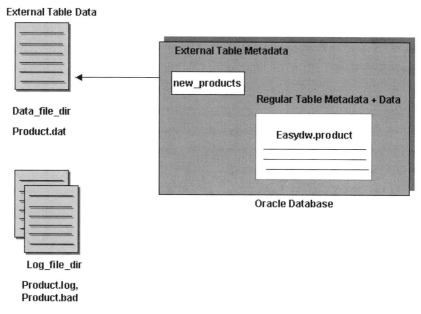

In Oracle 9*i*, there was only one type of access driver, called ORACLE_LOADER, which provides read-only access to flat files. In Oracle Database 10*g*, a new ORACLE_DATAPUMP access driver is introduced; provides greater performance, as we have already discussed, and new features, which we will discuss later. The access driver is specified in the TYPE clause on the CREATE EXTERNAL TABLE statement.

The following example shows the SQL to create an external table. In the CREATE TABLE statement, the ORGANIZATION EXTERNAL clause is used to specify the table as external, and the TYPE clause to specify the type of access driver and which begins the description of the structure of the file stored on disk. The metadata describing the column names and data types is listed and looks very similar to what is stored in a SQL*Loader control file. The locations of the datafile, log file, and bad files are specified here, and in this example we specify that each field be separated by a comma and optionally enclosed in a single quote. By specifying the PARALLEL clause, the data will be loaded in parallel.

```
CREATE TABLE new_products
(product_id          VARCHAR2(8),
 product_name        VARCHAR2(30),
 category            VARCHAR2(4),
 cost_price          NUMBER (6,2),
```

```
        sell_price              NUMBER (6,2),
        weight                  NUMBER (4,2),
        shipping_charge         NUMBER (5,2),
        manufacturer            VARCHAR2(20),
        supplier                VARCHAR2(10))
  ORGANIZATION EXTERNAL
  (TYPE ORACLE_LOADER
     DEFAULT DIRECTORY data_file_dir
     ACCESS PARAMETERS
          (RECORDS DELIMITED BY NEWLINE
           CHARACTERSET US7ASCII
           BADFILE log_file_dir:'product.bad'
           LOGFILE log_file_dir:'product.log'
           FIELDS TERMINATED BY ','
                  OPTIONALLY ENCLOSED BY "'")
     LOCATION  ('product.dat')
  )
  REJECT LIMIT UNLIMITED PARALLEL;
```

A portion of the data file, product.dat is shown in the following example. Each field is separated by a comma and optionally enclosed in a single quote. As the data is read, each field in the input file is mapped to the corresponding columns in the external table definition. As the data is read, it is converted from the data type of the input file to the data type of the column in the database, as necessary.

```
'SP1000', 'Digital  Camera','ELEC', 45.67, 67.23, 15.00, 4.50, 'Ricoh','Ricoh'
'SP1001', 'APS  Camera','ELEC', 24.67, 36.23,5.00, 4.50, 'Ricoh','Ricoh'
'SP1010', 'Camera','ELEC', 35.67, 47.89, 5.00,4.50, 'Agfa','Agfa'
```

After executing the CREATE TABLE command shown previously, the metadata for the NEW_PRODUCTS table is stored in the database. The table is as follows:

```
SQL> DESCRIBE new_products;

Name                      Null?      Type
----------------------    --------   -------------
PRODUCT_ID                           VARCHAR2(8)
PRODUCT_NAME                         VARCHAR2(30)
CATEGORY                             VARCHAR2(4)
COST_PRICE                           NUMBER(6,2)
SELL_PRICE                           NUMBER(6,2)
WEIGHT                               NUMBER(4,2)
SHIPPING_CHARGE                      NUMBER(5,2)
MANUFACTURER                         VARCHAR2(20)
SUPPLIER                             VARCHAR2(10)
```

The USER_EXTERNAL_TABLES dictionary view shows which external tables have been created, along with a description of them. The USER_EXTERNAL_LOCATIONS dictionary view shows the location of the datafile.

```
SQL> SELECT * FROM USER_EXTERNAL_TABLES;

TABLE_NAME        TYPE_OWNER TYPE_NAME
---------------   ---------- -------------------------------
DEFAULT_DIRECTORY_OWNER DEFAULT_DIRECTORY_NAME
----------------------- ------------------------------
REJECT_LIMIT                                 ACCESS_TYPE
----------------------------------------- -----------
ACCESS_PARAMETERS
-----------------------------------------------------------
PROPERTY
----------
NEW_PRODUCTS      SYS          ORACLE_LOADER
SYS                     DATA_FILE_DIR
UNLIMITED                                     CLOB
RECORDS DELIMITED BY NEWLINE
        CHARACTERSET US7ASCII
        BADFILE log_file_dir:'product.bad'
        LOGFILE log_file_dir:'product.log'
        FIELDS TERMINATED BY ',' OPTIONALLY ENCLOSED BY "'"
ALL


SQL> SELECT * FROM USER_EXTERNAL_LOCATIONS;

TABLE_NAME      LOCATION      DIR DIRECTORY_NAME
-------------   ------------  --- ------------
NEW_PRODUCTS    product.dat   SYS DATA_FILE_DIR
```

Accessing Data Stored in an External Table

After defining the external table, it can be accessed using SQL, just as if it were any other table in the database, although the data is actually being read from the file outside the database. A portion of the output is as follows:

```
SQL> SELECT * FROM NEW_PRODUCTS;
```

PRODUCT ID	PRODUCT_NAME	CATE	COST PRICE	SELL PRICE	WEIGHT	SHIPPING CHARGE	MANUF	SUPPLIER
SP1000	Digital Camera	ELEC	45.67	67.23	15	4.5	Ricoh	Ricoh
SP1001	APS Camera	ELEC	24.67	36.23	5	4.5	Ricoh	Ricoh
SP1010	Camera	ELEC	35.67	47.89	5	4.5	Agfa	Agfa

Loading Data From an External Table

The next example will use the INSERT/SELECT statement to load the data into the PRODUCT dimension table. It is very easy to perform transformations during the load using SQL functions and arithmetic operators. In this example, after the datafile was created, the cost of fuel rose, and our shipping company increased the shipping rates by 10 percent. In this example, data is loaded into the EASYDW.PRODUCT table by selecting the columns from the NEW_PRODUCTS external table. The shipping charge is multiplied by 1.1 for each item as the data is loaded.

```
SQL> INSERT INTO easydw.product
         (product_id, product_name, category,
          cost_price, sell_price, weight,
          shipping_charge, manufacturer, supplier)
      SELECT product_id, product_name, category,
             cost_price, sell_price, weight,
             (shipping_charge * 1.10),
             manufacturer, supplier
      FROM new_products;
```

The data has now been loaded into the EASYDW.PRODUCT table, and we can see here that the shipping charge increased from $4.50 to $4.95 for the items displayed.

```
SQL> select * from easydw.product;
```

PRODUCT ID	PRODUCT_NAME	CATE	COST PRICE	SELL PRICE	WEIGHT	SHIPPING CHARGE	MANUF	SUPPLIER
SP1000	Digital Camera	ELEC	45.67	67.23	15	4.95	Ricoh	Ricoh
SP1001	APS Camera	ELEC	24.67	36.23	5	4.95	Ricoh	Ricoh
SP1010	Camera	ELEC	35.67	47.89	5	4.95	Agfa	Agfa

Loading Data in Parallel Using External Tables

Another advantage of using external tables is the ability to load the data in parallel without having to split a large file into smaller files and start multiple sessions, as you must do with SQL*Loader. The degree of parallelism is set using the standard parallel hints or with the PARALLEL clause when creating the external table, as shown previously. The output of an EXPLAIN PLAN shows the parallel access, as follows:

```
SQL> EXPLAIN PLAN FOR
       INSERT INTO easydw.product
           (product_id, product_name, category,
            cost_price, sell_price, weight,
            shipping_charge, manufacturer, supplier)
       SELECT product_id, product_name, category,
              cost_price, sell_price, weight,
              (shipping_charge * 1.10),
              manufacturer, supplier
       FROM new_products;
```

The utlxplp.sql script is used to show the EXPLAIN PLAN output with the columns pertaining to parallel execution, which have been edited and highlighted for readability. Chapter 10 provides more of an explanation on how to read parallel execution plans.

```
SQL> @c:\oracle\product\10.1.0\db_1\rdbms\admin\utlxplp.sql
```

```
PLAN_TABLE_OUTPUT
------------------------------------------------------------------------------------
```

Id	Operation	Name	Rows	Bytes	Cost (%CPU)	Time
0	INSERT STATEMENT		8168	781K	13 (0)	00:00:01
1	PX COORDINATOR					
2	PX SEND QC (RANDOM)	:TQ10000	8168	781K	13 (0)	00:00:01
3	PX BLOCK ITERATOR		8168	781K	13 (0)	00:00:01
4	**EXTERNAL TABLE ACCESS FULL**	**NEW_PRODUCTS**	**8168**	**781K**	**13 (0)**	**00:00:01**

Using Data Pump External Tables to Move and Load Data

Data Pump external tables are another fast method available to us for moving data between databases; now we can actually write to the external file during the creation of the external table, which we could not do with the ORACLE_LOADER access driver. We will demonstrate this with an example.

First, let's create our external table based on the current PURCHASES table. To do this we will use a database directory object called xt_dir, where our external data file, called purch_xt.dmp, will reside.

```
CREATE TABLE purchases_xt ORGANIZATION EXTERNAL
( TYPE ORACLE_DATAPUMP
  DEFAULT DIRECTORY xt_dir
  LOCATION ('purch_xt.dmp')
)
AS SELECT * FROM purchases;
```

This statement is creating the Data Pump dump file, purch_xt.dmp, as the external table PURCHASES_XT is being created. Once it has been created, you can select from this table just like any other however, because it is now an external table, after the initial CREATE statement it is not possible to perform any further alterations to the records. Any subsequent DELETE, INSERT or UPDATE operations will result in an Oracle error, as illustrated here.

```
SQL> desc purchases_xt
 Name                            Null?    Type
 ------------------------------- -------- -----------------------
 PRODUCT_ID                      NOT NULL VARCHAR2(8)
 TIME_KEY                        NOT NULL DATE
 CUSTOMER_ID                     NOT NULL VARCHAR2(10)
 SHIP_DATE                                DATE
 PURCHASE_PRICE                           NUMBER(6,2)
 SHIPPING_CHARGE                          NUMBER(5,2)
 TODAY_SPECIAL_OFFER                      VARCHAR2(1)

SQL> SELECT count(*) FROM purchases_xt;

  COUNT(*)
----------
     94619

SQL> SELECT * FROM purchases_xt WHERE rownum < 3;


PRODUCT   TIME_KEY   CUSTOMER_I SHIP_DATE PURCHASE SHIPPING T
ID                                        PRICE    CHARGE
--------- ---------- ---------- --------- -------- -------- -
SP1001    01-JAN-03  AB123899   01-JAN-03    36.23      4.5 N
SP1011    01-JAN-03  AB123897   01-JAN-03    47.89      4.5 N

SQL> UPDATE purchases_xt SET purchase_price=37  WHERE
product_id='SP1001';
UPDATE purchases_xt SET purchase_price=37  WHERE
product_id='SP1001'
      *
ERROR at line 1:
ORA-30657: operation not supported on external organized table
```

We can now move this Data Pump formatted dump file from our specified directory to another server and access it from another database to use it as the basis of a new external table. This time, however, to create our external table we will need to specify the columns explicitly, as shown here.

```
CREATE TABLE purchases_xt2
 (product_id           VARCHAR2(8) ,
  time_key             DATE ,
  customer_id          VARCHAR2(10) ,
  ship_date            DATE,
  purchase_price       NUMBER(6,2),
  shipping_charge      NUMBER(5,2),
  today_special_offer VARCHAR2(1)
 )
ORGANIZATION EXTERNAL
(
 TYPE ORACLE_DATAPUMP
 DEFAULT DIRECTORY xt_dir
 LOCATION ('purch_xt.dmp')
 );

Table created.

SQL> SELECT count(*) FROM purchases_xt2;

  COUNT(*)
----------
     94619
```

By using a Data Pump external table, we have reaped the benefit of the performance improvements from Data Pump for both the writing of the dump file and also the reading of it on the target database. In addition, the syntax of the commands for creating this version of an external table is very succinct and readable.

Because the creation of the initial external table and the dump file can use a CREATE TABLE AS SELECT operation, we also have the capability to perform filtering with a WHERE clause and use joins when the external table is created. This can form a powerful mechanism for being selective and controlling the data that is transferred to the external table. For example, for transferring the data from a refreshed warehouse schema into a data mart, which requires a smaller subset of the fact data, the data is filtered with a WHERE clause when the external table is created.

5.4.5 Loading the Warehouse Using Transportable Tablespaces

The fastest way to move data from one Oracle database to another is using **transportable tablespaces**. Transportable tablespaces provide a mechanism to move one or more tablespaces from one Oracle database into another.

Rather than processing the data a row at time, the entire file or set of files is physically copied from one database and integrated into the second database by importing the metadata describing the tables from the files themselves. In addition to data in tables, the indexes can also be moved.

Because the data is not unloaded and reloaded, just detached, it can be moved quickly. In Oracle 9*i*, you could only transport tablespaces between Oracle databases that were on the same operating system. In Oracle Database 10*g*, this limitation is removed, and transportable tablespaces can be moved between different operating system platforms—for example, from Windows to Linux.

Transportable tablespaces can be used to move data from the operational database to the staging area if you are using an Oracle database to do your staging. Transportable tablespaces are also useful to move data from the data warehouse to a dependent data mart.

Figure 5.15 shows the steps involved in using transportable tablespaces.

These steps are as follows:

1.   Create a new tablespace.

2.   Move the data you want to transfer into its own tablespace.

3.   Alter the tablespace to read-only.

4.   Use the export utility to unload the metadata describing the objects in the tablespace.

5.   If moving between different operating systems, then convert the files using RMAN (this conversion step can alternatively be performed on the target platform after step 6).

6.   Copy the datafiles and export dump file containing the metadata to the target system.

7.   Use the import utility to load the metadata descriptions into the target database.

8.   Alter the tablespace to read/write.

9.   Perform transformations.

10.   Move the data from the staging area to the warehouse fact table.

This section will discuss steps 1–8. In the following sections, we'll look at steps 9 and 10.

Figure 5.15   *Transportable Tablespaces in Oracle Database 10g*

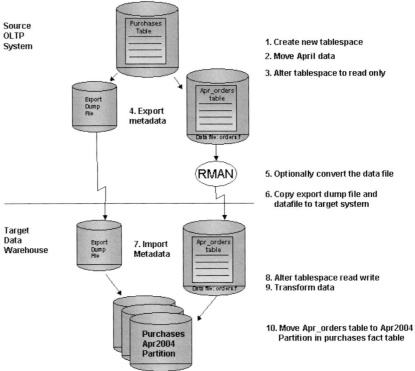

One of the sources for data in the EASYDW Warehouse is an Oracle Database 10*g* order-entry system. In this example, the order-entry system has a record for every order stored in the ORDERS table. At the end of April, all the orders for April 2004 will be copied into a new table, called APR_ORDERS, in the ORDERS tablespace stored in the datafile "orders.f."

Here are the steps that are required to transport a tablespace from one database to another. In our example, our source OLTP system is on Linux and our target warehouse system is on a Windows platform.

Step 1: Create a Tablespace in the OLTP System

Choose a name that is unique on both the source and target system. In this example, the tablespace ORDERS is created, and its corresponding datafile is "orders.f."

```
SQL> CREATE TABLESPACE orders
     DATAFILE 'C:\ORACLE\PRODUCT\10.1.0\ORADATA\EASYDW\orders.f'
     SIZE 5M REUSE
     AUTOEXTEND ON
     DEFAULT STORAGE
     (INITIAL 64K PCTINCREASE 0 MAXEXTENTS UNLIMITED);
```

Step 2: Move the Data for April 2004 into a Table in the Newly Created Tablespace

In this example, a table is created and populated using the CREATE TABLE AS SELECT statement. It is created in the ORDERS tablespace. In this example, there are 3,720 orders for April.

```
SQL> CREATE TABLE oltp.apr_orders TABLESPACE orders
     AS
     SELECT * FROM purchases
     WHERE ship_date BETWEEN to_date('01-APR-2004', 'dd-on-yyyy')
                         AND to_date('30-APR-2004', 'dd-mon-yyyy');

SQL> SELECT COUNT(*) FROM apr_orders;

  COUNT(*)
----------
      3720
```

Each tablespace must be self-contained and cannot reference anything outside the tablespace. If there were a global index on the April ORDERS table, it would not be self-contained, and the index would have to be dropped before the tablespace could be moved.

Step 3: Alter the Tablespace So That It Is Read-Only

If you do not do this, the export in the next step will fail.

```
SQL> ALTER TABLESPACE orders READ ONLY;
```

Step 4: EXPORT the Metadata

By using the Data Pump expdp command, the metadata definitions for the orders tablespace are extracted and stored in the export dump file "exp-dat.dmp."

```
expdp system/manager TRANSPORT_TABLESPACE=orders
DIRECTORY=data_file_dir
DUMPFILE=expdat.dmp
```

When transporting a set of tablespaces, you can choose to include referential integrity constraints. However, if you do include these, you must move the tables with both the primary and foreign keys.

Hint: When exporting and importing tablespaces, be sure to use an account that has been granted the EXP_FULL_DATABASE role.

The following code is a copy of the run-time information generated by the export. Only the tablespace metadata is exported, not the data.

```
$ expdp system/magic9 transport_tablespaces=orders
directory=data_file_dir dumpfile=expdat.dmp


Export: Release 10.1.0.2.0 - Production on Saturday, 10 July, 2004 8:01


Copyright (c) 2003, Oracle. All rights reserved.


Connected to: Oracle Database 10g Enterprise Edition Release 10.1.0.2.0 - Production
With the Partitioning, OLAP and Data Mining options
Starting "SYSTEM"."SYS_EXPORT_TRANSPORTABLE_01":  system/********
transport_tablespaces=orders directory=data_file_dir dumpfile=expdat.dmp
Processing object type TRANSPORTABLE_EXPORT/PLUGTS_BLK
Processing object type TRANSPORTABLE_EXPORT/TABLE
Processing object type TRANSPORTABLE_EXPORT/TABLE_STATISTICS
Processing object type TRANSPORTABLE_EXPORT/TTE_POSTINST/PLUGTS_BLK
Master table "SYSTEM"."SYS_EXPORT_TRANSPORTABLE_01" successfully
loaded/
unloaded*********************************************************************
**
Dump file set for SYSTEM.SYS_EXPORT_TRANSPORTABLE_01 is:
  /home/oracle/tt/expdat.dmp
Job "SYSTEM"."SYS_EXPORT_TRANSPORTABLE_01" successfully completed at 08:04
```

Step 5: Convert the Datafiles (Optional)

If you are transporting between different platforms and the endian formats of your platforms are different, you will need to convert the data files. The endian nature of your platform is the format in which multibyte data is stored. Big endian platforms store the most significant byte in the lowest address and little endian platforms store it in the highest address.

Oracle provides some tables and a simple query to determine the endian nature of your source and target platforms.

```
SELECT d.PLATFORM_NAME, tp.ENDIAN_FORMAT
FROM   V$TRANSPORTABLE_PLATFORM tp,
       V$DATABASE d
WHERE  tp.PLATFORM_NAME = d.PLATFORM_NAME;
```

When the query is run on the source Linux platform database, we see that the platform uses little endian format.

```
PLATFORM_NAME                            ENDIAN_FORMAT
---------------------------------------- --------------
Linux IA (32-bit)                        Little
```

When the query is run on the target warehouse database, we see that it is also little endian.

```
PLATFORM_NAME                            ENDIAN_FORMAT
---------------------------------------- --------------
Microsoft Windows IA (32-bit)            Little
```

If the endian format were different on the two platforms, then conversion would be required. In our example, even though both of our platforms are of the same endian format, we will still demonstrate the step for the conversion, which uses the Recovery Manager utility RMAN.

```
$ rman target /

Recovery Manager: Release 10.1.0.2.0 - Production
 Copyright (c) 1995, 2004, Oracle. All rights reserved.
 connected to target database: ORCL (DBID=1058909169)

RMAN> convert tablespace orders
2> to platform 'Microsoft Windows IA (32-bit)'
3> FORMAT '/home/oracle/tt/%N_%f' ;
Starting backup at 10-JUL-04
using target database controlfile instead of recovery catalog
allocated channel: ORA_DISK_1
channel ORA_DISK_1: sid=244 devtype=DISK
channel ORA_DISK_1: starting datafile conversion
input datafile fno=00005 name=/u01/app/oracle/oradata/orcl/
orders.f
converted datafile=/home/oracle/tt/ORDERS_5
channel ORA_DISK_1: datafile conversion complete, elapsed time:
00:00:01
Finished backup at 10-JUL-04
```

The conversion format mask '%N_%f' that was used will create a file name in the directory specified using the original tablespace name (%N) and the file id number on the database (%f).

If the conversion is performed on the source system, then RMAN can reference the tablespaces by logging on to the database, but if the conversion is performed after the files are transported to the warehouse server, then RMAN can no longer access the database to use the tablespace names. In this case, a slightly different format must be adopted, where the datafile names are used, as follows:

```
RMAN> CONVERT DATAFILE
2> '/u01/app/oracle/oradata/easydw/orders.f'
3> TO PLATFORM='Microsoft Windows IA (32-bit)'
4> FROM PLATFORM='Linux IA (32-bit)';
```

Step 6: Transport the Tablespace

Now copy the data file, ORDERS_5, and the export dump file, exp-dat.dmp, to the physical location on the system containing the staging database. You can use any facility for copying flat files, such as an operating system copy utility or FTP. These should be copied in binary mode, since they are not ASCII files.

In our example, ORDERS_5 was copied to c:\oracle\product\10.1.0\ oradata\easydw\ORDERS_5 on the for the EASYDW warehouse database using FTP.

Step 7: Import the Metadata

By importing the metadata, you are plugging the tablespace into the target database, which is why you should take care to place it in the correct directory that is appropriate to your database. Note that we have also specified that the tablespace contents be remapped from the OLTP schema used on the source database to the EASYDW schema on our warehouse database.

```
impdp easydw/easydw@easydw TRANSPORT_DATAFILES=c:\oracle\product\
10.1.0\oradata\easydw\ORDERS_5 DIRECTORY=tt2 DUMPFILE=expdat.dmp
logfile=log_file_dir:imporders2004.log  REMAP_SCHEMA=(oltp:easydw)
```

Check the run-time information or import log to ensure that no errors have occurred. Note that only the transportable tablespace metadata was imported.

```
Import: Release 10.1.0.2.0 - Production on Saturday, 10 July, 2004 8:45

Copyright (c) 2003, Oracle. All rights reserved.
;;;
Connected to: Oracle Database 10g Enterprise Edition Release 10.1.0.2.0 - Production
With the Partitioning, OLAP and Data Mining options
Master table "EASYDW"."SYS_IMPORT_TRANSPORTABLE_01" successfully loaded/unloaded
Starting "EASYDW"."SYS_IMPORT_TRANSPORTABLE_01":  easydw/********@easydw
TRANSPORT_DATAFILES=c:\oracle\product\10.1.0\oradata\easydw\ORDERS_5 DIRECTORY=tt2
DUMPFILE=expdat.dmp logfile=log_file_dir:imporders2004.log
REMAP_SCHEMA=(oltp:easydw)
Processing object type TRANSPORTABLE_EXPORT/PLUGTS_BLK
Processing object type TRANSPORTABLE_EXPORT/TABLE
Processing object type TRANSPORTABLE_EXPORT/TABLE_STATISTICS
Processing object type TRANSPORTABLE_EXPORT/TTE_POSTINST/PLUGTS_BLK
Job "EASYDW"."SYS_IMPORT_TRANSPORTABLE_01" successfully completed at 08:45
```

Check the count to ensure that the totals match the OLTP system.

```
SQL> SELECT COUNT(*) FROM orders;

  COUNT(*)
----------
      3720
```

Step 8: Alter the Tablespace to Read/Write

Alter the ORDERS tablespace so that it is in read/write mode. You are ready to perform your transformations!

```
SQL> ALTER TABLESPACE orders READ WRITE;
```

As you can see by following these steps, the individual rows of a table are never unloaded and reloaded into the database. Thus, using transportable tablespaces is the fastest way to move data between two Oracle databases.

5.4.6 Loading the Dimensions Using SQL MERGE

When loading new data into existing dimension tables, you may need to add new rows and make changes to existing rows. In the past, special programming logic was required to differentiate a new row from a changed row, which typically involved separate INSERT and UPDATE statements. A new capability was added in Oracle 9*i*, which makes this process much easier: the SQL MERGE. This says that if a row exists, update it; if it doesn't exist, insert it. This is often called an **upsert** operation.

In the following example, new data is added to the customer dimension. The input file has both new customers who have been added and changes to existing customer data. In this case, there is no need to retain the old customer information, so it will be updated. An external table, named CUSTOMER_CHANGES, is created for the file containing the updates to the customer dimension.

```
CREATE TABLE easydw.customer_changes
(customer_id              VARCHAR2(10),
 gender                   VARCHAR2(1),
 tax_rate                 NUMBER,
 city                     VARCHAR2(15),
 state                    VARCHAR2(10),
 region                   VARCHAR2(15),
 postal_code              VARCHAR2(10),
 country                  VARCHAR2(20),
 occupation               VARCHAR2(15))
ORGANIZATION EXTERNAL
(TYPE ORACLE_LOADER
      DEFAULT DIRECTORY  data_file_dir
      ACCESS PARAMETERS
        ( records delimited by newline
          characterset us7ascii
          badfile log_file_dir:'cus_changes.bad'
          logfile log_file_dir:'cust_changes.log'
          fields terminated by ','
          optionally enclosed by "'")
      LOCATION ('customer_changes.dat')
)
REJECT LIMIT UNLIMITED NOPARALLEL;
```

Instead of using an insert statement to load the data, the MERGE statement is used to load the data. The MERGE statement has two parts. When the customer_id in the customer table matches the customer_id in the customer_changes table, the row is updated. When the customer_ids do not match, a new row is inserted.

```
MERGE INTO easydw.customer c
USING easydw.customer_changes cc
ON (c.customer_id = cc.customer_id)
WHEN MATCHED THEN UPDATE SET
      c.city=cc.city, c.state=cc.state,
      c.postal_code=cc.postal_code,
```

```
            c.gender=cc.gender, c.country=cc.country,
            c.region=cc.region, c.tax_rate=cc.tax_rate,
            c.occupation=cc.occupation
WHEN NOT MATCHED THEN INSERT
            (customer_id, city, state, postal_code,
             gender, region, country, tax_rate,
             occupation)
        VALUES
            (cc.customer_id, cc.city, cc.state, cc.postal_code,
             cc.gender, cc.region, cc.country, cc.tax_rate,
             cc.occupation) ;
```

Before merging the customer changes, we had 500 customers.

```
SQL> SELECT COUNT(*) FROM customer;

  COUNT(*)
----------
       500
```

Once the external table is created, we can use SQL to look at the customer_changes data file. The first two are rows that will be updated. The first customer was previously an astronomer and is now returning to work as an astrophysicist. The second customer moved from postal region W1 1QC to W1-2BA. The last two rows are new customers who will be inserted.

```
SQL> SELECT * FROM customer_changes;

CUSTOMER_I G TAX_RATE CITY       STATE      REGION   POSTAL_COD COUNTRY OCCUPATION
---------- - -------- ---------- ---------- -------- ---------- ------- -----------
AB123459   M        5 Phoenix    AZ         AmerWest 85001      USA     Astro-Physicist
AB123460   F       15 London     London     EuroWest W1-2BA     UK      Engineer
AA114778   M       40 Reading    Berkshire  EuroWest RG1 1BB    UK      Astronomer
AA123478   F       25 Camberley  Surrey     Eurowest GU14 2DR   UK      DB Consultant
```

Looking at the following portion of the customer dimension, we can see the rows where the CUSTOMER_ID column matches the CUSTOMER_ID column in the CUSTOMER_CHANGES external table. These rows will be updated.

```
SQL> SELECT * FROM customer;

CUSTOMER_I CITY      STATE    POSTAL_COD G REGION    COUNTRY TAX_RATE OCCUPATION
---------- -------   ------   ---------- - --------- ------- -------- -----------
AB123459   Phoenix   AZ       85001      M AmerWest  USA            5 Astronomer
AB123460   London    London   W1 1QC     F EuroWest  UK            15 Engineer
```

After the MERGE, we now have 502 customers. A portion of the output, just the rows that have changed from the customer table, is displayed here.

```
SQL> SELECT COUNT(*) FROM customer;

  COUNT(*)
----------
       502

SQL> SELECT * FROM customer;
```

CUSTOMER_I	CITY	STATE	POSTAL_COD	G	REGION	COUNTRY	TAX_RATE	OCCUPATION
AB123459	Phoenix	AZ	85001	M	AmerWest	USA	5	Astro-Physicist
AB123460	London	London	W1-2BA	F	EuroWest	UK	15	Engineer
AA114778	Reading	Berkshire	RG1-1BB	M	EuroWest	UK	40	Astronomer
AA123478	Camberley	Surrey	GU14 2DR	F	Eurowest	UK	25	DB Consultant

In this example, the MERGE statement was used with external tables. It can also be used with any user tables. By using the MERGE statement we avoid multiple passes of our source data required for separate INSERT and UPDATE statements; therefore, there is a significant potential saving in terms of I/O and processor resources.

We can also use the MERGE statement and omit either the INSERT or the UPDATE clauses. For example, if, in our warehouse, we are not allowed to change data that is historical and can only insert new data, we can then omit the UPDATE part of the MERGE statement, as follows:

```
MERGE INTO easydw.customer c
USING easydw.customer_changes cc
ON (c.customer_id = cc.customer_id)
WHEN NOT MATCHED THEN INSERT
     (customer_id, city, state, postal_code,
      gender, region, country, tax_rate, occupation)
   VALUES
     (cc.customer_id, cc.city, cc.state, cc.postal_code,
      cc.gender, cc.region, cc.country,
      cc.tax_rate, cc.occupation) ;
```

In addition, MERGE also provides the capability to conditionally execute the INSERT or UPDATE clauses on a record-by-record basis. For example, you'll notice that one of our records to be updated, as well as a new record to be inserted, has the postal code in an illegal format using a hyphen "-" separator. We can add a conditional clause to both the update and the insert parts of the merge, so that records with a hyphen are not merged, as follows:

```
MERGE INTO easydw.customer c
USING easydw.customer_changes cc
ON (c.customer_id = cc.customer_id)
WHEN MATCHED THEN UPDATE SET
      c.city=cc.city, c.state=cc.state,
      c.postal_code=cc.postal_code,
      c.gender=cc.gender, c.country=cc.country,
      c.region=cc.region, c.tax_rate=cc.tax_rate,
      c.occupation=cc.occupation
  WHERE cc.postal_code not like '%-%'
WHEN NOT MATCHED THEN INSERT
      (customer_id, city, state, postal_code,
       gender, region, country, tax_rate, occupation)
    VALUES
      (cc.customer_id, cc.city, cc.state, cc.postal_code,
       cc.gender, cc.region, cc.country,
       cc.tax_rate, cc.occupation)
  WHERE cc.postal_code not like '%-%' ;
```

Now we have only one record inserted (AA123478), which had a valid postal code in the change record, but our existing record (AB123460) was not updated with its change; it had a bad postal code and remains W1 1QC.

CUSTOMER_I	CITY	STATE	POSTAL_COD	G	REGION	COUNTRY	TAX_RATE	OCCUPATION
AA123478	Camberley	Surrey	GU14 2DR	F	Eurowest	UK	25	DB Consultant
AB123459	Phoenix	AZ	85001	M	AmerWest	USA	5	Astro-Physicist
AB123460	London	London	W1 1QC	F	EuroWest	UK	15	Engineer

Finally, under certain circumstances, we can also use the MERGE statement to delete rows in our target table. When the update fires (because the match clause succeeds), we can add an additional clause to delete the matched records when an additional delete criteria succeeds. For example, let's assume that our legacy system for the customer data cannot add a new field to the table to indicate that a record has been deleted and instead the delete flag is encoded into the tax rate. If the tax rate is −1, then the record is deleted on the source system. Our new MERGE statement now looks like this:

```
MERGE INTO easydw.customer c
USING easydw.customer_changes cc
ON (c.customer_id = cc.customer_id)
WHEN MATCHED THEN UPDATE SET
     c.city=cc.city, c.state=cc.state,
     c.postal_code=cc.postal_code,
     c.gender=cc.gender, c.country=cc.country,
     c.region=cc.region, c.tax_rate=cc.tax_rate,
     c.occupation=cc.occupation
  DELETE WHERE (cc.tax_rate=-1)
WHEN NOT MATCHED THEN INSERT
     (customer_id, city, state, postal_code,
      gender, region, country, tax_rate, occupation)
   VALUES
     (cc.customer_id, cc.city, cc.state, cc.postal_code,
      cc.gender, cc.region, cc.country,
      cc.tax_rate, cc.occupation) ;
```

If the update match succeeds, then the new delete criteria is tested; if this also succeeds, then the customer record is deleted. Note, however, that this is a delete under special circumstances and only the rows that are updated are candidates for the delete.

The operation that MERGE performs is one of the most common in warehouse ETL: insert if it does not exist; otherwise, update. Therefore, instead of having to do this using a number of passes of your data, MERGE enables you to perform this operation with one call to the database and one pass over your data. A very useful feature in the warehouse!

5.5   Transformations inside the Oracle Database

Section 5.3 introduced transformations and discussed choosing the optimal place to perform the transformations. We've seen examples of transforming the data while loading it using both SQL*Loader and external tables. This section will discuss performing transformations inside the Oracle server. If you are doing transformations in the Oracle data warehouse, you typically load data into temporary staging tables, transform the data, then move it to the warehouse detail fact tables.

When using transportable tablespaces, as shown in the previous section, the data was moved from the OLTP system to the staging area in the Oracle warehouse. Data that was loaded using external tables or SQL*Loader, can be further transformed in a staging area inside the Oracle server. Oracle Database 10*g* provides tools that can be used to implement transformations in SQL, PL/SQL, or Java stored procedures.

In this section, we will first look at the SQL to perform the following simple transformations.

- Remove the hyphen from the product id and increase the shipping charges by 10 percent.
- Check for invalid product_ids.
- Look up the warehouse key, and substitute it for the PRODUCT_ID.

We will look at a new SQL feature to use regular expressions for searching and manipulating character data. Then, we will rewrite the first transformation as a table function.

5.5.1 Transformations That Cleanse Data and Derive New Data

The SQL UPDATE statement using built-in functions can be used to perform some simple transformations. Continuing with our example, the APR_ORDERS table must be cleansed. Some of the PRODUCT_ID'S contain a hyphen, which needs to be removed. The fuel costs have increased, so we must add 10 percent to the shipping charges. Both of these operations can be done in one step using the UPDATE statement. A few of the rows are shown here before they are transformed.

```
SQL> SELECT * FROM apr_orders;

PRODUCT  TIME_KEY   CUSTOMER SHIP_DATE PURCHASE SHIPPING TODAY_SPECIAL
    ID              ID                 PRICE    CHARGE   OFFER
-------  ---------  -------- --------- -------- -------- -------------
SP1001   02-APR-04 AB123457 02-APR-04   28.01     5.45 N
SP-1000  01-APR-04 AB123456 01-APR-04   67.23     5.45 N
SP-1000  01-APR-04 AB123457 01-APR-04   67.23     5.45 N
```

The SQL multiplication operator, *, will be used to update the shipping charge, and the REPLACE function will be used to replace the hyphen, '-' with an empty quote, '', thus removing it. The modified fields are highlighted. The shipping charge has increased from 5.45 to 6. The hyphen has been removed from the PRODUCT_ID.

```
SQL> UPDATE apr_orders
     SET shipping_charge = (shipping_charge * 1.10),
         product_id=REPLACE(product_id, '-','');
```

PRODUCT ID	TIME_KEY	CUSTOMER ID	SHIP_DATE	PURCHASE PRICE	SHIPPING CHARGE	TODAY_SPECIAL OFFER
SP1001	02-APR-04	AB123457	02-APR-04	28.01	6	N
SP1000	01-APR-04	AB123456	01-APR-04	67.23	6	N
SP1000	01-APR-04	AB123457	01-APR-04	67.23	6	N

Processing With More Power: The REGEXP Functions

In Oracle Database 10*g*, a powerful set of text search and replace functions are introduced; these use regular expressions and significantly improve our capability to search on, and process, character data.

The new regular expressions extend our ability to define the rules for the types of strings we are searching for and are also used in functions to manipulate character data. This provides us with a new, powerful mechanism for parsing more sophisticated strings in order to validate our warehouse data. It also gives us greater control and flexibility with the operations to transform and reorganize our source data to make it conform to the warehouse rules and representation.

Prior to Oracle Database 10*g*, the fundamental ability to process textual strings in the database was limited by relatively simple search and replace functionality—for example, the LIKE operator and the INSTR, SUBSTR, and REPLACE functions, which are really just based on either string matching or simple wildcards. Even with the facility to define new, more powerful functions in PL/SQL and call them from INSERT, UPDATE, and SELECT clauses we still have the burden of creating the functions in the first place. Having a more powerful set of text search and manipulation functions as standard is extremely valuable in the warehouse.

Let's look at an example, the criteria LIKE '%CARD%' searches for any string of characters (represented by '%') followed by the string 'CARD' followed by another string of any characters (the second '%'). We can also use the underscore character '_' to represent a single character wildcard. But other than that, this is more or less our standard search capability.

Regular Expression Basics and Searching

But what is a regular expression? Regular expressions operate by giving certain characters special meaning, which, when used in conjunction with normal characters, enables us to define an expression that represents the string we want to search for. Often these special characters are called **metacharacters**. For example, '%' and '_' in our previous simple example are the two metacharacters that we had prior to Oracle Database 10*g*.

Some of the basic metacharacters in regular expressions are:

.	A single character match
^	The start of a line or string
$	The end of a line or string
*	Repeat the pattern 0 or more times
?	Repeat the pattern 0 or 1 times
+	Repeat the pattern 1 or more times
{m}	Repeat the pattern m times
{m,}	Repeat the pattern at least m times
{m,n}	Repeat the pattern m times but not more than n times

If you are familiar with UNIX systems, you will recognize and feel comfortable with many of the constructs used in Oracle regular expressions, which are based on the POSIX rules.

Let's take a simple example based on the following table and rows.

```
SQL> CREATE TABLE regexp (chardata varchar2(50));

SQL> INSERT INTO regexp VALUES ('A theory concerning');

1 row created.

SQL> INSERT INTO regexp
     VALUES ('the origin of the universe, is the Big ');

1 row created.

SQL> INSERT INTO regexp VALUES ('Bang.');

SQL> COMMIT;
Commit complete.
```

Now let's see how we define a search condition using the wildcard character '*':

```
SQL> SELECT * FROM regexp
     WHERE regexp_like (chardata, '*the*');

CHARDATA
--------------------------------------------------
A theory concerning
the origin of the universe is the
```

The '*' metacharacter represents any string of characters, so we have specified a criteria for any record where the CHARDATA column data contains the string 'the'. The REGEXP_LIKE function can actually take three parameters, as follows:

```
REGEXP_LIKE(search_string, pattern_string, match_parameter)
```

In our example, we have already seen how *search_string* and *pattern_string* are used, but the *match_parameter* provides some extra functionality to add to the power and flexibility of REGEXP_LIKE. This parameter can take a small set of values, which changes the matching behavior:

'i'   case-insensitive matching

'c'   case-sensitive matching

'm'   allows the period '.' to match the new line character

'n'   allows the *search_string* to represent or contain multiple lines

Without this, Oracle treats each record as a separate line; by specifying 'n' Oracle will interpret *search_string* as containing multiple lines.

If we want to find the record where 'the' occurs only at the start of the line, then we use the '^' character, which represents the start of the line:

```
SQL> SELECT * FROM regexp
     WHERE regexp_like (chardata, '^the*');

CHARDATA
-------------------------------------------------
the origin of the universe is the
```

So if we combine the use of the '.' to match any single character with the '{}' repetition capability, we can show how we can easily construct a regular expression to find a single character between 'B' and 'g' and exactly two characters between the 'B' and 'g'.

```
SQL> SELECT * FROM regexp
     WHERE regexp_like(chardata, 'B.{1}g');
```

```
CHARDATA
-------------------------------------------------
the origin of the universe, is the Big

SQL> SELECT * FROM regexp
     WHERE regexp_like(chardata, 'B.{2}g');

CHARDATA
-------------------------------------------------
Bang.
```

To take another example to demonstrate the power of regular expressions, a construct for use in the pattern string is one to specify lists by bracketing the list values using '[' and ']'. For example, to find the records that contain the characters 'y' and 'v', the following list would be used, '[yv]'. Now the real power of lists is where predefined lists are provided. For example, lists representing all alphanumeric characters, all uppercase characters, or control characters enable these sets of characters to be referenced in one clear construct.

Regular Expressions and Substrings

We have shown the basic forms of regular expressions, and you can see that very powerful searching capability can be defined with their use. But there is also a REGEXP version equivalent to the existing INSTR function, called REGEXP_INSTR, which can tell us at what position our pattern occurs in the search string. For example:

```
SQL> SELECT regexp_instr(chardata, 'B.{1}g')
     FROM regexp
     WHERE regexp_like(chardata, 'B.{1}g') ;

REGEXP_INSTR(CHARDATA,'B.{1}G')
-------------------------------
                             36
```

Similarly, there is also a new regular expression version of the familiar SUBSTR functions. For example, to extract the substring that we just identified in the preceding example:

```
SQL> SELECT regexp_substr(chardata, 'B.{2}g')
     FROM regexp
     WHERE regexp_like(chardata, 'B.{2}g') ;

REGEXP_SUBSTR(CHARDATA,'B.{2}G')
-------------------------------
Bang
```

If we had used '1' instead of '2', then we would have extracted the string 'Big' from our other record.

Regular Expressions to Manipulate Data

Finally, let's take a look at the REGEXP_REPLACE function, which extends the REPLACE functionality. Now that we understand regular expressions a bit better, we will take an example that is closer to a warehouse parsing and manipulation requirement and add some data to our table: U.S. phone numbers. Some of our phone numbers are arriving with the area code in parentheses, which is not the required format for our warehouse. By using REGEXP_REPLACE, we can define a regular expression that matches the parenthesized phone number and removes the parentheses.

This example will take a bit more explaining; it is also demonstrating another powerful feature of the regular expression implementation called **back references**, where subexpressions in our pattern string can be separately referenced.

In our REGEXP_REPLACE() call, we have actually defined five subexpressions, as follows, to parse the string '(123)-456-7890':

```
SQL> SELECT regexp_replace('(123)-456-7890',
                           '(\()(.*)(\))-(.*)-(.*)',
                           '\2-\4-\5') AS transformed_string
     FROM dual ;


TRANSFORMED_STRING
------------------
123-456-7890
```

Where each of the five subexpressions is defined as follows:

- (\()   is the '(' character, where we have used the backslash to remove the special meaning
- (.*)   for any string of characters
- (\))   is the ')' character, from which we have also removed any special meaning
- (.*)   any string of characters
- (.*)   any string of characters

The hyphens act as themselves and are not our subexpressions. Therefore, in our replace string, we can refer to these subexpressions and reorder them or even remove them entirely from our resulting string. The string '\2-\4-\5' in our example means take the seconds, fourth, and fifth sub-expressions and separate them with hyphens.

To run our new phone number transformation function using the data within our table we will first add a few records containing some new numbers.

```
SQL> INSERT INTO regexp VALUES ('123-456-7890');

1 row created.

SQL> INSERT INTO regexp VALUES ('(111)-222-3333');
1 row created.

SQL> INSERT INTO regexp VALUES ('333-444-5555');

1 row created.

SQL> COMMIT;

Commit complete.

SQL> SELECT regexp_replace(chardata,
                    '(\()(.*)(\))-(.*)-(.*)',
                    '\2-\4-\5') AS transformed_string
     FROM regexp;

TRANSFORMED_STRING
-----------------------------------------
A theory concerning
the origin of the universe, is the Big
Bang.
123-456-7890
111-222-3333
333-444-5555
```

Hence, REGEXP_REPLACE has restructured just the strings that match our regular expression, removed the parenthesis to make it conform to our warehouse representation, and left alone all of the other records that don't match. Now, if you consider how to code that operation using normal SQL functions, you can see that regular expressions are very powerful. We have only touched the tip of the iceberg with some simple examples, but the REGEXP functions use a succinct and convenient notation to encompass some very useful functionality for our warehouse transformations.

5.5.2   Validating Data Using a Dimension

Often the incoming data must be validated using information that is in the dimension tables. While this is not actually a transformation, it is discussed here, since it is often done at this stage prior to loading the warehouse tables. In our example, we want to ensure that all the PRODUCT_ID'S for the April orders are valid. The PRODUCT_ID for each order must match a PRODUCT_ID in the product dimension.

This query shows that the April data does have an invalid PRODUCT_ID, where there is no matching PRODUCT_CODE in the product dimension. Any data that is invalid should be corrected prior to loading it from the staging area into the warehouse.

```
SQL> SELECT DISTINCT product_id FROM apr_orders
        WHERE product_id NOT IN (SELECT product_id FROM product);


PRODUCT_ID
----------
SP1036
```

Note that in many actual warehouse systems, the warehouse designer sometimes makes a conscious decision to map unknown natural dimension codes (SP1036 in our previous example) to a dimension record representing "unknown." For example, if the product surrogate key is in incrementing integer sequence from 1, then the unknown dimension new records are mapped to a record with the id -1. With this technique, we are always able to map our new source products to a product dimension record, and, consequently, the referential integrity constraints can always be activated, however, there is a necessary cleanup step required when the true dimensional record arrives in the warehouse.

5.5.3   Looking up the Warehouse Key

Now that we have cleansed the PRODUCT_ID column, we will modify it to use the warehouse key. For the next example, a PRODUCT_CODE has been added to the product table; this will be used to look up the PRODUCT_ID, which is the surrogate key for the warehouse. Figure 5.4 showed the use of surrogate keys in the warehouse. A portion of the product dimension is displayed.

```
SQL> SELECT PRODUCT_ID, PRODUCT_CODE FROM PRODUCT;

PRODUCT_ID PRODUCT_CODE
---------- ------------
         1 SP1000
         2 SP1001
         3 SP1010
         4 SP1011
         5 SP1012
```

In this next transform, we are going to use the PRODUCT_ID in the APR_ORDERS table to look up the warehouse key from the PRODUCT dimension. The PRODUCT_ID column in the APR_ORDERS table will be replaced with the warehouse key.

```
SQL> SELECT * FROM APR_ORDERS;
```

PRODUCT ID	TIME_KEY	CUSTOMER ID	SHIP_DATE	PURCHASE PRICE	SHIPPING CHARGE	TODAY_SPECIAL OFFER
SP1001	01-APR-04	AB123456	01-APR-04	28.01	6	Y
SP1001	01-APR-04	AB123457	01-APR-04	28.01	6	Y
SP1061	01-APR-04	AB123456	01-APR-04	28.01	8.42	Y
SP1062	01-APR-04	AB123457	01-APR-04	28.01	3.58	Y

```
SQL> UPDATE APR_ORDERS A
     SET A.PRODUCT_ID = (SELECT P.PRODUCT_ID
                         FROM PRODUCT P
                         WHERE A.PRODUCT_ID = P.PRODUCT_CODE);

4 rows updated.
```

Note that the original PRODUCT_ID'S have been replaced with the warehouse key.

```
SQL> SELECT * FROM APR_ORDERS;
```

PRODUCT ID	TIME_KEY	CUSTOMER ID	SHIP_DATE	PURCHASE PRICE	SHIPPING CHARGE	TODAY_SPECIAL OFFER
2	01-APR-04	AB123456	01-APR-04	28.01	6	Y
2	01-APR-04	AB123457	01-APR-04	28.01	6	Y
54	01-APR-04	AB123456	01-APR-04	28.01	8.42	Y
55	01-APR-04	AB123457	01-APR-04	28.01	3.58	Y

5.5.4   Table Functions

The results of one transformation are often stored in a database table. This table is then used as input to the next transformation. The process of transforming and storing intermediate results, which are used as input to the next transformation, is repeated for each transformation in the sequence.

The drawback to this technique is performance. The goal is to perform all transformations so that each record is read, transformed, and updated only once. Of course, there are times when this may not be possible, and the data must be passed through multiple times.

A **table function** is a function whose input is a set of rows and whose output is a set of rows, which could be a table—hence, the name table function. The sets of rows can be processed in parallel, and the results of one function can be pipelined to the next before the transformation has been completed on all the rows in the set, eliminating the need to pass through the data multiple times.

Table functions use Oracle's object technology and user-defined data types. First, new data types must be defined for the input record and output table. In the following example, the PURCHASES_RECORD data type is defined to describe the records in the PURCHASES table.

```
SQL> CREATE TYPE purchases_record as OBJECT
(product_id                VARCHAR2(8),
 time_key                  DATE,
 customer_id               VARCHAR2(10),
 ship_date                 DATE,
 purchase_price            NUMBER(6,2),
 shipping_charge           NUMBER(5,2),
 today_special_offer       VARCHAR2(1));
```

Next, the PURCHASES_TABLE data type is defined. It contains a collection of PURCHASES_RECORDS, which will be returned as output from the function.

```
SQL> CREATE TYPE purchases_table
     AS TABLE of purchases_record;
```

Next, define a type for a cursor variable, which will be used to pass a set of rows as input to the table function. Cursor variables are pointers, which hold the address of some item instead of the item itself. In PL/SQL, a pointer is created using the data type of REF. Therefore, a cursor variable has the data type of REF CURSOR. To create cursor variables, you first define a REF CURSOR type.

```
SQL> CREATE PACKAGE cur_pack
     AS TYPE ref_cur_type IS REF CURSOR;
     END cur_pack;
```

Here is our table function, named TRANSFORM, which performs the search and replace, removing the hyphen from the PRODUCT_ID and increasing the shipping charge. There are some things that differentiate it from other functions. The function uses PIPELINED in its definition and PIPE ROW in the body. This causes the function to return each row as it is completed, instead of waiting until all rows are processed. The input to the function is a cursor variable, INPUTRECS, which is of type ref_cur_type, defined previously. The output of the function is a table of purchase records of type PURCHASES_TABLE, defined previously. The REF CURSOR, INPUTRECS, is used to fetch the input rows, the transformation is performed, and the results for each row are piped out. The function ends with a RETURN statement, which does not specify any return value.

```
CREATE OR REPLACE FUNCTION
            transform(inputrecs IN cur_pack.ref_cur_type)
RETURN purchases_table
PIPELINED
IS
   product_id                VARCHAR2(8);
   time_key                  DATE;
   customer_id               VARCHAR2(10);
   ship_date                 DATE;
   purchase_price            NUMBER(6,2);
   shipping_charge           NUMBER(5,2);
   today_special_offer       VARCHAR2(1);
BEGIN
LOOP
   FETCH inputrecs INTO product_id, time_key,customer_id,
     ship_date,purchase_price,shipping_charge,
     today_special_offer;

   EXIT WHEN INPUTRECS%NOTFOUND;

   product_id := REPLACE(product_id, '-','');
   shipping_charge :=(shipping_charge+shipping_charge*.10);
   PIPE ROW(purchases_record(  product_id,
           time_key,
           customer_id,
```

```
                    ship_date,
                    purchase_price,
                    shipping_charge,
                    today_special_offer));
END LOOP;
CLOSE inputrecs;
RETURN;
END;
```

We've rolled back the changes from the previous transforms and are going to do them again using the table function instead. Here is the data prior to being transformed.

```
SQL> SELECT * FROM apr_orders;

PRODUCT TIME_KEY  CUSTOMER SHIP_DATE PURCHASE SHIPPING TODAY_SPECIAL
   ID                ID              PRICE    CHARGE OFFER
------- --------- -------- --------- -------- -------- ----------
SP-1001 01-APR-04 AB123456 01-APR-04    28.01    5.45 Y
SP-1001 01-APR-04 AB123457 01-APR-04    28.01    5.45 Y
SP1061  01-APR-04 AB123456 01-APR-04    28.01    8.42 Y
SP1062  01-APR-04 AB123457 01-APR-04    28.01    3.58 Y
```

To invoke the function, use it as part of a SELECT statement. The TABLE keyword is used before the function name in the FROM clause. The changes are shown in bold in the following code. For example:

```
SQL> SELECT * FROM
     TABLE(transform(CURSOR(SELECT * FROM apr_orders)));

PRODUCT TIME_KEY  CUSTOMER SHIP_DATE PURCHASE SHIPPING TODAY_SPECIAL
   ID                ID              PRICE    CHARGE OFFER
------- --------- -------- --------- -------- -------- ----------
SP1001  01-APR-04 AB123456 01-APR-04    28.01       6 Y
SP1001  01-APR-04 AB123457 01-APR-04    28.01       6 Y
SP1061  01-APR-04 AB123456 01-APR-04    28.01    9.26 Y
SP1062  01-APR-04 AB123457 01-APR-04    28.01    3.94 Y
```

If we needed to save the data, the following example shows creating a table to save the results of the table function.

```
SQL> CREATE TABLE TEST
     AS SELECT * FROM TABLE(transform(CURSOR(SELECT * FROM
apr_orders)));

Table created.
```

5.5.5 Transformations That Split One Data Source into Multiple Targets

Sometimes transformations involve splitting a data source into multiple targets, as illustrated in Figure 5.16. The multitable INSERT statement facilitates this type of transformation.

Figure 5.16 *Multitable Insert*

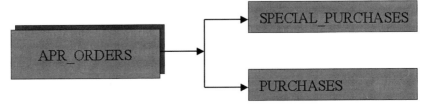

In the following example, the APR_ORDERS will be split into two tables. All orders that took advantage of today's special offer will be written to the SPECIAL_PURCHASES table. All regular sales will be written to the PURCHASES table. This information could be used to target future advertising. A new table, SPECIAL_PURCHASES, has been created with the same columns as the APR_ORDERS and PURCHASES tables.

The INSERT statement specifies a condition, which is evaluated to determine which table each row should be inserted into. In this example, there is only one WHEN clause, but you can have multiple WHEN clauses if there are multiple conditions to evaluate. If no WHEN clause evaluates to true, the ELSE clause is executed.

By specifying FIRST, Oracle stops evaluating the WHEN clause when the first condition is met. Alternatively, if ALL is specified, all conditions will be checked for each row. ALL is useful when the same row is stored in multiple tables.

```
SQL> INSERT FIRST WHEN today_special_offer = 'Y'
     THEN INTO special_purchases
     ELSE INTO purchases
     SELECT * FROM apr_orders;

15004 rows created.
```

The four rows with today_special_offer = 'Y' have been inserted into the SPECIAL_PURCHASES table. The remaining rows have been inserted into the PURCHASES table.

```
SQL> SELECT COUNT(*) FROM purchases;

  COUNT(*)
----------
     15000

SQL> SELECT COUNT(*) FROM special_purchases;

  COUNT(*)
----------
         4
```

From the following queries, we can see that the data has been split between the two tables. Purchases made with the value of N in TODAY_SPECIAL_OFFER are stored in the PURCHASES table. Those with the value of Y are stored in the SPECIAL_PURCHASES table.

```
SQL> SELECT DISTINCT(today_special_offer) FROM purchases;

TODAY_SPECIAL_OFFER
-------------------
N

SQL> SELECT DISTINCT(today_special_offer) FROM special_purchases;

TODAY_SPECIAL_OFFER
-------------------
Y
```

5.5.6   Moving Data from a Staging Table into the Fact Table

Once the data has been transformed, it is ready to be moved to the warehouse tables. For example, if the orders data for January 2005 has been moved into temporary staging tables in the warehouse, then, once the data has been cleansed and transformed, it is ready to be moved into the purchases fact table, as shown in Figure 5.17.

Figure 5.17   *Moving Data from a Staging Table into the Fact Table*

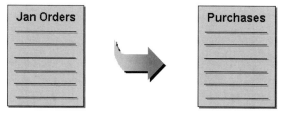

Staging table   Purchases fact table

When the fact table is partitioned, new tablespaces are created for the datafile and indexes, a new partition is added to the fact table, and the data is moved into the new partition. The steps are illustrated using the EASYDW example.

Step 1: Create a New Tablespace for the Jan Purchases and the Jan Purchases Index

Since the purchases table is partitioned by month, a new tablespace will be created to store the January purchases. Another tablespace is created for the indexes.

```
CREATE TABLESPACE purchases_jan2005
DATAFILE
'C:\ORACLE\PRODUCT\10.1.0\ORADATA\EASYDW\purchasesjan2005.f'
SIZE 5M REUSE AUTOEXTEND ON
DEFAULT STORAGE (INITIAL 64K NEXT 64K PCTINCREASE 0
                MAXEXTENTS UNLIMITED)

CREATE TABLESPACE purchases_jan2005_idx
DATAFILE
'C:\ORACLE\PRODUCT\10.1.0\ORADATA\EASYDW\purchasesjan2005_IDX.f'
SIZE 3M REUSE AUTOEXTEND ON
DEFAULT STORAGE (INITIAL 16K NEXT 16K PCTINCREASE 0
                MAXEXTENTS UNLIMITED)
```

Step 2: Add a Partition to the Purchases Table

The PURCHASES table is altered, and the purchases_jan2005 partition is created via an add partition operation.

```
SQL> ALTER TABLE purchases ADD PARTITION purchases_jan2005
VALUE LESS THAN (to_date('01-feb-2005', 'dd-mon-yyyy'))
PCTFREE 0 PCTUSED 99 STORAGE (INITIAL 64k NEXT 64k PCTINCREASE 0)
TABLESPACE purchases_jan2005;
```

Figure 5.18 shows the new partition that has been added to the PUR-CHASES table (this page can be accessed from the standard Tables page for EASYDW tables, clicking on the *View* button for the PURCHASES table, and scrolling down the resultant page—there is actually more information above and below than we have shown—the Options information extends further down the page). For the corresponding PURCHASE_PRODUCT_INDEX, you can view the index in a similar fashion by selecting *Indexes* on the *Administration* tab, selecting the indexes for

Figure 5.18   *Viewing a Table's Partitions Using Enterprise Manager*

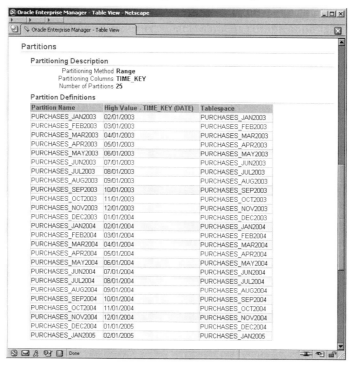

EASYDW and, again, selecting the *View* button. The presentation for the index information is similar to that shown for the table.

Step 3: Move the table into the new partition

There are a variety of ways to move the data from one table to another in the same database:

- Exchange Partition (when the fact table is partitioned)

- Direct Path Insert

- Create Table as Select

Moving Data Using Exchange Partition

The ALTER TABLE EXCHANGE PARTITION clause is generally the fastest way to move the data of a nonpartitioned table into a partition of a partitioned table. It can be used to move both the data and local indexes from a staging table into a partitioned fact table. The reason it is so fast is because the data is not actually moved; instead, the metadata is updated to reflect the changes.

If the data has not previously been cleansed, it can be validated to ensure it meets the partitioning criteria, or this step can be skipped using the WITHOUT VALIDATION clause. Figure 5.19 shows moving the data from the APR_ORDERS staging table into the PURCHASES fact table using exchange partition.

Figure 5.19   *Exchange Partition*

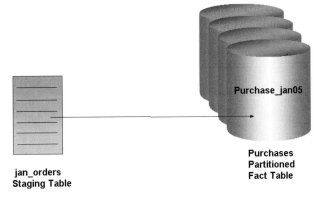

jan_orders
Staging Table

Purchases
Partitioned
Fact Table

The following example shows moving the data from the JAN_ORDERS into the PURCHASES_JAN2005 partition of the EASYDW.PURCHASES table.

```
SQL> ALTER TABLE easydw.purchases
     EXCHANGE PARTITION purchases_jan2005 WITH TABLE jan_orders
     WITHOUT VALIDATION;
```

Assuming that the PURCHASES_JAN2005 partition was newly created and empty at the start, then, after exchanging the partition, it will be full and there will be no rows left in the JAN_ORDERS table. The JAN_ORDERS table can now be dropped.

```
SQL> SELECT * FROM jan_orders;

no rows selected

SQL> DROP TABLE jan_orders;
Table dropped.
```

We discuss table partition operations more extensively in Chapter 11 where we also look at the Enterprise Manager screens to support these operations.

Moving Data Between Tables Using Direct Path Insert

If the fact table is not partitioned, you can add more data to it by using direct path insert. A direct path insert enhances performance during insert operations by formatting and writing data directly into the datafiles without using the buffer cache. This functionality is similar to SQL*Loader direct path mode.

Direct path insert appends the inserted data after existing data in a table; free space within the existing table is not reused when executing direct path operations. Data can be inserted into partitioned or nonpartitioned tables, either in parallel or serially. Direct path insert updates the indexes of the table.

In the EASYDW database, since the purchases table already exists and is partitioned by month, we could use the direct path insert to move the data into the table. Direct path INSERT is executed when you include the APPEND hint and are using the SELECT syntax of the INSERT statement.

```
SQL> INSERT /*+ APPEND */ INTO easydw.purchases
     SELECT * FROM jan_orders
```

In our example, the purchases fact table already existed, and new data was added into a separate partition.

Hint: Be sure you have disabled all reference constraints before executing the direct load insert. If you do not, the append hint will be ignored, no warnings will be issued, and a conventional insert will be used. Plus, the insert will take a long time if there is a lot of data. Conventional path is used when using the INSERT...with the VALUES clause even if you use the APPEND hint.

Creating a New Table Using Create Table As Select

If the detail fact table does not yet exist, you can create a new table selecting a subset of one or more tables using the CREATE TABLE AS SELECT statement. The table creation can be done in parallel. You can also disable logging of redo. In the following example, TEMP_PRODUCTS is the name of the staging table. After performing the transformations and data cleansing, the products table is created by copying the data from the TEMP_PRODUCTS table.

```
SQL> CREATE TABLE products
     PARALLEL NOLOGGING
     AS
     SELECT * FROM temp_products;
```

5.6 Postload Operations

After the data is loaded, you may need to validate its quality, reenable constraints and triggers, rebuild indexes, update the cost-based optimizer statistics, and refresh the materialized views prior to making the data available to the warehouse users. Some of these tasks have been discussed previously in this chapter.

5.6.1 Step 1: Gather Optimizer Statistics for the Tables

Run the DBMS_STATS package to update the optimizer statistics on any tables where you have added a significant amount of data. Statistics can be gathered for an index, index partition, table, partition or subpartition, and a materialized view.

Since we added an entire partition to the purchases fact table, the following example will gather statistics for the purchases_jan2005 partition.

```
SQL> EXECUTE DBMS_STATS.GATHER_TABLE_STATS('easydw','purchases',
'purchases_jan2005',DBMS_STATS.AUTO_SAMPLE_SIZE);
```

5.6.2 Step 2: Verify the Dimensions

If using summary management, run the DBMS_OLAP.VALIDATE_ DIMENSION procedure for each dimension to verify that the hierarchical, attribute, and join relationships are correct. It can also be used to determine if any level columns in a dimension are NULL. You can either verify the newly added rows or all the rows. Any exceptions are logged in the table MVIEW$_EXCEPTIONS, which is created in the user's schema.

In the following example, the product dimension (parameter 1) in the EASYDW schema (parameter 2) is verified for correctness. All rows will be validated (parameter 3 is set to false), and we'll check for nulls (parameter 4 is set to true).

```
SQL> EXECUTE
dbms_olap.validate_dimension('product','easydw',false,true);

SQL> SELECT * FROM mview$_exceptions;

no rows selected
```

5.6.3   Step 3: Refresh the materialized views

After loading the new data into the PURCHASES table, the
PRODUCT_SUM materialized view became stale. It only contains information for the existing data and must be refreshed to incorporate the newly
loaded data. The operations and options for refreshing materialized views is
discussed extensively in Chapter 7.

5.6.4   Step 4: Gather Optimizer Statistics for the Materialized Views

Next, update the optimizer statistics on any materialized views that may
have significantly changed in size. If you used Oracle Enterprise Manager
to refresh your materialized views, you have the option of analyzing the
materialized view by using the *Analyze* button on the Materialized View
General tab.

   To gather optimizer statistics outside of Oracle Enterprise Manager, use
the DBMS_STATS package. In this example, table statistics will be gathered from the PRODUCT_SUM materialized view in the EASYDW
schema.

```
SQL> EXECUTE
DBMS_STATS.GATHER_TABLE_STATS('easydw','product_sum');
```

5.6.5   Step 5: Back up the Database Table, or Partition

Back up the database, table or partition after the load is complete, if you
used the UNRECOVERABLE option. Since media recovery is disabled for
the table being loaded, you will not be able to recover in the event of media
failure. Refer to Chapter 12 for a discussion on backup techniques.

5.6.6   Step 6: Publish the Data

Notify the users about which data has been loaded the previous day and is
ready for their use.

5.7 Using Tools for the ETL process

Several tools are available on the marketplace to help automate parts of the ETL process, including Oracle Warehouse Builder and tools from Informatica, AbInitio, Ascential, and Sagent. These tools provide the mechanisms to connect to the heterogeneous data sources, generally to either relational databases or flat files, and perform the data extraction functions. They control the transfer of data across a network, provide data transformation services, data cleansing capabilities, and load the data into your data warehouse. We discuss Oracle Warehouse Builder in more detail in Chapter 13.

5.8 Summary

In this chapter, we looked at the ETL process. Various techniques were discussed to identify rows that changed on the source system as part of the extraction process, and both synchronous and asynchronous forms of Change Data Capture were introduced. A number of types of transformations that are common to a data warehouse were discussed. Examples were shown performing transformations during the load process, using staging tables inside the Oracle database, and using the new regular expression functionality. Techniques used to load the warehouse were illustrated, including SQL*Loader, Data Pump, external tables, and transportable tablespaces. Moving data from the staging system to the warehouse tables can be done using a variety of techniques, such as exchange partition, direct path insert, or create table as select. In Chapter 13, we'll look at Oracle Warehouse Builder, which uses many of the functions discussed in this chapter, to help you load your data warehouse.

In the next chapter, we will discuss more about how to query the data we have taken so much care in loading.

6

Querying the Data Warehouse

6.1 Introduction

A data warehouse is primarily used to organize data so queries about the business can be answered quickly. As data warehouses grow in size, it is not uncommon to find a fact table several gigabytes or even terabytes in size. In order to obtain fast query response, it is extremely important for the database to retrieve and process such large amounts of data efficiently.

In Chapter 4, we discussed several physical design techniques, including partitioning, compression, and bitmapped indexing, that are suited for data warehouses. In this chapter, we'll look at query optimizations, such as partition pruning, partition-wise join, and star transformation, that are specifically designed to improve query performance in a data warehouse. We will also describe how to use parallel execution for queries.

Finally, we will discuss several SQL functions that are useful for decision-support applications to answer business queries, which typically perform computations such as period-over-period comparisons and cumulative aggregations. These SQL functions allow users to express complex queries simply and process them efficiently. We will also look at the new spreadsheet technology in Oracle Database 10*g*.

We will begin with the query optimizer, which is the heart of query processing in a database.

6.2 The Query Optimizer

Anyone who has worked with a database is familiar with the query optimizer. The job of the optimizer is to determine a plan to execute a query in the fastest possible time. For instance, the optimizer may decide to use an index, or, if the table is small, it might be faster to perform a full table scan. The query optimizer in Oracle Database 10*g* is known as the **cost-based optimizer**.

The cost-based optimizer uses various statistics, such as the cardinality of the table (i.e., number of rows), number of distinct values of a column and the distribution of column values, to determine the method and the cost of accessing a table. The method used to access a table is called its **access path** and can use one or more **access structures**, such as indexes and materialized views, or scan the entire table. The optimizer first identifies for each table, the access path with the least cost. It then determines the cheapest way to join the tables, includes the cost of other operations such as sorts, and in this manner picks the strategy to execute the query with the cheapest cost. We refer to this strategy as the **query execution plan** and the cost is a measure of how much I/O, CPU time, and memory will be required to execute the query using this execution plan. To use the cost-based optimizer effectively, statistics describing the cardinality and data distribution must be collected for each table, index, and materialized view. Chapter 11 will describe the use of the DBMS_STATS package to collect statistics and will explain how you can set up automatic statistics collection. Note that if a table does not have statistics, Oracle Database 10*g* employs a feature called dynamic sampling, which will automatically sample the data to collect statistics. This is also discussed in Chapter 11.

Note: Prior to Oracle Database 10*g*, there was an alternative approach of using the rule-based optimizer; however, this is not suitable for a data warehouse, and, in fact, starting in Oracle Database 10*g*, the rule-based optimizer is no longer supported by Oracle.

Next, we will talk about some of the features of the cost-based query optimizer and how they work for queries in a data warehouse. We will begin by reviewing the EXPLAIN PLAN facility to view the query execution plan generated by the query optimizer. This will be used extensively by the examples in this book.

6.2.1   EXPLAIN PLAN

Oracle provides several tools to display the execution plan. You can use the **autotrace** option of SQL*Plus to display the plan when you execute the query. Alternatively, to just get the query plan without executing the query, you can use EXPLAIN PLAN. The output of EXPLAIN PLAN is placed in a table called the PLAN_TABLE. Before you can start using EXPLAIN

PLAN, you must create the PLAN_TABLE in the schema where you will execute the query by running the script ORACLE_HOME/rdbms/admin/ utlxplan.sql. You can also ask EXPLAIN PLAN to place the output in some other table, but it must have the same columns as the PLAN_TABLE. To display the plan you would use the script ORACLE_HOME/rdbms/ admin/utlxpls.sql.

Let us look at the output of an EXPLAIN PLAN statement. The output consists of the access path for each table, the cost of the access path, and the *estimated* number of rows retrieved. The plan output is indented so that tables that are being joined are shown at the same level of indentation; operations that are performed earlier are indented further.

```
EXPLAIN PLAN FOR
SELECT t.month, t.year, p.product_id,
       SUM (purchase_price) as sum_of_sales,
       COUNT (purchase_price) as total_sales,
       COUNT(*) as cstar
FROM time t, product p, purchases f
WHERE t.time_key = f.time_key AND
      f.product_id = p.product_id
GROUP BY t.month, t.year, p.product_id;


PLAN_TABLE_OUTPUT
-----------------------------------------------------------------------
Plan hash value: 419515211
-----------------------------------------------------------------------
```

Id	Operation	Name	Rows	Bytes	Cost	Psta	Pstp
0	SELECT STATEMENT		3936	169K	494		
1	SORT GROUP BY		3936	169K	494		
*2	HASH JOIN		81167	3487K	121		
3	TABLE ACCESS FULL	TIME	731	12427	3		
*4	HASH JOIN		81167	2140K	115		
5	INDEX FULL SCAN	PRODUCT_PK	164	1148	1		
6	PARTITION RANGE ALL	_INDEX	81167	1585K	111	1	24
7	TABLE ACCESS FULL	PURCHASES	81167	1585K	111	1	24

```
-----------------------------------------------------------------------
Predicate Information (identified by operation id):
-----------------------------------------------------------------------
   2 - access("T"."TIME_KEY"="F"."TIME_KEY")
   4 - access("F"."PRODUCT_ID"="P"."PRODUCT_ID")
20 rows selected.
```

In this example, the innermost operation is a hash join between the tables, PURCHASES and PRODUCT (rows 4–7). Note that an index, PRODUCT_PK_INDEX (row 5), is used to access the table, PRODUCT. The output of this is joined with the table, TIME, using a hash join (rows 2–4). The final operation is a sort in order to perform the GROUP BY. The plan display also shows the predicates being applied during each operation. In the previous examples, the predicates being applied are the join predicates. Later in this chapter, we will discuss partition pruning, wherein Oracle will automatically avoid scanning partitions that are not needed by the query. The PARTITION RANGE clause (row 6) indicates the first and last partitions being scanned. The keyword ALL means that no partition pruning was done and all 24 partitions were scanned, which is shown by column values 1 for Pstart and 24 for Pstop. The plan also shows information about temporary space and estimated time for each operation, which are not shown here due to lack of space. The plan hash value shown at the top is used by various tuning tools to uniquely identify a specific execution plan for a query.

EXPLAIN PLAN can also be used to display the detailed query plan involving parallel execution, which we will discuss later in Chapter 10.

Next, we will discuss various query optimization techniques used to efficiently process queries in a data warehouse. We will start with the basic join methods used by the query optimizer, and then discuss some advanced techniques, such as star transformation, partition pruning, and partition-wise join.

6.2.2   Join Method Basics

One of the most common operations in a query is a join between two tables. A join operation combines data from two or more tables, based on a condition (known as the join predicate) involving columns from the tables.

The Oracle query optimizer uses one of the following three join methods to execute a join.

- Nested Loops Join
- Sort-Merge Join
- Hash Join

Nested Loops Join

In nested loops join, one table is chosen as the outer table and the other as the inner table. For each row in the outer table, all matching rows that satisfy the join condition in the inner table are found. A nested loop join can be extremely efficient if the inner table has an index on the join column and there are few rows in the outer table. However, if indexes are missing it can also be a very resource- and time-intensive method of performing joins.

Sort-Merge Join

A sort-merge join is useful when joining two large tables or when the join is based on an inequality predicate. In a sort-merge join, the data from each table is sorted by the values of the columns in the join condition. The sorted tables are then merged, such that each pair of rows with matching columns is joined. If there is an index on the join columns of either table, the optimizer may use it to directly retrieve the data in sorted order, thereby avoiding the sort for that table.

Hash Join

Given the ad hoc nature of decision-support queries, it is not always possible for the DBA to index all the columns the users may use to join tables together. Hash joins are especially useful when there are no indexes on the columns being joined and hence are a very commonly seen join technique in a data warehouse.

In a hash join, a hashing function is applied to the join columns of the smaller table to build a hash table. Then, the second table is scanned, and its join columns are hashed and compared with the hash table to look for matching rows. A hash join performs best if the hash table can fit entirely into memory. If the hash table does not fit into memory, then parts of it need to be written to disk, causing multiple passes over the data, which is not very efficient. Hash joins can only be used for joins based on equality predicates (i.e., table1.column1 = table2.column2).

How to Pick the Join Method?

You may be wondering how you would pick the join method—fortunately, you don't need to pick one! The query optimizer will automatically choose the most efficient join method for each join within a query. In some cases, usually due to bad statistics or a skewed data distribution, the query optimizer may choose the incorrect join method. So it is extremely important to have accurate statistics on the data. It is possible to explicitly specify a join method to use by including an optimizer hint in the query; however, this is not recommended. Instead, we recommend running the SQL Tuning Advisor, described in Chapter 10, to tune slow-running queries. This will attempt to correct any mistakes made by the query optimizer and thereby improve the execution plan.

Another important point to note is that sort and hash joins are memory-intensive operations and may require temporary space if not enough memory is available. Chapter 10 also describes the PGA Memory Advisor, which can be used to automatically tune memory for these operations.

Next, we will look at some advanced query optimization techniques used in a data warehouse.

6.2.3   Star Transformation

A star query is a typical query executed on a star schema. Each of the dimension tables is joined to the fact table using the primary-key/foreign-key relationship. If the fact table has bitmapped indexes on the foreign-key columns, Oracle can optimize the performance of such star queries using an algorithm known as the **star transformation**. Star transformation is based on combining bitmapped indexes on the fact table columns that correspond to the dimension tables in the query. First, bitmapped indexes are used to retrieve the necessary rows from the fact table. The result is then joined to the dimension tables to get any columns required in the final answer.

If your data warehouse has a star schema, you should enable star transformation. This is done by setting the initialization parameter, STAR_TRANSFORMATION_ENABLED, to TRUE. Alternatively, you can use the STAR_TRANSFORMATION hint on queries that join the fact and dimension tables. The optimizer will weigh the execution plans, with and without star transformation, and pick the most efficient plan.

Suppose there were bitmapped indexes on each of the foreign-key columns of the PURCHASES table (i.e., CUSTOMER_ID, TIME_KEY, and PRODUCT_ID). The following example shows a query that can benefit from star transformation. This query joins the fact (PURCHASES) table and dimension tables (PRODUCT, TIME, CUSTOMER) in a star schema and has selections on each of the dimension tables (MONTH = 200301, and STATE = 'MA', and CATEGORY = 'HDRW'), representing a small fraction of the entire data.

```
EXPLAIN PLAN FOR
SELECT c.city, t.quarter, p.product_name,
       SUM(f.purchase_price) sales
FROM purchases f, time t, customer c, product p
WHERE f.time_key = t.time_key and
      f.customer_id = c.customer_id and
      f.product_id = p.product_id and
      t.month = 200301 and c.state = 'MA' and
      p.category = 'HDRW'
GROUP BY c.city, t.quarter, p.product_name;
```

The execution plan is as follows:

```
-------------------------------------------------------------
|ID | Operation                    | Name     |Rows| Bytes|Cost|
-------------------------------------------------------------
|  0| SELECT STATEMENT             |          |  54| 3834| 715|
|  1|  SORT GROUP BY               |          |  54| 3834| 715|
|* 2|   HASH JOIN                  |          | 328|23288| 712|
|* 3|    TABLE ACCESS FULL         |PRODUCT   |  54| 1188|   2|
|* 4|    HASH JOIN                 |          | 984|48216| 709|
|  5|     MERGE JOIN CARTESIAN     |          |   3|   78|   4|
|* 6|      TABLE ACCESS FULL       |CUSTOMER  |   1|   12|   2|
|  7|      BUFFER SORT             |          |   1|   14|   2|
|* 8|       TABLE ACCESS FULL      |TIME      |   1|   14|   2|
|  9|     TABLE ACCESS BY INDEX ROWID|PURCHASES|7030| 157K| 703|
| 10|      BITMAP CONVERSION TO ROWIDS|       |    |     |    |
| 11|       BITMAP AND             |          |    |     |    |
| 12|        BITMAP MERGE          |          |    |     |    |
| 13|         BITMAP KEY ITERATION |          |    |     |    |
|*14|          TABLE ACCESS FULL   |CUSTOMER  |   1|   12|   2|
|*15|          BITMAP INDEX RANGE SCAN|CUST_IDX|   |     |    |
| 16|        BITMAP MERGE          |          |    |     |    |
| 17|         BITMAP KEY ITERATION |          |    |     |    |
|*18|          TABLE ACCESS FULL   |TIME      |   2|   28|   2|
|*19|          BITMAP INDEX RANGE SCAN|TIME_IDX|   |     |    |
| 20|        BITMAP MERGE          |          |    |     |    |
| 21|         BITMAP KEY ITERATION |          |    |     |    |
|*22|          TABLE ACCESS FULL   |PRODUCT   |  54| 1188|   2|
|*23|          BITMAP INDEX RANGE SCAN|PROD_IDX|   |     |    |
-------------------------------------------------------------
```

To understand how star transformation works, notice that the rows corresponding to category = 'HDRW' can be retrieved using the following subquery (this is also known as a semijoin):

```
SELECT *
FROM purchases
WHERE product_id IN (SELECT product_id
                     FROM product
                     WHERE category = 'HDRW');
```

This query is executed to retrieve the product ids corresponding to the HDRW category, and then the PROD_IDX bitmapped index on PUR-CHASES.PRODUCT_ID is used to retrieve the rows from the PUR-CHASES table corresponding to these product id values. In star transformation, similar subqueries are generated for each of the dimension tables to obtain a bitmap for the rows of the PURCHASES table corresponding to that dimension table. Next, these bitmaps are combined using a bitmap AND operation into a single bitmap. This is shown in the execution plan in rows 10 through 23. This bitmap is then used to retrieve the relevant rows from the PURCHASES tables. Finally, a join is done back to the dimension tables (shown in plan rows 0 through 9) to obtain the other column values (CITY, QUARTER, and PRODUCT_NAME). Note that if the query did not select any columns from the dimension table, then the optimizer will not need to perform this join back. Star transformation turns out to be efficient when the fact table is large, because only a small subset of the table (in our example 7,030 rows out of 421K rows in the PURCHASES table) is now involved in the join.

Hint: Creating bitmapped indexes on foreign-key columns in the fact table will allow the optimizer to consider star transformation for your star queries.

A bitmapped join index can also be used instead of a combination of bitmapped indexes. Star transformation is also possible if only some of the foreign key columns have bitmapped indexes.

6.2.4   Partition Pruning

In Chapter 4, we mentioned that if a table is partitioned, the query optimizer could determine if a certain query can be answered by reading only specific partitions of the table. This can dramatically reduce the amount of data read to answer a query and hence speed up the query execution. This feature is known as **Partition Elimination** or **Dynamic Partition Pruning**.

We will now look at examples of partition pruning with different types of partitioning.

Range Partitioning

In range partitioning, data is partitioned into nonoverlapping ranges of data. In this case, the optimizer can perform partition pruning if the query has range, IN list, or LIKE predicates on the partition keys. For example, in the EASYDW schema, the PURCHASES table is partitioned on the TIME_KEY column, such that each partition corresponds to one month's data. The following query asks for sales of November and December 2003. The optimizer will therefore eliminate from its search all partitions except those containing these two months.

```
EXPLAIN PLAN FOR
SELECT t.time_key, SUM(f.purchase_price) as sales
FROM purchases f, time t
WHERE f.time_key = t.time_key
  AND t.time_key BETWEEN TO_DATE('1-Nov-2003', 'DD-Mon-YYYY')
  AND                    TO_DATE('31-Dec-2003', 'DD-Mon-YYYY')
GROUP BY t.time_key;
```

Id	Operation	Name	Rows	Cost	Pstart	Pstop
0	SELECT STATEMENT		62	15		
1	SORT GROUP BY		62	15		
*2	HASH JOIN		585	14		
*3	INDEX FAST FULL SCAN	TIME_PK_				
		INDEX	62	2		
4	PARTITION RANGE ITERATOR		6893	11	11	12
*5	TABLE ACCESS FULL	PURCHASES	6893	11	11	12

```
Predicate Information (identified by operation id):
---------------------------------------------------
  2 - access("F"."TIME_KEY"="T"."TIME_KEY")
  3 - filter("T"."TIME_KEY"<=TO_DATE('2003-12-31 00:00:00',
                            'yyyy-mm-dd hh24:mi:ss') AND
             "T"."TIME_KEY">=TO_DATE('2003-11-01 00:00:00',
                  'yyyy-mm-dd hh24:mi:ss'))

  5 - filter("F"."TIME_KEY"<=TO_DATE('2003-12-31 00:00:00',
                            'yyyy-mm-dd hh24:mi:ss'))
20 rows selected.
```

Note that the output of EXPLAIN PLAN includes columns Pstart and Pstop, which indicate the range of partitions used to answer the query. Note that for multicolumn range partitioning, only predicates on the first column in the partition key are used for partition pruning.

Hash Partitioning

Hash partitioning allows partition pruning only when a query involves equality or IN-list predicates on the partitioning column. This is because with hash partitioning, the values are distributed randomly among partitions and so contiguous values may not fall into a single partition.

List Partitioning

If a table is list partitioned, the optimizer can perform partition pruning if the query asks for a range or list of partition-key values. For instance, the REGIONAL_SALES table in Chapter 4 (Figure 4.3) is partitioned by states in each region. Now, if a query asks for sales for states NH, MA, CT, CA, AZ, the optimizer can prune all partitions except the Northeast and West.

```
EXPLAIN PLAN FOR
SELECT store_number, dept_number, SUM(sales_amount) as q1_sales
FROM regional_sales
WHERE state in ('NH', 'MA', 'CT', 'CA', 'AZ')
GROUP BY store_number, dept_number;
```

```
-------------------------------------------------------------------
|Id|Operation             |Name          |Rows|Cost|Pstart| Pstop|
-------------------------------------------------------------------
| 0|SELECT STATEMENT      |              | 500|   4|      |      |
| 1| SORT GROUP BY        |              | 500|   4|      |      |
| 2|  PARTITION LIST INLIST|             | 500|   3|KEY(I)|KEY(I)|
|*3|   TABLE ACCESS FULL  |REGIONAL_SALES| 500|   3|KEY(I)|KEY(I)|
-------------------------------------------------------------------
```

```
Predicate Information (identified by operation id):
---------------------------------------------------
   3 - filter("STATE"='AZ' OR "STATE"='CA' OR "STATE"='CT' OR
             "STATE"='MA' OR "STATE"='NH')
```

In case of a query with IN operator, you will see the KEY(I) term in the Pstart and Pstop columns in the output of EXPLAIN PLAN, rather than actual partition numbers.

Also note that in some cases the actual partitions to be accessed are determined only during the execution of the query, in which case you also will not see actual partition numbers but instead see the value KEY in the Pstart and Pstop columns in the EXPLAIN PLAN output.

Composite Partitioning

For a composite-partitioned table, in addition to pruning at the partition level, the optimizer can also prune subpartitions within the partitions using predicates on the subpartitioning columns. This can further reduce the data accessed to answer a query.

For example, suppose we have a table, SALES, composite-partitioned using range partitioning on SALE_DATE and list subpartitioning on STATE. The following query asks for total sales for NH, MA, and CT states for a range of sales dates. The optimizer will determine that this query can be answered quickly by reading the partitions for February and March. Further, within these two partitions, only the first subpartition needs to be accessed. The Pstart and Pstop values in the output of EXPLAIN PLAN show the range of partitions used to answer the query, in this case partitions 2 and 3.

Note that KEY keyword in the last line of the output indicates that the actual subpartition numbers will be determined at query execution time.

```
EXPLAIN PLAN FOR
SELECT store_number, dept_number, SUM(sales_amount) as q1_sales
FROM sales
WHERE sale_date between TO_DATE('15-Feb-2003', 'DD-Mon-YYYY')
  AND TO_DATE('15-Mar-2003', 'DD-Mon-YYYY')
  AND state in ('NH', 'MA', 'CT')
GROUP BY store_number, dept_number;
```

```
--------------------------------------------------------------------
|Id| Operation                |Name |Rows|Cost| Pstart | Pstop  |
--------------------------------------------------------------------
|0 | SELECT STATEMENT          |     | 1  | 41 |        |        |
|1 |  SORT GROUP BY            |     | 1  | 41 |        |        |
|2 |   PARTITION RANGE ITERATOR|     | 1  | 40 |   2    |   3    |
|3 |    PARTITION LIST INLIST  |     | 1  | 40 | KEY(I) | KEY(I) |
|4 |     TABLE ACCESS FULL     |SALES| 1  | 40 |  KEY   |  KEY   |
--------------------------------------------------------------------
```

```
Predicate Information (identified by operation id):

---------------------------------------------------
4 - filter((("STATE"='CT' OR "STATE"='MA' OR "STATE"='NH') AND
           "SALE_DATE">=TO_DATE('2003-02-15 00:00:00',
                'yyyy-mm-dd hh24:mi:ss') AND

           "SALE_DATE"<=TO_DATE('2003-03-15 00:00:00',
                'yyyy-mm-dd hh24:mi:ss'))
```

If the query optimizer chooses an index to access the table, then, in addition to pruning on table partitions, Oracle will also prune index partitions. If the index is local and hence partitioned identically to the table, then Oracle will only access the index partitions corresponding to the table partitions being accessed. If the index is global and partitioned differently than the table, Oracle can still eliminate index partitions that are not needed provided there is a predicate on the partitioning key of the index.

Partition pruning is one of the many benefits of partitioning and can provide huge performance gains in a data warehouse. When designing your queries, include predicates on partitioning columns whenever possible to obtain the benefits of partition pruning.

6.2.5   Partition-Wise Join

When the tables being joined are partitioned, the optimizer may choose to perform a **partition-wise join**. Rather than performing a large join between two tables, the join operation is broken up into a series of smaller joins between the partitions or subpartitions. These smaller joins can be executed in parallel, which can make the entire join operation significantly faster. Note that a partition-wise join can use any of the join methods discussed earlier—sort merge, hash, or nested loops join. Recall that a hash join performs best when the hash tables fit into memory—with a partition, wise join, hash joins can be made more efficient, because the hash tables for each partition are much smaller and hence more likely to fit into memory.

A **full partition-wise join**, illustrated in Figure 6.1, can be done when the tables being joined are equipartitioned on the join key in the query. Equipartitioning means that the two tables have identical partitioning criteria (i.e., partition method and partition bounds), which means that there is a correspondence between the partitions (or subpartitions) or one table with the partitions (or subpartitions) of the other. So every partition (or subpartition) of the first table needs to be joined only to its corresponding partition (or subpartition) in the other table. In Figure 6.1, the PURCHASES and ORDERS tables are both partitioned by a date column, and each partition contains data for a month. In a full partition-wise join

Figure 6.1   *Full Partition-Wise Join*

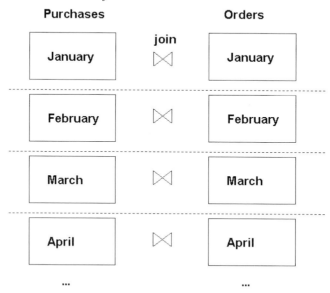

between these two tables, using the partition keys as the join columns, the January partition of PURCHASES will be joined to the January partition of ORDERS, the February partition of PURCHASES will be joined to the February partition of ORDERS, and so on. When executing the query in parallel, each piece of the join (separated by the dotted lines in the figure) can be executed on a separate processor.

If only one of the tables is partitioned on the join key, a **partial partition-wise join** can be done when executing the query in parallel. The table that is not partitioned by the join key is dynamically partitioned to match the partitioning criteria of the partitioned table. Each pair of partitions from the two tables is now joined, as in a full partition-wise join.

The decision to perform a partition-wise join or any of its variants is taken by the optimizer based on the cost of the execution plan. Note that if the query only requires some of the partitions of any table, then only those partitions will participate in the partition-wise join. Thus, a query execution can benefit from both partition pruning and partition-wise joins.

In this section, we mentioned executing queries in parallel. We will discuss the important technique of parallel execution in more detail next.

6.3   Parallel Execution

Many operations in a data warehouse involve processing large amounts of data. Bulk loads, large table scans, creating indexes and materialized views, sorting, and joining data from multiple tables can all take a considerable amount of time. Parallel execution can be used to reduce the time it takes to execute these operations.

With parallel execution certain SQL statements can be divided transparently into smaller concurrently executing operations. By dividing the work among several processes on different processors, the statement can be completed faster than with only a single process.

In Oracle, parallel execution is performed using a parallel execution coordinator process and a pool of parallel execution servers. The Oracle process that handles the user's query becomes the coordinator process for that query. The coordinator process partitions the work to be done among the required number of parallel execution servers. It ensures that the load is balanced among the processes and redistributes work to any process that may have finished before the others. The coordinator receives the results from the parallel execution servers and assembles them into the final result. For example, in Figure 6.2, parallel execution is used to concurrently read partitions for four months from a table—for example, to calculate total sales.

Figure 6.2   *Parallel Query*

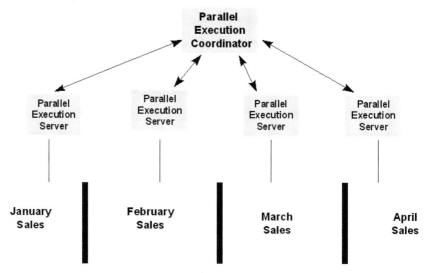

The operation to be executed in parallel is divided up into smaller units, known as **granules** of parallel execution. A granule corresponds to the work performed assigned to each parallel execution server. If a table or index is partitioned, the granule can be a partition or a subpartition. Alternatively, the granule can be a range of physical data blocks. Oracle will automatically determine the best granule to use to parallelize a statement.

6.3.1   SQL Statements That Can Be Parallelized

Many operations can benefit from parallel execution. SELECT statements with various operations, such as joins, aggregation, sorts, set operations (e.g., UNION and UNION ALL), and SELECT DISTINCT, can use parallel execution. Partition pruning and partition-wise join in conjunction with parallel execution can provide huge performance improvements.

DML statements—INSERT, UPDATE, DELETE, and MERGE—can be done in parallel on partitioned as well as nonpartitioned tables. You must use the ALTER SESSION ENABLE PARALLEL DML in the session to allow DML statements to be parallelized. Bulk loads done using SQL*Loader can be parallelized using the PARALLEL=TRUE option.

Parallel execution is also possible for DDL statements, such as CREATE TABLE, CREATE INDEX and CREATE MATERIALIZED VIEW, and partition maintenance operations, such as TRUNCATE, EXCHANGE, MERGE, and SPLIT PARTITION.

PL/SQL functions, user-defined aggregates, and table functions issued as part of SQL statements can also be parallelized.

6.3.2 Setting up Parallel Execution

At database startup, Oracle will start as many parallel execution servers as specified by the PARALLEL_MIN_SERVERS initialization parameter. These are available for use by any parallel operation. The query coordinator obtains the required number of parallel execution servers from the pool when needed to execute a parallel operation. When processing is complete, the coordinator returns the parallel execution servers to the pool. If there are a large number of concurrent users executing parallel statements, additional parallel execution servers can be created. The initialization parameter, PARALLEL_MAX_SERVERS, specifies the maximum number of server processes to create. When they are no longer needed, the parallel execution servers that have been idle for a period of time are terminated. The pool is never reduced below the PARALLEL_MIN_SERVERS parameter.

The number of units into which a statement gets divided is known as the **degree of parallelism** (DOP). You can set the DOP when creating or altering a table, index, or materialized view using the PARALLEL clause in the DDL statement, as shown in the following example:

```
-- set DOP to 4 for a table
ALTER TABLE purchases PARALLEL 4;
```

For a given query the DOP of the query is defined as the maximum DOP of all tables and indexes involved in the execution of the query. You can override the value of DOP for a SQL statement with the PARALLEL hint or by setting it for the entire session using the ALTER SESSION FORCE PARALLEL statement. This is shown in the following examples.

```
--set DOP to 6 for a session for parallel DML or query
ALTER SESSION FORCE PARALLEL DML PARALLEL 6;
ALTER SESSION FORCE PARALLEL QUERY PARALLEL 6;

-- set DOP to 2 for just this SQL statement
SELECT /*+ PARALLEL (2)*/ * FROM purchases;
```

If the DOP is not specified using the previous methods, Oracle will calculate it automatically using the number of CPUs or number of partitions. For good performance, the number of partitions should be a multiple of the

DOP. Otherwise, some parallel execution servers may remain idle waiting for others to complete a certain operation before beginning the next one.

During query execution, Oracle will try to use the requested degree of parallelism, but if several queries are competing for resources, it may adjust it to a lower value. Note that Oracle may use up to 2 × DOP number of execution servers for a query. If no parallel execution servers are available, the operation will execute serially. Sometimes a parallel operation cannot be executed efficiently unless a certain number of servers are available. The initialization parameter, PARALLEL_MIN_PERCENT, is used to specify the minimum percentage of requested parallel execution servers needed for the operation to succeed. If this percentage is not met, Oracle will return an error and you need to try the operation again later.

You may be wondering how to go about setting the different parallel execution parameters. Fortunately, since Oracle 9*i*, you can just set one initialization parameter, **PARALLEL_AUTOMATIC_TUNING** to TRUE, which will automatically set good defaults for all parallel execution–related parameters based on available resources on your system.

6.3.3 Hardware Requirements for Parallel Execution

It is important to have the right hardware and system characteristics to get the benefits of parallel execution. The system must have adequate spare CPU time, memory, and I/O bandwidth to allow parallel execution. In Chapter 3, we discussed various hardware and storage architectures for a warehouse. SMP, MPP, and Cluster architectures make parallel execution possible. Obviously, uni-processor machines cannot make use of parallel processing, since there is only one CPU.

When using Oracle Real Application Clusters technology (RAC), parallel execution of a query may distribute the work across slave processes running on multiple database instances. Oracle will determine at run time whether to run the query on a single instance or multiple instances to keep internode communication to a minimum. Also, when possible, Oracle will try to assign a node to work on a tablespace or partition that is on a local device for that node—this is known as **affinity**. Using affinity improves performance by reducing the communication overhead and I/O latency, because a node only accesses local devices, and also by ensuring that multiple nodes do not try to access the same device at the same time.

In this chapter, so far we have discussed several query execution techniques that improve query performance in a data warehouse. Next, we will delve into SQL language features that Oracle provides specially for data warehousing applications. The following section would be most useful to application developers and readers who need to write SQL to issue business queries. If you use an end-user tool such as Discoverer, you may skip over the detailed SQL examples in this section.

6.4 SQL Features for Querying the Data Warehouse

The primary purpose of building a data warehouse is to obtain information about your business so that you can improve business processes and better understand the buying habits of your customers.

For instance, you may need to answer questions such as:

- What were the top-10 selling products this year?

- How do the sales this year compare against last year?

- What are the cumulative sales numbers for each month this year?

- What are the sales numbers for each region and subtotals for each city within it?

This type of analysis is referred to as **business intelligence** or **decision support** analysis. Although these questions sound quite simple, the SQL queries needed to answer these questions can be extremely complex. These queries are very hard to optimize and may require multiple scans over the data. They may perform poorly or may require application layer processing. A few years ago, several database vendors started an initiative to provide SQL extensions to concisely represent these types of queries and execute them efficiently. The extensions are now part of the SQL99 standard. Oracle's BI tools, such as Discoverer, which are tightly integrated with the database, take advantage of the SQL functions in the database to deliver high performance for end-user queries.

The SQL extensions for business intelligence can be broadly classified into three categories—extensions for aggregation; such as calculating totals and subtotals; functions for analysis, such as finding the top-N products or cumulative sales and spreadsheet-like functionality for modeling (statistical analysis functions). We will provide a detailed look at each of these SQL extensions.

6.4.1 SQL Extensions for Aggregation

Aggregation is the most basic operation in a business intelligence query. Suppose we wanted to know the total sales by month for the current year. In this example, we are summing up the detailed data for each day, to give the total sales for each month. An operation where many detailed rows are combined using an operator such as SUM, to give a single value, is called aggregation. We have already seen several examples of aggregation in this chapter. You can recognize aggregation in a SQL query when you see a GROUP BY clause or operators such as SUM, AVG, COUNT, MIN, MAX, STDDEV, and VARIANCE.

The GROUP BY clause allows you to perform aggregation at a single level within a dimension, such as by month or by year. However, often you may want to see totals and subtotals in the same query—for instance, total sales by each month and further by quarter and by year. In the past, these types of operations were done using report-writing tools. Now, you can perform such multilevel aggregations within the database using the CUBE, ROLLUP, and GROUPING SETS operators. The ROLLUP operator is used to compute subtotals along a dimension hierarchy, and the CUBE operator is used to compute aggregations across all possible combinations for a set of GROUP BY columns (we refer to each combination as a **grouping**). The GROUPING SETS operator is used to compute aggregates for only specific groupings. By executing these aggregations within the database, they can be executed in parallel and benefit from the various query optimizations discussed earlier.

CUBE, ROLLUP, and GROUPING SETS can be used with all the supported aggregate operators in Oracle and also with other analysis functions discussed later in this chapter.

We will now take a detailed look at these extensions.

CUBE

The CUBE operator computes aggregates for all possible combinations of the columns in the GROUP BY clause. For example, suppose you wanted to analyze the sales of your products according to the product category and the year and also see total sales by category, by year, and a grand total. This corresponds to a CUBE operation, as shown in the following example.

```
SELECT p.category, t.year, SUM(purchase_price) total_sales
FROM product p, purchases f, time t
WHERE p.product_id = f.product_id AND
      t.time_key = f.time_key
GROUP BY CUBE (p.category, t.year);
```

```
CATE         YEAR            TOTAL_SALES
----      ----------     -------------------
ELEC        2003             9380600.38      <- (category, year)
ELEC        2004             9515598.19
HDRW        2003              105098.69
HDRW        2004              105130.03
MUSC        2003              107026.10
MUSC        2004              106399.30
ELEC                        18896198.60      <-  (category)
HDRW                          210228.72
MUSC                          213425.40
            2003             9592725.17      <-  (year)
            2004             9727127.52
                            19319852.70      <-  (grand total)

12 rows selected.
```

As we can see, the answer to this query includes the total sales for the four groupings—(CATEGORY, YEAR), (CATEGORY), (YEAR)—and a grand total. We have highlighted with arrows the first row in each group.

As the number of columns increases, computing the CUBE operator can consume a lot of time and space. Notice that the number of groupings for a CUBE with two columns is four, with three columns eight, and so on. Often, you are only interested in totals along a specific dimension, which is accomplished by the ROLLUP operator.

ROLLUP

The ROLLUP operator is useful for totaling data across a hierarchical dimension such as time. In a ROLLUP, you specify a list of columns and Oracle performs GROUP BY on steadily smaller subsets of the list, working from the rightmost column toward the left.

We will illustrate this operator using the following example, which computes the ROLLUP operation for category, year columns. To compute ROLLUP, we first group by (CATEGORY, YEAR) and then group by (CATEGORY), thereby aggregating over the rightmost column, YEAR, and finally produce a grand total. We have highlighted the first row of each grouping in the output with arrows.

```
SELECT p.category, t.year, SUM(purchase_price)
FROM product p, purchases f, time t
WHERE p.product_id = f.product_id AND
      t.time_key = f.time_key
GROUP BY ROLLUP (p.category, t.year);
```

```
CATE       YEAR SUM(PURCHASE_PRICE)
----  ---------- --------------------
ELEC       2003          9380600.38    <-  (category, year)
ELEC       2004          9515598.19
HDRW       2003           105098.69
HDRW       2004           105130.03
MUSC       2003           107026.10
MUSC       2004           106399.30
ELEC                    18896198.60    <-  (category)
HDRW                      210228.72
MUSC                      213425.40
                       19319852.70    <-  (grand total)

10 rows selected.
```

To ROLLUP along a hierarchy correctly, we must order the columns from the highest to the lowest level of the hierarchy from left to right. For instance, to ROLLUP along a time hierarchy the column ordering would be (YEAR, MONTH, DAY).

If we compare the output of the CUBE and ROLLUP, you will notice that ROLLUP only computes some of the possible combinations of groupings in a CUBE. In the previous example, the grouping (YEAR) is present in the CUBE but not in the ROLLUP output. The output of a CUBE always includes the output of a ROLLUP. The ROLLUP is thus a much simpler and more efficient operation: for two columns, a rollup produces three groupings, for three columns, four, and so on.

GROUPING SETS is a generalization of the ROLLUP operator that allows you to specify which particular groupings you would like to compute.

GROUPING SETS

In a data warehouse, aggregating data involves accessing a lot of detail data and therefore, to avoid repeating such expensive computations, it is common practice to precompute and store aggregations using materialized views. Now, if we were to store the result of a CUBE operator, computing all possible groupings, the space requirements could get too large. It is not uncommon for the output of a CUBE to be several times larger than the size of the fact table! This problem is overcome by using GROUPING SETS, which provide the capability to selectively compute only interesting combinations of groupings instead of the entire CUBE. Note that even though we introduced GROUPING SETS in the context of stored aggregates, it is a normal SQL operator and can be used in any query, just like the CUBE or ROLLUP operators.

For example, suppose we only wanted to calculate sales for the following groupings—(CATEGORY, YEAR), (CATEGORY, STATE), (YEAR, REGION)—and the grand total of sales, denoted by (). We choose not to calculate other combinations such as the detailed sales for each category, year, and state. This is accomplished in the following SQL query using a GROUPING SETS operator.

```
SELECT p.category as cat, t.year, c.region, c.state as st,
       SUM(f.purchase_price) sales
FROM product p, purchases f,  time t, customer c
WHERE p.product_id = f.product_id AND
       t.time_key = f.time_key AND
       c.customer_id = f.customer_id AND
       c.country = 'USA' and c.region in ('AmerWest', 'AmerSouth')
GROUP BY GROUPING SETS ((p.category, c.state),
                        (t.year, c.region),
                        (p.category, t.year),());
```

CAT	YEAR	REGION	ST	SALES	
ELEC			AZ	1198445.49	<- (category, state)
ELEC			CA	1392898.24	
ELEC			TX	1186616.83	
HDRW			AZ	15466.29	
HDRW			CA	12912.08	
HDRW			TX	12739.71	
MUSC			AZ	12771.05	
MUSC			CA	14870.83	
MUSC			TX	14886.50	
	2003	AmerWest		1317728.13	<- (year, region)
	2003	AmerSouth		604485.20	
	2004	AmerWest		1329635.85	
	2004	AmerSouth		609757.84	
ELEC	2003			1880405.77	<- (category, year)
ELEC	2004			1897554.79	
HDRW	2003			20229.97	
HDRW	2004			20888.11	
MUSC	2003			21577.59	
MUSC	2004			20950.79	
				3861607.02	<- (grand total)

Note that ROLLUP is a special case of GROUPING SETS. For example, ROLLUP(CATEGORY, YEAR) is equivalent to GROUPING SETS ((CATEGORY, YEAR),(CATEGORY), ()).

You may specify multiple GROUPING SETS in a query. This offers a concise notation to specify a cross-product of groupings across multiple dimensions. For example, suppose we would like to compute sales for each product category along the (STATE, REGION) columns in the customer dimension and along the (YEAR, QUARTER) columns in the time dimension. Instead of specifying all combinations of groupings involving these four columns, we could simply use the following query. This is known as **concatenated grouping sets**.

```
SELECT p.category as cat, t.quarter as quart, t.year,
       c.state as st, c.region, SUM(f.purchase_price) sales
FROM   purchases f, time t, customer c, product p
WHERE  p.product_id = f.product_id AND
       t.time_key = f.time_key AND
       c.customer_id = f.customer_id AND
       c.country = 'USA' and c.region in ('AmerWest', 'AmerSouth')
GROUP BY p.category,
         GROUPING SETS (c.state, c.region),
         GROUPING SETS (t.quarter, t.year);
```

CAT	QUART	YEAR	ST	REGION	SALES	
ELEC	200301		AZ		130219.58	<- (quarter,state)
ELEC	200302		AZ		154613.90	
ELEC	200303		AZ		153216.43	
....						
HDRW	200402		TX		1770.71	
HDRW	200403		TX		1504.32	
HDRW	200404		TX		1661.02	
...						
ELEC	200301			AmerWest	296382.05	<- (quarter,region)
ELEC	200302			AmerWest	329691.54	
ELEC	200303			AmerWest	338017.87	
...						
MUSC	200401			AmerSouth	1833.39	
MUSC	200402			AmerSouth	1661.02	
MUSC	200403			AmerSouth	1817.72	
...						
ELEC		2003	AZ		596005.79	<- (year, state)
ELEC		2004	AZ		602439.70	
...						
MUSC		2003	TX		7599.95	
MUSC		2004	TX		7286.55	
ELEC		2003		AmerWest	1289725.84	<- (year, region)
ELEC		2004		AmerWest	1301617.89	
...						
MUSC		2004		AmerSouth	7286.55	

150 rows selected.

The CATEGORY column that is outside the GROUPING SETS is present in all the groupings. Thus, the previous query computes the four groupings: (CATEGORY, QUARTER, STATE), (CATEGORY, QUARTER, REGION), (CATEGORY, YEAR, STATE), and (CATEGORY, YEAR, REGION).

GROUPING and GROUPING_ID Functions

We have seen how CUBE, ROLLUP, and GROUPING SETS operators all compute multiple levels of aggregations in one query. Now the problem is that in order to display the result appropriately for the end user, your application needs to know which rows in the answer correspond to which level. This is where the GROUPING and GROUPING_ID, functions come in handy. The SQL functions, GROUPING and GROUPING_ID provide a mechanism to identify the rows in the answer that correspond to each level of aggregation.

The following query illustrates the behavior of the GROUPING() function.

```
SELECT t.year, p.category as cat,
       SUM(f.purchase_price) sales,
       GROUPING(t.year) grp_y, GROUPING(p.category) grp_c
FROM product p, purchases f, time t
WHERE p.product_id = f.product_id AND
      t.time_key = f.time_key
GROUP BY ROLLUP (t.year, p.category);

    YEAR        CAT              SALES GRP_Y GRP_C
    -----  ---------  ---------------- ----- -----
    2003        ELEC        9380600.38     0     0   <- (year,category)
    2004        ELEC        9515598.19     0     0
    2003        HDRW         105098.69     0     0
    2004        HDRW         105130.03     0     0
    2003                     107026.10     0     0 *
    2004                     106399.30     0     0
    2003                    9592725.17     0     1 * <- (year)
    2004                    9727127.52     0     1
                          19319852.70     1     1   <- (grand total)

10 rows selected.
```

For each grouping, the function GROUPING(CATEGORY) returns a value 0 if the CATEGORY column is in the group and 1 otherwise. Similarly, GROUPING(YEAR) returns a value 0 if the YEAR column is in the group and 1 otherwise. Thus, each level of aggregation can be identified from the values of the GROUPING function. The group (YEAR, CATEGORY) has grouping function values (0,0); the group (YEAR) has grouping function values (0,1). Note that the grand total row can be easily identified as the row where each grouping function column has the value 1.

The GROUPING function also serves another purpose. In the output of CUBE or ROLLUP, the rows that correspond to higher level of aggregation have value NULL for the columns that have been aggregated away. The

GROUPING function can be used to distinguish this NULL from actual NULL values in the data itself. For example, look carefully at the two rows in the preceding output, marked with an asterisk. Both these rows have a value NULL in the TIME_KEY column. The first of these corresponds to products where the value of product category was unavailable (NULL). In the second one, we have aggregated away the category values and hence this row corresponds to aggregation at the year level. The GROUPING function distinguishes these two similar-looking rows. In the first case, the GROUPING(CATEGORY) is 0; in the second, it is 1.

Instead of using GROUPING for each column, you can use GROUPING_ID with all the columns together, as follows:

```
SELECT t.year, p.category as cat,
       SUM(f.purchase_price) sales,
       GROUPING_ID(p.category,t.year) gid
FROM product p, purchases f, time t
WHERE p.product_id = f.product_id AND
    t.time_key = f.time_key
GROUP BY ROLLUP (t.year, p.category);
```

```
    YEAR       CAT            SALES        GID
    -----  ---------  ----------------  ---------
    2003       ELEC        9380600.38          0    <- (year, category)
    2004       ELEC        9515598.19          0
    2003       HDRW         105098.69          0
    2004       HDRW         105130.03          0
    2003                    107026.10          0
    2004                    106399.30          0
    2003                   9592725.17          1    <- (year)
    2004                   9727127.52          1
                          19319852.70          3    <- (grand total)

10 rows selected.
```

If you concatenate the outputs of all the individual GROUPING functions, you create a binary number, which represents the complete grouping information for each row. The GROUPING_ID function performs this task and returns the decimal number corresponding to this binary value. Thus, in the previous example, if GROUPING(CATEGORY) is 0 and GROUPING(YEAR) is 1, then GROUPING_ID(CATEGORY, YEAR) is the binary number formed by 01, which is the decimal number 1. For the grand total row, GROUPING(CATEGORY) is 1 and GROUP-ING(YEAR) is 1; hence, the GROUPING_ID(CATEGORY, YEAR) is the binary number 11, which is the decimal number 3. The GROUPING_ID is thus a much more compact representation than individual GROUPING functions but is not as straightforward to interpret as separate GROUPING functions on each column.

In addition to the built-in aggregate functions, such as SUM or AVG, you can define your own custom aggregate functions, which we will discuss next.

User-Defined Aggregates

Some applications, usually financial ones, may use proprietary aggregation algorithms that cannot be computed using the built-in SQL aggregate operators. Or the data representation may be complex, involving objects or LOB columns. In such situations, you can define custom aggregate functions, which can be used in SQL queries just like regular aggregates.

User-defined aggregates are part of Oracle's extensibility framework. To define a user-defined aggregate, you must first define a type that implements the ODCIAggregate interface. You then declare a function that uses this type to perform aggregation. The implementation of the aggregate functions can be in any procedural language, such as C, PL/SQL, or Java.

The ODCIAggregate interface consists of the following functions:

- ODCIAggregateInitialize() initializes the aggregate value at the start of processing.

- ODCIAggregateIterate() updates the aggregate for new row of data.

- ODCIAggregateTerminate() returns the aggregate value and ends processing.

- ODCIAggregateMerge() is used to support parallel computation of the aggregation. The aggregate is computed on different pieces of the data and finally the ODCIAggregateMerge() is called to combine the results. The PARALLEL_ENABLE clause must be specified on the aggregate function to enable this.

For instance, suppose you have a proprietary sales forecasting algorithm that takes the sales numbers for the past five years and comes up with an estimate for sales for the next year. You can define a user-defined aggregate for this as follows. The SalesForecastFunction type implements the ODCI-Aggregate interface. (We omit the implementation here for lack of space. Please see the Appendix for instructions to obtain the full example.) The function SalesForecast() is declared as an aggregate function using the Sales-ForecastFunction.

```
CREATE OR REPLACE TYPE SalesForecastFunction AS OBJECT (
  data number,
  STATIC FUNCTION ODCIAggregateInitialize
                  (ctx IN OUT SalesForecastFunction)
      RETURN number,
  MEMBER FUNCTION ODCIAggregateIterate
                  (self  IN OUT SalesForecastFunction,
                   value IN number) RETURN number,
  MEMBER FUNCTION ODCIAggregateTerminate
                  (self IN OUT SalesForecastFunction,
                   returnValue OUT number,
                   flags IN number) RETURN number,
  MEMBER FUNCTION ODCIAggregateMerge
                  (self IN OUT SalesForecastFunction,
                   ctx2 IN OUT SalesForecastFunction)
                  RETURN number
);
/

CREATE OR REPLACE TYPE BODY SalesForecastFunction
IS
…
END;
/

CREATE or REPLACE FUNCTION SalesForecast(x number) RETURN number
PARALLEL_ENABLE AGGREGATE USING SalesForecastFunction;
/
```

This function can then be used in a SQL query in place of any aggregate, as follows. You can also use the DISTINCT flag to remove duplicate column values prior to aggregation.

```
SELECT p.category, SUM(f.purchase_price) sales,
       SalesForecast(f.purchase_price) as salesforecast
FROM purchases f, product p
WHERE f.product_id = p.product_id
GROUP BY p.category;

CATE        SALES  SALESFORECAST
----  ----------- -------------
ELEC  33327213.90   36659935.30
HDRW   2962332.61    3258565.87
MUSC   3223204.06    3545524.47
```

Hint: Before you implement a user-defined aggregate, check if your aggregate can be handled by existing SQL aggregates, since they would give better performance. The CASE function can be used to handle a wide variety of complex computations.

If aggregation were all we needed, life would be simple. However, business intelligence queries usually involve more complex analysis than just aggregation. For example, if you wanted to find the top-selling products or compare sales of one month with the previous one, you will need to use SQL functions for analysis; these are discussed next.

6.4.2 SQL Functions for Analysis

The analytical functions in Oracle provide very powerful SQL constructs to represent many typical decision-support queries. By using the analytical functions in the database, these calculations can take advantage of parallelism and other optimization techniques in the database.

Analytical functions fall into many categories, some of which are:

- Ranking functions can be used to answer queries for top-N items, such as: What were the top-10 best-selling products this year? Examples of ranking functions include RANK, DENSE_RANK, and NTILE.

- Moving window aggregates can be used to answer queries such as: What were the cumulative sales for Asia for each month this year? These functions calculate quantities, such as cumulative sum or moving average, that involve continuous computations over a period of time.

- Reporting aggregates can be used to see the aggregated value side by side with the detailed rows that contributed to it. You would use a reporting aggregate if you wanted to compare sales of each product with the average sales of all products.

- Lag and Lead functions can be used to do period-over-period comparisons—for example, comparing sales of one year to the previous year.

We will now look at these SQL functions in more detail with some examples.

Ranking Functions

Ranking functions allow you to answer queries such as: Who are my top 15 percent customers? or What were my worst- or best-selling products? Take, for example, that we are trying to streamline our product line and would like to take the 10 worst-selling products off the market at the end of the year. To answer this question, we must first compute the sales for each product and order the products according to their sales (least sales first) and finally pick the first 10.

The following SQL statement identifies the worst-selling 10 products using the RANK function. The RANK function assigns ranks from 1 to N, skipping ranks in case of ties. Thus, if there were two products with the same sales with rank 3, then the next rank would be 5.

```
SELECT *
FROM
(SELECT p.product_id p_id, SUM(f.purchase_price) as sales,
        RANK() OVER (ORDER BY SUM(f.purchase_price)) as rank
 FROM purchases f, product p
 WHERE f.product_id = p.product_id
 GROUP BY p.product_id)
WHERE rank <= 10;


P_ID        SALES       RANK
--------  ----------  ----------
SP1247     7082.84        1
SP1264     7145.52        2
SP1220     7223.87        3   <- tie for rank 3
SP1260     7223.87        3
SP1224     7239.54        5
SP1245     7302.22        6
SP1262     7333.56        7
SP1238     7364.90        8
SP1256     7380.57        9
SP1243     7474.59       10
SP1257     7474.59       10

11 rows selected.
```

This query has two parts—an inner subquery ranks the products by their sales and the outer query selects the rows corresponding to the first 10 ranks. Let us concentrate on the inner subquery for the moment. If you ignore the RANK function, this subquery simply performs the familiar aggregation SUM(f.purchase_price) to determine the total sales for each product. The RANK function then ranks the result according to the ordering criteria SUM(f.purchase_price) (i.e., the sales for that product).

If, instead of the worst-selling products, you wanted to determine the best-selling products, you simply need to change the ORDER BY clause from the default (ascending) to descending using the DESC keyword. However, you need to be aware of a small nuance due to NULL values. In the SQL ORDER BY clause, you can specify whether NULL values should be ordered before (FIRST) or after (LAST) any non-null values. NULLS LAST is the default for ascending order and NULLS FIRST for descending order. Obviously, in our case, we don't want products with NULL sales (perhaps they were damaged and had to be written off) to appear first in the list, so we must specify NULLS LAST. The resulting SQL is as follows:

```
SELECT p.product_id p_id, SUM(f.purchase_price) as sales,
       RANK() OVER (ORDER BY SUM(f.purchase_price)
                       DESC NULLS LAST) as rank
FROM purchases f, product p
WHERE f.product_id = p.product_id
GROUP BY p.product_id;
```

```
P_ID          SALES    RANK
--------  ---------  ------
SP1052    675785.37       1
SP1056    669445.92       2
SP1036    668178.03       3
SP1040    665642.25       4
SP1060    655499.13       5
...
SP1300        56.02     164
SP1255                  165 <- nulls last
```

A variant of RANK is the DENSE_RANK function that assigns contiguous ranks *despite* ties. For instance, if two products had the same rank, 3, DENSE_RANK would assign the next rank to be 4. Thus, the DENSE_RANK function does not skip ranks, whereas the RANK function does. The following query illustrates the difference between RANK and DENSE_RANK. We could have decided to use one or the other depending on the business policy.

```
SELECT p.product_id p_id, SUM(f.purchase_price) as sales,
       RANK() OVER (ORDER BY SUM(f.purchase_price)) as rank,
       DENSE_RANK() OVER (ORDER BY SUM(f.purchase_price)) as drank
FROM purchases f, product p
WHERE f.product_id = p.product_id
GROUP BY p.product_id;
```

```
P_ID            SALES      RANK       DRANK
--------     ----------  ----------  ----------
SP1247        7082.84        1           1
SP1264        7145.52        2           2
SP1220        7223.87        3           3      <- tie for rank 3
SP1260        7223.87        3           3
SP1224        7239.54        5           4      <- note the difference
SP1245        7302.22        6           5
...
```

All analytical functions follow a similar syntax, consisting of the OVER() clause, which can include an ORDER BY condition. To understand analytic functions better, it helps to remember that these functions are applied *after* the WHERE, GROUP BY, and HAVING clauses of the query have been computed and before ORDER BY and SQL Model clauses (explained in section 6.4.5). Consequently, any aggregate functions such as SUM(f.purchase_price), computed by the query, are available as ordering criteria to the analytical function.

PARTITION BY Clause

Now that we have computed the worst-selling products overall, we would like to identify the worst-selling products in each product category. This can be achieved by making a slight change to the OVER() clause in the earlier example, to include the PARTITION BY clause, as follows:

```
SELECT p.category, p.product_id, SUM(f.purchase_price) as sales,
       RANK() OVER (PARTITION BY p.category
                    ORDER BY SUM(f.purchase_price)) as rank
FROM purchases f, product p
WHERE f.product_id = p.product_id
GROUP BY p.category, p.product_id;
```

```
CATE PRODUCT_       SALES      RANK
---- --------    ----------  ----------
ELEC SP1078      11695.32        1
ELEC SP1065      11820.27        2
ELEC SP1063      11823.29        3
ELEC SP1066      11845.26        4
...
HDRW SP1220       7223.87        1
HDRW SP1224       7239.54        2
HDRW SP1238       7364.90        3
...
MUSC SP1247       7082.84        1
MUSC SP1264       7145.52        2
MUSC SP1260       7223.87        3
...
164 rows selected.
```

In this example, the query first computes the sales for each product. The PARTITION BY clause then divides the result into groups according to the CATEGORY column. Note that we must select category in the GROUP BY clause so that it is available to the PARTITION BY clause. Finally, for each category, the RANK function assigns a rank to the products within that category, ordered according to their sales. The rank is reset to 1 within each product category. Figure 6.3 illustrates the computation of RANK with the PARTITION BY clause.

Figure 6.3   *PARTITION BY clause*

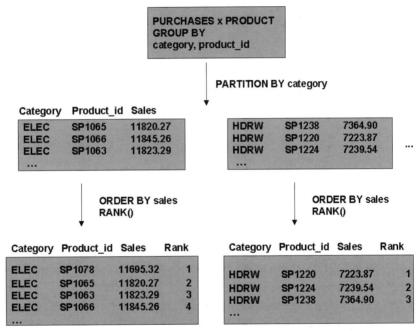

You can use the RANK function multiple times using different PARTITION and ORDER BY expressions in the same query. Note that the PARTITION BY clause used by analytical functions is completely unrelated to partitioning for tables, discussed in Chapter 4.

Relative Ranking Functions

In the previous section, we computed the worst-selling products, however, we did not get a sense of the relative standing of a product with respect to all of the products. For instance, if we had 1,000 products, then a rank of 10 would be pretty close to the top of the worst-selling list. However, if we only had 15 products, then a rank of 10 is not that bad—in fact, if we removed the 10 worst-selling products from our store, we would have eliminated 75 percent of our products, which may not be what we set out to do! The analytical functions PERCENT_RANK, CUME_DIST, and NTILE give us a way to interpret where any given product stands in comparison to the entire set. You can think of these functions as *relative* ranking functions whereas RANK and DENSE_RANK are *absolute* ranking functions. Relative ranking functions help us understand the placement of values in the distribution of data, so they are also known as **distribution** functions.

Suppose we wanted to answer the question: Show me the 25 percent worst-selling products with sales less than $7,500? To answer this question we need to compute the NTILE(4) of sales within each product category. The NTILE(N) function orders the data using a specified criterion and then divides the result into N buckets, assigning the bucket number to all rows in each bucket. Thus, NTILE(4) assigns a number (also called the quartile) between 1 and 4 to each row. You can use quartile to determine whether a value falls within the ranges of 0–25 percent, 25–50 percent, 50–75 percent or 75–100 percent with respect to all values in the set. You may be familiar with the term *percentile* used to compare test scores for school admissions. This is a special case of the NTILE function where N is 100, so if a student is in the 98 percentile, then only 2 percent of students performed better than this student.

The following query answers the business question we posed earlier. The 25 percent worst-selling products correspond to the first quartile—that is, those with an NTILE value of 1 (marked with an asterisk in the following output). Note that the condition sales < 7,500 specified in the HAVING clause will be evaluated *before* the analytical function.

```
SELECT p.category, p.product_id, SUM(f.purchase_price) as sales,
       NTILE(4) OVER (PARTITION BY p.category
                      ORDER BY SUM(f.purchase_price)) as quartile
FROM purchases f, product p
WHERE f.product_id = p.product_id
GROUP BY p.category, p.product_id
HAVING SUM(f.purchase_price) < 7500;

CATE PRODUCT_      SALES   QUARTILE
---- --------   ---------- ----------
HDRW SP1220      7223.87          1   *
HDRW SP1224      7239.54          2
HDRW SP1238      7364.90          3
MUSC SP1247      7082.84          1   *
MUSC SP1264      7145.52          1   *
MUSC SP1260      7223.87          2
MUSC SP1245      7302.22          2
```

```
MUSC SP1262        7333.56           3
MUSC SP1256        7380.57           3
MUSC SP1243        7474.59           4
MUSC SP1257        7474.59           4
```

The buckets generated by the NTILE(4) function all have almost the same number of rows: The function allocates rows so the count per bucket differs by no more than one. However, the range between the lowest and highest value in each bucket may differ. This is called an **equiheight** histogram.

Note that with NTILE(4), you only got a coarse distribution of the product, such as whether it was in the top 25 percent, the bottom 50 percent, and so on. Instead, if you wanted to see the finer-grained ranking of each product relative to the whole set, you could use a high number, such as 1,000, as the argument to NTILE or use the CUME_DIST or PERCENT_RANK functions.

The CUME_DIST function computes the cumulative distribution of product sales, which answers the question: What percentage of products have sales less than a given product? For instance, in the following example, 37.5 percent of products have sales *value* less than or equal to SP1260 in the music category. PERCENT_RANK answers the question: What percentage of products *rank* lower than a given product based on their total sales? For instance, in the following example, 28.5 percent of products rank lower than SP1260.

```
SELECT p.category, p.product_id, SUM(f.purchase_price) as sales,
       CUME_DIST() OVER (PARTITION BY p.category
                    ORDER BY SUM(f.purchase_price)) as cume_dist,
       PERCENT_RANK() OVER (PARTITION BY p.category
                    ORDER BY SUM(f.purchase_price)) as pct_rank
FROM purchases f, product p
WHERE f.product_id = p.product_id
GROUP BY p.category, p.product_id
HAVING SUM(f.purchase_price) < 7500 ;
```

CATE	PRODUCT_	SALES	CUME_DIST	PCT_RANK	
HDRW	SP1220	7223.87	.333333333	0	
HDRW	SP1224	7239.54	.666666667	.5	
HDRW	SP1238	7364.90	1	1	
MUSC	SP1247	7082.84	.125	0	
MUSC	SP1264	7145.52	.25	.142857143	
MUSC	SP1260	7223.87	.375	.285714286	*
MUSC	SP1245	7302.22	.5	.428571429	
MUSC	SP1262	7333.56	.625	.571428571	

```
MUSC SP1256        7380.57          .75    .714285714
MUSC SP1243        7474.59            1    .857142857
MUSC SP1257        7474.59            1    .857142857
```

Both these functions are calculated with respect to all the elements in the set and have a value between 0 and 1. To convert to a percentage, you simply need to multiply it by 100. One characteristic of PERCENT_RANK is that the first value will always be 0 (since there are no ranks lower than the first rank!), and the last value will always be less than or equal to 1. On the other hand, CUME_DIST will always have the first entry greater than 0 and the last entry equal to 1. Note that in case of a tie (i.e., when two rows have the same value of sales), they will get the identical value of CUME_DIST and PCT_RANK—for example, the last two rows, SP1243 and SP1257 in the preceding output. If you are interested, PERCENT_RANK of an element with rank R is computed as (R–1) / (Total Ranks–1) and CUME_DIST of an element with value V is computed as (Number of values before V in the given order) / (Total number of values).

Note that the examples in this section use the PARTITION BY clause, which means that the analytical function would be applied to each partition, or in this case each product category.

Other functions in the RANK family are FIRST_VALUE, LAST_VALUE, and ROW_NUMBER. All of these provide different ways to choose data from ordered groups.

WIDTH_BUCKET Function

We have seen how we can do comparative analysis using ranking functions. Another common form of comparative analysis is frequency distribution (i.e., to classify items into different categories based on some quantity and then count how many would fall into each category). For instance, we would like to classify products that have sales between $0 and $100,000 into five equal-sized buckets, as shown in Figure 6.4.

Figure 6.4   *WIDTH_BUCKET Bucket Distribution*

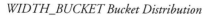

This type of classification called as an **equiwidth** histogram, because each bucket has roughly the same range but can have differing number of rows. The WIDTH_BUCKET function can be used to generate this classification, as shown in the following example. This function takes a range (in this example, 0–10,000) and number of buckets (in this example, four) and assigns a bucket from 1 to 4 to each value. Any values lower than the lower bound will go into an underflow bucket, numbered 0, and any values higher than the upper bound go into an overflow bucket, numbered 5. To get the frequency distribution, we have an outer query that counts all values with a given bucket number using a GROUP BY on the width_bucket value. We also show the minimum and maximum actual sales value, in each bucket.

```
SELECT width_bucket, min(sales) , max(sales), COUNT(*)
FROM
(SELECT  p.product_id, SUM(f.purchase_price) as sales,
        WIDTH_BUCKET(SUM(f.purchase_price), 0, 100000, 4)
                       as width_bucket
FROM purchases f, product p
WHERE f.product_id = p.product_id
GROUP BY p.product_id)
GROUP BY width_bucket;
```

WIDTH_BUCKET	MIN(SALES)	MAX(SALES)	COUNT(*)
1	56.02	24854.91	95
2	25333.81	37236.57	30
3	73531.50	4783.10	4
4	75252.45	83387.85	9
5	573086.28	675785.37	26
			1 <- no sales

From this analysis, we can tell that most of our products (95) had total sales less than $25,000. We also see that we have a significant number of products (26) that had total sales over $100,000. Note also that products with NULL sales value do not get counted in this analysis and get a bucket number NULL.

This type of analysis can also be used to concisely report statistics such as customer demographics or income-level surveys. The WIDTH_ BUCKET function only allows you to create buckets of equal sizes. If you need a more customized distribution of buckets, you should take a look at the CASE expression discussed in section 6.4.4.

Period-over-Period Comparison Functions—LAG and LEAD

Period-over-period comparisons, such as comparing sales to those a year ago, are often part of business reporting. The two simple analytic functions, LAG and LEAD, allow you to perform such comparisons. For instance, suppose we need to compare monthly sales to the sales six months ago. In this case we would use the LAG function, as shown in the following query:

```
SELECT t.month, SUM(f.purchase_price) as monthly_sales,
       LAG(SUM(f.purchase_price),6)
            OVER (ORDER BY t.month) as sales_6_months_ago
FROM purchases f, time t
WHERE f.time_key = t.time_key
GROUP BY t.year, t.month;

    MONTH MONTHLY_SALES SALES_6_MONTHS_AGO
---------- ------------- ------------------
    200301       747376.33
    200302       677746.09
    ...
    200306       847609.93
    200307       905908.19       747376.33  <- LAG(sales,6) = 200301
    200308       762608.21       677746.09
    ...
    200401       883351.03       905908.19
    200402       841068.94       762608.21
    200403       779704.31       745532.66
    200404       833190.58       886877.84
    200405       906714.58       733383.72
    200406       736279.04       754124.30
    200407       758762.01       883351.03  <- LAG(sales,6) = 200401
    200408       900208.87       841068.94
    200409       732996.94       779704.31
    ...
```

For each row returned by a query, LAG and LEAD functions provide the values at a row at a known offset from the current row. In this example, since each row corresponds to one month, the term *6 months ago* would translate to a LAG offset of 6. For example, LAG(sales,6) for July 2004 is the sales for January 2004. Similarly, monthly sales last quarter would translate to LAG(sales,3) and monthly sales for the following year would translate to LEAD(sales, 12).

Note that if the lagging (or leading) row specified by the function is not present, LAG (or LEAD) returns the NULL value or a default you specify. In the EASYDW data warehouse, we keep data for two years, 2003 and 2004, and hence LAG(sales,6) for 200301 through 200306 will have a value of NULL, because data for six months prior is unavailable.

These functions are extremely simple to use and very powerful. Without these functions, such apparently simple computations would require a join of a table to itself, possibly multiple times, or a number of subqueries, which would make the query extremely inefficient.

Window Aggregate Functions

One of the most powerful tools provided by the analytical functions is to aggregate over a moving window. These functions allow you to answer questions such as: What are the cumulative sales numbers for each month this year? Window aggregate functions let you compute a function such as SUM over a specified window of rows relative to the current row.

The following example calculates the monthly cumulative sales for the year 2003. The query first computes the SUM(purchase_price) (i.e., sales for each month in 2003). Then, for each month, it sums up the sales for all months up to and including the current month. This is indicated by the expression SUM(SUM(f.purchase_price)). Note that the ORDER BY clause indicates how to order the rows to determine the window; in this example the window is determined by the order of the months. The ROWS UNBOUNDED PRECEDING clause specifies that the window is all rows before and including the current row. A window specified using number of rows preceding or following the current row is known as a **physical window**.

```
SELECT t.month, SUM(f.purchase_price) as sales,
       SUM(SUM(f.purchase_price))
           OVER (ORDER BY t.month ROWS UNBOUNDED PRECEDING)
             as cumulative_sales
FROM purchases f, time t
WHERE f.time_key = t.time_key and t.year = 2003
GROUP BY t.month;
```

MONTH	SALES	CUMULATIVE_SALES
200301	747376.33	747376.33
200302	678003.47	1425379.80
200303	899322.05	2324701.85
200304	871402.28	3196104.13
200305	758742.80	3954846.93
200306	848080.03	4802926.96
200307	906190.25	5709117.21
200308	762764.91	6471882.12
200309	745689.36	7217571.48
200310	887175.57	8104747.05
200311	733383.72	8838130.77
200312	754594.40	9592725.17

Another common example of a moving window function is a moving average. In the next example, we are computing, for each month, the moving average of the sales for that month and the two months preceding it. This is specified by the ROWS 2 PRECEDING clause.

```
SELECT t.month, SUM(f.purchase_price) as sales,
       AVG(SUM(f.purchase_price))
            OVER (ORDER BY t.month ROWS 2 PRECEDING) as mov_avg
FROM purchases f, time t
WHERE f.time_key = t.time_key and t.year = 2003
GROUP BY t.month;
```

MONTH	SALES	MOV_AVG
200301	747376.33	747376.330
200302	678003.47	712689.900
200303	899322.05	774900.617
200304	871402.28	816242.600
200305	758742.80	843155.710
200306	848080.03	826075.037
200307	906190.25	837671.027
200308	762764.91	839011.730
200309	745689.36	804881.507
200310	887175.57	798543.280
200311	733383.72	788749.550
200312	754594.40	791717.897

If, instead, we wanted the window to include the current month and two months following it, the window expression would simply change to ROWS 2 FOLLOWING.

Specifying a Logical Window

One of the most common moving window analyses is a time-series analysis, where the ordering expression is a date. For this special case, you can specify the window using logical entities such as INTERVAL DAY, MONTH, or YEAR. Such window expressions are called **logical windows** and are only allowed when the ORDER BY expression has a numeric, date, or interval data types. For instance, suppose you wanted to know the daily sales totaled over a moving five-day window including two days before and two days after the current date. The SQL to answer this query is as follows. The window is specified using a RANGE BETWEEN clause and INTERVAL DAY expressions for the upper and lower bounds.

```
SELECT t.time_key, SUM(f.purchase_price) as sales,
       SUM(SUM(f.purchase_price)) OVER (ORDER BY t.time_key
       RANGE BETWEEN INTERVAL '2' DAY PRECEDING AND
                     INTERVAL '2' DAY FOLLOWING) as sales_5_day
FROM purchases f, time t
WHERE f.time_key = t.time_key and t.year = 2003
GROUP BY t.time_key
HAVING SUM(f.purchase_price) < 25000;
```

```
TIME_KEY         SALES  SALES_5_DAY
---------  -----------  -----------
01-JAN-03    23345.03     71195.91
02-JAN-03    24572.88     94636.72
03-JAN-03    23278       119209.60                     ---
04-JAN-03    23440.81    119142.57                      |
05-JAN-03    24572.88    118010.50  <- current row |logical window
06-JAN-03    23278      1193058.00                      |
07-JAN-03    23440.81    119142.50                     ---
08-JAN-03    24572.88    118010.50
09-JAN-03    23278       119305.38
10-JAN-03    23440.81    119142.57
...
27-JAN-03    23278        72423.76
29-JAN-03    24572.88     71128.88                     ---
30-JAN-03    23278        69999.47  <- current row | logical window
01-FEB-03    22148.59     70191.14                     ---
03-FEB-03    24764.55     68977.70
...
152 rows selected.
```

In this example, the computation for the date 5-Jan-03 consists of sales from five consecutive dates from 3-Jan-03 through 7-Jan-03. However, the calculation for 30-Jan-03 consists only of three dates: 29-Jan-03, 30-Jan-03, and 01-Feb-03, because dates 28-Jan-03 and 31-Jan-03 are missing. Instead, if this were a physical window, the window would have included 27-Jan-03 and 01-Feb-03, which is not really what we want. This highlights an important issue with using physical windows, which is that a physical window is good only if you have *dense* data (i.e., no gaps in the ordering values). Fortunately, the Oracle Database 10*g* provides a solution to this problem, which is what we will discuss next.

Converting Sparse Data into Dense Form

A logical window can only be used for a restricted set of data types. A physical window is often the most convenient for time-series calculations, such as comparing year over year or quarterly sales. However, as mentioned earlier if the data is not dense we cannot use a physical window for analysis. For instance, the following query shows sales for each product by month. In this example, a product, CD LX1 was not sold in February 2003, and so the result would be missing a row for 200302, CD LX1. Therefore, a physical window expression such as a three-month moving average would give incorrect results.

```
SELECT t.month, p.product_name, SUM(f.purchase_price) as sales
FROM purchases f, time t, product p
WHERE f.time_key = t.time_key
  AND f.product_id = p.product_id
GROUP BY p.product_name, t.month;
```

```
   MONTH PRODUCT_NAME             SALES
---------- ---------------   ----------
   200301 CD LX1               485.77
                                        <- missing 200302
   200303 CD LX1               470.10
   200304 CD LX1               313.40
   200305 CD LX1               313.40
   200306 CD LX1               313.40
   200307 CD LX1               470.10
   200308 CD LX1               501.44
   200309 CD LX1               470.10
   200310 CD LX1               250.72
   200311 CD LX1                56.70
   ...

3417 rows selected.
```

Would it not be easier if, instead of having no row, we had a "dummy" row for 200302, CD LX1 with sales of 0? We could then simply use a physical window, such as ROWS PRECEDING 1, for the previous month or ROWS FOLLOWING 1 for the next month. Oracle Database 10*g* introduced a new operation, known as a PARTITION OUTER JOIN, which can be used to convert sparse data into dense data, thus enabling the use of physical windows even with sparse data. Before we discuss, let us briefly review what an outer join is.

OUTER JOIN

In this chapter, we have seen several queries where we calculate the total sales by product. The joins used in these examples were **inner** joins, where rows appear in the result only if the joining column value is present in both tables. However, if we also wanted to see those products that did not sell at all, we would need to use an outer join. These products would have PRODUCT_ID values that appear in the PRODUCT table but not in the PURCHASES table. For such rows, a NULL value is output instead of columns in the PURCHASES table. The SQL statement for this query is as follows. As you can see, this query has two rows marked with an asterisk, corresponding to products that did not sell, which would not be in the inner join. These extra rows are called the **antijoin**.

```
SELECT p.product_name, SUM(f.purchase_price) as sales
FROM purchases f RIGHT OUTER JOIN product p
  ON (f.product_id = p.product_id)
GROUP BY p.product_name;
```

PRODUCT_NAME	SALES
APS Camera	17064.33
CD LX1	7772.32
...	
XYZ	56.02
Tents Half Dome 1999	*
Tents Half Dome 2000	*

Note that this query uses a RIGHT OUTER JOIN clause, which is the ANSI standard syntax for a join. Here the join is represented in the FROM clause rather than in the WHERE clause, which is an Oracle specific syntax. An outer join can be a LEFT OUTER JOIN or RIGHT OUTER JOIN. The RIGHT OUTER JOIN between PURCHASES and PRODUCT gave us rows from the PRODUCTS (right) table, which had no corresponding rows in the PURCHASES (left) table. If we used a LEFT OUTER JOIN in the previous example, we would get those rows in the PURCHASES (left) table, for which PRODUCT_ID was not in the PRODUCTS (right) table. For instance, these may be transactions for discontinued or special products or maybe where the actual products sold was not known.

Now that we know what an outer join is, we can see how the partition outer join is used.

Partition Outer Join

Recall the problem we are trying to solve: We would like to find sales by product and month for each product; if there were no sales for that product in some month, we would like to generate a row with sales of 0 for that product and month. This is done by the following SQL statement, which uses the PARTITION OUTER JOIN. The PARTITION OUTER JOIN is an extension of the outer join where the outer join is done against each partition identified by a PARTITION BY clause. (Note that we are talking about the PARTITION BY clause shown in Figure 6.5 and not physical data partitioning.) We will explain this SQL in more detail in a moment, but for now notice that rows marked with an asterisk indicate that we have filled in the missing rows with a sales value of 0.

```
SELECT v2.month, v1.product_name, nvl(v1.sales,0)
FROM
(SELECT t.month, p.product_name, SUM(f.purchase_price) as sales
 FROM purchases f, time t, product p
 WHERE f.time_key = t.time_key
   AND f.product_id = p.product_id
 GROUP BY p.product_name, t.month) v1 PARTITION BY (product_name)
```

```
RIGHT OUTER JOIN
(SELECT DISTINCT t.month
 FROM time t) v2
ON v1.month = v2.month;

   MONTH PRODUCT_NAME                      NVL(V1.SALES,0)
---------- ------------------------------ ---------------

   200301 CD LX1                                   485.77
   200302 CD LX1                                        0 *
   200303 CD LX1                                   470.10
   200304 CD LX1                                   313.40
   200305 CD LX1                                   313.40
   200306 CD LX1                                   313.40
   200307 CD LX1                                   470.10
   200308 CD LX1                                   501.44
   200309 CD LX1                                   470.10
   200310 CD LX1                                   250.72
   200311 CD LX1                                   156.70
   200312 CD LX1                                        0 *
   ...

3816 rows selected.
```

Now let us try to understand this query. The query has two views in the FROM clause, v1 and v2. The first view, v1, is simply the query for sales by product and month we saw earlier. The second view, v2, obtains the distinct values of month in the table, TIME. The PARTITION BY clause on

Figure 6.5   *PARTITION OUTER JOIN*

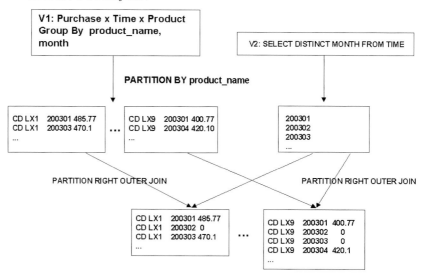

PRODUCT_NAME will take the result of v1 and divide it into partitions one for each product. The query then joins each such partition of v1 to the view v2 using a RIGHT OUTER JOIN. For each product, the antijoin portion will correspond to rows (months) from v2 that do not join with any rows in the partition of v1 for that product. This exactly corresponds to the months where there were no sales for the particular product! The expression nvl(sales,0) will put a value of 0, rather than NULL for such rows. And, Voilà—we have converted the sparse data into a dense form. Figure 6.5 can help visualize this PARTITION OUTER JOIN operation.

If you are wondering why we need the PARTITION OUTER JOIN and cannot do this with just an OUTER JOIN, remember that we would be joining v1 and v2 on month. As long as every value of month in v2 appears in v1 *for some product*, a simple outer join will be same as an inner join and will leave the result of v1 unchanged. If some value of month does not appear in v1 at all, it means that in this month we did not sell *any* products at all, which is *not* what we were looking for in this example! The interested reader may find it to be an instructive exercise to use outer joins to find those months where we did not sell *any* products and those products that did not sell in *any* month. Hint: The query is very similar to the example given here but you do not need the PARTITION OUTER join to do this.

Reporting Aggregates

Continuing on with our product analysis, suppose we want to answer the question: What is the percentage contribution of each product category to the overall sales? You can visualize this result as a pie chart, with each slice being sales of one product category. To generate this pie chart, what we need to compute is the ratio of each product category's sales to the total sales of all categories combined.

You will find that with conventional SQL it is very cumbersome to do this type of calculation. This is because when you ask for a simple aggregate such as SUM or MAX in SQL, you lose the individual rows contributing to the aggregate. Only one row, which is the aggregate, is returned. So you will need to do two queries: one to get the sales for each individual category and another to compute the total sales of all categories and then calculate the ratio within the application outside of SQL. Reporting aggregates solve this problem by reporting the computed aggregate value *side by side* with all the detail rows that contributed to it.

The following query uses a reporting aggregate to answer our question. In this example, the aggregate sales is a regular aggregate, whereas sales_total is a reporting aggregate that computes the total sales for all products. You can identify a reporting aggregate by its use of an OVER() clause. Notice how the same value 19312425.1 appears in all the rows. To generate the pie chart we simply use the ratio between sales and total_sales for each category, computed as ratio_sales in this example.

```
SELECT category, SUM(f.purchase_price) as sales,
       SUM(SUM(f.purchase_price)) OVER () as sales_total,
       SUM(f.purchase_price)/SUM(SUM(f.purchase_price)) OVER()
          as ratio_sales
FROM product p, purchases f
WHERE f.product_id = p.product_id
GROUP BY p.category;
```

CATE	SALES	SALES_TOTAL	RATIO_SALES
ELEC	18896198.6	19312425.1	.978447733
HDRW	210228.72	19312425.1	.010885672
MUSC	205997.82	19312425.1	.010666595

In fact, there is a built-in reporting aggregate called RATIO_TO_ REPORT, which does this particular computation automatically. Thus, we could have written the query as follows to get the same ratio as the previous query:

```
SELECT category, RATIO_TO_REPORT(SUM(f.purchase_price))
                          OVER () as ratio_sales
FROM product p, purchases f
WHERE f.product_id = p.product_id
GROUP BY p.category;
```

CATE	RATIO_SALES
ELEC	.978447733
HDRW	.010885672
MUSC	.010666595

The preceding examples used an empty OVER() clause, which simply means that the reporting aggregate is being computed without any PARTITION BY clause (i.e., over all rows). However, as with other analytical functions, you can use the PARTITION BY clauses to divide the data into partitions before computing the reporting aggregate. For example, if we wanted to see the products whose sales are below the average sales in their category, we would use the following query:

```
SELECT *
FROM (SELECT p.category, p.product_id prod_id,
             SUM(f.purchase_price) prod_sales,
             AVG(SUM(f.purchase_price))
                 OVER (PARTITION BY p.category) category_avg
      FROM product p, purchases f
      WHERE f.product_id = p.product_id
      GROUP BY p.category, p.product_id)
WHERE prod_sales < category_avg;
```

```
CATE PROD_ID  PROD_SALES CATEGORY_AVG
---- -------- ---------- ------------
ELEC SP1000     34085.61   170237.033
ELEC SP1001     17064.33   170237.033
ELEC SP1010     22699.86   170237.033

...

HDRW SP1217      7740.98   7786.24889
HDRW SP1220      7223.87   7786.24889
HDRW SP1221      7552.94   7786.24889

...

MUSC SP1242      7772.32   7922.99308
MUSC SP1243      7474.59   7922.99308
MUSC SP1244      7740.98   7922.99308

...
```

In this example, the inner query computes the sales of each product as a regular aggregate and the average sales for each category as a reporting aggregate using the PARTITION BY category. The outer query then simply selects the products with sales below the category average.

First and Last Functions

While we are streamlining our product portfolio, we have decided to revamp our pricing model as well and to do so we must determine how prices affect our sales. For instance, we would like to find the number of purchases made for the costliest and cheapest products in each category. This involves first ranking all products, by their selling price, picking the cheapest and costliest products and then aggregating using COUNT(*) all the purchases made for these products. The FIRST and LAST aggregation functions allow you to do such operations in a concise manner, as illustrated in the following query. In our example, we find that total sales for the costliest items are about the same as for the cheaper ones.

```
SELECT p.category cat, SUM(f.purchase_price) total_sales,
       MIN(p.sell_price) cheap_prod,
       COUNT(*) KEEP (DENSE_RANK FIRST
                      ORDER BY p.sell_price) cheap_sales,
       MAX(p.sell_price) costly_prod,
```

```
            COUNT(*) KEEP (DENSE_RANK LAST
                         ORDER BY p.sell_price) costly_sales
FROM purchases f, product p
WHERE f.product_id = p.product_id
GROUP BY p.category;
```

CAT	TOTAL_SALES	CHEAP_PROD	CHEAP_SALES	COSTLY_PROD	COSTLY_SALES
ELEC	18896198.60	24.99	13888	1267.89	12770
HDRW	210228.72	15.67	13416	15.67	13416
MUSC	205997.82	15.67	13620	15.67	13620

Note that the ranking of an item as FIRST or LAST is done using the DENSE_RANK function we discussed earlier.

A common use of FIRST and LAST is to return the value of a column other than the column used to order the group. For instance, you can order by column A yet return the MIN(column B). This approach increases query performance by avoiding subqueries or other processing that is required without FIRST and LAST. The FIRST and LAST functions can also be used as reporting aggregates.

Inverse Percentile

Previously, we mentioned the CUME_DIST function, which can be used to determine the cumulative distribution of a quantity, also known as its percentile. Given this distribution, an inverse percentile function looks up the data value that corresponds to a given percentile value in an ordered set of rows. You can use this to ask the question—what product falls into the 50th percentile?

To illustrate this function, we will use the output of the following query, which we saw previously. Recall that the rows are ordered by SUM(purchase_price) and each row is assigned a value between 0 and 1.

```
SELECT p.category, p.product_id, SUM(f.purchase_price) as sales,
       CUME_DIST() over (PARTITION BY p.category
                         ORDER BY SUM(f.purchase_price))
                  as cume_dist
FROM purchases f, product p
WHERE f.product_id = p.product_id
GROUP BY p.category, p.product_id
HAVING SUM(f.purchase_price) < 7500 ;
```

```
CATE PRODUCT_     SALES  CUME_DIST
---- -------- ---------- ----------
HDRW SP1220     7223.87 .333333333
HDRW SP1224     7239.54 .666666667  <-  PERCENTILE_DISC(0.5)
```

```
HDRW SP1238      7364.90            1

MUSC SP1247      7082.84          .125
MUSC SP1264      7145.52          .25
MUSC SP1260      7223.87          .375
MUSC SP1245      7302.22          .5   <-   PERCENTILE_DISC(0.5)
MUSC SP1262      7333.56          .625
MUSC SP1256      7380.57          .75
MUSC SP1243      7474.59            1
MUSC SP1257      7474.59            1
```

There are two flavors of inverse percentile. PERCENTILE_DISC assumes that the sales values are discrete and returns the value that corresponds to the nearest CUME_DIST value greater than the percentile specified. PERCENTILE_CONT assumes that the values are continuous and returns the interpolated value corresponding to the given percentile. In the previous example, the sales value that corresponds to PERCENTILE_DISC(0.5) for the HDRW category is 7239.54 and for MUSC category it is 7302.22.

The following example illustrates the use of the inverse percentile functions. This example returns the median sales amount for products within each category. Note that PERCENTILE_DISC and PERCENTILE_CONT functions always return a single data value. An ORDER BY criterion must be specified and must consist of a single expression.

```
SELECT p.category, p.product_id, SUM(f.purchase_price) as sales,
       PERCENTILE_DISC(0.5) WITHIN GROUP
            (ORDER BY SUM(f.purchase_price))
             OVER (PARTITION BY p.category) as pct_disc,
       PERCENTILE_CONT(0.5) WITHIN GROUP
            (ORDER BY SUM(f.purchase_price))
             OVER (PARTITION BY p.category) as pct_cont
FROM purchases f, product p
WHERE f.product_id = p.product_id
GROUP BY p.category, p.product_id
HAVING SUM(f.purchase_price) < 7500;
```

```
CATE PRODUCT_      SALES   PCT_DISC   PCT_CONT
---- --------  ---------- ---------- ----------
HDRW SP1220      7223.87    7239.54    7239.54
HDRW SP1224      7239.54    7239.54    7239.54
HDRW SP1238      7364.90    7239.54    7239.54
MUSC SP1247      7082.84    7302.22    7317.89
MUSC SP1264      7145.52    7302.22    7317.89
MUSC SP1260      7223.87    7302.22    7317.89
MUSC SP1245      7302.22    7302.22    7317.89
MUSC SP1262      7333.56    7302.22    7317.89
MUSC SP1256      7380.57    7302.22    7317.89
MUSC SP1243      7474.59    7302.22    7317.89
MUSC SP1257      7474.59    7302.22    7317.89
```

In this example, PERCENTILE_DISC and PERCENTILE_CONT have been used as reporting aggregates.

Hypothetical RANK and Distribution Functions

Business intelligence often involves what-if analysis, where you make a hypothetical change to the business and analyze its impact. For instance, we are introducing a new product in the HDRW category and have a projected sales figure of $7,600 based on market surveys. Based on this information, we would like to know how this product would rank among other products in its category. Oracle provides a family of hypothetical rank and distribution functions for this purpose. With these functions, you can ask to compute the RANK, PERCENT_RANK, or CUME_DIST of a given value, as if it were hypothetically inserted into a set of values.

To illustrate this, we will use the following query, showing the sales for different products in the HDRW category in ascending order of sales and their respective ranks.

```
SELECT p.product_id, SUM(f.purchase_price) sales,
       RANK() OVER (ORDER BY SUM(f.purchase_price)) as  rank
FROM purchases f, product p
WHERE f.product_id = p.product_id and p.category = 'HDRW'
GROUP BY p.product_id;
```

```
PRODUCT_       SALES        RANK
--------    ----------   ----------
SP1220       7223.87          1
SP1224       7239.54          2
SP1238       7364.90          3
SP1221       7552.94          4
SP1222       7568.61          5
SP1237       7568.61          5
SP1239       7568.61          5
                    <- Insert hypothetical value 7600.00
SP1230       7646.96          8
SP1235       7725.31          9
SP1217       7740.98         10
SP1223       7787.99         11
SP1233       7787.99         11
SP1218       7819.33         13
...
```

Now, suppose we want to find the hypothetical rank of a product with sales of $7,600. From the previous output, we can see that this value, if inserted into the data would get a rank of 8. The following query asks for the hypothetical rank:

```
SELECT RANK(7600.00)
       WITHIN GROUP (ORDER BY SUM(f.purchase_price)) as hrank
FROM purchases f, product p
WHERE f.product_id = p.product_id and p.category = 'HDRW'
GROUP BY p.product_id;

    HRANK
----------
        8
```

Hypothetical rank functions take an ordering condition and a constant data value to be inserted into the ordered set. The way to recognize a hypothetical rank function in a query is the WITHIN GROUP clause and a constant expression within the RANK function. Similarly, you can use CUME_DIST or PERCENT_RANK to find the distribution or percentile of a quantity inserted hypothetically into a result.

Statistical Analysis Functions

Statistical analysis is a key tool for business intelligence. Business decisions may often be influenced by relationships between various quantities. For instance, earlier we wanted to know if the price of an item influences how many items are sold. A common technique used in such analyses is **linear regression** analysis, which is a statistical technique used to quantify how one quantity affects or determines the value of another. The idea is to fit the data for two quantities along a straight line, as accurately as possible. This line is called the **regression line**. Some of the quantities of interest are the slope of the line, y-intercept of the line and the coefficient of determination (which is how closely the line fits the points). Oracle provides various diagnostic functions commonly used for this analysis, such as standard error and regression sum of squares.

The linear regression functions are all computed simultaneously in a single pass through the data. They can be treated as regular aggregate functions or reporting aggregate functions.

The following example illustrates the use of some of these functions. Here, we are analyzing, for each manufacturer, whether the price of a product has a relationship to the number of items sold. To do so we compute the slope, intercept, and coefficient of determination of the regression line for the quantities sell_price and total_purchases.

```
SELECT manufacturer,
       REGR_SLOPE(sell_price, total_purchases) slope,
       REGR_INTERCEPT(sell_price, total_purchases) intercept,
       REGR_R2(sell_price, total_purchases) coeff_determination
```

```
FROM
(
SELECT p.manufacturer , p.product_id,
       f.purchase_price sell_price,
       count(f.purchase_price) as total_purchases
FROM purchases f, product p
WHERE f.product_id = p.product_id
GROUP BY p.manufacturer, p.product_id, f.purchase_price
)
GROUP BY manufacturer;


MANUFACTURER          SLOPE     INTERCEPT  COEFF_DETERMINATION
---------------    ----------   ----------  -------------------
Dell               2.39415728   89.6207996          0.946392646
RTG               -.00712584    35.922917           0.000745027
Ricoh              .86111111   -369.35333                     1
...
```

From this analysis, we can see that a straight line can closely model the relationship between selling price and total purchases for the products manufactured by Dell but not for those made by RTG.

Oracle also provides aggregate functions to compute other quantities of interest to a linear regression analysis, such as covariance of a population (COVAR_POP) or sample (COVAR_SAMP) and correlation (CORR) between variables.

DBMS_STATS_FUNC Package

In Oracle Database 10*g*, there is a new package, DBMS_STATS_FUNC, that includes several statistical functions. One function that is particularly convenient is the SUMMARY function, which computes several useful statistics, such as mode, median, TOP 5, and so on, on a given column in a table. The results are returned in a PL/SQL record of type SummaryType.

The following example shows the SUMMARY function on the PURCHASE_PRICE column of the PURCHASES table and prints the values that correspond to various quantiles and the median.

```
set serveroutput on;
DECLARE
  srec dbms_stat_funcs.summaryType;
BEGIN
  dbms_stat_funcs.summary(p_ownername=>'EASYDW',
                          p_tablename=>'PURCHASES',
                          p_columnname=>'PURCHASE_PRICE',
                          s=>srec);
  dbms_output.put_line('Quantile 5   => ' || srec.quantile_5);
  dbms_output.put_line('Quantile 25  => ' || srec.quantile_25);
  dbms_output.put_line('Median       => ' || srec.median);
```

```
    dbms_output.put_line('Quantile 75  => '  ||  srec.quantile_75);
    dbms_output.put_line('Quantile 95  => '  ||  srec.quantile_95);
END;
/

Quantile 5   => 15.67
Quantile 25  => 15.67
Median       => 24.99
Quantile 75  => 72.87
Quantile 95  => 1267.89

PL/SQL procedure successfully completed.
```

Other functions in this package allow you to test if your data conforms to a particular distribution, such as Uniform, Exponential, Poisson, or Normal. Detailed explanation of these statistical concepts can be found in any textbook on statistics and is beyond the scope of this book.

CASE Expression

Earlier, we saw how we can generate a frequency distribution using the WIDTH_BUCKET function. However, instead of equally sized buckets, if we wanted a more customized classification, you could use a CASE expression. The CASE expression allows you to return different expressions based on various conditions. The simple CASE statement is identical to a DECODE statement, where you can return different values depending on the value of an expression. The searched CASE statement allows you more flexibility, as illustrated by this example:

```
SELECT f.product_id,  SUM(f.purchase_price) as sales,
       CASE WHEN SUM(f.purchase_price) > 150000 THEN 'High'
            WHEN SUM(f.purchase_price)
                 BETWEEN 100000 and 150000 THEN 'Medium'
            WHEN SUM(f.purchase_price)
                 BETWEEN 50000 and 100000 THEN 'Low'
            ELSE 'Other'  END  as sales_value
FROM purchases f
GROUP BY f.product_id;

PRODUCT_      SALES SALES_VALUE
-------- ---------- -----------
SP1023    75252.45     Low
SP1024    82136.25     Low
...
SP1053   613658.76     High
SP1054   654231.24     High
...
SP1268     7584.28     Other
SP1269    14197.02     Other

164 rows selected.
```

You can use the CASE expression anywhere you use a column or expression, including inside aggregate functions. The combination of aggregates and CASE expressions can be used to compute complex aggregations and for what-if analysis. For instance, suppose we wanted to provide free shipping on orders greater than $50. However, for customers who live in California the minimum order would be $100 and for customers who live in the United Kingdom the minimum order would be $250, and they would only get 10 percent off shipping. The following statement computes the current and projected shipping costs paid by a customer:

```
SELECT AVG(f.shipping_charge) as current_avg_shipcosts,
       AVG(CASE WHEN c.state = 'CA' and f.purchase_price > 100
                   THEN 0
               WHEN c.country = 'UK' and f.purchase_price > 250
                   THEN  0.9 * f.shipping_charge
               WHEN f.purchase_price > 50 THEN 0
               ELSE f.shipping_charge
           END) projected_shipping_costs
FROM purchases f, customer c
WHERE f.customer_id = c.customer_id;

CURRENT_AVG_SHIPCOSTS PROJECTED_SHIPPING_COSTS
--------------------- ------------------------
          4.55426569                2.45110852
```

Thus, we can see that with this scheme, on the average, customers will end up paying around $2 less for shipping.

WITH Clause

Even with all the analytical functions, business intelligence queries could be very complex and contain complex subqueries. In fact, the same subquery can appear multiple times in the query. The WITH clause, introduced in Oracle 9*i*, can improve the readability of such complex queries and also improve performance for queries needing repeated computation.

For example, suppose we wanted to determine for each product category the month for which the sales were the highest. One way of doing this is by using the following query:

```
SELECT s.category, s.month, s.monthly_prod_sales
FROM (SELECT p.category, t.month,
             SUM(f.purchase_price) as monthly_prod_sales
      FROM product p, purchases f, time t
      WHERE f.product_id = p.product_id
        AND f.time_key = t.time_key
      GROUP BY p.category, t.month) s
```

```
WHERE s.monthly_prod_sales
  IN (SELECT MAX(v.monthly_sales)
      FROM (SELECT p.category, t.month,
                   SUM(f.purchase_price) as monthly_sales
            FROM product p, purchases f, time t
            WHERE f.product_id = p.product_id
              AND f.time_key = t.time_key
            GROUP BY p.category, t.month) v
      GROUP BY v.month);
```

We can see that this is a very complex SQL statement, and, moreover, the subqueries with alias s and v are identical. The WITH clause can be used to simplify such queries, as we will demonstrate shortly.

The WITH clause allows you to name a subquery and then subsequently use the name instead of that sub-query within a statement. If the same sub-query appears multiple times in a query, then Oracle will automatically materialize that subquery into a temporary table and reuse it when executing the query. The temporary table will live only for the duration of the query and will be automatically deleted when the execution is complete.

Let us rewrite the preceding SQL statement to use the WITH clause. First, we will pull out the common subquery and give it a name, such as PRODUCT_SALES_BY_MONTH. Then, wherever we used this subquery before, we will instead use this name, resulting in the following statement:

```
WITH  product_sales_by_month             <- name the subquery
AS
(
 SELECT p.category, t.month,
        SUM(f.purchase_price) as monthly_prod_sales
 FROM  product p, purchases f, time t
 WHERE f.product_id = p.product_id
   AND f.time_key = t.time_key
 GROUP BY p.category, t.month
)
SELECT s.category, s.month, s.monthly_prod_sales
FROM    product_sales_by_month s          <- use name here
WHERE   s.monthly_prod_sales
   IN (SELECT MAX(v.monthly_prod_sales)
       FROM product_sales_by_month v       <- use name here
       GROUP BY v.month);
```

This makes the query execute more efficiently, since Oracle can choose to materialize the result of the subquery into a temporary table and reuse it in both places, thereby saving repeated computation. Also, the query is now much easier to read. The careful reader may have noted that this particular query could also have been done efficiently using reporting aggregates, discussed previously, or using the FIRST or LAST functions of Section First and Last Functions, as also discussed previously. Analytical functions provide great flexibility in expressing business queries.

6.4.3   The SQL Model Clause

Every one of us has used a spreadsheet such as Excel to perform calculations. Often, calculations that may be extremely simple to do in a spreadsheet can be surprisingly difficult and slow in SQL. For example, you can add the second column of the third row to the fifth column of the fifth row as C2 + E5. This is very cumbersome to do in conventional SQL. Some such calculations could be performed with SQL but not without using several self-joins and union operations with abysmal performance. The underlying reason for this is that a spreadsheet allows you to address every row and column of data and use it in a formula. Conventional SQL completely lacks this very simple but extremely powerful interrow and intercell calculation functionality. Hence, it is not uncommon to find that many businesses pull data out of the database into myriad spreadsheets just to perform calculations required for modeling their business performance or revenue forecasts. When it is time to upgrade the accounting model, all users of the spreadsheets must be notified to use the newer version. Even a small discrepancy could lead to serious accounting inconsistencies. In this era of financial accounting scandals, compliance laws are getting stricter and so managing their accounting procedures is becoming a major concern for businesses.

Oracle Database 10*g* introduced a new feature known as the SQL Model Clause, which adds this calculation capability into SQL. The SQL Model Clause gives you all the power of a conventional spreadsheet. Some of the benefits of this feature are as follows:

- Within this clause you can address the result of a query as if it were a multidimensional array. In fact, instead of the ordinal addressing scheme (using row and column number) in a spreadsheet, you use dimension values. For example, instead of saying C5 or D3, which can be very error-prone, you can simply say sales[May] or purchases[March].

- Calculations are done in the database and therefore have the added benefit of a scalable data processing engine, which can optimize and parallelize the calculations.

■ The result of calculations done using the model produce rows like any SQL query and so you can do further processing on this result or save it into a table.

■ Last, but not least, you can store the model itself in the same database as the data, using a view. So when it is time to change the model, just change the view and all users automatically run with the newer model!

Let us now look at how to do a simple calculation.

A Simple Calculation

The following query calculates the total sales by each month and produces an additional row for "Holidays," which gives the total sales for November and December. This is quite like a calculation you may have done in a spreadsheet previously.

```
SELECT month_name, sales
FROM (SELECT t.month, t.month_name, SUM(f.purchase_price) sales
      FROM purchases f, time t
      WHERE f.time_key = t.time_key AND t.year = 2003
      GROUP BY t.month, t.month_name)
MODEL
MAIN holiday_sales_model
DIMENSION BY (month_name)
MEASURES (sales)
RULES
(sales['Holidays'] = sales['November'] + sales['December']);


MONTH_NAME       SALES
----------  ----------
January     747376.33
February    677690.07
March       899008.65
April       870947.85
May         758257.03
June        847609.93
July        905908.19
August      762608.21
September   745532.66
October     886877.84
November    733383.72
December    754124.30
Holidays   1487508.02  <- new row computed by the model clause
```

The SQL looks quite complex and has a lot of new syntax; however, we will break it down into simpler pieces as we move along. The careful reader will notice that the answer to this calculation has a value of "Holidays" under month, which obviously did not come from the month table. This row was created by execution of the RULES section of the model clause. The rule defines a calculation to add the sales for November and December and assign it under a new value, "Holidays." This type of calculation is referred to as a **calculated member**. The notation sales['November'] is used to identify a specific element in the result of the query. The quantity, sales, which is used in numerical calculations, is called a **measure** and is conceptually the same as a measure from a fact table. The elements within square brackets, specified within the **DIMENSION BY** clause, are called **dimensions**. In this example, we have a single dimension, month. For those of you who have worked with a MOLAP product or even arrays in any programming language, this notation should be very intuitive to you. Finally, notice that the MODEL has an optional name, holiday_sales_model.

In addition to this, a model clause can also specify a **PARTITION BY** clause. This is the same concept as we discussed previously. If a PARTITION clause is present, the calculation is done for each partition. If it is not present, the entire query is treated like one partition.

Figure 6.6   *SQL Model Clause Operation*

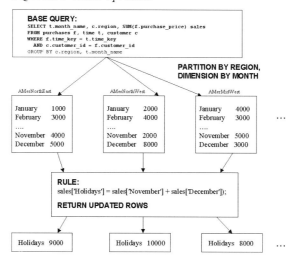

Figure 6.6 shows the operation of a model pictorially. Imagine the result of the query without the model clause. For each partition created by the partition by clause, picture an array of the measure columns, addressed by dimensions. Rules are then applied to each array to produce the calculations.

The following example shows the SQL query for Figure 6.6. As in the previous example, the query shown in the figure calculates the sales for the holiday season for each region. After applying the model clause, you can choose to return only the new rows that were inserted or updated by the rules using the RETURN UPDATED ROWS option. If not specified, the default behavior is RETURN ALL ROWS, which will return the rows from the original query in addition to those computed by the rules.

```
SELECT region, month_name, sales
FROM (SELECT t.month_name, c.region, SUM(f.purchase_price) sales
      FROM purchases f, time t, customer c
      WHERE f.time_key = t.time_key
        AND c.customer_id = f.customer_id
      GROUP BY c.region, t.month_name)
MODEL
RETURN UPDATED ROWS                     <- returns only the updated rows
MAIN holiday_sales_model
PARTITION BY (region)
DIMENSION BY (month_name)
MEASURES (sales)
RULES
(sales['Holiday'] = sales['November'] + sales['December'])
ORDER BY region;

REGION            MONTH_NAME      SALES
---------------   ----------   ----------
AMerNorthEast     Holiday       207454.07
AmerMidWest       Holiday       435140.11
AmerNorthEast     Holiday       611232.13
AmerNorthWest     Holiday       185404.61
AmerSouth         Holiday       197293.73
AmerWest          Holiday       435254.48
EuroWest          Holiday      1027255.94
```

Note that the SQL Model Clause is executed after the SELECT, WHERE GROUP BY, and HAVING clauses but before the ORDER BY clause. Hence, any aggregates and analytic functions computed by the query may be used in the DIMENSION BY, PARTITION BY, and MEASURES clauses of the SQL Model Clause. One restriction with the SQL Model clause is that the query block containing the model clause must not contain any aggregation in the SELECT list, so we need to use a subquery (or view) in the FROM clause to do the aggregation.

Hint: If you have several SQL models that use the same base query, you could create a materialized view for this query (see Chapter 7) to avoid repeat computation. Further, you can create regular database views to store the definition of each model.

Now that we understand the basics, let us see what else we can do with RULES.

More about RULES

The SQL Model Clause uses an array-like notation to identify an element at a given row and column in the result of the query. This is called a **cell-reference.** There can be several different ways of addressing cells, as we shall see. Each RULE is an assignment expression, where the cell(s) referenced on the left-hand side of the = are assigned the result of the expression on the right-hand side. Thus, in the previous example, the rule assigns to the cell sales['Holiday'] the value of sales['November'] + sales['December'].

For the following examples, we will define a view, which computes sales by month and region, which we will use as our base query.

```
CREATE VIEW sales_region_month
AS
SELECT t.month, t.month_name, c.region, t.year,
       SUM(f.purchase_price) sales
FROM purchases f, time t, customer c
WHERE f.time_key = t.time_key
  AND c.customer_id = f.customer_id
GROUP BY t.month, t.month_name, c.region, t.year;
```

Cell Referencing

A cell-reference that uses only constant values of each dimension to identify a cell is called a **positional** reference. For instance, if the model had DIMENSION BY (month_name), then sales['November'] is a positional reference. Similarly, if the model clause had DIMENSION BY (region, month_name), then sales['Northeast', 'January'] is also a positional reference. The ordering of dimensions is specified by the DIMENSION BY clause.

On the other hand, you can use a **symbolic** reference, where you specify an expression involving each dimension column. For example, sales[month IN ('January', 'February'), region IN ('NorthEast', 'NorthWest')]. This actually translates into four cells: sales['NorthEast', 'January'], sales['NorthEast', 'February'], sales['NorthWest', 'January'], and sales['NorthWest', 'February']. Note that when a cell reference expression refers to one cell, for example, sales['November']—it is called a **single-cell** reference. When it refers to multiple cells—for example, sales[month in ('November', 'December')], it is called **multicell** reference.

In any cell-reference on the left hand side of a rule, you can use the ANY keyword as a wildcard to refer to all values of a dimension, as illustrated in the following example. The CV function on the right-hand side refers to the current value of the dimension on the left-hand side. This shorthand notation allows us to specify the same rule for all region values, rather than repeating the rule for each region value. In this example, the rule computes, for every region, the percentage growth in sales in that region in the year 2004, compared with the sales in that region in 2003.

```
SELECT region, year, sales
FROM (SELECT region, year, SUM(sales) as sales
      FROM sales_region_month
      GROUP BY region, year)
MODEL
RETURN UPDATED ROWS
MAIN sales_growth_2004
DIMENSION BY (region, year)
MEASURES (sales)
RULES
(sales[region IS ANY, 2004]
= (sales[CV(region), 2004] - sales[CV(region), 2003])*100
  /sales[CV(region), 2003])
ORDER BY region;
```

REGION	YEAR	SALES
AMerNorthEast	2004	1.734760870
AmerMidWest	2004	1.103745720
AmerNorthEast	2004	1.529564870
AmerNorthWest	2004	2.465897740
AmerSouth	2004	.872252952
AmerWest	2004	.903655293
EuroWest	2004	1.466177920

If your rule requires multiple-cell references on the right-hand side to compute a single-cell value on the left-hand side, you must use an aggregation operator to collapse the multiple values to a single value. For instance, in the previous example, if you wanted to compute sales growth for all regions combined, you would use the following rule. The SUM operator is used to aggregate the multicell reference on the right-hand side to one value, which is then assigned to sales['All Regions', 2004]. Note that the ANY keyword here is used to specify all values for the region on the right-hand side.

```
sales['All Regions', 2004] = (SUM(sales) [region IS ANY, 2004]] -
SUM(sales) [region IS ANY, 2003)]) *100/SUM(sales) [region IS ANY, 2003]
```

UPDATE versus UPSERT

In the case of positional references used on the left-hand side, the rules can have either UPDATE or UPSERT semantics. With UPSERT semantics, if the cell does not exist, it is inserted; otherwise, the existing value is updated. However, if the rule is specified with UPDATE semantics, the cell is updated only if it already exists; otherwise, no action is taken. For instance, suppose we had a rule that computed sales['All Regions'] as the sum of sales of each region. If we specified update semantics for this rule, then unless there already exists a cell named 'All Regions', this rule will not do anything, as shown in the following example! If, on the other hand, we had a region value called 'All Regions', its value would have been updated.

```
SELECT region, sales
FROM (SELECT region, SUM(sales) as sales
      FROM sales_region_month
      GROUP BY region)
MODEL
RETURN UPDATED ROWS
MAIN holiday_sales_model
DIMENSION BY (region)
MEASURES (sales)
RULES UPDATE                               <- update semantics
(sales['All Regions'] = SUM(sales) [region is ANY])
ORDER BY region;


no rows selected                           <- does nothing
```

Alternatively, if you used the upsert semantics, you would get a new row for "All Regions" as shown in the following example.

```
SELECT region, sales
FROM (SELECT region, SUM(sales) as sales
      FROM sales_region_month
      GROUP BY region)
MODEL
RETURN UPDATED ROWS
MAIN holiday_sales_model
DIMENSION BY (region)
MEASURES (sales)
RULES UPSERT                               <-  upsert semantics
(sales['All Regions'] = SUM(sales) [region is ANY])
ORDER BY region;


REGION                SALES
--------------- ----------
All Regions     19312425.1
```

Note that while symbolic references are a powerful construct in a model clause, if you specify a symbolic reference on the left-hand side of a rule, you will only get UPDATE semantics, even if you say RULES UPSERT. This can be cumbersome in some cases. One case when you may want UPSERT semantics with a symbolic reference is as a shorthand notation to combine multiple identical or similar rules into one rule. Fortunately, this can be achieved using the FOR keyword, as shown in the example that follows.

```
SELECT region, month_name,sales
FROM (SELECT region, month_name, sales
      FROM sales_region_month
      WHERE year = 2003)
MODEL
RETURN UPDATED ROWS
MAIN holiday_sales_model
DIMENSION BY (region, month_name)
MEASURES (sales)
RULES UPSERT
(sales[FOR region IN ('AmerNorthEast', 'AmerMidWest'), 'Winter']
= SUM(sales) [CV(region),
             month_name IN ('November', 'December',
                            'January', 'February', 'March')],
 sales[FOR region IN ('AmerWest', 'AmerSouth'), 'Winter']
= SUM(sales) [CV(region),
             month_name IN ('January', 'February')])
ORDER BY region, month_name;


REGION            MONTH_NAME      SALES
---------------   ----------   ----------
AmerMidWest       Winter       539398.81
AmerNorthEast     Winter       747304.58
AmerSouth         Winter        81210.68
AmerWest          Winter       182327.29
```

Instead of writing the same rule for each region separately, we have written one rule. If you omitted the FOR keyword in the rules, you will get no rows returned.

Hint: To get UPSERT semantics with a symbolic reference on the left-hand side of a rule, use the FOR keyword. Note that the use of the ANY keyword in the left-hand side of a rule precludes UPSERT semantics for that rule.

Rule Ordering

If your SQL model specifies multiple rules, there may be dependencies among the rules. You can specify the AUTOMATIC ORDER option to indicate that Oracle should automatically determine in which order to apply the rules. In the following example, we want to compute the total sales for Americas, and Europe, and also the grand total. We can see that RULE 1 depends on RULE 2 and RULE 3, and by specifying AUTO-

MATIC ORDER we let Oracle decide to first evaluate RULES 2 and 3 and then RULE 1.

```
SELECT region, sales
FROM (SELECT region, SUM(sales) sales
      FROM sales_region_month
      WHERE year = 2003
      GROUP BY region)
MODEL
RETURN UPDATED ROWS
MAIN holiday_sales_model
DIMENSION BY (region)
MEASURES (sales)
RULES AUTOMATIC ORDER
(sales['Total']
     = sales['TotalAmericas']
     + sales['TotalEurope'],                  <- RULE 1
 sales['TotalAmericas']
     = SUM(sales)[region like 'Amer%'],       <- RULE 2
 sales['TotalEurope']
     = SUM(sales)[region like 'Eur%'])        <- RULE 3
ORDER BY region;
```

```
REGION              SALES
---------------  ----------
Total           8938839.16
TotalAmericas   5758817.19
TotalEurope     3180021.97
```

On the other hand, you can also specify that the rules must be executed in the order specified, using the SEQUENTIAL ORDER option.

Iteration

The rules in a SQL Model Clause can be applied multiple times. You can specify the exact number of iterations to apply the rules or specify that the rules be applied until a given stopping condition is satisfied. You can use the ITERATION_NUMBER keyword in a rule to refer to the current iteration number. Note that ITERATION_NUMBER starts from 0. The following example shows a sales forecasting model for 10 years. It iterates the rule 10 times. Each iteration computes the forecast for the next year using the values computed in the previous iteration.

```
SELECT year, sales
FROM (SELECT year, SUM(sales) sales
      FROM sales_region_month
      WHERE year = 2003
      GROUP BY year)
```

```
MODEL
RETURN ALL ROWS
MAIN forecast_over_10_years
DIMENSION BY (year)
MEASURES (sales)
RULES ITERATE (10)                      <- # of iterations
(sales[2003+ITERATION_NUMBER+1]
 = sales[2003+ITERATION_NUMBER] * 0.15
 + AVG(sales)[year in (2003+ITERATION_NUMBER,
                       2003+ITERATION_NUMBER-1)]);
```

YEAR	SALES
2003	9589380.8
2004	11027787.9
2005	11962752.5
2006	13289683.1
2007	14619670.3
2008	16147627.3
2009	17805792.9
2010	19647579.0
2011	21673822.8
2012	23911774.3
2013	26379564.7

Instead of the number of iterations, you can also specify a condition such that the iteration stops when that condition is satisfied.

In the following section, we will look at couple of complex examples of using the SQL Model Clause.

Some Examples of the SQL Model Clause

The first example uses the SQL Model Clause to do a pivot operation. This is a very common operation in decision-support applications. In a pivot operation, you take the dimension values along one column of data and convert them into columns in a report. This is useful to display a result in a cross-tabulation along two or more dimensions. For example, the following query combines the monthly sales for each region by quarter and then pivots the result so that each quarter appears as a column. We have declared a measure variable, Q1sales, Q2sales, and so on, for sales of each quarter. The rules assign values to each of these measures for each region. Recall that the ANY keyword precludes the upsert semantics for rules. Hence, we use the existing cell for the month January, since we are really only interested in the final values.

```
SELECT region, Q1sales, Q2sales, Q3sales, Q4sales
FROM
(SELECT region,month_name, Q1sales, Q2sales, Q3sales, Q4sales
 FROM (SELECT region, month_name, SUM(sales) sales
       FROM sales_region_month WHERE year = 2003
       GROUP BY region, month_name)
MODEL
RETURN ALL ROWS
MAIN holiday_sales_model
DIMENSION BY (region, month_name)
MEASURES (sales,
          0 as Q1sales, 0 as Q2sales, 0 as Q3sales, 0 as q4sales)
RULES AUTOMATIC ORDER
(
Q1sales[region is ANY, 'January']
       = SUM(sales)[CV(region), month_name
                    IN ('January', 'February', 'March')],
Q2sales[region is ANY, 'January']
       = SUM(sales)[CV(region), month_name
                    IN ('April', 'May', 'June')],
Q3sales[region is ANY, 'January']
       = SUM(sales)[CV(region), month_name
                    IN ('July', 'August', 'September')],
Q4sales[region is ANY, 'January']
       = SUM(sales)[CV(region), month_name
                    IN ('October', 'November','December')]
)
) WHERE month_name = 'January'
ORDER BY region;

REGION            Q1SALES     Q2SALES     Q3SALES     Q4SALES
---------------   ----------  ----------  ----------  ----------
AMerNorthEast     168666.12   163446.74   164542.86   153829.90
AmerMidWest       336162.46   352213.10   340611.21   329105.92
AmerNorthEast     447266.04   477220.90   464554.97   471557.18
AmerNorthWest     158393.71   163313.59   147821.03   148383.75
AmerSouth         140683.64   162605.99   151958.09   149237.48
AmerWest          303449.22   336507.99   345210.40   332560.52
EuroWest          769453.86   821506.50   799350.50   789711.11
```

The next example uses a SQL Model Clause to compute the net sales for the year 2003 for various states based on different state tax rates. This example uses a feature called a REFERENCE model to identify the sales tax rates for each state. The reference model also uses the DIMENSION BY and MEASURE clauses; however, its cells cannot be modified and hence it serves the purpose of a read-only lookup table which can be used in the calculations in the main model. The reference model cannot have a PARTITION by clause.

```
SELECT year, state, sales, net_sales
FROM (SELECT t.year, c.state, SUM(f.purchase_price) sales
      FROM purchases f, time t, customer c
      WHERE f.time_key = t.time_key
        AND c.customer_id = f.customer_id
        AND c.country = 'USA'
      GROUP BY t.year, c.state)
MODEL
REFERENCE state_tax_model
       ON (SELECT distinct state, tax_rate FROM customer)
       DIMENSION BY (state) MEASURES (tax_rate) IGNORE NAV
MAIN
DIMENSION BY (year, state)
MEASURES (sales, 0 as net_sales) IGNORE NAV
RULES SEQUENTIAL ORDER
(net_sales[ANY, ANY] =  sales[CV(year), CV(state)] *
               (1 - state_tax_model.tax_rate[CV(state)]/100));
```

YEAR	STATE	SALES	NET_SALES
2004	AZ	616558.37	585730.45
2004	CA	713077.48	656031.28
2004	CT	627492.12	596117.51
2004	IL	740107.36	703101.99
2004	MA	661769.99	628681.49
2004	NH	628569.43	628569.43
2004	NY	632996.61	588686.85
2004	OH	632975.22	601326.46
2004	TX	609757.84	609757.84
2004	WA	633149.16	633149.16
2003	AZ	610124.46	579618.24
2003	CA	707603.67	650995.38
2003	CT	613003.5	582353.32
2003	IL	740373.37	703354.70
2003	MA	650485.62	617961.34
2003	NH	622458.88	622458.88
2003	NY	625136.71	581377.14
2003	OH	617719.32	586833.35
2003	TX	604485.2	604485.20
2003	WA	617912.08	617912.08

The IGNORE NAV option allows you to treat missing cell values as 0 for purposes of calculations. For instance, the CUSTOMERS table does not store states with no tax rate, and this option will set the cells for tax rates for these states to 0.

We have only skimmed the surface of what we can do with the SQL Model Clause, but we can already see the power it can bring to business intelligence applications. Obviously, there are a lot of concepts and new syntax to learn here and it may take you some time to master it; however, once you do, you will find that this feature can indeed be very convenient and useful. So the next time you plan to use a spreadsheet, consider using the SQL Model Clause instead and reap the benefits of a scalable and more manageable modeling solution.

6.5   Summary

In this chapter, we looked at several features in the Oracle database for querying and analysis in a data warehouse. Oracle provides several mechanisms to improve query performance, such as star transformation, partition-wise join, partition pruning, and parallel execution. Complex aggregation and reporting needs can be met through the new aggregation and analytical functions in the database. The new SQL Model Clause can be used instead of conventional spreadsheets for calculations and modeling applications.

With good physical design and proper use of these querying features, a data warehouse can deliver excellent query performance for large amounts of data. In the next chapter, we will discuss materialized views, which are indispensable when it comes to boosting query performance in a data warehouse.

Summary Management

7.1   **Summary Tables**

A common technique used in data warehouses is to precompute and store results of frequent queries. This is especially beneficial when the queries involve aggregation, because the result is usually much smaller than the detailed data used to produce the result. An example of such a query is a monthly sales report for a business. Since multiple users are interested in the total sales of each product for each month, the data would be selected, joined, sorted, and aggregated over and over again for each user. Rather than wasting resources reexecuting the same query repeatedly the result could be precomputed and saved in a table. Such precomputed results are often called **summaries** or **summary tables**.

Figure 7.1 shows a summary containing the total number of items sold for each month of the year. Summary tables are usually much smaller than

Figure 7.1   *Summary Table*

Detail Sales Transactions

Date	Customer	Product
1/5/02	Smith	Book
1/6/02	Jones	Tent
2/5/02	Smith	Book
2/5/02	Mills	Book
3/5/02	Smith	Film
3/7/02	Mills	Book
3/5/02	Smith	Film
4/1/02	Smith	Book
4/2/02	Jones	Book
4/3/02	Smith	Tent
4/3/02	Jones	Tent
5/5/02	Peters	Book
5/6/02	Smith	Book
6/1/02	Jones	Book
6/5/02	Smith	Tent
6/6/02	Jones	Tent
6/5/02	David	Tent

Total Sales by product, by month

Month	Product	Qty Sold
1/02	Book	1
1/02	Tent	1
2/02	Book	2
3/02	Book	1
3/02	Film	2
4/02	Book	2
4/02	Tent	2
5/02	Book	2
6/02	Book	1
6/02	Tent	3

the tables containing the detail data. In this example, 17 rows of detailed sales transaction data are summarized into 10 rows. Depending on the data, the reduction in size and therefore the improvement in query performance can be quite significant.

Oracle 8*i*, with its **summary management** feature, made a huge advance in the way people used summary tables by letting the database manage and use summaries *transparently*. Summary tables in Oracle are called **Materialized Views**.

7.1.1 Why Do You Need Summary Management?

To understand why summary management is needed, let us first look at some of the tasks involved in managing summary tables.

A summary is the precomputed result of a SQL query. Once a summary has been created, the result of the query can be obtained from the summary. A summary can also be used to answer other related queries. For instance, if we were interested in the total sales of each product for each year, the result can be obtained by adding the months for that year together, since months roll up into years. To use a summary, the query has to be modified somehow to reference that summary. In some situations this would mean that application SQL must be modified. Alternatively, users must be informed of the existence of summarized data and trained on which summary tables to use for each particular query. Thus, while summary tables improve query performance, managing these summaries can be quite a task.

As new detail data is loaded into the warehouse, the data in the summary is no longer synchronized with the detail tables. When this happens, the summary is said to be **stale**. Figure 7.2 shows a stale summary. In order to bring it up-to-date with the detail data, the stale summary must be **refreshed**. A summary can be rebuilt when new data is loaded into the warehouse. This is known as **complete refresh.** In some cases, it is possible to **incrementally refresh** the summary with only the new or changed data. Before summary management with Oracle 8*i*, refreshing summaries involved complex, custom-built procedures.

Choosing which summaries to create requires an understanding of the workload—which types of questions users are asking and how often the same information is being requested. The number of possible summary tables that could be created is very large. Since summaries consume disk space and take time to refresh, it is important to select few summaries that produce the most performance benefits.

Figure 7.2 *Stale Summary*

Detail Sales Transactions

Date	Customer	Product
1/5/02	Smith	Book
1/6/02	Jones	Tent
2/5/02	Smith	Book
2/5/02	Mills	Book
3/5/02	Smith	Film
3/7/02	Mills	Book
3/5/02	Smith	Film
4/1/02	Smith	Book
4/2/02	Jones	Book
4/3/02	Smith	Tent
4/3/02	Jones	Tent
5/5/02	Peters	Book
5/6/02	Smith	Book
6/1/02	Jones	Book
6/5/02	Smith	Tent
6/6/02	Jones	Tent
6/5/02	David	Tent
7/1/02	Smith	Book
7/2/02	Jones	Book
7/2/02	David	Tentk

Total Sales by product, by month

Month	Product	Qty Sold
1/02	Book	1
1/02	Tent	1
2/02	Book	2
3/02	Book	1
3/02	Film	2
4/02	Book	2
4/02	Tent	2
5/02	Book	2
6/02	Book	1
6/02	Tent	3

← New detail data not yet in summary

In other words, before using summaries, the following questions must be addressed:

1. What is the best set of summaries to create?

2. Do users have to be aware of summaries? If so, how will the users know which summaries exist and when to use them? If summaries are later determined not to be that useful and are dropped, users also need to know about this.

3. As the detail data changes, how will the summaries be kept up-to-date?

Oracle's Summary Management has the answer to all these questions.

7.1.2 Summary Management with Oracle

Summary management provides a complete environment to manage and use summary tables. With this feature, summaries can be created directly in the Oracle database. Mechanisms are provided to keep your summaries up-to-date with changes in underlying data. Further, Oracle will transparently rewrite your queries to use these summaries, so users do not have to be aware of the summaries. Summary management in Oracle includes the following components:

- A database object, known as a **Materialized View**, which stores precomputed results, such as a summary table.

- A mechanism to refresh the materialized views using either **Complete** or **Incremental Refresh**.

- **Query Rewrite**, which transparently rewrites SQL queries to use materialized views.

- A database object called **Dimension,** which provides an ability to declare hierarchical relationships, such as rollups in the data, to assist query rewrite.

- **The SQL Access Advisor,** a tool that can recommend which materialized views to create.

Let us see how summary management answers the questions we had posed earlier:

1. **What is the best set of summaries to create?** Using the SQL Access Advisor you can easily determine the materialized views to create for a given set of queries to fit a specified amount of space.

2. **Do users have to be aware of summaries?** Once the materialized views have been created and enabled for query rewrite, queries will automatically use these materialized views. A significant benefit of this is that the end users and database applications no longer need to be aware of the existence of the summary tables. Query rewrite in Oracle is not limited to star schemas or queries with aggregation. Any client tool can take advantage of this feature in the database server to provide aggregate navigation capabilities. For instance, Oracle Discoverer uses the summary management features in the Oracle database to improve query response time.

3. **How are summaries kept up-to-date?** Summary management provides procedures for complete and fast refresh, so that the materialized views can be updated when new detail data is loaded

into the warehouse. This eliminates the need to write customized refresh programs.

In this chapter, we will discuss how to create and refresh materialized views. The dimension object is described in Chapter 8, query rewrite is discussed in Chapter 9, and the SQL Access Advisor is described in Chapter 10.

7.2 Creating a Materialized View

A **Materialized View** (MV) is a database object that precomputes and stores the result of a SQL query, akin to a summary table. Note that a summary is typically an aggregate query; however, materialized views can be created for any query—for example, one just involving a join. In this respect, a materialized view is quite similar to a conventional view. The difference is that by materializing the view, you save the results in the database. In the remainder of this chapter, we will use the term *materialized view* instead of summary.

Hint: Materialized views can also be used for replication of data. Before Oracle 8*i*, such materialized views were called snapshots. Materialized views include all the features that were available with snapshots and more. In this book, we will only focus on the application of materialized views to data warehousing.

A materialized view is created using the **CREATE MATERIALIZED VIEW** SQL statement. The following example creates a materialized view named MONTHLY_SALES_MV, which contains the total sales of each product for each month.

```
CREATE MATERIALIZED VIEW MONTHLY_SALES_MV
PCTFREE 0 TABLESPACE summary
STORAGE (initial 64k
         next 64k pctincrease 0)        <- storage parameters
BUILD IMMEDIATE                          <- when to populate it
REFRESH FORCE                            <- how to refresh it
ON DEMAND                                <- when to refresh it
ENABLE QUERY REWRITE                     <- use in query rewrite or not
AS                                       <- query result it contains
SELECT t.month, t.year, p.product_id,
       SUM (f.purchase_price) as sum_of_sales,
       COUNT (f.purchase_price) as total_sales,
```

```
        COUNT(*) as cstar
FROM time t, product p, purchases f
WHERE t.time_key = f.time_key AND
      f.product_id = p.product_id
GROUP BY t.month, t.year, p.product_id;
```

The materialized view definition specifies the following properties, highlighted with arrows in the example:

- How to physically store the materialized view (i.e., the storage clause).

- When to populate it—immediately upon creation or later. Or, if it is an existing table that must be registered as a materialized view.

- How to refresh it when data in the underlying detail tables has changed.

- When to refresh it—at the end of each transaction or when explicitly requested.

- Whether to use it for query rewrite or not.

- A SELECT statement, which describes the contents of the materialized view.

We will now explain each clause of the materialized view creation statement in detail.

7.2.1 Naming the Materialized View

As with any database object, a materialized view has a name and a schema that owns it. It is good practice to follow a naming convention for materialized views, so that you can easily identify them later and differentiate them from tables and views. For example, you could use the suffix _MV when naming materialized views.

7.2.2 The Physical Storage for the Materialized View

The materialized view has a storage specification where you can specify the tablespace to store the data in, the initial allocation size and the size, of its extents. The syntax and semantics of the storage specification are the same as for any other object in the database

In the MONTHLY_SALES_MV example, the materialized view is being placed in the tablespace called MVIEW, its first extent will be 64K, and all subsequent extents will be 64K.

7.2.3 When Should the Materialized View Be Populated with Data?

The materialized view definition describes when you would like the materialized view to be populated with data. If you specify BUILD IMMEDIATE (the default), as in the example, the materialized view is populated immediately upon creation. If you specify BUILD DEFERRED, then the materialized view will be populated when you perform the refresh operation. If you have an existing summary table that you would like to manage using Oracle's summary management, you can use the ON PREBUILT TABLE clause. This indicates to the database that the existing table should be treated like a materialized view and makes it available to query rewrite, if desired.

Hint: A materialized view is not considered by query rewrite until it has been populated with data

7.2.4 How Should the Materialized View Be Refreshed?

As new detail data is periodically loaded into the data warehouse, the materialized views have to be refreshed to reflect the changes. Four refresh options are available:

- Complete
- Fast
- Force
- Never

A materialized view can be completely rebuilt by specifying REFRESH COMPLETE. Or, it can be incrementally updated by specifying the REFRESH FAST option. It is usually faster to perform a fast refresh than a complete refresh; however, if there are a lot of changes, it may be faster to perform a complete refresh. The REFRESH FORCE option (the default), means that Oracle will perform a fast refresh if possible and only do a COMPLETE refresh if necessary. Materialized views that use the NEVER REFRESH option will never be refreshed by any of the procedures supplied by Oracle. This option can be useful if you have custom-built refresh procedures or would like to store some historical data that must not be updated. The materialized view MONTHLY_SALES_MV, in our example, is created using the REFRESH FORCE clause, which means that Oracle will decide whether to perform fast or complete refresh.

7.2.5 When should the Materialized View be refreshed?

As the underlying detail data changes, the materialized views that are based on those detail tables become stale and no longer reflect the results of summarizing all the detail data. The most common ways of refresh are ON COMMIT or ON DEMAND (the default).

If your business is such that it requires the materialized view be kept up-to-date with the detail data at the transaction level, the materialized view can be refreshed at the end of each transaction by specifying the ON COMMIT option. This is rarely used in a data warehouse.

Hint: Adding materialized views with the ON COMMIT option will lengthen the time required to commit a transaction, because the materialized views must be refreshed as part of the commit processing.

On the other hand, with ON DEMAND refresh you must manually request that the materialized view be refreshed using procedures in the DBMS_MVIEW PL/SQL package. ON DEMAND refresh allows you to control when the materialized view will be refreshed. This is useful in a warehouse, where new data is loaded in a batch after which the materialized views must be refreshed.

You can also specify that a materialized view be refreshed on a periodic schedule by specifying a start date and subsequent refresh intervals using the START WITH and NEXT clauses.

The facilities for refreshing materialized views will be discussed later in the chapter.

7.2.6 Enabling the Materialized View for Query Rewrite

One of the major benefits of using Oracle's summary management is query rewrite. Once a materialized view has been registered as being eligible for use by query rewrite, Oracle will transparently rewrite user queries to access the data in the materialized view, without the need for any application changes. If you would like the materialized view to be considered for query rewrite, then it must be defined with the clause ENABLE QUERY REWRITE, as shown in the example. If you don't want a materialized view to be used for query rewrite, use the DISABLE QUERY REWRITE clause (the default).

7.2.7 Specifying the Contents of the Materialized View

The materialized view definition includes a SELECT statement, which describes its contents. The tables referenced in a materialized view's query are referred to as **detail** tables or **base** tables of the materialized view.

A typical query for a materialized view used in a data warehouse includes the following:

- A WHERE clause, which joins the fact table and one or more dimension tables. In this example, the fact table, PURCHASES, is joined with the dimension tables, TIME and PRODUCTS. The WHERE clause may also contain selection criteria to restrict the data in the materialized views.

- One or more aggregate operators. In our example, COUNT is used to obtain the total sales. You can include any of the built-in aggregate operators in Oracle, such as SUM, MIN, MAX, AVG, COUNT(*), COUNT, COUNT(DISTINCT x), VARIANCE, and STDDEV. You can also use analytical functions, moving window aggregates, and user-defined aggregates, which were discussed in Chapter 6.

- A GROUP BY clause. In the example, we are counting the total items sold by the columns YEAR, MONTH, and PRODUCT_ID. You can also use the CUBE, ROLLUP, or GROUPING SETS features described in Chapter 6.

The materialized view, MONTHLY_SALES_MV, discussed in the preceding example was a materialized view involving aggregation. A materialized view can also be used to join two or more tables *without* any aggregation. Such a materialized view is used to precompute expensive joins and can be used in lieu of a bitmapped join index (see Chapter 4). A bitmapped join index is useful for star queries and will work better than materialized views if you want to compute combinations of selections against the index keys. On the other hand, a materialized view can be used to answer a wider class of queries using query rewrite.

The next example shows a materialized view that is used to compute the join between two tables, PURCHASES and CUSTOMER, without any aggregation.

```
CREATE MATERIALIZED VIEW customer_purchases_mv
BUILD IMMEDIATE
REFRESH COMPLETE
AS
SELECT c.gender, c.occupation, f.purchase_price
FROM purchases f, customer c
WHERE f.customer_id = c.customer_id;
```

In general a materialized view can be defined using an arbitrarily complex SQL query; however, the fast refresh and query rewrite capabilities would be limited. For example, the following materialized view, which stores the sales for customers who spent the most money in our store in the year 2003, contains a HAVING clause with a subquery.

```
CREATE MATERIALIZED VIEW customers_maxsales2003_mv
ENABLE QUERY REWRITE
AS
SELECT c.customer_id, SUM(f.purchase_price) AS dollar_sales
FROM purchases f, customer c
WHERE f.customer_id = c.customer_id
GROUP BY c.customer_id
HAVING SUM(f.purchase_price)
    IN (SELECT max(f.purchase_price) dollar_sales
        FROM purchases f, time t
        WHERE f.time_key = t.time_key
          AND t.year = 2003
        GROUP BY f.customer_id);
```

However, as we will see later, this materialized view cannot be incrementally refreshed.

7.2.8 Creating a Materialized View in Enterprise Manager

You can use Oracle Enterprise Manager to create and edit materialized views by following the *Materialized Views* link from the *Warehouse* section of the *Administration* page (see Figure 2.16 in Chapter 2). When you get to the *Materialized Views* screen, click the *Create* button to bring up the screen shown in Figure 7.3. Here, we are creating a materialized view named MONTHLY_SALES_MV.

Figure 7.3   *Creating a Materialized View in Oracle Enterprise Manager*

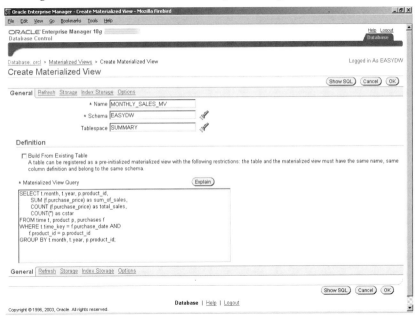

All the options for a CREATE MATERIALIZED VIEW statement may be specified via this graphical interface. It is also possible to collect statistics on the materialized view upon creation.

7.2.9 Using Summary Management with Existing Summary Tables

If you already have a data warehouse with summaries stored in regular database tables and do not want to completely recreate them, summary management can still be used to manage them and to perform query rewrite.

To register your summary table with summary management, create a materialized view using the ON PREBUILT TABLE clause. If you specify the ENABLE QUERY REWRITE clause, the materialized view can be used for query rewrite.

For example, suppose you have a table named MONTHLY_ CUSTOMER_SALES, which summarizes the amount each customer spent each month, as represented by the following query:

```
SELECT t.year, t.month, c.customer_id,
      SUM(f.purchase_price) as dollar_sales
FROM time t, purchases f, customer c
WHERE f.time_key = t.time_key AND
     f.customer_id = c.customer_id
GROUP BY t.year, t.month, c.customer_id;
```

The MONTHLY_CUSTOMER_SALES table is described as follows:

```
describe monthly_customer_sales;

Name                                        Null?   Type
------------------------------------------- -------- ------------
YEAR                                                 NUMBER(4)
MONTH                                                NUMBER(2)
CUSTOMER_ID                                          VARCHAR2(10)
DOLLAR_SALES                                         NUMBER
```

If you would like to use this table as a materialized view and make it eligible for query rewrite, you can issue the following statement:

```
CREATE MATERIALIZED VIEW monthly_customer_sales
ON PREBUILT TABLE
ENABLE QUERY REWRITE
AS
SELECT t.year, t.month, c.customer_id,
      SUM(f.purchase_price) AS dollar_sales
FROM time t, purchases f, customer c
WHERE f.time_key = t.time_key AND
     f.customer_id = c.customer_id
GROUP BY t.year, t.month, c.customer_id;
```

The ON PREBUILT TABLE clause creates the necessary metadata for the data in the existing table, which allows it to be used by query rewrite and to be refreshed using Oracle's supplied refresh procedures.

Hint: When creating the materialized view using an existing table, the materialized view must have the same name as the table.

A word of caution when creating materialized views with the PRE-BUILT clause—Oracle will not verify that the data in the existing table corresponds to the result of the query used to define the materialized view. You must ensure that the contents of the existing table correctly represent the summarization of the detail data. Otherwise, you may see incorrect results with query rewrite.

Hint: For query rewrite to use a materialized view with the PREBUILT option, you must set the initialization parameter QUERY_REWRITE_INTEGRITY level to TRUSTED or STALE_TOLERATED, as explained in Chapter 9.

7.2.10 Partitioning the Materialized View

You can partition a materialized view as you would a table, using any of the partitioning methods described in Chapter 4. In a warehouse, it is common to partition materialized views in the same way as the fact table. Range-List partitioning may also be a good way to partition a materialized view when it contains multiple dimensions, such as time (range) and geography (list).

In the following example, the materialized view is partitioned using range partitioning:

```
CREATE MATERIALIZED VIEW Q12003_SALES_MV
PARTITION by RANGE(time_key)
(
    partition purchases_jan2003
        values less than (TO_DATE('01-FEB-2003', 'DD-MON-YYYY'))
        tablespace purchases_jan2003,
    partition purchases_feb2003
        values less than (TO_DATE('01-MAR-2003', 'DD-MON-YYYY'))
        tablespace purchases_feb2003,
    partition purchases_mar2003
        values less than (TO_DATE('01-APR-2003', 'DD-MON-YYYY'))
        tablespace purchases_mar2003
)
BUILD IMMEDIATE
REFRESH FORCE
```

```
ON DEMAND
ENABLE QUERY REWRITE
AS
SELECT t.time_key, p.product_id,
       SUM(f.purchase_price) as sum_of_sales
FROM time t, product p, purchases f
WHERE t.time_key = f.time_key AND
      f.product_id = p.product_id AND
      t.time_key BETWEEN TO_DATE('01-JAN-2003', 'DD-MON-YYYY') AND
                         TO_DATE('31-MAR-2003', 'DD-MON-YYYY')
GROUP BY t.time_key, p.product_id;
```

Partitioning a materialized view can speed up refresh, because refresh can now use parallel DML. We will see later how some partitioning techniques may allow a materialized view to take advantage of optimizations during refresh. Partitioning also enables queries that use the materialized view to take advantage of optimizations such as partition pruning.

7.2.11   Indexing the Materialized View

You can also build indexes on your materialized view to improve the performance of your queries. The techniques used to index materialized views are similar to those for any table.

In the following example, a concatenated index is created on the grouping columns of the MONTHLY_SALES_MV materialized view, shown earlier in this chapter. Also, bitmapped indexes are created on the grouping columns. These indexes will improve performance of queries that get rewritten to use the materialized view.

```
CREATE INDEX easydw.products_by_month_concat_index
ON MONTHLY_SALES_MV  (month, year, product_id)
pctfree 5
tablespace indx
storage (initial 64k next 64k pctincrease 0) ;

CREATE BITMAP INDEX easydw.total_products_by_month_index
ON monthly_sales_mv (month, year);

CREATE BITMAP INDEX easydw.total_products_by_id_index
ON monthly_sales_mv (product_id);
```

Oracle automatically creates an index on materialized views with aggregates to speed up fast refresh. To suppress creation of this index, use the NO INDEX clause in the CREATE MATERIALIZED VIEW statement.

> **Hint:** You could use the SQL Access Advisor tool, discussed in Chapter 10, to determine the best materialized views and indexes on materialized views to create for your application.

7.2.12   Security of Materialized Views

Some information in the data warehouse may have restricted access, and it is important to ensure that the appropriate security policies are implemented regarding access to materialized views. You may want to allow users access to a materialized view, but not allow them to see the underlying detail data. For example, you may allow a user to see the average salary by department, but not to see an individual employee's salary. On the other hand, you want to ensure that materialized views and query rewrite are not used as a mechanism for bypassing security. As with all database objects, Oracle provides a privilege model for creating and altering materialized views.

To create a materialized view in a user's own schema, the user must have the CREATE MATERIALIZED VIEW privilege. To create a materialized view in another user's schema, the creator must have the CREATE ANY MATERIALIZED VIEW privilege. The owner of the schema where the materialized view will be placed must have the CREATE TABLE and CREATE INDEX privilege and must be able to execute the materialized view's defining query.

> **Hint:** It is helpful to remember that most privilege checks for a materialized view are applied to the owner of the schema in which the materialized view is placed. The creator only needs the CREATE/ALTER (or CREATE/ALTER ANY) MATERIALIZED VIEW privilege. Also, the privilege checks are applied during creation and altering and not during query rewrite.

To enable a materialized view for query rewrite, the owner of the materialized view must have the QUERY REWRITE object privilege on any tables (referenced in the materialized view) that are outside the owner's schema. Alternatively, the owner must have the GLOBAL QUERY REWRITE system privilege.

To refresh a materialized view in another schema, the user issuing the refresh procedure must have the ALTER ANY MATERIALIZED VIEW privilege.

To create a materialized view with REFRESH ON COMMIT option, the owner must have the ON COMMIT object privileges on all tables (referenced in the materialized view) outside the schema or have the ON COMMIT system privilege.

In the following example, the user EASYDW is granted the following privileges to create materialized views and to allow these to be used for query rewrite.

```
-- Add privileges
GRANT select any table to easydw;
GRANT execute any procedure to easydw;


-- Add privileges for materialized views and query rewrite
GRANT create materialized view to easydw;
GRANT drop materialized view to easydw;
GRANT alter materialized view to easydw;
GRANT global query rewrite to easydw;
```

7.3   Refresh

As new data is loaded into the warehouse, any materialized view based on that data must be updated. This operation is known as **refresh**.

In section 7.2, we discussed the two refresh policies—ON COMMIT and ON DEMAND in the context of creating a materialized view. To recap, refresh can be performed ON COMMIT or ON DEMAND. A materialized view with the refresh ON COMMIT option is automatically refreshed at the end of every transaction that updates the detail tables. A materialized view with the ON DEMAND refresh option must be explicitly refreshed using procedures in the DBMS_MVIEW package.

The frequency of refresh determines how recent the data in the materialized view is with respect to the detail data. The refresh operation can be very time consuming depending on the amount of data involved. You must carefully determine your refresh policy based on available resources and your application's need for current data. If your application needs the materialized view to be synchronized with the detail data at all times, choose the ON COMMIT option. With this option, Oracle will automatically refresh the materialized view when the changes to detail data get committed. If your warehouse gets new data only once a day during a specified maintenance window, deferring the refresh until then would be the right choice.

The refresh policy must be chosen when creating the materialized view; however, it can be altered at a later time by issuing an ALTER MATERIALIZED VIEW statement.

7.3.1 Using the DBMS_MVIEW Refresh Procedures

Oracle provides three procedures for ON DEMAND refresh in the DBMS_MVIEW–supplied PL/SQL package:

- DBMS_MVIEW.REFRESH
- DBMS_MVIEW.REFRESH_DEPENDENT
- DBMS_MVIEW.REFRESH_ALL_MVIEWS

If you want to refresh all your materialized views, typically after bulk loading new detail data into the warehouse, you can use the DBMS_MVIEW.REFRESH_ALL_MVIEWS procedure. If you have materialized views that are refreshed at different times—for example, some weekly and others monthly—you can specify a list of materialized views to refresh using the DBMS_MVIEW.REFRESH procedure. If you want to refresh all materialized views that are based on a particular detail table that has changed, use the DBMS_MVIEW.REFRESH_DEPENDENT procedure, specifying the detail table.

Before we look at some examples of using these procedures, let us briefly look at some of the parameters that can be specified to control the behavior of refresh:

- **method**: Recall that at the time of creating the materialized view, you specify a default refresh method of COMPLETE, FAST, or FORCE. You may override this refresh method when issuing the refresh command by specifying the method parameter as C (complete), F (fast), or ? (force). If you don't specify it, the refresh method given at the time of creating the materialized view will be used. In Oracle Database 10g, you can also specify a special method, P, which requests that refresh should be done using Partition Change Tracking, which is discussed in detail in section 7.3.4. Note that at the time of writing, there is no syntax to choose Partition Change Tracking as a refresh method when creating the materialized view.

- **atomic_refresh**: If atomic_refresh is specified (default), all operations during refresh are performed within one transaction, which means that any error will rollback the entire refresh operation. Otherwise, Oracle may choose to partially commit some of the work done during refresh.

    The setting of this parameter can have some effect on refresh performance, as we will discuss in section 7.3.5.

- **refresh_after_errors**: When refreshing multiple materialized views, this parameter indicates whether or not refresh should stop if it encounters an error, or if it should continue on to the next materialized view. The default behavior is to stop when the first error is encountered. Note that if the atomic_refresh parameter is set to TRUE, then any errors will roll back the refresh, regardless of the setting of the refresh_after_errors parameter.

- **nested:** This parameter is used to control the refresh of nested materialized views and will be described in section 7.3.6.

Hint: There are several other parameters, such as rollback_segment, push_deferred_rpc, heap_size, purge_option, and parallelism, that are specific to replication and should not be used in a data warehouse.

The first example shows the use of the REFRESH_ALL_MVIEWS procedure. Here, the refresh method is not specified, which means each materialized view will be refreshed using the method specified when creating it. The bind variable, :failures will return the number of failed refreshes. (You can identify the materialized views that failed to refresh using the last_refresh_date field in the dictionary view, USER_MVIEWS, or from the error messages in the Oracle alert.log file.)

```
VARIABLE failures number;
EXECUTE DBMS_MVIEW.REFRESH_ALL_MVIEWS(:failures);
```

In the following example, the materialized view MONTHLY_SALES_MV, defined earlier as REFRESH FORCE, is being refreshed using COMPLETE refresh:

```
EXECUTE DBMS_MVIEW.REFRESH('MONTHLY_SALES_MV', 'C');
```

In the following example, the REFRESH procedure is used to refresh two materialized views, MONTHLY_SALES_MV and Q12003_SALES_MV, using atomic_refresh.

```
EXECUTE DBMS_MVIEW.REFRESH('MONTHLY_SALES_MV, Q12003_SALES_MV',
                             atomic_refresh=>TRUE);
```

The following statement can be used to refresh FORCE (as indicated by refresh method of ?) all materialized views that have changed when the CUSTOMER table is updated. We have requested that the refresh should continue even after errors. On completion of this procedure, the :failures bind variable will indicate the number of failed refreshes.

```
EXECUTE DBMS_MVIEW.REFRESH_DEPENDENT(:failures, 'customer', '?',
                                 refresh_after_errors=>true);
```

7.3.2 Using Enterprise Manager for Refresh

Alternatively, you can use Oracle Enterprise Manager to refresh your materialized views. From the *Administration* page (see Chapter 2, Figure 2.16), click on the *Materialized Views* link and then search for the materialized view you want to refresh. Once you find the materialized view, click on the link for its name and you will get the screen shown in Figure 7.4.

Figure 7.4   *Refreshing a Materialized View in Oracle Enterprise Manager*

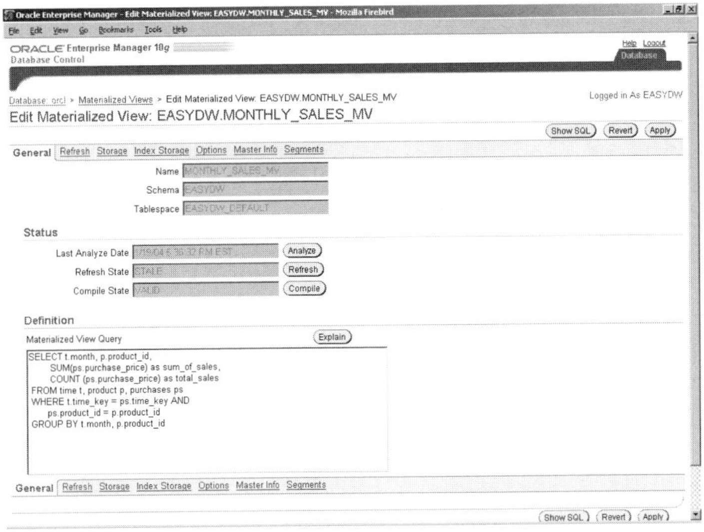

In this page, you can check the refresh status of the materialized view by looking at the *Refresh State* field. If the materialized view is STALE, you can refresh it by pressing the *Refresh* button.

To get an accurate picture of the refresh state, the *Compile State* field must say VALID. If it says *NEEDS_COMPILE*, it means that some internal metadata needs to be updated, and you must press the *Compile* button to validate the materialized view first.

Pressing the *Refresh* button will bring up a refresh options screen (as shown in Figure 7.5) from which you can choose the refresh type, such as fast or complete, and choose to optionally update the statistics on the materialized view after refresh. Pressing the *OK* button will refresh the materialized view.

Figure 7.5   *Refreshing a Materialized View in Oracle Enterprise Manager—Options*

Once the refresh has completed, you can once again check the status of the materialized view in the *Refresh State* field, shown in Figure 7.4.

7.3.3   Fast Refresh

As the volume of data in a warehouse increases, rebuilding the entire materialized view after each new data load can get prohibitive. Oracle provides the capability to refresh materialized views without a complete rebuild. This is known as **fast** refresh. There are two mechanisms for fast refresh—either using materialized view logs, described in the next section, or using Partition Change Tracking, which is described in section 7.3.4.

Fast Refresh Using Materialized View Logs

One way to fast refresh a materialized view is by capturing the individual changes done to the detail tables by DML statements (INSERT, UPDATE, DELETE, and MERGE statements) and then applying these changes to the materialized view. A materialized view log is a mechanism used to capture these changes and must be created on each of the detail tables of the materialized view. During fast refresh, Oracle will use the materialized view log to identify the changes that have occurred since the last refresh and apply them to the materialized view. Once all materialized views have been refreshed to include the changes, the relevant rows will be automatically purged from the materialized view log. You must never modify the materialized view log manually, as you will be forced to completely rebuild the materialized view.

You may be concerned about the overhead of materialized view logs on the transaction issuing the DML statements. While this may indeed be a problem for a transaction-processing system, in a data warehouse this is not a major issue, because DML statements are not heavily used. The more typical method used to load new data is using a bulk load using SQL*Loader or using an INSERT /*+ APPEND */ statement. Fortunately, the individual changes made by these methods are not recorded in the materialized view log but are tracked internally in a compressed fashion.

Materialized View Log Options

A materialized view log can be created with several options; depending on the materialized views you need to be fast refreshed, you will need one or more of these options. Some of these options include:

- ROWID, which will log the rowids of the rows changed by DML statements.
- INCLUDING NEW VALUES clause, which indicates that both the old and new version of a row changed by an update statement should be logged.
- SEQUENCE, which causes a sequence number to be logged for each change.

Hint: You must create the materialized view logs before creating the materialized views; otherwise, you will have to completely refresh the materialized views once before fast refresh can be performed.

The following example shows a fast refreshable materialized view along with the materialized view logs on its detail tables. Note that for a materialized view with aggregates, the options ROWID, SEQUENCE, and INCLUDING NEW VALUES must be specified for the materialized view logs. If you omit the SEQUENCE option, you can still get fast refresh but only under specific conditions (i.e., either when only one detail table has been changed or when only inserts have been performed). Also, all detail table columns referenced in the materialized view's query must be included in the materialized view log.

```
CREATE MATERIALIZED VIEW LOG on time
       WITH ROWID, SEQUENCE (time_key, month, year)
       INCLUDING NEW VALUES;

CREATE MATERIALIZED VIEW LOG on purchases
       WITH ROWID, SEQUENCE (time_key, product_id,
                             purchase_price)
       INCLUDING NEW VALUES;

CREATE MATERIALIZED VIEW LOG on product
       WITH ROWID, SEQUENCE (product_id)
       INCLUDING NEW VALUES;

CREATE MATERIALIZED VIEW monthly_sales_mv
 PCTFREE 0 TABLESPACE summary
 STORAGE (initial 64k next 64k pctincrease 0)
 BUILD IMMEDIATE
 REFRESH FAST
 ON DEMAND
 ENABLE QUERY REWRITE
 AS
 SELECT t.month, t.year, p.product_id,
        SUM (ps.purchase_price) as sum_of_sales,
        COUNT (ps.purchase_price) as total_sales, COUNT(*)
 FROM time t, product p, purchases ps
 WHERE t.time_key = ps.time_key AND
       ps.product_id = p.product_id
 GROUP BY t.month, t.year, p.product_id;
```

The next example shows a materialized view without aggregation that is fast refreshable with the ON COMMIT option. To make this type of a materialized view fast refreshable, the materialized view logs only need to have the ROWID option. However, you must include a ROWID column for each table in the SELECT clause of the materialized view. In this example, we are assuming that the materialized view logs for PRODUCT and PURCHASES, created earlier for the MONTHLY_SALES_MV, are available.

```
CREATE MATERIALIZED VIEW LOG on customer WITH ROWID;

CREATE MATERIALIZED VIEW product_customer_mv
BUILD IMMEDIATE
REFRESH FAST ON COMMIT
AS
SELECT c.rowid r1, c.gender, p.rowid r2, p.product_id,
       f.rowid r3, f.purchase_price
FROM purchases f, product p, customer c
WHERE f.customer_id = c.customer_id
  AND f.product_id  = p.product_id;
```

Hint: There is only one materialized view log on a given table, and this materialized view log is used for all materialized views that reference that table. Therefore, be sure to specify options to satisfy all the materialized views. If you use the SQL Access Advisor to determine which materialized views to create, the appropriate materialized view logs will also be recommended for you.

Using Oracle Enterprise Manager to Define Materialized View Logs

You can use Oracle Enterprise Manager to create and edit your materialized view logs, as shown in Figure 7.6. You get to this screen by clicking on the *Materialized View Logs* link on the Administration page and then clicking on the *Create* button. The first step is to enter the table name, such as EASYDW.CUSTOMER. Note that you can only specify the name of the table on which the materialized view log is being defined—the name of the materialized view log itself is automatically determined by Oracle and cannot be modified by the user. Pressing the *Go* button will give you a list of available columns. From this list, you can choose the columns you would like to add to the materialized view log. Once you have made your choices, you can click the *Show SQL* button to see the SQL command or click *OK* to create the materialized view log.

Figure 7.6 *Creating a Materialized View Log in Oracle Enterprise Manager*

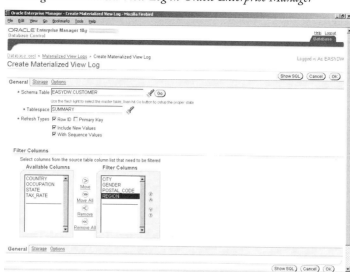

Other Requirements for Fast Refresh

In addition to requiring materialized view logs on the detail tables, the defining query of a materialized view to be fast refreshed must adhere to certain rules. For example, if the materialized view contains an aggregate operator, it must also include some additional supporting aggregates—if the materialized view had SUM(x) or AVG(x), it must also have COUNT(x); if it had STD-DEV(x), it must also include SUM(x), COUNT(x), and SUM(x * x). In the previous section, we saw an example of the PRODUCT_CUSTOMER_MV, where we needed to include ROWID columns for the detail tables in the materialized views.

Rather than trying to remember such detailed rules for when a particular materialized view is fast refreshable, we would recommend that you simply use the EXPLAIN_MVIEW and TUNE_MVIEW tools provided for this purpose. The EXPLAIN_MVIEW tool will explain which operations (such as fast refresh or query rewrite) the materialized view can or cannot support and the reasons why not. The TUNE_MVIEW tool will suggest modifications to the materialized view to fix any problems reported by EXPLAIN_MVIEW. These tools will be discussed later in this chapter.

7.3.4   **Partition Change Tracking**

Partitioned tables are a common feature in a warehouse. In Chapter 5, we saw the use of partitioning to load data into the warehouse. In Chapter 6, we discussed how partitioning can help improve query performance using partition pruning.

Oracle 9*i* introduced a new feature known as **Partition Change Tracking (PCT)**. With this feature, whenever any DML or partition maintenance operation occurs to a partitioned detail table referenced by a materialized view, Oracle keeps track of the updated partitions. Then, during refresh, Oracle can identify which portion of the materialized view corresponds to the updated partitions in the detail tables, and recompute only that portion of the materialized view. This is referred to as **PCT refresh.**

Figure 7.7 shows a conceptual picture of how data changes are tracked in Partition Change Tracking. In this example, the PURCHASES table is partitioned by month into Jan2002, Feb2002, and Mar2002 partitions.

Figure 7.7   *Partition Change Tracking*

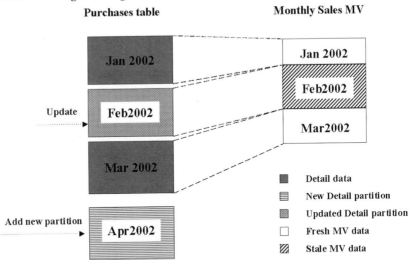

The materialized view MONTHLY_SALES_MV stores the total sales for each month. The materialized view is defined in such a way that there is a correspondence between the partitions of the PURCHASES table and the data in the materialized view, as shown by the dotted lines. (We will discuss how to create such a materialized view shortly.) If the Feb2002 partition is updated, only the corresponding portion of the materialized view is stale. During refresh, only the portion of the materialized view that refers to the stale partition needs to be refreshed and hence the refresh can be much faster.

When and How to Perform PCT Refresh

You may be wondering why you should learn about Partition Change Tracking when you can refresh using materialized view logs. There are three main reasons why you may consider using PCT refresh:

1. If you have performed any partition maintenance operations, such as adding a new partition or dropping an old one, then fast refresh using materialized view logs is not possible. In this situation, which is quite common when loading data into the fact table, you will be forced to perform a complete refresh—unless your materialized view supports PCT.

2. Some materialized views do not allow fast refresh with materialized view logs—for example, if the materialized view included analytical functions such as RANK, discussed in Chapter 6. However, the materialized view may still support PCT refresh.

3. If a lot of changes have been done to the partitioned detail table, PCT refresh may perform *much faster* than fast refresh using materialized view logs.

If you specified refresh FAST or FORCE either when creating the materialized view or using the DBMS_MVIEW procedures, Oracle Database 10*g* will automatically determine the best refresh method to use. However, if your materialized view supports PCT, you can explicitly request PCT refresh using the DBMS_MVIEW procedure, as follows:

```
EXECUTE DBMS_MVIEW.REFRESH('monthly_sales_mv', 'P');
```

Next, we will discuss how to create a materialized view that can support PCT refresh.

Creating a Materialized View That Supports PCT Refresh

One of the advantages of PCT is that the materialized view itself does not have to be partitioned at all! To allow PCT, the materialized view must have at least one partitioned detail table, which may be partitioned by Range,

List, Range-Hash or Range-List composite partitioning. The partition key must consist of a single column.

There are three techniques that can be used to define a materialized view so that it can be refreshed using PCT refresh. Each of these techniques provides a mechanism to associate a row in the materialized view with a specific table partition.

■ **Join dependency expression:** The materialized view includes a join between the partitioned table and another table using the partitioning key, and a column from the latter table is included in the SELECT clause of the materialized view. This technique is new in Oracle Database 10*g*, and several materialized views may automatically satisfy this condition.

■ **Partition key**: The partition key of the partitioned detail table is included in the SELECT clause of the materialized view.

■ **Partition marker:** A special column known as the partition marker, using the DBMS_MVIEW.PMARKER() function, is included in the SELECT clause of the materialized view.

We will illustrate how each of these techniques can be used.

Join Dependency Expression

Consider the MONTHLY_SALES_MV materialized view used in several examples in this chapter. This materialized view stores the total sales for each product by month. Suppose we used partition maintenance operations to load new data into the PURCHASES table at the end of each month and hence would like to refresh this materialized view using PCT refresh after data loads.

```
CREATE MATERIALIZED VIEW monthly_sales_mv
AS
SELECT t.month, t.year, p.product_id,
       SUM (ps.purchase_price) as sum_of_sales,
       COUNT (ps.purchase_price) as total_sales, COUNT(*)
FROM time t, product p, purchases ps
WHERE t.time_key = ps.time_key AND
      ps.product_id = p.product_id
GROUP BY t.month, t.year, p.product_id;
```

It so happens that this materialized view automatically supports PCT using a join dependency expression. To see why, recall that in the EASYDW schema, the PURCHASES table is partitioned by TIME_KEY. In this materialized view, the partitioned table, PURCHASES, is joined to the table, TIME, using the partitioning-key column, TIME_KEY. As long as the materialized view's SELECT list now includes a column or expression from table, TIME, PCT will be supported on this materialized view. Here, the table TIME is said to be a **join-dependent table** and the column or expression from TIME, which is included in the materialized view, is known as a **join dependency expression**. The best way to determine if your materialized view supports PCT in this manner is to use the EXPLAIN_MVIEW procedure, discussed in section 7.4.

Now, suppose we had another materialized view, REGIONAL_ SALES_MV, which had the total sales by region.

```
CREATE MATERIALIZED VIEW regional_sales_mv
AS
SELECT c.region, SUM(ps.purchase_price) as sum_of_sales,
       COUNT (ps.purchase_price) as total_sales
FROM customer c, purchases ps
WHERE c.customer_id = ps.customer_id
GROUP BY c.region;
```

In this materialized view, join dependency is not possible, because the joining keys (CUSTOMER_ID and PRODUCT_ID) are different from the partitioning key (TIME_KEY). In this case, you can use either the partition key or partition marker methods, described next.

Partition Key

The simplest way to modify the REGIONAL_SALES_MV to allow PCT refresh is to include in it the partition key of the PURCHASES table. The resulting materialized view, REGIONAL_SALES_PARTKEY_MV, will appear as follows:

```
CREATE MATERIALIZED VIEW regional_sales_partkey_mv
AS
SELECT c.region, ps.time_key,
       SUM (ps.purchase_price) as sum_of_sales,
       COUNT (ps.purchase_price) as total_sales
FROM customer c, purchases ps
WHERE c.customer_id = ps.customer_id
GROUP BY c.region, ps.time_key;
```

Note that this materialized view has the TIME_KEY column (shown underlined), in the SELECT and the GROUP BY clauses.

Hint: If the materialized view has a GROUP BY clause, the partition key must be included in both the SELECT and the GROUP BY clauses; otherwise, it is not a legal SQL query.

Let us compare the contents of this modified materialized view with the original one, by selecting from the two materialized views, as follows:

```
SELECT * FROM regional_sales_mv;

REGION          SUM_OF_SALES TOTAL_SALES
--------------- ------------ -----------
AmerNorthEast     1314778.48        5658
AmerMidWest       2731175.27       10849
AmerNorthEast     3752117.44       16370
...
7 rows selected.

SELECT * FROM regional_sales_partkey_mv;


REGION          TIME_KEY  SUM_OF_SALES TOTAL_SALES
--------------- --------- ------------ -----------
AMerNorthEast   04-JAN-03      4536.39          17
AMerNorthEast   05-JAN-03      2950.63          11
AMerNorthEast   06-JAN-03      4412.16          16
...
810 rows selected.
```

You will notice that for each region there is a row for every value of TIME_KEY. Thus, even though this materialized view is supposed to have *total sales* for each region, the inclusion of the TIME_KEY column has resulted in it having *daily sales* for each region. In other words, including the partition key has significantly increased the size of the materialized view from 7 rows to 810 rows!

Including a partition key is suitable provided the partition key has only a few distinct values, which means that including it will not have a significant impact on the size of the resulting materialized view. In our case, the partition key is TIME_KEY and so a more appropriate alternative may be to use a partition marker, discussed next.

Partition Marker

A partition marker is an alternative to using the partition key and results in a much smaller materialized view than one using a partition key. The following example shows the regional sales materialized view in the previous example, except that instead of the TIME_KEY, it includes a special function, DBMS_MVIEW.PMARKER.

```
CREATE MATERIALIZED VIEW regional_sales_marker_mv
REFRESH FORCE
AS
SELECT c.region, DBMS_MVIEW.PMARKER(ps.rowid) as pmark,
       SUM(ps.purchase_price) as sum_of_sales,
       COUNT (ps.purchase_price) as total_sales
FROM customer c, purchases ps
WHERE c.customer_id = ps.customer_id
GROUP BY c.region, DBMS_MVIEW.PMARKER(ps.rowid);
```

Let us now select the data from this materialized view as follows:

```
select * from regional_sales_marker_mv;
REGION            PMARK  SUM_OF_SALES  TOTAL_SALES
--------------- ---------- ------------ -----------
AmerWest          50539    101431.57          431
AmerWest          50540     80895.72          414
AmerWest          50541    121121.93          465
...
168 rows selected.
```

The partition marker function produces a different value for each partition, but all rows in the same partition get the same value. Thus, by including the partition marker in the SELECT (and GROUP BY clause), for each region you will get at most as many rows as the number of partitions. In the EASYDW data warehouse, we have two years of data, partitioned by month, and so we have 24 partitions. Thus, for each region, we will get 24 rows. Therefore, while the original REGIONAL_SALES_MV had seven rows (for seven regions), the modified REGIONAL_SALES_MARKER_MV will now have 7 * 24 = 168 rows. This is still preferable to the 810 rows with the partition key.

To summarize, first check if your materialized view already supports PCT using a join dependency expression. If this is not the case, include the partition key if there are few distinct values in each partition. If there are many distinct values for the partition key, such as time_key, use a partition marker instead, to keep the materialized view to a reasonable size.

PCT can only track changes done to a partitioned table if the materialized view satisfies the conditions (using one of the previous techniques) for *that specific* table. In other words, if the materialized view had multiple partitioned tables, for each of those tables you must have the partition key, partition marker, or a join dependency expression in the materialized view. You could use different techniques for each table—for example, if you had two partitioned tables, CUSTOMER and PURCHASES, you could use partition marker for one and partition key for the other, as appropriate. Note that if changes have occurred to any nonpartitioned tables or partitioned tables not enabled for PCT, you will not be able to perform a PCT refresh.

7.3.5 Refresh Performance

Good performance of materialized view refresh is extremely crucial because of the limited maintenance windows available in data warehouses today. Here are some tips for getting the best performance out of your refresh procedures.

Optimizer Statistics

In order to get good refresh performance, it is important to have accurate statistics on the data. The package DBMS_STATS should be used to gather optimizer statistics on the detail tables after each data load and prior to creating or refreshing the materialized views. It is also important to gather statistics on the materialized views themselves—both upon creation and after refresh. This will ensure that the optimizer has accurate statistics during refresh and when optimizing queries that are rewritten to use materialized views.

Set the Parameter atomic_refresh to FALSE

We mentioned that DBMS_MVIEW refresh procedures have a parameter known as atomic_refresh. If this parameter is set to TRUE (which is the default), all operations during refresh are performed as a single atomic transaction. This means that in case of a failure, the entire refresh operation will be rolled back. However, to achieve this, the refresh operation has to disable use of some operations, such as parallel execution and bulk inserts, which are critical to refresh performance in a data warehouse. Therefore, we recommend you use the atomic_refresh setting of FALSE. In the worst case of a failure, you may have to refresh the particular materialized view with a complete refresh; however, refresh performance will be much better in general.

Another benefit of setting atomic_refresh to FALSE is that when doing a complete refresh, Oracle Database 10*g* will automatically disable all indexes on the materialized view prior to refresh and rebuild them after the refresh. This is much faster than maintaining the indexes during refresh.

Use PCT Refresh and Partitioned Materialized Views

It can be advantageous to enable PCT on your materialized views so that you can avoid a complete refresh in many situations. Although PCT does not require that the materialized view be partitioned, if the materialized view is partitioned on the partition key or the join dependency expression used to enable PCT, this can further improve PCT refresh performance. This is because Oracle can use some optimizations during refresh. Note that to take advantage of these optimizations, the atomic_refresh parameter must be set to FALSE.

Use Parallel Execution

Using parallel execution during refresh can significantly improve performance. To do so, you must include the PARALLEL clause when creating the materialized view and enable parallel DML (as discussed in Chapter 6) in the session performing refresh.

Build and Refresh Multiple Materialized Views Using REFRESH_ALL

In Oracle Database 10*g*, significant enhancements have been made to allow refresh of multiple materialized views simultaneously. If you specify multiple materialized views in the DBMS_MVIEW procedures and use the atomic_refresh parameter setting of FALSE, Oracle can refresh multiple materialized views concurrently. Note that to do so, the initialization parameter JOB_ QUEUE_PROCESSES must be set to a nonzero value, indicating how many refreshes can proceed simultaneously. When refreshing multiple materialized views, Oracle Database 10*g* will automatically determine the best order to refresh the materialized views. It will take into account dependencies among the materialized views, the degree of parallelism needed for each refresh, and the number of available job processes, so as to provide the best refresh performance.

To take advantage of this feature, when you first create materialized views, use the BUILD DEFERRED option rather than BUILD IMMEDIATE. You can then use REFRESH_ALL to concurrently populate all the materialized views. Similarly, when refreshing materialized views in the data warehouse, use the DBMS_MVIEW.REFRESH_ALL or DBMS_MVIEW.REFRESH_DEPENDENT procedures.

When refreshing multiple materialized views, you can see the status of jobs using the DBA_JOBS dictionary view, as shown in the following example:

```
SELECT what job_description, this_date, total_time
FROM dba_jobs
WHERE what like '%REFRESH%';

JOB_DESCRIPTION                     THIS_DATE TOTAL_TIME
----------------------------------- --------- ----------
BEGIN DBMS_SNAPSHOT.REFRESH_MV      12-JUN-04       1725
 ('MV_RF$JPIPE_007F01880001',2
,'EASYDW','CUSTOMER_PURCHASES_
MV2','?','',0,6,1); END;
```

Enable Query Rewrite during Refresh

Performance of complete refreshes and PCT refreshes can be significantly improved by using query rewrite during refresh. In Chapter 9, we will discuss query rewrite and also see how you can use it to speed up refresh.

7.3.6 Nested Materialized Views

All the materialized views we have seen so far are based on queries involving detail tables; however, it is also possible to create materialized views using queries involving other materialized views. Recall that a materialized view is a stored result and hence can be used in lieu of a table. A materialized view that is based on another materialized view is known as a **nested materialized view**. In the following example, the materialized view QUARTERLY_SALES_MV is created using the MONTHLY_CUST _SALES_MV.

```
CREATE MATERIALIZED VIEW monthly_cust_sales_mv
ENABLE QUERY REWRITE
AS
SELECT t.year, t.quarter, t.month, c.customer_id,
      SUM(f.purchase_price) AS dollar_sales
FROM time t, purchases f, customer c
WHERE f.time_key = t.time_key AND
      f.customer_id = c.customer_id
GROUP BY t.year, t.quarter, t.month, c.customer_id;

CREATE MATERIALIZED VIEW quarterly_sales_mv
ENABLE QUERY REWRITE
AS
SELECT m.year, m.quarter, SUM(m.dollar_sales) AS dollar_sales
FROM monthly_cust_sales_mv m
GROUP BY m.year, m.quarter;
```

Why Use Nested Materialized Views?

You can use nested materialized views as shown in our previous example to compute the aggregates at a higher level in a hierarchy from a lower level—for example, from month to quarter. Similarly, if several of your materialized views need to use the same join in their defining queries but different aggregates, you could separate the join into one materialized view and then build different aggregate materialized views using this common materialized view. This may provide you better performance for materialized view creation and complete refresh, because you only need to compute the join once.

Another reason to use nested materialized views is to improve your fast refresh capabilities. Often, there is some complex clause in the materialized view's defining query that may make it not fast refreshable. In such cases, it may be possible to split the materialized view into two or more *simpler* materialized views, *some* of which are fast refreshable. The refresh performance of this *partially* fast refreshable group of materialized views may be much better than a complete refresh. For example, consider the following materialized view, SALES_MV1, that uses a subquery to find the customers who spent the most money in our store in January 2003.

```
CREATE MATERIALIZED VIEW sales_mv1
ENABLE QUERY REWRITE
AS
SELECT c.customer_id, SUM(f.purchase_price) AS dollar_sales
FROM purchases f, customer c
WHERE f.customer_id = c.customer_id
GROUP BY c.customer_id
HAVING SUM(f.purchase_price)
    IN (SELECT max(f.purchase_price) dollar_sales
        FROM purchases f, time t
        WHERE f.time_key = t.time_key
          AND t.month_name = 'January'
          AND t.year = 2003
        GROUP BY f.customer_id);
```

Ordinarily, this materialized view is not fast refreshable using either materialized view logs or using PCT, because of the subquery in the HAVING clause. Now, let us split this materialized view as follows into two fast refreshable materialized views.

```
CREATE MATERIALIZED VIEW sales_submv1
REFRESH FAST
ENABLE QUERY REWRITE
AS
SELECT c.customer_id, SUM(f.purchase_price) AS dollar_sales,
COUNT(f.purchase_price) as cnt_sales, COUNT(*) cstar
FROM purchases f, customer c
WHERE f.customer_id = c.customer_id
GROUP BY c.customer_id;

CREATE MATERIALIZED VIEW sales_submv2
REFRESH FAST
ENABLE QUERY REWRITE
AS
SELECT f.customer_id, max(f.purchase_price) max_sales
FROM purchases f, time t
WHERE f.time_key = t.time_key
  AND t.month_name = 'January' and t.year = 2003
GROUP BY f.customer_id;
```

The first, SALES_SUBMV1, computes the result of SALES_MV1 without including the subquery—in other words, the sales by customer. The second one, SALES_SUBMV2, computes the result of the subquery itself—in other words, the maximum amount spent by any customer in January 2003. These two materialized views are much simpler and are fast refreshable. We can now write SALES_MV1 in terms of SALES_SUBMV1 and SALES_SUBMV2, as follows:

```
CREATE MATERIALIZED VIEW sales_mv1
REFRESH COMPLETE
ENABLE QUERY REWRITE
AS
SELECT customer_id, dollar_sales
FROM sales_submv1
WHERE dollar_sales IN (SELECT max_sales FROM sales_submv2);
```

Note that the resulting materialized view still includes a subquery and cannot be fast refreshed directly; however, its complete refresh would be much faster.

This may sound very complicated, but there are two simple tools that will assist you in modifying your materialized view! The EXPLAIN_MVIEW utility, discussed section 7.4 will tell you if your materialized view is not fast refreshable for some reason. The TUNE_MVIEW utility, discussed in section 7.5 will automatically split your materialized view, if needed, into nested materialized views to maximize its fast refresh capabilities. Before we look at these tools, let us briefly discuss how to refresh nested materialized views.

Refreshing Nested Materialized Views

The DBMS_MVIEW refresh procedures can be used to refresh nested materialized views. When using the REFRESH procedure, if you set the parameter **nested** to TRUE, then any underlying materialized view is refreshed first before refreshing the nested materialized view. This parameter is new in Oracle Database 10*g*.

For instance, in the following example, referring to the nested materialized views created in the preceding section, Oracle will first refresh SALES_SUBMV1 and SALES_SUBMV2 before refreshing the nested materialized view, SALES_MV1.

```
execute dbms_mview.refresh('sales_mv1', nested=>TRUE);
```

Similarly, when using REFRESH_DEPENDENT, if nested is set to TRUE, Oracle will refresh all nested materialized views dependent on the table. For instance, if REFRESH_DEPENDENT is issued on the table TIME, as follows, Oracle will refresh SALES_SUBMV1, SALES_SUBMV2, and SALES_MV1. If nested had been set to FALSE, only SALES_SUBMV2 would be refreshed, since only this materialized view refers directly to the TIME table.

```
execute dbms_mview.refresh_dependent(:failures,'time',
nested=>TRUE);
```

If the procedure REFRESH_ALL is used, Oracle will automatically determine the dependencies among all the materialized views and refresh them in the correct order.

7.4   **EXPLAIN_MVIEW Utility**

As we have seen so far, in order to get the most benefit out of a materialized view, the materialized view must conform to some rules. For instance, you may need to create materialized view logs to make fast refresh possible or add a partition marker to allow Partition Change Tracking. The EXPLAIN_MVIEW interface is designed to help you determine what these rules are. Before creating the materialized view, you can run its defining query through the EXPLAIN_MVIEW utility. If a capability such as fast refresh is not possible, EXPLAIN_MVIEW will point out the offending construct or the missing columns. You now have the opportunity to fix these problems before expending precious resources to create the materialized view. EXPLAIN_MVIEW is invoked via the PL/SQL procedure DBMS_MVIEW.EXPLAIN_MVIEW or by using Oracle Enterprise Manager.

The DBMS_MVIEW.EXPLAIN_MVIEW PL/SQL procedure comes in two flavors:

- You can provide the procedure, the name of an existing materialized view, and it will display the refresh and query rewrite capabilities of the materialized view.

- You can provide the procedure with the SELECT statement that defines the materialized view and it will project its capabilities, if it has been created.

Prior to using this procedure, you must create the MV_CAPABILITIES_TABLE table in the current schema by running the utlxmv.sql script found in the ORACLE_HOME/rdbms/admin directory. The results of EXPLAIN_MVIEW will be placed in this table. EXPLAIN_MVIEW also has interfaces to return the results in a PL/SQL varray rather than in a table.

The output of EXPLAIN_MVIEW first lists all the capabilities of a materialized view and whether each one is possible (Y) or not (N). It then presents detailed information regarding each capability and the reason, if any, why it is not possible, as we will demonstrate in the next section.

7.4.1 Running EXPLAIN_MVIEW procedure

In the following example, we illustrate the first flavor of the EXPLAIN_MVIEW utility, which uses the SELECT statement of the materialized view, yet to be created. To illustrate how EXPLAIN_MVIEW can be used, we have deliberately introduced two problems with the materialized view logs—first, we have dropped the materialized view log on the PRODUCT table, and, second, we have removed the INCLUDING NEW VALUES clause from the materialized view log on the TIME table.

```
DROP MATERIALIZED VIEW LOG on PRODUCT;

ALTER MATERIALIZED VIEW LOG on TIME EXCLUDING NEW VALUES;
BEGIN
  dbms_mview.explain_mview (
    'SELECT t.month, t.year, p.product_id,
            SUM (f.purchase_price) as sum_of_sales,
            COUNT (f.purchase_price) as total_sales,
            COUNT(*) as cstar
     FROM time t, product p, purchases f
     WHERE t.time_key = f.time_key AND
           f.product_id = p.product_id
     GROUP BY t.month, t.year, p.product_id');
END;
/
```

The following query shows the output of the procedure:

```
SELECT capability_name, possible p, related_text obj,
       msgtxt   explanation
FROM MV_CAPABILITIES_TABLE;
```

CAPABILITY_NAME	P	OBJ	EXPLANATION
PCT	Y		
REFRESH_COMPLETE	Y		
REFRESH_FAST	Y		
REWRITE	Y		
PCT_TABLE	N	TIME	relation is not a partitioned table
PCT_TABLE	N	PRODUCT	relation is not a partitioned table
PCT_TABLE	Y	PURCHASES	
REFRESH_FAST_AFTER_INSERT	N	EASYDW.PRODUCT	the detail table does not have a materialized view log
REFRESH_FAST_AFTER_INSERT	N	EASYDW.TIME	mv log must have new values
REFRESH_FAST_AFTER_ ONETAB_DML	N		see the reason why REFRESH_FAST_

			AFTER_INSERT is disabled
REFRESH_FAST_AFTER_ANY_DML	N		see the reason why REFRESH_FAST_ AFTER_INSERT is disabled
REFRESH_FAST_PCT	Y		
REWRITE_FULL_TEXT_MATCH	Y		
REWRITE_PARTIAL_TEXT_MATCH	Y		
REWRITE_GENERAL	Y		
REWRITE_PCT	N		general rewrite is not possible or PCT is not possible on any of the detail tables
PCT_TABLE_REWRITE	N	TIME	relation is not a partitioned table
PCT_TABLE_REWRITE	N	PRODUCT	relation is not a partitioned table
PCT_TABLE_REWRITE	N	PURCHASES	PCT is enabled through a join dependency

From this output, we can see that the PCT_TABLE capability for the PURCHASES table is possible because of a join dependency (because of the column month from the TIME table, which is joined to PURCHASES using the partition key). The TIME table is not partitioned, and hence PCT refresh is not possible if this table has been updated.

Fast refresh may be possible in some situations and not others. Hence, the fast refresh capabilities are presented at three levels, so if the first one is not possible, the remaining ones are also not possible and so on:

- REFRESH_AFTER_INSERT (only inserts were done to the tables)

- REFRESH_AFTER_ONETABDML (only one table is modified at a time)

- REFRESH_AFTER_ANY_DML (there is no restriction on the type of DML)

The output of EXPLAIN_MVIEW indicates that the materialized view log on the TIME table was missing the INCLUDING NEW VALUES clause, and hence fast refresh using materialized view logs is not possible.

EXPLAIN_MVIEW also indicates if query rewrite has been enabled and if it is possible in general or only using text match mode.

Hint: To find out the detailed reasons why a particular query did not rewrite using a certain materialized view, use the EXPLAIN_REWRITE utility, which is discussed in Chapter 9.

Let us now correct the problems with the materialized view logs and re-run the utility. You can see that fast refresh is now possible, as indicated by REFRESH_FAST_AFTER_INSERT Y.

```
CREATE MATERIALIZED VIEW LOG on product
        WITH ROWID, SEQUENCE (product_id)
INCLUDING NEW VALUES;

ALTER MATERIALIZED VIEW LOG on TIME including new values;

BEGIN
  dbms_mview.explain_mview (
    'SELECT t.month, t.year, p.product_id,
            SUM (f.purchase_price) as sum_of_sales,
            COUNT (f.purchase_price) as total_sales,
            COUNT(*) as cstar
     FROM time t, product p, purchases f
     WHERE t.time_key = f.time_key AND
           f.product_id = p.product_id
     GROUP BY t.month, t.year, p.product_id');
END;
/

SELECT capability_name, possible
FROM MV_CAPABILITIES_TABLE
WHERE capability_name LIKE 'REFRESH%';

CAPABILITY_                        P
------------------------------     -
REFRESH_COMPLETE                   Y
REFRESH_FAST                       Y
REFRESH_FAST_AFTER_INSERT          Y
REFRESH_FAST_AFTER_ONETAB_DML      Y
REFRESH_FAST_AFTER_ANY_DML         Y
REFRESH_FAST_PCT                   Y
```

If you wanted to look at the capabilities of an existing materialized view—for example, MONTHLY_SALES_MV—you would use EXPLAIN_MVIEW, as follows:

```
EXECUTE dbms_mview.explain_mview('EASYDW.MONTHLY_SALES_MV');
```

The output will be similar to that shown in the previous example.

7.4.2 Using Oracle Enterprise Manager to run EXPLAIN_MVIEW

The CREATE MATERIALIZED VIEW screen in Oracle Enterprise Manager (Figure 7.3) has an *Explain* button, which can be clicked to run EXPLAIN_MVIEW. This allows you to immediately identify and correct any problems with the materialized view. Figure 7.8 is the screen showing the output of EXPLAIN_MVIEW.

Figure 7.8　*EXPLAIN_MVIEW in Oracle Enterprise Manager*

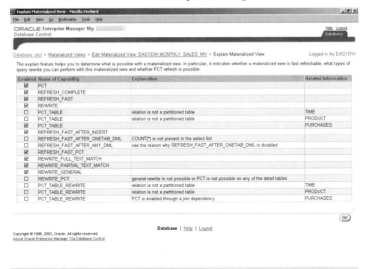

You can also issue EXPLAIN_MVIEW on an existing materialized view by using the *Explain* button shown in Figure 7.4.

The EXPLAIN_MVIEW utility will identify the capabilities of a materialized view and point out which ones are missing. The TUNE_MVIEW tool, which is discussed next, can then be used to fix the materialized view to enhance its capabilities.

7.5   **TUNE_MVIEW Utility**

The TUNE_MVIEW utility is new in Oracle Database 10*g* and is available using the DBMS_ADVISOR.TUNE_MVIEW procedure. (There is no graphical interface for this utility at this time.) You supply to it the SQL for the materialized view to be created and it will fix the defining query of the materialized view so that it is fast refreshable and supports as many types of query rewrite as possible. In order to achieve fast refresh, the materialized view may be modified to include additional columns or decomposed into several simpler fast refreshable nested materialized views (see section 7.3.6). Additionally, TUNE_MVIEW will also recommend materialized view logs if they are necessary for fast refresh.

To illustrate this utility, consider the following materialized view statement:

```
CREATE MATERIALIZED VIEW monthly_cat_sales_mv
REFRESH FAST ON DEMAND
ENABLE QUERY REWRITE
AS
SELECT distinct p.category, t.month
FROM product p, purchases ps, time t
WHERE ps.product_id = p.product_id
  AND ps.time_key = t.time_key;
```

If we run EXPLAIN_MVIEW on it, we will see that the DISTINCT keyword has made this materialized view not fast refreshable. It may not be obvious to you how to modify this materialized view to make it fast refreshable.

```
BEGIN
  dbms_mview.explain_mview (
   SELECT distinct p.category,  t.month
   FROM product p, purchases ps, time t
   WHERE ps.product_id = p.product_id
     AND ps.time_key = t.time_key;
   );
END;
/

SELECT capability_name, possible p,  msgtxt  explanation
FROM MV_CAPABILITIES_TABLE
WHERE CAPABILITY_NAME LIKE 'REFRESH%';
```

```
CAPABILITY_NAME                  P    EXPLANATION
------------------------------   -    -----------------------
REFRESH_COMPLETE                 Y
REFRESH_FAST                     N
REFRESH_FAST_AFTER_INSERT        N    DISTINCT clause in select
                                        list in mv

REFRESH_FAST_AFTER_INSERT        N    DISTINCT clause in select
                                        list in mv

REFRESH_FAST_AFTER_INSERT        N    one or more joins present
                                      in mv

REFRESH_FAST_AFTER_ONETAB_DML    N    see the reason why REFRES
                                      H_FAST_AFTER_INSERT is
                                      disabled

REFRESH_FAST_AFTER_ANY_DML       N    see the reason why REFRES
                                      H_FAST_AFTER_ONETAB_DML
                                      is disabled

REFRESH_FAST_PCT                 N    see the reason why REFRES
                                      H_FAST_AFTER_INSERT is
                                      disabled
```

Now, let us pass this materialized view to TUNE_MVIEW. To indicate to TUNE_MVIEW that we would like to optimize the materialized view for fast refresh and/or query rewrite, the CREATE MATERIALIZED VIEW statement must include the REFRESH FAST and/or ENABLE QUERY REWRITE clauses, respectively. The results of the analysis are saved under a user-specified taskname identifier and will consist of the SQL for the modified materialized view(s) and any required materialized view logs. If you do not specify REFRESH FAST, then TUNE_MVIEW will not recommend materialized view logs.

```
DECLARE
  taskname  varchar2(20);
BEGIN
  taskname := 'MY_TUNE_MVIEW_TASK';

 dbms_advisor.tune_mview(taskname,
   'CREATE MATERIALIZED VIEW monthly_sales_mv
    REFRESH FAST ON DEMAND
    ENABLE QUERY REWRITE
    AS
    SELECT distinct p.category, t.month
    FROM product p, purchases ps, time t
    WHERE ps.product_id = p.product_id
      AND ps.time_key = t.time_key');
END;
/
```

We can now generate a SQL script for this analysis, which can later be executed to create the materialized view. To generate this script, you must specify a database DIRECTORY object where the script will be placed and you must have been granted write privileges to that directory, as shown in the following example:

```
CREATE DIRECTORY TUNE_RESULTS AS '/oracle/scripts';

BEGIN
 DBMS_ADVISOR.CREATE_FILE
 (DBMS_ADVISOR.GET_TASK_SCRIPT('MY_TUNE_MVIEW_TASK'),
                               'TUNE_RESULTS',
                               'mv_create.sql');
END;
/
```

An excerpt from the script is shown below:

```
Rem   SQL Access Advisor: Version 10.1.0.1 - Production
Rem
Rem   Username:          EASYDW
Rem   Task:              MY_TUNE_MVIEW_TASK
Rem   Execution date:
Rem

set feedback 1
set linesize 80
set trimspool on
set tab off
set pagesize 60

whenever sqlerror CONTINUE

ALTER MATERIALIZED VIEW LOG FORCE ON
    "EASYDW"."PRODUCT"
    ADD ROWID, SEQUENCE("PRODUCT_ID","CATEGORY")
    INCLUDING NEW VALUES;

CREATE MATERIALIZED VIEW EASYDW.MONTHLY_SALES_MV
REFRESH FAST WITH ROWID
ENABLE QUERY REWRITE
AS
SELECT EASYDW.PRODUCT.CATEGORY C1, EASYDW.TIME.MONTH C2,
       COUNT(*) M1 FROM EASYDW.PURCHASES,
       EASYDW.PRODUCT, EASYDW.TIME
WHERE EASYDW.PRODUCT.PRODUCT_ID = EASYDW.PURCHASES.PRODUCT_ID
  AND EASYDW.TIME.TIME_KEY = EASYDW.PURCHASES.TIME_KEY
GROUP BY EASYDW.PRODUCT.CATEGORY, EASYDW.TIME.MONTH;
…
```

We can see that the utility has modified the materialized view definition to convert the DISTINCT keyword to an equivalent GROUP BY clause (underlined) and has added a COUNT(*) aggregate, which makes it fast refreshable. It has also recommended the necessary changes to the materialized view logs.

Because TUNE_MVIEW may create several materialized views to achieve fast refresh of the given materialized view, it is advisable to also generate an UNDO script from TUNE_MVIEW, which can be used to remove the materialized views as a group, when no longer needed.

```
BEGIN
DBMS_ADVISOR.CREATE_FILE
(DBMS_ADVISOR.GET_TASK_SCRIPT('MY_TUNE_MVIEW_TASK', 'UNDO'),
                            'TUNE_RESULTS',
                            'mv_undo.sql');
END;
/
```

With TUNE_MVIEW, a novice materialized view user can now very easily take advantage of all the powerful and even the most advanced features of materialized views without having to deal with the complexity.

7.6   Summary

In this chapter, we discussed how materialized views could be used to precompute the results of frequently asked queries. Summary management in Oracle provides a complete framework to manage materialized views. Fast refresh and Partition Change Tracking allows materialized views to be kept up-to-date when your warehouse gets loaded. Tools such as EXPLAIN_MVIEW and TUNE_MVIEW make it extremely simple to create and use materialized views.

In the next two chapters, we will discuss two more key components of summary management—dimensions and query rewrite.

8

Dimensions

In Chapter 7, we described materialized views, which can be used to pre-compute and store results of frequently used queries. A major benefit of doing this is that you can use query rewrite to transparently rewrite queries to use these materialized views, thus significantly reducing the query response time. One important type of metadata for query rewrite is a database object called a dimension, which allows you to declare relationships in your data warehouse and allows the optimizer to rewrite more queries to use materialized views. In this chapter, we will discuss how to create dimensions as part of the logical design of your data warehouse. In Chapter 9, we will then discuss how these dimensions can be used by query rewrite.

8.1   Concepts

In Chapter 2, we discussed the logical design of a data warehouse, using a schema based on a dimensional model such as a star or a snowflake. The relationships between tables in this logical model are typically represented in the data warehouse using referential integrity constraints. Constraints usually signify join relationships between fact and dimension tables, with primary keys on the dimension tables and foreign keys on the fact tables. Another type of a logical relationship in a dimensional model is a **hierarchy**, which expresses rollup or aggregation relationships within the columns of a dimension table. The concept of a hierarchy is commonly used by analysis tools to roll up data from a finer to a coarser level of granularity and to drill down to see more detail. For example, a time hierarchy, shown in Figure 8.1, may indicate that data at a daily grain can be aggregated to a monthly level and from the monthly to the yearly level.

Figure 8.1   *Concept of a Hierarchy : Time*

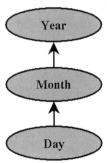

The **dimension** database object can be used to define logical relationships within and across dimension tables, such as hierarchies, which often cannot be expressed using referential integrity constraints.

In particular, dimensions are used to define the following types of relationships:

- The hierarchical relationships among the columns within dimension tables, such as the one in Figure 8.1. The hierarchy may be contained within a single dimension table in case of a star schema and within multiple dimension tables in a normalized snowflake schema. For example, in a snowflake schema, there may be separate dimension tables for day and month. The dimension object supports both these models. Each column that participates in a hierarchy is called a **level**.

- Functional dependencies between two columns in a dimension table. A **functional dependency** from column A to B means that for every value of A, there is only one value of B. So if you know the value of A, then you can determine the value of B. This is useful for looking up the value of one column based on the value of another column in the table. For example, given a state, we can determine the tax rate. This type of relationship is also referred to as an **attribute** relationship.

Defining a dimension to declare hierarchical relationships in the data makes it possible for the optimizer to rewrite more queries to use materialized views. It also allows tuning tools, such as the SQL Access Advisor, to recommend the best set of materialized views to create and the best OLAP analysis tools to perform rollup and drill-down operations.

Note that a dimension is a metadata object, such as a constraint, and should not be confused with a dimension table, which stores data. However, unlike a constraint, which can be automatically checked and validated, relationships declared by a dimension are not automatically verified when the dimension is created. They are assumed to be "trusted" information supplied by the DBA. The significance of this will become clearer in Chapter 9, when we discuss how dimensions are used by query rewrite. In the remainder of this chapter, when we say dimension or dimension object, we refer to the metadata object and not to a dimension table.

8.2   Creating a Dimension

Designing dimensions should be part of the logical design of your data warehouse. Once the dimension tables have been created, you can create DIMENSION objects, using the CREATE DIMENSION SQL statement. Within the CREATE DIMENSION statement, hierarchical relationships are described using the HIERARCHY clause, and functional dependencies are defined using the ATTRIBUTE clause.

As with other database objects, you need certain privileges to manage dimensions. To create a dimension in your own schema, you must have the CREATE DIMENSION privilege, and to create one in someone else's schema, you must have the CREATE ANY DIMENSION privilege. You must also have SELECT access to any tables referenced in the dimension. We assume that the EASYDW user has been granted the following privileges, allowing it to create, alter, and drop dimensions.

```
GRANT create any dimension to easydw;
GRANT alter any dimension to easydw;
GRANT drop any dimension to easydw;
```

We will now look at the specifics of the CREATE DIMENSION statement and how it can be used to define hierarchies and attributes.

8.2.1   Defining a Dimension with a Single Hierarchy

In the EASYDW schema, we have a geography hierarchy within the CUSTOMER table, where postal codes roll up into cities, which roll up into states, which, in turn, roll up into countries. One technique that makes it easy to construct the CREATE DIMENSION statement is to draw a bubble diagram, such as the one in Figure 8.2, showing these rollup rela-

Figure 8.2   *Bubble Diagram for a Geography Dimension*

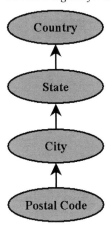

tionships within a hierarchy. The direction of the arrows indicates how rollup can be done.

To convert the diagram in Figure 8.2 into a SQL dimension definition, each bubble in the diagram becomes a LEVEL in the dimension, as shown in the following example:

```
CREATE DIMENSION geography_dim
LEVEL postal_code IS customer.postal_code
LEVEL city       IS customer.city
LEVEL state      IS customer.state
LEVEL country    IS customer.country
HIERARCHY loc_rollup (
        postal_code     CHILD OF
        city            CHILD OF
        state           CHILD OF
        country
     );
```

Each level is specified using a name and the underlying column in the dimension table. For example, the level named CITY corresponds to the column CITY in the CUSTOMER table. The relationships between the levels are described with the HIERARCHY clause. The hierarchy is also given a name, LOC_ROLLUP in our example. The bubbles with arrows coming out of them in Figure 8.2 are described with the CHILD OF clause. In our example, postal code rolls up into city; therefore, postal_code is a CHILD OF city. City rolls up into state; therefore, city is a CHILD OF state and so on.

Hint: Note that in the HIERARCHY clause you must use level names rather than the underlying column names.

Note that the definition of a hierarchy signifies that for any value of a child column in a hierarchy, there must be one and only one value of its parent column. In our customer table, a postal code is unique to any given city; therefore, it satisfies this rule. For example, postal code 02134 is in the city of Boston. The code 02134 refers to addresses in Boston only; it cannot also be used to refer to addresses in San Francisco.

8.2.2 Defining a Dimension with Multiple Hierarchies

Sometimes it may be possible to logically roll up the same data in different ways. In our sample schema, EASYDW, as in many businesses, we use both a regular calendar and a fiscal calendar. In the regular calendar, days roll up into months, which roll up into years. In the fiscal calendar, days roll up into weeks, which roll up into fiscal quarters. This type of a logical model can also be represented in the dimension object by defining multiple hierarchies.

Figure 8.3 shows a diagram for this TIME dimension. It contains two hierarchies, describing the two ways by which the data can be rolled up from the TIME_KEY (i.e., daily) level, using the regular and the fiscal calendars.

Figure 8.3 *Bubble Diagram for the Time Dimension*

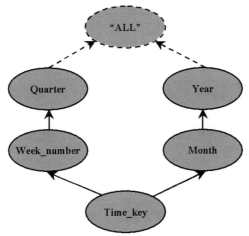

In the CREATE DIMENSION statement, each way of rolling up the data will be described using a HIERARCHY clause, as shown in the following example. The two hierarchies are called CALENDAR_ROLLUP and FISCAL_ROLLUP. Each arrow coming out of a bubble in Figure 8.3 is described in a CHILD OF clause. There are two arrows coming out of the TIME_KEY bubble, and hence there are two CHILD OF statements, one in each hierarchy. From a given date (TIME_KEY), the FISCAL_ROLLUP hierarchy tells us the week and fiscal quarter this date is in and the other, CALENDAR_ROLLUP, tells us the month and year.

```
CREATE DIMENSION time_dim
 LEVEL time_key    IS time.time_key
 LEVEL month       IS time.month
 LEVEL quarter     IS time.quarter
 LEVEL year        IS time.year
 LEVEL week_number IS time.week_number
 HIERARCHY calendar_rollup (
              time_key   CHILD OF
              month      CHILD OF
              year
          )
 HIERARCHY fiscal_rollup (
              time_key    CHILD OF
              week_number CHILD OF
              quarter
          );
```

At the top of every bubble diagram is the special level "ALL," representing the "grand total" level for that dimension. All levels of a hierarchy can be rolled up to ALL. We don't always define the ALL level in the CREATE DIMENSION statement explicitly.

Again, for each value of a child column in a hierarchy, there is only one parent value. Any given date—for example, 21-Mar-2003—falls into one and only one fiscal week and in a specific quarter.

8.2.3 Defining a Dimension with Attributes

In a dimension definition, the ATTRIBUTE clause is used to define any functional dependencies between columns within the same table that are not hierarchical in nature.

In the EASYDW schema, in the PRODUCT table we have two columns, PRODUCT_ID and PRODUCT_NAME, such that given a PRODUCT_ID, there is only one PRODUCT_NAME. The following example shows the definition of a dimension with the attribute clause, representing this relationship. Note, however, that this relationship is true only in one direction (i.e., it does not mean that given the PRODUCT_NAME we can determine the PRODUCT_ID).

```
CREATE DIMENSION product_dim
 LEVEL product_id   IS product.product_id
 LEVEL category     IS product.category
 HIERARCHY merchandise_rollup (
                  product_id   CHILD OF
                  category
                )
 ATTRIBUTE product_id DETERMINES (product_name)
 ATTRIBUTE prod_manufacturer
          LEVEL product_id DETERMINES (manufacturer);
```

In the ATTRIBUTE clause, the name on the left side of the DETERMINES keyword should be a level name—for example, PRODUCT_ID. To the right of the DETERMINES keyword are the dependent columns—for example, PRODUCT_NAME. Note that you can either specify multiple dependent columns within the same attribute clause or specify different attribute clauses for each one—both ways convey equivalent semantics.

Note that you can also specify a name for the attribute relationship; however, this is optional. To do this, you need to use the extended clause with the LEVEL keyword. For example, in the preceding example, the relationship between PRODUCT_ID and MANUFACTURER is given a name, PROD_MANUFACTURER.

8.2.4 Defining a Dimension with Normalized Tables

If you have a snowflake or other normalized schema, then your hierarchy may refer to columns in multiple dimension tables. The CREATE DIMENSION statement allows you to declare such relationships as well. Figure 8.4 shows a bubble diagram for a normalized TIME dimension. The bubbles and bold arrows define the rollup relationships as before. The dotted rectangles represent the tables where the levels come from. The dotted arrows show how the tables join to each other. In this example, there is a separate table for time, week, month, quarter, and year. The TIME table joins to the WEEK table using the join condition time.week_number = week.week_number and to the MONTH table using the condition time.month = month.month.

Figure 8.4   *A Normalized Dimension*

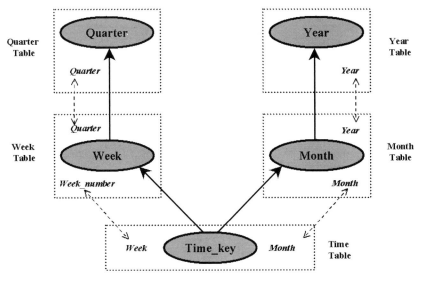

To convert this diagram to a CREATE DIMENSION statement, you would first define a level for each of the bubbles, specifying both the table name and column name for that level. For example, the level WEEK corresponds to the column WEEK.WEEK_NUMBER, which is the WEEK_NUMBER column from the WEEK table. Next, you would define your hierarchy using the level names as before. Finally, you would specify any joins that must be performed when traversing up the hierarchy using the JOIN KEY clause. Thus, you would get the following CREATE DIMENSION statement:

```
CREATE DIMENSION time_dim
 LEVEL time_key IS time.time_key
 LEVEL month    IS month.month
 LEVEL quarter  IS quarter.quarter
 LEVEL year     IS year.year
 LEVEL week     IS week.week_number
 HIERARCHY calendar_rollup (
                 time_key CHILD OF
                 month    CHILD OF
                 year
                 JOIN KEY time.month REFERENCES month
                 JOIN KEY month.year REFERENCES year
          )
 HIERARCHY fiscal_rollup (
                 time_key CHILD OF
```

```
                           week      CHILD OF
                           quarter
                           JOIN KEY time.week_number  REFERENCES week
                           JOIN KEY week.quarter REFERENCES quarter
               )
     ATTRIBUTE time_key DETERMINES time.day_of_the_week
     ATTRIBUTE time_key DETERMINES month.month_name;
```

In the fiscal_rollup hierarchy in this example, the join key, TIME.WEEK_NUMBER column, is used to join the table TIME to the WEEK level in the WEEK table.

Hint: In a normalized dimension, remember to qualify column names with the table name; otherwise, you may get an error.

You can also specify attribute clauses in a normalized dimension. For example, the level TIME_KEY determines the column DAY_OF_THE_WEEK from the TIME table and the column MONTH_NAME from the MONTH table.

As discussed in Chapter 2, normalized dimension tables incur the overhead of extra joins during query processing and hence must be used with care.

8.2.5   Creating Dimensions with Oracle Enterprise Manager

You can use Oracle Enterprise Manager as an alternative to SQL to manage dimensions. To create a new dimension, from the *Administration* page, select the *Dimensions* link and click the *Create* button. You will see a screen such as the one shown in Figure 8.5. You need to name the dimension and identify which schema it will reside in. In our example, we are creating a dimension, EASYDW.TIME_DIM. We recommend that you use an appropriate naming convention to easily identify dimensions in the database and to differentiate them from dimension tables.

The screen in Figure 8.5 has several tabs for creating levels, hierarchies, and attributes for the dimension. Each tab will have an *Add* button, which you can use to create the requisite levels, hierarchies, and attributes. For example, Figure 8.6 shows the levels tab, where you can see several levels we have created.

Figure 8.5   *Creating a Dimension*

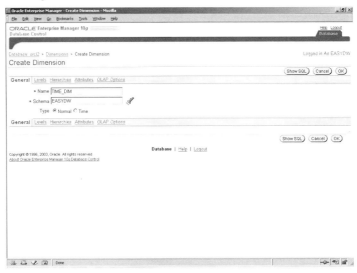

At any stage, you can see the current SQL statement for the dimension by pressing the *Show SQL* button. Figure 8.7 shows the screen for adding a new level.

Figure 8.6   *Creating a Dimension—the Levels Tab*

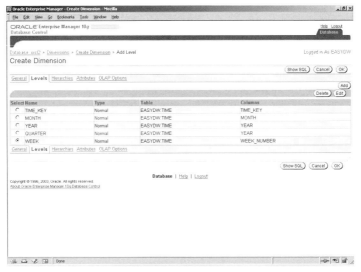

Figure 8.7 *Creating a Dimension—Adding a Level*

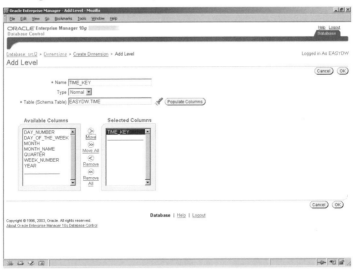

You must name the level and choose a table, which must be in the form of schema.tablename—for example, EASYDW.TIME. If you are creating a normalized dimension, then different levels could come from different tables. Once you pick a table, press the *Populate Columns* button to see the table columns in the *Available Columns* list. Click on the *Move* arrow keys to choose the columns for the level. In Figure 8.7, we are creating a level named TIME_KEY, based on the TIME_KEY column from the EASYDW.TIME table. Once you are done filling in all the information and press the *OK* button, the newly created level will now show up.

Once you have added all the levels, you can move on to creating hierarchies. Figure 8.8 shows the screen to create a new hierarchy, where we are adding a hierarchy named CALENDAR_ROLLUP.

To build the hierarchy, use the *Move* keys to move levels from the *Available Levels* list to the *Selected Levels* list. One important point to note is that you must correctly order the levels in the *Selected Levels* list to reflect the hierarchy. The columns in the *Selected Levels* list are ordered from the highest to the lowest level in the hierarchy.

Hint: You must ensure that the levels in the hierarchy are in the correct order; otherwise, you may get unexpected results when you use this dimension with query rewrite. Before creating the dimension, you can use the *Show SQL* button in Figure 8.5 to see the SQL statement with the hierarchy definition.

Figure 8.8　*Creating a dimension—Adding a Hierarchy*

Finally, if you would like to create any attributes, click on the *Attributes* tab in Figure 8.5 and you will get a screen such as that in Figure 8.9. In this example, we are creating an attribute named MONTH_NAME. You must choose the level for which the attribute is being defined (MONTH in our

Figure 8.9　*Creating a Dimension—Adding an Attribute*

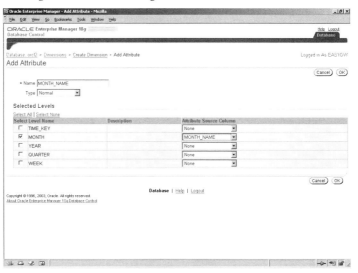

example) and choose, from the drop-down box, the column the attribute determines (MONTH_NAME in our example).

Note that when you first go to the *Attributes* tab, you will find two pre-defined attributes, called long-description and short-description, which are used by the OLAP Option. You can edit these attributes from the *OLAP Options* tab, which we will discuss in Chapter 15.

Once you have created all the levels, hierarchies, and attributes, press the *OK* button in Figure 8.5 to create the dimension.

8.3   Describing a Dimension

As we can see, a dimension definition can be quite involved, and before Oracle Database 10g, there was no easy way to examine the structure of a dimension from SQL*Plus. This has been rectified in Oracle Database 10g, which provides a convenient way to view a dimension with a call to the procedure DBMS_DIMENSION.DESCRIBE_DIMENSION. The following example shows the PRODUCT_DIM dimension we had defined earlier:

```
set serveroutput on;
execute dbms_dimension.describe_dimension('EASYDW.product_dim');

DIMENSION EASYDW.PRODUCT_DIM
LEVEL CATEGORY IS EASYDW.PRODUCT.CATEGORY
LEVEL PRODUCT_ID IS EASYDW.PRODUCT.PRODUCT_ID
HIERARCHY MERCHANDISE_ROLLUP (
PRODUCT_ID CHILD OF
CATEGORY
)
ATTRIBUTE PROD_MANUFACTURER LEVEL PRODUCT_ID
         DETERMINES EASYDW.PRODUCT.MANUFACTURER
ATTRIBUTE PRODUCT_ID LEVEL PRODUCT_ID
         DETERMINES EASYDW.PRODUCT.PRODUCT_NAME

PL/SQL procedure successfully completed.
```

8.4   Validating a Dimension

One of the major differences between referential integrity constraints and dimensions is that the relationships declared by the dimension are not automatically checked or enforced by Oracle. In order to get accurate results with query rewrite, you must ensure that these relationships are correct. For example, if you incorrectly defined a dimension to indicate that weeks roll up into months, when they actually did not, you may get incorrect data when rolling up data from weekly to the monthly level. To help ensure that the data in the dimension table actually conforms to the dimension definition, Oracle provides a procedure named DBMS_DIMENSION.VALIDATE_DIMENSION. This procedure should be run every time new data is loaded into your dimension tables to ensure data integrity.

Hint: Prior to Oracle Database 10*g*, the dimension validation procedure was in the DBMS_OLAP package. This has now been subsumed by the VALIDATE_DIMENSION procedure in the new DBMS_DIMENSION package.

For example, suppose we had the following customer dimension.

```
CREATE DIMENSION customer_dim
  LEVEL customer IS customer.customer_id
  LEVEL city     IS customer.city
  LEVEL state    IS customer.state
  HIERARCHY  customer_zone (
                    customer CHILD OF
                    city     CHILD OF
                    state
             )
  ATTRIBUTE city DETERMINES postal_code
  ATTRIBUTE customer DETERMINES (gender, occupation);
```

According to this dimension, town determines the postal_code, and every city should have a unique postal code. Now suppose some bad data got inserted into the customer table. The postal code for Boston was mistyped as 01210 instead of 01201.

```
INSERT INTO customer (customer_id, city, state,
                      postal_code, gender, region,
                      country, tax_rate, occupation)
VALUES ('AB130000', 'Boston', 'MA',
       '01210', 'F', 'AmerNorthEast', 'USA', 0.05, 'Doctor');

INSERT INTO customer (customer_id, city, state,
                      postal_code, gender, region,
                      country, tax_rate, occupation)
VALUES ('AB130001', 'Boston', 'MA',
       '01210', 'F', 'AmerNorthEast', 'USA', 0.05, 'Doctor');

COMMIT;
```

If we run DBMS_DIMENSION.VALIDATE_DIMENSION, it will verify the integrity of the data and detect that there is a discrepancy in the HIERARCHY and ATTRIBUTE relationships declared by the CUSTOMER_DIM dimension.

```
variable stmt_id varchar2(30);

execute :stmt_id := 'CUST_DIM_VAL';
execute dbms_dimension.validate_dimension ('EASYDW.CUSTOMER_DIM',
                                    FALSE, TRUE, :stmt_id);
```

Any exceptions found are placed in the DIMENSION_EXCEPTIONS table. You must create this table *prior to* running the procedure, by executing the script utldim.sql from the rdbms/admin directory.

```
SELECT distinct owner,table_name,dimension_name,relationship
FROM dimension_exceptions
WHERE statement_id = :stmt_id;

OWNER       TABLE_NAME DIMENSION_NAME       RELATIONSHIP
----------  ---------- -------------------- -------------------
EASYDW      CUSTOMER   CUSTOMER_DIM         ATTRIBUTE
```

The BAD_ROWID column of DIMENSION_EXCEPTIONS gives the table rowids with the discrepancy (i.e., all rows corresponding to the violated relationship). In our example, it would return all rows corresponding to the city of Boston. We can now look at the actual data values by looking up the customer table, as follows. We can see that the CUSTOMER_ID values, AB130000 and AB130001, have mismatched values for CITY and POSTAL_CODE with respect to the remaining data.

```
SELECT customer_id, city, state, postal_code FROM customer
WHERE rowid IN (SELECT bad_rowid FROM dimension_exceptions
            WHERE statement_id = :stmt_id);

CUSTOMER_I CITY             STATE      POSTAL_COD
---------- ---------------- ---------- ----------
AB123410   Boston           MA         01201
AB123420   Boston           MA         01201
AB123440   Boston           MA         01201
AB123450   Boston           MA         01201
AB123470   Boston           MA         01201
...
AB130000   Boston           MA         01210     <- bad data
AB130001   Boston           MA         01210
```

It is extremely important that the relationships declared by the dimension are valid; otherwise, you may see unexpected results when using query rewrite.

8.5   Summary

In this chapter, we have discussed a new metadata object called a dimension, which allows you to declare logical relationships between columns of your dimension tables. With dimensions, you can represent hierarchies and attribute relationships in your data. We also discussed procedures to validate a dimension to ensure that the underlying data conforms to the dimension definition.

In the next chapter, we will look at how query rewrite can be used to transparently rewrite queries with materialized views. We will also see how dimension objects can significantly enhance the ability of the optimizer to rewrite a large number of queries using few materialized views.

9

Query Rewrite

In Chapter 7, we described materialized views, which can be used to pre-compute and store results of frequently used queries. A major benefit of doing this is that you can use query rewrite to transparently rewrite queries to use these materialized views, thus significantly reducing the query response time. With this feature, queries that used to take hours to return results can now return them in minutes or even instantly.

As with indexes, materialized views and query rewrite should be considered an essential part of query tuning in a data warehouse. Just as the query optimizer considers all available indexes when determining the fastest way to answer the query, it also considers any available materialized views that may have already precomputed part or all of the answer to the query. This means that no application changes are needed in order to use materialized views. If the optimizer determines that the materialized view is insufficient to answer the query, it uses the detail data. Therefore, end users do not have to be aware of the existence of materialized views and hence they can be created and modified without impacting users.

In this chapter, we will describe various techniques used by Oracle to rewrite queries using materialized views.

9.1   Setting up Query Rewrite

There are three steps that must be followed to enable queries to be rewritten to use materialized views.

- The materialized views must be created with the ENABLE QUERY REWRITE clause, discussed in Chapter 7.

■ The initialization parameter QUERY_REWRITE_ENABLED must be set to TRUE. This is the default in Oracle Database 10*g*.

```
-- enable query rewrite
ALTER SESSION SET QUERY_REWRITE_ENABLED=TRUE;
```

■ The initialization parameter QUERY_REWRITE_INTEGRITY must be set to an appropriate level for the application. This parameter indicates to the optimizer what type of metadata information (e.g., dimensions) may be used to rewrite queries. We will discuss this parameter in detail later in this chapter.

Query rewrite uses the cost-based optimizer, which automatically compares the cost of the query execution plan with and without query rewrite and uses the one with the lower cost. To ensure that the optimizer makes the correct choices, you need to collect statistics both on the detail tables involved in the query and on the materialized views using the DBMS_STATS package.

Occasionally, your application may require that the query must only use the materialized view and must never use the base tables. In such cases, you can override the optimizer's cost-based decision making by setting the QUERY_REWRITE_ENABLED parameter to FORCE. In this mode, if there is a materialized view that satisfies the query, the optimizer will use it without comparing the cost of the plan with and without rewrite. You can disable query rewrite by setting this parameter to FALSE.

9.1.1   How Can We Tell If a Query Was Rewritten?

To determine if the query was rewritten, we use the EXPLAIN PLAN utility (described in Chapter 6) to look at the query execution plan. Specifically, if the query was rewritten, the output of EXPLAIN PLAN will include the special operation, **MAT_VIEW REWRITE**, and the name of the materialized view used to rewrite the query. If you find that query rewrite is not occurring as expected, you should use the DBMS_MVIEW.EXPLAIN_REWRITE, utility discussed later in this chapter, to diagnose the problem.

9.2 Types of Query Rewrite

Oracle supports several types of query rewrite transformations, allowing a single materialized view to be used to answer several queries. We will illustrate several of these in the following sections, including:

- SQL text match
- Aggregate rollup
- Join-back
- Computing aggregates from other aggregates
- Filtered data
- Rewrite using dimensions and constraints

Our first few examples will use the following materialized view, which computes the sum of sales and total sales for products by month.

```
CREATE MATERIALIZED VIEW monthly_sales_mv
 ENABLE QUERY REWRITE
 AS
 SELECT t.year, t.month, p.product_id,
        SUM (ps.purchase_price) as sum_of_sales,
        COUNT (ps.purchase_price) as total_sales
 FROM time t, product p, purchases ps
 WHERE t.time_key = ps.time_key AND
       ps.product_id = p.product_id
 GROUP BY t.year, t.month, p.product_id;
```

9.2.1 SQL Text Match

The simplest type of query rewrite is when the SQL text of the materialized view's defining query exactly matches that of the incoming query. The text match is not case-sensitive and ignores any comments and whitespace differences.

The execution plan that follows shows that the optimizer chose to access the materialized view MONTHLY_SALES_MV via a full table scan.

```
-- exact text match
EXPLAIN PLAN FOR
SELECT t.year, t.month, p.product_id,
```

```
        sum (ps.purchase_price) as sum_of_sales,
        count (ps.purchase_price) as total_sales
FROM time t, product p, purchases ps
WHERE t.time_key   = ps.time_key AND
      ps.product_id = p.product_id
GROUP BY t.year, t.month, p.product_id;


PLAN_TABLE_OUTPUT
-------------------------------------------------------------------
|Id| Operation                    |Name             | Rows  |Cost|
-------------------------------------------------------------------
| 0| SELECT STATEMENT             |                 | 3522  |  7|
| 1|  MAT_VIEW REWRITE ACCESS FULL|MONTHLY_SALES_MV | 3522  |  7|
-------------------------------------------------------------------
```

Oracle will also try a text match starting from the FROM keyword of the query. This allows for differences in column ordering in the SELECT list and computation of expressions. In the following example, SUM(purchase_price) and COUNT(purchase_price) have been used to compute the average, and, also, the order of columns in the SELECT list is changed. You can see from the execution plan that the materialized view has been used to rewrite this query.

```
EXPLAIN PLAN FOR
SELECT t.month, p.product_id,  t.year,
       AVG(ps.purchase_price) avg_of_sales
FROM time t, product p, purchases ps
WHERE t.time_key = ps.time_key AND
      ps.product_id = p.product_id
GROUP BY t.year, t.month, p.product_id;


PLAN_TABLE_OUTPUT
-------------------------------------------------------------------
|Id| Operation                    |Name             | Rows  |Cost|
-------------------------------------------------------------------
| 0| SELECT STATEMENT             |                 | 3522  |  7|
| 1|  MAT_VIEW REWRITE ACCESS FULL|MONTHLY_SALES_MV | 3522  |  7|
-------------------------------------------------------------------
```

If the text of the query and materialized view does not match, Oracle will then compare the join conditions, GROUP BY clauses, and aggregates in the query and materialized view to determine if the query can be rewritten using the materialized view. We will illustrate these rules in the following sections.

9.2.2 Aggregate Rollup

An **aggregate rollup** occurs when the aggregates in the materialized view can be further aggregated to supply the aggregates requested by the query. A simple example of this is when the query contains only some of the grouping columns from the materialized view. For instance, the following query asks for the sum of sales and total number of sales by product and year. The materialized view contains the sum of sales by product by year and month. During query rewrite, the monthly sales are added together to compute the yearly totals.

```
-- rollup over month column
EXPLAIN PLAN FOR
SELECT t.year, p.product_id,
       SUM (ps.purchase_price) as sum_of_sales,
       COUNT (ps.purchase_price) as total_sales
 FROM time t, product p, purchases ps
 WHERE t.time_key = ps.time_key AND
       ps.product_id = p.product_id
 GROUP BY t.year, p.product_id;


PLAN_TABLE_OUTPUT
```

Id	Operation	Name	Rows	Cost
0	SELECT STATEMENT		232	9
1	SORT GROUP BY		232	9
2	MAT_VIEW REWRITE ACCESS FULL	MONTHLY_SALES_MV	3522	7

When a rollup occurs, the rewritten query will contain a GROUP BY clause, as shown in the previous execution plan.

A more interesting case of rollup is when your data has a hierarchy described by a dimension object. In this case, query rewrite can roll up data from a lower level to a higher level in the hierarchy. We will explain this in more detail in section 9.2.7.

9.2.3 Join-back

For query rewrite to occur, all the columns in the query must either appear in the materialized view or must be derivable from some column in the materialized view. In the latter case, the materialized view must be joined to the base table to obtain the required column. This is called a **join-back**. In the simple case, for a join-back to occur, the materialized view must contain either the primary key or the rowid of the detail table.

For instance, suppose, in addition to the sum of sales by product id, we would also like to see the product name. The column PRODUCT_ID is the primary key of the PRODUCT table; therefore, the following query, asking for PRODUCT_NAME, can be answered using the MONTHLY_SALES_MV materialized view and using a join-back. The optimizer's plan shows that the query has been rewritten to use the materialized view MONTHLY_SALES_MV with a join to the PRODUCT table. The predicate information printed by EXPLAIN PLAN can be used to see that the join-back is done using the PRODUCT_ID column in the materialized view.

```
-- join-back to product table using primary key constraint
EXPLAIN PLAN FOR
SELECT t.year, t.month, p.product_name,
       SUM (ps.purchase_price) as sum_of_sales
FROM time t, product p, purchases ps
WHERE t.time_key = ps.time_key AND
      ps.product_id = p.product_id
GROUP BY t.year, t.month, p.product_name;


PLAN_TABLE_OUTPUT
------------------------------------------------------------------
|Id| Operation                    | Name            |Rows |Cost|
------------------------------------------------------------------
|  0| SELECT STATEMENT             |                 | 3522|   4|
|  1|  SORT GROUP BY               |                 | 3522|   4|
|* 2|   HASH JOIN                  |                 | 3522|   1|
|  3|    TABLE ACCESS FULL         | PRODUCT         |  164|    |
|  4|    MAT_VIEW REWRITE ACCESS FULL| MONTHLY_SALES_MV | 3522|    |
------------------------------------------------------------------
Predicate Information (identified by operation id):
---------------------------------------------------
   2 - access("P"."PRODUCT_ID"="MONTHLY_SALES_MV"."PRODUCT_ID")
```

The advantage of using the materialized view with a join-back, even though there is an extra join, is that this join is likely to be based on a smaller number of records and so will be usually much faster than using the detail data.

9.2.4 Computing Other Aggregates in the Query

Aggregates in the query can be computed from different aggregates in the materialized view. We have already seen a simple example of this in the SQL text match section, where SUM and COUNT were used to compute the AVG. However, the power of query rewrite comes from the fact that many different transformations can be combined together. For instance, in the following query, we want to know the average purchase price of each item by year. The materialized view has the sum and count of the purchase price at the monthly level. The average can be computed by first doing a rollup of months to years and then dividing the sum by the count of the purchase price. The query is therefore rewritten to use the MONTHLY_SALES_MV materialized view.

```
-- aggregate computability
EXPLAIN PLAN FOR
SELECT t.year, p.product_id, AVG(ps.purchase_price) as ave_sales
FROM time t, product p, purchases ps
WHERE t.time_key = ps.time_key AND
ps.product_id = p.product_id
GROUP BY t.year, p.product_id;
```

```
PLAN_TABLE_OUTPUT
----------------------------------------------------------------
|Id| Operation                    | Name            |Rows  |Cost|
----------------------------------------------------------------
|  0| SELECT STATEMENT             |                 | 232  |  9 |
|  1|  SORT GROUP BY               |                 | 232  |  9 |
|  2|   MAT_VIEW REWRITE ACCESS FULL| MONTHLY_SALES_MV | 3522 |  7 |
----------------------------------------------------------------
```

To compute aggregates in the query with a rollup, the materialized view may need to contain additional aggregates. For instance, to roll up AVG, the materialized view must have SUM and COUNT or AVG and COUNT.

9.2.5 Filtered Data

The materialized view MONTHLY_SALES_MV defined previously contained data for all products for each month and year. Sometimes you may only want to summarize data for a certain product or year or have separate materialized views for each region. In this case, the materialized view will only contain a subset of data indicated by a selection condition in the WHERE clause of its query. Sophisticated query rewrites are possible with one or more such materialized views. Oracle will determine if the data in the query can be answered by a materialized view by analyzing and comparing the WHERE clauses of the materialized view and the query.

The following materialized view contains sum of sales and the total number of sales for the electronics category for the months from January 2003 through June 2003.

```
CREATE MATERIALIZED VIEW sales_elec_1_6_2003_mv
 ENABLE QUERY REWRITE
 AS
 SELECT t.month, t.year, p.product_id,
        SUM(ps.purchase_price) as sum_of_sales,
        COUNT (ps.purchase_price) as total_sales
 FROM time t, product p, purchases ps
 WHERE t.time_key = ps.time_key AND
       ps.product_id = p.product_id AND
       p.category = 'ELEC' AND
       t.month >= 200301 AND t.month <= 200306
 GROUP BY t.month, t.year, p.product_id;
```

This materialized view can be used to answer the following query, which requests the sum of sales and number of sales for the Electronics category for May 2003. The predicate information section, which is output by EXPLAIN PLAN shows the predicates applied during each step of the execution plan. From this, we can see that the MV data is filtered to select only the row for May 2003.

```
EXPLAIN PLAN FOR
SELECT t.month, p.product_id,
       SUM(ps.purchase_price) as sum_of_sales,
       COUNT (ps.purchase_price) as total_sales
 FROM time t, product p, purchases ps
 WHERE t.time_key = ps.time_key AND
       ps.product_id = p.product_id AND
       p.category = 'ELEC' AND t.month = 200305
 GROUP BY t.month, t.year, p.product_id;

PLAN_TABLE_OUTPUT
-----------------------------------------------------------------
|Id|Operation                  |Name                     |Rows|Cost|
-----------------------------------------------------------------
| 0|SELECT STATEMENT           |                         | 100|   2|
|*1| MAT_VIEW REWRITE ACCESS FULL|SALES_ELEC_1_6_2003_MV| 100|   2|
-----------------------------------------------------------------
Prdicate Information (identified by operation id):
-----------------------------------------------------------------

  1 - filter("SALES_ELEC_1_6_2003_MV"."MONTH"=200305)
```

A query can have additional conditions not mentioned in the materialized view. For instance, in the following query, we are looking for monthly sales of digital camera products in the electronics category for Jan 2003. The materialized view has all products within this category and we can determine the PRODUCT_NAME from PRODUCT_ID using a join-back. Hence, the query will be rewritten to use the materialized view with a join to the product table.

```
EXPLAIN PLAN FOR
SELECT t.month, SUM(ps.purchase_price) as sum_of_sales,
       COUNT (ps.purchase_price) as total_sales
 FROM time t, product p, purchases ps
 WHERE t.time_key = ps.time_key AND
       ps.product_id = p.product_id AND p.category = 'ELEC' AND
       t.month = 200301 AND product_name  = 'Digital  Camera'
GROUP BY t.month;


PLAN_TABLE_OUTPUT
-------------------------------------------------------------
|Id|Operation                       |Name                |Row|Cst|
-------------------------------------------------------------
| 0|SELECT STATEMENT                |                    | 1| 5|
| 1| SORT GROUP BY NOSORT           |                    | 1| 5|
|*2|  HASH JOIN                     |                    | 1| 5|
|*3|   TABLE ACCESS FULL            |PRODUCT             | 1| 2|
|*4|   MAT_VIEW REWRITE ACCESS FULL|SALES_ELEC_1_6_2003_MV| 96| 2|
-------------------------------------------------------------


Predicate Information (identified by operation id):
-------------------------------------------------------------
  2 -
access("P"."PRODUCT_ID"="SALES_ELEC_1_6_2003_MV"."PRODUCT_ID")
  3 - filter("PRODUCT_NAME"='Digital  Camera')
  4 - filter("SALES_ELEC_1_6_2003_MV"."MONTH"=200301)
```

This example illustrates how two rewrite mechanisms can be applied together—namely, join-back and filtered data.

9.2.6 Rewrite Using Materialized Views with No Aggregation

The examples in the previous sections all involve materialized views with aggregation. Materialized views are sometimes used to precompute expensive joins and may not involve any aggregation. Query rewrite can use such materialized views to rewrite queries, which may or may not contain aggregation.

Consider the following materialized view, which stores the information about purchases made by customers, including the customer gender and occupation. This materialized view has a join between the CUSTOMER and PURCHASES table but no aggregation.

```
CREATE MATERIALIZED VIEW customer_purchases_mv
ENABLE QUERY REWRITE
AS
SELECT c.gender, c.occupation, f.purchase_price
FROM purchases f, customer c
WHERE f.customer_id = c.customer_id;
```

The following query, which asks for the purchases made by doctors, can be answered using this materialized view.

```
EXPLAIN PLAN FOR
SELECT c.gender, f.purchase_price
FROM purchases f, customer c
WHERE f.customer_id = c.customer_id
   AND c.occupation = 'Doctor';
```

```
PLAN_TABLE_OUTPUT
-----------------------------------------------------------------
|Id|Operation                     |Name                  |Cost|
-----------------------------------------------------------------
| 0|SELECT STATEMENT              |                      | 54|
| 1| MAT_VIEW REWRITE ACCESS FULL|CUSTOMER_PURCHASES_MV |    |
-----------------------------------------------------------------

Prdicate Information (identified by operation id):
---------------------------------------------------
   1 - filter("CUSTOMER_PURCHASES_MV"."OCCUPATION"='Doctor')
```

The same materialized view can also be used to answer the following query, which asks for the total purchases made by women.

```
EXPLAIN PLAN FOR
SELECT c.occupation, SUM(f.purchase_price)
FROM purchases f, customer c
WHERE f.customer_id = c.customer_id
   AND c.gender = 'F'
GROUP BY c.occupation;
```

```
PLAN_TABLE_OUTPUT
-------------------------------------------------------------
|Id|Operation                        |Name                |Cost|
-------------------------------------------------------------
|  0|SELECT STATEMENT                 |                    |62  |
|  1|  SORT GROUP BY                  |                    |62  |
|  2|   MAT_VIEW REWRITE ACCESS FULL|CUSTOMER_PURCHASES_MV|53  |
-------------------------------------------------------------

Predicate Information (identified by operation id):
---------------------------------------------------
   2 - filter("CUSTOMER_PURCHASES_MV"."GENDER"='F')
```

Note that even though the materialized view does not contain aggregation, it can still be used to answer a query with aggregation.

All the query rewrites we have seen so far have not required any additional information from the user. However, to get the most out of query rewrite, you must inform query rewrite about relationships between data columns using constraints and dimensions.

9.2.7 Rewrite Using Dimensions

One of the powerful features of query rewrite is the ability for a single materialized view to be used to satisfy a wide range of queries. The Dimension object, discussed in Chapter 8, is extremely useful in this respect. By allowing you to declare relationships within columns of dimension tables, it provides query rewrite with information to roll up from a lower to a higher level of a hierarchy. For example, suppose your users want to know the sum of sales by day, month, or year. You could create three materialized views to answer these queries, or you could create one at the level of day and then define a dimension object that contains a hierarchy to show the relationship between time, month and year. Now, when the query asks for data at the month level, the materialized view at the daily level will be used to roll up the data to the monthly level.

Using the HIERARCHY Clause

Consider the following definition for a TIME dimension. The HIERARCHY clause tells query rewrite that the TIME_KEY rolls up into WEEK_NUMBER, which, in turns, rolls up into QUARTER. This means that if we knew the TIME_KEY value for some row in the TIME table, we know which week it belonged to. Similarly, if we knew the MONTH (say January 2004), we know which YEAR it belonged to: 2004.

```
CREATE DIMENSION time
  LEVEL time_key           is time.time_key
  LEVEL month              is time.month
  LEVEL quarter            is time.quarter
  LEVEL year               is time.year
  LEVEL week_number        is time.week_number
  HIERARCHY fiscal_rollup (
           time_key              CHILD OF
           week_number           CHILD OF
           quarter )
  HIERARCHY calendar_rollup(
           time_key              CHILD OF
           month                 CHILD OF
           year);
```

Suppose our materialized view MONTHLY_SALES_MV was defined to report the total sales by product and month, as shown in the following code. Note that we have **not** included the year column in the materialized view.

```
CREATE MATERIALIZED VIEW monthly_sales_mv
 ENABLE QUERY REWRITE
 AS
 SELECT t.month, p.product_id,
        SUM(ps.purchase_price) as sum_of_sales,
        COUNT (ps.purchase_price) as total_sales
 FROM time t, product p, purchases ps
 WHERE t.time_key = ps.time_key AND
       ps.product_id = p.product_id
 GROUP BY t.month, p.product_id;
```

In the following query, we want to know the total sales by product by year. Since we have a materialized view with the total sales by product by month, and months can be rolled up into years, as specified in the calendar_rollup hierarchy in the time dimension, the optimizer will rewrite the query to use the materialized view, MONTHLY_SALES_MV. Note that in order to determine the YEAR value for the MONTH, a join-back is done from the materialized view to the TIME table.

```
-- rollup to higher LEVEL in the HIERARCHY
EXPLAIN PLAN FOR
SELECT t.year, p.product_id,
       COUNT (ps.purchase_price) as total_sales
FROM time t, product p, purchases ps
WHERE t.time_key = ps.time_key AND
      ps.product_id = p.product_id
```

```
GROUP BY t.year, p.product_id;
PLAN_TABLE_OUTPUT
-----------------------------------------------------------------
|Id| Operation                     |Name            |Rows |Cost|
-----------------------------------------------------------------
|  0| SELECT STATEMENT              |                |    2|  11|
|  1|  SORT GROUP BY                |                |    2|  11|
| *2|   HASH JOIN                   |                | 4990|   9|
|  3|    VIEW                       |                |   34|   4|
|  4|     SORT UNIQUE               |                |   34|   4|
|  5|      TABLE ACCESS FULL        |TIME            |  731|   3|
|  6|      MAT_VIEW REWRITE ACCESS FULL|MONTHLY_SALES_MV| 3522|   4|
-----------------------------------------------------------------
```

Using the ATTRIBUTE Clause

When defining a data warehouse, the dimension object is often overlooked, because its value to query rewrite is not fully appreciated. However, a dimension object gives you tremendous query rewrite power at no extra cost. We have already seen how query rewrite can take advantage of the HIERARCHY clause to rewrite several queries with one materialized view. Query rewrite can also make use of the ATTRIBUTE clause of dimension. In the following example, we want to know the sum of sales by customer based on gender and occupation.

```
SELECT c.gender, c.occupation,
       SUM(ps.purchase_price) as sum_of_sales
FROM purchases ps,  customer c
WHERE c.customer_id = ps.customer_id
GROUP BY c.gender, c.occupation;
```

We could have put the columns GENDER and OCCUPATION into a materialized view. But we know that given the CUSTOMER_ID, we can find information such as the customer's name, gender, and occupation. Such relationships within a table that are not hierarchical in nature are defined by the ATTRIBUTE clause in a dimension.

Suppose we have the following dimension, which defines the relationships within the customer table.

```
CREATE DIMENSION customer_dim
  LEVEL customer IS customer.customer_id
  LEVEL city     IS customer.city
  LEVEL state    IS customer.state
HIERARCHY  customer_zone
  ( customer CHILD OF
```

```
      city      CHILD OF
      state )
ATTRIBUTE customer DETERMINES (customer.gender,
                                customer.occupation);
```

Now that we have this dimension object, we only need to include the CUSTOMER_ID in the materialized view.

```
CREATE MATERIALIZED VIEW cust_sales_mv
ENABLE QUERY REWRITE
AS
SELECT c.customer_id, SUM(ps.purchase_price) as sum_of_sales,
       COUNT (ps.purchase_price) as total_sales
FROM customer c, purchases ps
WHERE c.customer_id = ps.customer_id
GROUP BY c.customer_id;
```

The execution plan of the query shows that the query was rewritten to use the materialized view. Note that a join-back was done to the customer table to retrieve the values of the OCCUPATION and GENDER columns.

```
PLAN_TABLE_OUTPUT
-----------------------------------------------------------------
| Id|Operation                       |Name         |Rows  |Cost |
-----------------------------------------------------------------
|  0 |SELECT STATEMENT                |             |    9 |    7|
|  1 |  SORT GROUP BY                 |             |    9 |    7|
| *2 |   HASH JOIN                    |             |  500 |    6|
|  3 |    MAT_VIEW REWRITE ACCESS FULL|CUST_SALES_MV|  500 |    2|
|  4 |    TABLE ACCESS FULL           |CUSTOMER     |  500 |    3|
-----------------------------------------------------------------
```

When designing your data warehouse, you should try to identify relationships between your dimension tables and define dimensions, wherever possible. This will lead to significant space savings and increase query rewrite opportunities, thereby improving your query performance.

Recall that the relationships declared by dimensions are not validated automatically by Oracle. Hence, to take advantage of dimensions, you must set the QUERY_REWRITE_INTEGRITY parameter to TRUSTED or STALE_TOLERATED, as we will discuss shortly in section 9.3.

9.2.8 **Rewrite Using Constraints**

In a data warehouse, constraints may be used to define the join relationships between the fact and dimension tables. Typically, a primary-key constraint is defined on the unique key column on each dimension table. A foreign-key constraint and a NOT NULL constraint are defined on each corresponding key in the fact table. For example, The EASYDW schema has primary-key constraints on each of the dimension tables: CUSTOMER, PRODUCT, and TIME. Also, there are foreign key and NOT NULL constraints on the foreign-key columns of the PURCHASES table that join to these dimension tables.

The relationship defined by these constraints indicates to query rewrite that a join between the PURCHASES table and, for example, the TIME table will produce exactly one row for every row in the PURCHASES table. Rows from the PURCHASES table cannot be lost during the join, because the NOT NULL and foreign key constraints mean that there **must** be a parent TIME record for every row in the PURCHASES table. Also, because of the primary-key constraint on TIME, each row in PURCHASES will join to a single parent TIME record and so no rows can be duplicated. Such a join is known as a **loss-less join,** because no rows in the PURCHASES table will be lost or duplicated by the join process.

The benefit of a loss-less join is that if a materialized view has more joins than the query, but the *extra* joins in the materialized view are *loss-less* joins, then the query can be rewritten using the materialized view. For instance, in the following example, the query does not have the TIME table. However, we can still rewrite the query with the MONTHLY_SALES_MV materialized view (which has tables PURCHASES, PRODUCT, and TIME). This is because the extra join in the materialized view, between tables PURCHASES and TIME, is a loss-less join.

```
EXPLAIN PLAN FOR
SELECT  p.product_id, SUM(ps.purchase_price) as sum_of_sales
FROM  product p, purchases ps
WHERE ps.product_id = p.product_id
GROUP BY p.product_id;

PLAN_TABLE_OUTPUT
-------------------------------------------------------------------
|Id |Operation                        |Name            | Rows  |Cost|
-------------------------------------------------------------------
|  0|SELECT STATEMENT                 |                |   164 |   6|
|  1| SORT GROUP BY                   |                |   164 |   6|
|  2|  MAT_VIEW REWRITE ACCESS FULL|MONTHLY_SALES_MV|  3522 |   4|
-------------------------------------------------------------------
```

Using the NOVALIDATE and RELY Clauses on Constraints

As described in Chapter 2, when a constraint is enabled, you can choose to have Oracle validate the integrity of the data. If you are concerned about the overhead of maintaining the constraint, or if you have already validated the data during the ETL process, you could use the NOVALIDATE clause to tell Oracle that the data has already been validated.

```
ALTER TABLE purchases ENABLE NOVALIDATE CONSTRAINT fk_customer_id;
```

An additional RELY clause should be used to tell Oracle that it can rely on the constraint being correct and can use it in query rewrite even when the constraint has not been validated. It allows the Database Administrator (DBA) to say: "Trust me. I've already checked the data validity. Query rewrite can rely on the relationship being correct."

```
ALTER TABLE purchases MODIFY CONSTRAINT fk_customer_id RELY;
```

Hint: Use constraints to define the relationship between your fact and dimension tables. Use the dimension object to declare the relationships within your dimension tables, such as a time or a region hierarchy.

As with dimensions, in order to use RELY constraints, you must set the QUERY_REWRITE_INTEGRITY parameter to TRUSTED. The next section explains this parameter in detail.

9.3   Query Rewrite Integrity Modes

We have mentioned the QUERY_REWRITE_INTEGRITY parameter several times in our examples. This parameter indicates to Oracle the extent to which the rewritten queries must reflect the data in the detail tables and what metadata can be used to rewrite queries. This parameter can take three values:

- **ENFORCED**: In this mode (which is the default), Oracle will guarantee that the rewritten query will return the same results as the original query when executed without query rewrite.

- **TRUSTED**: In this mode, Oracle will use data and relationships that have been "blessed" by the DBA—namely, dimension objects, RELY constraints, and materialized views created from PREBUILT tables. Oracle does not validate that the relationships declared by the dimension are indeed valid in the data or that a prebuilt table is the same as the materialized view's query.

- **STALE_TOLERATED**: In this mode, Oracle will use stale materialized views, which may not contain the very latest data, because they have not yet been refreshed. This is appropriate if the business users do not need to have the most up-to-date data in order to perform their analyses.

You must decide what query rewrite integrity level is appropriate for your application. In the following sections, we will discuss the differences between the three modes and the motivation behind using one versus the other.

9.3.1 Comparing ENFORCED and TRUSTED Modes

Setting the parameter to ENFORCED guarantees that you will see the same results from using the materialized view or querying the detail tables. You are probably thinking that this is the best mode to use! However, the problem is that this mode also requires that all defined relationships, such as constraints, be validated. This can be a huge overhead in a data warehouse. Another issue with the ENFORCED mode is that dimension objects are not used. This greatly limits the power of query rewrite, and you may need a large number of materialized views to answer all your queries. For example, the query rewrites with dimensions shown in section 9.2.7 will never occur in ENFORCED mode. Also, you cannot use materialized views defined using the PREBUILT TABLE clause, unless they have been completely rebuilt.

Unlike ENFORCED mode, in TRUSTED mode constraints are used even though they are not validated, provided they have the RELY clause and dimensions are also considered. Therefore, in a warehouse you will more likely use the TRUSTED mode.

A note of caution: Query rewrite in TRUSTED mode depends on the integrity of your dimension and constraint definitions. Does each product in the product table roll up to one and only one category, as specified in your dimension definition? Does each product in the PURCHASES table have a corresponding product_id in the products table, as specified by your referential integrity constraints? If your data does not reflect the relationships defined by the constraint or dimension, then you may get unexpected results. The same holds for materialized views on prebuilt tables: If the prebuilt table does not reflect the materialized view's query accurately, then results can be unexpected.

The last mode is STALE_TOLERATED, and it is even more relaxed than the TRUSTED mode, as discussed in the next section

9.3.2   Comparing TRUSTED and STALE_TOLERATED Modes

The STALE_TOLERATED mode also allows use of trusted relationships like the TRUSTED mode. However, the key difference with the STALE_TOLERATED mode is that it allows use of materialized views even if they are stale. In both TRUSTED and ENFORCED modes, the optimizer will use the detail table if necessary but will never return stale data.

Hint: You can determine if a materialized view is FRESH or STALE by using the STALENESS column of the catalog view USER_MVIEWS.

Most of the time, you would like to get the result the fastest way possible, rewriting your queries to use materialized views. However, if your materialized views have become stale and no longer represent the summarization of all your detail data, depending on your application, you may prefer to get the results from the detail tables until you can perform your next refresh. If so, then the TRUSTED mode is the right choice.

On the other hand, if the results obtained from a materialized view are "close enough" for your application, you may want to use the materialized view even if it is stale. For example, to determine the month-over-month growth rate of on-line sales, you do not need every single sales transaction in the materialized view. As long as the data is reasonably recent, you could still get an answer that was close enough. Or, if the application knew that the missing data was beyond the scope of the query, it may still want to use the materialized view. For instance, if the missing data is for the last month but your query does not need it, you can use the materialized view. Or, it may be appropriate to use the materialized view when the fact table is stale, but not when a dimension is updated. The decision to use stale data or not should be made after consulting business users who would be using the data for analysis.

If you would like the optimizer to use the materialized view even if it is stale, set the QUERY_REWRITE_INTEGRITY parameter to STALE_TOLERATED.

Hint: When first testing a materialized view to see if query rewrite will occur, set QUERY_REWRITE_INTEGRITY to STALE_TOLERATED, because if the query does not rewrite in this mode, it will not rewrite in any other mode. Once you know it works, you can try setting the parameter mode to your desired level.

The following example shows the difference between the two integrity modes STALE_TOLERATED and TRUSTED (or ENFORCED) with regard to stale data. Suppose we introduced a new product code, SP1300 and inserted two new rows into the purchases fact table corresponding to it.

```
INSERT INTO product VALUES ('SP1300', 'XYZ', 'ELEC', '75.0',
                            '100.0', 15, 4.50, 'ABC', 'UVW');
COMMIT;

INSERT INTO purchases VALUES ('SP1300','1-FEB-2003',
        'AB123456','1-FEB-2003', 28.01, 4.50, 'Y');

INSERT INTO purchases VALUES ('SP1300','2-FEB-2003',
        'AB123457','1-FEB-2003', 28.01, 4.50, 'Y');
COMMIT;
```

The MONTHLY_SALES_MV materialized view is now stale, which means all the data in the detail table is not reflected in the materialized view.

```
SELECT staleness FROM user_mviews
WHERE mview_name = 'MONTHLY_SALES_MV';

STALENESS
---------
STALE
```

Suppose we had the following query, which requests sales by month for product SP1300. If you set QUERY_REWRITE_INTEGRITY to STALE_TOLERATED, then we see that no rows are returned in the result. This is because the materialized view was created before the new rows were inserted and so the data about SP1300 is not in the materialized view.

```
ALTER SESSION SET QUERY_REWRITE_INTEGRITY=STALE_TOLERATED;

SELECT t.month, p.product_id,
       SUM(ps.purchase_price) as sum_of_sales,
       COUNT(ps.purchase_price) as total_sales
FROM time t, product p, purchases ps
WHERE t.time_key = ps.time_key AND
      ps.product_id = p.product_id
GROUP BY t.month, p.product_id
HAVING p.product_id = 'SP1300';

no rows selected
```

The execution plan shows that the materialized view was indeed used for this query.

```
PLAN_TABLE_OUTPUT
-------------------------------------------------------------------
|Id|Operation                    | Name             | Rows  |Cost|
-------------------------------------------------------------------
|0 | SELECT STATEMENT            |                  |   21  |  4|
|1 |   MAT_VIEW REWRITE ACCESS FULL| MONTHLY_SALES_MV |   21  |  4|
-------------------------------------------------------------------
```

On the other hand, if you set the QUERY_REWRITE_INTEGRITY to TRUSTED, Oracle will use the detail tables, PURCHASES, PRODUCT, and TIME, rather than the materialized view and the sales numbers include the new rows we just inserted.

```
ALTER SESSION SET QUERY_REWRITE_INTEGRITY=TRUSTED;

SELECT t.month, p.product_id,
       SUM(ps.purchase_price) as sum_of_sales,
       COUNT(ps.purchase_price) as total_sales
FROM time t, product p, purchases ps
WHERE t.time_key = ps.time_key AND
      ps.product_id = p.product_id
GROUP BY t.month, p.product_id
HAVING p.product_id = 'SP1300';

    MONTH PRODUCT_  SUM_OF_SALES TOTAL_SALES
---------- -------- ------------ -----------
    200302 SP1300          56.02           2
```

The execution plan indicates that the materialized view was **not** used for this query.

```
PLAN_TABLE_OUTPUT
-------------------------------------------------------------------
|Id|Operation             |Name             | Rows  |Cost |
-------------------------------------------------------------------
|0 |SELECT STATEMENT      |                 |     1 |  143|
|1 | FILTER               |                 |       |     |
|2 |  SORT GROUP BY       |                 |     1 |  143|
|3 |   HASH JOIN          |                 | 81169 |  121|
|4 |    TABLE ACCESS FULL |TIME             |   731 |    3|
|5 |    HASH JOIN         |                 | 81169 |  115|
|6 |     INDEX FULL SCAN  |PRODUCT_PK_INDEX |   164 |    1|
|7 |     PARTITION RANGE ALL|               | 81169 |  111|
|8 |      TABLE ACCESS FULL|PURCHASES       | 81169 |  111|
-------------------------------------------------------------------
```

To summarize, in a data warehouse it is recommended to use either TRUSTED or STALE_TOLERATED modes. Use the TRUSTED mode if your applications require up-to-date data at all times. If you can tolerate a materialized view that does not contain all the latest data, use the STALE_TOLERATED mode instead, to get the most benefit. Note that when using either of these modes, you must ensure that all the data satisfies the relationships declared in the RELY constraints and dimensions; otherwise, you may get unexpected results.

9.4   **Query Rewrite and Partition Change Tracking**

In Chapter 7, we discussed the Partition Change Tracking (PCT) feature, which allows materialized views to be fast refreshed after partition maintenance operations. PCT also increases the query rewrite capabilities of the materialized view. As discussed in the previous section, when a detail table is updated, the materialized view becomes stale and cannot be used by query rewrite in ENFORCED or TRUSTED integrity levels. However, if the detail table is partitioned and the materialized view supports PCT on that table, Oracle can determine which portion of the materialized view is fresh and which is not. Now, if a query can be answered by using only the fresh portion of the materialized view, query rewrite will use the materialized view. For example, in Figure 7.7, in Chapter 7, the data for Feb 2002 was updated, and a new partition with data for Apr 2002 was added. The fresh portion of the materialized view corresponds to the Jan 2002 and Mar 2002 data. If a query only required data for these partitions, the materialized view can be used. The materialized view cannot be used for Feb 2002 (updated partition) or Apr 2002 (new partition).

Query rewrite is supported when PCT is enabled using either the partition key or partition marker techniques described in Chapter 7. Query rewrite currently does not take advantage of PCT using the join dependency technique.

9.4.1   Query Rewrite with PCT Using Partition Key

Consider the following materialized view containing sales data for products. The PURCHASES table is partitioned by TIME_KEY, which is included in the materialized view.

```
CREATE MATERIALIZED VIEW product_category_sales_mv
 ENABLE QUERY REWRITE
 AS
 SELECT ps.time_key, p.category,
        SUM(ps.purchase_price) as sum_of_sales
 FROM   product p, purchases ps
 WHERE ps.product_id = p.product_id
 GROUP BY ps.time_key, p.category;
```

If we query the view USER_MVIEWS, we will see that the materialized view is FRESH.

```
SELECT staleness FROM user_mviews
WHERE mview_name = 'PRODUCT_CATEGORY_SALES_MV';


STALENESS
----------
FRESH
```

The PURCHASES table has data through Dec 2004, so the materialized view only contains data through Dec 2004. Now, suppose we added a new partition to the PURCHASES table and loaded data for Jan 2005.

```
ALTER TABLE purchases ADD PARTITION purchases_jan2005
        values less than (TO_DATE('01-02-2005', 'DD-MM-YYYY'));

INSERT INTO purchases VALUES ( 'SP1063','2-JAN-2005',
        'AB123457','7-JAN-2005', 28.01, 4.50, 'N');

INSERT INTO purchases VALUES ( 'SP1064','2-JAN-2005',
        'AB123457','8-JAN-2005', 28.01, 4.50, 'N');

COMMIT;
```

If we query the view user_mviews now, we will see that the materialized view is STALE.

```
SELECT staleness FROM user_mviews
WHERE mview_name = 'PRODUCT_CATEGORY_SALES_MV';

STALENESS
----------
STALE
```

Now consider the following query, which asks for the sum of sales for the last quarter of 2004: October through December 2004. The optimizer will determine that the query only needs to access partitions for Oct, Nov, and Dec 2004 of the PURCHASES table. Since the materialized view is enabled for partition change tracking for this table, Oracle will track that the materialized view is fresh with respect to these partitions. Hence, it can rewrite with the materialized view, as shown in the following execution plan.

```
EXPLAIN PLAN FOR
SELECT ps.time_key, p.category,
       SUM(ps.purchase_price) as sum_of_sales
FROM   product p, purchases ps
WHERE  ps.product_id = p.product_id and
       ps.time_key  BETWEEN TO_DATE('01-10-2004', 'DD-MM-YYYY')
                       AND TO_DATE('31-12-2004', 'DD-MM-YYYY')
GROUP BY ps.time_key, p.category;


PLAN_TABLE_OUTPUT
-----------------------------------------------------------------
|Id |Operation                      |Name                     |Cost|
-----------------------------------------------------------------
|  0|SELECT STATEMENT               |                         |  3|
|  1| MAT_VIEW REWRITE ACCESS FULL|PRODUCT_CATEGORY_SALES_MV|  3|
-----------------------------------------------------------------

Predicate Information (identified by operation id):
---------------------------------------------------
1 - filter("PRODUCT_CATEGORY_SALES_MV"."TIME_KEY">=
        TO_DATE('2004-10-01 00:00:00','yyyy-mm-ddhh24:mi:ss')
        AND "PRODUCT_CATEGORY_SALES_MV"."TIME_KEY"<=
        TO_DATE('2004-12-31 00:00:00','yyyy-mm-dd hh24:mi:ss'))
```

On the other hand, a query that requests the sum of sales for Oct 2004 through Mar 2005 cannot be answered using the materialized view.

9.4.2 Query Rewrite Using PCT with Partition Marker

Query rewrite can also take advantage of partition change tracking using the partition marker. The following query illustrates how rewrite can be used if the PRODUCT_CATEGORY_SALES_MV had a partition marker for the PURCHASES table instead of the partition key (TIME_KEY).

```
CREATE MATERIALIZED VIEW product_category_sales_mv
ENABLE QUERY REWRITE
AS
SELECT DBMS_MVIEW.PMARKER(ps.rowid) pmarker, p.category,
       SUM(ps.purchase_price) as sum_of_sales
FROM  product p, purchases ps
WHERE ps.product_id = p.product_id
GROUP BY DBMS_MVIEW.PMARKER(ps.rowid), p.category;
```

The following query asks for data for the last quarter of 2004. Note that for rewrite to work, the bounds specified by the filter condition must match exactly with partition boundaries.

```
EXPLAIN PLAN FOR
SELECT p.category,
       SUM(ps.purchase_price) as sum_of_sales
FROM  product p, purchases ps
WHERE ps.product_id = p.product_id and
      ps.time_key  >= TO_DATE('01-10-2004', 'DD-MM-YYYY')
  AND ps.time_key  < TO_DATE('01-01-2005', 'DD-MM-YYYY')
GROUP BY p.category;

PLAN_TABLE_OUTPUT
-------------------------------------------------------------------
|Id|Operation                     |Name                     |Cost |
-------------------------------------------------------------------
| 0|SELECT STATEMENT              |                         |   3|
| 1| SORT GROUP BY                |                         |   3|
|*2|  MAT_VIEW REWRITE ACCESS FULL|PRODUCT_CATEGORY_SALES_MV|   2|
-------------------------------------------------------------------

Predicate Information (identified by operation id):
---------------------------------------------------
   2 - filter("PRODUCT_CATEGORY_SALES_MV"."PMARKER"=52520 OR
             "PRODUCT_CATEGORY_SALES_MV"."PMARKER"=52521 OR
             "PRODUCT_CATEGORY_SALES_MV"."PMARKER"=52522)
```

As we can see, partition change tracking is a very useful technique—not only to speed up refresh of your materialized views but also to improve the ability of the optimizer to rewrite queries with those materialized views.

Oracle query rewrite is a very powerful feature but with this power comes some complexity. The next section explains how you can identify and fix common problems in query rewrite.

9.5 Troubleshooting Query Rewrite with EXPLAIN_REWRITE

In the examples in this chapter, we have used EXPLAIN PLAN to see if a query was rewritten to use a materialized view. However, sometimes you may find that the query did not rewrite with the materialized view as you had expected. In some cases, the reason is extremely trivial, such as the parameter QUERY_REWRITE_ENABLED not being set to TRUE. In other cases, the reason could be more subtle, such as a constraint that was not present or validated or some column required by the query not being present in the materialized view. The rules governing query rewrite can be extremely complex and the reasons for not using a materialized view may not be obvious. To diagnose the reasons for such missed rewrites, you should use the PL/SQL procedure DBMS_MVIEW.EXPLAIN_REWRITE.

To use EXPLAIN_REWRITE, you provide the query and, optionally, the materialized view it is supposed to rewrite with. The procedure will tell you if the query will use that materialized view and, if not, then the reason for not doing the rewrite. Prior to using the procedure, you must create a table named REWRITE_TABLE in your schema, using the script utlxrw.sql in the rdbms/admin directory. The results of EXPLAIN_REWRITE are placed in this table. There is also a varray interface, which allows you to access the results through a PL/SQL program instead.

We will now illustrate how to use this utility. In the first example, the user forgot to set the QUERY_REWRITE_ENABLED parameter to TRUE. To diagnose the problem you issue EXPLAIN_REWRITE and select the results from the REWRITE_TABLE. The message column in the REWRITE_TABLE indicates the reason why query rewrite did not happen with the materialized view, specified in the MV_NAME column.

```
BEGIN
dbms_mview.explain_rewrite('
SELECT t.month, t.year, p.product_id,
       SUM (ps.purchase_price) as sum_of_sales,
       COUNT (ps.purchase_price) as total_sales
 FROM time t, product p, purchases ps
 WHERE t.time_key = ps.time_key AND
 ps.product_id = p.product_id
 GROUP BY t.month, t.year, p.product_id', 'MONTHLY_SALES_MV');
END;
/

SELECT mv_name, message FROM rewrite_table;

MV_NAME                        MESSAGE
------------------------        ------------------------------------
MONTHLY_SALES_MV               QSM-01001: query rewrite not enabled
```

EXPLAIN_REWRITE can be used to check why a specific materialized view was not used to rewrite the query. For example, consider the following query, which is asking for the total sales by quarter, which is not possible to compute using the MONTHLY_SALES_MV because the QUARTER column is not in the materialized view.

```
BEGIN
dbms_mview.explain_rewrite('
SELECT p.product_id, t.quarter,
       SUM (ps.purchase_price) as sum_of_sales,
       COUNT(ps.purchase_price) as total_sales
 FROM  product p, purchases ps, time t
 WHERE p.product_id = ps.product_id
   AND t.time_key = ps.time_key
 GROUP BY p.product_id, t.quarter', 'MONTHLY_SALES_MV');
END;
/

SELECT mv_name, message FROM rewrite_table;

MV_NAME                        MESSAGE
----------------------         ------------------------------------
MONTHLY_SALES_MV               QSM-01082: Joining materialized
                               view, MONTHLY_SALES_MV, with
                               table, TIME, not possible

MONTHLY_SALES_MV               QSM-01102: materialized view,
                               MONTHLY_SALES_MV, requires join
                               back to table, TIME, on column,
                               QUARTER
```

The EXPLAIN_REWRITE output clearly indicates that it is not possible to do the rewrite because of the missing quarter column.

Sometimes query rewrite may be possible with the requested materialized view; however, there may be a more optimal materialized view that can be used. Suppose we create a materialized view, PRODUCT_SALES_EXACT_MATCH, for the following query, matching its text exactly. Query rewrite now uses this materialized view instead, since it is more optimal. EXPLAIN_REWRITE will tell you that this is the case.

```
BEGIN
dbms_mview.explain_rewrite('
SELECT p.product_id,
       SUM(ps.purchase_price) as sum_of_sales,
       COUNT(ps.purchase_price) as total_sales
 FROM  product p, purchases ps, time t
 WHERE p.product_id = ps.product_id
   AND t.time_key = ps.time_key
 GROUP BY p.product_id', 'MONTHLY_SALES_MV');
END;
/

SELECT mv_name, message FROM rewrite_table;

MV_NAME                          MESSAGE
-------------------------        ------------------------------------
MONTHLY_SALES_MV                 QSM-01009: materialized view,
                                 PRODUCT_SALES_EXACT_MATCH, matched
                                 query text
```

EXPLAIN_REWRITE can also be used with very large queries by declaring them using a character large object (CLOB) data type.

9.6 Advanced Query Rewrite Techniques

In the preceding sections, we have discussed the most commonly used types of query rewrites. In this section, we will discuss some advanced topics in query rewrite. If you are just getting familiar with query rewrite, the preceding sections may be enough to get you started and you can come back to the remainder of this chapter as you get more familiar with using it.

9.6.1 Optimizer Hints for Query Rewrite

Ordinarily, the query optimizer will automatically decide whether or not to rewrite a query, and if there are several materialized views that are eligible to rewrite the query, it will pick the best one. You can, however, influence this behavior using the following optimizer hints:

- **REWRITE(mv)** hint request the optimizer to use a specific materialized view.

- **NO_REWRITE** hint to not use query rewrite for the query.

- **REWRITE_OR_ERROR** to throw an error when it is not possible to rewrite.

For instance, suppose we had two eligible materialized views: MONTHLY_SALES_MV, which computes sum of sales by month, and YEARLY_SALES_MV, which computes the sum of sales by year. If we wanted to know the sum of sales by year, as shown in the following query, you would expect query rewrite to pick the latter, since it would read less data.

```
SELECT t.year, p.product_id, SUM(ps.purchase_price) sum_of_sales
FROM time t, product p, purchases ps
WHERE t.time_key = ps.time_key AND
      ps.product_id = p.product_id
GROUP BY t.year, p.product_id;

PLAN_TABLE_OUTPUT
```

Id	Operation	Name	Rows	Cost
0	SELECT STATEMENT		329	2
1	MAT_VIEW REWRITE ACCESS FULL	YEARLY_SALES_MV	329	2

You could, however force query rewrite to use MONTHLY_SALES_MV with a hint.

```
SELECT /*+ REWRITE(monthly_sales_mv) */ t.year, p.product_id,
       SUM(ps.purchase_price) as sum_of_sales
FROM time t, product p, purchases ps
WHERE t.time_key = ps.time_key AND
      ps.product_id = p.product_id
GROUP BY t.year, p.product_id;
```

Id	Operation	Name	Rows	Cost
0	SELECT STATEMENT		2	11
1	SORT GROUP BY		2	11

```
|*2|    HASH JOIN                    |           |  4990|   9|
| 3|      VIEW                       |           |    34|   4|
| 4|        SORT UNIQUE              |           |    34|   4|
| 5|          TABLE ACCESS FULL      |TIME       |   731|   3|
| 6|      MAT_VIEW REWRITE ACCESS FULL|MONTHLY_SALES_MV| 3522|   4|
------------------------------------------------------------------
```

Forcing an Error When Query Rewrite Is Not Possible

For some applications, query rewrite is critical to achieve good performance; it is preferable for a query to fail rather than execute against the detail data, because it may take too long to complete. In Oracle Database 10g, you can specify the REWRITE_OR_ERROR hint to force the query to fail if query rewrite is not possible. In the following example, the query asking for the sum of sales by day cannot rewrite against the available monthly or yearly summaries and hence will fail.

```
SELECT /*+ REWRITE_OR_ERROR */ t.time_key,
       SUM(ps.purchase_price) as sum_of_sales
FROM time t, product p, purchases ps
WHERE t.time_key = ps.time_key AND
      ps.product_id = p.product_id
GROUP BY t.time_key, p.product_id;

ORA-30393: a query block in the statement did not rewrite
```

9.6.2 Query Rewrite and Bind Variables

You may use bind variables in your queries to allow the query plan to be shared by multiple invocations of the query. However, in certain cases, use of bind variables can prohibit query rewrite. First of all, when the optimizer makes its decisions to rewrite a query, the bind variable values are generally not available. Further, the bind values can change for subsequent executions, without again going through the query rewrite process. Therefore, if the value of the bind variable could influence the correctness of query rewrite, then the query will not be rewritten.

For example, consider the following query, which asks for total sales for a specific product by month. This query has a bind variable on PRODUCT_ID. Now, if we had a materialized view with all product values, such as MONTHLY_SALES_MV defined earlier, the optimizer could safely use query rewrite for this query, regardless of the actual value of the bind variable, as shown in the execution plan.

```
EXPLAIN PLAN FOR
SELECT t.month, p.product_id,
        SUM(ps.purchase_price) as sum_of_sales,
        COUNT (ps.purchase_price) as total_sales
 FROM time t, product p, purchases ps
 WHERE t.time_key = ps.time_key AND
        ps.product_id = p.product_id AND
        p.product_id = :1
 GROUP BY t.month, p.product_id;


PLAN_TABLE_OUTPUT
---------------------------------------------------------------
|Id|Operation                        |Name            |Rows |Cost|
---------------------------------------------------------------
| 0|SELECT STATEMENT                 |                |  35|   4|
| 1| MAT_VIEW REWRITE ACCESS FULL|MONTHLY_SALES_MV|  35|   4|
---------------------------------------------------------------


Predicate Information (identified by operation id):
-----------------------------------------------
    1 - filter("MONTHLY_SALES_MV"."PRODUCT_ID"=:1)
```

However, recall the materialized view SALES_ELEC_1_6_2003_MV, defined earlier in section 9.2.5, which only has data for the ELEC category for the months January through June 2003. Suppose we had the following query instead; with a bind variable for the CATEGORY value, the optimizer cannot safely determine if your query can be answered using the materialized view. For example, if the bind variable :1 had the value MUSC, then the materialized view would not contain the data and query rewrite is not possible. However, if the value were ELEC, query rewrite would be possible. Because the actual value of the bind variable is not available when the decision to rewrite the query is made, the optimizer is unable to use the materialized view, as indicated by the execution plan output.

```
EXPLAIN PLAN FOR
SELECT t.month, t.year, p.product_id,
        SUM(ps.purchase_price) as sum_of_sales,
        COUNT (ps.purchase_price) as total_sales
 FROM time t, product p, purchases ps
 WHERE t.time_key = ps.time_key AND
        ps.product_id = p.product_id AND
        p.category = :1 AND
        t.month >= 200301 and t.month <= 200306
 GROUP BY t.month, t.year, p.product_id;
```

```
PLAN_TABLE_OUTPUT
---------------------------------------------------------------
| Id  | Operation                  | Name      | Rows  |Cost |
---------------------------------------------------------------
|   0 | SELECT STATEMENT           |           |  6628 |  207|
|   1 |  SORT GROUP BY             |           |  6628 |  207|
|*  2 |   HASH JOIN                |           |  6628 |  122|
|*  3 |    TABLE ACCESS FULL       | PRODUCT   |    55 |    2|
|*  4 |    HASH JOIN               |           | 20004 |  119|
|*  5 |     TABLE ACCESS FULL      | TIME      |   181 |    3|
|   6 |     PARTITION RANGE ITERATOR|          | 80790 |  113|
|   7 |      TABLE ACCESS FULL     | PURCHASES | 80790 |  113|
---------------------------------------------------------------
```

Instead of bind variables, if the previous query had literal values, such as ELEC, Oracle may internally replace these values with bind variables known as **internal bind variables**. This allows queries differing only in these literal values to reuse or share compiled execution plans. This reuse of execution plans is called **cursor sharing** in Oracle. (To enable this feature the initialization parameter CURSOR_SHARING must be set to a value other than EXACT.) Just as with user-specified bind variables, the decision to rewrite the query may depend on the value of the internal bind variable. The difference here is that unlike user-specified bind variables, Oracle knows the values of internal bind variables at the time of query rewrite and so the query will be rewritten as expected. However, because the query plan now depends on the value of the literal, you may not see the expected amount of cursor sharing you may have otherwise seen.

To summarize, if your application would like to use query rewrite, you must carefully design the use of bind variables in your queries, otherwise you may not be able to take full advantage of query rewrite.

9.6.3 Query Rewrite with Complex SQL Constructs

The examples discussed so far used the more common constructs in SQL, such as joins, selections, and aggregation operators. However, query rewrite can also work in the presence of complex SQL expressions, including set operators, subqueries in the FROM clause, analytical functions, and GROUPING SETS.

Set Operators

A set operator is a SQL operation such as UNION ALL, UNION, MINUS, and INTERSECT. If a query has multiple subqueries, such as in a UNION ALL, the optimizer will try to rewrite each branch of the UNION

ALL individually using a simple materialized view. In addition, Oracle Database 10*g* supports query rewrite using a materialized view with the set operators. If the query has a UNION ALL, then query rewrite will try to match each branch in the query with appropriate branches in the materialized view. This is best illustrated with an example.

The following materialized view has a UNION ALL with two branches. Each branch also has a special column known as a **subselect marker**, which is required by query rewrite to identify rows for each branch. The marker can be any constant column (numeric or string) with a distinct value for each branch of the UNION ALL operation. In this example, the marker column has been aliased as *um*.

```
CREATE MATERIALIZED VIEW muscelec_mv
ENABLE QUERY REWRITE
AS
SELECT 'M' um, p.product_id, p.manufacturer,
       SUM(ps.purchase_price)
FROM purchases ps, product p
WHERE ps.product_id = p.product_id AND p.category = 'MUSC'
GROUP BY p.product_id, p.manufacturer
UNION ALL
SELECT 'E' um, p.product_id, p.manufacturer,
      SUM(ps.purchase_price)
FROM purchases ps, product p
WHERE ps.product_id = p.product_id AND p.category = 'ELEC'
GROUP BY p.product_id, p.manufacturer;
```

The following query can now be rewritten with this materialized view. Note that the order of the branches for ELEC and MUSC in the query has been reversed and one of the branches has an additional selection.

```
EXPLAIN PLAN FOR
SELECT p.product_id, SUM(ps.purchase_price)
FROM purchases ps, product p
WHERE ps.product_id = p.product_id AND p.category = 'ELEC'
GROUP BY p.product_id
UNION ALL
SELECT  p.product_id, SUM(ps.purchase_price)
FROM purchases ps, product p
WHERE ps.product_id = p.product_id AND p.category = 'MUSC' AND
      p.manufacturer = 'ABC'
GROUP BY p.product_id;
```

```
PLAN_TABLE_OUTPUT
----------------------------------------------------------------
| Id  | Operation                 | Name        | Rows  |Cost |
----------------------------------------------------------------
|   0 | SELECT STATEMENT          |             |  112  |   4|
|   1 |  UNION-ALL                |             |       |    |
|*  2 |   MAT_VIEW REWRITE ACCESS FULL| MUSCELEC_MV |  111  |   2|
|*  3 |   MAT_VIEW REWRITE ACCESS FULL| MUSCELEC_MV |    1  |   2|
----------------------------------------------------------------
```

Unlike UNION ALL, other set operators, UNION, MINUS, and INTERSECT, are not commutative (cannot be reordered) and do not preserve duplicates in the query. So for a query to be rewritten, it must match the materialized view exactly.

Subqueries in the FROM Clause

Applications often need to use subqueries in the FROM clause due to security reasons (e.g., they do not want to expose table names) or because the query is dynamically generated by a tool. If a query has sub-queries in the FROM clause, the optimizer can replace subqueries with the underlying tables and then query rewrite can take place as usual. In addition, in Oracle Database 10*g*, query rewrite will look for materialized views that have the identical subquery in the FROM clause (i.e., the text of the subquery in the query and materialized view match exactly). If any such matching materialized views are found, all the normal rules of query rewrite will then be checked. The subquery can be arbitrarily complex.

For example, suppose we have a materialized view, as follows, that contains the total sales by category for the manufacturer ABC:

```
CREATE MATERIALIZED VIEW prodcat_sales_mv
 ENABLE QUERY REWRITE
 AS
 SELECT v.category, SUM(ps.purchase_price) as sum_of_sales
 FROM   (SELECT * FROM product p
 WHERE p.manufacturer = 'ABC') v, purchases ps
 WHERE ps.product_id = v.product_id
 GROUP BY v.category;
```

Now, the following query, which is asking for the total sales for the ELEC category for the manufacturer ABC, can be rewritten to use this materialized view.

```
EXPLAIN PLAN FOR
SELECT v.category, SUM(ps.purchase_price) as sum_of_sales
 FROM  (SELECT * FROM product p
 WHERE p.manufacturer = 'ABC') v, purchases ps
 WHERE ps.product_id = v.product_id and v.category = 'ELEC'
 GROUP BY v.category;


PLAN_TABLE_OUTPUT
---------------------------------------------------------------
|Id|Operation                     |Name           |Rows |Cost|
---------------------------------------------------------------
| 0|SELECT STATEMENT              |               |   1|   2|
| 1| MAT_VIEW REWRITE ACCESS FULL|PRODCAT_SALES_MV|   1|   2|
---------------------------------------------------------------
```

Multiple Occurrences of a Table in the FROM Clause

Occasionally, queries may need to include the same table multiple times in the FROM clause. For instance, in the following query, we are finding the total monthly sales for orders that took at most one week to ship. We are using two date columns from the PURCHASES table: TIME_KEY and SHIP_DATE. So in order to determine any auxiliary information for that date, such as WEEK_NUMBER, MONTH, from the TIME dimension table, you will need to join with TIME separately for each of these columns.

```
EXPLAIN PLAN FOR
SELECT ot.month, SUM(ps.purchase_price) as sum_of_sales
FROM  purchases ps, time ot, time st
WHERE ps.time_key = ot.time_key AND ps.ship_date = st.time_key
  AND st.week_number ñ ot.week_number <= 1
GROUP BY ot.month;
```

In Oracle Database 10*g*, query rewrite can automatically analyze the joins in the query and correctly match multiple instances of tables with their corresponding instances in a materialized view. So the preceding query can rewrite with the following materialized view (we have deliberately changed table aliases to rule out any simple text match rewrite).

```
CREATE MATERIALIZED VIEW sameweek_sales_mv
ENABLE QUERY REWRITE
AS
SELECT od.month ord_mon, sd.month ship_mon,
       od.week_number ord_week, sd.week_number ship_week,
       SUM(ps.purchase_price) as sum_of_sales
FROM  purchases ps, time od, time sd
```

```
WHERE ps.time_key = od.time_key AND ps.ship_date = sd.time_key
GROUP BY od.month, sd.month, sd.week_number, od.week_number;
```

The following execution plan shows the query rewritten:

```
PLAN_TABLE_OUTPUT
----------------------------------------------------------------
| Id  | Operation                          | Name              |Cost|
----------------------------------------------------------------
|   0 | SELECT STATEMENT                   |                   |  3|
|   1 |  SORT GROUP BY                     |                   |  3|
|*  2 |   MAT_VIEW REWRITE ACCESS FULL|    | SAMEWEEK_SALES_MV |  2|
----------------------------------------------------------------

Predicate Information (identified by operation id):
----------------------------------------------------------------
  2 - filter("SAMEWEEK_SALES_MV"."SHIP_WEEK"-
             "SAMEWEEK_SALES_MV"."ORD_WEEK"<=1)
```

So for all practical purposes, query rewrite will work as if the multiple occurrences were different tables.

Grouping Sets

The SQL aggregation operators, CUBE, ROLLUP, and GROUPING SETS, described in Chapter 6, provide a mechanism to compute multiple levels of aggregation in a single query. You can create a materialized view using a query with these operators to store multiple levels of aggregation, instead of separate materialized views for each level. Query rewrite can be used to rewrite a query that asks for any of these levels of aggregation.

The following example shows a materialized view with grouping sets that computes the sum of sales for the 3 groupings: (category, time_key), (category, time_key, state), and (time_key, country). Note that the materialized view must have a GROUPING_ID or GROUPING function on the group by columns to distinguish rows that correspond to different groupings.

```
CREATE MATERIALIZED VIEW sales_mv
ENABLE QUERY REWRITE
AS
SELECT p.category,  t.time_key, c.country, c.state,
       SUM(f.purchase_price) sales,
       GROUPING_ID(p.category, t.time_key, c.country, c.state) gid
FROM product p, purchases f,  time t, customer c
WHERE p.product_id = f.product_id AND
      t.time_key = f.time_key AND
```

```
            c.customer_id = f.customer_id
GROUP BY GROUPING SETS ((p.category, t.time_key),
                        (p.category, t.time_key, c.state),
                        (t.time_key, c.country));
```

This materialized view can be used to rewrite a query that asks for any grouping that is present in the materialized view or one that can be derived using a rollup. For example, the following query, which asks for total sales by category and time_key, can be rewritten to use the SALES_MV materialized view.

```
EXPLAIN PLAN FOR
SELECT p.category, t.time_key, SUM(f.purchase_price) sales
FROM product p, purchases f, time t, customer c
WHERE p.product_id = f.product_id AND
      t.time_key = f.time_key AND
      c.customer_id = f.customer_id
GROUP BY p.category, t.time_key;
```

From the predicate information in the EXPLAIN PLAN output, we see that rewrite was done by selecting rows for the grouping (p.category, t.time_key), which corresponds to gid = 3.

```
PLAN_TABLE_OUTPUT
----------------------------------------------------------------
| Id  | Operation                   | Name     | Rows  |Cost |
----------------------------------------------------------------
|   0 | SELECT STATEMENT            |          | 2194  |   18|
|*  1 |   MAT_VIEW REWRITE ACCESS FULL| SALES_MV | 2194  |   18|
----------------------------------------------------------------

Predicate Information (identified by operation id):
---------------------------------------------------
   1 - filter("SALES_MV"."GID"=3)
```

If the query itself has multiple groupings, Oracle will try to find a materialized view that satisfies all the groupings. If Oracle cannot find a single materialized view to answer a GROUPING SETS query, it will try to rewrite each grouping separately. (Note that a query with GROUPING SETS can be expressed using a UNION ALL of queries with the individual groupings.) As a result, several materialized views may get used to rewriting the query and some groupings may remain unrewritten and use the detail data.

The next query cannot be rewritten using SALES_MV alone. The grouping (p.category, t.time_key) is present in the SALES_MV materialized view, and the grouping (t.time_key, c.state) can be derived using a rollup of (p.category, t.time_key, c.state). However, the grouping (p.category, c.country, t.year) is not present in this materialized view.

```
EXPLAIN PLAN FOR
SELECT p.category,  t.time_key, c.country, t.year, c.state,
 SUM(f.purchase_price) sales
FROM product p, purchases f,  time t, customer c
WHERE p.product_id = f.product_id AND
      t.time_key = f.time_key AND
      c.customer_id = f.customer_id
GROUP BY GROUPING SETS ((p.category, t.time_key),
                        (t.time_key, c.state),
                        (p.category, c.country, t.year));
```

PLAN_TABLE_OUTPUT

```
-------------------------------------------------------------------
| Id  | Operation                      | Name     | Rows  |Cost |
-------------------------------------------------------------------
|   0 | SELECT STATEMENT               |          | 16052 | 189|
|   1 |  VIEW                          |          | 16052 | 189|
|   2 |   UNION-ALL                    |          |       |    |
|   3 |    SORT GROUP BY               |          |     6 | 150|
|*  4 |     HASH JOIN                  |          | 80569 | 129|
|   5 |      TABLE ACCESS FULL         | CUSTOMER |   500 |   3|
|*  6 |      HASH JOIN                 |          | 80569 | 122|
|   7 |       TABLE ACCESS FULL        | TIME     |   731 |   3|
|*  8 |       HASH JOIN                |          | 80679 | 116|
|   9 |        TABLE ACCESS FULL       | PRODUCT  |   164 |   2|
|  10 |        PARTITION RANGE ALL     |          | 81171 | 111|
|  11 |         TABLE ACCESS FULL      | PURCHASES| 81171 | 111|
|  12 |    SORT GROUP BY               |          | 13852 |  22|
|* 13 |     MAT_VIEW REWRITE ACCESS FULL| SALES_MV | 13852 |  18|
|* 14 |     MAT_VIEW REWRITE ACCESS FULL | SALES_MV |  2194 |  18|
-------------------------------------------------------------------
Predicate Information (identified by operation id):
---------------------------------------------------
   4 - access("C"."CUSTOMER_ID"="F"."CUSTOMER_ID")
   6 - access("T"."TIME_KEY"="F"."TIME_KEY")
   8 - access("P"."PRODUCT_ID"="F"."PRODUCT_ID")
  13 - filter("SALES_MV"."GID"=2)
  14 - filter("SALES_MV"."GID"=3)
```

The EXPLAIN PLAN output shows that rewrite was done using SALES_MV for two groupings (gid = 3 and gid = 2) and using the detail tables for grouping (p.category, c,county, t.year).

If we had another simple materialized view, SALES_MV2 (not shown here), that had the missing grouping (p.category, c.county, t.year), the optimizer would use it to rewrite the remaining grouping, as shown in the following execution plan.

```
PLAN_TABLE_OUTPUT
-----------------------------------------------------------------
| Id  | Operation                        | Name     | Rows  |Cost |
-----------------------------------------------------------------
|   0 | SELECT STATEMENT                 |          | 16059 |   42|
|   1 |  VIEW                            |          | 16059 |   42|
|   2 |   UNION-ALL                      |          |       |     |
|   3 |    MAT_VIEW REWRITE ACCESS FULL  | SALES_MV2|    13 |    2|
|   4 |     SORT GROUP BY                |          | 13852 |   22|
|*  5 |      MAT_VIEW REWRITE ACCESS FULL| SALES_MV | 13852 |   18|
|*  6 |      MAT_VIEW REWRITE ACCESS FULL| SALES_MV |  2194 |   18|
-----------------------------------------------------------------

Predicate Information (identified by operation id):
---------------------------------------------------
   5 - filter("SALES_MV"."GID"=2)
   6 - filter("SALES_MV"."GID"=3)
```

Analytical Functions

Oracle Database 10*g* supports limited query rewrite with the analytical functions, which were discussed in Chapter 6. If an analytical function in the query matches exactly with one in the materialized view, and the query and the materialized view aggregate at the same level (i.e., there is no need for a rollup), then query rewrite can occur. For example, the following materialized view includes the RANK() function and contains the ranks for products, ordered by their total sales, with the worst-selling products first.

```
CREATE MATERIALIZED VIEW rank_mv
ENABLE QUERY REWRITE
AS
SELECT p.product_id p_id, SUM(f.purchase_price) as sales,
       RANK() over (ORDER BY SUM(f.purchase_price)) as rank
FROM purchases f, product p
WHERE f.product_id = p.product_id
GROUP BY p.product_id;
```

The following query, asking for the 10 worst-selling products, can now rewrite against this materialized view.

```
EXPLAIN PLAN FOR
SELECT * FROM
(SELECT p.product_id p_id,
       RANK() over (ORDER BY SUM(f.purchase_price)) as rank
 FROM purchases f, product p
 WHERE f.product_id = p.product_id
 GROUP BY p.product_id)
WHERE rank < 10;


PLAN_TABLE_OUTPUT
-------------------------------------------------------------
| Id  | Operation                   | Name     | Rows |Cost |
-------------------------------------------------------------
|   0 | SELECT STATEMENT            |          |    9 |   2 |
|*  1 |   MAT_VIEW REWRITE ACCESS FULL| RANK_MV |    9 |   2 |
-------------------------------------------------------------


Predicate Information (identified by operation id):
---------------------------------------------------
   1 - filter("RANK_MV"."RANK"<10)
```

If the analytical function is not present or does not match the one in the materialized view, but the underlying aggregate is present in the materialized view, then query rewrite can happen. In this case, the analytical function will be computed from the aggregate in the materialized view. This is indicated by a **window sort** operation in the execution plan. In the following example, the query computes the DENSE_RANK() and also computes RANK() in descending order.

```
EXPLAIN PLAN FOR
SELECT p.product_id p_id,
       DENSE_RANK() over (ORDER BY SUM(f.purchase_price)) as drank,
       RANK() over (ORDER BY SUM(f.purchase_price) DESC) as
rev_rank
FROM purchases f, product p
WHERE f.product_id = p.product_id
GROUP BY p.product_id;
```

Since SUM(purchase_price) is present in the materialized view, query rewrite takes place, as shown in the following execution plan.

```
PLAN_TABLE_OUTPUT
-----------------------------------------------------------------
| Id  | Operation                      | Name    | Rows  |Cost |
-----------------------------------------------------------------
|  0  | SELECT STATEMENT               |         |  165  |    4|
|  1  |  WINDOW SORT                   |         |  165  |    4|
|  2  |   WINDOW SORT                  |         |  165  |    4|
|  3  |    MAT_VIEW REWRITE ACCESS FULL| RANK_MV |  165  |    2|
-----------------------------------------------------------------
```

9.6.4 Query Rewrite Using Nested Materialized Views

In Chapter 7, we discussed how nested materialized views could be used to share common joins across several materialized views or to materialize different levels in a hierarchy. After a query has been rewritten using a materialized view, the optimizer will check if it can be further rewritten using a nested materialized view. To illustrate this, consider the following query, which asks for total product sales.

```
EXPLAIN PLAN FOR
SELECT p.product_id, SUM(ps.purchase_price) as ave_sales
FROM product p, purchases ps
WHERE ps.product_id = p.product_id
GROUP BY p.product_id;
```

In section 9.2.8, we saw how this query can be rewritten using MONTHLY_SALES_MV. Now, suppose we had a nested materialized view on top of this materialized view, which computed the total sales by product_id as follows:

```
CREATE MATERIALIZED VIEW YEARLY_PROD_SALES_MV
ENABLE QUERY REWRITE
AS
SELECT m.product_id, SUM(m.sum_of_sales) as yearly_sales
FROM monthly_sales_mv m
GROUP BY m.product_id;
```

After the query has been rewritten using the MONTHLY_SALES_MV materialized view, the optimizer will further rewrite this query to use YEARLY_PROD_SALES_MV, as illustrated in the following execution plan output.

```
PLAN_TABLE_OUTPUT
---------------------------------------------------------------
| Id  | Operation                | Name                 |Cost|
---------------------------------------------------------------
|  0  | SELECT STATEMENT         |                      |   2|
|  1  |  MAT_VIEW REWRITE ACCESS FULL| YEARLY_PROD_SALES_MV |   2|
---------------------------------------------------------------
```

Thus, the answer to the query is directly obtained from the smaller YEARLY_PROD_SALES_MV nested materialized view without using the larger intermediate MONTHLY_SALES_MV materialized view.

9.6.5 Rewrite Equivalences

The optimizer can rewrite a query using a materialized view, provided it can determine that the answer is contained in the materialized view. However, to do so, it can only rely on available metadata in the database. Sometimes it may be not possible to rewrite the query in general, but with some specific application knowledge, it may indeed be possible to rewrite the query. Oracle Database 10*g* has a new feature called **rewrite equivalence**, which allows you to declare an alternative equivalent form of a given query. You can use this feature to do a user-defined query rewrite using your application knowledge. To use this feature you must use the procedure DBMS_ADVANCED_REWRITE.DECLARE_REWRITE_EQUIVALENCE to declare to Oracle that two statements are identical. We will illustrate this concept with an example.

Suppose we had the following materialized view, which computes a monthly sales forecast using the user-defined aggregate function, SalesForecast(), which was discussed in Chapter 6.

```
CREATE MATERIALIZED VIEW SALES_FORECAST_MV
ENABLE QUERY REWRITE
AS
SELECT t.month, t.year,
       SalesForecast(ps.purchase_price)  sales_forecast
FROM time t, purchases ps
WHERE t.time_key = ps.time_key
GROUP BY t.month, t.year;
```

Some simple query rewrites are possible with user-defined aggregates—for example, you can use this materialized view to return the precomputed sales forecast by month. However, it is not possible to do a rollup of a user-defined aggregate—for instance, from monthly to yearly level. In other words, if we wanted to calculate the sales forecast on a yearly basis, we would ordinarily have to use the detail data or create a separate materialized view for it.

Now, suppose that, because of the nature of this aggregate function, it is possible to roll up to a yearly level by simply doing a SUM over the monthly forecasts. Obviously, this is not generally true with all user-defined aggregates; however, in this specific case, we know this to be the case based on "insider" knowledge of its implementation. In this case, we can declare a rewrite equivalence, as follows:

```
BEGIN
SYS.DBMS_ADVANCED_REWRITE.DECLARE_REWRITE_EQUIVALENCE (
    'SALES_FORECAST_ROLLUP',
    'SELECT t.year, SALESFORECAST(ps.purchase_price) sales_forecast
    FROM time t, purchases ps
    WHERE t.time_key = ps.time_key
    GROUP BY t.year',
    'SELECT year, SUM(sales_forecast) yearly_forecast
    FROM sales_forecast_mv
    GROUP BY year'
);
END;
/
```

This procedure has three required parameters: a name (which can later be used to drop or edit the equivalence), a source statement, and a destination statement. With this declaration, if you now ask the query on the source statement, Oracle will automatically use the equivalent query specified by the destination statement.

Hint: The optimizer only uses rewrite equivalences provided the QUERY_REWRITE_INTEGRITY parameter is set to the TRUSTED or STALE_TOLERATED modes.

In our example, if we issue the query on the yearly level, it will be transparently replaced with the query using the SALES_FORECAST_MV, as shown in the following execution plan. Thus, we have done a user-defined query rewrite!

```
EXPLAIN PLAN FOR
SELECT t.year, SALESFORECAST(ps.purchase_price)  sales_forecast
FROM time t, purchases ps
```

```
WHERE t.time_key = ps.time_key
GROUP BY t.year;

PLAN_TABLE_OUTPUT
-----------------------------------------------------------
| Id  | Operation               | Name              |Cost|
-----------------------------------------------------------
|  0  | SELECT STATEMENT        |                   |  3 |
|  1  |   SORT GROUP BY         |                   |  3 |
|  2  |     MAT_VIEW ACCESS FULL| SALES_FORECAST_MV |  2 |
-----------------------------------------------------------
```

Hint: If there is a choice between using a rewrite equivalence and a materialized view to rewrite a query, the optimizer will prefer the equivalence to the materialized view.

When declaring the equivalence, if you set the parameter *validate* to true, Oracle will execute both the source and destination queries and verify that they return the same results or otherwise give an error. However, as the underlying data changes, it is possible that the two statements may no longer return identical results. Oracle will not check the validity of the equivalence as the data changes. It is up to the user who created the equivalence to ensure that the two queries are equivalent for the application; otherwise, it may produce unexpected results. You can check the validity of the equivalence at any time by issuing the procedure DBMS_ADVANCED_REWRITE.VALIDATE_ REWRITE_EQUIVALENCE.

As you can see, this is an extremely powerful feature; hence, this package is owned by SYS and its use is not enabled by default. The DBA needs to explicitly grant access to the package to trusted users who can create these equivalences, as follows:

```
GRANT EXECUTE ON DBMS_ADVANCED_REWRITE TO <user>;
```

You can disable a rewrite equivalence using the following procedure:

```
EXECUTE DBMS_ADVANCED_REWRITE.ALTER_REWRITE_EQUIVALENCE
          ('SALES_FORECAST_ROLLUP', mode=>'disabled');
```

Rewrite equivalences should only be used if absolutely necessary and should be made available only to the most advanced users of query rewrite.

Incorrect use of this powerful feature can wreak havoc, since users could get unexpected or bogus results.

9.6.6 Using Query Rewrite during Refresh

Another new feature in Oracle Database 10*g* is using query rewrite when populating or refreshing a materialized view. This means that to populate or refresh one materialized view, Oracle will try to reuse the precomputed data in another materialized view, using query rewrite. This can be much quicker than refreshing the materialized view directly from the detail data! For example, if you had a materialized view at a monthly grain and another one at a daily grain, Oracle can use the materialized view at the daily grain to refresh the monthly one.

Note that only fresh materialized views will be used for query rewrite during refresh so that the materialized view being refreshed always sees the most up-to-date data. In addition, by default query rewrite will be performed with the QUERY_REWRITE_INTEGRITY parameter setting of ENFORCED, which means trusted relationships such as dimensions will not be used by query rewrite. However, if you would like to have refresh use the QUERY_REWRITE_INTEGRITY setting of TRUSTED, you may specify the USING TRUSTED CONSTRAINTS clause on the CREATE MATERIALIZED VIEW statement, as shown in the following example.

```
CREATE MATERIALIZED VIEW product_category_sales_mv
REFRESH FORCE
USING TRUSTED CONSTRAINTS        <- constraints clause
 ENABLE QUERY REWRITE
 AS
 SELECT ps.time_key, p.category,
        SUM(ps.purchase_price) as sum_of_sales
 FROM   product p, purchases ps
 WHERE ps.product_id = p.product_id
 GROUP BY ps.time_key, p.category;
```

If you do not specify this clause, the default clause is USING ENFORCED CONSTRAINTS.

This allows refresh to take advantage of trusted information, such as RELY constraints, dimensions, and materialized views on prebuilt tables, to rewrite the internal queries issued during refresh. Note, however, that, as discussed in section 9.3, it is the DBA's responsibility to guarantee correctness of the trusted information; otherwise, your materialized view could have incorrect data.

> **Hint:** To enable use of query rewrite during refresh, set the initialization parameter, QUERY_REWRITE_INTEGRITY, to TRUE in the session performing the refresh.

When refreshing materialized views, it is recommended that you refresh multiple materialized views simultaneously and enable query rewrite. This allows Oracle Database 10g to optimize the ordering of the refresh operations such that it can make best use of query rewrite during refresh. For example, if you have two materialized views, one at a monthly level and one at a daily level, Oracle will first refresh the materialized view at a daily grain and then use this materialized view to refresh the one at a monthly grain, using query rewrite.

Using query rewrite during refresh can significantly improve performance of refreshing your materialized views.

9.7 Summary

Summary management in Oracle provides a very powerful set of tools to improve query performance in your warehouse. With query rewrite, the queries will be transparently rewritten to use the materialized views. We have seen how you can use the same materialized view to rewrite a large class of queries, thereby reducing the space and maintenance resources required for materialized views. We have also seen how to troubleshoot problems with query rewrite and how to use query rewrite to improve performance of refreshing the materialized views.

This brings us to the question: How do you know which materialized views to create? Determining the optimal set of materialized views to create for a large number of queries can be tricky, and, if not done correctly, the disk space requirements and refresh overhead could soon get prohibitive. Fortunately, Oracle Database 10g provides a tool called the SQL Access Advisor, which is designed to choose the best set of materialized views and indexes for an application.

The next chapter discusses the SQL Access Advisor and various other query techniques and tools to tune query performance in a data warehouse.

10

Tuning Query Performance

Query performance tuning is an ongoing process, which is needed throughout the life cycle of any database application. A data warehouse is no exception, and, in fact, good query performance is extremely crucial to the success of any data warehouse. It is important when the application is first designed that the SQL statements are well written and all requisite access structures, such as indexes and materialized views, are created to obtain good execution plans. However, even after the application is deployed, as the data and query workload changes, you will find that you will need to tune the SQL and modify the access structures periodically in order to meet your performance goals.

There are many different reasons why a query may perform poorly. Performance issues may arise due to resource constraints such as inadequate memory or inadequate processing resources. Over time the data distribution may change and the current execution plan may not be optimal. A DBA faces a challenging task of constantly monitoring performance, identifying poorly performing queries, determining the reason for the poor performance, and finally fixing the problem. Therefore, performance tuning can be a very difficult and time-consuming task for even the most experienced DBA.

Fortunately, with Oracle Database 10*g*, the task of performance tuning is greatly simplified by using several new tools available for this purpose. In this chapter, we will take a look at various aspects of tuning query performance in a data warehouse and the tuning tools available in Oracle Database 10*g*.

10.1 Monitoring Performance

The first step in tuning query performance is to be able to monitor the database and identify queries that are not performing adequately. Oracle

Figure 10.1   *Performance Page in Oracle Enterprise Manager*

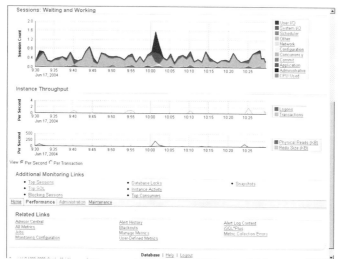

Database 10*g* Enterprise Manager provides a simple interface to monitor such queries. Figure 10.1 shows the *Performance* page of Oracle Enterprise Manager, which monitors various metrics of performance for the database, such as the waiting sessions, user versus system I/O and instance throughput. To get to this page, after logging into Oracle Enterprise Manager, click on the *Performance* link at the top of the initial (*Home*) page.

Figure 10.2   *Top SQL Page*

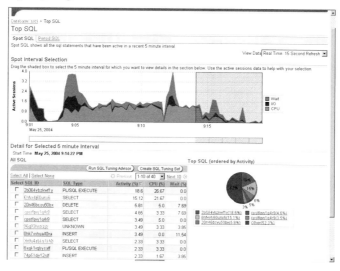

Near the bottom of this page is a link called *Top SQL*, which will bring you to the page shown in Figure 10.2. On this page, you can monitor the SQL statements that consumed (or are currently consuming) significant resources in the database. The graph on the top shows the CPU, I/O, and Wait activity in the system over time. The shaded box on the graph corresponds to a five-minute window, and the table below the graph displays the SQL statements that were executed in that window. Click on the rectangle below the graph to move the shaded box to pick a specific five-minute window you are interested in. The page will automatically refresh every 15 seconds by default, though this can be altered by changing the value in the *View Data* box in the top right of the screen.

The table below the graph in Figure 10.2 shows the SQL statements sorted by a statistic such as by percentage of CPU consumed. Click on the links in the SQL ID column to view the detailed SQL statement, its execution plan, and statistics, as shown in Figure 10.3. From this page it is possible to peruse the execution history and tuning history of the SQL statement.

Figure 10.3   *SQL Details*

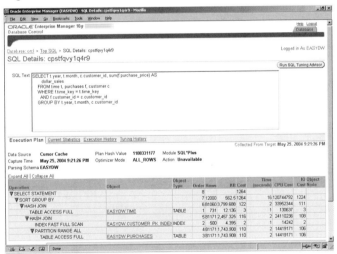

10.1.1   SQL Tuning Sets

Once you have identified the poorly performing SQL, you can create a collection, called a **SQL Tuning Set**, to save these SQL statements persistently in the database. The benefit of creating this collection is that you can keep track of your problematic SQL over a period of time and can use it as input to the tuning tools, SQL Access Advisor and SQL Tuning Advisor, which we will discuss in sections 10.3 and 10.4 respectively.

A SQL Tuning Set can be created either using Oracle Enterprise Manager or by the DBMS_SQLTUNE PL/SQL package.

Creating a SQL Tuning Set in Oracle Enterprise Manager

To create a SQL Tuning Set simply select one or more statements from the table in Figure 10.2, and press the *Create SQL Tuning Set* button to bring up the screen shown in Figure 10.4. Here you can provide a name and description for the SQL Tuning Set and then press *OK* to create it.

Figure 10.4   *Creating a SQL Tuning Set*

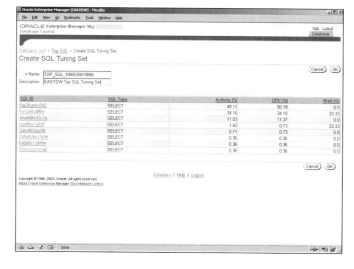

The available SQL Tuning Sets will then be listed in the screen shown in Figure 10.5. From this page, we can manage the SQL Tuning Sets and also run the SQL Access and SQL Tuning Advisors.

Creating a SQL Tuning Set Using the DBMS_SQLTUNE Package

SQL Tuning Sets can also be created using the DBMS_SQLTUNE package. The DBMS_SQLTUNE package allows you to create SQL Tuning Sets from the SQL Cache, or any user table as long as it includes some specific columns. In Chapter 5, we discussed how SQL Table functions can be used in the FROM clause instead of an actual table. The SQL Tuning Set procedures provide built-in table functions that allow you to load a workload from the SQL Cache (also called the **Cursor Cache**), from the **Automatic**

Figure 10.5   *Listing of SQL Tuning Sets*

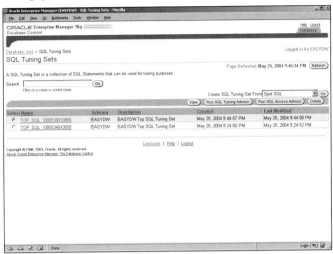

Workload Repository (described in Chapter 11), or from any user table with the SQL statements.

Hint: In order to use the DBMS_SQLTUNE package to create SQL Tuning Sets, you must be familiar with programming using PL/SQL cursors and SQL Table functions.

To avoid creating the SQL Tuning Set with too many statements, you can specify a filter condition restricting the SQL statements to be considered. You can also specify up to three ranking measures used to prioritize (i.e., order) the SQL statements and then request that only the top-N statements or only the ones contributing up to a certain percentage of the ranking measures should be included. When creating a SQL Tuning Set from the SQL Cache, you can use any column from the V$SQL view as a filter condition, and the numeric ones can be used as ranking measures. This should become clearer from the following example, which shows how to create a SQL Tuning Set from the SQL Cache:

```
DECLARE
    sqlsetname   VARCHAR2(30);
    sqlsetcur    dbms_sqltune.sqlset_cursor;
BEGIN
    sqlsetname := 'MY_STS_WORKLOAD';
    dbms_sqltune.create_sqlset(sqlsetname, 'SQL Cache STS');
```

```
    OPEN sqlsetcur FOR
      SELECT VALUE(P)
      FROM TABLE(
      dbms_sqltune.select_cursor_cache(
              'SQL_TEXT like ''%purchases%''',
              NULL,
              'CPU_TIME', NULL, NULL,        -- ranking measures
              NULL, 10)                      -- limit to 10
      ) P;
    dbms_sqltune.load_sqlset(sqlsetname, sqlsetcur);
end;
/
```

In this example, the CREATE_SQLSET procedure creates a SQL Tuning Set with the given name (MY_STS_WORKLOAD) and description (SQL Cache STS). The OPEN statement opens a cursor using the built-in table function, SELECT_CURSOR_CACHE. We have specified a filter, which says that the SQL_TEXT must include the word "purchases," a ranking measure as CPU_TIME, and a maximum limit of 10 statements.

You can now view the SQL Tuning Set by either using the list in Oracle Enterprise Manager (Figure 10.5) or by using the dictionary views, DBA_SQL_SET and DBA_SQLSET_STATEMENTS, as follows:

```
select substr(name,1,15) name,substr(owner,1,6) owner,
       substr(sql_text,1,30) description, sql_id
from dba_sqlset d, dba_sqlset_statements s
where id = sqlset_id and name = 'MY_STS_WORKLOAD';


NAME            OWNER  SQL_TEXT                  SQL_ID
--------------- ------ ------------------------- -------------
MY_STS_WORKLOAD EASYDW SELECT t.month, t.year, p  4bw858yjjbl1x
MY_STS_WORKLOAD EASYDW SELECT count(distinct pro  4rt9sqw6tnrzz
MY_STS_WORKLOAD EASYDW SELECT sqlset_row (sql_id  5ts120q1a40b5
MY_STS_WORKLOAD EASYDW SELECT VALUE(P) FROM TABL  5z0pw0x58fj88
MY_STS_WORKLOAD EASYDW SELECT VALUE(P) FROM TABL  5zs8b269g338s
...
10 rows selected.
```

This is a very powerful interface and can be used when you need more functionality and flexibility than are available in the graphical interface in Oracle Enterprise Manager.

10.2 Advisor Central

Oracle Database 10*g* Enterprise Manager includes several tools called **advisors** to aid in performance tuning of the system. The advisors can be launched from a number of locations within Enterprise Manager. However, the most convenient way to find and run any advisor is to follow the *Advisor Central* link, which can be found at the bottom of the ***Performance*** page in Figure 10.1.

Hint: The performance tuning tools require the tuning pack of Oracle Enterprise Manager.

Figure 10.6 shows the Advisor Central page, where you can find links to the following advisors related to query performance tuning:

- SQL Access Advisor, which gives advice on index and materialized views
- SQL Tuning Advisor, which identifies problems such as missing statistics, possibly bad SQL construction, and so on.
- Memory Advisor, for tuning SGA and PGA memory

Figure 10.6 *Advisor Central*

Additional advisors, such as Segment Advisor and ADDM, are discussed separately in Chapter 11.

Hint: To run the advisors in Oracle Database 10*g* you must be granted the ADVISOR system privilege, which you will already have if you have the DBA role.

Many of the advisors in Oracle Database 10*g*, including the SQL Access Advisor and the SQL Tuning Advisor, use a common container known as an **Advisor Task** to store their tuning parameter settings and the results. On the Advisor Central page, you can monitor currently executing advisor tasks and press the *View Result* button in Figure 10.6 to look at recommendations of completed tasks.

Hint: By default, a task will be automatically deleted after 30 days, but you can change the expiration date by using the *Change Default Expiration* button.

We will now look at each of the advisors in detail, starting with the SQL Access Advisor.

10.3 SQL Access Advisor

One of the most critical aspects of tuning any query is to ensure that it is making use of appropriate access structures such as indexes and materialized views. In Chapter 4, we discussed various indexing techniques for a data warehouse, and in Chapter 9, we saw how you could use a materialized view to answer many different queries using query rewrite. Determining the optimal set of materialized views and indexes to create for the application's workload of queries is often a difficult exercise. The materialized views must work cooperatively with indexes defined on the base tables and may also need additional indexing. If not done correctly, the application may be slowed down and you could be wasting space and incur overhead to maintain unnecessary structures. The SQL Access Advisor in Oracle Enterprise Manager is an invaluable tool for this purpose. This tool will take a given workload of SQL statements and recommend the ideal set of materialized view and indexes for that workload.

The SQL Access Advisor is available as a wizard in Oracle Enterprise Manager. We recommend using the graphical interface; however, if you prefer to use the command-line interface, you could use the DBMS_ADVISOR PL/SQL package. We will illustrate both of these mechanisms.

Hint: In the previous versions of Oracle, there was a tool called the Summary Advisor, which only recommended materialized views but no indexes. This tool has now been replaced by the SQL Access Advisor, which also recommends indexes.

Figure 10.7 shows the overall flow of the SQL Access Advisor.

Figure 10.7   *SQL Access Advisor Flow*

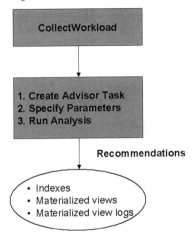

The SQL Access Advisor takes as input a workload of SQL statements and some optional tuning parameters. It recommends indexes, materialized views, and any materialized view logs to make the recommended materialized views fast refreshable (see Chapter 7). As mentioned in section 10.2, the analysis parameters and the recommendations resulting from the analysis are stored in an Advisor Task and can be monitored from the Advisor Central page (see Figure 10.6). Note that many of these steps are transparently done for you by the Oracle Enterprise Manager wizard; therefore, you do not need to even know these details unless you plan to use the PL/SQL procedures.

The workload used by the SQL Access Advisor can come from one of the following sources:

1. **A SQL Tuning Set**: In section 10.1.1, we discussed how to collect SQL statements from the Top SQL page into a SQL Tuning Set. Once you have created a SQL Tuning Set, you can specify it as a workload source to the SQL Access Advisor.

2. **The SQL Cache**: This consists of the current contents of the SQL Cache.

3. **A user-specified table**: The workload table may be a table in any schema, which contains the text of the SQL statements.

4. **A Hypothetical Workload**: The SQL Access Advisor can generate hypothetical SQL statements using dimension and constraint information from a schema. This can be very useful when you are designing your application schema and cannot run the queries yet.

5. **An Oracle 9*i* Summary Advisor Workload:** If you have used the Summary Advisor in Oracle 9i and have some existing workload, you can reuse this workload for the SQL Access Advisor. To do this, you must provide the SQL Access Advisor with the workload id of the Summary Advisor workload. Note that this option is not available in the graphical interface.

We will now walk through the various steps of the SQL Access Advisor wizard in Oracle Enterprise Manager.

10.3.1   SQL Access Advisor Wizard

The SQL Access Advisor can be launched from the Advisor Central page shown in Figure 10.6. Alternatively, it may be launched by specifying a SQL Tuning Set as a workload source and then pressing the ***Run SQL Access Advisor*** button in Figure 10.5.

Choosing a Workload Source

If the SQL Access Advisor is launched from Advisor Central, you will first see the screen shown in Figure 10.8, where you must choose a workload source. (When the SQL Access Advisor is launched directly on a SQL Tuning Set, this screen is skipped.)

In Figure 10.8, we have decided to specify a user-defined workload that is contained in the table EASYDW.USER_WORKLOAD. The table used

Figure 10.8   *SQL Access Advisor: Choosing a Workload Source*

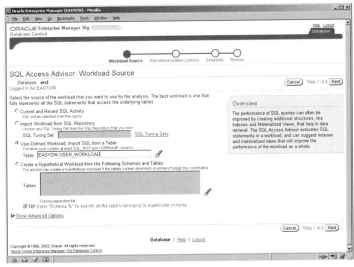

for a SQL Access Advisor workload can be any user table but must have columns, as shown in the following example:

```
CREATE TABLE user_workload
( MODULE                VARCHAR2(48),
  ACTION                VARCHAR2(32),
  BUFFER_GETS           NUMBER,
  CPU_TIME              NUMBER,
  ELAPSED_TIME          NUMBER,
  DISK_READS            NUMBER,
  ROWS_PROCESSED        NUMBER,
  EXECUTIONS            NUMBER,
  OPTIMIZER_COST        NUMBER,
  LAST_EXECUTION_DATE   DATE,
  PRIORITY              NUMBER,
  SQL_TEXT              CLOB,
  STAT_PERIOD           NUMBER,
  USERNAME              VARCHAR2(30) )
```

Although this table has many columns, only a couple of them are mandatory columns—namely, the sql_text, which is the complete text of the SQL statement, and the username, which is the name of the user who will execute that SQL statement. The PRIORITY column is a user-settable priority for each SQL statement (1 = HIGH, 2 = MEDIUM, or 3 = LOW). The analysis will make trade-offs in favor of the high-priority SQL statements. If not specified, all statements are treated on an equal footing. All other columns are optional but provide useful statistics for the analysis and will improve the quality of the recommendations.

Alternatively, we can choose the workload source to be a SQL Tuning Set, the current contents of the SQL Cache, or a hypothetical workload generated from a given set of schemas and tables.

At the bottom of Figure 10.8 is a link named *Show Advanced Options*. Clicking on this link will allow you to set additional options, as shown in Figure 10.9.

Figure 10.9   *SQL Access Advisor: Specifying Workload Filtering Options*

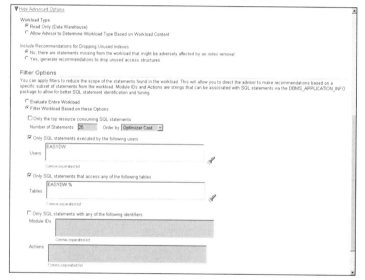

Here, you can indicate whether the workload is for a primarily read-only application; in this case, the analysis will ignore the impact of index and materialized view maintenance. Otherwise, the SQL Access Advisor will try to identify the maintenance impact from the DML statements in the workload. Unless you are in the initial design phase of the application, it is wise to allow the Advisor to consider the maintenance impact.

Hint: In order for the SQL Access Advisor to correctly consider maintenance impact of the recommended indexes and materialized views, the workload must include a representative sample of DML statements, such as INSERT, UPDATE, DELETE, and MERGE.

It is also possible to specify if the SQL Access Advisor should consider dropping existing access structures and replacing them with new ones. If you are unsure if your workload covers all relevant SQL for the application, you should choose not to recommend dropping any access structures.

When using a workload source such as the SQL cache, it is possible to have a large number of SQL statements not interesting to the application you are trying to tune. In order to achieve a more focused tuning, it is advisable that you should specify various criteria to narrow down the relevant SQL statements in the workload. By restricting the workload in this manner, the SQL Access Advisor can work in a more focused manner and thereby its analysis would be faster.

In the example, shown in Figure 10.9, we have specified that only SQL statements executed by the user EASYDW and containing tables in the EASYDW schema should be considered for analysis. You could also specify that the top-N most resource consuming SQL be analyzed, or that only SQL from a certain application (specified using the MODULE and ACTION attributes) should be considered.

Specifying Tuning Parameters

Once the workload has been chosen, press the *Next* button to proceed to the screen shown in Figure 10.10, where you can pick various recommendation options for the SQL Access Advisor, as follows.

Figure 10.10 *SQL Access Advisor: Recommendation Options*

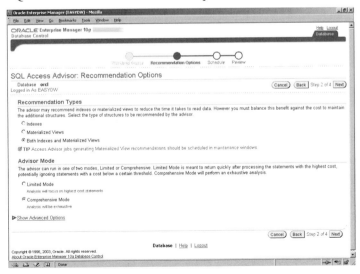

Recommendation Types: The SQL Access Advisor can recommend Indexes, Materialized Views, or both. If the *Indexes* option is chosen, it will recommend either B*tree or bitmap indexes. If the *Materialized Views* option is chosen, it will recommend materialized views and also any materialized view logs required for fast refresh. If both *Indexes* and *Materialized Views* are chosen, it will recommend all of these, as well as indexes on the materialized views.

Advisor Mode: The SQL Access Advisor has two modes: *Limited* and *Comprehensive*. In the comprehensive mode, it will perform an exhaustive analysis of the entire workload; however, this can take significantly longer to run, depending on the size of the workload. If you would like a quick analysis of the workload, you can specify the limited mode; however, you may not get the best possible recommendations. Use the comprehensive mode as much as possible, unless you have a really large workload.

If you click the *Show Advanced Options* link in Figure 10.10, you can set some additional recommendation options, as shown in Figure 10.11. The advanced options allow you to specify a storage limit (in megabytes) that the recommended access structures should fit within (if created) and also to pick the tablespace and schema where any recommended materialized views and indexes should reside. Note that this information is used when implementing the recommendations, as we will see later.

Figure 10.11   *SQL Access Advisor: More Recommendation Options*

Generating Recommendations

Pressing the *Next* button will bring up the screen shown in Figure 10.12, where you can name the advisor task that will contain the results of the analysis. It's worth choosing a sensible name, because you will need this to retrieve your recommendations from Advisor Central, especially if you wish to come back at a later date and review them. The analysis can be scheduled to execute immediately or at a specified later date.

Figure 10.12   *SQL Access Advisor: Schedule*

On pressing the *Next* button, you will see the review screen shown in Figure 10.13, where you can see all your choices at a glance. To make any changes, go back to the previous screens by using the *Back* buttons.

Once you are satisfied with the settings, you click the *Submit* button, which will bring you back to Advisor Central; from here you can monitor the status of your job (see Figure 10.6).

Hint: You will need to click the Refresh button on the top right corner in Figure 10.6 to check if the status has changed.

Figure 10.13   *SQL Access Advisor: Review Page*

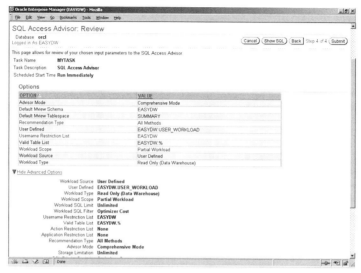

Viewing the Results of the Analysis

Once the status of the task in Advisor Central indicates *Completed*, you can select the task and click the *View Result* button, which will bring you to the recommendations page, shown in Figure 10.14.

Figure 10.14   *SQL Access Advisor: Recommendations*

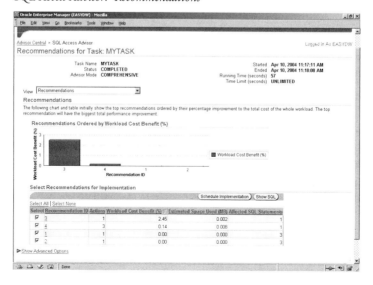

There are two ways to view the results of the SQL Access Advisor:

- **Recommendations View**: This view shows each recommendation, consisting of indexes and/or materialized views, along with the estimated performance improvement obtained from that recommendation.

- **SQL Statement View**: This view shows each SQL statement in the workload along with the specific recommendation for that statement and the performance improvement for that statement.

Hint: To switch between these two views choose the required view from the drop-down box labeled *View* in Figure 10.14. We will look at each of these views in detail.

Recommendations View

Figure 10.14 shows the recommendations view, where you can see a bar graph of the estimated improvement in your workload for each recommendation. You can also see the estimated space required to implement that recommendation and the number of SQL statements benefited by that recommendation.

Each **recommendation** consists of a series of **actions** to CREATE new materialized views or indexes or to DROP or RETAIN existing ones. There may also be actions to CREATE or ALTER materialized view logs for the recommended materialized views. You can see the actions for each recommendation by clicking on the link in the *Recommendation ID* column for that recommendation. For example, recommendation ID 4, shown in Figure 10.15, consists of a materialized view and two associated materialized view logs. There is also an auxiliary action to gather statistics on the materialized view once it is created. You can also see the SQL statement(s) that it benefits.

The text of the materialized view can be seen by clicking on the *CREATE MATERIALIZED VIEW* link in the *Action* column. Or you can see the SQL for all the actions in a recommendation by clicking the *Show SQL* button in Figure 10.14. The SQL for Recommendation ID 4 is shown in Figure 10.16.

Recommendation ID 3 consists of an index, as shown in Figure 10.17. Clicking on the *CREATE INDEX* link will show the detailed columns in the index key.

Figure 10.15   *SQL Access Advisor: Recommendation Details*

Figure 10.16   *SQL Access Advisor: Recommendation SQL*

In both Figure 10.15 and Figure 10.17, you can edit the names of the recommended structures and the tablespace and schema where they reside.

Figure 10.17 *SQL Access Advisor: Index Recommendation*

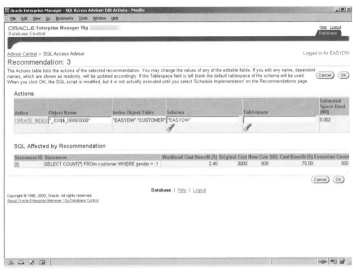

SQL Statement View

The alternate way to view the recommendations is by the SQL statements in the workload, as shown in Figure 10.18.

Figure 10.18 *Recommendation: SQL View*

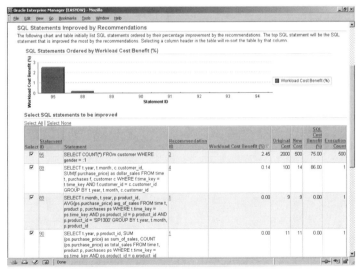

This view shows the SQL statements that contribute the most improvement in the overall performance of the workload. It also shows the original optimizer cost (as shown by an EXPLAIN PLAN) and the estimated reduction in cost (and thereby increase in performance), if the recommendation were implemented. For example, SQL statement ID 95 was improved by 75 percent. Just as in the recommendations view, you can see the detailed actions in the recommendation by clicking on the links in the *Recommendation ID* column.

Implementing the Recommendations

To choose the recommendation(s) you would like to implement simply click on the check boxes in the *Select* column in Figure 10.14. Creating the access structures can be time consuming and therefore you may want to schedule the implementation during an appropriate maintenance window. Pressing the *Schedule Implementation* button will bring you to the page shown in Figure 10.19, where you can specify parameters to schedule the implementation. Once you press the *Submit* button, the implementation job will be scheduled and you will be returned to the *Advisor Central* page where the status of the job can be monitored.

Figure 10.19   *SQL Access Advisor: Schedule Implementation*

As we have seen, the SQL Access Advisor wizard is extremely simple to use, and, with a few simple choices, you can tune your application for materialized views and indexes. Next, we will take a brief look at the command-line interface for the SQL Access Advisor.

10.3.2 DBMS_ADVISOR PL/SQL Package

The SQL Access Advisor can also be run using the PL/SQL procedures in the DBMS_ADVISOR package. The flow for using the command-line interface is the same as the graphical interface. The following example shows the various steps involved in running the SQL Access Advisor on a workload from the SQL Cache.

Step 1: Creating a Workload Named MY_WORKLOAD

The first step is to invoke the CREATE_SQLWKLD procedure to create a workload object, which will store the SQL statements in the workload. In this example we are creating a workload object named MY_WORKLOAD.

```
variable workload_name varchar2(255);
execute :workload_name := 'MYWORKLOAD';
execute dbms_advisor.create_sqlwkld(:workload_name);
```

Step 2: Specifying Workload Parameters for Filtering

You can also specify various criteria to narrow down the workload using the SET_SQLWKLD_PARAMETER procedure. For example, you can specify that the statements in the SQL Cache should be ordered using their ELAPSED_TIME, and only the top-10 statements should be considered.

```
execute dbms_advisor.set_sqlwkld_parameter(:workload_name,
                                'ORDER_LIST',
                                'ELAPSED_TIME');
execute dbms_advisor.set_sqlwkld_parameter(:workload_name,
                                'SQL_LIMIT', 10);
```

Step 3: Load Workload Statements

The next step is to load the SQL statements into the workload. We are loading the workload from the SQL Cache. The filter parameters described in step 2 will be used to determine the statements being loaded.

```
variable saved_stmts number;
variable total_stmts number;
variable failed_stmts number;

execute dbms_advisor.import_sqlwkld_sqlcache(:workload_name,
                                'APPEND', 2,
                                :total_stmts,
                                :saved_stmts,
                                :failed_stmts);
```

Step 4: Create a SQL Access Advisor Task and Set Parameters

The next step is to use the CREATE_TASK procedure to create a SQL Access Advisor Task to store the analysis parameters and the recommendations. This is the time to set various parameters such as whether the execution should be INDEX_ONLY and whether the analysis should be limited or comprehensive.

```
variable task_id number;
variable task_name varchar2(255);

execute :task_name := 'MYTASK';
execute dbms_advisor.create_task('SQL Access Advisor',
                                 :task_id, :task_name);

execute dbms_advisor.set_task_parameter(:task_name,
                                        'EXECUTION_TYPE',
                                        'INDEX_ONLY');
```

Step 5: Create a Link between Workload and Task

Once both the workload and the task are created, they must be linked using the ADD_SQLWLKD_REF procedure.

```
execute dbms_advisor.add_sqlwkld_ref(:task_name, :workload_name);
```

Step 6: Execute the Task to Generate Recommendations

Finally, execute the task to generate the recommendations. To obtain a SQL script for the recommended access structures, use the GET_TASK_SCRIPT procedure. This can be run later to create the access structures. Note that you must specify a DIRECTORY object (in this example, ADVISOR_RESULTS) where the script will be placed and you must have write permissions on this directory object.

```
execute dbms_advisor.execute_task(:task_name);

execute dbms_advisor.create_file(
   dbms_advisor.get_task_script(:task_name),
   'ADVISOR_RESULTS', 'advisor_script.sql');
```

The following is an excerpt from a SQL Access Advisor script:

```
Rem   SQL Access Advisor: Version 10.1.0.1 - Production
Rem
Rem   Username:        EASYDW
Rem   Task:            MYTASK
Rem   Execution date:  19/06/2004 23:59
```

```
Rem

…
CREATE BITMAP INDEX "EASYDW"."_IDX$$_0188000E"
    ON "EASYDW"."CUSTOMER"
    ("GENDER")
    COMPUTE STATISTICS;
…
```

10.3.3 Templates

The PL/SQL command-line interface provides some features not available in the graphical user interface. One useful feature is templates, which allow you to define a model task, which can then be used as a starting point for other tasks. To create a template, use the same procedure as creating a task and set various analysis parameters. Then, when you need to create a new task with the same parameters, you just create the task from the template.

The following example shows how to create a template named MY_TEMPLATE and then use it to create a new task named MY_TASK.

Step1: Defining a Template

To create a template, use the CREATE_TASK procedure but set the *is_template* parameter to TRUE. In this example, the template sets up the default naming conventions for the recommended materialized views and indexes.

```
variable template_name varchar2(30);
execute :template_name := 'MY_TEMPLATE';
execute dbms_advisor.create_task
    ('SQL Access Advisor',:template_id,
     :template_name,is_template=>'TRUE');

execute dbms_advisor.set_task_parameter(:template_name,
                                'INDEX_NAME_TEMPLATE',
                                'SH_IDX$$_<SEQ>');

execute dbms_advisor.set_task_parameter(:template_name,
                                'MVIEW_NAME_TEMPLATE',
                                'SH_MV$$_<SEQ>');
```

Step2: Create a Task Using the Template

Now we can use this template to create a task by specifying the *template* parameter in the CREATE_TASK procedure.

```
variable task_id number;
execute dbms_advisor.create_task
    ('SQL Access Advisor', :task_id,
     'MY_TASK', template=>'MY_TEMPLATE');
```

10.3.4   **Quick_Tune**

Another procedure available via the command-line interface but not in the graphical user interface is the ability to analyze a single SQL statement for materialized views and indexes using the QUICK_TUNE procedure. This is a useful tool if you have a problematic SQL query that needs to be resolved immediately and you do not have the time to collect an entire workload and analyze it. Note that if you would like to set any recommendation options for QUICK_TUNE, you must first create a template and then pass it to this procedure.

The following example shows how to run the QUICK_TUNE procedure to analyze a single SQL statement. We use the template MY_TEMPLATE, defined earlier.

```
variable task_name varchar2(255);
variable sql_stmt varchar2(4000);

BEGIN
   :sql_stmt := ' SELECT count(distinct product_id) as num_cust
                  FROM  purchases f, customer c
                  WHERE f.customer_id = c.customer_id and
                        c.gender = :1'

   :task_name   := 'MY_QUICKTUNE_TASK';
   dbms_advisor.quick_tune('SQL Access Advisor',
                           :task_name, :sql_stmt,
                       template=>'MY_TEMPLATE');
END;
/
```

Once the procedure completes, you can generate a script just like we did with the previous example.

Unfortunately, due to limited space, we cannot discuss all the procedures in the DBMS_ADVISOR package in detail.

The next section discusses the SQL Tuning Advisor, which is a tool that complements the SQL Access Advisor to tune SQL statements.

10.4   **SQL Tuning Advisor**

It is not always possible to create a new access structure to fix a long-running query. Perhaps it would take too long to create the index or it is not possible to do so except during the maintenance window. Or maybe the problem is that there is a skew in the data distribution, which causes the optimizer to pick a bad execution plan. There may be alternative ways to express the query that are more efficient. In these situations, when you need a quick fix targeted at a specific SQL statement, you should try the SQL Tuning Advisor.

The SQL Tuning Advisor takes as input one or more SQL statements (or a SQL Tuning Set) and gives recommendations to fix each SQL statement using one of the following techniques:

- Identifying if a table has changed significantly and its statistics are no longer accurate.

- Identifying potential problems in the way the SQL is written. For example, a query may be missing a join condition between two tables, leading to an extremely expensive Cartesian product.

- Identifying if the internal estimates used by the cost-based optimizer are off the mark and creating a corrective structure known as a ***Profile***.

The SQL Tuning Advisor is available as a graphical user interface in Oracle Enterprise Manager and as a command-line interface in the DBMS_SQLTUNE PL/SQL package. We will review both these interfaces.

10.4.1 SQL Tuning Advisor in Enterprise Manager

The SQL Tuning Advisor has a simple one-page graphical user interface in Oracle Enterprise Manager. This Advisor can be launched from the *Top SQL* page, discussed in section 10.1 (see Figure 10.2), by selecting one or more SQL statement(s) and pressing the *Run SQL Tuning Advisor* button. Alternatively, it is possible to first create a SQL Tuning Set and then launch the SQL Tuning Advisor on it from the screen in Figure 10.5. Once you launch it, you will get a screen similar to the one in Figure 10.20.

As with the SQL Access Advisor, the SQL Tuning Advisor stores its inputs and recommendations in an Advisor Task, for which you may provide a name and description. We recommend you provide a meaningful name or description so you can identify the task in Advisor Central at a later time.

The SQL Tuning Advisor has two modes of analysis: *Limited* and *Comprehensive*. In the limited mode, it will spend around one second per statement and do a very quick analysis to look for major problems such as missing statistics. Typically, you would want to run it in the comprehensive

Figure 10.20   *The SQL Tuning Advisor*

mode, where it will attempt to check the optimizer's cost estimates, check for possible problems in the SQL, look for better execution plans, and so on. In the comprehensive mode, you can specify a maximum time limit for the analysis.

The Advisor can be run immediately or scheduled to run later using the scheduling mechanism in Oracle Enterprise Manager. If you ask to run it immediately, you will get a screen (not shown here) showing the progress of the Advisor until it completes. If you schedule it for later, you can monitor its progress from the Advisor Central page, shown in Figure 10.6, just as you did for the SQL Access Advisor.

Figure 10.21 shows the summary of the recommendations of the SQL Tuning Advisor. For each SQL statement, there will be a check mark indicating the type(s) of recommendations produced. Select any one SQL statement and press the *View Recommendation* button to see its detailed recommendation. We will now look at a couple of these recommendations.

Figure 10.22 shows a recommendation for restructuring a SQL statement. Recommendations in this category require the user to change the SQL text to a *different* statement, which is *not generally equivalent* to the original one, but, based on application knowledge, *may* perform better. For example, suppose a UNION operator were present in the SQL. It is possible that the query would not produce any duplicates (which can only be determined by the application developer), and hence a UNION ALL oper-

Figure 10.21 *SQL Tuning Advisor Recommendation Summary*

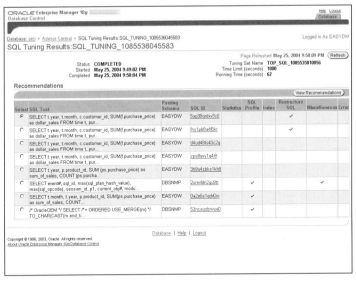

ator could be used instead and would be much faster. Another common problem is a missing join between two tables, which could be an oversight on the part of the application developer.

Figure 10.22 *SQL Tuning Recommendation: Restructure SQL*

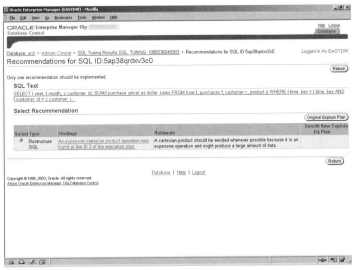

Hint: To implement a Restructure SQL type of recommendation, you must be able to physically modify the application or script that launched that SQL statement. Also, care should be taken to ensure that the new SQL produces the same result as the original one, based on your application knowledge.

Note that the SQL Tuning Advisor does not recommend transformations that could transform a SQL into another, better-performing but *semantically equivalent* SQL statement. This is because the cost-based optimizer will automatically and transparently do these transformations whenever applicable! One example of such a transformation is query rewrite using materialized views, which we discussed in Chapter 9.

Profiles

Another type of recommendation produced by the SQL Tuning Advisor is a **profile**, which keeps track of various statistics on the table, as well as predicates and joins in a SQL statement, to assist the optimizer in producing a better execution plan. These statistics are collected by actually running the query on a sample of the data, and by verifying if the optimizer's estimates match the values found during actual execution. There could be many reasons why the optimizer might produce a bad plan—for example, data skew or stale statistics. The SQL profile will provide information that will allow the optimizer to correct its past mistakes. Once a profile is implemented by pressing the *Implement* button in Figure 10.23, the optimizer will then automatically use the improved estimates to produce a more efficient execution plan.

Hint: You must implement the profile for the new execution plan to take effect.

Note that sometimes the SQL Tuning Advisor may indicate that a very critical index is missing on a SQL statement. However, this is a very limited analysis and should not be considered as advice to implement the index right away. You should instead run the SQL Access Advisor on that SQL Tuning Set to obtain the comprehensive access structure advice.

Figure 10.23 *SQL Tuning Recommendation: Create Profile*

10.4.2 The DBMS_SQLTUNE PL/SQL Package

In section 10.1.1, we saw how the DBMS_SQLTUNE package can be used to create a SQL Tuning Set. This package also provides PL/SQL procedures to run the SQL Tuning Advisor and to create and manage SQL profiles.

The SQL Tuning Advisor can be run either on a single SQL statement or on a SQL Tuning Set. The following example illustrates how to run this advisor on a single SQL statement. Begin by first using the CREATE_TUNING_TASK procedure to create a task, supplying the SQL statement, and then call EXECUTE_TUNING_TASK to analyze the statement.

```
variable  task_name    varchar2(30);
declare
  sql_stmt     varchar2(4000);
begin
  -- prepare task to tune
  sql_stmt :=
   'SELECT p.product_id,
         SUM(ps.purchase_price) as sum_of_sales,
         COUNT (ps.purchase_price) as total_sales
   FROM product p, purchases ps
   WHERE ps.customer_id
      not in (select customer_id
              from customer where country = ''US'')
   GROUP BY p.product_id';
```

```
task_name
    := dbms_sqltune.create_tuning_task(sql_text=>sql_stmt);
-- execute the task created above
dbms_sqltune.execute_tuning_task(:task_name);
end;
/
```

The recommendations and any modified query execution plans can then be viewed using the REPORT_TUNING_TASK function, as shown in the following example.

```
set long 3000
select dbms_sqltune.report_tuning_task(:task_name)
from dual;


----------------------------------------------------------------
GENERAL INFORMATION SECTION
----------------------------------------------------------------
Tuning Task Name    : TASK_497
Scope               : COMPREHENSIVE
...


FINDINGS SECTION (2 findings)
----------------------------------------------------------------
1- SQL Profile Finding (see explain plans section below)
--------------------------------------------------------
A potentially better execution plan was found for this statement.

  Recommendation (estimated benefit: 81%)
  ---------------------------------------
  Consider accepting the recommended SQL profile.
    execute :profile_name :=
        dbms_sqltune.accept_sql_profile(task_name =>'TASK_497');
...
```

If the recommendation includes a SQL profile, as in the preceding example, you can use the ACCEPT_SQL_PROFILE procedure to accept the recommendation and create the profile. The next time the SQL statement is executed, the optimizer will use this profile to adjust its estimates when determining an execution plan.

Hint: The REPORT_TUNING_TASK function returns the report as a CLOB column, and hence you must set the long parameter in SQL*Plus and use a SELECT statement to display this column.

Instead of a single statement, if you would like to tune a SQL Tuning Set, you must pass the name of a SQL Tuning Set to the CREATE_TUNING_TASK procedure. The remaining steps are identical to the preceding example.

We have seen how the SQL Access Advisor and SQL Tuning Advisor help find and fix problems with the query performance. However, even with the most optimal plan the performance may be poor if there is a problem during the SQL statement execution. In the next two sections, we will discuss two common problems: insufficient memory and parallel execution problems that can affect query performance.

10.5 Memory Advisor

Good memory configuration is extremely important in the data-intensive applications typical of a data warehouse. The total available physical memory on your system must be properly split between the Operating System, Oracle Shared Global Area (SGA), Process Global Area (PGA), and any other applications running on the system. The SGA is shared by all Oracle server processes. Among other things, the SGA contains the buffer cache, which caches data blocks, and the shared pool, which caches dictionary metadata and compiled cursors. PGA is a separate private memory used by each Oracle server process. PGA memory is used for complex SQL operations, such as sorts, hash joins, and bitmap merges. PGA is also used as buffers for bulk loads and other processing such as PL/SQL and Java. If available physical memory is insufficient to satisfy all these needs, it will result in the Operating System writing pages to disk to free up memory (known as thrashing), causing performance to degrade rapidly.

Oracle Database 10*g* includes advisors to help tune both PGA and SGA memory. Oracle Enterprise Manager provides a graphical interface to these tools.

10.5.1 Tuning PGA Memory

PGA memory is the most critical memory parameter for the resource-intensive queries found in a data warehouse. In a data warehouse, PGA memory is used by SQL operations, such as sorts, hash joins, bitmap merges, and bulk loads. The amount of PGA memory used by each operation is called its **work area.** Due to the memory-intensive nature of these operations, tuning the work areas is very crucial to ensure good query performance. If enough memory is not available, intermediate data may need to be written to temporary segments on disk, which can slow down performance significantly. Prior to Oracle 9*i*, in order to tune query performance, the DBA had to tune various initialization parameters, such as SORT_AREA_SIZE, HASH_AREA_SIZE, CREATE_BITMAP_AREA_SIZE, and BITMAP_MERGE_AREA_SIZE, to get good performance. However, this was a very difficult and time-consuming process because, the ideal values for these parameters may vary from query to query and may depend on the load on the system. Oracle 9*i* introduced the automatic PGA memory management feature to ease this burden. Additionally, in Oracle Database 10*g* the PGA advisor can be used to determine the ideal memory size setting for the system.

Automatic PGA memory management will automatically balance the work area sizes across SQL statements so as to make best use of available memory. The DBA only needs to specify the total amount of memory available for the database instance by setting the initialization parameter, PGA_AGGREGATE_TARGET. To enable automatic memory management the initialization parameter WORKAREA_SIZE_POLICY must be set to AUTO (setting it to MANUAL will revert back to manual memory management).

Hint: The automatic PGA memory management is not available when you use the shared server–based operation in Oracle. For a data warehouse, the number of connections is usually not an issue; hence, it is recommended to use the dedicated server model.

Before we discuss how to tune PGA memory, let us learn how to monitor the PGA memory usage.

Monitoring PGA Memory Usage

The amount of PGA memory allocated and used by each Oracle server process can be seen in the V$PROCESS view, as follows. The PGA_USED_MEM column represents the memory currently in use, PGA_ALLOC_MEM column is total memory currently allocated by the process (some of it may be freed but not yet returned to the operating system), and PGA_MAX_MEM is the maximum ever allocated by that process. In a well-tuned system, every process should be allocating adequate memory but no more than necessary.

```
SELECT spid, pga_used_mem, pga_alloc_mem, pga_max_mem
FROM v$process;
```

```
SPID         PGA_USED_MEM PGA_ALLOC_MEM PGA_MAX_MEM
------------ ------------ ------------- -----------
340               132552        198880      198880
341               135056       3371624     3371624
343              4349880       7570468     7570468
...
```

The memory used by the work area of SQL statements is seen in the V$SQL_WORKAREA view. You can join to V$SQL to get the complete text for the SQL statements. (We have edited the following output to show only part of the text for lack of space.)

```
SELECT sql_text, operation_type,
       estimated_optimal_size estsize, last_memory_used
FROM v$sql_workarea w, v$sql s
WHERE w.address = s.address
AND parsing_schema_id = USERENV('SCHEMAID') ;
```

```
SQL_TEXT          OPERATION_TYPE    ESTSIZE LAST_MEMORY_USED
---------------   --------------    ------- ----------------
SELECT t.month,   GROUP BY (SORT)     56320            49152
SELECT t.month,   HASH-JOIN          874496           628736
...
```

While a query execution is in progress, you can monitor the work area usage in the V$SQL_WORKAREA_ACTIVE view.

```
-- shows the current workarea usage during an execution
SELECT operation_type, work_area_size, expected_size,
       actual_mem_used
FROM v$sql_workarea_active;
```

```
OPERATION_TYPE WORK_AREA_SIZE EXPECTED_SIZE ACTUAL_MEM_USED
-------------- -------------- ------------- ---------------
HASH-JOIN            1087488       1086464          628736
```

Complex SQL operations need adequate work area memory; otherwise, the operation may need to spill over to temporary segments on disk. The **optimal** memory size is one that allows the entire operation to be performed entirely in memory. If memory is somewhat less than optimal, then one or more extra passes over the data may be required. A **one-pass** operation is the next best to the optimal and will perform reasonably well and as work area sizes get larger, may be the typical case. However, a **multipass** operation will severely degrade performance and should be avoided as much as possible.

Hint: A well-tuned system should have a high percentage of optimal and one-pass executions and very few, if any, multipass executions.

The view V$SQL_WORKAREA_HISTOGRAM can be used to find the distribution of optimal, one-pass, and multipass query executions in your system. The view shows the number of optimal, one-pass, and multipass executions for different ranges of work area sizes. For example, in the following query, most executions use work area sizes under 2MB and are able to execute with the optimal amount of PGA memory. There is one query with work areas between 4 and 8 MB, which needed a one-pass execution and two queries with work areas between 8 and 16 MB, which needed a multi-pass execution.

```
SELECT LOW_OPTIMAL_SIZE LOW, HIGH_OPTIMAL_SIZE HIGH,
       OPTIMAL_EXECUTIONS OPT, ONEPASS_EXECUTIONS Onepass,
       MULTIPASSES_EXECUTIONS multipass
FROM V$SQL_WORKAREA_HISTOGRAM
WHERE TOTAL_EXECUTIONS != 0;
```

LOW	HIGH	OPT	ONEPASS	MULTIPASS
2048	4095	4712	0	0
65536	131071	44	0	0
131072	262143	23	0	0
262144	524287	20	0	0
524288	1048575	178	0	0
1048576	2097151	34	0	0
4194304	8388607	0	1	0
8388608	16777215	0	0	2

Now that we understand how to monitor PGA memory usage and identify any multipass executions, let us see how we go about tuning it.

Tuning PGA_AGGREGATE_TARGET

As we mentioned earlier, available physical memory on a system running Oracle must be distributed among the Operating System, SGA, and PGA. For a data warehouse, a good rule of thumb is to set the PGA_AGGREGATE_TARGET *initially* to about 40 percent to 50 percent of available physical memory and then tune it based on execution of a real workload.

Oracle Database 10*g* will continuously monitor how much PGA memory is being used by the entire instance by collecting statistics during executions of queries. This information can be seen in the V$PGASTAT view.

Using these statistics, it estimates how the performance would vary if the PGA_ AGGREGATE_TARGET were set to different values. This information is published in the V$PGA_ TARGET_ADVICE view and can be used to tune the PGA_AGGREGATE_TARGET parameter.

Hint: Set the initialization parameter STATISTICS_LEVEL to TYPICAL (default) or ALL; otherwise, the V$PGA_TARGET_ADVICE view is not available.

The following query shows the various statistics in V$PGASTAT:

```
SELECT   * FROM V$PGASTAT;
NAME                                          VALUE UNIT
--------------------------------------------- ------------
aggregate PGA target parameter             15728640 bytes
aggregate PGA auto target                   4194304 bytes
global memory bound                          786432 bytes
total PGA inuse                            16775168 bytes
total PGA allocated                        50482176 bytes
maximum PGA allocated                      59011072 bytes
total freeable PGA memory                   6094848 bytes
PGA memory freed back to OS                23986176 bytes
total PGA used for auto workareas            460800 bytes
maximum PGA used for auto workareas         1323008 bytes
total PGA used for manual workareas               0 bytes
maximum PGA used for manual workareas        529408 bytes
over allocation count                           426       <- non zero
bytes processed                            69940224 bytes
extra bytes read/written                   62337024 bytes
cache hit percentage                          60.87 percent <- too low

16 rows selected.
```

The first step is to look at the top two lines of this output: the aggregate PGA target parameter, which is the current setting of PGA_ AGGREGATE_TARGET, and the aggregate PGA auto target, which Oracle has calculated as the total memory it can use for SQL work areas. The difference is the estimated memory needed for other processing, such as PL/SQL, and is not tuned by the automatic memory management feature. In our example, the PGA_AGGREGATE_TARGET is 15.7MB, and the total amount available for work areas is 4.2MB. Note that if you find the auto target is much smaller than the PGA_AGGREGATE_TARGET, as is the case in our example, this is *one* indication that there is not enough PGA memory for work areas and you may need to increase it.

To confirm whether your PGA_AGGREGATE_SETTING is too small, you should look at two quantities - the **cache hit percentage** and the **overallocation count**, underlined in the preceding output. The cache hit percentage indicates the percentage of work areas that operated with an optimal allocation of memory. The overallocation count indicates how many times Oracle had to step over the user-defined limit for PGA_AGGREGATE_TARGET, because there was not enough memory available. In a well-tuned system, the overallocation count should be zero, meaning the available PGA memory was sufficient, and the cache hit percentage should be over 80 percent, meaning most queries execute with the optimal amount of memory. If you find that your cache hit percentage is too low or the overallocation count is nonzero, you have insufficient PGA memory. In our example, the cache hit ratio is 61 percent, which is low, and the overallocation count is 426, which is not good.

In these cases you should look at the V$PGA_TARGET_ADVICE view for advice. The view shows the projected values of the cache hit percentage and the overallocation count for various memory sizes. For each memory size, the FACTOR column shows which factor of the current memory setting it is. For example, the row where the FACTOR column is 1 is the current setting, in our example 15.7MB.

```
select PGA_TARGET_FOR_ESTIMATE PGA_TARGET, PGA_TARGET_FACTOR
FACTOR,
       ESTD_PGA_CACHE_HIT_PERCENTAGE CACHE_HIT_PCT,
       ESTD_OVERALLOC_COUNT OVERALLOC_CNT
from v$pga_target_advice;


PGA_TARGET    FACTOR CACHE_HIT_PCT OVERALLOC_CNT
----------    ------- ------------- -------------
  11796480      .75            50            23
  15728640        1            61            23 <-current setting
  18874368      1.2            61            23
  22020096      1.4            65             2
  25165824      1.6            70             1
  28311552      1.8            80             0 <-minimal needed
   3145728        2            85             0
  47185920        3            87             0
  62914560        4            88             0 <-optimal
  94371840        6            88             0
 125829120        8            89             0

11 rows selected.
```

When tuning PGA memory, you must ensure that the PGA_AGGREGATE_TARGET is *at least* set to a value where the overallocation count is zero. Otherwise, there is simply not enough memory for all the work areas. In this example, the minimum memory setting where overallocation count goes to zero is around 28MB. Further, notice that as you increase memory size, the cache hit ratio value increases rapidly up to a point (88 percent for around 63MB in the previous output), and after that it starts to increase more slowly. This point is the optimal value of PGA memory. You must ideally set your PGA memory at or close to this optimal value.

You can see a graphical representation of this view in Oracle Enterprise Manager. From the Advisor Central page (Figure 10.6), if you follow the *Memory Advisor* link and then click on *PGA* link, you will see the screen shown in Figure 10.24, which shows the current PGA settings and usage.

Figure 10.24 *PGA Memory Advisor*

From this page, if you click on the *Advice* button, you will see a line graph as shown in Figure 10.25 with the memory size setting on the X-axis and the cache hit percentage on the Y-axis. You will find that the initial part of the line graph indicates the threshold below which you will see nonzero overallocation count. The optimal value of memory is where this line starts to taper off. The vertical line shows the current setting of the PGA_AGGREGATE_TARGET parameter and can be moved to choose a new setting for this parameter. Once you have chosen a new value, you simply press the *OK* button and the change will be made.

Figure 10.25   *PGA Target Advice in Oracle Enterprise Manager*

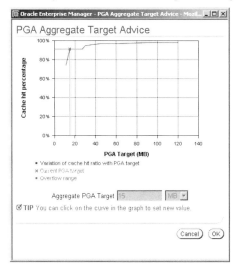

Hint: At all times, you must ensure that there is adequate physical memory on your system to accommodate increases in the PGA memory for all users. If not, then you will need to decrease the SGA memory size, which may not always be desirable. Increasing PGA memory size without available physical memory means that there will be thrashing, which will only slow the system down.

In the next section, we will discuss how to set the value for the SGA memory.

10.5.2   SGA Memory Advisor

SGA memory is accessible across all Oracle processes and is used to store various internal control structures, such as compiled cursors and dictionary entries (known as the shared pool), and the buffer cache. The SGA memory setting is not as critical as the PGA in a data warehouse application; however, in any system, it is important to have sufficient SGA memory for smooth functioning. One component of the SGA, known as the large pool, can be important if you are using parallel execution, which was discussed in Chapter 6. Also, you should ensure that you are not allocating too much shared memory, which takes away valuable physical memory that can be used for PGA instead.

Following the *Memory Advisor* link from *Advisor Central*, you will come to the SGA Memory Advisor page, shown in Figure 10.26. Here you can see at a glance the allocation of SGA between various pools, such as buffer cache, Java pool, large pool, and so on. On this page you can set the *Maximum SGA Size* parameter, which will determine the total shared memory allocated when the database starts up. Later, as the database is running, you can adjust the sizes of the individual components, as long as the total does not exceed the specified maximum.

Figure 10.26 *SGA Memory Advisor*

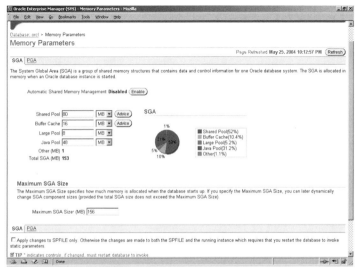

Oracle Database 10*g* has an **Automatic Shared Memory Management** feature, which will automatically and dynamically size the various components of the shared memory to adapt to the current workload. To enable this feature, click the *Enable* button, near the top of Figure 10.26. Note, however, that if you use the automatic feature, you will no longer be able to use the Advisor, since the system will automatically make the changes for you.

You can click the *Advice* buttons to get advice on setting the shared pool and the buffer cache sizes.

Shared Pool Advice

Increasing the shared pool size will improve the time taken to compile a SQL statement. Hence, the shared pool size advice is in the form of a graph, shown in Figure 10.27, with the shared pool size on the X-axis and the expected savings in parse time on the Y-axis. The optimal value is the knee of this graph (i.e., where the graph tapers off). The vertical line shows the current setting of the shared pool, and you can click on the curve to change this setting.

Figure 10.27   *Shared Pool Size Advice*

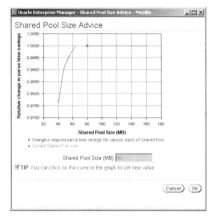

Buffer Cache Advice

The buffer cache is used to cache frequently used data blocks from disk into memory, thereby speeding up queries. In a data warehouse, many queries involve scanning entire tables, and increasing the size of the buffer cache does not usually speed up these scans. (This is because as new blocks get loaded they displace the earlier blocks and so the next query that needs that earlier block will need to get it from the disk again.) Also, loading of data using SQL*Loader or Parallel DML uses PGA memory and not SGA. So, typically, the size of the buffer cache in a data warehouse would be small compared with that in an OLTP system. You can use the buffer cache advice shown in Figure 10.28, to correctly size your buffer cache so you do not waste too much memory. In this graph, the Y-axis shows the decrease in physical disk blocks read as you increase the buffer cache size shown on the X-axis. Again, the optimal value is around the knee of the graph (i.e., where it starts to flatten out) and you can choose the new setting by clicking on the graph.

Hint: Automatic Shared Memory Management must be <u>disabled</u> in order to see the shared pool and buffer pool advice.

Figure 10.28   *Buffer Cache Advice*

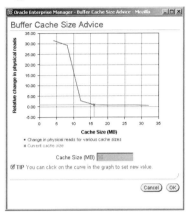

It must be said that, as with all tuning tasks, memory configuration is an iterative process and depends on the workload; therefore, you may need to repeat this process a few times before you get to the optimal settings. However, once you start using automatic PGA and SGA advisors, this process is very straightforward and will ensure that you get the best performance out of your queries.

10.6   Troubleshooting Parallel Execution

Parallel execution is one of the most useful features for good query performance in a data warehouse. However, sometimes you may find that your query did not perform as expected even with parallel execution. First and foremost, it is imperative that you have accurate statistics on your tables. If the data has changed significantly and statistics are not updated, the query plan may no longer be optimal. If statistics are not the problem, it may be that the optimizer did not generate a parallel execution plan for your query. It is also possible that resource constraints forced the query to be executed serially.

In this section, we will discuss some of the problems that can occur with parallel execution and how to identify and fix them.

10.6.1   Using EXPLAIN PLAN to Display Parallel Plans

The first step when troubleshooting parallel execution is to check for possible problems with the query plan. You can use the EXPLAIN PLAN facility (discussed in Chapter 6) to display the parallel query execution plan. Note that you must use the script utlxplp.sql to display the plan. The following example shows the parallel execution plan for the same query used in Chapter 6. We have formatted the plan to show only columns related to parallel execution, for lack of space.

```
EXPLAIN PLAN FOR
SELECT t.month, t.year, p.product_id,
       SUM (purchase_price) as sum_of_sales,
       COUNT (purchase_price) as total_sales,
       COUNT(*) as cstar
FROM time t, product p, purchases f
WHERE t.time_key = f.time_key AND
      f.product_id = p.product_id
GROUP BY t.month, t.year, p.product_id;
```

```
-------------------------------------------------------------------
|Id|Operation                  |Name     |   TQ |IN-OUT|PQDistrib|
-------------------------------------------------------------------
| 0|SELECT STATEMENT           |         |      |      |         |
| 1|PX COORDINATOR             |         |      |      |         |
| 2| PX SEND QC (RANDOM)       |:TQ10003 |Q1,03| P->S |QC (RAND)|
| 3|  SORT GROUP BY            |         |Q1,03| PCWP |         |
| 4|   PX RECEIVE              |         |Q1,03| PCWP |         |
| 5|    PX SEND HASH           |:TQ10002 |Q1,02| P->P |HASH     |
| 6|     HASH JOIN             |         |Q1,02| PCWP |         |
| 7|      PX RECEIVE           |         |Q1,02| PCWP |         |
| 8|       PX SEND BROADCAST   |:TQ10000 |Q1,00| P->P |BROADCAST|
| 9|        PX BLOCK ITERATOR  |         |Q1,00| PCWC |         |
|10|         TABLE ACCESS FULL |TIME     |Q1,00| PCWP |         |
|11|      HASH JOIN            |         |Q1,02| PCWP |         |
|12|       PX RECEIVE          |         |Q1,02| PCWP |         |
|13|        PX SEND BROADCAST  |:TQ10001 |Q1,01| P->P |BROADCAST|
|14|         PX BLOCK ITERATOR |         |Q1,01| PCWC |         |
|15|          INDEX FAST FULL SCAN|PRODUCT|Q1,01| PCWP |         |
|  |                           |_PK_INDEX|      |      |         |
|16|         PX BLOCK ITERATOR |         |Q1,02| PCWC |         |
|17|          TABLE ACCESS FULL|PURCHASES|Q1,02| PCWP |         |
-------------------------------------------------------------------
```

The first thing to note is that if you ignore the rows prefixed with a PX, the plan is the same as the serial plan seen earlier in Chapter 6! The PX rows for each operation indicate how that operation has been parallelized. For instance, the PX BLOCK ITERATOR row for id 16 indicates that the scan of the PURCHASES TABLE has been parallelized at the block granule. The TQ column and the :TQxxxx names refer to communication pipes between the query coordinator process and the parallel execution servers. The IN-OUT columns indicate which processes are involved in the communication at each stage. The important thing to note for this column is that as long the value is P->P, PCWC, or PCWS it implies that operation is in parallel. However, if you see P->S or no value at all, it means that at that point the operation is serial. Typically, you will see P->S when the coordinator collects results from all the slaves. This column can be used to check if your plan is using parallel execution throughout or if some operation is being unexpectedly serialized. If you find that an operation that can be parallelized, such as a table scan, a join, or a sort, is executing serially, then there may be a problem with the execution plan.

If you find that an operation is serial where it could be parallel, check your parallel execution setup and ensure that the tables and indexes have statistics. Check if some user-defined function or aggregate (discussed in Chapter 6) is preventing parallel execution. Run the SQL Tuning Advisor to see if your query can be tuned further. For instance, if your query involves subqueries, it may be possible to express the query using a join instead.

Finally, the last column in the plan display, PQ Distrib, is the method used by parallel execution to distribute rows of a table among the slaves: broadcast, meaning all rows are sent to all slaves; hash, meaning a hash function is used to distribute the rows; and random, meaning the rows are distributed randomly among the slaves. If the table data is skewed so that there are more rows with one value than another, or if there are very few distinct values, then this can result in some slaves having more work to do than others. In this case, the PX_DISTRIBUTE hint can be used to alter the distribution method chosen by the optimizer.

If the query plan looks good, then the problem is likely due to lack of some resource.

10.6.2 Problems Due to Resource Constraints

You can find some useful execution statistics in various dynamic performance views such as V$SYSSTAT, V$PX_SESSION and V$PX_PROCESS_SYSSTAT.

Hint: Corresponding to every V$ view is a GV$ view. The V$ views only give statistics for the current instance. If you are using Real Application Clusters, you will have multiple instances and will need to use the GV$ views. The GV$ views give the statistics for all the instances and therefore have an extra column, INST_ID.

The view V\$SYSSTAT keeps cumulative statistics about the Oracle instance from the time of database startup. The following query can be used to query the statistics related to parallel execution. From this you can tell if your queries are being parallelized with the desired degree of parallelism or if they are being downgraded due to resource contention. If you find this to be the case, you may need to limit the number of concurrent users or identify whether there is some high-load SQL statement that is taking up a lot of the parallel execution servers. In the following output, the rows marked with an asterisk indicate that some statements did not execute with the requested degree of parallelism.

```
SELECT ss.value, ss.name
FROM v$sysstat ss
WHERE UPPER(ss.name) like '%PARALLEL%'
   or UPPER(ss.name) like '%PX%';

     VALUE NAME
---------- ------------------------------------------------
         5 DBWR parallel query checkpoint buffers written
         8 queries parallelized
         0 DML statements parallelized
         0 DDL statements parallelized
         8 DFO trees parallelized
         4 Parallel operations not downgraded
         0 Parallel operations downgraded to serial
         0 Parallel operations downgraded 75 to 99 pct
       * 1 Parallel operations downgraded 50 to 75 pct
       * 1 Parallel operations downgraded 25 to 50 pct
       * 3 Parallel operations downgraded 1 to 25 pct
    151171 PX local messages sent
    151084 PX local messages recv'd
         0 PX remote messages sent
         0 PX remote messages recv'd
15 rows selected.
```

The V\$PX_SESSION view can be used to figure out which parallel execution servers are working together on a query. QCSID is the session id of the coordinator and there is one row for each slave process, with SID being the session id of the slave process. One useful piece of information in this view is the requested and actual degree of parallelism for the operation. If the requested degree is more than the actual, then you have a resource shortage. In this example, the requested degree is 8 and the actual degree is 7, which indicates a shortage of parallel execution servers.

```
SELECT QCSID, SID, DEGREE "Degree", REQ_DEGREE "Req Degree"
FROM V$PX_SESSION
ORDER BY QCSID, QCINST_ID, SERVER_GROUP, SERVER_SET;
```

```
     QCSID          SID      Degree Req Degree
---------- ---------- ---------- ----------
       142        122          7          8
       142        140          7          8
       142        124          7          8
       ...
```

Finally, the V$PX_PROCESS_SYSSTAT gives information about the status of the parallel execution servers and statistics about memory and buffer allocations. The Highwater, or HWM, figures represent the maximum concurrent usage for that resource and give you an idea whether the resource is being maximally used at the present time. Specifically, if the Servers Highwater value is equal to PARALLEL_MAX_SERVERS, it means that all the parallel execution server processes were in use concurrently at some point in time. In this case, you should consider increasing this parameter, if you have the processing capacity.

```
select * from V$PX_PROCESS_SYSSTAT;

STATISTIC                            VALUE
------------------------------ ----------
Servers In Use                          28
Servers Available                        2
Servers Started                         34
Servers Shutdown                         4
Servers Highwater                       30
Servers Cleaned Up                       0
Server Sessions                         92
Memory Chunks Allocated                  9
Memory Chunks Freed                      2
Memory Chunks Current                    7
Memory Chunks HWM                        9
Buffers Allocated                     1234
Buffers Freed                          856
Buffers Current                        378
Buffers HWM                            387
```

Oracle recommends configuring the LARGE_POOL_SIZE parameter when using parallel execution. This memory pool is used to store the message buffers for communication between parallel execution processes. If the product of Buffers HWM and the initialization parameter PARALLEL_MESSAGE_BUFFER_SIZE is much less than the parameter LARGE_POOL_SIZE, you should consider increasing this parameter setting.

You should also consider using the Oracle Resource Manager to create resource plans to limit resource usage for each user or application. We cannot stress enough that for parallel execution to be effective, it is important to have sufficient hardware capacity; otherwise, no amount of tuning can improve your performance.

10.7   Plan Stability

You have successfully tuned and deployed your data warehouse application and everything is running perfectly. Then you apply a new patch to the underlying database and suddenly everything slows down and the users start complaining. What happened? Well, the most likely explanation is that the optimizer chose a different strategy for the query execution, which it believes is better but in reality is worse. This can happen for many reasons, including skewed data distribution, different optimizer statistics, or a new default setting for some initialization parameter. Thus, anytime you do a software upgrade, or after statistics get updated, there is a risk that a query execution plan may change and the query may take longer to run.

To mitigate this problem, Oracle has a feature called **plan stability**. This allows you to create an object called a **stored outline** for a SQL statement, which keeps a record of the execution plan for that query. When a query is issued, if there is an outline for that query, Oracle will try to reproduce the same execution plan as stored in the outline.

10.7.1   Creating an Outline

You can instruct Oracle to create outlines for all SQL statements or for specific SQL statements. Outlines can be grouped together into **categories** to better organize and manage them.

The schema where outlines will be created must have the CREATE ANY OUTLINE system privilege.

To create stored outlines for all SQL statements you must set the parameter CREATE_STORED_OUTLINES to TRUE or specify a category name to group the outline into. In the following example, we are setting the category name to EASYDW_CAT.

```
ALTER SESSION SET CREATE_STORED_OUTLINES = easydw_cat;
```

Once you set this, outlines will automatically be created for every SQL statement and associated with the given category (if specified). This is an easy way to create the outlines, but it may result in a large number of outlines. Typically, just before upgrading to a new database version, you would turn this parameter on, leave the application running for some period of time to create outlines, and then turn the parameter off by setting CREATE_STORED_OUTLINES to false.

Alternatively, you can create stored outlines for specific SQL statements using the CREATE OUTLINE statement. In the following example, we are creating an outline named CUST_OUTLN under the category CUST_PURCHASES_CAT.

```
CREATE OUTLINE cust_outln FOR CATEGORY cust_purchases_cat
ON
SELECT count(distinct product_id) as num_cust
FROM  purchases f, customer c
WHERE f.customer_id = c.customer_id and
      c.gender = 'F';
```

10.7.2 Using an Outline

To use stored outlines, you must set the parameter USE_STORED_OUTLINES to true or to a category name (which you specified when you created the outlines). When Oracle compiles a SQL statement, it looks to see if there is an outline for a query with *exactly* the same text as the query. If it finds one, then the information stored in the outline is used to control the execution plan generated for the query.

```
ALTER SESSION SET USE_STORED_OUTLINES = easydw_cat;
```

To check if a query used an outline, you can run the EXPLAIN PLAN utility to see the execution plan of the query. The output will indicate the name of the outline used, if any. You can also view the available outlines and their usage using the USER_OUTLINES dictionary view, as shown in the following example.

```
NAME        USED    SQL_TEXT
----------  ----    ------------------------------
CUST_OUTLN  USED    SELECT count(distinct product_id
```

Hint: Using an outline does not guarantee that you will get the identical execution plan. For example, if the outline referred to an index that was later dropped, you would obviously not be able to use the execution plan using that index. Also, some initialization parameter settings may take precedence over outlines—for example, if you set query_rewrite_enabled to false, Oracle will not use a materialized view even if you had an outline using it.

As you can see, plan stability is extremely simple to use and can be a very valuable tool to ensure that query performance remains predictable. After your application has been tuned adequately, consider creating some outlines for your important queries. Once they have been created and stored in the database, it is not necessary that you use them all the time. Instead, they can be kept in case of emergency and enabled only in the event of performance degradation. Outlines are also useful when building applications that are deployed at a number of sites to ensure the same query execution plan is chosen for all users.

10.8 Summary

In this chapter, we discussed various aspects of query performance tuning. Oracle Database 10*g* provides tuning tools such as the SQL Access Advisor and SQL Tuning Advisor, which can be invaluable assistants to a DBA in simplifying the ongoing tasks of performance tuning. With these tools you can create index and materialized views to speed up your queries and also improve the optimizer's ability to create good execution plans, using profiles. We also discussed how you could find and fix some common parallel execution problems and tune the PGA memory so that the queries execute with the optimal memory required. Finally, we discussed how you can use plan stability to keep the query performance predictable over time.

Query performance tuning is just one of the tasks faced by a DBA when managing a warehouse. Chapter 11 looks at the larger scope of managing a data warehouse and the tools and features Oracle Database 10*g* provides for this purpose.

Managing the Warehouse

11.1 What Has to Be Managed

Once the warehouse has been created and is populated with data, it is very important to ensure that it is correctly managed. The warehouse must be configured for optimal performance and availability. Disk, memory, and CPU resources must be managed effectively. In this chapter, we will describe some of the tasks involved in managing a data warehouse and provide advice on how to execute them.

We will make use of the various GUI tools provided in Oracle Enterprise Manager (OEM) to manage our database. There are alternative methods to this approach, but we are sure you will agree that using OEM makes managing the database considerably easier.

This chapter will first provide an introduction to OEM and then discuss various tasks, such as reorganizing the warehouse, gathering optimizer statistics, maintaining security, and monitoring space usage.

11.2 Managing Using Oracle Enterprise Manager

With Oracle Database 10*g*, Enterprise Manager changed significantly from the Java-based GUI tool to an easily accessible interface accessed via any browser on your wide area network. There are two named variants of Enterprise Manager: Database Control and Grid Control.

For managing an individual database and its ASM storage, EM Database Control is used, and this is the version that we are using predominantly in this chapter. EM Database Control is installed as standard with the database.

For managing multiple databases, application servers, and ASM storage components in your enterprise environment, Enterprise Manager Grid Control is used. EM Grid Control is installed from a separate installation CD.

EM Database Control provides a subset of the functionality that is present in EM Grid Control.

Therefore, from one lightweight browser you can manage your entire system, no matter where the components may be located. This is an extremely powerful capability, and you should remember that what we are describing here could be used not only for the data warehouse database but also for other Oracle databases—from versions 8.1.7 and above, Oracle Application Server 10*g*, and ASM storage on your network. In this section, we'll take a look at some of the concepts and steps required to start using OEM.

11.2.1 The Enterprise Manager Console

Before we launch into a more detailed examination of the new Enterprise Manager, it is worth mentioning that we still have the old Java GUI EM console to handle certain aspects of managing our environment.

The Java EM Console is installed from the Client CD and still has the same familiar interface from its Oracle 9*i* version. With the Oracle Database 10*g* version, you will find that some of the tools have been removed to the browser version, such as the import and export wizards, backup wizard, the events and job scheduling tools, and the ability to create warehouse dimensions and cubes. For handling the following product areas you will still need to use the Console.

- Streams

- Advanced replication

- Advanced queues

- XML database

- Spatial

None of these components is crucial to a data warehouse, so you can manage the warehouse environment exclusively using the browser-based interface.

11.2.2   Overview of Enterprise Manager

EM Database Control, which we have been using so far, is for administering and managing an individual Oracle Database 10*g* at a time. As we have seen in previous chapters, you simply point your browser at the URL for the instance on a server that you wish to administer. The deployment is shown in Figure 11.1.

Figure 11.1   *Enterprise Manager Database Control*

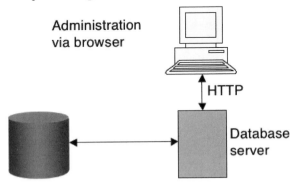

The URL for Database Control is shown in the following code, and the default port number is 5500. If you have multiple Oracle 10*g* databases on your server, then EM will be configured to use a different port number for each database. For example, the second database may be configured to use port 5501.

```
http://<server name>:port/em
```

The background tasks for the database console can be manually started and stopped from the operating system command line, using the Enterprise Manager command-line utility, emctl, as follows:

To start the console:

```
emctl start dbconsole
```

Or to stop the console:

```
emctl stop dbconsole
```

On a Windows system, Enterprise Manager uses a Windows service for operation. The Windows service name is OracleDBConsole<sid>, where

<sid> is that for your database. For example, the service for the EASYDW database is OracleDBConsoleeasydw. The service will be configured during installation to start automatically at system startup.

However, if we want to be managing and administering a number of databases, and also other components such as Oracle Application Server 10*g*, then we need to use Enterprise Manager 10*g* Grid Control.

Enterprise Manager Grid Control is designed to run in a three-tier architecture.

- The **console**, which is accessed using a browser, provides the graphical user interface on the client system.

- The **management service** (OMS), which provides administrative functions, such as executing jobs and events, runs in the middle tier.

- The **management agents**, which monitor the various targets on the servers, such as the database and ASM instances, start and stop them and gather performance data.

All information required to manage and administer the environment is stored in the OEM repository, which can be part of any Oracle database or in a separate Oracle database, which is used exclusively for Enterprise Manager. It is where the management service stores the information it needs to manage the network configuration, the events to monitor, jobs to run, and the administrator accounts.

The various components in EM Grid Control are shown in Figure 11.2. To manage a server and the different components deployed on it, you must have a management agent deployed. This is done as part of an installation separate from that for the database itself. In Figure 11.2, we have shown just two types of servers with agents deployed:

- A server with two database instances and an ASM instance

- A server with a Oracle Application Server 10*g* instance

Of course, via EM Grid Control you can administer as many servers and components as you have agents deployed

Figure 11.2   *Enterprise Manager Grid Control Deployment*

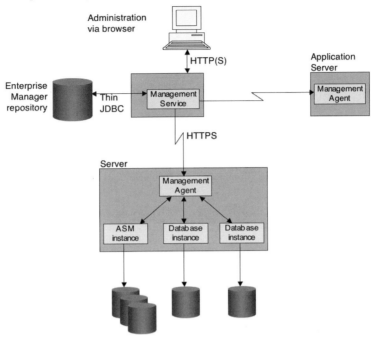

The Grid Control management service communicates with the agents via secure https. Your browser can communicate with the management service either via a nonsecure or a secure https connection. Considering the importance of your enterprise environment, we recommend you always use the secure https URL.

For EM Grid Control, the secure URL is different from the one for Database Control. For Grid Control, the default URL is:

```
https://<server name>:port/em
```

where the default port number is 7777.

To control the management service we again use the emctl command-line utility. To start the management service we execute the following from the operating system command line:

```
emctl start oms
```

The management agent must similarly be started and this is done as follows:

```
emctl start agent
```

We will continue looking at the new interface and features in the Enterprise Manager for now and have a further look at the extensions for Grid Control later in the chapter.

11.2.3 Enterprise Manager Database Control

In Chapter 2, we have already touched upon how to access the EM login screen via the browser. When you logon to EM Database Control, you have the option of logging on as a normal user, an operator, or as SYSDBA. Each has different levels of privileges, and certain administration functions will not be available from all login types. For example, if you want to change the value of certain initialization parameters, such as shared_pool_size, then you will need to be logged on as a privileged SYSDBA account. We will assume that a DBA account is being used and point out any differences when we come across them.

When you have logged in, you are presented with the *Home* screen, shown in Figure 11.3, which provides you with a basic summary and status of your database operation. It is grouped into separate areas, and, if you scroll down further, you will see other areas, such as the *Alerts* section, where you can easily see if there are any critical alerts and notifications for your attention. We will look at alerts in more detail later in the chapter. The home page is also an active display. On the top right of the screen there is the *View Data* field, where you can switch from a manual refresh to a regular one every 60 seconds.

Even further down the screen (which isn't shown), there is a section for *Job Activity* and *Critical Patch Advisories*. We will look at jobs later in this chapter. The new patch advisory feature uses an Oracle Metalink connection, configured in OEM to determine whether or not any new patches have been released by Oracle and need to be installed on your system.

Enterprise Manager has four different home tab areas, which are accessed from the links at the top left of the screen. These are:

- Home
- Performance
- Administration
- Maintenance

Figure 11.3 *Launching Oracle Enterprise Manager*

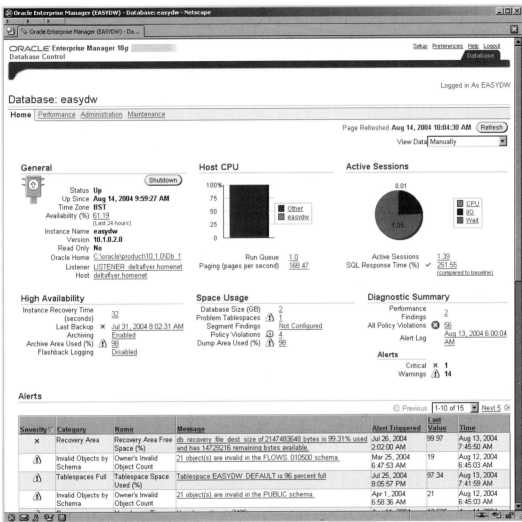

Home

The *Home* page is the initial login Home page with the summary information, where critical alerts and warnings are flagged for the administrator's attention.

Performance

The *Performance* screen provides a new graphical user interface to show the performance and operation of the system and visually highlight problem areas. Various links by the graphs enable drill down, so that the administrator can analyze the system and focus in on any problem areas and even drill down to identify the SQL or other activity that is causing the problem. This is a very powerful new area and set of screens for assisting the administrator in problem identification and resolution.

We discussed various SQL tuning tools available from the *Performance* page in Chapter 10.

Administration

The *Administration* screen is the area that we have visited quite frequently during the course of this book. It is the main launch area to specific screens for administering the objects and other activities in the database. For example, we can administer the instance, monitor the memory usage, and change the initialization parameters from the *Instance* section. Or we can monitor and control the use of resources among our consumers in the database in the *Resource Manager* section.

From the work that we have done in the preceding chapters, you should now be quite comfortable with the look and feel of these administration screens, so, instead of reviewing each area, later in the chapter we will focus on some new areas, such as the *Scheduler*.

Maintenance

The *Maintenance* screen consists of three main areas for *Utilities, Backup & Recovery,* and *Deployments.* The *Utilities* section includes some areas that we have already talked about in Chapter 5, such as import and export and SQL*Loader. It also contains some other very useful features, such as *Online Redefinition,* which we will discuss later and Chapter 12 is dedicated to backup and recovery, and software upgrades is discussed in Chapter 17.

Finally, at the bottom of the screen, we have a small section on related links, which will take us to other important areas of Enterprise Manager. You will find the *Related Links* section is common to each of the four Home screens described previously.

11.2.4 Enterprise Manager Grid Control

Enterprise Manager Grid Control enables us to view the status of all of the components in our enterprise grid, including the host servers, the databases, the application servers, and the storage instances. EM enables us to drill down from the enterprise perspective to look at any aspect of the individual operation of these components. In this section, we will provide a brief overview of what we mean by this.

When we log on to EM Grid Control, our initial view and Home page is very different from what we are used to with EM Database Control. The EM Grid Control *Home* screen is shown in Figure 11.4.

Hint: Figure 11.4 shows the use of a drop-down list. Drop-down lists are a key feature used in Enterprise Manager screens for finding more options or actions that can be performed.

In Enterprise Manager, **targets** are components that you monitor or configure via Enterprise Manager. In the expanded drop-down list shown in Figure 11.4, we can see how the Grid Control interface enables us to view all component targets in our environment. The drop-down list demonstrates the comprehensive nature of what can be monitored and administered, such as databases, application servers, and ASM storage.

Notice that in Figure 11.4, we have a main tab menu at the top of the screen showing the following options:

- Home
- Targets
- Deployments
- Alerts
- Jobs
- Management System

For certain selections from this tab menu, a secondary menu, as shown in Figure 11.5, is displayed. The submenu for *Targets* contains entries for the different types of targets that can be administered; they are:

Figure 11.4   *Enterprise Manager Grid Control Screen*

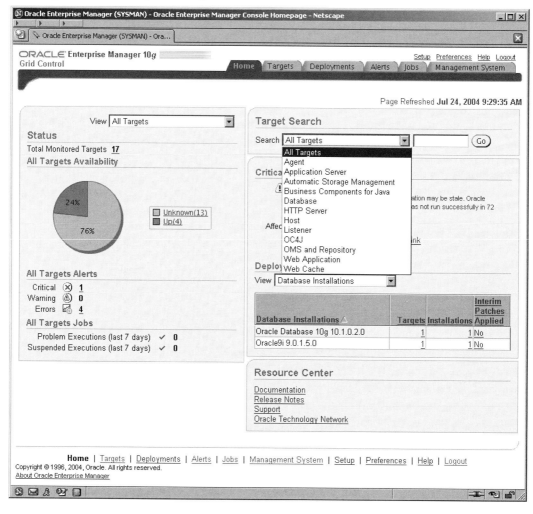

- Hosts

- Databases

- Application Servers

- Web Applications

- Groups

- All Targets

But to enable us to monitor and manage a target, Enterprise Manager must first know about it. To do this we must direct EM to discover the targets. This operation only needs to be performed once for a new server. Go to the top of the main *Hosts* screen, shown in Figure 11.5, select the *Targets* tab at the top, and then select *Hosts* from the submenu. Once the Management Agent on the new host has started talking to the Management Service, then your new host will appear in the list on the *Hosts* screen. Select the host on which you want EM to discover the targets and click on the *Add* button.

Figure 11.5 *Enterprise Manager Target Hosts Screen*

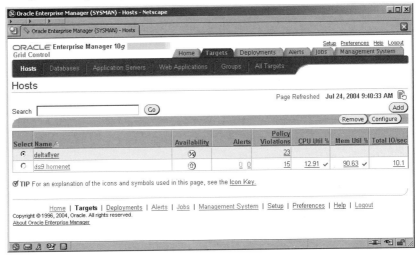

On the next screen (not shown) enter the name of the host and click the *Continue* button. This will start a task, which may take a few minutes to execute, where the EM management service is talking to the agent that is deployed on the new host. The agent examines its host environment and the targets that are deployed on it—for example, database instances or ASM instances—and communicates the findings back to the management service. These are then displayed in the *Targets Discovered* screen, shown in Figure 11.6.

By clicking the *OK* button you accept the discovered targets and the metadata for these is written to the OMS repository. You are now able to access and drill down to manage these target components directly from the EM screens. For example, by selecting the *Targets* tab and *Hosts* subtab at the top of the screen, you will see the *Hosts* screen shown in Figure 11.5.

Figure 11.6   *Enterprise Manager Host Discovery Results*

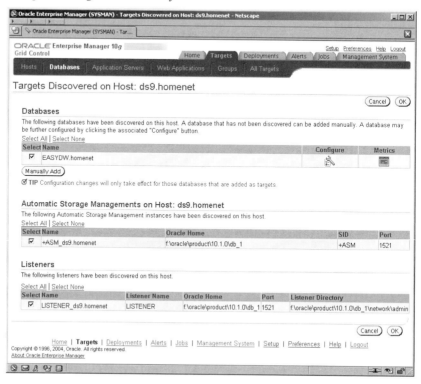

Clicking on the name of a host in the list will navigate you to the host's *Home* page for which there are four separate screens for the host: *Home*, *Performance*, *Targets*, and *Configuration*. By clicking on the *Targets* link, you will see a list of all of the targets on that host that are monitored by EM, as shown in Figure 11.7.

You can now click on the name of any of these targets to navigate to specific screens for the administration of that type of target. In Chapter 3, we have already seen some of the screens for administering an ASM instance. Alternatively, if the database name is clicked (which is third in our list), we navigate to the now very familiar EM Database Control Home pages for that database.

There is much, much more to Grid Control than we have space for in this chapter, so we have only provided a quick glimpse of its capabilities here. Grid Control is not just about the ability to monitor, diagnose, and control—though, as we have seen at the database level, it is a very impor-

Figure 11.7   *Enterprise Manager Navigating to Host Targets*

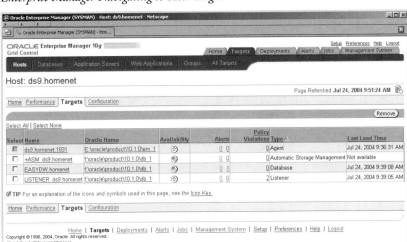

tant component—it is also about the ability to control resources across the grid.

11.2.5   Enterprise Manager Administrators

To perform certain operations, an Enterprise Manager administrator account is required. An administrator account is a database account that has been enabled within Enterprise Manager to perform administration tasks. Database and normal Enterprise Manager accounts are not administrators by default. Enterprise Manager has two types of administrator accounts: regular administrators and super administrators, who have additional privileges.

A super administrator is created when Enterprise Manager is installed and configured. This is the SYSMAN account and, depending upon the password option you selected during database creation (see Figure 2.7), will either have your common password for key accounts or a specifically chosen one. Go to the *Administration* screen and select the *Administrators* link, which takes you to the *Administrators Setup* screen, shown in Figure 11.8 from where we can manage the administrators' accounts.

When we click the *Create* button, we can create a new administrator in the screen shown in Figure 11.9, where an existing database account can be selected and granted the privileges to be an administrator in Enterprise Manager. The Super Administrator is creating an account with the user

Figure 11.8   *The Administrators Setup Screen*

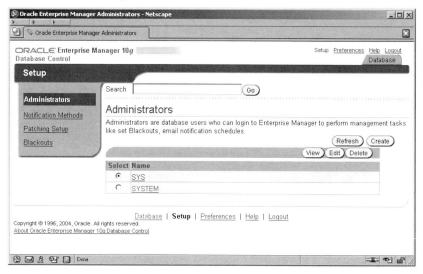

name of EASYDW, for the DBA of the EASYDW data warehouse. Note that this is not a Super Administrator account, because we have not selected that option.

Figure 11.9   *Creating An Enterprise Manager Administrator Account*

11.2.6   Creating and Using Groups

Earlier, we spoke of the issues surrounding managing multiple databases, and this applies equally to other targets in our grid, such as application servers and ASM instances. The purpose of a group is to allow you to logically associate the different targets in your environment to assist with the issues surrounding managing multiple targets. The Oracle grid in an enterprise environment can manage many different separate systems. For example:

- Warehouse databases

- Warehouse ASM instances

- Application Servers

- Source OLTP servers and databases

- HR and payroll servers and databases

There are many other Oracle systems typically required for the running of the business that fall into this list.

In a large enterprise environment, we often require some way to group these together to help us better understand and appreciate the organization of the grid that we are administering. A group can consist of targets of the same type—for example, all databases—or it can consist of targets of different types, such as the database, ASM instances, and application servers for the warehouse. Some examples of ways that we may want to define the groups are:

- A functional requirement—for example, all targets for the data warehouse

- A geographical split for example, a group for the systems in the North-east United States and another for the systems in the United Kingdom.

- An area of individual responsibility for example, the systems which are the responsibility of a particular administrator

You can only create and administer groups from EM Grid Control and not EM Database Control, because it is Grid Control that has the management framework for the administration of multiple targets.

To create a group, go to the *Targets* tab at the top of the Grid Control *Home* screen and select the *Group* subtab below it. The resulting screen (not shown) lists all of the groups that have been defined. To create a new group, choose the type of group and click the *Go* button. There are three types of groups that can be created:

- **Group**, which can either be for mixed or for all the same type of targets.

- **Database Group**, which is only for database targets

- **Host Group**, which is only for host server targets

We have chosen to create a general group, which can contain targets of mixed types, the range of which you can see from the displayed drop-down list in Figure 11.10. On this screen you enter the name of the group, Easy Shopping Inc. When a target type is selected, the list is refreshed to display all available targets of that type, which you can then select and move to the *Selected Targets* list.

Figure 11.10   *Creating a Group*

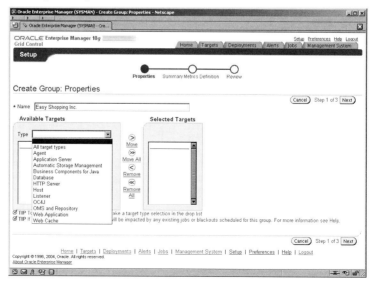

On the next screen of the wizard (not shown), you can define which metrics are to be collected and used for the group. This screen displays the metrics that are applicable to each type of target in the group. When the choice of metrics has been made, the minimum, maximum, and average of these for the targets are used for the alerts and warnings on the group's Home page (see Figure 11.11).

Figure 11.11   *The Enterprise Manager Group For Easy Shopping Inc.*

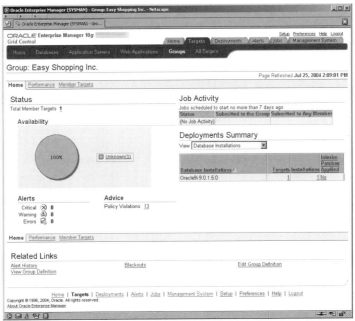

In Figure 11.11, we can see our group, called Easy Shopping Inc., which represents our warehouse. The screen is a summary display of key information about the hosts that make up our group. This is one of the powerful visual features of creating a group, because you can instantly look at the screen and see the state of your system. From this screen we may drill down and focus on different aspects of the various targets in the group by navigating to the *Member Targets* screen.

You may be saying to yourself: This is all very well, but what is the point? Later in the chapter, we will describe metrics, alerts, and warnings in more detail, and when these are combined with the group concept, you have a very powerful management environment.

Groups simplify the management of a complex environment by enabling the environment to be subdivided into logical groups, which serve a similar purpose. You can create as many groups as you like to assist with the management of your environment.

11.2.7   Scheduling Jobs

Data warehouses require a great deal of maintenance, because data is continually being loaded. You could write scripts to perform these tasks and remember to run them, or you could use the Scheduler in Enterprise Manager to automatically run your jobs at the designated time.

The Oracle Database 10g Scheduler

The new Scheduler facility in Oracle Database 10*g* provides the ability to define jobs that must be run in order to manage your data warehouse. These jobs can be placed in a library and scheduled automatically by EM to run at the specified time.

First, we need some simple definitions to help us understand the process:

- The **Program**. This is the actual executable that we want to run.

- The **Job**. This is metadata that defines how a program is to be run. It defines the argument values for the execution of the program.

- The **Schedule**. This specifies when the job is executed. The schedule also defines whether or not, and how, the job repeats its execution.

Before we can create a job, we must first create a program that we want to run. A program can be a PL/SQL block, a stored procedure, or an operating system executable outside of the database. We will base our example on a small program to collect schema statistics. As we have seen in the previous chapters, the ability of the database optimizer to select the best access plan to get the data to answer the queries depends on statistics having been collected on our schema objects.

We will now create a program that gathers the statistics for a schema and for this we will use a simple PL/SQL stored procedure, which takes the schema name as its single parameter and calls a standard procedure, called GATHER_SCHEMA_STATS, in the package DBMS_STATS.

```
CREATE OR REPLACE PROCEDURE gather_schema_stats
    (schema_name IN VARCHAR2)
AS
BEGIN
  dbms_stats.gather_schema_stats(schema_name);
END;
/
```

To create a program, click the *Programs* link under the Scheduler section on the *Administration* screen and you will get a screen that contains a list of programs. Click the *Create* button on the right to get to the *Create Program* screen shown, in Figure 11.12, where we can define our program. Name your program and make sure that it is owned by EASYDW and that it is enabled. For our example, we have decided to use a naming convention with a _P suffix for the programs and _J suffix for the jobs. Make sure that you have clicked the *Yes* radio button so that the program is enabled.

Now you have to specify the type of the program; in this example we are going to create one for a stored procedure. When you click on the *Type* box to select STORED_PROCEDURE, the screen layout will change to the screen shown and will contain extra fields that are specific to that program type. If the default procedure name shown isn't the one for our stored procedure, then click the *Select Procedure* button. This will display a new screen (not shown), which enables you to select the GATHER_SCHEMA_STATS procedure in the EASYDW schema.

We will create our program as a stored procedure in order to demonstrate how the arguments work. In Figure 11.12, you can see that the single

Figure 11.12   *Creating a Program*

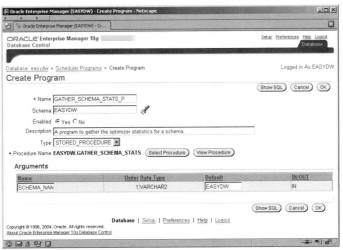

argument for our stored procedure has been displayed. At this point, we have the opportunity to provide a default value for the argument, which will be used if the program is invoked without any value at all. Enter EASYDW into the *Default* field.

Our program is ready to be created, and, if you click on the *Show SQL* button, you will see the screen shown in Figure 11.13, which Enterprise Manager is going to execute. This involves three calls to procedures in the DBMS_SCHEDULER package to create metadata about the program and the arguments and then to enable the program.

Figure 11.13   *SQL to Create a Program*

Click *Return* to go back to the *Create Program* screen and then *OK* to create the program.

Now that we have created the program, we need to define the job that will execute it. In the *Administration* screen in the *Scheduler* section, click on *Jobs* to get to the *Scheduler Jobs* screen and then click the *Create* button to see the *Create Jobs* screen, shown in Figure 11.14.

Figure 11.14   *Creating a Job*

In the same fashion as when we created the program, the *Job* screen defaults to fields for the command that are relevant to a PL/SQL block. Changing the command type will refresh the screen with fields appropriate to that type. In our example to gather schema statistics, we could have entered the call to the DBMS_STATS package directly into the PL/SQL block in this screen. However, this wouldn't have helped demonstrate how programs and arguments are used by the Scheduler, which is why we are using a program.

Once you have completed the *Name, Owner,* and *Description fields,* click on the *Change Command Type* button and you will see the small screen shown in Figure 11.15 for selecting the program to be associated with this job.

Figure 11.15   *Selecting the Program for the Job*

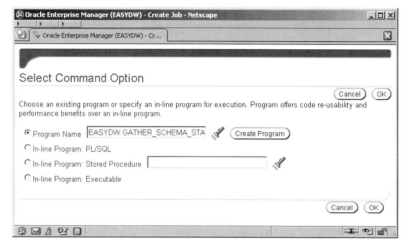

Select the *Program Name* radio button and the program that we just created and click *OK.* Figure 11.16 shows that the *Command* section now reflects our program with its single argument. If we fill in the *Value* field with EASYDW, then, whenever this job is run, it will gather statistics for the EASYDW schema.

There are two other screen tabs associated with creating a job. The first is to specify the schedule that is used for executing the job. Click on the *Schedule* link. The resulting screen, similar to that shown in Figure 11.17, enables us to specify whether or not the job should reexecute on a repeating basis and if so, when it repeats. Assuming that our warehouse will be refreshed every night, we would want the optimizer statistics to be collected daily at the end of that refresh task, just before the warehouse starts to be used for the business day. Click on the *Repeat* field and select *By Days,* and the resulting screen will be similar to that shown in Figure 11.17.

In Figure 11.17, there are four different ways to define the schedule for our new job, specified by the *Schedule Type* field.

Figure 11.16   *Setting the Job-Specific Parameters*

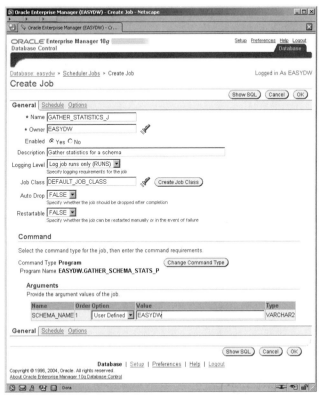

- **Standard**, where you can create a specific schedule, as shown in Figure 11.17.

- **Use Predefined Schedule**, where the job uses a predefined and stored schedule. With this type, the stored schedule name is simply selected for use.

- **Standard, using PL/SQL for repeated intervals** where a PL/SQL expression (e.g., "SYSDATE + 1" is the Enterprise Manager suggestion) is used to define the repeat interval.

- **Use Predefined Window**, where a predefined window of operation can be used as a schedule. A job starts when the window opens and can be forced to stop when the window closes.

The remaining schedule fields on the screen change to be appropriate to the schedule type selected. We are using the standard schedule type. Simi-

Figure 11.17   *Setting the Schedule for the Job*

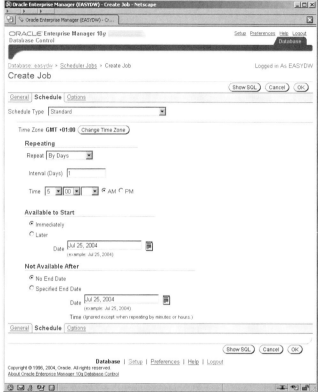

larly, the fields required to define the repeat schedule will change and be appropriate to the *Repeat* field value that is selected. The *Available to Start* and *Not Available After* parameters enable us to specify the boundaries within which our repeating schedule will operate. There is actually a lot of sophistication in how the schedule may be defined via this screen.

The definition of our job is almost complete. Clicking the *Options* link enables some more controls on the job execution, such as job priority, to be set, as shown in Figure 11.18.

We don't really need to set any of these for our job, though we should possibly consider setting the *Priority.* This defaults to *Medium,* but we may want to consider a higher priority to ensure that our statistics gathering completes, so we have raised its priority slightly to *High.* Clicking *OK* will create our job and return us to the *Scheduler Jobs* screen, where we can see our new job listed, as shown in Figure 11.19.

Figure 11.18 *Setting the Options for the Job*

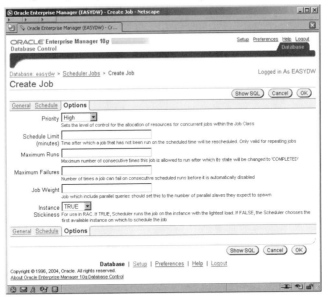

Figure 11.19 *The Confirmed Created Job*

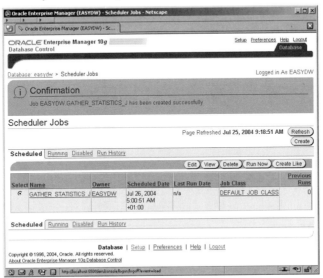

From this screen there are a number of links for tabs to display the jobs we have:

- Scheduled
- Currently executing
- Marked as disabled
- Already executed

We can use these lists to manage, edit, and monitor our jobs. For example, if we now wanted to disable the job that we have just created, we would click on its name, GATHER_STATISTICS, in the *Name* field in the *Scheduled* list and change the *Enabled* flag. Once the screens are refreshed, the job will have disappeared from the *Scheduled* list and appeared in the *Disabled* list. In a similar fashion, those jobs in the *Run History* list can be drilled into to examine their execution status and their results.

Enterprise Manager Job System

Distinct from the new Oracle Database 10*g* Scheduler jobs and programs that we've just discussed, there is another EM Job screen, which can be accessed by following the *Jobs* link in the *Related Links* section at the bottom of the four main Home pages.

The *Job Activity* screen shown in Figure 11.20 enables information about all EM jobs and current and previous executions to be searched for and examined. At the bottom of the screen, you can follow the link to the *Job Library*. The title of Jobs is used for both these EM Job screens and those for the new Oracle Database 10*g* Scheduler section, but these are actually two separate areas. You will notice that different jobs submitted by different parts of EM will utilize either these EM Job screens or the new Oracle Database 10*g* Scheduler job screens. For example, backup jobs will be listed in the *Results* section of this EM *Job Activity* screen; however, the new Segment Advisor jobs will be listed in the *Run History* list of the Scheduler *Jobs* screen.

Figure 11.20 shows the *Job Activity* screen. By clicking on the job *Name* field in the *Results* section, the jobs can be drilled into. This will display new screens (not shown) containing information on the job's execution, its individual steps, and the output logs from these steps—with further information on any error that may have occurred. For example, the backup jobs listed in Figure 11.20 show a problem that was caused by lack of space in the disk area where the backups were being written to.

Figure 11.20   *Enterprise Manager Job Activity Screen*

To create a job, select the type of job that you want to create from the *Create Job* field on the right and click *Go*. The screen shown in Figure 11.21 will appear, which is where you describe the details for this job. In this example, we are again creating the job to collect the EASYDW schema statistics. First, we name the job and state upon which database it is to be performed. We can also define the accounts and passwords required for the job's execution on both the server and the database, if necessary. Enterprise Manager has stored preferred credentials for our current login account, and this section allows us to override these defaults should we need to.

Although this example features a database task, other options are available from the drop-down list on destination type.

All jobs may be kept in the job library for reuse. Therefore, if you wish to retain the job, now is a good time to click on the button at the top of the screen to *Save to Library*.

Figure 11.21   *Creating a Job*

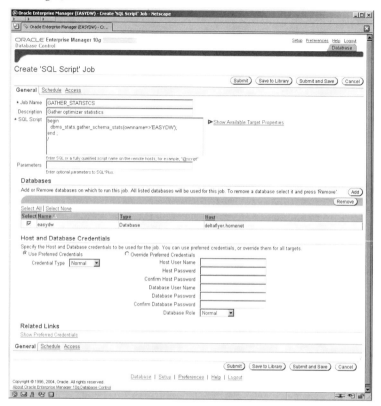

The jobs form a library for reuse and can also be used by other user accounts. It is easy to see that a sophisticated suite of reusable components can be created. The other links on this page enable the job to be scheduled, and the *Access* link displays a screen where access to the new job can be granted to other administrators.

The examples in this section have shown a database operation and job. Alternatively, a job could be an operating system task that needs to be performed for managing the warehouse, such as ensuring that files are copied from one system to another prior to loading the warehouse.

The number of jobs that we can submit by both of the job mechanisms described in this chapter is quite extensive, and, once they are defined and as long as we are backing up our database, we have a comprehensive set of tasks that is safe and that can never be lost.

11.3 Monitoring the Warehouse

Oracle Database 10*g* introduces new tools for monitoring the performance of your data warehouse, diagnosing and providing recommendations for correcting any problems. The new components associated with this are the **Automatic Workload Repository (AWR)** and the **Automatic Database Diagnostic Monitor (ADDM)**.

A database administrator may be barraged daily with questions about the performance of the warehouse. How do we make this SQL run faster? What is the problem? Where is the bottleneck? What do I look at to solve this one? These may be questions that your users have asked or they may be ones that you have asked yourself when something executes and grinds the database to a halt. The examination of what is happening on the database and where to look for information to resolve it comes from experience and knowledge. Similarly, the ability to know how to correct the problem without disrupting other aspects of the system often requires a knowledgeable Oracle person. On many occasions, solving one issue just uncovers another or can cause a problem elsewhere if care is not taken. Hence, the task of problem diagnosis and resolution can be a time-consuming and iterative process, which can take up quite a bit of a DBA's time.

With the new AWR and ADDM components, Oracle Database 10*g* is addressing the perennial problem of assisting with the collection of the myriad data about the operation of the database and the analysis of this data to identify problem areas. AWR collects and stores the statistics and ADDM uses them to diagnose problems with the database performance. Oracle Database 10*g* is also providing new options and EM performance screens to increase the administrator's ability to focus on the causes, and then EM assists with the correction and deployment of the solution.

11.3.1 Automatic Workload Repository (AWR)

The Automatic Workload Repository is a repository of the statistics and information about the operation of the Oracle Database 10*g*. To be able to understand what is happening as the database operates is a prerequisite to being able to analyze and resolve any problems that may occur; in order to be able to understand something, we must first have information about it. AWR is the repository of the information that enables us to understand the database operation. The statistics gathered are an enhanced superset of those used by Statspack in prior versions of the database. AWR is used by a number of other components in the database, such as the EM Performance screens and ADDM (which is discussed in the next section).

By default, every 30 minutes AWR collects detailed performance statistics and derived metrics on the operation of the database and stores these in the database. These are known as **snapshots**. The operation of AWR is designed and optimized to be an integral part of the database and not an operation that sits on top of it utilizing resources. Consequently, this integral aspect of the design and optimization minimizes the impact on the database operation and performance.

AWR is configurable and there are a number of parameters that control its operation. For example, the 30-minute collection frequency, which we have already mentioned, can be adjusted, as can the default seven days used to purge old snapshots. The AWR screens can be accessed by going to the *Administration* screen and clicking on the *Automatic Workload Repository* link in the *Workload* section. The resulting AWR screen, shown in Figure 11.22, enables you to view the general information about the AWR, such as the retention period and frequency that the snapshot is taken.

Figure 11.22   *Enterprise Manager AWR Information*

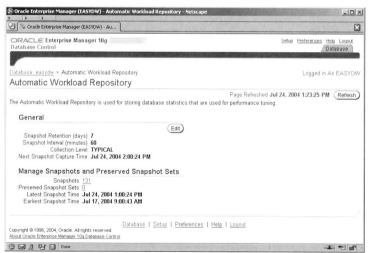

By clicking on the snapshot id number, the *Snapshots* page is displayed, where you can further control and manage snapshots. For example, you can use the snapshots to create a SQL Tuning Set (as described in Chapter 10) or create a set of preserved snapshots for future reference to use as the basis of a baseline for other metrics operations.

By clicking the *Edit* button on the AWR screen, the *Edit Settings* screen (not shown) is displayed, where you can adjust the retention period for the snapshots and the frequency with which they are taken—or even turn the snapshots off all together.

AWR and the comprehensive nature of the statistics that are collected underpin both the monitoring features of the EM performance screens (which are accessed from the *Performance* Home page) and the diagnostic capability that is possible with ADDM, which we will look at next.

11.3.2 Automatic Database Diagnostic Monitor (ADDM)

ADDM is Oracle's "expert DBA in a box." It is a diagnostic engine that runs after every snapshot collection and analyzes the collected data to identify possible problems and recommend corrective actions. Principally, ADDM focuses on potential problem areas that are consuming a lot of database time and resources. It drills down to identify the underlying cause and creates a recommendation, with an estimate of the associated benefit.

First, we need to define the range of snapshots that we want ADDM to analyze. To launch ADDM, start at *Advisor Central* and in the list of Advisors click on *ADDM*. The resulting screen (not shown) enables you to specify the start and end snapshots and then create an ADDM task to analyze these snapshots.

To define the snapshot range, click on the *Period Start Time* radio button and then on one of the little camera icons under the graph. This specifies the start of your snapshot range. Then click on the *Period End Time* radio button and click on a camera icon for a later snapshot time. When you click the *OK* button, an ADDM task is created and executed. This task analyzes the data in AWR between your start and end points and provides you with a list of performance findings, as shown in Figure 11.23.

The *Performance Analysis* section, as shown in Figure 11.23, displays a list of the ADDM findings based on the snapshots that you specified. The ADDM findings are prioritized by the estimated impact on the system, as shown by the *Impact (%)* column on the left. Due to the different sets of metrics that ADDM analyzes, it also categorizes the findings, as shown by the *Recommendation* column on the right. For example, in the analysis findings we have shown in Figure 11.23, the highest impact is one involving potentially badly performing SQL. In the second finding, ADDM has discovered that the buffer cache is undersized and that the database configuration should be adjusted.

Figure 11.23   *Enterprise Manager ADDM*

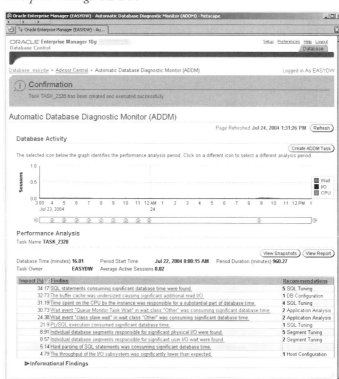

Note the two buttons on the right-hand side, which will enable you to view the information on the individual snapshots and also generate a very detailed HTML report of the finding.

In Figure 11.24, you can see the result from clicking on the *View Snapshots* button in Figure 11.23, which contains details of the snapshots involved. By clicking on the *Report* link, you generate the comprehensive and user friendly HTML report.

From the list of the ADDM findings shown in in Figure 11.23, you can click on the *Finding* links for one of the findings categories that are displayed, and this takes you to other screens, which enable further drilling—even right down to the piece of nonperforming SQL or other cause of a problem. For example, by drilling down on a SQL statement that ADDM has identified, you get to the *SQL Details* screen (not shown), where there are different sections to enable you to examine more thoroughly the cause of the problem. These areas are:

Figure 11.24 *Enterprise Manager ADDM Snapshot Details*

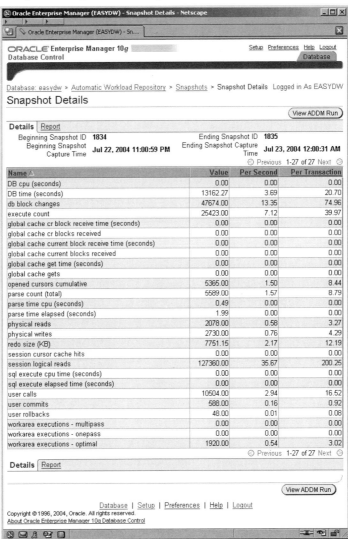

- the execution plan for the SQL

- the execution statistics

- the execution history

- the tuning history of recommendations that have already been generated for the SQL

From any of these four screens, you can then invoke the SQL Tuning Advisor (described in Chapter 10) to provide recommendations on how to correct the SQL.

This ability to drill down from the general to the specific is an approach adopted in many places within Enterprise Manager in order to facilitate the identification of a problem. For example, the graphs on the main *Performance* Home page, shown in Figure 11.25, operate in a similar fashion and use the historical snapshot data. The approach here is that the graphs display a larger block of color to indicate a possible problem area. You can then drill down using the links on the right-hand side to further identify the causes of the problems.

We have only touched upon the power of the new EM interface in order to demonstrate the functionality and importance of ADDM and AWR. These new features provide a very comprehensive set of monitoring and recommendation technologies, which appear in many aspects of the database operation and the management approach by EM. To assist with the normal day-to-day tasks in administering the warehouse, it will pay significant dividends for the DBA to explore and get a good understanding of these new features.

11.3.3   Using Alerts

One of the problems for anyone managing a database is knowing when certain events occur. For example, suppose a tablespace fills up and has no free space remaining. Wouldn't you like to know immediately that it has happened rather than wait for the calls from your users, who are complaining that the system is no longer available?

An alert is a notification that occurs when a metric, about which you have instructed the database to collect information, goes above a threshold target that you have set. Within Enterprise Manager, there are many alerts that are defined as standard and you see an example of these every time you log into Enterprise Manager in the *Alerts* section of the *Home* page. But you can also define your own alerts, which will allow you to monitor custom aspects of your data warehouse and be notified when certain events occur.

To manage these metrics, thresholds, and alerts, click on the *Manage Metrics* link in the *Related Links* section and you will get the screen shown in Figure 11.26. This screen lists the standard precreated metrics, as well as the custom ones, the thresholds that will trigger an alert, and the operator that defines the boundary criteria for the threshold. For example, the first metric in the list in Figure 11.26 is *Archive Area Used*, which is monitoring

Figure 11.25 *Enterprise Manager Performance Screen*

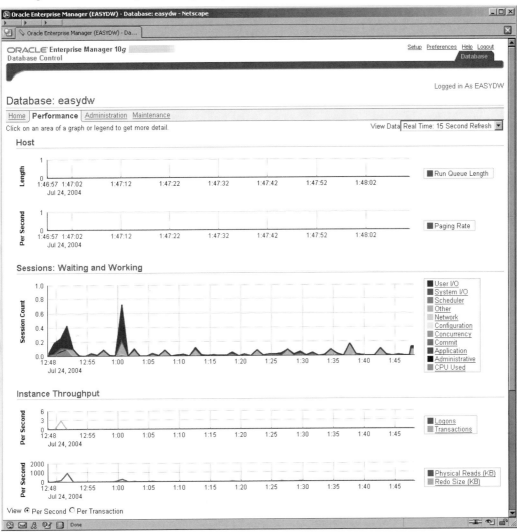

the disk space used by the archived redo logs; when it exceeds the 80 percent threshold, an alert is issued. When this occurs, you will see this alert on the Home page when you logon to Enterprise Manager.

The thresholds and actions can be adjusted by clicking the *Edit Threshold* button, where a screen very similar to the one shown in Figure 11.27 is displayed, but this time the fields *Warning Threshold*, *Critical Threshold*, and *Response Action* are editable.

Figure 11.26   *Enterprise Manager Manage Metrics Screen*

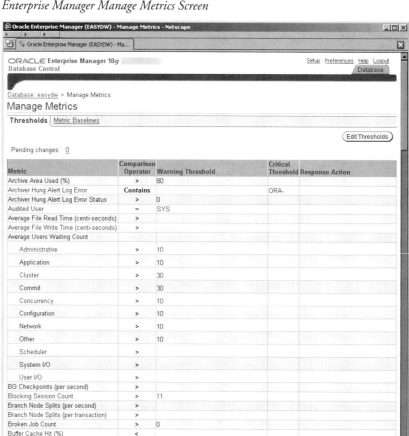

The *Response Action* field can be any operating system command, which includes calling custom programs and scripts. It is executed by the Management Agent running on the server, and this field is one of those that only superuser administrators can edit.

We can also define our own metrics on which a threshold can be based. On the *Administration* screen in the *Related Links* area, click on the *User-Defined Metrics* link at the bottom and then click the *Create* button to go to the *Create User-Defined Metric* screen, shown in Figure 11.28.

Figure 11.27   *Enterprise Manager Threshold Screen*

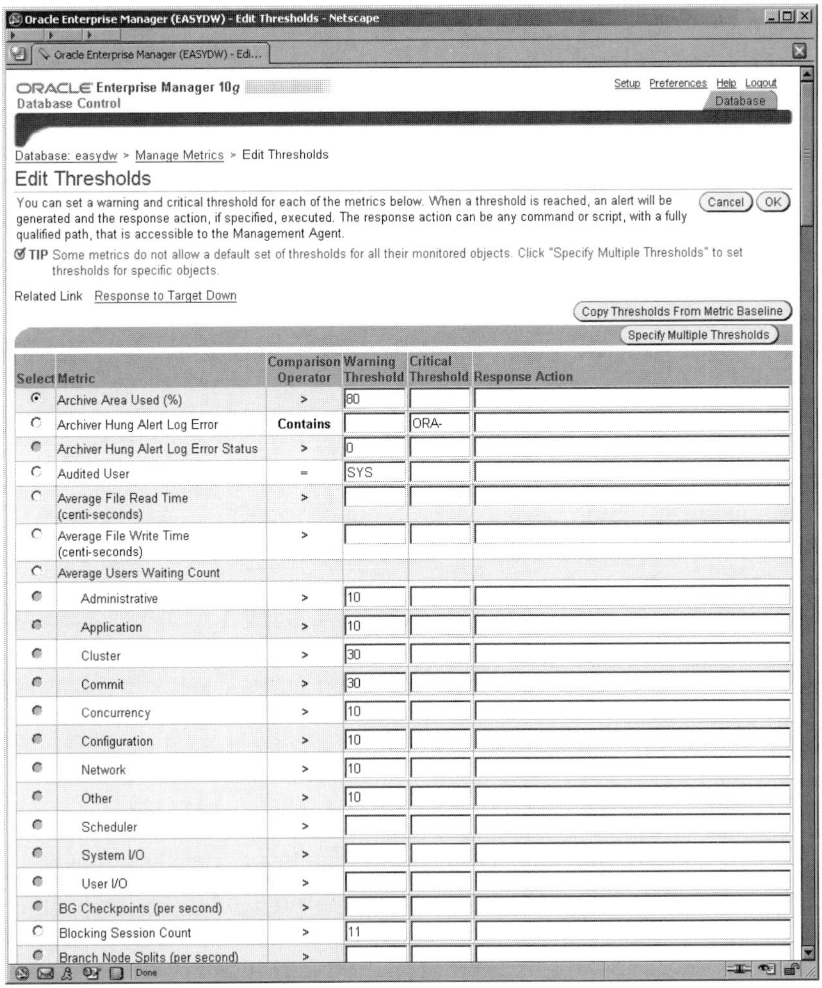

In the screen in Figure 11.28, we need to be able to express our metric in terms of either a SQL statement or a call to a function. To execute this code, we will also need to provide a database account name and password. In our example, we are using some SQL to read the database data dictionary to test if there are any materialized views that have the status NEEDS_COMPILE with a refresh date more than two days old. You can then specify the warning and critical conditions and the action to be performed. Our example will raise a warning if the OLD_AND_STALE value is returned from executing the SQL.

Figure 11.28   *Enterprise Manager User-Defined Metric Screen*

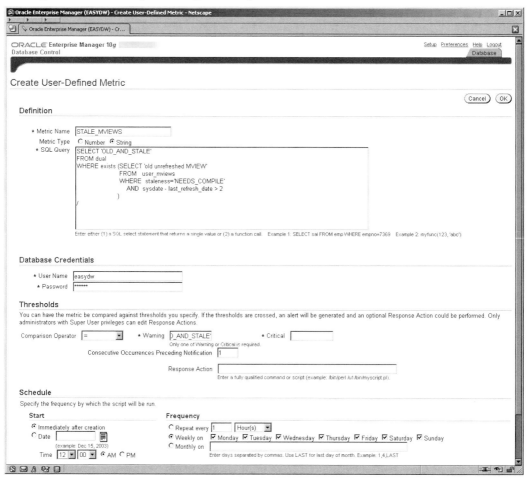

A useful feature here is the field in the *Thresholds* section to specify the number of consecutive times that the warning or critical threshold may be met prior to an alert being issued. This provides some control over temporary or transitory occurrences, which you may not want to be alerted about, but enables persistent ones to be flagged.

Here we have just scratched the surface of what is possible with metrics and thresholds. Much of the power of these features underpins the strength of the new monitoring and alert capability in Oracle Database 10*g* and is enhanced by the capability to customize for your own environment. Hopefully, this introduction will encourage you to investigate this area further and implement it as part of your data warehouse management procedures.

11.4 Reorganizing the Warehouse

Reorganizing a database, irrespective of whether it is a data warehouse or a database used for transaction processing–style systems, is not a task to be undertaken lightly. Unfortunately, in a data warehouse, the time required to reorganize can become a serious issue, due to the high data volumes involved. Therefore, it shouldn't be necessary to reorganize the database entirely, but minor changes may be necessary.

11.4.1 Why Reorganize?

Reorganizations can occur for a variety of reasons, such as:

- The business needs change
- A regular archiving of data
- The government changes the rules
- Changes are required to the database design
- Improve performance
- The characteristics of the data were not as predicted
- The integration of another company's computer system following an acquisition

A change in the business requirements from the system is almost impossible to predict, and one solution to the problem may be to create a data mart rather than restructure the entire data warehouse.

The most probable reasons that we will need to reorganize are to improve performance, database changes, and archiving. Changing the physical implementation of the tables can certainly make a significant difference to the performance. Changing a table to be partitioned is a good example, but there may be more subtle changes, such as changing a column data type, which could also be required.

Careful reviewing of the database design and physical implementation can help overcome the need for later changes to the design and schema. If necessary, asking for an external review by an experienced data warehouse designer can be a good mechanism to identify potential problems as early as possible. One of the problems with data warehouses is that what may seem a good design at the outset may prove unsuitable in the long term, due to the large volumes of data involved. Therefore, try to minimize the likelihood of this occurring by using techniques such as partitioning.

Some reorganization may be planned. If you want to keep your data warehouse somewhat constant in size and not let it grow indefinitely, you may decide to keep only a few years of data. When new data is added, old data is archived and removed. This is called a *rolling window operation* and is discussed later in the book. The two major types of reorganization used in a data warehouse are partition operations and on-line reorganization, which we will look at in the next sections.

11.4.2   Partition Maintenance

Some of the structural changes required by the data warehouse can be achieved by using partition operations. In this section, we will look at some of the most common partition maintenance operations, including the following:

- Adding and dropping partitions
- Exchanging a partition
- Splitting and merging partitions
- Coalescing a partition
- Truncating a partition
- Moving a partition

We will provide the full examples using SQL and also present the EM screens where the operation can also be performed. Where these are multiple-step operations, we will only demonstrate one of the steps in EM.

These operations are performed from the Edit Table screen EM following the *Partitions* link. When a partition has been chosen, a selection is made from the *Actions* box, which contains a list of the operations that can be performed on the partition when the *Go* button is clicked.

Rolling Window Partition Maintenance

When the warehouse is first created, there may be little or no historic data with which to populate it. Therefore, for the first 18 to 24 months, new data continues to be added every month until the required system limits are met. Then, when the data warehouse is full, every month the old data is backed up and removed to make room for new data. Without partitions, the operation to delete the old data would have to scan all of the large fact tables to identify and delete the records, which is very time consuming. The faster alternative to this problem is to drop the partition containing the old data and create a new partition for the new data, as shown in Figure 11.29.

Figure 11.29 *Partition Maintenance*

This technique is applicable only if the data is partitioned on a date or on a partition key that infers a date (i.e., that is time sequential, such as an absolute month number, for example, 200412 for December 2004). Therefore, if you decide upon another partitioning scheme, such as a code, this type of maintenance operation would not be possible. For example, it would be impossible to use with a hash partitioning mechanism, because you have no control over which partition Oracle will place the records into.

The SQL commands to perform the tasks are as follows. First, the old partition containing the data for sales for the month of January 2000 is dropped.

```
ALTER TABLE easydw.purchases
    DROP PARTITION purchases_jan00;
```

Next, the new partition for the data for sales for the month of December 2004 is created. The first step is to create the tablespace where the data will reside.

```
CREATE TABLESPACE purchases_dec04
DATFILE 'C:\ORACLE\PRODUCT\10.1.0\ORADATA\EASYDW\PURCHASESdec2004.f'
   SIZE 5m REUSE AUTOEXTEND ON DEFAULT STORAGE
   (INITIAL 16k    NEXT 16k
    PCTINCREASE 0 MAXEXTENTS UNLIMITED);
```

The next step is to alter the table definition to create the new partition for December 2004 data in the new PURCHASES_DEC2004 tablespace.

```
ALTER TABLE easydw.purchases
   ADD PARTITION purchases_dec2004
      VALUES LESS THAN (TO_DATE('01-01-2005',
                                'DD-MM-YYYY'))
      PCTFREE 0 PCTUSED 99
      STORAGE (INITIAL 64k NEXT 16k PCTINCREASE 0)
      TABLESPACE purchases_dec2004 ;
```

Of course, with this mechanism we had to drop the old tablespace in which the PURCHASES_JAN00 resided; otherwise, we would eventually end up with a collection of empty tablespaces that are not being used.

A slight variation of this technique is one where our tablespace names do not reflect the contents of the data they are holding. In Figure 11.30, we have named our partitions 1 through 60—instead of calling them after the data they hold, such as PURCHASES_JAN00. By using this approach, the tablespaces can then be reused. As we drop the old partition, it frees up the tablespace and then we simply reuse it to contain the new partition, as shown in Figure 11.30.

Figure 11.30   *Rolling Window with Tablespace Reuse*

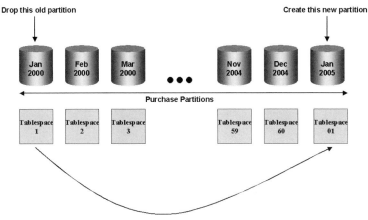

Exchanging a Partition

After a new partition is added to a table, data already can be loaded into it. Various techniques to load data were described in Chapter 5. If the data is in a table in the database, the fastest way to move the data into the new partition is by using exchange partition. This is used to move data from a non-partitioned table into a partition of a partitioned table. Exchange partition can also be used to convert a partition into a nonpartitioned table or between various types of partitioned tables. The following example shows moving the data from the DEC_ORDERS table into the PURCHASES_DEC2004 partition of the EASYDW.PURCHASES table.

```
ALTER TABLE easydw.purchases
   EXCHANGE PARTITION purchases_dec2004
   WITH TABLE dec_orders;
```

Most of the partition operations that we are going to look at in this chapter can be performed from Enterprise Manager by editing a partitioned table. From the *Administration* screen go to the *Schema* section and click on the *Tables* link. Select the PURCHASES table, and click on the *Edit* button to navigate to the *Edit Table* screen, and click on the *Partitions* link. This screen will show you a list of the partitions in the PURCHASES table. The *Actions* pick list on the right-hand side contains the list of operations that can be performed on a partition. Select *Exchange* from this list, click the *Go* button, and the screen shown in Figure 11.31 appears.

Select the nonpartitioned table that you want to exchange with the selected partition. In our example, the table is DEC_ORDERS but it only contains records for December 2004.

Hint: The partitioned and nonpartitioned tables must have the same structure and definition.

The reason that this operation is very quick is because no data movement is actually involved; Oracle is simply exchanging the metadata about the objects within the data dictionary. So the table's metadata is redefined to be that of the partition of the PURCHASES table and the partition's metadata is redefined to be that of the DEC_ORDERS table.

Merging Partitions

Partitions can be merged, either by merging into a wholly new partition or into an existing partition.

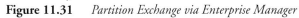

Figure 11.31   *Partition Exchange via Enterprise Manager*

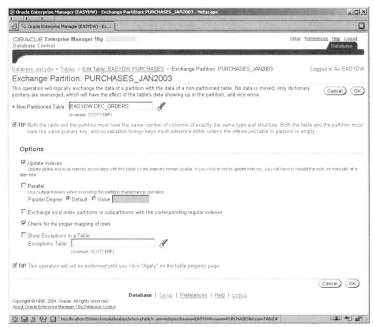

One technique often used by designers is to keep the first six months of data in monthly partitions, and then after that, store the data in quarterly partitions. By using the MERGE PARTITION option, the data can be easily moved to the new partition, as shown in the following code.

If we wanted to combine the data for April through July 2004 into a partition for the second quarter, we could merge the partitions. First, a new tablespace is created to store the Q2 purchases.

```
CREATE TABLESPACE purchases_q2_2004
   DATAFILE
'C:\ORACLE\PRODUCT\10.1.0\ORADATA\EASYDW\PURCHASESQ22004.f'
      SIZE 5M
      REUSE AUTOEXTEND ON
      DEFAULT STORAGE
         (INITIAL 64K NEXT 64K
          PCTINCREASE 0 MAXEXTENTS UNLIMITED);
```

In our example, there are three partitions that have to be merged, but the MERGE PARTITION command only allows us to merge two partitions at a time. Since only adjacent partitions can be merged, we will begin with merging May and June and then the resultant partition with April. If a table is partitioned by range, only adjacent partitions can be merged. Therefore, we can merge April and May or May and June but cannot merge April and June.

The new partition inherits the upper bound of the two merged partitions. Therefore, the two partitions with the highest ranges need to be merged first (May and June), into the Q2 partition. The following example merges the May and June partitions and stores them in the newly created tablespace called PURCHASES_Q2_2004. The PURCHASES_Q22004 partition is automatically added to the PURCHASES table.

```
ALTER TABLE purchases
        MERGE PARTITIONS purchases_may2004,purchases_jun2004
        INTO PARTITION purchases_q22004
        TABLESPACE purchases_q2_2004 ;
```

Next, the partition with the lowest range, PURCHASES_APR2004, is merged into the PURCHASES_Q22004 partition, as follows:

```
ALTER TABLE purchases
        MERGE PARTITIONS purchases_apr2004,
                        purchases_q22004
        INTO PARTITION purchases_q22004
        TABLESPACE purchases_q2_2004 ;
```

After this operation, the PURCHASES table contains one partition, shown in Figure 11.32, which is showing the partitions section of the *View Table* screen for PURCHASES. Upon completion of the merge operation, the old partitions are automatically dropped from the PURCHASES table. The high value for the new PURCHASES_Q22004 partition is July 01, 2004.

This operation can also be performed by Enterprise Manager. On the *Edit Table, Partitions* screen, select the PURCHASES_MAY2004 partition, select the *Merge* action, click the *Go* button, and you are then presented with the screen shown in Figure 11.33, where you select the other partition with which you wish to merge.

The operation is then repeated to merge the new partition for Q22004 with the partition for APR2004.

When merging partitions, both the data and the indexes are merged. The index partitions for April, May, and June were automatically dropped and were replaced by a new index partition for Q2. In the following query,

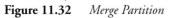

Figure 11.32   *Merge Partition*

Figure 11.33   *Partition Merge via Enterprise Manager*

there is a new index partition, PURCHASES_Q22004, for the indexes on the PURCHASES table.

```
SELECT index_name, partition_name, status
FROM   user_ind_partitions;

INDEX_NAME               PARTITION_NAME     STATUS
-----------------------  -----------------  --------
PURCHASE_SPECIAL_INDEX   PURCHASES_Q22004   UNUSABLE
PURCHASE_CUSTOMER_INDEX  PURCHASES_Q22004   UNUSABLE
PURCHASE_PRODUCT_INDEX   PURCHASES_Q22004   UNUSABLE
PURCHASE_TIME_INDEX      PURCHASES_Q22004   UNUSABLE
```

The new index partitions are unusable and must be rebuilt, as shown in the following example.

```
ALTER INDEX purchase_product_index
   REBUILD PARTITION purchases_q22004 ;
ALTER INDEX purchase_time_index
   REBUILD PARTITION purchases_q22004 ;
ALTER INDEX purchase_special_index
   REBUILD PARTITION purchases_q22004 ;
ALTER INDEX purchase_customer_index
   REBUILD PARTITION purchases_q22004 ;
```

Splitting Partitions

If a partition becomes too big, it may need to be split to help maintenance operations complete in a shorter period of time or to spread the I/O across more devices. A partition can be split into two new partitions. If the PURCHASES table was originally partitioned by quarter, and sales significantly exceeded expectations resulting in a very large partition, the partition could be split up into three monthly partitions. Tablespaces are first created for PURCHASES_APR2004, PURCHASES_MAY2004, and PURCHASES_JUN2004.

In the following example, all rows with PURCHASE_DATE less than or equal to May 1, 2004, will be split into the PURCHASES_APR2004 partition. The remaining rows will remain in the PURCHASES_Q22004 partition. The April purchases will be stored in the PURCHASES_APR2004 tablespace.

```
ALTER TABLE purchases
SPLIT PARTITION purchases_q22004
    AT (TO_DATE('01-MAY-2004','dd-mon-yyyy'))
    INTO (PARTITION purchases_apr2004
         TABLESPACE purchases_apr2004,
        PARTITION purchases_q22004) ;
```

After the split operation, there are two partitions. Next, the remaining rows in the partition, PURCHASE_Q22004, are split into the May and June partitions.

```
ALTER TABLE purchases
SPLIT PARTITION purchases_q22004
    AT (TO_DATE('01-JUN-2004','dd-mon-yyyy'))
    INTO (PARTITION purchases_may2004
            TABLESPACE purchases_may2004,
          PARTITION purchases_jun2004
            TABLESPACE purchases_jun2004) ;
```

The data has been repartitioned, and the PURCHASES_Q22004,z partition automatically dropped, as shown in Figure 11.34.

Figure 11.34   *Split Partition*

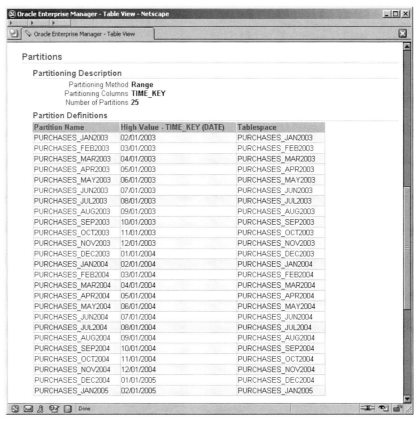

Figure 11.35   *Splitting Partitions via Enterprise Manager*

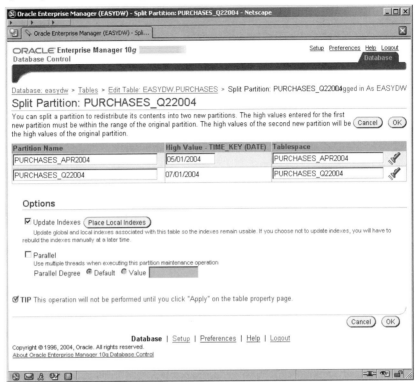

This operation is performed from EM via the *Edit Table, Partition* screen, for the PURCHASES table, as shown in Figure 11.35, by selecting the *Split* action. The use of the screen to perform this operation is much more intuitive and less error prone than performing the operation by hand with SQL commands.

Clicking the *OK* button returns you to the *Partitions* screen, with check boxes against the partition to indicate that the actual split operation is pending. Repeat the operation again on the PURCHASES_Q22004 partitions to split it for the May and June partitions. When the *Apply* button is clicked, the two pending split partition operations are actually performed.

Any partitions of the local indexes corresponding to the PURCHASES_ Q22004 partition have been dropped. In their place are new local index partitions for the new table partitions.

```
SELECT INDEX_NAME, PARTITION_NAME, STATUS
FROM   USER_IND_PARTITIONS;

INDEX_NAME                  PARTITION_NAME      STATUS
----------------------      ------------------  --------
PURCHASE_SPECIAL_INDEX      PURCHASES_APR2004   UNUSABLE
PURCHASE_CUSTOMER_INDEX     PURCHASES_APR2004   UNUSABLE
PURCHASE_SPECIAL_INDEX      PURCHASES_JUN2004   UNUSABLE
PURCHASE_SPECIAL_INDEX      PURCHASES_MAY2004   UNUSABLE
PURCHASE_CUSTOMER_INDEX     PURCHASES_JUN2004   UNUSABLE
PURCHASE_PRODUCT_INDEX      PURCHASES_APR2004   UNUSABLE
PURCHASE_TIME_INDEX         PURCHASES_APR2004   UNUSABLE
PURCHASE_CUSTOMER_INDEX     PURCHASES_MAY2004   UNUSABLE
PURCHASE_PRODUCT_INDEX      PURCHASES_JUN2004   UNUSABLE
PURCHASE_PRODUCT_INDEX      PURCHASES_MAY2004   UNUSABLE
PURCHASE_TIME_INDEX         PURCHASES_JUN2004   UNUSABLE
PURCHASE_TIME_INDEX         PURCHASES_MAY2004   UNUSABLE
```

Any unusable indexes must be rebuilt, as follows, for the APR2004 partition.

```
ALTER INDEX purchase_product_index
    REBUILD PARTITION purchases_apr2004 ;
ALTER INDEX purchase_time_index
    REBUILD PARTITION purchases_apr2004 ;
ALTER INDEX purchase_customer_index
    REBUILD PARTITION purchases_apr2004 ;
ALTER INDEX purchase_special_index
    REBUILD PARTITION purchases_apr2004 ;
```

Coalescing Hash Partitions

Range and list partitions can be merged, but hash partitions cannot; they must be coalesced. Rather than determining which partition a row is stored in by comparing the value of the partitioning key with the table's partitioning criteria, as is done for range or list partitioning, the partition is determined by applying a hash function.

Merging partitions in effect reduces the number of partitions by one. When the number of partitions changes, the hash function must be reapplied to redistribute the data. Coalescing the partitions does this.

The following example shows the creation of a hash-partitioned table with 10 partitions.

```
CREATE TABLE easydw.hash_purchases
 (product_id                 varchar2(8),
  time_key                   date,
  customer_id                varchar2(10),
  purchase_date              date,
```

```
        purchase_time                    number(4,0),
        purchase_price                   number(6,2),
        shipping_charge                  number(5,2),
        today_special_offer              varchar2(1))
PARTITION BY HASH(product_id)
PARTITIONS 10;
```

To reduce the number of partitions by one, issue the following command.

```
ALTER TABLE easydw.hash_purchases COALESCE PARTITION;
```

This, in effect, drops a partition.

Likewise, a hash-partitioned table cannot be split when it becomes too big. To increase the number of partitions in a hash-partitioned table, alter the table and add a partition to it.

Truncating Partitions

Sometimes we need to remove all the rows in a partition. For example, we may only keep 18 months of data and, once a month, we need to remove that old data. Rather than delete each row individually, we can use the TRUNCATE PARTITION option, which rapidly removes the data.

To remove all the rows from a partition, but not the partition itself, use TRUNCATE partition. This is much faster than deleting each row in the partition individually. Any local indexes for the partition, such as the EASYDW.PURCHASE_TIME_INDEX, are also truncated. Prior to truncating the partition, there are 3,847 rows in the PURCHASES_JAN2003 partition.

```
SELECT COUNT(*) FROM purchases
WHERE time_key
        BETWEEN TO_DATE('01-JAN-2003', 'dd-mon-yyyy')
            AND TO_DATE('31-JAN-2003', 'dd-mon-yyyy') ;

  COUNT(*)
----------
      3847
```

```
ALTER TABLE PURCHASES TRUNCATE PARTITION purchases_jan2003;
```

After truncating the partition, all rows have been deleted.

```
SELECT COUNT(*) FROM purchases
```

```
WHERE time_key
        BETWEEN TO_DATE('01-JAN-2003', 'dd-mon-yyyy')
            AND TO_DATE('31-JAN-2003', 'dd-mon-yyyy') ;

  COUNT(*)
----------
         0
```

The EM screen for this operation is shown in Figure 11.36; it is a confirmation screen, which provides some useful options and control over the truncate operation. When a truncate command is performed, it deletes the rows, but you can specify whether the freed-up space is retained by the partition or returned to the containing tablespace.

Be warned that the truncation operation is actually a DDL operation, which effectively commits immediately and does not create any undo infor-

Figure 11.36   *Partition Truncation via Enterprise Manager*

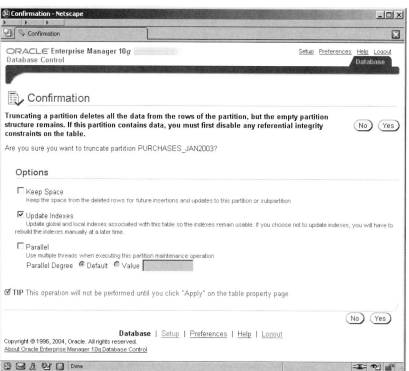

mation. So once you click the *Yes* button, you confirm the operation and lose your data.

Moving Partitions

A partition can be moved from one tablespace to another. For example, if the January partition on the PURCHASES table had been incorrectly created in EASYDW_DEFAULT tablespace, it would need to be moved to the PURCHASES_JAN2003 tablespace to be consistent with the database design conventions. The following command could be used.

```
ALTER TABLE purchases
    MOVE PARTITION purchases_jan2003
    TABLESPACE purchases_jan2003 ;
```

Hint: A NOLOGGING clause can be specified after the tablespace name; that causes the operation not to create redo logs and results in better performance. After performing NOLOGGING operations, don't forget to take a backup, since you will not be able to recover in the event of media failure.

This task can also be performed in EM, where you are asked simply to specify the target tablespace. It also provides the option to update the indexes and choose the degree of parallelism to be used for the move operation.

Partitions Facilitate Management

Most of the management operations that can be performed at a table level can also be performed on an individual partition or subpartition of a table. Partitions or subpartitions can be backed up, exported, restored, and recovered without affecting the availability of the other partitions or subpartitions. To best manage each partition or subpartition independently, they should each be stored in their own tablespace. Each tablespace should be stored on one or more separate storage devices.

Summary management and the query optimizer make use of the fact that the data is partitioned in choosing the optimal strategy for executing a query or refreshing a materialized view. Partition Change Tracking (PCT) for materialized views, which was discussed in Chapter 7, keeps track of which partitions have been updated after a partition maintenance operation and recomputes only that portion of the materialized view when it is refreshed. Partition Change Tracking also increases the query rewrite capabilities of the materialized view by rewriting queries to use the partitions of the materialized view that are not stale. If a table is partitioned, the query optimizer can use partition elimination or partition pruning to determine if a certain query can be answered by reading only specific partitions.

Hint: The examples shown in this section have performed partition maintenance operations on a table, but don't forget that partitions are also used on indexes, so you will have to create and maintain the corresponding index partitions. Also in these examples we've used partitions, but the operations are equally valid on subpartitions as well.

11.4.3 Index Changes

Probably one of the aspects of the design that will be changed is the indexes. New ones will be created, and existing ones will be modified. In a data warehouse, there is a temptation to create more indexes, because of the lack of updates to the system. However, you should consider the impact all of these indexes will have on the data load time.

If you need to rebuild an index for any reason, it is suggested that you use the ALTER INDEX REBUILD statement, which should offer better performance than dropping and recreating the index.

Many table maintenance operations on partitioned tables invalidate global indexes and they are marked UNUSABLE. You must then rebuild the entire global index or, if partitioned, all of its partitions. To avoid this you can include the UPDATE GLOBAL INDEXES clause in the ALTER TABLE statement for the maintenance operation. Specifying this clause tells Oracle to update the global index at the time it executes the maintenance operation DDL statement.

Hint: By partitioning the data, you can perform maintenance on specific index partitions rather than on the entire index.

11.4.4 Online Redefinition of Tables

With the increased importance of our data warehouse to the business can come the increased requirement for it to be constantly available; when it is not actually open to the users, it will need to be refreshed. These activities can seriously reduce the available window in which to perform maintenance operations. In a data warehouse with very large tables, these operations can be quite time consuming to perform. Gone are the days when the warehouse was only needed 9 to 5 and then there were these long batch windows and periods when maintenance could be performed. Now data warehouses are being used 24 hours a day, and it is becoming increasingly difficult to find time to perform maintenance operations.

However, Oracle has online redefinition, which enables tables to be rebuilt and restructured and data to be transformed while the tables are fully on-line and accessible to the users of the database.

The benefits and features of online redefinition are:

- The ability to change the table to or from a partitioned structure

- To improve space utilization

- To modify the storage characteristics of the table

- To change a normal table to or from an index-organized table

- To Automatically copy dependant objects on the table, such as triggers, constraints, and indexes (new in 10*g*)

- Dependant stored procedures do not require recompilation (new in 10*g*)

- To free unused space within the table segments back to the tablespace (new in 10*g*)

- To convert data types such as longs to LOBs (new in 10*g*)

In spite of all the care and attention spent during the design and deployment of our warehouse, there can still be the occasional table that is created but does not operate quite as anticipated. This could be due to a number of reasons, such as:

- The table has become much larger than expected by the volume metrics on which the warehouse designer based physical table design, and it now needs to be partitioned.

- The update activity on the table was not as expected during analysis and has caused the underlying physical storage to be used inappropriately.

In our first example, changing a large table to be partitioned enables easier management and performance improvements to the queries that access it—for example, to make use of partition elimination or partition-wise joins. A persistent problem that exists with table partition operations is that it is not possible to convert an unpartitioned table into a partitioned table. There is no SQL operation to do this. All of the partition operations that we discussed earlier in the chapter are only possible if the table was originally implemented as a partitioned table.

In the second example for storage problems, unanticipated update DML activity can cause a problem called **row chaining**, which causes a row to become stored in more than one disk block and consequently require two I/O operations to retrieve it.

Correcting these types of problems typically requires that the table be dropped, rebuilt, and reloaded to restructure it or improve the space utilization. But if the table has constraints or triggers on it, then the opportunity to drop the table in order to rebuild it in this fashion is significantly reduced.

Online redefinition enables these changes to the table structure and storage to be performed without needing to drop the table. During the operation the table remains available and in use by the users.

There are two ways to use on-line redefinition: from within Enterprise Manager or by invoking the DBMS_REDEFINITION package directly. We will start by looking at the Enterprise Manager approach, but because this currently only offers a limited subset of what is possible via the package, we will then look at an example that calls the package directly.

Online Redefinition via Enterprise Manager

Within Enterprise Manager, the on-line redefinition wizards can be accessed by going to the *Maintenance* screen and clicking on the *Reorganize Objects* link. On the first screen of the wizard (not shown), you need to decide which path through the wizard you want to take to reorganize the objects:

- By schema
- By tablespace

Either route enables you to specify the objects within the schema or tablespace that you want to reorganize.

Figure 11.37   *The Enterprise Manager Reorganize Objects Options Screen*

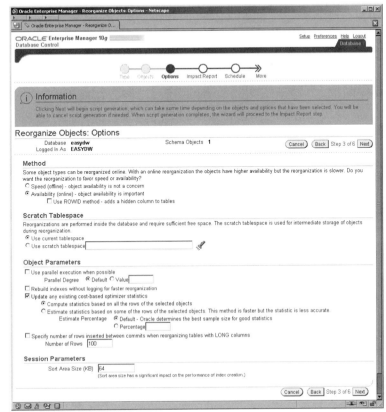

The wizard is very easy to use and very self-explanatory. One of the important screens is the *Options* screen, shown in Figure 11.37, which requires further explanation.

There are two methods by which the objects can be rebuilt:

- Offline, which results in the objects being unavailable

- Online, which ensures that the objects are available during the redefinition process

The online method requires the tables to have some form of unique identifier, such as a primary key, rowid, or unique index. If one is not present, then you will need to tick the check box for the ROWID method.

As part of the redefinition process, temporary objects will need to be built; therefore, the tablespace reorganization method needs to use a separate scratch tablespace.

There are two final sections on the *Options* screen shown in Figure 11.37: *Object Parameters* and *Session Parameters*, which enable you to fine-tune the execution of the redefinition. In these sections, you can control the degree of parallelism to be used, which can be important for large objects. Similarly, when indexes are being rebuilt, if the check box to build without generating redo logs is selected, a performance gain can be achieved for large indexes. However, be careful when selecting NOLOGGING, because this can prevent database recovery in the event of media failure; taking a backup is advised.

When the *Next* button, shown in Figure 11.37, is clicked, the wizard analyzes the objects and dependencies that you have selected and displays an impact report (not shown) of its findings. Examples of the types of findings detected are insufficient tablespace or no primary key on a table for an on-line redefinition method. After viewing the report, you then have the option to go back and make corrections using the *Back* button or progress to the *Schedule* screen by pressing the *Next* button.

The final two steps of the wizard are to specify the schedule for when you want the reorganization performed (this screen is not shown) and to make a final review of the process that you have defined via the wizard. On the *Review* page, which is shown in Figure 11.38, the scripts that are generated by Enterprise Manager are displayed.

The scripts produced in Figure 11.38 are either:

- A summary showing the steps required and the packaged procedures called
- The full script, which is detailed PL/SQL and includes much more code for controlling each step of the operation

It is the full script that is actually executed. The summary script, however, is very useful as a starting point for understanding more about the steps required for the redefinition operation.

Clicking on the *Submit Job* button, shown in Figure 11.38, will submit the job to the job queue for execution according to the schedule that you defined.

Figure 11.38   *The Enterprise Manager Reorganize Objects Options Review Screen*

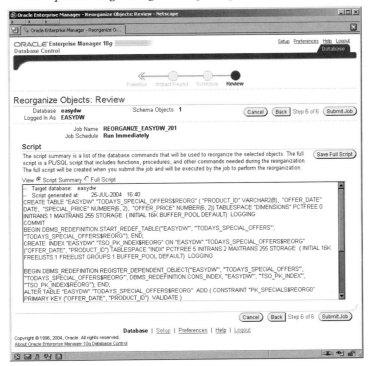

Online Redefinition Using the DBMS_REDEFINITION Package

From the initial part of the script shown in Figure 11.38, it is clear that a number of steps are required for redefining an object; these are performed by executing various procedures in the DBMS_REDEFINITION package.

Before attempting to redefine a table, you should use the procedure DBMS_REDEFINITION.CAN_REDEF_TABLE() to check if a redefinition is possible. This is because, at the time of writing, there is a limitation with the DBMS_REDEFINITION package in that it is not possible to reorganize a table that has materialized views on it.

We will illustrate the use of this feature with an example. Suppose the CUSTOMER table is currently not partitioned. However, as the business grows, this table has grown significantly in size and so we would now like to reorganize it to use list partitioning on the STATE column. Further, we would like to change the OCCUPATION column from a VARCHAR2(15) to a VARCHAR2(20). Finally, in order to support some more detailed analysis of the postal code for U.K. addresses, we want to restructure it from a single column into two columns. We will split it on the first space it may contain into OUTER and INNER parts, as follows:

- If the postal code contains a space, then the OUTER part will be assigned the characters preceding the first space and the INNER part will be assigned the characters following the first space.

  For example, W1 1QC becomes OUTER=W1 and INNER=1QC

- If the postal code contains no space, then it is assigned to the OUTER column and the INNER column is null.

  For example, 73301 becomes OUTER=73301 and INNER=NULL

To perform the split of the postal code we need to define two PL/SQL functions to perform the operations, as follows:

```
CREATE OR REPLACE
FUNCTION outer(postal_code IN VARCHAR2)
RETURN VARCHAR2
IS
BEGIN
  IF instr(postal_code, ' ') = 0
  THEN return (postal_code);
  ELSE return (substr(postal_code,
                      1,
                      instr(postal_code, ' ')-1)) ;
  END IF ;
END ;

CREATE OR REPLACE
FUNCTION inner(postal_code IN VARCHAR2)
RETURN VARCHAR2
IS
BEGIN
  IF instr(postal_code, ' ') = 0
  THEN return (null);
  ELSE return (substr(postal_code,
                      instr(postal_code, ' ')+1)) ;
  END IF ;
END ;
```

To redefine the CUSTOMER table, while allowing users to still query and update the data, we need to do the following.

Step 1: Create an Interim Table

Create the interim table showing how you would like the redefined table to look. Note that the interim table will need to have a name different from the actual table you are redefining.

```
CREATE TABLE customer_interim
(
 CUSTOMER_ID           VARCHAR2(10) NOT NULL,
 CITY                  VARCHAR2(15),
 STATE                 VARCHAR2(10),
 POSTAL_CODE_OUTER     VARCHAR2(10),
 POSTAL_CODE_INNER     VARCHAR2(10),
 GENDER                VARCHAR2(1),
 REGION                VARCHAR2(15),
 COUNTRY               VARCHAR2(20),
 TAX_RATE              NUMBER,
 OCCUPATION            VARCHAR2(20)
)
PARTITION BY LIST(state)
(
  PARTITION northeast VALUES ('NH', 'VT', 'MA', 'RI', 'CT'),
  PARTITION southeast VALUES ('NC', 'GA', 'FL'),
  PARTITION northwest VALUES ('WA', 'OR'),
  PARTITION midwest   VALUES ('IL', 'WI', 'OH'),
  PARTITION west      VALUES ('CA', 'NV', 'AZ'),
  PARTITION otherstates VALUES (DEFAULT)
);
```

Step 2: Start the Redefinition Process

Call the START_REDEF_TABLE procedure providing the name of the table to be redefined and the interim table.

```
BEGIN
 dbms_redefinition.start_redef_table
   (uname=>'EASYDW',
    orig_table=>'CUSTOMER',
    int_table=>'CUSTOMER_INTERIM',
    col_mapping=>'customer_id customer_id, '
              ||'city city, '
              ||'state state,'
              ||'outer(postal_code) postal_code_outer,'
              ||'inner(postal_code) postal_code_inner,'
              ||'gender gender, '
              ||'region region, '
              ||'country country, '
              ||'tax_rate tax_rate, '
              ||'occupation occupation'
   );
END;
```

Once you have done this, the interim table will be instantiated with the contents of the original table.

Currently, the Enterprise Manager wizard does not support the more complex table redefinitions that we are performing—for example, where new columns are added, dropped or column values are transformed. These types of operations require a mapping and transformation between the columns on the original table and the columns on the interim table and are performed by using the COL_MAPPING parameter.

The COL_MAPPING parameter takes a list of comma-separated pairs of columns. The first column in each pair is the original table column, or a function on the original table column. The second column in a pair is the destination column in the interim table to which we are mapping. In our example, outer(POSTAL_CODE) from the original table is mapping to POSTAL_CODE_OUTER in the interim table.

If the column mapping parameter isn't supplied, then it is assumed that all columns map with their names unchanged to columns in the interim table.

Step 3: Create the Dependant Objects

For each dependent object, such as grants, triggers, constraints, and indexes:

- If the object is the same on the interim table as it is on the table being redefined, then call the COPY_TABLE_DEPENDENTS procedure to automatically create it on the interim table.

- If it is different on the interim table, then manually create it and call the REGISTER_DEPENDENT_OBJECT procedure. This registers and associates the two names of the object as applied on the two tables. This enables the objects to be correctly renamed upon completion of the redefinition.

In our example, all dependent objects are the same on the interim table, so we are using the COPY_TABLE_DEPENDENTS procedure, as follows:

```
set serveroutput on

DECLARE
   num_errors number;
BEGIN
```

```
num_errors:= 0;
dbms_redefinition.copy_table_dependents
   (uname=>'EASYDW',
    orig_table=>'CUSTOMER',
    int_table=>'CUSTOMER_INTERIM',
    num_errors=>num_errors);
dbms_output.put_line
   ('Number of errors:'||to_char(num_errors));
END;
```

Step 4: Synchronize the Tables

Call the SYNC_INTERIM_TABLE procedure, which will synchronize any DML performed on the original table with the interim table. Any changes done to the original table, while it is being redefined, will be automatically tracked by Oracle and applied to the interim table.

```
BEGIN
  dbms_redefinition.sync_interim_table
     (uname=>'EASYDW',
      orig_table=>'CUSTOMER',
      int_table=>'CUSTOMER_INTERIM');
END;
```

Step 5: Finish the Redefinition

Call the FINISH_REDEF_TABLE procedure to finish the redefinition. Finishing the redefinition ensures that all of the indexes, grants, and triggers are on the redefined table, and the referential integrity constraints and triggers are enabled.

```
BEGIN
  dbms_redefinition.finish_redef_table
     (uname=>'EASYDW',
      orig_table=>'CUSTOMER',
      int_table=>'CUSTOMER_INTERIM');
END;
```

Step 6: Gather Statistics on the Redefined Table

```
BEGIN
  dbms_stats.gather_table_stats(ownname=>'easydw',
                                tabname=>'customer',
                                cascade=true
                                );
END;
```

> **Hint:** If the on-line redefinition operation fails for any reason, then the ABORT_REDEF_TABLE procedure must be called; this cleans up all the dependent objects so you can start again.

Our table structure has now changed, and, if we look at a subset of the new postal code columns, we can see that they have been correctly transformed and contain their new values.

```
SQL> desc customer
 Name                      Null?    Type
 ------------------------- -------- ----------------
 CUSTOMER_ID               NOT NULL VARCHAR2(10)
 CITY                               VARCHAR2(15)
 STATE                             VARCHAR2(10)
 POSTAL_CODE_OUTER                 VARCHAR2(10)
 POSTAL_CODE_INNER                 VARCHAR2(10)
 GENDER                            VARCHAR2(1)
 REGION                            VARCHAR2(15)
 COUNTRY                           VARCHAR2(20)
 TAX_RATE                          NUMBER
 OCCUPATION                        VARCHAR2(20)

SQL> SELECT postal_code_outer outer, postal_code_inner inner
       FROM customer;

OUTER      INNER
---------- ----------
10001
W1         1QC
W1         1QC
W1         1QC
10001
W1         1QC
73301
W1         1QC
```

We think you will agree that the on-line redefinition feature is a very useful and powerful tool to assist the administrator with the long-term management of the warehouse tables.

11.4.5   Online Segment Shrink

As the tables in our warehouse undergo INSERT, UPDATE and DELETE operations, the underlying space in the tablespace segments can become less efficient and space can become unusable. A new feature in Oracle Database

10*g*, called on-line segment shrink, enables this space to be reclaimed from a table and reassigned back to the tablespace for reuse.

In previous versions of the database, this operation would have involved a costly rebuild of the table, which would mean that it became unavailable. However, in Oracle Database 10*g* the operation can be performed while the table and indexes are on-line and fully available for use.

Via SQL, segment shrinkage can be performed by simply altering the table, index, or materialized view by using the SHRINK SPACE command. For example:

```
ALTER MATERIALIZED VIEW product_sum SHRINK SPACE;
```

Hint: To perform the shrink space operation, the owning tablespace must be set for automatic segment management, and tables and materialized views must be altered to enable row movement.

In Enterprise Manager, one of the new advisors is the Segment Advisor, which can be accessed from *Advisor Central*. This advisor will analyze objects you specify, either those owned by a schema or those residing in the same tablespace, and provide a report of the space usage and what can be reclaimed. It then enables you to schedule the job on the objects that you have selected for shrinkage.

Rather than a hit and miss manual approach for finding out where space can be effectively recovered, the Segment Advisor provides a very quick and easy method to access and perform this operation.

11.5 Refreshing the Warehouse

An extremely important management task is refreshing the warehouse with the latest data. This is a management task that is usually performed overnight with the data presented in batches. As was described earlier, frequently the data has to be cleansed and transformed before it can be loaded. Chapter 5 described various techniques that can be used for loading the new data into the warehouse.

Throughout this book, we have seen extensive use of Oracle Enterprise Manager for managing and controlling many of our management tasks. Depending on how complex your tasks are and on the data dependencies, you may prefer to use your own techniques. Otherwise, you could place the jobs on the Scheduler queue and come in the next day to see that everything has run smoothly. For example, it is not uncommon to receive data loads from various sources at different times. If there are dependencies between the data, then you may have to control that within your own management suites. Alternatively, Oracle Warehouse Builder performs complex scheduling of its various tasks by use of Oracle Workflow.

Once the data has been loaded into the warehouse, the materialized views must be refreshed. Depending on the number of materialized views, this could also take a significant amount of time.

An OEM job could be created to refresh the materialized views. Executing the DBMS_MVIEW.REFRESH_ALL_MVIEWS procedure could refresh all of the materialized views. Alternatively, you could use the DBMS_MVIEW.REFRESH_DEPENDENT option to request that it refresh only materialized views dependent on certain tables. Or you can call the refresh procedure and specify which materialized views are to be refreshed. Specific details on how to refresh materialized views were described in Chapter 7.

11.6   Gathering Optimizer Statistics

Missing or stale optimizer statistics are often the cause of suboptimal query performance. The cost-based optimizer uses statistics such as the cardinality of the table, number of distinct values of a column, and the data distribution to determine the cost of an access path. The cost is a measure of how much I/O, CPU time, and memory will be required to execute the query. To use the cost-based optimizer effectively, statistics describing the cardinality and data distribution must be collected for each table, index, and materialized view.

11.6.1   Automatic Statistics Collection

Previously, to automate the gathering of statistics for a table meant enabling the monitoring of DML activity for that table using the MONITORING keyword in the CREATE or ALTER TABLE command. Then the GATHER STALE option in the GATHER_DATABASE_STATS procedure was used to gather statistics for just those tables whose contents had changed significantly.

Starting with Oracle Database 10*g*, the MONITORING and NOMONITORING keywords have been deprecated, and now statistics collection is performed automatically and is controlled by the

STATISTICS_LEVEL initialization parameter. When this parameter is set to BASIC, the monitoring and automatic statistics collection is disabled, and when set to TYPICAL (the default), it is enabled. Monitoring tracks the insert, update, and delete activity on the tables and maintains the information in the SGA; it then periodically updates this information into the data dictionary.

Finally, there is an automatic statistics collection job that is available "out of the box" with the Scheduler. Only the user SYS can see and configure this job. Log on to Enterprise Manager as SYS and navigate to the *Administration* page, and click the *Jobs* link in the *Scheduler* section; this will display the *Scheduler Jobs* page where the GATHER_STATS_JOB will be listed. This job is scheduled using one of two windows:

- WEEKNIGHT_WINDOW for weekdays from 10:00 P.M. to 6:00 A.M.
- WEEKEND_WINDOW from midnight Saturday morning for 48 hours

11.6.2 Manual Statistics Collection

You can, of course, still manually perform statistics collection. Two methods are available:

- Via Enterprise Manager using the Gather Statistics wizard
- Via the DBMS_STATS package

To access the wizard go to the *Maintenance* Home screen and, in the *Utilities* section, click on the *Gather Statistics* link. This displays a five-step wizard, which enables a job to be defined and scheduled to collect statistics on:

- Schemas
- Tables
- Indexes
- Table partitions
- Index partition
- The whole database

Alternatively, you can use the DBMS_STATS package directly. For example, to use the DBMS_STATS package to collect statistics on all tables and indexes in the EASYDW schema, issue the following query:

```
EXECUTE DBMS_STATS.GATHER_SCHEMA_STATS ('EASYDW');
```

If you are just interested in a specific table—PURCHASES, for example—you can use the following statement. This will gather statistics on the table, its columns, and indexes.

```
EXECUTE DBMS_STATS.GATHER_TABLE_STATS ('EASYDW', 'PURCHASES');
```

The table and column statistics can be viewed by querying the USER_TABLES and USER_TAB_COLS dictionary views, as follows:

```
-- table statistics
SELECT num_rows, blocks, avg_row_len, last_analyzed
FROM   user_tables
WHERE  table_name = 'PURCHASES';

  NUM_ROWS     BLOCKS AVG_ROW_LEN LAST_ANAL
---------- ---------- ----------- ---------
     94619        567          42 13-JUL-04

-- column statistics
SELECT column_name, num_distinct, num_nulls, avg_col_len
FROM   user_tab_cols
WHERE  table_name = 'PURCHASES';

COLUMN_NAME         NUM_DISTINCT NUM_NULLS AVG_COL_LEN
------------------- ------------ --------- -----------
PRODUCT_ID                   165         0           7
TIME_KEY                     762         0           8
CUSTOMER_ID                  500         0           9
SHIP_DATE                    762         0           8
PURCHASE_PRICE                 9         0           5
SHIPPING_CHARGE                3         0           4
TODAY_SPECIAL_OFFER            2         0           2
```

To collect statistics for the index, CUSTOMER_INDEX, use the following statement:

```
EXECUTE DBMS_STATS.GATHER_INDEX_STATS
            ('easydw', 'purchase_customer_index');
```

Statistics should be gathered after data is loaded and again whenever changes made to the data are likely to have altered the distribution. This ensures that the cost-based optimizer has up-to-date data to base its decision upon. When partitioned tables are used, only the newest partition or sub-partition to which rows have been added needs to be analyzed for statistics. For example, if a new partition for Jan 2005 was added to the purchases table, statistics can be collected for the newly added partition, as follows:

```
ALTER TABLE purchases
  ADD PARTITION purchases_jan2005
  VALUES LESS THAN (TO_DATE('01-02-2005',
                           'DD-MM-YYYY'));

INSERT /*+APPEND */  INTO purchases ...

EXECUTE DBMS_STATS.GATHER_TABLE_STATS
      ('easydw', 'purchases', 'purchases_jan2005');
```

11.6.3   Collecting System Statistics

System statistics such as CPU speed and number of I/Os per second give an indication of the resource availability in the system. Oracle Database 10*g* considers system statistics in determining the execution plan. This allows the optimizer to make smarter decisions when several users are contending for the same resources. System statistics can be collected using the DBMS_STATS.GET_SYSTEM_STATS procedure.

As with all statistics, it is important that the system statistics give the optimizer an accurate picture of the system load. Statistics could be collected for different periods during the day—for example, during normal business hours and during after-hours reporting activities. Statistics can be saved using the EXPORT_SYSTEM_STATS procedure and later imported into a database using the IMPORT_SYSTEM_STATS procedure.

11.6.4   Dynamic Sampling

In the Oracle Database 10*g*, a feature known as **dynamic sampling** can be used by the optimizer when statistics on a table are absent. With dynamic sampling, the optimizer automatically collects statistics by sampling the data before optimizing the query. Dynamic sampling is useful for queries whose tables do not have statistics collected or when the statistics are too old.

To enable dynamic sampling, the initialization parameter, OPTIMIZER_DYNAMIC_SAMPLING, must be set to a value greater than 1. The optimizer will perform dynamic sampling if there is more than one table in the query and some of the tables have no statistics and no indexes. Note that dynamic sampling will incur some overhead during query optimization and hence must be used with care. In a data warehouse, it is always a good practice to collect statistics on all your tables as part of your housekeeping procedures and to keep them current.

11.7 Parallel Management Tasks

Throughout this book, the typically large size of the data warehouse means that tasks can take a very long time to complete. So far, we have considered some techniques for improving performance, but there is a very useful one that is worth mentioning again: the ability to run operations in parallel.

Parallel execution is most useful for operations that access significant amounts of data, including queries, index creation, bulk inserts, updates and deletes, aggregations, and data movement. At the time of writing, most operations can be run in parallel, including:

- Parallel query—queries and subqueries in SELECT statements.
- Parallel DDL—including:
  - CREATE TABLE AS SELECT, CREATE INDEX, and ALTER INDEX REBUILD
  - For partitioned tables: ALTER TABLE MOVE, SPLIT, COALESCE
  - For partitioned indexes: ALTER INDEX REBUILD or SPLIT
- Parallel DML—INSERT, UPDATE, DELETE, multitable insert
- SQL*Loader and external tables

Parallel operations require accurate statistics to perform optimally and correct use of the initialization parameters to ensure that parallel operations properly utilize the database resources. Chapter 6 discussed in detail the configuration of the database to use parallelism and its use to improve query performance, and Chapter 5 showed examples of loading data in parallel. Similar techniques are used to execute DDL statements in parallel.

11.8 Maintaining Security

One should not forget the security of the data in a data warehouse. In many respects, warehouse data should probably be more secure than production data, because its value to your competitors could be enormous. Imagine if one of your users started earning spare cash by running reports against your data or if an employee left the company with information from the data warehouse. If you are laughing at the last statement, please don't; although it is very rare, it actually does happen.

The level of security in your data warehouse will depend on what you think is appropriate for your system. Some sites may prefer to have the warehouse open for read-only queries, but restrict management tasks such as creating summary data to the administration team.

We have already seen, in Chapter 2, how we can protect individual tables by specifying explicitly who may access the tables using the GRANT and REVOKE commands.

Another technique is to create a role, assign privileges to that role, and then grant that role to a user. Roles can either be created via SQL or by going to the Administration screen and following the Roles link in the Security section, which will take you to the Roles screen. Here you will see a list of all of the existing roles in the database and from where you can perform a number of actions to create and administer roles and view to which users the role has been granted.

Click the Create button and you will navigate to the General tab of the Create Role screen, shown in Figure 11.39, where the name of our new role, EASY_USER, is entered.

Figure 11.39 *Creating a Role*

Security isn't limited only to tables; it can be placed on a wide range of database objects. Clicking on the links on this page displays specific screens that enable objects of that type to be granted to our new role. For example, to grant privileges on EASYDW tables to this role, click on the *Object Priv-*

ileges link and you will see a screen similar to that shown in Figure 11.40. We have already granted the SELECT privilege on the PRODUCT and CUSTOMER tables to the role by choosing the object type, which in this example is a table, and clicking the *Add* button. The subsequent simple screen (not shown) enables you to find the objects and assign the privileges.

Figure 11.40　　*Create Role: Grant Object Privileges*

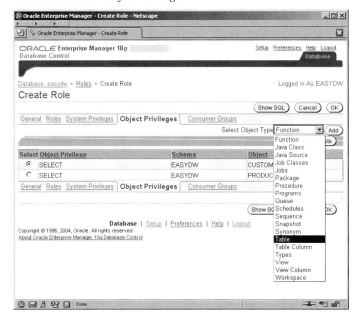

Figure 11.40 also shows the range of objects for which privileges can be granted. The screens for granting the other privilege types to the role operate in a similar fashion.

For those of you who do not want to use Enterprise Manager to create the role—for example, if you want to perform this at a later time—the *Show SQL* button will display a screen that shows the commands to implement this role.

Once the role has been defined, it can be allocated to a user, as shown in Figure 11.41. From the *Administration* screen go to the *Security* section, follow the *Users* link, and navigate to the *Edit Users* screen. Select the user account and click on the *Roles* link. By clicking on the *Modify* button you can assign the new EASY_USER role in the subsequent screen. The *Admin Option* shown here designates whether or not the user that you are assigning the role to can grant that to another user. For our warehouse security, check-

Figure 11.41 *Allocating a Role to a User*

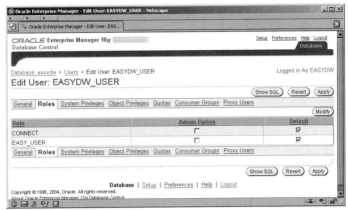

ing the *Admin Option* box would allow access to the warehouse to be granted to users outside of the administrator's control and is not a good idea.

Roles are an extremely powerful feature in Oracle and can save an immense amount of time in not having to allocate lots of individual privileges to a user.

11.8.1 Virtual Private Database

Applications that are deployed on the Internet and make information available to customers, suppliers, employees, or other users need to provide access control at a very fine level of granularity. An on-line banking system needs to ensure that customers can only see transactions for their accounts, and not anyone else's account. A self-service human resources application may let employees see their own records and modify their marital status, address, and phone number, but not their salary. The same application may provide managers with the ability to read and modify the records of all employees who work for them.

As companies are increasing focus on their core competencies, they may outsource other tasks, such as human resources, customer support, and payroll. When designing an application that provides hosting services, the data for each company must be kept separate and secure from each other.

Traditionally, access has been controlled at the object level. The data security policy determines which users have access to which schema objects, and which types of actions are allowed for each object. For example, a user may be able to select from a table, but not insert, update, or delete the rows in the table. If you wanted to allow a user access to a subset of rows in a table, a view could be created and the user granted access to the view. If you have a self-service application, where each employee in a large company had access to the rows containing his or her own personal data in the human resources database, each employee would have to have his or her own view. However, the number of views quickly becomes unwieldy. If you want to allow access to employee data for a certain group of users only through the human resources application, and not for adhoc queries, views do not give you this capability.

Another way to implement data security is with Virtual Private Database (VPD) and fine-grained access control. VPD provides row level security, for all applications. Associating one or more security policies with a table or view creates the Virtual Private Database. Any access to a table with an attached security policy causes the invocation of a function that implements the policy. The function returns an access condition in the form of a WHERE clause, which is appended to the user's SQL statement, thus dynamically modifying the user's data access. For example, in the EASYDW warehouse, we could allow each customer to see information about his own order history on-line. When a customer issues SELECT * FROM PUR-CHASES, the function would add his or her customer_id to the WHERE clause, resulting in the following query.

```
SELECT * FROM PURCHASES WHERE customer_id = 'AB123459'
```

Often, you want to control access based on some attributes about the user, such as job code, department, location, or whether he or she is a customer or partner. An *application context* is created to do this. Upon logging into the database, the application context is associated with the user's session. Each application can have its own application context, with each having different attributes.

After creating the application context, the PL/SQL functions to implement the security policies are created. The function determines the WHERE clause to return, based on the user's application context.

The PL/SQL package DBMS_RLS, is used to administer the security policies and apply them to the appropriate tables. Using this package, you can add, drop, enable, disable, and refresh the policies you create.

Many of the Oracle applications make use of VPD to provide fine-grained access control.

11.9 Monitoring Space Usage

A very important piece of information for the DBA is to know how much space is available in the data warehouse. One technique to avoid running out of space is to create the datafiles with autoextend and to define an unlimited number of extents. However, this won't help you if the disk actually fills up.

Therefore, as part of your routine monitoring of the data warehouse, you should check for free space. This could be done by simply navigating to the *Tablespaces* screen, where this information is shown by default, or you may prefer to simply query the Oracle metadata in the data dictionary for this information. Figure 11.42 shows an example of the space utilization for the EASYDW database.

Figure 11.42   *Tablespace Space Utilization*

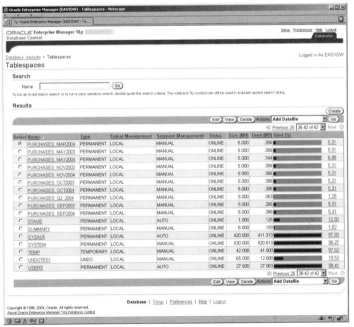

In Figure 11.42, the *Used (%)* graph display for each tablespace enables a very quick visual check of how much space has been used in the tablespace. In our example, we can see that SYSAUX, SYSTEM, TEMP, and USERS are very nearly full; this may cause a problem for any operations that cause an object in these tablespaces to grow in size. However, this screen does not quite show the full story, because, you will recall from Chapter 2 (see Figure 2.21), the datafiles for a tablespace can be set to auto extend when they are nearly full. We will need to click on the tablespace name link and drill down to the data file to verify the exact status.

But manually checking this on a daily basis is a chore and prone to error; with Oracle Database 10*g*, this type of operation is now performed automatically. To look at this further, click on the *All Metrics* link in the *Related Links* of the Home pages to display the screen shown in Figure 11.43.

Figure 11.43   *Tablespace Utilization Metrics*

Clicking on the + icon to the right of the *Tablespace Full* metric expands the category to show the space used by the metric. From here you can drill down further to values collected and thresholds set for each tablespace and even further to displays and values for each tablespace.

When the tablespace full warning or critical thresholds are crossed, an alert will be generated and displayed in the *Alert* section on the database *Home* page. Notification mechanisms can also be defined by email or by paging the DBA on duty to correct this issue.

11.9.1 Automated Space Management

Summarized here are several features and enhancements in the database that simplify space management. Some of these features are outside the scope of this book, but we have listed the relevant chapters where we discuss certain features in more detail.

- Locally managed tablespaces eliminate the need for periodically reorganizing tablespaces to reclaim fragmented space.

- Tablespaces can be created with the SEGMENT SPACE MANAGEMENT AUTO clause to automate the management of free space inside a database segment, such as a table or index.

- Automatic undo management eliminates the need to manage rollback segments manually.

As discussed in Chapter 3, Oracle Managed Files (OMF) can be used to create and delete files, as they are needed for the datafiles, on-line logs, and control files, eliminating the need to directly manage the files. All you need to do is specify the location of where you would like the files stored.

The Flash Recovery Area is new in Oracle Database 10*g* and is an area on disk that is used to contain database backups stored to disk, as well as for a new type of log file, called flashback logs. When the Flash Recovery Area is configured, the Oracle database will automatically manage the disk space utilization. The Flash Recovery Area is discussed in more detail in Chapter 12, and the flashback feature in Chapter 17.

11.9.2 Resumable Space Allocation

Long-running operations that update or add new data to the database can fail when they run out of space. Reexecuting the procedure could take a long time, particularly if it was almost complete when it failed. A feature introduced in Oracle 9*i*, resumable statements, makes it possible to intervene and correct errors in the middle of an operation. When the problem that caused the failure is fixed, the operation is automatically resumed.

A resumable statement is suspended when one of the following errors occurs:

- Out of space
- Maximum extents reached
- User space quota exceeded

The following operations are resumable:

- SELECT statements that run out of temporary space (for sort areas)
- DML statements—INSERT, UPDATE, and DELETE
- Import/Export
- SQL*Loader
- DDL statements—CREATE TABLE ... AS SELECT, CREATE INDEX, ALTER INDEX ... REBUILD, ALTER TABLE ... MOVE PARTITION,
- ALTER TABLE ... SPLIT PARTITION, ALTER INDEX ... REBUILD PARTITION, ALTER INDEX ... SPLIT PARTITION, CREATE MATERIALIZED VIEW, and CREATE MATERIAL-IZED VIEW LOG

Resumable mode must be enabled for a session. Optionally, you can specify a time-out period. If the error condition is not fixed within that time period, it will abort. You can also specify a name, which can help identify the session that has been suspended in the USER_RESUMABLE or DBA_RESUMABLE views. The following statement sets the time-out period for 3,600 seconds, or one hour, and assigns the name data warehouse load to resumable statements for the session.

```
SQL> ALTER SESSION
    ENABLE RESUMABLE
    TIMEOUT 3600 NAME 'data warehouse load';
```

SQL*Loader and the Import and Export utilities provide the same options as command-line parameters.

When a resumable statement is suspended, the error is reported in the alert log. The system also internally generates an AFTER SUSPEND system event. Users can register triggers for this event at both the database and schema level. The triggers can be used to notify the DBA when a statement is suspended, so corrective action can be taken.

Information about the status of resumable statements can be seen by looking at the DBA_RESUMABLE or USER_RESUMABLE views, as shown in the following example. The data warehouse load was suspended, because there was inadequate space to extend the PURCHASE_PRODUCT_INDEX.

```
SQL> SELECT STATUS, TIMEOUT, START_TIME,
        SUSPEND_TIME,  NAME, ERROR_MSG
FROM DBA_RESUMABLE

STATUS     TIMEOUT START_TIME        SUSPEND_TIME       NAME
---------  ------- ----------------  -----------------  --------
SUSPENDED 3600     08/16/04 06:27:56 08/16/04 14:01:05  data
warehouse load


ERROR_MSG
---------
ORA-01683: unable to extend index EASYDW.PURCHASE_PRODUCT_INDEX
partition PURCHASES_JUL04 by 2 in tablespace INDX
```

When a statement is suspended the session invoking the statement is put into a wait state. A row is inserted into the V$SESSION_WAIT as seen in the following example.

```
SQL> SELECT EVENT, STATE FROM V$SESSION_WAIT;

EVENT                                            STATE
------------------------------------------------ -------------
statement suspended, wait error to be cleared    WAITING
```

When space is added, the session will automatically resume. If space is not added within the time-out period, an error will occur.

11.10 Other Management Issues

We have already seen a number of management tasks. The ones specified here are by no means an exhaustive list, and there may very well be ones that are not mentioned here that may be applicable in your environment. There are also some additional tasks that you may want to consider.

11.10.1 Building a Test System

When you suggest the construction of a test system, it is not uncommon for many people to throw their hands up in the air and say, "impossible." But you should stop for a moment and consider the implication on your business if you don't have a test system. When a test system exists, it can be used for a variety of reasons, such as:

- Testing new software releases
- Timing data loads
- Evaluating management task times
- Practicing management tasks
- Testing scripts before executing in production
- Assessing impact of maintenance tasks (e.g., index rebuild)
- Determining query response times

Many people think that a test system has to be identical to the production system, but, in a warehouse, that is usually impossible. Therefore, what is required is a scaled-down version of the warehouse that is representative of the real warehouse. Ideally, numbers obtained from it should scale easily so that you can determine what the effect would be on your production warehouse.

Data inside the warehouse should, whenever possible, be representative of the real data. It may be that, to obtain the desired effect, you may have to extract data from the real warehouse and then load it into the test warehouse.

The various uses for a test system will now be discussed.

11.10.2 Testing New Software

Once a database becomes a critical component in the business, and the information supplied from it is used to make critical business decisions, no one wants to jeopardize the business by introducing new software that may have problems. Therefore, if you have a test system, you can check that all of the important parts of the database software that you use are the same. The range of items to test could be extensive. For example, you will want to check that queries use the same optimizer strategy as before. If they have changed, then you should create outlines to ensure consistency of query response times.

However, you should always ensure, when using outlines, that performance will not degrade when a new version of Oracle is installed; it could improve due to an optimizer change, so always check for the current strategy.

Another important check to make is that key features that you rely on still function the same. For example, if you rely heavily on partition operations to maintain the data in your warehouse, then check that they still work.

Utilities you rely on should also be checked to see that no changes have occurred that cause them to change their behavior.

If a script is created that contains all of these important tasks, then each time you upgrade the software, you have only to run the scripts and check the results. Therefore, considerable effort will be required to construct the scripts the first time. Once completed, however, they can be run repeatedly and you will know that everything that is important to your environment will have been checked.

11.10.3 Timing Data Loads

The test system provides an ideal opportunity to determine the load time for data and to practice any data cleansing that may be required. Generally, the fastest way to load data into an Oracle 9*i* data warehouse is by using the utility SQL*Loader via the direct path method. But, you may want to compare the performance with external tables, particularly if you also need to perform transformations.

Hint: Don't forget to check the logs from any SQL*Loader jobs in case any problems occurred during the run, such as constraints not being enabled.

11.10.4 Evaluating/Practicing Management Tasks

Now is also an ideal opportunity to practice and try out all of those management tasks before they are done in production. When it comes to testing backup and recovery processes, using very small databases initially and then moving on to the full size once you are sure that all of the procedures are working correctly will save time.

11.10.5 Determine Query Response Times

The test system provides an ideal opportunity to see the data warehouse in use before all the users are given access. Even with a limited user audience, you will be surprised that you will find queries that do not perform well.

Therefore, you now have time to diagnose the cause of the poor performance and resolve the problem by adding a new index, for example, or creating a materialized view to make the query perform faster.

In a test environment, it is unlikely that you will see an exact reproduction of usage of the data warehouse. Nevertheless, problems will still surface and it is easier to fix them now before the pressure comes with users demanding reports yesterday!

11.11 Summary

In this chapter, we have taken a look at some of the tasks required to manage a warehouse, examined many of the new features available in Oracle Database 10g to help with this, and used Oracle Enterprise Manager to simplify management of our warehouse. Ongoing tasks, including monitoring space usage, were discussed, and techniques for periodic reorganization using partition maintenance operations and on-line redefinition were introduced. Developing a test system and a business continuity plan are important considerations.

Hopefully, you can begin to appreciate what is involved in managing a database. Many of the tasks described here apply equally to a traditional OLTP database. It's often the size of the data warehouse that makes the task different. Remember that it is better to manage now than not at all. Even something as simple as failing to monitor space usage could have disastrous results, usually when you can least afford the time to correct them.

12

Backup and Recovery

12.1 Strategy

One of the most important management tasks for any database is taking backups of the data. It may seem obvious, but you will be surprised how many companies jeopardize their business by taking backups infrequently, by not taking care of their backup tapes, or by not testing their backup and recovery strategy.

A data warehouse has a couple of major characteristics that influence the backup strategy:

- The size of the data warehouse
- The historical, and therefore static, nature of most of the data in the warehouse.

A data warehouse by its very nature is a repository of historical records, which, generally, once loaded, are not subsequently altered. Therefore, once this load has been performed and backed up, it is unnecessary for it to participate in any subsequent backup operation. For example, if our data warehouse holds five years of data, it may be only the partitions for the current month that are updated on a nightly basis. This is less than 2 percent of the warehouse data that is changing and therefore needs to be backed up.

In addition, the problems with scheduling the backup of a data warehouse are slightly different from backing up a typical production system. Since warehouses usually receive large loads of data at scheduled times, typically overnight, backups have to be scheduled along with this work. Plus, we have the added complication of deciding how to back up the database.

Why is this a problem? Well, normally, a database is backed up in its entirety, but that may not be possible with your data warehouse, especially if it is particularly large (multiple terabyte size). Therefore, incremental backups and backups of one or more tablespaces may be more practical. Careful management of your backup location, or of the backup tapes, is critical; otherwise, you could find yourself unable to rebuild the data warehouse.

In the next sections, we are going to look at the common backup and recovery strategies and their applicability to the data warehouse; we will also discuss a new feature in Oracle Database 10*g*, called the Flash Recovery Area, which is a disk backup area.

12.1.1   Methods of Performing a Backup and Recovery

In this section, we will look at the different forms of backup and recovery that are possible on the Oracle database and their business implications.

Backup

There are a number of types of backup that can be performed on an Oracle database.

Logical Backup

A logical backup is an export to an operating system file of the database or objects in the database, such as schema object definitions, and the contents of the objects, such as tables and indexes. It provides a snapshot of the schema and its data at the time of the export, and reimporting can be used to restore that snapshot.

However, using export and import is not advised as the sole basis of a warehouse backup strategy on any but the smallest of data warehouses. For example, exporting the whole database would be prohibitively time consuming for a large data warehouse and would use a lot of disk space. In addition, recovery by reimport could also take an inordinate amount of time. Furthermore, it is not possible to easily export just the changed data for either the fact tables or the dimensions. This could result in the scripts to control a backup, which must be selective on the data being exported, being complex and difficult to write.

However, a logical backup can still play a very useful role. It can still be necessary or convenient to take an export snapshot of part of our data warehouse schema. For example, the dimension tables, which tend to be significantly smaller than the fact tables, could be exported more conveniently and may provide a supplement to the other backup mechanisms. If we know that a dimension table has not changed appreciably, it may be markedly quicker and easier to reimport the table from the logical backup and rerun the processes to reapply any changes to the data.

During a logical backup, we do not want changes occurring to the data that may result in a transactionally inconsistent backup. If Data Pump export is used, as discussed in Chapter 5, the use of the flashback feature ensures that a transactionally consistent view of the data is obtained.

Physical Backup

A physical backup involves backing up the actual files that form the database and are necessary for its recovery (i.e., the datafiles, control files, and redo log files).

There are two modes of physical backup that can be performed:

- *Cold*, or *off-line*, backup, which is performed when the database has been shut down in a consistent state or is not operating in archive log mode. The database must be shut down consistently (i.e. using shutdown modes immediate or normal); the database files and control file are backed up and then the database is restarted. During a cold backup, the database is not accessible to the users and this can be a major limiting factor.
- *Hot*, or *on-line*, backup, which is performed while the database is in archive log mode, open to read and write activity, and accessible to the users.

Furthermore, there are two other considerations when performing a physical backup concerning how copies of the datafiles are made.

- Full backup, which backs up all used blocks in the database data files
- Incremental backups, which backs up only those blocks in the database that have changed since the last full or incremental backup

Incremental Backups

We mentioned earlier that a type of backup that is very useful for a data warehouse is one that does not have to back up all of the datafiles. The *incremental backup* allows us to back up only the parts of the database datafiles that have changed.

Oracle incremental backups have the concept of backup levels, of which there are two: level 0 and level 1. A level 0 incremental backup acts as the base for subsequent incremental backups and is similar to a full backup in that it copies all blocks that contain data. (The only difference between a level 0 incremental backup and a full backup is that a full backup cannot act as the base of an incremental backup strategy.)

The level 1 backup has two types:

- *Differential*, which copies all blocks changed since the last level 0 or level 1 backup

- *Cumulative*, which copies all blocks changed since the last level 0 backup

Cumulative level 1 incremental backups, therefore, contain all of the previous level 1 backups back to the last level 0 incremental backup. They are better for recovery purposes, because only the one incremental backup needs to be applied.

Figure 12.1 shows how each of the differential incremental level 1 backups only backs up the changes occurring since the preceding level 1 or level 0 backup.

A level 0 incremental backup (i.e., a full backup of all used blocks to use as a baseline) is taken on Saturday, and then each day at close of business up

Figure 12.1   *Differential Incremental Backups*

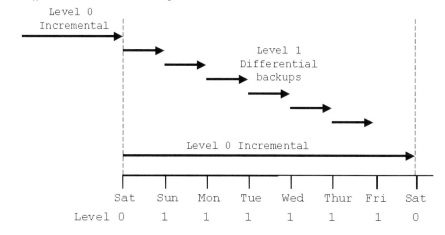

to Friday, a level 1 differential backup is taken. This backs up all of the blocks that have changed since the preceding day's level 1 backup. Therefore, after Friday's backup, all of the changed blocks are held on six incremental backup files. On the following Saturday, a new full level 0 backup is taken and the cycle repeats.

Now, let's compare this with using a cumulative incremental backup strategy. A level 1 cumulative backup taken on the same schedule will incorporate all of the changes back to the preceding level 0 backup. To clarify how this is different from the differential level 0 backup, refer to Figure 12.2.

Figure 12.2   *Cumulative Incremental Backups*

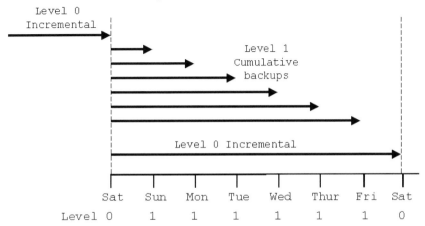

A cumulative backup on Sunday backs up the changes since the preceding level 0 incremental backup on Saturday. The cumulative backup on Monday backs up the changes on Monday and the changes on Sunday. On each day, the cumulative incremental backup will back up all changes since the last level 0. Therefore, after Friday's backup, all of the changed blocks are held on just one incremental backup file. On Saturday, a new level 0 incremental backup is taken and the cycle repeats.

Block Change Tracking

In order to track which blocks have changed for an incremental backup, Oracle tracks the system change number (SCN). Each block in an Oracle database contains the system change number (SCN) of the most recent change to a block. When performing an incremental backup, Oracle must read each block in a file and compare the block's SCN with the SCN of the preceding backup. If the SCN is greater, then the block has changed and is backed up. This method does rely on reading every block to get its SCN number and hence can be slow. However, one of the new features in Oracle Database 10*g* is block change tracking, which uses a special tracking file to record the location of all changed blocks in the database. The backup process can then use this file when performing an incremental backup rather than reading all of the datafiles. The file enables the backup to more quickly identify the location of the changed blocks and back them up resulting in a much more efficient incremental backup.

Hint: Block change tracking records changed blocks even if no redo log is generated. It should, therefore, be used after performing NOLOGGING operations—for example, during data load operations, for which you may still want to backup incrementally.

Another particularly important new feature in Oracle Database 10*g* is the ability to merge the incremental backup into the full backup copy of the database, so that the full backup files then contain the up-to-date backup. Full backups are a lengthy process, because they are backing up all blocks that have ever been used; incremental backups usually take a significantly shorter amount of time, because they are backing up just the changed blocks. Effectively, this new feature means that we can obtain a full backup in about the same time that is taken to perform an incremental backup of our database.

Considering the size of a typical data warehouse, copying the entire datafile every time that a backup is required can be a significant overhead in terms of time, processing requirements, and space requirements of the backup media. To only have to back up the datafiles for the partitions that have changed or, even better, the blocks in those files that have changed, can result in considerable savings.

Restore and Recovery

To restore a database or parts of the database, such as a tablespace, is to retrieve the backed up files from the backup media and make them available to the database. For example, the whole database can be restored from a full backup by restoring the datafiles and control files. It will, therefore, still have the same data as it had at the time the backup was taken.

We could also restore the database by restoring the level 0 backup and then restoring and applying the incremental differential level 1 backups. This will update the blocks in the correct sequence and therefore result in the database files being brought up-to-date. Applying a single cumulative level 1 backup will be quicker than applying the multiple differential level 1 backups. For example, if we have to perform a restore due to some form of system failure and get the database back quickly, then time is our enemy and this is when we least need a lengthy process. Consider the backup strategy that involves a weekly full backup on Saturday night with daily differential incremental backups, as shown in Figure 12.1. If the system fails on a Friday, then to restore the database would necessitate restoring the level 0 backup and then restoring and applying each of the five differential incremental backups in turn, which could take a considerable amount of time.

This is where the new incremental merge option in Oracle Database 10*g* is a very important feature. Now, our base level 0 backup files contain an up-to-date backup so that all that is required is to restore the most recent merged level 0 backup. In our weekly backup strategy example, just the merged level 0 backup must be restored, and this method removes the need to apply the incremental backups. A considerable saving on both the speed of the backup and the speed of the restore!

However, restoring the database only resets it to the state at the time that the backup was made. In our example backup strategy, this means the time that the incremental or full backup was actually taken at the end of the day. This would result in losing any transactions that occurred during the day after the backup. This is where databases that operate in archive redo log mode have the advantage of being able to be recovered.

To recover the database, or part of the database, is to recover to a point in time using the archived redo logs. By applying the transaction changes in the redo logs to the restored database files, the datafiles are rolled forward to a required point in time.

Applying the redo logs in this fashion effectively repeats the transactions contained in the log files. We can roll forward to a selected point in time and then open the recovered files to make them accessible and usable on the database again. We do not necessarily have to perform a complete recovery, which would be to the most recent point in time. For example, if we are recovering due to a faulty program writing incorrect data into our tables, then we will want to recover to just before that program commences its transaction. This is known as an incomplete recovery or point-in-time recovery.

Running the database in archive log mode provides significant advantages. The data warehouse could still have other transactions, which we want to preserve, occurring at other times on the database. For example, the database may also be used for a number of other repositories, such as Oracle Enterprise Manager, Oracle Discoverer and Oracle Warehouse Builder. If we run the database in archive log mode, then changes to the data in these repositories can be recovered without needing to reenter any of the transactions.

Oracle backup and recovery is performed using Recovery Manager (RMAN). RMAN handles the administrative work associated with the backup and recovery operations and catalogs the metadata about the backup files and the activities performed. We will now look at the new Flash Recovery Area feature for performing backups to disk; in the remainder of the chapter, we will discuss how backup and recovery are managed and performed via Oracle Enterprise Manager using RMAN.

12.1.2   Simplifying Recovery with Flash Recovery Area

Traditionally, backup was done to a slow medium such as tape. However, with the advent of low-cost disk storage devices, it is much easier and faster to do backups to disk. Unlike with a tape backup, restoring data from a disk backup can be a very quick operation. However, the process of managing the disk space for backups and determining which files to keep and discard can be an onerous task for a DBA. Oracle Database 10*g* has a new feature called the Flash Recovery Area, which can greatly simplify the management of all recovery related files. By setting up the *Flash Recovery Area* and some simple policies, RMAN can now automatically manage all of the backup and recovery files with no DBA intervention.

The Flash Recovery Area is a unified storage area that contains all the recovery related files for the Oracle database, including redo logs, RMAN backups, and data and control file backups. Creating a Flash Recovery Area simplifies the process of managing recovery related files, such as naming backup files, determining which ones to keep and removing files when they are no longer necessary. In addition, the Flash Recovery Area is used to contain a new type of file, called the **flashback logs**, which are used by the new Oracle Database 10*g* flashback feature discussed in more detail in Chapter 17. The Flash Recovery Area uses the Oracle Managed Files (OMF) feature, discussed in Chapter 3, to manage the files.

At this point it is worth reiterating a golden rule of backup, which is particularly relevant when we are backing up to disk. What is being backed up (i.e., the database data, control, and redo log files) must reside on separate disks to the backup destination—that is the Flash Recovery Area. This prevents any form of media failure causing the loss of both the source database files and the backup files. Furthermore, also backing up to tape, which is then held off site, enables recovery from any disaster that affects the whole data center, such as fire or flood.

Setting up the Flash Recovery Area

The Flash Recovery Area can be set up by simply setting up two initialization parameters, as follows:

- **DB_RECOVERY_FILE_DEST**: This parameter specifies the default location for all recovery-related files, which can be a directory on a file system or an ASM disk group (see Chapter 3). By using ASM, you can automatically provide redundancy for files stored in the Flash Recovery Area.
- **DB_RECOVERY_FILE_DEST_SIZE**: Specifies (in bytes) the maximum space to be used by the recovery files created in the recovery area location. The Flash Recovery Area size should be large enough to include a copy of all the datafiles, control files, any incremental backups (created using RMAN), on-line redo logs, and archive logs that have not yet been archived to tape.

Hint: When creating a database using the Database Configuration Assistant, you will be asked if you would like to set up the Flash Recovery Area, as shown in Chapter 2, Figure 2.10.

Use of the Flash Recovery Area for backups to disk has the advantage that you set the location, size to be used, and retention policy; Oracle manages the storage area on disk. Files no longer needed are eligible for deletion. If you don't use a Flash Recovery Area, then you must manage the disk area manually.

12.2 Backup

In this section, we will discuss the various techniques you can use to back up your data warehouse. However, it is important to realize that, if your data warehouse is very large, taking a full backup of it may be almost impossible due to time and other constraints.

The following types of backups will be discussed:

- Full backups
- Incremental backups performed as a custom backup
- Tablespace backups

12.2.1 Creating a Backup Configuration

The first step toward defining our backup environment is to create a backup configuration. The backup configuration is a set of defaults used for backup operations. It determines where the backup is to be stored and what the backup medium is to be (tape or disk). It enables customizations to be defined and saved for reuse.

In Enterprise Manager, on the *Maintenance* screen in the *Backup/Recovery* section, there are a number of options for performing and managing your backup and recovery. Start by selecting *Configure Backup Settings,* where you can specify default values for your backup operations, as shown in Figure 12.3.

This screen contains three sections for defining the defaults for your backup, and they are used when you create the backup job if you don't specifically override them. The three groups of settings that can be defined are:

- Device
- Backup set
- Policy

On the *Device* screen, shown in Figure 12.3, there are check boxes in the disk and tape sections for an important option in Oracle Database 10*g*: to instruct RMAN to compress the backup files as they are archived to the destination area. This feature assists in the management of large volumes and enables better space utilization and more backup files to be stored.

Another new and important option in Oracle Database 10*g* is the option to compress the backup set as it is being written to disk or tape. With writing to the disk-based Flash Recovery Area, being able to compress the backup set can have significant benefits in saving and managing the space.

Figure 12.3 *Configure Backup Settings*

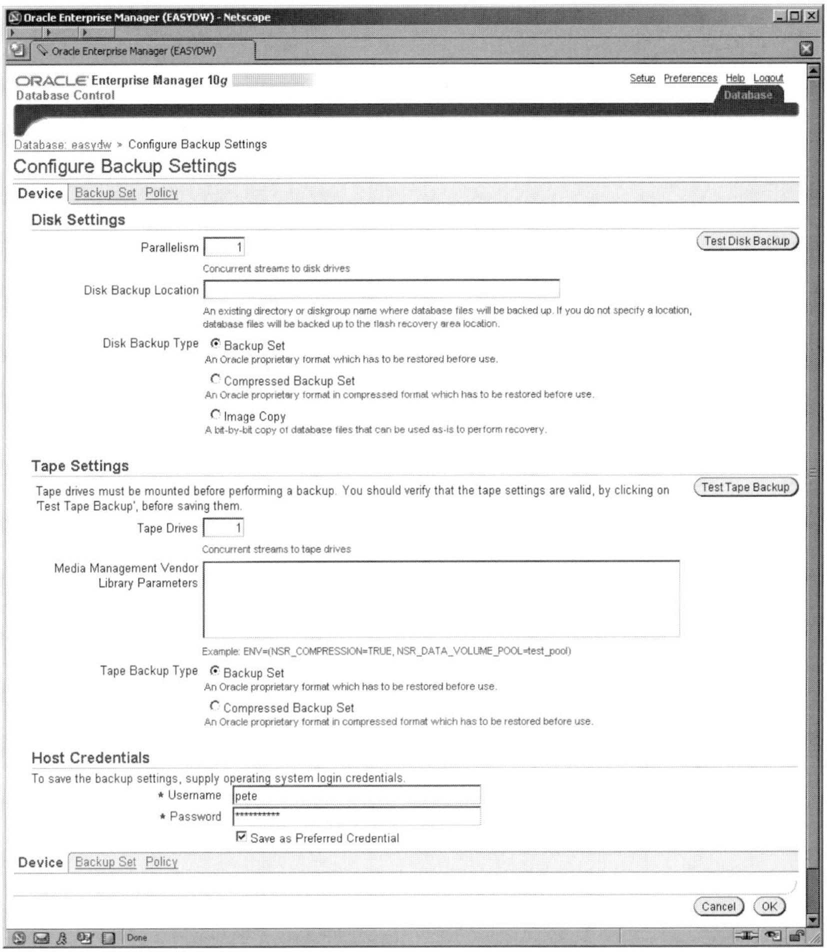

Also on the *Device* screen, you can define the degree of parallelism to be used when the backup is performed, as well as the disk location for the backup. By default the disk location is the Flash Recovery Area, but here you can override the default to use a different disk location. Similarly, you can provide default settings if you are backing up directly to tape.

In our examples in this section, the backup will go to disk, but, in a data warehouse, it will probably also have to go to tape. For example, a disaster recovery plan may mandate off-site storage on tape. To store backups on tape, RMAN requires the installation of a media management library available from another company such as Legato or Veritas. Refer to Oracle's Backup Solutions Partners Program for the current list of certified vendors.

When backing up to tape, it is extremely important to ensure that the physical labels placed on the tapes match the contents. Too many times we have seen customer problems, where it is impossible to recreate the database from the backups because the labels on the tapes do not match the actual tape contents. Sloppy management practices such as this could mean that you lose your entire data warehouse.

Whenever you take a full backup of the system, do not discard the previous full backup set, because, if there were a problem with the current backup, you would lose your entire data warehouse. Therefore, save as many full backup sets as is possible before you recycle the tapes.

On the *Configure Backup Settings* screen, use the appropriate test button to test the disk or tape device's configuration. For example, for a disk-based backup, clicking the *Test Disk Backup* creates a BACKUPSET directory. This is created under the named directory for your database in the Flash Recovery Area. In the BACKUPSET directory, the new directory is named by the current date (e.g., 2004_07_18). Once tested, we know our configuration is correct.

On the *Policy* screen, shown in Figure 12.4, you can define various additional settings for your backup, such as how long the backup sets are to be retained.

This screen provides a good indication of changes that have been implemented with Oracle Database 10*g* to ease the backup management task. For example, under the *Retention Policy* section, there are options to define which backup sets must be kept in order to meet the backup and recovery strategy for your system; these are then automatically used when a backup is performed.

Note the *Optimize* check box in the *Backup Policy* section. If this is selected so that backups are executed using the optimization feature, then RMAN avoids creating identical copies of files that have not changed since the last backup. However, if backup files are aged out by the retention policy, then RMAN will take a new copy.

12.2.2 Full Backups

The size of your data warehouse will determine how frequently a full backup is taken. Even if your warehouse is huge, a backup should always be taken periodically.

Figure 12.4 *Configure Backup Settings Policy*

One of the tools provided in Oracle Enterprise Manager is the backup wizard, where you can:

- Define a predefined backup strategy
- Customize your own strategy

To start a backup, go to the *Backup/Recovery* section on the *Maintenance* screen and click on the *Perform Backup* link.

Predefined Backup Strategy

Here we will see how to set up a predefined backup strategy. The first question asked by the wizard, illustrated in Figure 12.5, is where is the destination of the backup is disk, tape, or both.

Figure 12.5   *Oracle Suggested Backup Strategy*

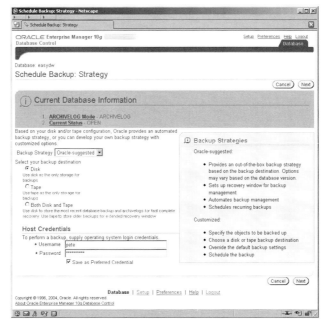

The next screen (not shown) summarizes the Oracle suggested backup policy. This is first to perform a full backup followed by an incremental daily backup.

Moving on to the next screen in the wizard, shown in Figure 12.6, enables the schedule for the backup job to be set. Don't forget that the first backup performed as part of the schedule is a full backup, which could be a very lengthy operation on a warehouse-sized database.

The definition of the backup procedure is almost complete. Click on *Next* and the screen in Figure 12.7 is displayed shown where we can review all of the options that we have selected. To change any of the values, press the *Back* key to return to the appropriate screen, and make the necessary modifications. At this point we can also view the RMAN script that has been generated.

Figure 12.6 *Predefined Backup Schedule*

Figure 12.7 *Reviewing the Backup Procedure*

Clicking on the *Submit Job* button completes the definition of the backup and submits the job, which will be placed on the Enterprise Manager job queue until it is time for it to run. Monitoring the job can be performed by going to the EM Home pages and clicking on the *Jobs* link in the *Related Links* section, where the screen illustrated in Figure 12.8 is displayed.

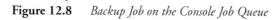

Figure 12.8   *Backup Job on the Console Job Queue*

12.2.3   **Incremental Backups**

An alternative to the Oracle suggested backup is to create a custom backup strategy. We will use the customized option to show how to perform a level 1 incremental backup.

Again, we start at the *Schedule Backup Strategy* screen shown in Figure 12.9, where a backup strategy of *Customized* is selected.

The first question asked by the wizard is the type of backup that you require. If *Whole Database* is selected, you will then have the choice of either backing up the entire database or taking an incremental backup. As we have already discussed, an incremental backup is very likely to be of interest to a data warehouse administrator, because it allows you to back up only the data that has changed, instead of the entire data warehouse.

Figure 12.9   *Type of Custom Backup*

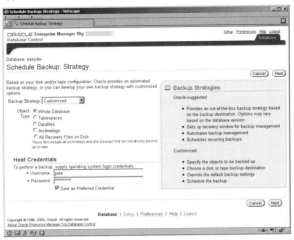

Depending on whether or not the database is running in archive log mode will determine the types of backup options available. In Figure 12.9, more options are available because archive log mode is enabled. With archive logging disabled, it is only possible to perform an off-line (cold) backup of the whole database which will necessitate it being automatically shut down first. Enabling archive logging means that the database, selected tablespaces, datafiles, or the archived logs can be backed up in on-line mode with the database still open to the users.

The steps in a custom backup are very similar to those we have seen previously; it uses a four-step wizard, so we won't show all screens because most of these are self-explanatory. However, in Figure 12.10 we show the *Options* screen for the customized approach.

Here we can control the type of backup that we want to perform. As we have already mentioned, a typical warehouse is going to be too large to perform a full backup following every single refresh, so normally we will want to perform incremental backups. However, to perform an incremental backup we must start with a baseline full backup position. The *Backup Type* field provides us with the ability to specify which backup we want to perform.

- Full backup
- Incremental backup

Figure 12.10   *Customized Backup Options for an Incremental Backup*

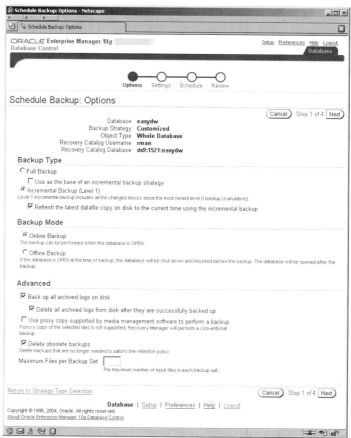

We can perform a full backup by selecting the *Full Backup* option and leaving the check box clear for use as the base of an incremental backup. This will just perform the full backup. However, if we select the check box as well, then a level 0 incremental backup is performed. It is the same full backup of all of the used database blocks, but, because it is the base of an incremental backup strategy, this is what we have previously defined as a level 0 incremental backup.

We have chosen the level 1 incremental backup on the basis that a prior backup operation has performed the full backup to use as a baseline. Note the check box under the *Incremental Backup* option; it specifies that the incremental backup is to be merged into the full backup image held in the Flash Recovery Area.

The other options we can specify on this screen are:

- Backup mode, for whether the backup is performed when the database is open or whether it is shut down first. The database must be in ARCHIVELOG mode for an on-line backup to be performed.
- Advanced options, which control the backup and retention policy for our archived logs and for the obsolete backups on disk.

Here we are backing up the archived redo logs and specifying that RMAN manage the logs by deleting those that are no longer required once they have been backed up. Similarly, we want any backups that are no longer required to be deleted. These options automate and simplify the backup procedure and the associated management tasks.

Figure 12.11   *The Custom Backup Job Name and Schedule Screen*

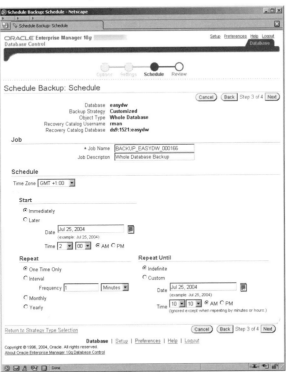

The remaining screens in the custom backup wizard enable us to specify the backup destination, disk or tape (which is step 2 and not shown), and specify the backup job name and schedule, as shown in Figure 12.11. Finally, there is a review screen (also not shown).

In Figure 12.11, we can rename the backup job to something that is more meaningful on our system, and we have full control of the start, stop, and frequency of operation of the job by the Scheduler. Once we have submitted the job in step 4 then, as before, we can always access it from the *Related Links* section of the OEM pages and click on the *Jobs* link.

12.2.4 Tablespace Backups

Another technique for backing up the database is a tablespace backup. Using this technique, you have the ability to back up a specific tablespace, which, in a data warehouse, could make for a very nice backup strategy.

This time, when we schedule a backup, as shown in Figure 12.9, we will choose *Customized* and select the *Tablespaces* radio button. The first step is to select the tablespaces that we want to back up. In Figure 12.12, we see one of the screens from the backup wizard asking us which tablespaces we want to back up. Tablespaces are added to the list using a separate screen, accessed via the *Add* button. In our example, we have selected the tablespace that contains the January 2005 data.

Figure 12.12 *Selecting a Tablespace to Back Up*

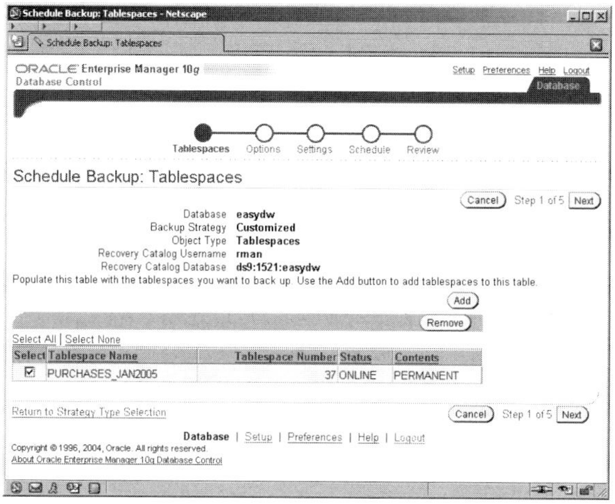

This screen is a good example of where designing the database for management should be considered during the initial construction process. If we can group our updates to the database by date, and we know that after a given point in time there will be no changes made within this tablespace, then, if we set the tablespace to be read-only and back it up, we can rest assured that we have captured the data in that tablespace. Since it will never change, we won't have to back it up again.

Changing the status of a tablespace to read-only is very simple. You can enter this SQL command:

```
ALTER TABLESPACE purchases_jan2005 READ ONLY;
```

Alternatively, go to the *Maintenance* screen and select *Tablespaces* from the *Storage* area, select the tablespace, and then click on the box on the right of the screen marked *Read Only*, as shown in Figure 12.13. Finally, clicking on the *Apply* button will make this a read-only tablespace. You can change it back to a read/write tablespace at any time.

Figure 12.13 *Making a Tablespace Read-Only*

Of course, it makes sense to periodically take full backups, just in case there are any problems with the backup files you have taken. Taking only tablespace backups is okay, but it still makes it possible for somebody to accidentally overwrite the tape containing all of the data for a given month.

12.2.5   Backup File Sizes

When a database is being built, designers are constantly aware of the size of the database. However, that information seems to get lost when people start thinking about backing up the database. Everyone tends to say, "Well it's 300 gigabytes so it will take x minutes to back up." What they forget to add is that the backup file will need y gigabytes of space.

In the examples shown here, we have used disks to store our backups. For a real data warehouse, however, you will be storing them on tape; so don't forget how many tapes you will require for the backup strategy you will be implementing. It has been known for sites to actually run out of tapes! Our Easy Shopping Inc. database is small, and the datafiles occupy approximately 1.5 gigabytes on a Windows XP system. In Figure 12.14, we can see the different sizes for the full backup files.

Figure 12.14   *Backup File Sizes*

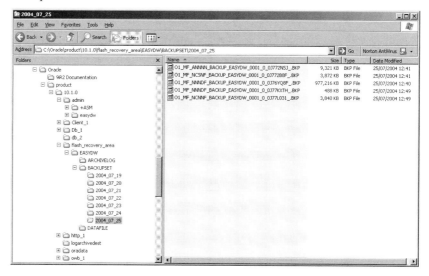

A full backup occupies a little less than 1GB, which is about 66 percent of the full size of the database. Therefore, you can see that you can save a significant amount of storage space by using the backup provided by Oracle Database 10*g*. If a backup were taken using the Operating System backup utility, which may or may not compress the file, then 1.5GB of storage would be needed, instead of 1GB.

The files resulting from an incremental backup will be even smaller than the full backup files, though the size will be dependent upon the update activity that has occurred in the database. Obviously, we can see that there is a big advantage in using the RMAN utility for backups.

It is easy to see that even for the incremental backups, the size of the files is going to be significantly less than that for the full warehouse. By taking incremental backups, you can make backups of your warehouse more frequently and not have to worry about when you are going to find the time to back up the entire warehouse. By using the new option to merge the incremental backup into the full backup files, you can significantly improve the recovery times.

One final reminder on this topic: during the testing of the data warehouse, don't forget to test your backup procedures and obtain some estimates of possible run times for backups. Then you can discuss your requirements with the operations department so that your management tasks can be included with all of the other work that has to be done.

12.3 The Recovery Catalog

Information describing your RMAN backups can be stored in the target database's control file or in a recovery catalog. The recovery catalog is a separate repository of information stored in a database schema; it contains backup and recovery information for one or more databases. The catalog schema should always reside in a database different from the data warehouse. You will recall that when EM Grid Control is used, it uses its own database, which contains the EM repository, and this database can also be used for the recovery catalog. Using a recovery catalog is a safer alternative than storing it in the control file alone, since the information is stored separately from the database. It also allows you to store information about all of your backups in a central place, which is a particularly flexible configuration when administering multiple databases using Grid Control.

12.3.1 Creating the Recovery Catalog

A recovery catalog should be stored in its own tablespace. In our example, the RMANREP tablespace is used. A new user, who will own the recovery catalog schema in the recovery catalog database, should be created. In the following example we have created a user called RMAN and granted it the appropriate privileges.

```
CREATE USER rman IDENTIFIED BY rmanrep
  DEFAULT TABLESPACE rmanrep TEMPORARY TABLESPACE temp
  QUOTA UNLIMITED ON rmanrep;
GRANT connect, resource TO rman;
GRANT recovery_catalog_owner TO rman;
```

The next step is to actually create the recovery catalog, which is achieved by running the RMAN utility. As soon as the RMAN prompt appears, as illustrated, connect to the database that will hold the catalog. Since you are using the syntax CONNECT CATALOG, an error message will appear saying that the recovery catalog is not installed. Ignore this message. Then issue the CREATE CATALOG command. Once complete, you are now ready to use the catalog.

```
C:\>rman

Recovery Manager: Release 10.1.0.2.0 - Production

Copyright (c) 1995, 2004, Oracle. All rights reserved.

RMAN> connect CATALOG rman/rmanrep

connected to recovery catalog database
recovery catalog is not installed

RMAN> CREATE CATALOG

recovery catalog created
```

12.3.2   Registering the EASYDW database with RMAN

Before a database can be included in the recovery catalog, it must be registered. Otherwise, you may see the message "RMAN-20001 Target database not found in recovery catalog." Do not be alarmed by the message.

To register the EASYDW database in the catalog, go to the *Backup/ Recovery* section on the *Maintenance* page and click on the *Configure Recovery Catalog Settings* link; you will see the screen shown in Figure 12.15.

Here you must specify where the recovery catalog is located (i.e., either on a known database or by entering the database access information directly) and you must also provide the catalog repository account username and password. In our example, the account is RMAN, which can be

Figure 12.15   *Recovery Catalog Information*

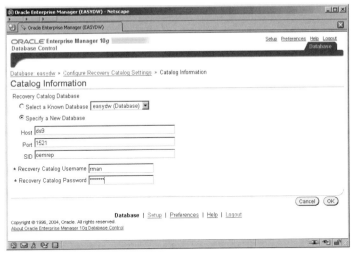

found on the OEMREP database on server DS9. On the next screen (not shown), it is simply a case of clicking the *Register Database* button to register our EASYDW database in the RMAN catalog.

As mentioned previously, the recovery catalog should always be placed in a database different from the one being backed up. Also, don't forget that the recovery catalog must also be backed up regularly because it is stored inside a database.

Oracle Enterprise Manager can be used to access the catalog to report on various backup information. The example in Figure 12.16 shows the *Manage Current Backups* screen accessed from the *Maintenance* home page, which lists the backup information stored in the catalog. A very pertinent piece of information is whether the backup is obsolete due to being replaced by a more recent backup.

From the screen in Figure 12.16, we are able to perform additional tasks to manage our backup sets by pressing the following buttons.

- *Catalog Additional Files* enables other backup pieces that have been made to disk to be registered in the catalog.

- *Crosscheck All* enables a job to be scheduled that will resynchonize the information about backups on disk with the information in the catalog.

Figure 12.16   *List of the Backup Contents of the Catalog*

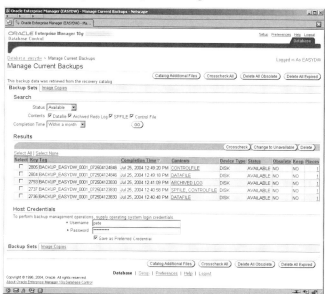

- *Delete All Obsolete* enables a job to be scheduled that will delete any obsolete backup sets—that is, both the actual backup set files on disk and the records within the catalog.

By clicking on the links in the *Contents* column, you can get more information from the catalog about the contents of what that backup set contains. For example, clicking on the datafile link for Key 2736 results in the screen shown in Figure 12.17.

Although this has been a brief introduction to the recovery catalog and how it is used by OEM, hopefully you can begin to see some of the benefits of using it, especially being able to see which backups exist. Using this information, you will see later how automatic recovery is possible, although, for a data warehouse, we may prefer to do it manually.

12.4 **Restore and Recover**

Restoring a database from a backup is a task that most DBAs probably fear. They are always concerned that the backup may fail, leaving them with no database. Unfortunately, unless you test every backup, you can never be sure that a backup file will actually work. If you can, it is a good idea to

Figure 12.17 *Contents of a Backup Set*

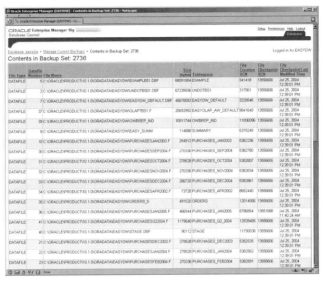

periodically restore your backup files onto a test system, so that you know that the files and your procedures are good.

Hint: If you are restoring during a serious database problem, try to restore to another location, so that, if the restore operation fails, you still have the original database.

One of the first problems you encounter when restoring a database is identifying which backup files to use. If you have been using the recovery catalog, then it is very simple, since it will automatically figure it out; otherwise, you will have to check your records to determine the correct backup file.

Don't forget that restoring a database could require a number of full and incremental backup files. This is when the RMAN recovery wizard is extremely useful, especially if you want to recover to the latest point in time. But, if we have been using the new Oracle Database 10*g* feature of rolling our incremental backups into our full backup, then only the full backup files are required.

The recovery wizard can be started by clicking on the *Perform Recovery* link in the *Backup/Recovery* section of the Maintenance home screen. The

screen shown in Figure 12.18 will appear, and you will be asked for the type
of restoration that is required.

Figure 12.18   *Perform Recovery: Restore Tablespace*

In Figure 12.18, we have the option of restoring the following by choosing from the Object Type drop-down list.

- The whole database
- Tablespaces
- Datafiles
- Archived logs
- Tables

The other parameter fields on the screen will alter, depending on the
type of object chosen to be specific to restoring that object type. For example, for the Datafiles option, the additional fields become a radio button
selection, allowing you to choose whether to:

- Restore datafiles, possibly to a new location

- Recover to a point in time (i.e., roll forward)

- Restore datafiles and recover

- Recover datafile blocks that are marked as corrupted

If *Tablespaces* is chosen, then one of the options shown in Figure 12.18 is the ability to recover to a specific point in time, such as to Monday at 11:30 A.M. Usually this type of recovery is unnecessary. If a specific problem corrupted the database, however, then you may want to restore to just prior to the job running against the database. In this example, we have chosen to restore a tablespace.

After selecting *Tablespaces* from the drop-down list, click on the radio button *Restore Tablespace,* then click the *Next* button and you will navigate to the *Tablespaces* screen. Here you will create the list of tablespaces that you want to restore.

The subsequent step illustrates the reason why you should be familiar with your backup and restoration procedure, because, after selecting which tablespaces should be restored, the *Perform Recovery* screen will appear, as shown in Figure 12.19. The wizard automatically selects the most recent backup.

Using this configuration, the wizard knows where the backup files are located and is given the information to access the recovery catalog.

The next screen in the wizard asks where the files are to be restored to, as illustrated in Figure 12.20, where a separate directory is being used that is not the directory containing the database files. Depending on the reason for the restore, you may want them to go to another location, which can be specified here. The other advantage of this screen is that it provides an opportunity to check which files are going to be restored.

Finally, you will see the *Review* screen, shown in Figure 12.21. Here you have the opportunity to perform a final check on all of the options that you have specified and to examine, and even alter, the generated RMAN script.

When you click the *Submit* button, your RMAN job is executed to perform the restore; when completed, you will see the status screen shown in Figure 12.22, where you can examine the RMAN log file

In this example we can see only a portion of the log, and the utility has automatically worked out which backup files were required. Here we used the recovery catalog to determine the required backup files, but the

Figure 12.19   *Recovery Configuration*

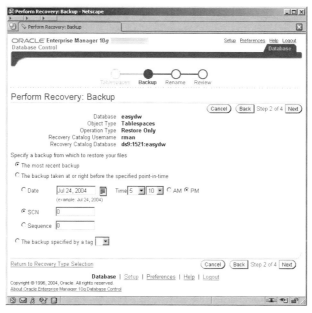

Figure 12.20   *Location of Data Files*

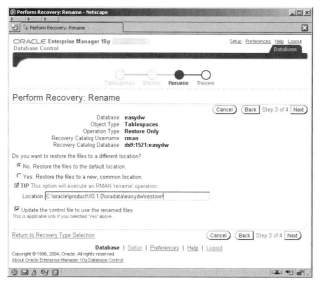

backup information is also recorded in the database control file, which can be used for some recovery operations. Although we have illustrated how to

Figure 12.21 *Perform Recovery: Restore Tablespace Review*

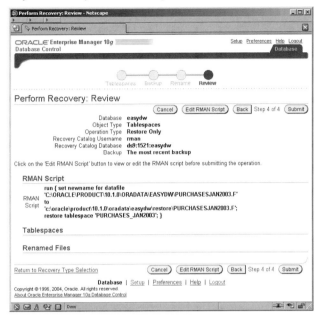

Figure 12.22 *RMAN Recovery Log*

recover a tablespace, the procedure is almost the same for a datafile or the entire database.

12.5 Summary

In this chapter, we have taken a look at some of the approaches and tasks required to protect our warehouse by backing it up. We have seen how RMAN is integral to the ease of performing this operation and how Enterprise Manager integrates with the recovery catalog to provide information on our backups.

Hopefully, this section has given you some idea of how to back up and recover an Oracle Database 10*g* data warehouse. This is such an extensive subject that it is highly recommended that you read the *Oracle Database 10g Backup and Recovery Manual* for detailed information on functionality, as well as many more ideas on how to design, create, and run backup-and-recovery operations.

Remember that deciding on, implementing, and testing the backup and recovery strategy is very important and should be performed at the outset of the warehouse project. Failure to back up the database could have disastrous results, usually when you can least afford the time.

13

Oracle Warehousing Tools

13.1 Which Tool

So far we have built and managed our database using the SQL*Plus interface or Oracle Enterprise Manager. But there are a number of tools available to the user, DBA, and designer to facilitate easy warehouse creation and access to information. We will now look at three of these tools, which are available from Oracle.

- Warehouse Builder
- Discoverer
- Reports

Oracle Warehouse Builder is a tool that helps the DBA design and manage the data warehouse, whereas Oracle Discoverer and Reports are end-user tools for querying your data warehouse.

13.2 Oracle Warehouse Builder

Oracle Warehouse Builder (OWB) is Oracle's tool for designing and deploying data warehouses, data marts, and business intelligence applications. It is part of the Oracle Developer Suite 10*g*, which includes products for application development, such as Jdeveloper, Designer, and Forms Developer. In the business intelligence (BI) area, it includes the products Oracle Discoverer which is described later in this chapter, Oracle Reports, and Oracle Warehouse Builder.

Building any type of application is not a task to be undertaken lightly; since there are so many steps to be completed when building our data warehouse and BI application, Oracle Warehouse Builder (OWB) is essential. It allows you to:

- Design and create the data flows between sources and targets
- Design, create, manage, update, and upgrade the data warehouse schema
- Manage and update the source definitions
- Import data source definitions
- Design and create the OLAP and ad hoc query environment
- Take advantage of Oracle Database 10*g* features
- Manage the deployment process
- Be another repository of the metadata for the warehouse structure, processes, and mappings (i.e., OWB can act as a design tool)
- Generate documentation from the metadata

Within OWB there is a **repository** stored in an Oracle database and this is where OWB keeps all of its metadata. The *OWB Client* is the main interface and is used to design and create the data warehouse and application.

A code generator is provided that creates the scripts from your design that are applied to the data. The OWB Browser Assistant can be used to view the design and reports from your browser, provided Oracle Application Server 10*g* has been installed.

You may be wondering why you should use a tool such as Oracle Warehouse Builder to design and create your data warehouse and associated application. Why not design it by hand? Yes, you could do that, but some of the benefits of using Warehouse Builder include:

- System design time is reduced, due to the GUI
- The design is held in one place, so everyone is guaranteed that he or she is not working with an out-of-date model
- The code generated by OWB is free from errors and works the first time
- The design can easily be changed or an ETL process modified and then a new module is generated for that change

Let us now look at how we would use OWB to design our data warehouse or data mart.

13.2.1 Setting up Warehouse Builder

Before your data warehouse can be designed using Warehouse Builder, a small amount of setup is required to create the repository that Warehouse Builder uses when designing your warehouse. When launching the OWB Repository Assistant, Figure 13.1 appears, which shows us the steps that have to be completed to set up our Warehouse Builder repository. Although there are quite a few steps, this entire process does not take very long, so you will soon be up and running Warehouse Builder.

Figure 13.1 *Warehouse Builder—Setup Steps*

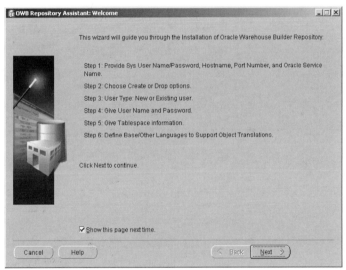

You can choose into which database the OWB repository will reside, and then you must connect using a user name that has the SYSDBA privilege. Then a user name and password must be supplied for the schema that will own the OWB repository. You must also specify which tablespace to use for repository data and also which language you would like to use. Click on *Finish*, and your repository is created. Now Oracle Warehouse Builder is ready to use.

13.2.2   Oracle Warehouse Builder Client

Once the Oracle Warehouse Builder repository has been built, it is time to start using this tool to design our data warehouse, where we can:

- Define the logical view of our warehouse schema

- Define data sources and targets

- Describe ETL processes, where we extract, transform and load

- Generate the SQL required to create the data warehouse and ETL processes

In OWB, your data warehouse is defined inside a *Project,* and the following five steps must be completed to build and implement a design:

1.   Create a project.

2.   Define the data sources and targets.

3.   Specify how data moves and its transformations.

4.   Validate and generate the design.

5.   Deploy and run the design.

The OWB client is the primary tool for building our design, and Figure 13.2 shows the console when it is first started.

Creating the project is very straightforward, as this involves simply starting the OWB client, selecting *Project* from the strip menu at the top, and then selecting *Create Project*. Give the project a name (our project is called EASYDW), supply an optional description and version number, and the project is created.

13.2.3   Data Sources and Targets

The next step is to define where the data for our warehouse will originate. Referring to the OWB Console in Figure 13.2, this could be a database or a file, and a module must now be created that tells us all about that source.

Figure 13.2   *OWB Client Console*

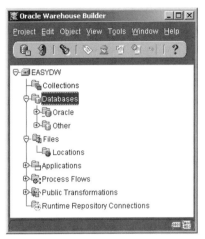

Oracle Database Source

Suppose that one of the sources for our Oracle database comes from our Order entry system, which is in an Oracle database. This source would be defined by right-clicking on *Oracle* under *Databases* and selecting *Create Oracle Module*. Figure 13.3 appears, where the module is named and we specify that it is a data source.

Figure 13.3   *Warehouse Builder—Creating a Module*

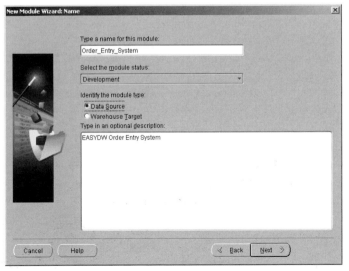

Hint: Spaces in the module name are not allowed if you are defining a physical object.

Since we specified that our data source is an Oracle Database, Figure 13.4 appears, where we must specify how to connect to this database. At this time a database link can be created, if one does not already exist, by clicking on the *New DB Link* button. At this time the link will be tested, so make sure that the database is accessible.

Figure 13.4   *Warehouse Builder—Creating an Oracle Database Source*

Next, we must specify where this data will be deployed; we have chosen the EASY_DATAW location. By clicking on the *Finish* button the source and target are now created.

Oracle Database Target

We also have to define the target for our design, which is where the design will be deployed. To achieve this the same process is used as for defining our sources. Therefore, this time in Figure 13.3, we would specify THE_EASYDW_DW, which is the name we want to give to our design, and click the radio button for Warehouse Target.

File Data Source

If there are any file data sources that will be input to our data warehouse, these can also be defined at this stage. Suppose that customers can also place orders via PDA devices. These orders are captured from the device and are currently stored in a file for subsequent processing into the system. This data source can be defined by right-clicking on *Files* in Figure 13.5 and then selecting *Create Flat File Module*. The details of this flat file are entered into the wizard, and the data source, PDA_SALES, has now been defined.

Figure 13.5   *Warehouse Builder—Defined Data Sources and Targets*

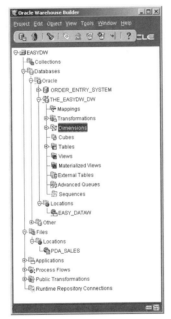

This process is repeated for every data source in our system, and OWB provides for several standard data sources, including, flat files, SAP, Oracle database, or other databases such as DB2.

After doing all of this work, it is extremely important to save it, because OWB does not automatically save your work. Therefore, whenever you are satisfied with the state of the objects, you must *Commit* the changes by either clicking on the commit icon or selecting *Commit* from the *Project* option on the strip menu at the top.

13.2.4 Defining the Tables in Our Data Warehouse

In the previous section, we defined the sources for our data and our data warehouse. Now is the time to define the tables that we require inside our data warehouse. This can be achieved by either defining the tables manually or importing them from another database.

Importing the table definitions illustrates how OWB can save on development time, because it can be quite time consuming and error prone defining the tables by hand. When you are defining these tables, which are going to be the sources for your data, its very important that they are defined exactly as they exist in your production system; otherwise, costly delays will incur when trying to resolve the data inconsistencies. If you have to define them by hand, then it's easy to make mistakes, which can subsequently delay implementation of your data warehouse.

The table definitions are imported by right-clicking on *Database* and selecting *Import*. The *Import Metadata Wizard* will appear for you to answer the questions as to what is to be imported—tables, sequences, and so on. Upon completion, Figure 13.6 appears, where we can see the tables that have been imported from another database.

Figure 13.6   *Warehouse Builder—Import a Table*

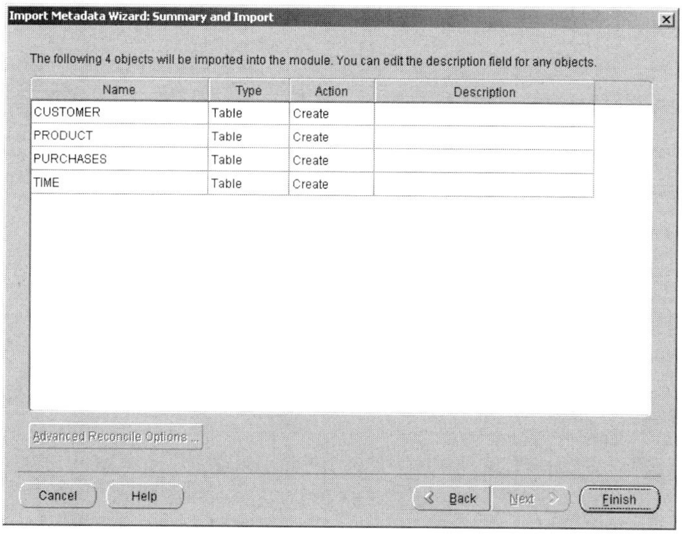

Some of the tables may have to be defined manually, and this can be achieved by double-clicking on THE_EASYDW_DW database source shown in Figure 13.5, then right-clicking on *Tables,* and then selecting *Create Table.* This will start the new table wizard; Figure 13.7 illustrates how the columns are specified. Here we have defined a new table called COUNTRY.

Figure 13.7   *Warehouse Builder—Manually Define a Table*

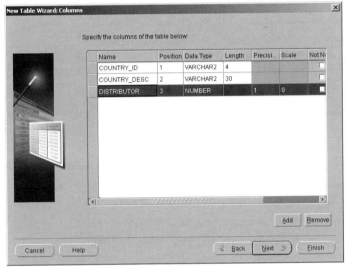

While using this wizard don't forget that you can also specify constraints, such as primary-key, foreign-key, and check constraints. When the definition is complete, click on the *Finish* button to complete the definition of our table.

13.2.5   Creating Dimensions

Typically, a data warehouse consists of tables, which can be fact and dimension tables; in the previous section, we saw how to physically create tables. At this stage in the development of our data warehouse, we probably only have a model, described in terms of facts and dimensions. OWB allows us to define these logical objects and then, when it is time to generate our design, OWB will physically create the tables to represent these facts and dimension.

A dimension is created in OWB by using the dimension wizard, which is selected by right-clicking on the *Dimension* object, shown in Figure 13.5, and selecting *Create Dimension.*

The process is very similar to the one we saw in Chapter 8 for creating a dimension. That is, you must name the dimension, define each level and its attributes, and then describe the hierarchy. In Figure 13.8, we see one of the dimension wizard screens where we are defining the hierarchy for our customer dimension.

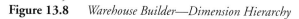

Figure 13.8   *Warehouse Builder—Dimension Hierarchy*

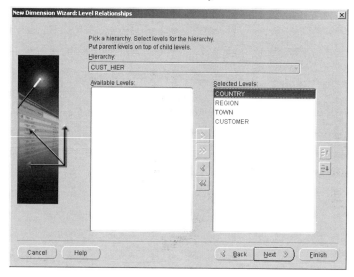

13.2.6 Creating a Cube

Once the dimensions have been created, the next step in our design process is to define one or more fact tables, which are known as cubes. In OWB a cube is a logical object in that only when the physical design is generated, does our cube become a physical table. It is created by right-clicking on *Cube* in Figure 13.5 and selecting *Create Cube*; the *New Cube Wizard* appears. One of the screens is shown in Figure 13.9, which is where the foreign keys for our cube are defined. In this example, OWB automatically offers a foreign key to each dimension that was previously defined.

The wizard also allows you to add measures and by clicking on the *Finish* button our cube is created.

At any time while the data warehouse is being defined, the various parts of the design can be validated by selecting the *Validate* option, described in section 13.2.8. Any problems, can be correctly immediately before proceeding to defining the next part of the design.

Figure 13.9 *Warehouse Builder—Cube Creation*

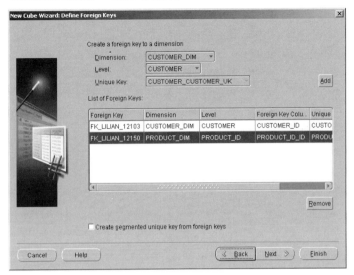

Hint: Validate your design and individual components frequently.

There are a number of other objects that can be defined but will not be described in this chapter. They include materialized views, external tables, sequences, and views.

13.2.7 Defining Source to Target Mappings

In Chapter 5, we saw that when data is being moved from one source to another, it often needs to undergo some transformations. In OWB we can define these transformations using functions, procedures, and packages.

The real power of Oracle Warehouse Builder starts to become apparent when we see how it can be used to define how data is moved from our sources, such as from our OLTP system into our data warehouse. In Chapter 5, we discussed the various techniques that we can use to load and perform transformations. Now, inside Oracle Warehouse Builder, by using its GUI interface, we can graphically represent these processes by defining a **mapping**. When the design is finally generated, OWB even creates the procedures required to transform and load the data, using the principles described in Chapter 5. Now we will look at just a few of the many different types of mappings that are possible.

Mapping a Source to a Target

A mapping is defined from the OWB client by right-clicking on *Mappings*, in Figure 13.5; selecting *Creating Mappings* gives the mapping a name and then the Mapping Editor appears, as shown in Figure 13.10. The first mapping that we are going to define is extracting information from our ORDER_ENTRY_SYSTEM and moving it into our data warehouse. OWB can also take information from flat files or from SAP, but we won't be showing here how that is done.

Figure 13.10   *Mapping Editor*

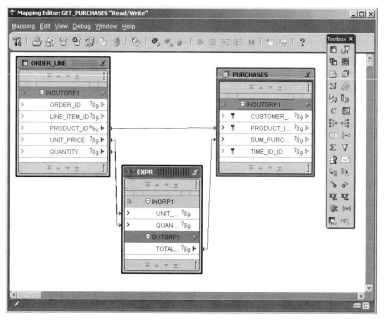

When the blank Mapping Editor appears, click on the *Mapping Table* icon (which is top left in the floating toolbar) and drag it onto the Editor. It now asks you where your table is to come from, and we are going to select the ORDER_LINE table from our source ORDER_ENTRY_SYSTEM, which we defined earlier. Then click on the *Mapping Cube* icon and select PURCHASES. Now in our Editor we have two tables: ORDER_LINE and PURCHASES.

The next step is to specify which items are to be moved from each table. First, we are going to move the item PRODUCT_ID from the ORDER_LINE table to the PURCHASES table. This is achieved by dragging a line from PRODUCT_ID in ORDER_LINE to PRODUCT_ID in

PURCHASES. In Figure 13.10, we can see the line that OWB has drawn between the two items.

Computing a Value

The next column to be defined in PURCHASES is the value of the order, and this can only be obtained by computing its value from two columns in the ORDER_ITEM table. To compute this value an intermediate expression box must be created, as illustrated in Figure 13.10.

Click on the *Expression* icon and drag that onto the Mapping Editor. An empty box appears with empty input and output groups. Take the two columns from ORDER_LINE, unit_price and quantity, and drag them over to the input group box. Now we have to use the right mouse button to add a new attribute in our output group, which we will call Total_Price. Do this by choosing *Edit* from the right mouse menu, and under the *Output Attribute* tab add the new attribute, called Total Price.

Then you select that item's properties and click on the expression box and the expression builder will appear, where you can specify how the attribute is to be computed, which in our case is to multiply the two numbers together. Then drag a line from TOTAL_PRICE to the column SUM_PURCHASES in PURCHASES to complete the mapping operation.

Hint: It's probably worth validating the design periodically so that you don't create mappings and transformations that are invalid.

Joining Tables to Obtain Data

Another common task that our warehouse designer has to perform is joining data from two or more tables to extract information that is used as input to another table. In Figure 13.11, we see a join that we have created between ORDER and ORDER_LINE to enable us to store one record in our data warehouse for the total value of the order. Note that the expression that we created in Figure 13.10 has now been used as input to the join.

Hint: When you have finished working on a part of the design, such as the expression to compute the value of the sales, you can minimize the box to give you more working space.

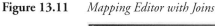

Figure 13.11   *Mapping Editor with Joins*

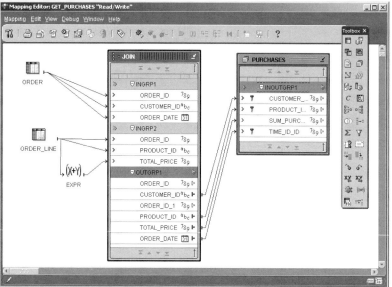

Key Lookup

Previously in this book we have described surrogate keys, where the natural keys used in the sources for your data warehouse are transformed into a key used by the data warehouse. In OWB we can define exactly how that transformation should occur by using the key lookup feature.

In Chapter 5, we described the process of converting the product code used in out OLTP system to a surrogate key in the data warehouse. In Figure 13.12, this has been implemented in OWB by showing that the column PRODUCT_ID from the join between ORDER and ORDER_LINE is input to the key lookup process. Although not visible, a mapping has been defined that states that PRODUCT_ID is to be matched to PRODUCT_CD. The resulting output is the column PRODUCT_ID, which is sent to the PURCHASES table.

Filtering Data

When data is being extracted from sources such as our OLTP system, there may be times when we do not want all of that data to be sent across to our data warehouse. In OWB, this is not a problem, because it allows us to filter the incoming data in a variety of ways.

Figure 13.12   *Product Key Lookup*

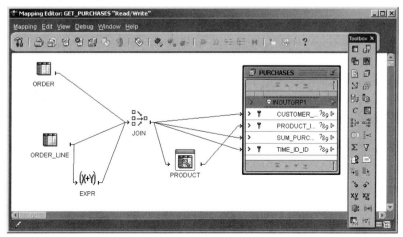

In Figure 13.13, we are filtering the items from the ORDER_LINE table according to criteria that we have specified. For example, we could say that we are only interested in certain products. Also see in our example how, after we have filtered the data, we are then applying the expression we defined in Figure 13.10 to the data that has passed through the filter.

Figure 13.13   *Filtering Source Data*

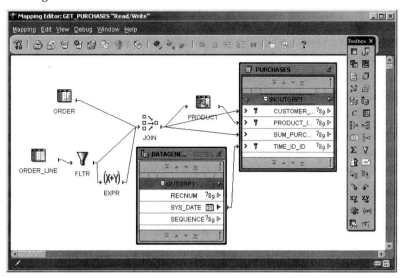

Using Data Generators

There may be times when, rather than extracting data from a source, the data must be automatically generated. OWB has this capability, and it can automatically create:

- Record number
- Sequence number
- System date

In Figure 13.13, we can see the system date being used to set the date for our order. This was achieved by dragging the *Data Generator* icon onto the Mapping Editor, and then selecting the item required and attaching it to PURCHASES.

Over these few pages, we have barely touched the surface on the types of transformations and mappings that are possible with Oracle Warehouse Builder. All of the icons shown in the toolbox in Figure 13.13 can be used to define your warehouse. Also, in these examples we have kept them simple, but in a real warehouse, they would be connected; we did start to show this in Figures 13.12 and 13.13 where the expression was being used as input to another stage in the loading process.

13.2.8   Validating the Design

Once the design is complete, or while it is being developed, it must be validated before Oracle Warehouse Builder can create all the components needed to build, load, and manage our data warehouse. You can validate each component individually, or the entire project, but it's probably easier to resolve problems if you validate each component as it is defined.

To validate any component, select *Object* from the strip menu at the top and then select *Validate,* or it can be selected by clicking on the right mouse button. In Figure 13.14, we can see that there are several errors with our design. We can't use SYS_DATE for the time in the purchases column and, more importantly, OWB has detected that the data types of the CUSTOMER_ID column are incompatible between the ORDERS system and the data warehouse. Therefore, we need to fix these problems before we can continue.

Figure 13.14 *Validating the Design*

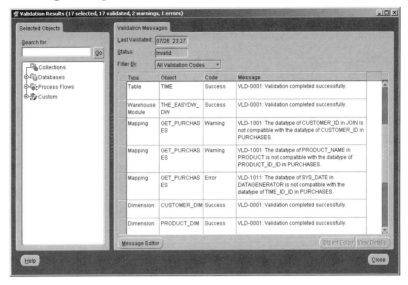

This illustrates the benefits of using a tool such as OWB, because with a complex design it is very easy to miss a problem such as the one in Figure 13.14 until very late in the day. We have known of systems where data type inconsistencies were only detected the first day someone tried to transfer data from the source system.

13.2.9 Generating the Design

Once the design has been validated, Oracle Warehouse Builder can now generate the design. From the OWB client, shown in Figure 13.5, we can generate each component individually or by selecting *Generate*. The generation process will run and OWB will create scripts that perform the following tasks:

- SQL for creating the database

- PL/SQL for executing within the database

- Procedures for loading the data

- SQL*Loader files for working with our flat files

In Figure 13.15, we can see the various components that OWB will generate. There are the schema objects, such as our PRODUCT table. By clicking anywhere on the PRODUCT line, everything that OWB created for the PRODUCT table is displayed in the lower part of the screen.

Figure 13.15   *Generating the Design*

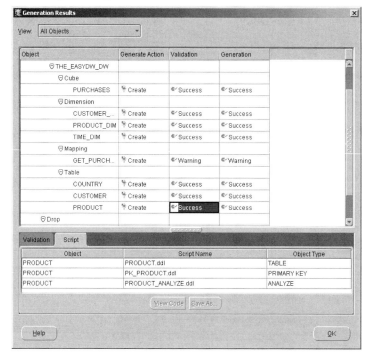

By clicking on the *Validation* tab, the validation messages are shown, and clicking on the *Script* tab lists all the scripts created for this object. To view the script, click on the script name and then click on *View Code*.

If we click on the *Mappings* tab, we would see that OWB has created a package for us to load the data, which we defined previously. By clicking on the *View Code* button, we can see part of this long procedure generated by OWB (Figure 13.16). Just look at where the slider bar is to see how much code OWB has created for us. The section of code we have shown here is part of the INSERT statement, but prior to this there are variable definitions and lots of other things that we would have had to write ourselves.

In this example, OWB has chosen to use a SQL INSERT statement, but since OWB has been designed to take advantage of features in the database,

Figure 13.16 *Code Generated by Oracle Warehouse Builder*

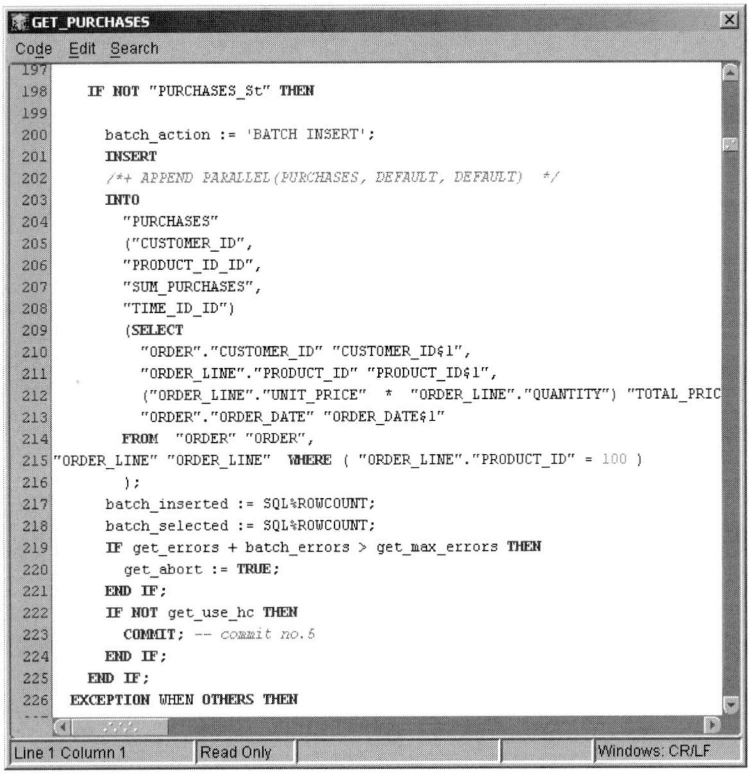

```
 GET_PURCHASES                                                          X

 Code  Edit  Search
 197
 198        IF NOT "PURCHASES_St" THEN
 199
 200           batch_action := 'BATCH INSERT';
 201           INSERT
 202           /*+ APPEND PARALLEL(PURCHASES, DEFAULT, DEFAULT)  */
 203           INTO
 204             "PURCHASES"
 205             ("CUSTOMER_ID",
 206             "PRODUCT_ID_ID",
 207             "SUM_PURCHASES",
 208             "TIME_ID_ID")
 209             (SELECT
 210               "ORDER"."CUSTOMER_ID" "CUSTOMER_ID$1",
 211               "ORDER_LINE"."PRODUCT_ID" "PRODUCT_ID$1",
 212               ("ORDER_LINE"."UNIT_PRICE" * "ORDER_LINE"."QUANTITY") "TOTAL_PRIC
 213               "ORDER"."ORDER_DATE" "ORDER_DATE$1"
 214           FROM  "ORDER" "ORDER",
 215 "ORDER_LINE" "ORDER_LINE"  WHERE ( "ORDER_LINE"."PRODUCT_ID" = 100 )
 216             );
 217           batch_inserted := SQL%ROWCOUNT;
 218           batch_selected := SQL%ROWCOUNT;
 219           IF get_errors + batch_errors > get_max_errors THEN
 220             get_abort := TRUE;
 221           END IF;
 222           IF NOT get_use_hc THEN
 223             COMMIT; -- commit no.6
 224           END IF;
 225         END IF;
 226       EXCEPTION WHEN OTHERS THEN

 Line 1 Column 1        Read Only                              Windows: CR/LF
```

it can therefore use statements such as MERGE, which we saw earlier in the code that it generates.

Vast amounts of time can be saved using OWB, because you no longer have to write the code needed to implement and load data into your warehouse. The code that OWB generates is optimized for the Oracle database and it works immediately. When was the last time you wrote a complex piece of code that worked the first time?

13.2.10 **Deploying the Design**

Now the time has come to implement our design, but before this can be completed, you must ensure that the runtime repository has been created on the system where your design will be deployed, because this is where all the information about your deployed system is stored. This task should have been completed when OWB was installed, but it can be performed at any time by running the OWB Runtime Assistant.

Launch the *Deployment Manager* from the OWB client by selecting *File* from the strip menu at the top and Figure 13.17 appears. Here we can see all the objects for our system, such as the PRODUCT table and the CUSTOMER_DIM dimension. To deploy an object, click in the *Deploy Action* box to specify the action required, which, in Figure 13.17, is create.

Figure 13.17   *Deployment Manager*

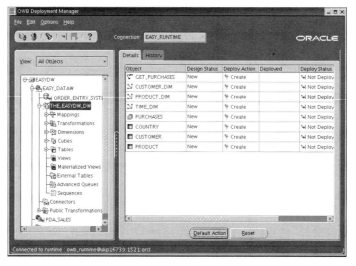

Once all appropriate actions have been set for the objects, to actually deploy them, click on *File* in the strip menu at the top and then select *Generate/Deploy*. A status bar will appear showing how deployment is progressing.

The next screen to appear is that shown in Figure 13.18, which is the predeployment report, where we can see the state of every object. Referring to TIME, it has completed validation, and by clicking on the *Script* tab, we can see all the scripts that will be generated.

Select the script, and then click on the *View Code* button to view the contents of any of those scripts. When you are satisfied with what is to be built, click on the *Deploy* button and your system will be generated.

The design has now been generated, and in Figure 13.19, which is a screen from Enterprise Manager, we can see the all the objects created by the deploy operation in our new schema, EASY_OWB.

Figure 13.18   *Deployment Manager—Predeployment Report*

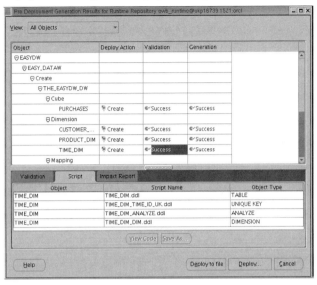

Figure 13.19   *Enterprise Manager Shows OWB Objects Deployed*

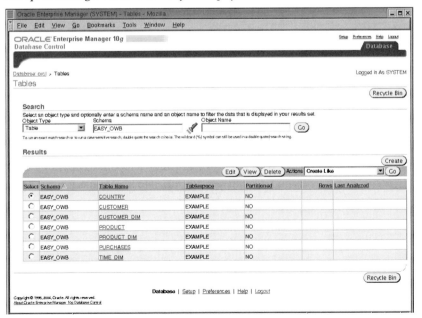

Returning to the Deployment Manager, we see that in Figure 13.20 that the status of all of our objects is displayed and that everything was successful except for the GET_PURCHASES mapping. OWB did tell us about this problem earlier, but we decided to deploy regardless, because it was not affecting the deployment of any other objects.

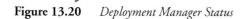

Figure 13.20   *Deployment Manager Status*

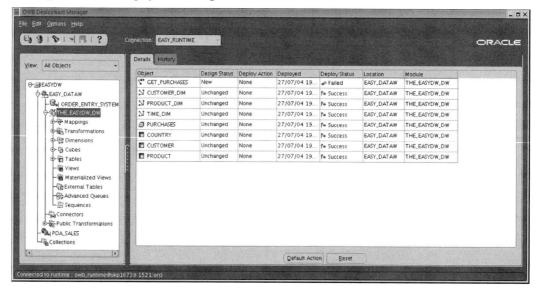

With virtually all of the system deployed, OWB allows us to go back to the OWB client, fix the problem with the GET_PURCHASES mapping, and then repeat the deploy process; however, this time it would only be performed on this object.

Configuring the Physical Design

Although we have generated a logical design, it is most likely that it does not include all of the physical aspects of our design, such as whether a table is partitioned and which indexes are needed. These physical components can be configured in OWB by selecting the module to be configured, right-clicking on the mouse, and selecting *Configure*. Figure 13.21 is displayed, which lists all of the properties that you can configure. In this example, for our COUNTRY table, we can see that an index has been defined, and the table is going to be stored in tablespace USERS.

Figure 13.21   *Configuring the Physical Design*

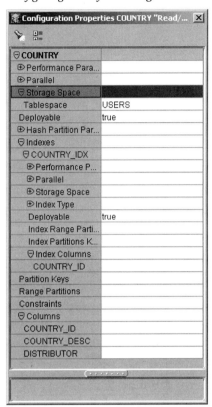

When defining indexes, OWB has the ability to automatically recommend bitmapped indexes; clicking on the Generate button shows these recommendations.

Normally, the physical design for the objects would be done prior to deployment. However, in our example we have created the EASYDW warehouse and then returned to OWB, defined more physical design attributes, and then redeployed.

Hopefully, you now have an appreciation of what OWB can do. This is a very powerful product and, over these few pages, we have only been able to highlight some of its features. What we have not covered here is how OWB can be managed using a browser and integrated into Oracle Portal.

There are many benefits from using tools such as Oracle Warehouse Builder. It provides a visual representation of your warehouse and, by using the various wizards that are available, it is easy to complete the tasks needed for building the warehouse. In addition when changes to the environment occur, you can visually see the impact of them and OWB can easily incorporate them into the environment. The Deployment Manager enables you to clearly see the state of all modules in the system and view the code for those modules.

Now that you have deployed the physical design to the database, you may want to enable this for a query tool. OWB has the capability of transferring the design metadata into a Discoverer environment, which is described in the next section. By doing this you can save yourself time and effort in creating the reporting solution on top of your logical design. A second benefit is the concentration of metadata in a single place, allowing you to reduce the maintenance efforts for your integrated solution.

Oracle Warehouse Builder provides a comprehensive environment for building and managing your data warehouse that could significantly reduce your development time and costs when its full potential is exploited.

13.3 Oracle Discoverer

Oracle Discoverer is an extremely popular tool for querying data warehouses and generating reports, because it is very easy and intuitive to use and has been designed for use by end users who are focused on the business aspects and not necessarily familiar with databases. Therefore, in order for these business users to be able to use Discoverer easily, some setup is required from the DBA group. But once this has been done, these end users should really like using this tool. There are four parts to Oracle Discoverer:

- Administrator
- Desktop
- Plus
- Viewer

Discoverer *Administrator* is the version that is used by the power user or analyst of the data warehouse to set up the environment for the general Discoverer users. The business end user will either use the *Desktop* or *Plus* version, because it has been designed especially for people who are not familiar with writing computer programs, as well as for anyone who is not familiar with SQL and prefers to deal with data using familiar business entities. For business users and others who may be concerned that they could change the data within the data warehouse, fear not, because Discoverer Viewer allows the user to only view predefined reports. The attraction of using Discoverer Viewer is that all users require to access the data is their PC and a browser.

Oracle Discoverer is also integrated with Oracle Portal, which we will learn more about later. From within Oracle Portal it is possible to set up Web pages that have direct access to Discoverer reports on our data, thus providing a very powerful and dynamic mechanism for displaying information.

Oracle Discoverer is part of Oracle Application Server and it can be run in one of two ways. When *Oracle Developer Suite* is installed, this provides access to Discoverer Administrator and Discoverer Desktop, which are the original, nonbrowser-based versions of Discoverer. Currently, Discoverer can only be configured using the Discoverer Administrator therefore, Oracle Developer Suite will have to be installed.

Discoverer requires some configuration, which will be described shortly, before it can be used by general users. Once this task is complete, it can then be queried using Discoverer Desktop; however, you may prefer to use one of the browser-based tools, Discoverer Viewer or Plus, due to the additional capabilities these offer because they are tightly integrated into Oracle Application Server. Some additional setup and configuration is required when Discoverer Viewer and Plus are used, but it is worth all the extra effort.

Oracle Discoverer can also be used to access data held in non-Oracle databases, using Oracle Heterogeneous Services. A single business area can be created that references data from these different data sources. Then, Discoverer functionality, such as report scheduling, query prediction, and use of analytical functions, can be used against this non-Oracle data.

13.3.1   Why Discoverer?

Before we learn how to set up Discoverer, let's first look at the types of reports that it can produce. Imagine logging on to the corporate Web site and having available to you reports containing the latest data from Discoverer, along with other company information. Figure 13.22 illustrates its capabilities with Oracle Portal, where we can see a list of all of the reports available to us in its only region on the screen. In another region, one of the reports is displaying its results in a pie chart. Since each user of the Portal can have his or her own customized view, it can greatly improve productivity and business efficiency.

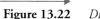

Figure 13.22   *Discoverer and Oracle Portal*

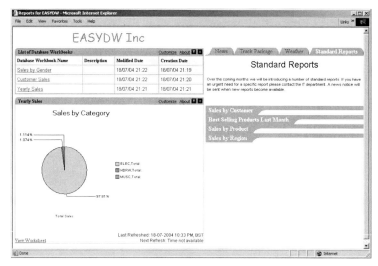

Query Using Discoverer Viewer

Many organizations run Discoverer independently, and Discoverer Viewer provides a user with the ability to access predefined reports and have the capability to modify those reports in a limited way. The advantage of this approach is that the user only needs a PC and a browser to access the data in the warehouse and the DBA can rest assured that users cannot change the data.

You can start Discoverer viewer from your browser using a URL such as:

```
http://easydw.com:7777/discoverer/viewer
```

A connection is made to this database, and a list of the available workbooks that we can attach to is presented. We select our workbook, EASYDW and the query contained within is immediately executed. In Figure 13.23, we can monitor the progress of our executing query, and when it has completed our report is displayed, as shown in Figure 13.24.

Since we defined this report as both a table and a graph, both versions are displayed in Figure 13.24. Note that at any time we can hide the graph or table by clicking on the *Data* or *Chart* option. The report shown here is the default generated by Discoverer, and I am sure you will agree that it is a very nice format, which is presented well and is easy to understand.

Figure 13.23 *Discoverer Viewer—Executing Our Query*

Inside a workbook there can be many reports. In Figure 13.24, we can see a list of those reports in the top left. Any of these reports can be run by simply clicking on the report name.

Figure 13.24 *Discoverer Viewer—Category Sales by Country*

One of the advantages of using Discoverer Viewer is that is the user is not able to change the data in the warehouse or generate new reports. However, there are limited customizations that can be done to this report, such as changing the sort order or table layout, or, by clicking on the *Presentation Options* items, as illustrated in Figure 13.25, changing how our report looks.

Figure 13.25　*Discoverer Viewer—Presentations Options*

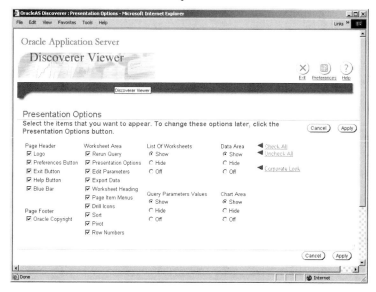

Dynamic Reports with Graphs

One of the features that makes Discoverer nice to use is the ability to group together a number of reports that can be easily run and customized to your own requirements. In the example shown here, we have a workbook called EASYDW and, referring to Figure 13.24, at the top left of the screen we can see a tab, with two entries on it, for each of the reports that are available:

- Yearly Sales
- Customer Sales

In Figure 13.24, we see both a table and a graph generated from data in our warehouse. When this report is run, the user is prompted to specify his or her criteria for which years the sales are to be displayed.

Drilling on the Data

When a report is produced, someone reading it may say that this is very interesting, but I need to know more about how this data is derived. For example, suppose the user is viewing the report shown in Figure 13.24 and sees that we sold many items in the United States, but how does that break down by state and is it more than we sold in the United Kingdom?

Figure 13.26   *Discoverer Viewer—Drill Down*

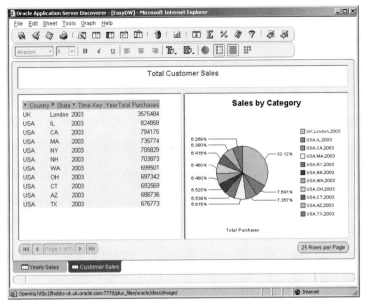

By clicking on *Country*, a drill-down list is displayed and State was selected; Figure 13.26 shows us the report with the data by state. Now we can see that we sold across a number of states, rather than in just one state, and U.K. sales are equivalent to selling in over four U.S. states.

Now that we have caught a glimpse of the types of reports, Discoverer can produce, we must return to setting up Discoverer, because, before you can use it, that setup we mentioned earlier must be performed.

13.3.2   Setting up the Environment

When a database is created, usually everything is named using terminology that is familiar to a computer-literate person, but for a typical end user it may look like a foreign language. Oracle Discoverer overcomes this problem by creating what is known as the *End-User Layer*. Here, all those technical computer terms are turned into a user-friendly environment so that it is easy for anyone to understand and access the information in the database. Therefore, this task has to be completed before anyone can access the database. This may seem like a lot of work, but, once completed, it will make it very easy for users to access all the information, thus saving countless phone calls to the IT department.

A major advantage of this approach is that it enables an organization to control exactly which data in the warehouse users can see how they see it, and, most importantly, they won't need to understand how to join data in order to query the data warehouse. To begin using Discoverer, first connect to your Oracle database.

Hint: You may prefer to create a special user for Discoverer and connect to your database using that user to ensure that the metadata is loaded under that user name.

End-User Layer

The first time the Discoverer Administrator is started, you will be asked to create an end-user layer (EUL), which consists of all the metadata that is needed by Discoverer; therefore, this task will be performed only once. Figure 13.27 shows the screen where you can manage the end-user layer, including creating a new one or deleting an existing one.

Figure 13.27   *Discoverer Administrator—Create an EUL*

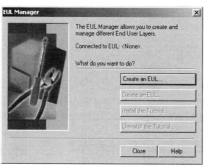

The wizard will then ask who will own the EUL. In our example, it would be EASYDW. Now click on the *Finish* button and the end-user layer is created. This process may take a few minutes, depending on the complexity of the schema that it has to analyze.

Business Area

Once the definition of the end-user layer is complete, a *Business Area* is named, where all of the information needed to query the warehouse must be defined. The purpose of the business area is to group information into business-oriented categories, such as Sales or Finance, which are familiar to end users. Business areas are the unit of access control and a user can be assigned to one or more business areas. Users will then have access to all of the objects within the assigned business area.

Within this business area, you will specify exactly which data a user may access, how that data may be joined, and describe data aggregations and new data items based on calculations on existing data items. Creating the business area will take some time, but it will reap significant benefits later.

When creating the business area, we must first specify the schemas from where data is to be made available to the end user, as illustrated in Figure 13.28. We can select any number of users from the list and also request that it only selects items from the list that match the pattern specified in the box. In our example, we have selected only the user, or schema EASYDW.

Figure 13.28   *Discoverer Administrator—Select the Schema*

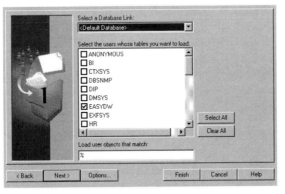

Once we know the schema from which the data will be available, we can then explicitly state from which tables or views we can retrieve data, as shown in Figure 13.29. Using our Easy Shopping Inc. example, we have given the users access to all of the five tables in this data warehouse.

Figure 13.29   *Discoverer Administrator—Select the Tables and Views*

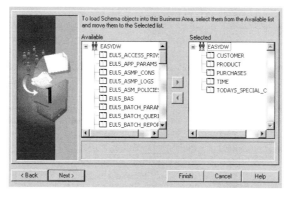

One extremely useful feature in Discoverer is the ability of the wizard to automatically create joins based on primary and foreign keys and create hierarchies from the data, as illustrated in Figure 13.30. By allowing the wizard to perform these tasks, there will be less setup work for you to do,

Figure 13.30   *Discoverer Administrator—Automatic Joins*

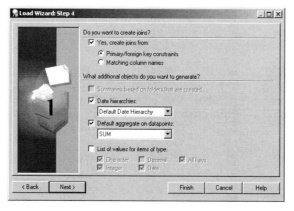

and by default these options are already selected. The advantage to the end users is that when they are constructing queries they won't need to know how to join the data, because Discoverer will know this from what was done at this stage. Therefore, end users require minimal computer design knowledge in order to construct reports in the database.

There is one final screen before the first stage in creating the business area is complete. In Figure 13.31, we must name the EUL and optionally

Figure 13.31   *Administrator—Naming the Business Area*

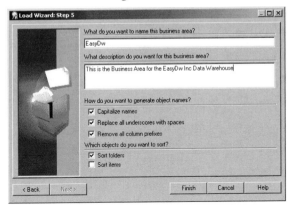

add a description to describe what is being held. Discoverer will also generate names for all of the objects, and in Figure 13.31 you can see the options available, such as capitalize or replace underscores with spaces.

Clicking on the *Finish* button, completes the first stage in creating our business area. A task list will appear, as shown in Figure 13.32, to help remind us of the steps to follow.

Figure 13.32   *Discoverer Administrator—Task List*

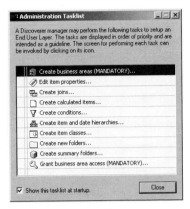

In Figure 13.33, we can see that part of the basic EUL screen in Discoverer from where everything can be managed. Discoverer has already identified that the table PURCHASES can be joined to the customer, product, and time table and that some computation may be applied to the column purchase price.

Figure 13.33　*Discoverer Administrator—Setting up the Business Area*

With the basic EUL is place, this is where the real work begins, since we can now set up the rest of the business area; although we have shown only the creation of one business area, you could create any number of business areas in your environment, each with its own unique set of data requirements.

Restricting the Visible Columns

By default, when access is given to a table, all the columns in that table are accessible. What is nice about Discoverer is that users can only access data via the business area. If the table and column are not given visibility by Discoverer, then the user will never even know that this data existed.

In Figure 13.33, we can see all the tables from the database that we have access to. Note that our table TODAYS_SPECIAL_OFFERS is now called *Todays Special Offer*, as a result of the naming change requested earlier. By default, the end user will have access to every column in those tables. If you click on the table name to expand it, all the columns in that table will appear. To remove any of those columns, simply click on the item using the right mouse button, and a drop-down list will appear. One of the items in that list is *Delete Item*. Simply select that option, and the item will be removed from the business area but not from the database.

Folders

Before moving on, there is some terminology that you should familiarize yourself with. In Discoverer, a table or view is known as a *folder*, and a column from the table is called an *item*. A folder can be one of two types:

- Simple, where it is based on a single database table or view

- Complex, where it can contain items from other folders and can be nested

An *item* corresponds to a column in a relational database. A simple item is based on a single column in the database, but an item can also be calculated or derived based on a formula using other items, functions, or operators.

Changing Item Details

The attributes of any of the items that you have selected may be modified by selecting that item, clicking on the right mouse button, and then selecting *Properties*. The window illustrated in Figure 13.34 will appear, and you can then modify whichever properties you like. In this example, we have changed the item's name from Supplier to Main Supplier, which means that our users can be presented with friendly meaningful names, rather than computer format names.

Figure 13.34   *Discoverer Administrator—Change the Item Details*

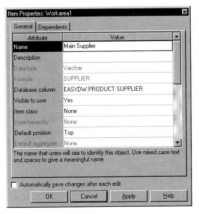

When the business area is first created, if the database has primary and foreign keys defined, then Discoverer will automatically create joins between those constraints. However, you can specify your own joins by selecting *Insert* from the strip menu and then *Joins*.

Creating New Items

Another feature that many DBA's may require is the ability to create new columns or items in the database by calculating their results from other columns.

A *calculation* creates a new item in the end-user layer. It will not add underlying columns to database tables and is used to create a new item where there is no underlying database column that contains the data required. Calculations can be simple, such as *weight * 4.54* or they can be complex mathematical or statistical expressions. For example, in Figure 13.35, a new column called Total Cost is created in the PURCHASES table by adding together the columns purchase price and shipping charges. You can create as many of these types of calculations as you require, and they will appear as an item for that table.

Figure 13.35   *Discoverer Administrator—Creating a Calculated Item*

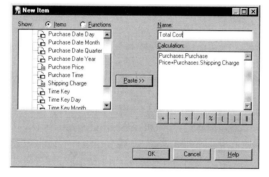

Creating Joins

When the EUL was first created, Discoverer tried to identify which joins to create from the primary- and foreign-key relationships that had already been defined. However, there may be times when additional joins are required and these can easily be created using the join wizard.

A *join* is created by clicking on *Create Joins* in the Discoverer Administrative Task List, which is shown in Figure 13.32, or from the Administration Work Area, shown in Figure 13.34, by clicking on *Insert* and then *Joins*; the wizard will then appear, as illustrated in Figure 13.36.

By using the wizard, give the join a name and then, from the drop-down list, select the table and columns to join on and the type of join. In our example in Figure 13.36, we have specified a join between the TODAYS SPECIAL OFFERS table and the PRODUCT table using the column PRODUCT_ID. The advantage of defining these joins now is that when a user writes a query, Discoverer will know how to join the data, so it's one less piece of information that our user has to supply; in this way we ensure that a meaningful join is being applied.

Figure 13.36   *Discoverer Administrator—Define a Join*

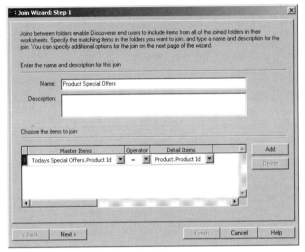

Click on the *Next* button to proceed to the second and final join wizard screen, where you can specify some more advanced options about the joins.

Hierarchies

We have already seen that hierarchies play an important role in our data warehouse. Although in Oracle we can create dimensions, at the time of writing, these are not used by Discoverer, and we must create our own dimensions, which are known in Discoverer as hierarchies. Hierarchies are very important in Discoverer, because if an item is in a hierarchy, then users can:

- Drill up, which changes the query to show a higher level of details

- Drill down, which shows more detail

This is how we were able to drill on our report shown earlier. A hierarchy is created by clicking on *Insert* in the menu at the top and then selecting

Hierarchy. First, you will be asked about the type of hierarchy you want to create: an item or a date. When the business area is first created, it is quite likely that Discoverer will automatically create a time-based hierarchy. Therefore, you will probably only have to create nontime-based hierarchies.

Figure 13.37 shows how easy it is to create the hierarchy by selecting the items and then defining the hierarchy relationship. In Figure 13.37, we have created a very simple hierarchy between PRODUCT_ID and CATEGORY.

Figure 13.37   *Discoverer Administrator—Defining a Hierarchy*

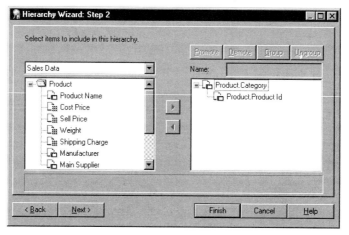

Hint: Click on the Hierarchy tab shown in Figure 13.34 to see all the hierarchies that Discoverer created automatically when the EUL was generated.

Item Classes—List of Values

When the end users are actually querying the data, there are times when it may be helpful to them if they can see a possible list of values. For example, suppose they want to pick out all of the electrical items. If they know which category they are represented in, then this will facilitate rapid query generation.

An *item class* can describe the hierarchical relationship between items, a list of values, alternative sort keys for items, and the display methods. Therefore, an item class defines all of the attributes for an item. Once an item class has been defined, it can then be assigned to other items, which share similar properties.

An item class is created by selecting *Insert* from the menu at the top and then *Insert Class* from the list or by clicking on the text in the Administration Task List, shown in Figure 13.32, the *Item Class Wizard* will now appear.

The first step is to define the type of item class, a *List of Values, Alternative Sort*, or *Drill to Details*, which is used to drill between a summary and the detail. Then all you have to select is the column containing the values and which tables will use it. When it is complete, click on the tab *Item Classes*, and the window shown in Figure 13.38 will appear.

Figure 13.38   *Discoverer Administrator—Item Class*

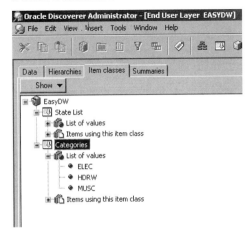

In this example, a list of values called Categories has been created from our products dimension table. If we expand the entry categories, the data warehouse can be queried, and all the different values will be displayed; in Figure 13.38, we can see some of the different categories for products that are sold. Here we only have a few items, but in the real world, where you may have a number of different values, you can omit this step of displaying the results.

When an item class is defined, you can also define the sort order for the data. In Figure 13.39, we have chosen to use the conventional alphabetical method, but that is not always suitable, so Discoverer will allow you explicitly to specify a logical order, such as N, S, E, W (North, South, East, West) rather than E, N, S, W.

Summaries

We have already seen the importance of creating and using materialized views in our data warehouse in Chapter 7. Discoverer allows you to create

Figure 13.39   *Discoverer Administrator—Creating a Summary*

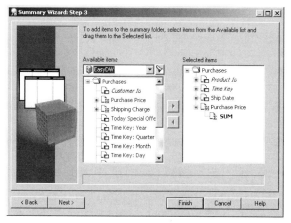

your materialized views, which Discoverer calls summaries, from its summary wizard, by:

- Using query performance statistics
- Manually creating the summary
- Registering a previously built summary

To create your summary, click on *Insert* in the menu at the top, and then select *Summary* and the summary wizard appears. Three types of summaries can be created:

- Specifying items in the end-user layer
- Recommendations based on query performance statistics
- Registering an existing summary table

Then the window shown in Figure 13.39 appears, where you select the folders and items from within those tables that are to appear in the summary. In our example, we have selected only the PURCHASES table, but you could select multiple tables. Then we have chosen four of the data items in that table. For the item purchase price, we have asked that this value be aggregated. You will see that Discoverer will automatically supply a range of functions for you to select when a function may be applied to an item. In Figure 13.39, for the item PURCHASE_PRICE, we have asked that the SUM function be applied to this item. Next, you are asked to specify which groups of items you require.

As we have seen, it is very important to ensure that the materialized views or summary contain the latest data. When defining your summary in Discoverer, you can specify how often it is to be refreshed. Remember that, as new data is added to the warehouse, the summaries must be maintained to reflect the latest data. In Figure 13.40, we can see that we have stated that this summary should be refreshed every day.

Figure 13.40   *Discoverer Administrator—Refreshing the Summary*

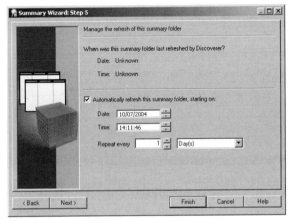

If you don't know which summaries to create, Discoverer can recommend them for you using its own summary wizard. In Figure 13.41, we can see one of the steps from the wizard, where we can select the summaries we require based on our space requirements. This wizard is very similar to summary management's own SQL Access Advisor, described in Chapter 10, but the recommendation process used by Discoverer is different from the one used by the Oracle SQL Access Advisor.

Creating either Discoverer summaries or materialized views is very important if you want to achieve the fastest query response time. Here, we have seen how to create summaries directly in Discoverer, but you can create materialized views, as discussed in Chapter 7, or use the SQL Access Advisor, which was described in Chapter 10. Irrespective of how the materialized view is created, Discoverer will still use it whenever possible.

Figure 13.41   *Discoverer Administrator—Summary Wizard*

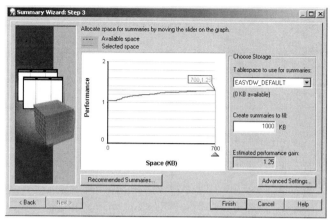

Security Issues

The final setup task is defining who may access the business area that you have just created. You can start this component by double-clicking on *Grant Business Area Access*, shown in Figure 13.42. A window will appear that will allow you to state which users can access a business area or which business areas a user can access. In Figure 13.42, we can see that the only user who will be granted access to our business area is EASYDW. Don't forget that although in this example we have enabled access via the user name, you can also grant access to the business area via the roles that may be given to a user. When you are satisfied that all the relevant access rights have been given, click on the *Apply* button to complete the changes.

Figure 13.42   *Administrator—Granting Access to the Business Area*

In Figure 13.43, our complete business area is shown. Expanding just the PURCHASES table, we can see all the items that are available to our users; the new calculation that we created, called Total Cost; and the functions that we can apply to that column. At the bottom of the window, we can see that joins have been created from the PURCHASES table to the PRODUCT and TIME table. Of course, not all the information can be displayed on this one window, so, to see the Hierarchies tab, you will have to click that tab. The same is true for item classes and summary information.

Figure 13.43 *Discoverer Administrator—Business Area*

We have now completed all of the basic setup tasks for using Discoverer. Don't forget to save all of your work, and please remember that the tool is much more comprehensive than we have shown in these few pages. For example, we haven't shown here that Discoverer fully supports the Oracle analytical functions to enable sophisticated analysis of the data. Now we can start using Discoverer Desktop, Viewer, or Discoverer Plus to retrieve data from our data warehouse.

13.3.3   Query Using Discoverer Plus

Once the environment has been set up for querying via Discoverer, you can now start either the Desktop edition or the Plus version, which has been designed for use via a browser. In this chapter, our examples will use the browser version, Discoverer Plus.

Reports in Discoverer are held in a workbook; therefore, the first step is to connect to the database where our workbooks reside. In Discoverer Plus, launch Plus from your browser using a URL such as:

```
http://easydw.com:7777/discoverer/plus
```

You will be presented with a list of the databases that you can connect to, as shown in Figure 13.44. Here we can see that we only have one database, called EASYDW.

Figure 13.44   *Discoverer Plus—List of Databases for Connection*

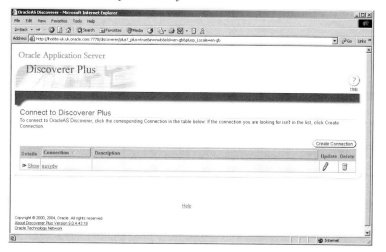

These connections will have been defined previously and consist of your user name and database name. Therefore, all you must supply is your password, and you will be asked whether to create or open an existing workbook. In Figure 13.45, we see the initial window, where we specify the workbook and how the results are to be displayed. Discoverer offers a range of display options, such as showing the data in tabular or a crosstab form. Using the crosstab format is ideal when you have multidimensional data to display.

Figure 13.45   *Discoverer Plus—Using a Workbook*

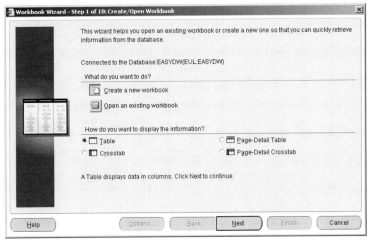

Now, it is time to specify exactly what is to be reported in this query. First, you must select the business area that was defined using the Administration edition, which determines the data that you may see. In our example, we have only the EASYDW business area, but there could be several areas to choose from.

Now we have to select the items from those folders. This is a simple process, involving moving them from the left window (available) to the right window (selected). In Figure 13.46, we have selected the item *category*

Figure 13.46   *Discoverer Plus—Selecting Data to Be Displayed*

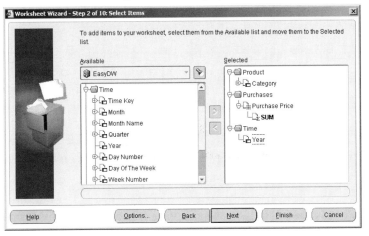

from the *product* folder, *purchase price* from the *purchases* folder, and the *year* from the *time* folder.

Next, we must specify the layout for our report. This is very easily achieved by dragging the columns to where you require them on the report. In Figure 13.47, we have specified our order as category, year, and price. Initially the year column was to the right of the purchase price column, but by simply dragging the year column, we can place it wherever we wish on the report. At this stage, we can only decide how the data is to be presented; we can specify formats and headings on another screen.

Figure 13.47   *Discoverer Plus—Table Layout*

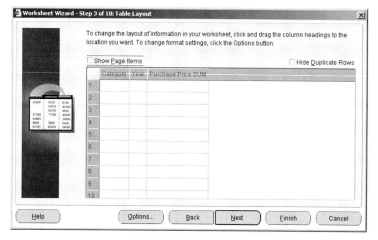

At this stage, by clicking on the *Options* button, Figure 13.48 will appear, and, in Discoverer, some very useful limits can be set on the query, such as preventing it from running longer than a specified period of time or only returning a limited number of rows.

For each item that will be displayed on our report, we can now specify how that data is to be formatted and the heading to be used on reports. In Figure 13.49, we have changed the heading for our sum on PURCHASE_PRICE to Total Sales. By clicking on the *Format Heading* button, the font and alignment options can be defined, and clicking on *Format Data* allows us to specify how the data is actually presented. In this example, we have decided that our total will have no decimal places.

Progressing through all of the steps in the wizard shows a number of other options that are available, but we will not show all of these steps here. For example, a condition can be specified to limit the results of our work-

Figure 13.48 *Discoverer Plus—Query Options*

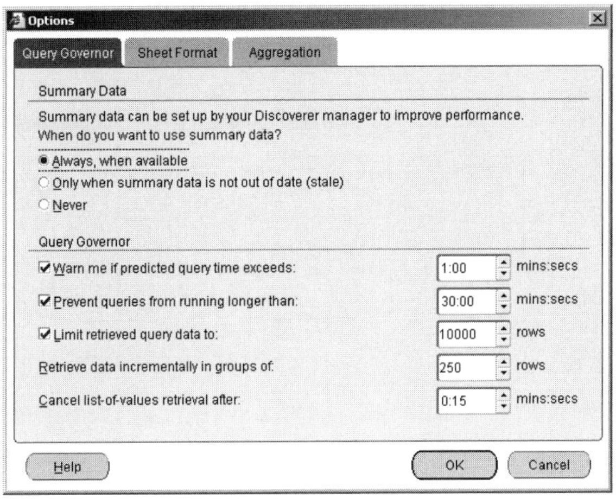

Figure 13.49 *Discoverer Plus—Format Headings*

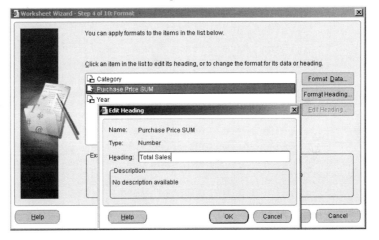

sheet to a specific criterion. There are some very extensive options available here, however, in this example we are going to view all of the data.

Step 6 in the wizard is specifying the sort order of our data, which is achieved by clicking on the *Add* button and selecting one of the available columns. In our example in Figure 13.50, we are sorting by year first and then category.

At this stage we could also add calculations to appear on our report, such as profit made by subtracting purchase price from cost price. In our

Figure 13.50   *Discoverer Plus—Sorting the Data*

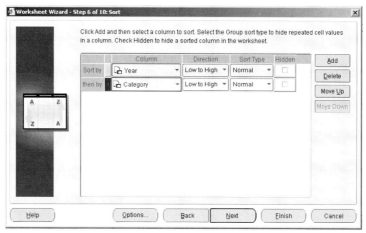

report today, we will not include any calculations. Another option is the ability to create a percentage point on any item on the report, which can be useful to help understand the data.

We have already said that we want to total the item purchase price, and in Figure 13.51 we can now add a total to this item as well. As you can see, there are a number of options available to us, such as whether we want a subtotal, the type of sum to perform, and how the data should be format-

Figure 13.51   *Discoverer Plus—Defining Totals*

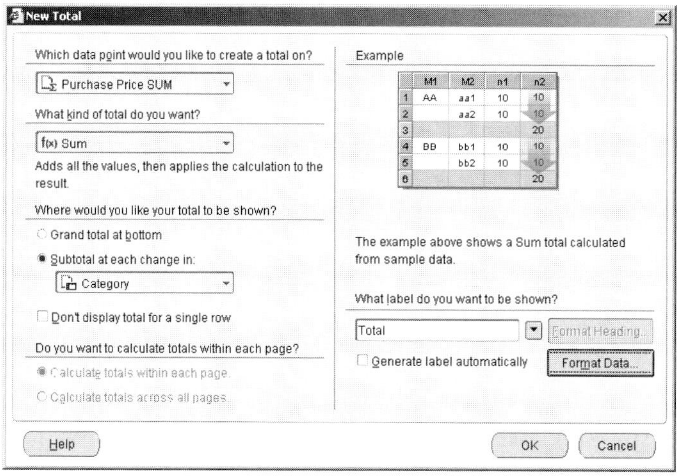

ted. Once again, we can create as many totals as we need for inclusion in our report.

The last step on the wizard is the ability to define a parameter so that the user of the report can be prompted to enter some value. In our example here, we want to see all of the data, but we could use this if, say, we wanted the ability to specify which years data we wanted.

Clicking on the *Finish* button will display our data. Discoverer will now query our data warehouse directly and show us the results, as shown in Figure 13.52. There we can see the total sales by category for a given year.

Figure 13.52   *Discoverer Plus—Report*

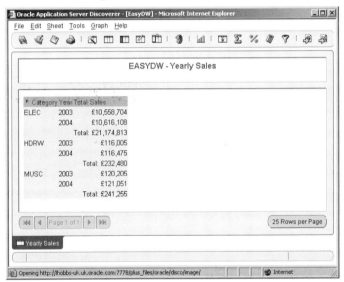

> **Hint:** You may have to format the cells of the report to see the data if the numbers are large, because, by default, it uses small numbers.

Note that in order to report this data, we did not have to specify how to join the tables that we selected, because the join information had already been specified in the business area. This is one of the really nice benefits of using Discoverer, because the end user does not have to know about relational joins. The person who created the business area using Discoverer Administration edition has done all of this work behind the scenes. Now all that the user has to do to get the report is select the data of interest, answer the questions on a few screens, and then click the *Finish* button to request the information.

Now that we have our report, we can customize it to our own requirements by either clicking on the items or selecting from the menu at the top. To change the format of our numbers, if we click on *Sheet* and then *Format*, the item can be amended.

If you are interested in how the report is being executed within the database, selecting *Sheet*, followed by *Show SQL*, will bring up the SQL Inspector box shown in Figure 13.53. Here you can either view the SQL used to execute the query by clicking on the SQL tab, or, as shown in Figure 13.53, the query execution plan. Here we can see that query rewrite has selected a materialized view to show the results of this query.

Figure 13.53   *Discoverer Plus—SQL Inspector*

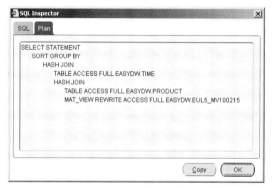

Now that we have our report, we may want to look at the data from a different perspective. Discoverer will automatically offer alternative drill down on the data; it's easy to see if this is possible, by looking for a sideways triangle beside a column.

In Figure 13.52, the column Category has one of these triangles beside it, and clicking on it displays the drop-down list shown in Figure 13.54. Now we have the ability to view the data either by category, or to drill down to the product level. Note that the user did not have to tell Discoverer

Figure 13.54   *Discoverer Plus—Drilling up/down the Data*

about how it could report on the data. All this information was previously defined during the setup, so once again the end user needs to know little about how the data is stored in order to get the information requireed.

In Figure 13.55, we now see our report with the information at the product level. Because we have a product hierarchy, we can change our report to total by product, instead of by category, simply by selecting product from the drop-down list. Hopefully, now you are beginning to appreciate the benefits of all the setup work that we completed using the Discoverer Administration edition.

Figure 13.55   *Discoverer Plus—Report at the Month Level*

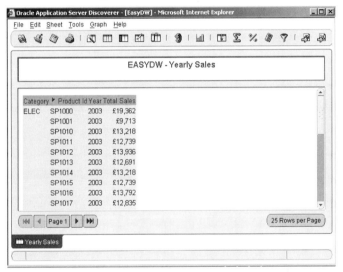

So far, we have only viewed our data in a traditional report format, but Discoverer Plus can also represent our data graphically. By answering a few questions using the *Graph Wizard,* which is started by clicking on the graph icon shown in Figure 13.55, it is possible to create a report similar to the one shown in Figure 13.56.

There are over a dozen different types of graphs available from within Discoverer Plus, and you can totally customise the output by adding your own titles and legends. We have decided to use a pie chart to represent our yearly sales, shown in Figure 13.57, which makes it easy for us to see that electrical items were the most popular item.

In this sample Discoverer report, we reported all of the data, but you can select a subset by specifying a condition. What is nice in Discoverer Plus is

Figure 13.56   *Discoverer Plus—Graph Wizard*

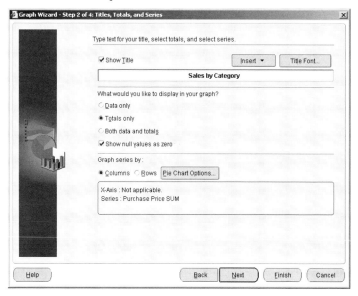

Figure 13.57   *Discoverer Plus—Graph of Yearly Sales*

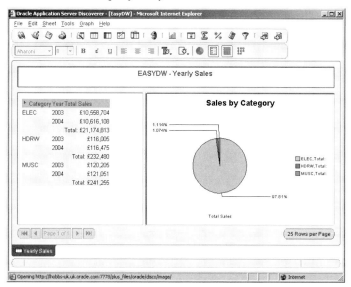

that you can set up a number of conditions and then select the ones you want for this report. In Figure 13.58, we see one of the screens where you specify these conditions.

Figure 13.58   *Discoverer Plus—Select Specific Data*

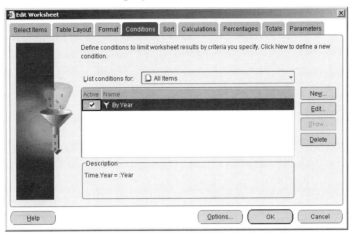

There is another screen where you specify the condition, which can be done using quite a complex expression. Here, we can see that we have one conditions defined so that we can select data for a year. Then, when we view the new report in Figure 13.59, we can see that when we restrict the view to just the sales for 2003, electrical is still by far our top-selling item.

Figure 13.59   *Discoverer Plus—Report Using Conditions*

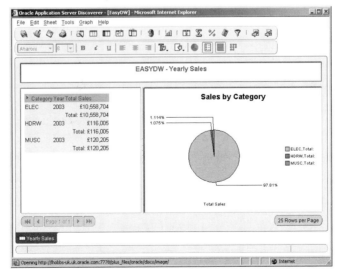

There are many more facilities available from Discoverer, but, hopefully, over these few pages, you can now see some of this tool's capabilities and how ideal this tool is for business-focused end users.

We will discuss Discoverer further in Chapter 14, when we describe how to integrate these reports into Oracle Portal, so that they can be run and viewed from within our browser as part of our Web content.

13.4   Oracle Reports 10*g*

We have just seen how reports can be generated using tools such as Oracle Discoverer. But if you are looking to create sophisticated reports, which accept data from a variety of sources, can use report templates, and can be published in a variety of formats, such as HTML and PDF, then consider using Oracle Reports 10*g*.

Oracle Reports 10*g* will accept data from a variety of sources, including Oracle Database, Oracle Express, Oracle OLAP, XML, JDBC, or even a simple text file. Reports can be presented in a variety of styles and can be enhanced by adding graphs, such as pie charts or bar charts. Each report can be based on predefined templates, or the Template Editor can be used to create your own templates, which means that you can define a standard layout and include, for example, your company logo. Once the report has been defined, it can then be sent to a number of different destinations, which include a file, a printer, email distribution list, or Oracle Portal for inclusion on your corporate Web site. However, the real power of Oracle Reports 10*g* comes when you can use its powerful Web publishing capabilities, which allow you to create JavaServer Pages (JSP)using Report Builder.

Let us now look at some of the types of reports that we can produce using Oracle Reports.

13.4.1   Creating a Report Using the Report Builder

A report can either be constructed manually or by using the *Report Wizard,* which we will use to guide us through the steps of creating a report. In Figure 13.60, we see one of the first screens, where we are asked to select the type of layout. Since our report is going to be published on our intranet, we have selected the *Create Web Layout* option. This means that a single report can have two formats, if required: one for paper and another for the Web.

Figure 13.60   *Oracle Reports—Select the Reporting Medium*

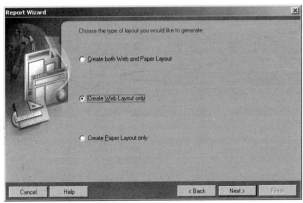

Our next step is to select the type of report we require, as shown in Figure 13.61, where there are a number of options to choose from; a thumbnail sketch of the style is presented next to each radio button. The title of this report will be *Monthly Sales by Manufacturer*, and the data will be presented in tabular format. Later, we will see examples of reports using the matrix option.

Figure 13.61   *Choosing the Style of Report and Title*

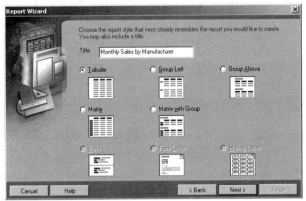

The next step is to define the source of the data; in Figure 13.62, we can see the ways that Oracle Reports allow us to query the data source. In this example, we have chosen to use SQL, but it could just as easily be a query to Oracle OLAP or JDBC.

Figure 13.62   *Oracle Reports—Selecting the Data Source*

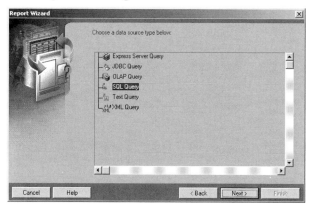

Since we are querying the database, in Figure 13.63 we see there are three methods available for defining the SQL. If you know SQL, then you can type it in manually; otherwise the SQL can be imported from a file, or the Query Builder can construct the query.

Figure 13.63   *Oracle Reports—Specifying the SQL Query*

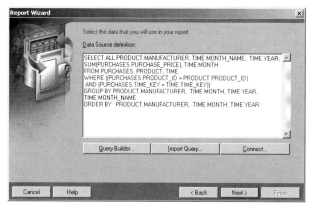

For users not familiar with SQL, use the *Query Builder,* because it makes defining SQL statements very easy and will certainly save you a lot of time, since all you have to do is select the tables to include in your report and then select the items that are to appear.

Oracle Reports automatically determine how to join the data and creates the required SQL when you leave the query builder. In Figure 13.64, we have selected the PRODUCT, TIME, and PURCHASES tables and have

Oracle Reports—Using the Query Builder

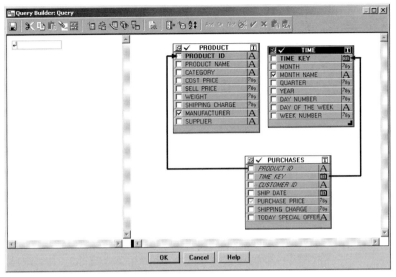

selected some columns from these tables. Note how Oracle Reports have determined how to join the PURCHASES table to the TIME and PRODUCT table.

Oracle Reports will now validate our SQL statement, and next we are asked which fields are to appear in the report. In Figure 13.65, we have selected manufacturer, the month name rather than a number, the year, and the total purchase price.

Oracle Reports—Columns to Display

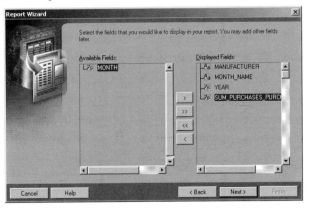

We can now select, in Figure 13.66, whether we require any totals to be computed for data. See how Oracle Reports give us buttons to request for sum, average, count, minimum, maximum, and %total.

Figure 13.66   *Oracle Reports—Calculate Totals*

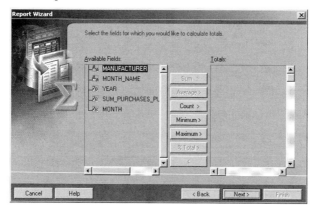

A nice feature in Oracle Reports is the ability to specify how wide the columns should be for our data and what our column headings should be. In Figure 13.67, we are given the option to specify these widths before our report is produced. At this time, column headings can also be defined therefore, we have taken the opportunity to change the heading for Month Name to Month and increase the size of the column for the Manufacturer .

Figure 13.67   *Oracle Reports—Specify the Column Widths*

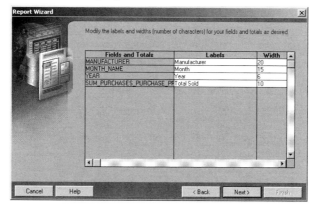

The layout for the report is determined by selecting one of the pre-defined templates, or you can define your own template. When you're done, click *Finish* and you are returned to the Report Builder. Once here you can save the report and then select *Program* followed by *Run Web Layout* to actually run the report. Figure 13.68 shows us the actual report as viewed from our browser.

Figure 13.68   *Oracle Reports—Final Report*

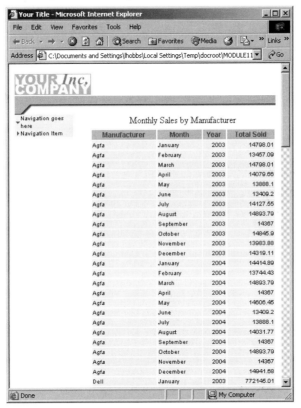

However, this is in its raw format, and it can be customized as required. Therefore, the report layout can be modified to include currency symbols, commas, and decimal points. Other possible changes include changing the fonts, bolding numbers, underline, or italicize text, and you can format numbers to represent a monetary value. You can even add your own logos, graphics, headings and footers, and construct company-specific templates for report layouts.

Report Builder has so many reporting capabilities that once its capabilities are appreciated, it soon becomes apparent how this extremely sophisticated reporting design tool can be used to produce flexible and powerful reports.

13.4.2   **More Oracle Reports Examples**

The report shown in Figure 13.68 is a very simple report and not that exciting, but it illustrates how to create a report. Let us now look at examples of some more reports that we have created using Oracle Reports from our EASYDW Data Warehouse.

Matrix Report

In Figure 13.69, we see an example of a report using the matrix with a group layout, where we can view the total amount that has been purchased for each of our manufacturers for the month of January.

Figure 13.69   *Oracle Reports—Matrix Report*

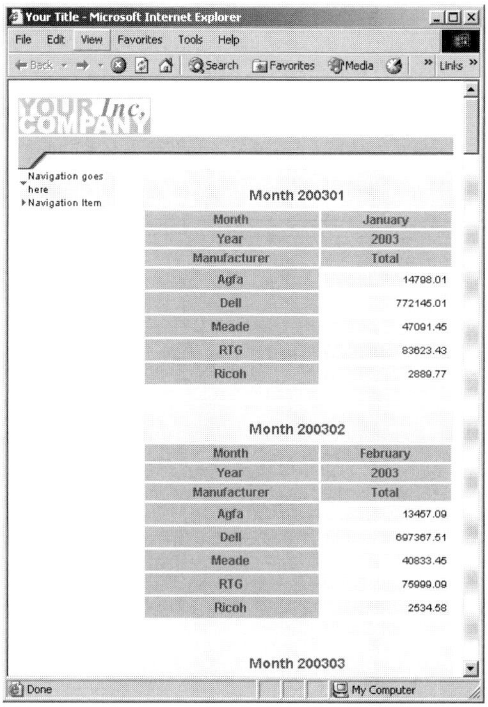

Conditional Report

The extensive capabilities of Oracle Reports begin to become apparent when we see how defining a condition on our report can be used to highlight when specified conditions have been reached. In Figure 13.70, we have chosen to highlight in red any customer who spent less than $250. We could even go further and specify a number of conditions, all highlighted with a different color. Therefore, customers spending less than $250 are in red, up to $1,000 in yellow, and over $1,000 in black. Unfortunately, in a black and white book we can't show this, so the red numbers are in italic.

Figure 13.70 *Oracle Reports—Conditional Report*

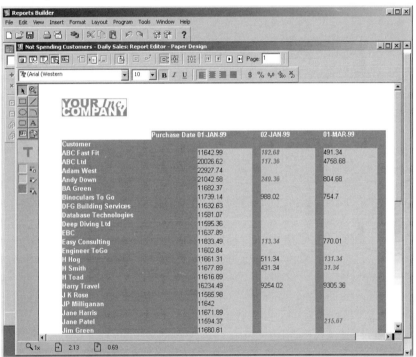

13.4.3 **Publishing the Report**

Once our report has been created, it can then be published in a number of formats. From within Report Builder, we can see the options by clicking *File,* then *Generate,* and a list of output formats is displayed, which includes, HTML, PDF, XML, RTF, and Text; we have already seen the HTML layout in Figures 13.68 and 13.69.

By selecting PDF and HTML formats, we have the ability to view the reports using a Web browser. Oracle Reports also allow you to deploy a report to:

- File
- Printer
- OracleAS Portal
- Email

Select the type of report that is required, and you will be prompted to specify where the report is to be stored. Optionally, you may also be prompted for database connection information. The report is then run immediately, and the report can be viewed from the location where it is stored.

The report can also be published in OracleAS Portal as a portlet, and we will learn more about publishing data this way in Chapter 14.

13.5 Summary

In this chapter, we have barely skimmed the surface of what is possible with these three data warehousing tools from Oracle. They are all very powerful and it is strongly recommended that you find out more about these tools; visit http://otn.oracle.com, where there will be demos showing the tools capabilities and very detailed documentation, tutorials, and best practices.

Data Warehousing and the Web

14.1 Overview

There was a time when, if you mentioned integrating the data warehouse with the Web, people would stare at you and ask, "Why on earth would you want to do that?" Most of us, when we first think of the Web, probably imagine checking out a company's product or placing an order, so what does that have to do with our data warehouse? Well, you may be very surprised at how important the Web could be to your data warehouse.

Today, as described in Chapter 1, applications and tools are evolving toward browser-based solutions. We saw in Chapter 13 that Discoverer Viewer is a browser-based tool for querying your data. Now, imagine tightly integrating that tool into the Web pages you are viewing, and an extremely powerful reporting environment is now available.

14.1.1 Internet and Intranet

To distinguish between an internal Web and the World-Wide-Web, the term *Internet* is used to describe the global connection of public computers. Often sitting behind the Internet is a company's own Web, called the *intranet*, which is only accessible to people within that organization; it is the intranet that we are primarily interested in.

Today, most companies have a presence on the World Wide Web, but what many people may not realise is that within the company there can be a huge internal Web site used by employees only. This is the Web site where all business is conducted, and Oracle is a good example of a company using its intranet to communicate and conduct internal business. For example, when an Oracle employee needs a new laptop or mobile phone, he or she accesses the internal procurement system and goes shopping similar to shopping on the Web. In some countries, payslips are only available on-line, as well as all end-of-year tax documents. Numerous reports, status documents, and product specifications are all accessed via Web-based systems using a browser such as Internet Explorer or Netscape. Therefore, information is quickly and easily available, provided he or she is connected to the corporate network, no matter where in the world the Oracle employee is located. Therefore, what does a company place on its intranet? Well, the possibilities are endless, and here are just a few ideas:

- Press releases
- Product information
- Software to download
- Payslips and HR systems
- Purchasing systems
- Telephone lists
- Sales information
- Historical data
- Trends and analysis
- Many different types of reports and documents

At first glance, this list looks like a typical Internet site, but it's the items such as sales information, historical data, and trends and analysis that differentiate it from the normal Internet and indicate a role for our data warehouse.

Before we look at how we can use this intranet, we must address a concern many people have when data is published on the Web, even if it is internal: Is it safe? Typically, company intranets are not connected to the Internet and can only be accessed by either being in a company office, by dialing in, or through a secure VPN connection when outside a company office. Therefore, the information is safe and protected from hackers. Of course, if you are concerned about security within your organization, then information can be protected so that only certain staff can review sensitive information.

Therefore, knowing that our data is safe, why would we want to consider putting our data warehouse on the company intranet? Well, before the intranet, if there was a report that a manager needed—say, sales by area for this month, he or she would have to request that report and then wait for the paper copy to arrive.

Now, the intranet changes all of that, because standard reports can be created and then published on the intranet for managers to review at a time that is convenient to them. Once they have been produced, reports can be made readily available to everyone, no matter location. No longer do you have to wait for them to arrive in the internal mail. If you are not in the office today but working from a hotel, home, or dialing in from some location, you can still review the report. You could even consider converting the report into, say, a spreadsheet, so that the data can be downloaded and manipulated locally.

By using this approach, reports don't have to be published on the Web. They can be configured so that they are regularly updated and always contain the latest information. When published in conjunction with tools such as Discoverer Viewer and Discoverer Plus, not only can the users get the report when they want it, but they are no longer restricted to getting a standard report. Now, tools such as Discoverer allow users some degree of customization of the report, such as only sales for the Southern area or store whose sales are less than $10,000.

Hopefully, now you are beginning to appreciate how the Web can help solve your report publishing and distribution problems and provide a mechanism for users to have access to the very latest information. For example, suppose you have a static report: You could automatically regenerate that report every hour and publish it on the Web or refresh it on demand as users request it. On-line interaction with reports has traditionally not been feasible with a data warehouse, because business intelligence queries can typically take hours to run. But now, with features such as summary management, described in Chapter 7, a query that used to take hours can be reduced to seconds. Thus, the reports using that data can be run more frequently.

Now that we have an appreciation of what the Web can do, there are several different ways in which it can interact with our data warehouse:

- It becomes the deployment platform for all your business intelligence information, using tools such as Oracle Discoverer and Reports.

- It becomes the platform where an application can be customized, using Oracle Personalization, thanks to data from our warehouse.

14.1.2   Oracle Software for the Data Warehouse

Oracle offers a complete solution that facilitates easy publishing of the data from your data warehouse onto your intranet or Internet, providing a complete customized experience. Everything that is needed to build this environment can be found within Oracle Application Server 10*g*, but this is a product that includes many different components. However, it is not necessary to install everything, because you only need to use the parts of the Application Server that you require. But be warned, once you discover what is possible, those other components could suddenly become very useful.

There are four components in Oracle Application Server 10*g* that will initially be of interest in our data warehouse:

- Portal
- Discoverer
- Reports
- Personalization

We will now look briefly at each of these products and see how they can help our data warehouse.

14.2   Oracle Application Server 10*g*

Hopefully, now you are beginning to appreciate how the Web can dramatically change how information is used and accessed by the data warehouse. Using Oracle Application Server 10*g* (OracleAS) to run all of your business intelligence applications provides you with the complete environment to run e-business intelligence.

Oracle Application Server 10*g*, provides all the technology stack that you need to build and implement e-business portals, Web services, and transaction-based applications. It supports all the Java, XML, and Web services industry standards and can be used to access both Oracle and non-Oracle data.

Included is Oracle's HTTP server, which is based on the Apache Web server. Following installation of OracleAS, which has already been configured, it is immediately ready for use. There is also a J2EE (Java 2 Enterprise Edition) environment, which is a Java platform designed for the development of applications up to enterprise-size businesses. By using J2EE technologies, you can create an application using Java server pages, servlets, and enterprise Java Beans.

- A *Java servlet* is a program, which, when it receives a request for information from the client, dynamically gets the information from the database, generates a response, which can be in HTML or XML, and sends that back to the client.
- *JAVAServer pages* help us develop our servlets, because they allow the developer to easily design and maintain dynamic Web pages by separating the dynamic content from the page layout.
- *Enterprise Java Beans* help developer by encapsulating business logic, so they don't have to write the code for these functions.

Within OracleAS, development is possible using Java, XML, Perl, and PL/SQL.

Oracle Application Server 10*g* actually comprises the following areas, which, as you can see are a very comprehensive list. Thankfully, you don't have to install all of them to use OracleAS.

Oracle HTTP Server	Web Server
OracleAS Portal	Build and administer portal applications
OracleAS Reports Services	Create reports
OracleAS Discoverer	Business intelligence reporting
OracleAS Personalization	Provides real-time personalization
OracleAS Containers for J2EE	J2EE run-time component
OracleAS TopLink	Store Java objects in database
OracleAS Web Services	Develop and deploy Web services
OracleAS Form Services	Web deployment for oracle forms
OracleAS Developer Kits	XML, Content Management, and MapViewer
OracleAS High Availability	Ensures application high availability
OracleAS Integration	Manages Enterprise Business processes
OracleAS Identity Management	Identity management infrastructure

OracleAS BPEL Process Manager	Deploy and manage BPEL processes
OracleAS Workflow	Manage workflows
OracleAS Wireless	Deploys wireless and voice applications
OracleAS Web Cache	Web caching and compression
OracleAS Java Object Cache	Manage local Java objects
Oracle Enterprise Manager	Web-based administration

Now, we will begin to see which components you may need to take the data warehouse to the Web. There are many ways that a Web site can be configured, and it's beyond the scope of this book to discuss them here, but typically Oracle Application Server 10g will be installed and running on a machine different from where your database is located.

By using this approach, an environment can be created where the hardware and operating systems can be configured to match the processing demands. The examples in this book were constructed with Oracle Application Server 10g running on a Windows machine and Oracle Database 10g running on Linux.

14.2.1   Why Set up a Portal?

When the Internet first became popular, a company would talk about their Web site, but now talks about its *portal*, where a portal is a Web site that offers a range of resources and services. A Web site devoted to a specific topic, such as the medical site WebMD (http://www.webmd.com/), is known as a vertical portal. But most portals cover a wide range of subjects, such as Yahoo (http://www.yahoo.com); these are known as horizontal portals.

The portal provides access to this wealth of information, and, typically, once you sign in, what you see is customized to meet your needs. For example, when an external visitor visits Oracle (http://myoracle.com), he or she will see a screen very similar to the one shown in Figure 14.1. However, when an Oracle employee signs in, he or she will see a completely different Web.

The Oracle employee will be presented with internal company information and access to a wide range of internal systems, such as email. The external visitor to the Web site will first be presented with the screen shown in Figure 14.2, where he or she invited to register for Oracle World and is presented with the latest news. Since this is a portal, users can now customize this page so that they only see and access information of interest to them.

Figure 14.1   *Signing in to the OracleAS Portal*

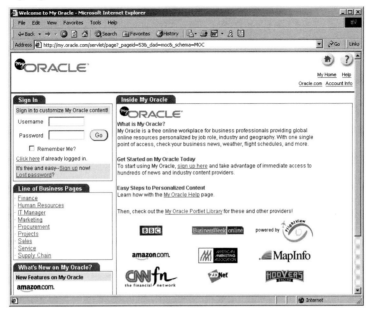

Figure 14.2   *OracleAS Portal—Standard View*

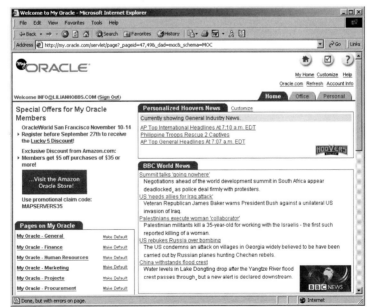

So why is a portal relevant to our data warehouse. Well, many companies are now realizing that they need a portal, which is a very sophisticated Web site. Using the tools available, a portal is not difficult to construct, and efficiency should increase because the portal provides customized access to the information companies need to do their jobs. Therefore, consider using a portal to bring the information from your data warehouse to its users. There are two products within OracleAS that make this possible: OracleAS Portal and Personalization.

14.2.2   OracleAS Portal

Oracle Application Server 10*g* includes OracleAS Portal, which is software that allows a portal to be developed quickly and easily. Since OracleAS Portal uses the single sign-on authentication, which is part of OracleAS, it provides the mechanism by which access to the information is controlled.

It's very easy to develop applications using OracleAS Portal, even if you are not an experienced developer. This is because it is a friendly, browser-based tool with many wizards; these can be used to quickly create a very comprehensive and professionally designed portal. Whenever information is being retrieved from the database or other sources, there are always wizards to help you specify the query, or you can define the SQL yourself. The benefits of using OracleAS Portal are:

- It has a framework that is extensible and that integrates all the Web resources.

- It uses the OracleAS single sign-on.

- It provides easy access to information.

- The contents can be personalized.

- It has comprehensive wizards to help build applications quickly and with minimal development knowledge.

- It uses a scalable architecture.

- It forms an integrated solution with OracleAS Reports and Discoverer.

- It information is published using portlets.

- It is a self-service publishing facility.

Although OracleAS Portal can create simple reports, it is also tightly integrated with Oracle Reports and Discoverer, and the information and reports produced by these tools can be published as a portlet.

Security is also not an issue; since OracleAS Portal is part of Oracle Application Server 10g, it uses single sign-on (SSO). Therefore, before anyone can access any information, he or she will have to log in, as illustrated in Figure 14.1; this will control exactly which pages a user can see within the portal.

In Figure 14.3, we can see all of the components that can be used to create our portal. Before access can be granted to any information, security must confirm that this is an authorized user. Once users have access to the pages in the portal, information is presented in regions. Within those regions, portlets can be used to present information from tools such as Discoverer. The pages used to present this information can use a template for consistent styling, and navigation is provided so the users can move around the portal quickly.

Figure 14.3   *An Overview of OracleAS Portal*

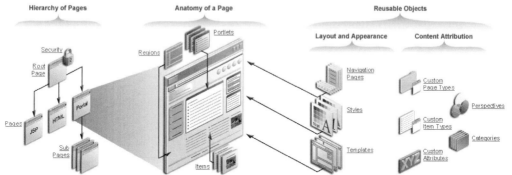

Before we discuss how to get started with Oracle Application Server, let's look at how easy it is to create Web pages in OracleASPortal. Figure 14.4 shows part of the graphical design tool for constructing our Web page. Although it may look a bit complex, it's actually quite straightforward to use. Regions are specified and then within that region information is placed such as text, a graphic or a link to Discoverer worksheets or the actual results from a report, such as this one from Discoverer can be displayed. Using this approach, Web pages can be quickly constructed, and, by using

Figure 14.4   *Creating the EASYDW Web Page in OracleAS Portal*

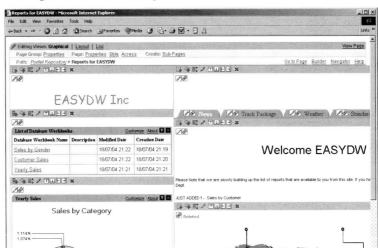

templates, a corporate look and feel can easily be incorporated into the design.

In Figure 14.4, we see how our page is being constructed. Regions have been defined for each of the areas on the screen and within those regions there are text, navigation tabs, and Discoverer portlets.

In Figure 14.5, we can see how our page will look when it is displayed in a browser. The page shown here is extremely simplistic and only shows a very small percentage of what is possible with OracleAS Portal.

Referring to Figure 14.5, on the left we can see links to some of the Discoverer reports we created in Chapter 13; one of the reports, Sales by Category, is displayed. The information from Discoverer is published here via what is known as a **portlet**. Once in the portal, these report contents do not have to remain static, since they can be automatically refreshed and republished with the new data. At the bottom of the window on the left, information is displayed about when the report was last refreshed and when it is due to be refreshed again. These are just some of the parameters that can be controlled when the page is constructed.

On the right side of the screen, there are tabs to select business processes, such as tracking a package, clicking on the News tab, or displaying

Figure 14.5 *The EASYDW Portal*

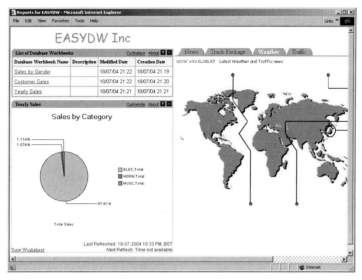

the latest company news and a graphic. When clicked, a tab can perform a number of tasks—from simply displaying text to running a report.

Hopefully, you can start to appreciate how this self-service publishing feature is of interest to our data warehouse users, because it allows them to publish and share documents. Therefore, we can use the portal to create a portlet, shown in Figure 14.4, where we can publish the information from our data warehouse. Using this approach to publish and retrieve information in our data warehouse means that any user within our organization, who has permission to access the data, can easily view it. He or she simply clicks on the tab or link and is taken to the report or graph of interest.

As you can see, by using OracleAS Portal, it is very easy to give users access to all the information they may require from their browser. Now that we have an appreciation of what is possible using Oracle Application Server 10*g*, let us now look at what is involved in setting up this environment.

14.2.3 Getting Started with Oracle Application Server 10*g*

Oracle Application Server 10*g* is an extremely comprehensive product, but, at the time of writing, the installation procedure, while straightforward, does involve a number of steps, so it shouldn't be attempted when only limited time is available.

In this section, some of the key points of the installation will be high-lighted, but it is highly recommended that the installation guides be read prior to installation.

In order to use the various components of Oracle Application Server, several software installations need to be performed. The first step involves installing the infrastructure, which is the second option on the installation screen. During this step, components such as Oracle Internet Directory and single sign-on are installed; these are needed by Oracle Application Server 10*g*.

Once this installation is complete, start the installation again and this time, select the first option. Now you can choose which parts of Oracle Application Server to install, and, once completed, everything should be up and running.

Hint: During the installation, you will be asked to specify several passwords so keep a careful note of these and the URLs listed at the end of the installation.

Administration of Oracle Application Server 10*g* is achieved via a browser, and the URL will depend on the available ports at installation time. In the example shown in Figure 14.6, the administration page was started by entering http://lhobbs-uk.uk.oracle.com:1812, where lhobbs-uk is the name of the server and uk.oracle.com is the domain.

Oracle Application Server is managed via its own database instance—for our EASYDW system it is known as iasdb3. By selecting the iasdb3 instance, the administration screen shown in Figure 14.6 appears. Here we can see that all the installed components, such as Discoverer and Portal, are running.

This screen is very useful, because from here the performance of the system can be monitored; we will return here shortly to perform some configuration tasks to use Discoverer.

14.3   Publishing Data on the Web

We have started to see how using the Web to publish information can be extremely powerful, so let us now look at how easy it is to achieve this from Oracle Discoverer and Oracle Reports using OracleAS Portal.

Figure 14.6   *Administering Oracle Application Server 10g*

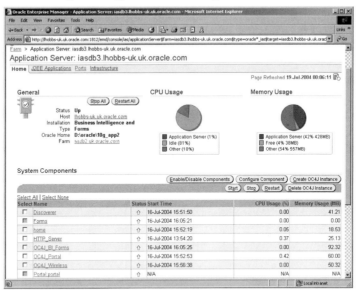

14.3.1   Discoverer

Oracle Discoverer is an extremely popular tool for querying data in the data warehouse, and only minimal extra configuration is required in order to publish reports on the Web.

Creating a Public Connection

Although users can have their own private connections to access Discoverer data, this could involve considerable administration, especially if there are many users. Therefore, for some general reports, *public connections* may be beneficial; these can be created by clicking on *Discoverer* in Figure 14.6 and then the screen shown in Figure 14.7 will appear.

Here, all the options for configuring Discoverer within Oracle Application Server are shown, and clicking on *Create Connection* will show a screen where the database connection information can be supplied; this was described in Chapter 13.

14.3.2   Publishing a Portlet

Information from Discoverer is shared via a portlet which has to be configured before it can be included in our portal. This is achieved in OracleAS

Figure 14.7   *Creating a Public Connection*

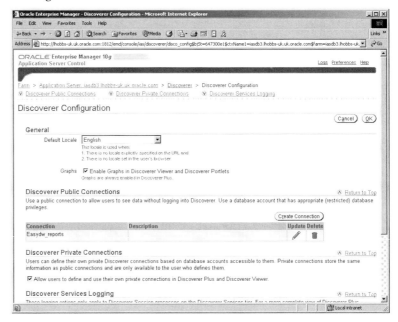

Portal from the *Portal Builder* screen, which is reached by clicking on the *Administer* tab. Register your *Remote Provider* here by completing the three steps in the wizard; your portlets will now be available for inclusion on your Web pages.

To include a portlet on your Web page click, on the *Add Portlet* icon, this is one of the options for the regions shown in Figure 14.4. This will take you

Figure 14.8   *Specifying Portlet Details*

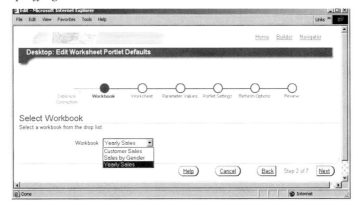

to the *Add Portlet* screen, where you select the portlet from the ones available. The next step is to specify exactly which information is to be displayed; this is achieved by clicking on the *Edit default* icon, shown in Figure 14.4.

A wizard will appear and will ask a number of questions. The first one will be to select the database connection, which could be the one specified earlier in Figure 14.7. Then Figure 14.8 will appear, which lists the workbooks available from this portlet. Select the one required and then continue with the remainder of the screens in the wizard; eventually it will return to design mode.

The data is now available from Discoverer, and clicking on the *View Page* link within OracleAS Portal will allow you to see exactly how the information will appear to the end user.

Although we have illustrated here how to publish a portlet from Discoverer, a very similar approach is used to embed an OracleAS Report.

14.3.3 Embedding a Static Report

In Chapter 13, we saw that in OracleAS Reports it was also possible to generate a static report, since sometimes it may be desirable to see a report at a specific point in time. These reports can also be embedded within our portal, and there are various ways in which they can be launched. In Figure 14.9, we have chosen to set up some tabs, which users are presented with when they click on the *Standard Reports* tab. Clicking on any of these tabs would display the report we produced in Chapter 13.

Figure 14.9 *Using Tabs to Launch a Static Report*

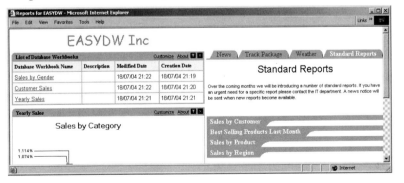

14.4 **Oracle Personalization**

So far, we have seen how we can use the portal to present and retrieve information, but it would be nice if we could extend this further and customize the information being presented. Then, users of the portal would see the information that is of interest to them; this can be achieved using OracleAS Personalization.

Have you noticed that when you visit some Web sites, they remember who you are? Then, the next time you visit, they start recommending specific products, making you aware of special offers they think you might be interested in, and even tailoring the products to suit your needs. If you have ever wondered how they do it, the answer is by using products such as Oracle Personalization and your data warehouse.

What OracleAS Personalization does, is take the information stored in the data warehouse about what customers do each time they visit our Web site—for example, which products did they buy, which pages did they visit, and when did they buy items. Then, using the data mining technology that is built into Oracle Database 10*g*, OracleAS Personalization makes recommendations to our customers as to what it thinks they will be interested in. By using Oracle Personalization, questions such as the following can be asked:

- Which product will our customer most likely buy?

- Which other items may be bought when customers buy this item?

- Which rating will a customer assign to a product?

- Which items on the Hot Pick list do we think our customer will purchase?

Once again, we are using all of the information in our data warehouse to not only benefit the customer, but hopefully benefit our business both financially and with respect to customer service.

14.5 The Data Warehouse and E-Business Intelligence

The Internet and company intranets are creating huge opportunities for organizations. For businesses, they are identifying new customers and providing the data to create promotional opportunities to encourage customers to switch their loyalties from other companies. Within a company, they are providing a flexible, easy-to-use, working environment. The data warehouse can be a key component in making your e-business successful. Why? Because it can help answer all those important questions to ensure that your business succeeds, such as:

- Which products do people buy?

- When are these products sold (time of year and time of day)?

- When is there a quiet time when systems can come off-line?

- Based on current sales, what do we predict our sales will be this time next year?

- How much will free shipping cost us?

By integrating your data warehouse with OracleAS Portal, customized information can be published to a wide community of users, from the person on the shop floor to senior executives within the organization, providing them with fast and easy access to the very latest information.

Hopefully, this chapter has given you an insight into how you can use the Web with your data warehouse. There are many ways it can be exploited, and we have barely touched the surface here with respect to the tools and techniques that are available.

OLAP

Once a data warehouse has been built, a business can deploy a host of business intelligence applications to derive full benefit from the data. These include ad hoc querying and reporting applications such as Discoverer and Reports, which were discussed in Chapter 13. These applications may be used by all levels of an organization to analyze data about the ongoing operation of the business. Other applications, such as demand planning, sales forecasting, corporate budgeting, and financial modeling, require specialized knowledge and algorithms to operate. These types of analyses are usually performed by a select few analysts or financial experts. A common aspect of business intelligence applications is that data is analyzed along multiple dimensions, such as product, geography, and time, and hence this type of analysis is generally referred to as Online Analytical Processing (OLAP).

15.1 Why Do We Need the Oracle OLAP Option?

Oracle Database 10g OLAP, which is an additional option in the Enterprise Edition of the database, provides a specialized storage and analysis model for OLAP within the database server. This is an alternative to using the SQL-based relational model provided by the Oracle database. To understand the motivation behind using this option, let us look at some of the operations commonly involved in OLAP and the different models that can be used to accomplish them.

15.1.1 OLAP Applications

Online Analytical Processing involves analysis along multiple dimensions. The most basic OLAP operations are aggregation and analysis, such as ranking (e.g., top-10 products), time-series calculations (e.g., moving average), and interrow calculations (such as period-over-period comparisons).

As we discussed in Chapter 6, these calculations can be done using SQL analytical functions. You can also use powerful end-user tools such as Discoverer to perform this analysis graphically. These types of operations when done using SQL may require multiple passes over the data and hence, with Oracle OLAP option, it may be possible to do these types of operations faster because the data storage format is optimized for analysis.

Other business applications, such as financial modeling, sales forecasting, what-if analysis, and budget allocation, require more specialized storage and analysis models and cannot be done efficiently using SQL. Let us review what each of these applications involves.

Forecasting: Forecasting, as the name suggests, involves predicting a quantity based on available historical figures—for instance, forecasting sales for the next quarter based on results of the past year. These applications use advanced statistical algorithms, such as linear and nonlinear regressions, single and double exponential smoothing, and the Holt-Winters method.

Allocation: Allocation, also known as reverse aggregation, is used to divide a quantity such as a budget or a quota into several parts. Allocation is an important part of business planning applications. For example, at the beginning of each quarter, each department head may be given a budget for purchasing new equipment, which must then be further apportioned among the managers within that department and so on.

Financial Calculations: These are calculations that can be conveniently done in a spreadsheet environment—for example, interest calculations and payment schedules.

Modeling: Modeling involves describing a quantity using a set of equations. The model can then be used to compute other quantities by plugging data into these equations. The equations may have an implied dependency order among them and can compute new values of dimensions and facts. For example, you may have a model to calculate the peak sales for different countries or regions based on different holiday months. With Oracle Database 10g, you can now also do some modeling using the SQL Model Clause.

What-if Analysis: What-if analysis, or scenario management, is a very important aspect of advanced analytical applications. It involves analyzing data under hypothetical scenarios to determine its impact on the business. For instance, how much will it cost the company if we were to close down some of our retail stores and start an online outlet store? What will be the impact on revenues if we made a change to our sales organization? What-if analysis requires a transactional model different from that provided by relational databases and SQL. Users must be able to change the structure and content of the data in a localized fashion within the session, without making it visible to the entire database. Further, the changes may be temporary and the user should be able to restore the data back to the way it was.

Regardless of the type of analysis being performed, OLAP typically involves analyzing data across multiple dimensions. The question then arises—what is the best way to store data to facilitate such multidimensional analysis?

15.1.2 ROLAP and MOLAP

Ever since the OLAP industry started, there has been an ongoing debate about the best way to store data for OLAP. One school of thought advocates storing and analyzing data using relational databases, which have long been known for their ability to scale to large amounts of data. This is known as Relational OLAP (**ROLAP**). In this case, analysis of data is done using SQL queries. All the SQL analytical features discussed in this book, especially in Chapter 6, would qualify as relational OLAP.

The other school of thought says that multidimensional data processing should be done using a specialized storage format (called a multidimensional database, or MDDB) designed to quickly answer OLAP queries. This is known as Multidimensional OLAP (**MOLAP**). The major benefit of MOLAP is that data is presented to the users in an intuitive multidimensional fashion that they can very easily access without needing to write complex and lengthy SQL. Further, because the storage format is optimized for multi-dimensional analysis, it may be possible to obtain much better performance than using SQL. Many vendors provide standalone MOLAP products as an alternative to the relational database. However, a major problem with this approach is that business data is typically stored in a relational database or data warehouse and must then be moved or replicated from the relational to the multidimensional database for analysis. This means that the data can never be up-to-date and can easily get out-of-sync. Further, standalone MOLAP products, being primarily focused on ease of analysis, may not provide the same level of security and reliability that a relational database does.

Sometimes ROLAP and MOLAP technologies are combined to varying degrees to perform Hybrid OLAP (**HOLAP**). This is done by storing some data in relational format and other data in multidimensional format as appropriate to the application. For example, you can store summarized information in the MDDB and then reach out to the relational database when you need to drill down to the detail-level data.

To summarize, both the relational and the multidimensional mechanisms have their merits, and the right choice depends on the application in question. In the past, most businesses had to invest in two products—a relational database for simple analysis and reporting needs and a specialized MOLAP product for advanced analysis and business planning applications. With Oracle Database 10*g*, there is no need to have two separate analysis products. You can choose to do either ROLAP, MOLAP, or a combination in the Oracle Database Server. Applications can either use the relational model using SQL or the multidimensional model provided by the Oracle OLAP Option.

15.1.3   Oracle OLAP

Ever since Oracle 8*i*, Oracle has been incorporating OLAP functionality into the database to support relational OLAP. In Chapter 6, we discussed analytical functions, such as RANK, aggregation operators, CUBE, ROLLUP and GROUPING SETS, and modeling features, such as SQL Model Clause, which allow users to do complex OLAP calculations through SQL. Materialized views and query rewrite allow you to preaggregate data so that queries can be answered quickly. Therefore, simple OLAP analyses can be performed within the database. However, as we discussed earlier, there are still some types of analyses, such as forecasting and allocation, that cannot be done in SQL.

Starting with Oracle 9*i*, Release 2, Oracle also supports multidimensional OLAP directly in the database. This is available via the OLAP Option of Database, Enterprise Edition. With the OLAP Option, the database can store data in a multidimensional format in an entity known as an **analytic workspace**. Further, there is a rich multidimensional calculation engine built into the database. Oracle OLAP provides several built-in algorithms for advanced OLAP analyses, such as forecasting, allocation, and modeling. Thus, you now have the full analytical capabilities provided by any traditional MOLAP products, with the added benefits of scalability, security, manageability, and reliability provided by a database management system. Data does not have to be moved into a separate database; hence, data consistency can be maintained easily and the time lag involved in making data available for analysis is reduced. Further, Oracle also provides a mechanism so you can access the multidimensional data using SQL. So any analyses that cannot be done in SQL can be performed in the analytic workspace, but the results can still be retrieved using SQL.

With the introduction of the Oracle OLAP Option, the calculation capabilities of Oracle's original MOLAP product, Oracle Express Server, are now integrated into the database server. Existing Oracle Express databases can be migrated to analytic workspaces in the database. The OLAP Option also supports a rich application development environment. Users can build Java applications using the standard JDeveloper tool. They can use OLAP APIs to access the multidimensional data and use reusable components known as BI Beans to create sophisticated graphical user interfaces. Oracle Warehouse Builder can be used to generate metadata required by OLAP APIs, and the multidimensional data can be queried using tools such as Discoverer—just like relational tables.

Most of the features described in this book deal with relational storage and queries. In this chapter, we will mostly focus on the multidimensional analysis model provided by the Oracle OLAP option.

15.2 Oracle OLAP Architecture

Oracle Database 10*g* OLAP provides a very flexible architecture for multidimensional analysis. It consists of the following components, shown in Figure 15.1.

- Analytic Workspaces for multidimensional storage
- OLAP Catalog to define multidimensional logical metadata model
- OLAP Analysis Engine to perform calculations
- Access to multidimensional data using:
    - OLAP DML command language
    - SQL Table functions
- Tools
    - Analytic Workspace Manager
    - Oracle Enterprise Manager
- Application Development Framework
    - Analytic Workspace Java API
    - OLAP Java API
    - DBMS_AW PL/SQL API
    - BI Beans in JDeveloper

Figure 15.1   *Oracle Database 10g OLAP Architecture*

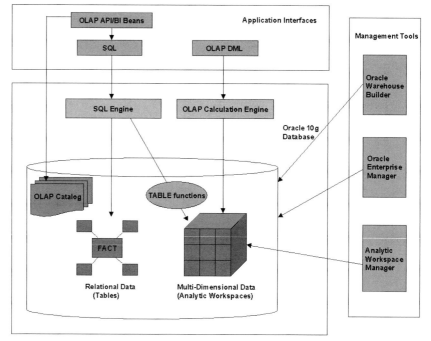

Analytic Workspaces: An analytic workspace is an entity that aggregates and stores data in a multidimensional format within the Oracle database. The relational counterpart to an analytic workspace is a materialized view or summary table, which is used to preaggregate data in a relational table. Unlike other database objects, an analytic workspace can be permanent or temporary for the duration of analysis. You may choose to use an analytic workspace when you need to use the advanced analytical capabilities of the OLAP calculation engine. Oracle Database 10*g* provides a tool known as **Analytic Workspace Manager**, which can be used to define, populate, and refresh analytic workspaces.

OLAP Analysis Engine: The OLAP Analysis Engine is a multidimensional calculation engine running inside the Oracle database server. It operates on data stored in analytic workspaces. It complements the analytical features provided by SQL with various calculation capabilities, such as forecasting, allocation, and modeling.

You can access analytic workspaces using either OLAP DML or SQL.

OLAP DML: The OLAP DML is powerful programming language that is used to load, manipulate and query data in analytic workspaces. It provides several operations such as aggregation, forecasting, regression analysis, numerical calculations and time-series manipulation. OLAP DML can be issued using a tool similar to SQL*Plus, known as the OLAP Worksheet. You can also issue OLAP DML using the Java OLAP API or the DBMS_AW PL/SQL package. If you are familiar with Oracle Express, you may recognize that OLAP DML is very similar to the SPL language. In fact, existing programs written for Oracle Express should work with only minor changes in OLAP DML.

SQL Access to Analytic Workspaces: Oracle provides a mechanism to access analytic workspace with SQL, using Table functions. This makes Oracle OLAP accessible to users who are unfamiliar with OLAP DML but are familiar with SQL. In Chapter 5, we saw how table functions can be used to perform various ETL functions for your data warehouse. A table function can perform any kind of computation underneath but finally produces its output as a set of rows. Hence, it can be used in SQL queries as if it were a table in a database. Because of this capability, if you have a table function that encapsulates the OLAP DML commands used to access the analytic workspace, SQL applications can then use it like a table in a query. Oracle provides a table function called OLAP_TABLE, which provides access to an analytic workspace.

While the analytic workspaces provide the physical storage model for multidimensional data, the OLAP Catalog describes the logical model for the multidimensional data.

OLAP Catalog: The OLAP Catalog imposes a multi-dimensional logical model on data in a relational schema. The OLAP Catalog consists of metadata entities like dimensions, levels, hierarchies, attributes, measures and cubes. Note that the underlying data may be stored in actual relational tables i.e. in a star or a snowflake schema, or alternatively, it may be stored in analytic workspaces and mapped into relational views using SQL. The model provided by the OLAP Catalog allows OLAP applications to access multi-dimensional data and relational data in a uniform fashion. The Analytic Workspace Manager tool uses this metadata to create an analytic workspace from a relational star schema.

Finally, Oracle OLAP provides a very sophisticated application development framework.

Programming APIs: As mentioned earlier, you can use OLAP DML, SQL, or PL/SQL (DBMS_AW package) to access the multidimensional data. Oracle also supports the OLAP API, which is a set of Java programming interfaces for OLAP. The OLAP API allows application developers to write programs to perform calculations and multidimensional selection and navigation through the data. Since it is Java based, the OLAP API provides a portable, object-oriented application development framework for OLAP applications. The objects being manipulated by OLAP API must first be defined in the OLAP Catalog. Java APIs are also available to define analytic workspaces.

UI Components: BI Beans are reusable components specially designed for rapid development of OLAP applications. You can create BI Beans using simple wizards in JDeveloper and store them persistently in the database itself. BI Beans can perform various operations, such as connecting to a database, forming analytical calculations, and displaying them in various graphical and tabular formats. These can then be used in Java or JSP applications that need analytical capabilities. BI Beans use the OLAP APIs to access data.

We will now discuss each of these components in detail. We will start by describing various concepts in the multidimensional storage model provided by analytic workspaces. In the subsequent sections, we will delve into the details of defining the metadata model, creating analytic workspaces, and querying them.

15.3 Analytic Workspaces

Analytic workspaces allow you to store data in a multidimensional form. As with relational tables, an analytic workspace is owned by a specific schema and uses an Oracle tablespace for storage. You can use analytic workspaces to store data that is used in calculations such as forecasting and allocations.

Hint: Existing Oracle Express databases can also be migrated into analytic workspaces in the Oracle database.

Analytic workspaces can be persistent or temporary, depending on your needs. If you need to perform a calculation but do not need to store the results, you can discard changes done within the analytic workspace at the end of the session. A temporary analytic workspace is often used for what-if analysis, where you want to try different hypothetical scenarios but not make all the changes persistent. Unlike relational tables, where changes done by DDL, such as adding a column, are automatically made visible throughout the database, all changes done within the analytic workspace are local to your session unless explicitly committed.

Now, let us look at the physical storage model used by analytic workspaces and see how it differs from the relational model.

15.3.1   The Multidimensional Model

Throughout this book, we have described how a data warehouse can be created and managed using relational tables. In this relational world, data is typically stored in a star or snowflake schema. The fact table stores various measures and quantities that you want to analyze with respect to each dimension. Dimension tables store the associated data about each dimension. To perform a calculation, queries must join the fact and dimension tables using appropriate predicates. The SQL Dimension object described in Chapter 8 can be used to define the hierarchical relationships between various columns in the dimension tables.

In a multidimensional format, such as an analytic workspace, there are no tables or columns. Instead, there are entities known as dimensions, relations, and variables.

Dimension: A dimension in the multi-dimensional model is simply a list of values. For instance, a city dimension may consist of the values Boston, London, and San Francisco. A geography dimension may consist of the values World, United States, Massachusetts, New Hamphire, UK, and London. Unlike a SQL dimension object, which defines a hierarchy within one or more dimension tables, a dimension in a multidimensional model does not itself imply any relationships. To specify any relationships between various values in the dimension, you must create a relation.

Relation: A relation stores the correspondence between a value in one dimension to another value in the same or another dimension. Note that relations can also declare a relationship between two values in the same dimension—these are called self-relations. Relations can be used to describe hierarchies in a multidimensional world.

You can think of the relationship defined by a relation as a **parent-child** dimension table in a relational schema, as illustrated by Figure 15.2. On the left is a typical geography dimension table, used in a relational star schema, where each level is stored in a separate column. This is sometimes referred to as a **level-based** dimension table. For instance, you have columns corresponding to the city, state, and region levels.

On the right is a parent-child dimension table, where all values are stored in the child column and parent column has the corresponding parent value. For example, suppose the child column contains values such as Bos-

Figure 15.2   *Level-based versus Parent-Child Dimension Tables*

City	State	Region
Boston	MA	NorthEast
Waltham	MA	NorthEast
Burlington	VT	NorthEast
San Francisco	CA	West
San Jose	CA	West
...		

Child	Parent
Boston	MA
Waltham	MA
Burlington	VT
San Francisco	CA
San Jose	CA
MA	NorthEast
VT	NorthEast
CA	West
NorthEast	N/A
...	

Level-based Dimension   **Parent-Child Dimension**

ton, San Francisco, and MA. For each value in the child column, there will be a corresponding value in the parent column. For instance, for the child value Boston, the parent value is MA. Unlike a level-based dimension table, where higher-level values are repeated for every lowest-level value, in a parent-child dimension every relationship is stored exactly once. This ensures that the dimension data is automatically validated.

Variable: A variable is used to store data and is equivalent to a fact table in a relational star schema. A variable is defined with respect to a specific set of dimensions. Figure 15.3 shows a *conceptual* version of how data is stored in a variable. In this example, the sales variable is dimensioned by geography and time. You can query the value of a variable for any values of the dimensions it is defined against. For instance, the sales value for United States for the year 2002 is $3,102. Notice that this is quite like a spreadsheet, where you can retrieve the value of any cell by simply specifying the row and column.

Figure 15.3 *Conceptual version of a Variable*

Sales Variable by Geography, Time

	Q1-2002	Q2-2002	Q3-2002	Q4-2002	YR-2002
BOSTON	132	144	111	555	942
WALTHAM	233	321	144	123	821
SAN FRANCISCO	164	135	153	145	597
SAN JOSE	234	134	142	232	742
MA	365	465	255	678	1763
CA	398	269	295	377	1339
UNITED STATES	763	734	550	1055	3102

Time Dimension

Geography Dimension

Sales (San Jose, Q4-2002) = 232

Sales (United States, YR-2002)= 3102

There are several advantages of this multidimensional storage format:

- It enforces referential integrity. For instance, if a variable is defined along customer and time dimension, every cell of the data will have some unique value of a customer and time. Also, relationships between dimension values are stored exactly once, and hence you will not end up with inconsistent data such as Boston, MA and Boston, CA.

- There is an implicit ordering between rows in the dimension that is defined at creation. This is unlike SQL, where you must explicitly add ORDER BY clauses to return values in a certain order.

- Users don't need to specify how to join the fact and dimension tables to get their answers. They can simply ask to report the variable for any dimension values, as in a spreadsheet. However, unlike a spreadsheet, you are not restricted to two dimensions.

- The data is presented to the application as "fully solved." Once the DBA sets up the analytic workspace with various calculations, the application users do not have to describe *how* to perform a calculation as part of the query. They just have to indicate *which* of the available calculations they would like and the calculation engine will take care of the details of computing it. The calculation may be a complex analytical function, a formula, or an aggregate. The data may be precomputed for performance or calculated on the fly; however, the application users do not have to know these details, they simply get the results they ask for.

15.3.2 Creating Analytic Workspaces

At this point, you may be wondering what is involved in creating and querying these analytic workspaces. You can use OLAP DML to create dimensions and variables and to load data into the analytic workspace. However, if you would like to use any of Oracle's tools, such as OLAP API or BI Beans, to manipulate data stored in an analytic workspace, you need to satisfy the following requirements:

- You must have a logical model defined in the OLAP Catalog.

- The analytic workspace itself must conform to a certain format known as the **database standard form**.

Sounds like quite a handful! Fortunately, in cases where the data is stored in a relational star or a snowflake schema, such as as the ones described in this book, a simple wizard in Oracle Enterprise Manager can be used to populate the OLAP Catalog from the relational schema. Once you have defined a relational cube in the OLAP Catalog, a wizard in the Analytic Workspace Manager can be used to build the analytic workspace in the standard form.

Hint: The database standard form for an analytic workspace is very complex, and manually creating the analytic workspace elements can be extremely tedious and error prone. It is strongly recommended that you use Analytic Workspace Manager and Oracle Enterprise Manager at least as starting points.

Oracle Database 10*g* also provides Java APIs to create analytic workspaces. These APIs do not require any preexisting metadata and do not require knowledge of OLAP DML. Due to limitations of space, we will not be discussing these APIs in this book.

In the next sections, as we discuss various other components of Oracle OLAP, we will walk you through the process of defining an analytic workspace from the EASYDW star schema. In section 15.4, we will describe the logical model defined in the OLAP Catalog and populate it using Oracle

Enterprise Manager. Then, in section 15.5, we will use the Analytic Workspace Manager tool to create and populate a sample analytic workspace in the standard form. Along the way, we will highlight any assumptions or restrictions imposed by these tools.

Finally, in section 15.6, we will give a brief tour of OLAP DML and illustrate some calculations using the standard form analytic workspace we created. This should help you understand how the multidimensional model can be used to perform analysis instead of, or to complement, the SQL features we have discussed elsewhere in this book.

15.4 The OLAP Catalog

The OLAP Catalog stores the *metadata* to specify the logical model for your data. The purpose of defining this metadata is to allow applications to access data using OLAP API or BI Beans. These APIs require that the data is accessible relationally using SQL and require a certain logical metadata model, which we will describe shortly.

The OLAP Catalog metadata can be used regardless of whether your data is in a relational or multi-dimensional format.

- If you have a relational schema, the OLAP Catalog simply defines a logical metadata model for this data, as is required by OLAP API and BI Beans. This metadata can also be used to generate a standard form analytic workspace using the Analytic Workspace Manager tool, which we will discuss in section 15.5.

- Alternatively, if you have data in a standard form analytic workspace, you can define relational views on top of the multi-dimensional data. The OLAP Catalog can then be defined on these relational views, which can then be used by the OLAP API to access the analytic workspace using SQL. The Analytic Workspace Manager provides wizards to automatically create the required relational views and OLAP Catalog metadata, to enable the analytic workspace for the OLAP API.

Thus, once the requisite metadata has been defined, you can use SQL, OLAP API, or BI Beans to access the data, regardless of whether the data is actually stored in a relational or multidimensional format.

The logical model provided by the OLAP Catalog consists of the following entities:

- **Dimensions:** Dimensions are used to express relationships, such as hierarchies, in your data. Dimensions consist of levels, hierarchies, and level attributes. Note that the SQL dimension object described in Chapter 8 is part of but *not* the complete metadata for an OLAP Catalog dimension. Also note that the dimension in the OLAP Catalog is not the same as the dimension described in section 15.3.1, which was used to store a list of values in the multidimensional storage format.

- **Measures:** A measure is a quantity that will be used in calculations, such as purchase price or cost.

- **Measure folders:** A measure folder, also known as a measure catalog, is a convenient place to keep related measures together.

- **Cube:** A cube defines how measures will be aggregated across one or more dimensions. In relational terms, it defines how to join your fact and dimension tables. A cube also specifies which hierarchies in the dimensions will be used to compute aggregations.

In the next section, we will discuss how to define OLAP metadata for a relational schema.

15.4.1 Defining OLAP Metadata for a Relational Schema

OLAP metadata can be defined from a relational schema in two ways:

- Using the CWM_OLAP_* and CWM2_OLAP_* packages
- Using Oracle Enterprise Manager or Oracle Warehouse Builder tools

The CWM_OLAP_* packages (henceforth referred to as CWM1) are APIs that correspond to the first version of the Common Warehouse Metadata model, also known as CWMLite. This model supports traditional dimension tables, as defined in a star or a snowflake schema. In order to use CWM1 your relational schema must satisfy the following conditions:

- The dimension table must be level-based and not parent-child (see Figure 15.2)

- If there are multiple hierarchies in a dimension, they must all start with the same base level. Hierarchies where this is not the case, are called **ragged hierarchies**.

- Dimension levels cannot have nulls. Hierarchies where levels can be nulls are called **skip-level** hierarchies.

- The fact table can only have data at the lowest level of the hierarchy. Fact tables where detail data and aggregated data are stored in the same table, known as **embedded-total** fact tables, are not supported.

A dimension defined using CWM1 in the OLAP Catalog consists of a SQL Dimension object (described in Chapter 8), with some additional descriptive attributes. Oracle Enterprise Manager also provides a graphical user interface to create CWM1 metadata. If you used Oracle Warehouse Builder to design the relational schema for your data warehouse, you can automatically generate metadata from it, according to the CWM1 specification.

The CWM2_OLAP_* packages (henceforth referred to as CWM2) are the second version of CWM1 and provide advanced features not supported by CWM1. If your relational schema has artifacts such as embedded-total fact tables, parent-child dimensions, ragged hierarchies, same value mapping to different levels in different hierarchies, and null values in level columns, you need to use CWM2. At the time of writing, there is no graphical user interface to create this metadata.

Both CWM1 and CWM2 metadata can be *viewed* in the Analytic Workspace Manager tool.

We will now illustrate the use of Oracle Enterprise Manager to generate OLAP metadata for the EASYDW schema.

Creating OLAP Metadata in Oracle Enterprise Manager

You can access the OLAP functionality in Oracle Enterprise Manager from the *Administration* page (see Chapter 2, Figure 2.16). On this page, in the *Warehouse* section, you will see links to *Cubes*, *OLAP Dimensions*, and *Measures*, which lead to simple wizards to create and edit dimensions, cubes, and measure folders.

We will define a cube containing the customer, product, and time dimensions using this interface. First, we must define the metadata for the dimensions involved in the cube and then specify the measures and the aggregation operators associated with the cube.

Let us start by going to the OLAP Dimensions page and search for dimensions under schema EASYDW, as shown in Figure 15.4. You will see listed here the SQL Dimension objects we had defined for use with query rewrite in Chapter 9.

Figure 15.4   *Dimensions in Oracle Enterprise Manager*

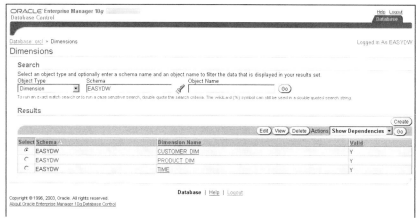

To generate the OLAP metadata for a dimension, select the dimension and click on the *Edit* button. You will get a page similar to the one we discussed in Chapter 8 (Figure 8.5) when creating a dimension—with tabs such as *General, Levels, Hierarchies*, and *Attributes*. The last tab is *OLAP Options* and, when you click on it, you will see a page similar to the one in Figure 15.5. In this figure, we have added OLAP options for the time dimension.

You should now fill in all the descriptive fields on this page, because OLAP API and BI Beans use this information to display various elements related to the dimension. If you press the *Show SQL* button, you can see the corresponding CWM API calls, as shown in Figure 15.6.

Returning to Figure 15.5, once you press *Apply*, the CWM metadata will be created. Be assured that your existing SQL dimension object will not be harmed in any way by doing this. Similarly, we can define OLAP metadata for the other two dimensions, Customer and Product. You can now use these dimensions to define your cube objects, as discussed next.

Figure 15.5 *Editing OLAP Options for a Dimension*

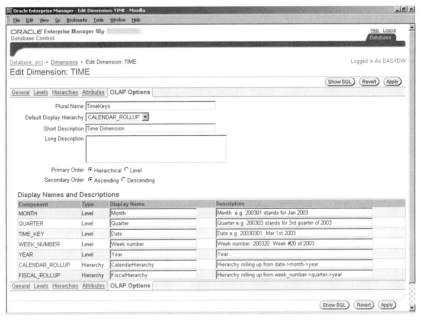

Figure 15.6 *CWM Metadata for a Dimension*

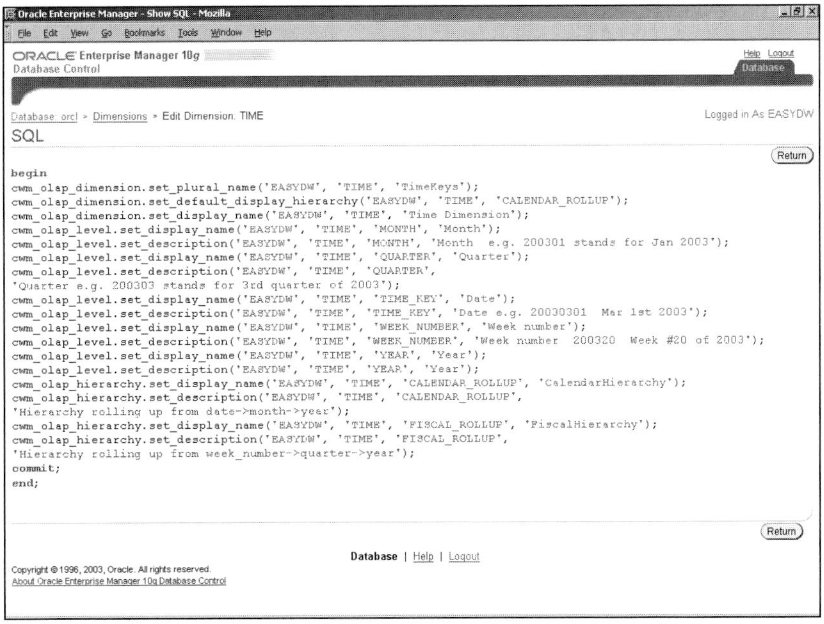

The cube is a metadata object that defines a relationship between the dimensions and measures. From the *Administration* page (Chapter 2, Figure 2.16), click on the *Cubes* link to get a page similar to Figure 15.4, except that the Object Type is Cubes. If you press the *Create* button, you will get the page shown in Figure 15.7. Here, you must specify a name for the cube and the schema where it should reside. You must also indicate the table that would serve as the fact table for this cube. In our example, we are creating the EASYDW_SALES cube using the PURCHASES fact table.

Figure 15.7   *Creating a Cube in Oracle Enterprise Manager*

Next, you must click on the *Dimensions* link and add dimensions to the cube, as shown in Figure 15.8. A cube must have at least one dimension. When adding a dimension to the cube, you must specify how the dimension table joins to the fact table, as well as the default hierarchy to be used to aggregate data along this dimension. In order to do so, after you have entered the dimension name, click the *Populate Property* button to see the available hierarchies and join key columns, from which you can then choose the ones for the cube. In our example, we have chosen the time dimension, with the hierarchy being CALENDAR_ROLLUP and the join keys being TIME_KEY columns in the dimension and fact tables.

Figure 15.8 *Adding Dimensions to a Cube*

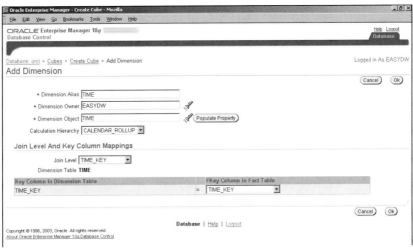

Clicking *OK* takes you back to the *Create Cube* page, where you will now see your new dimension in the list. For our example, assume that we have added two more dimensions, CUSTOMER_DIM, and PRODUCT_ DIM to the cube. The next step is to define measures—click the *Measures* tab and on the next screen click the *Add* button; you will see the screen as shown in Figure 15.9. This step is easy—you just need to pick the fact table columns that you want to use for analysis.

Figure 15.9 *Add a Measure to the Cube*

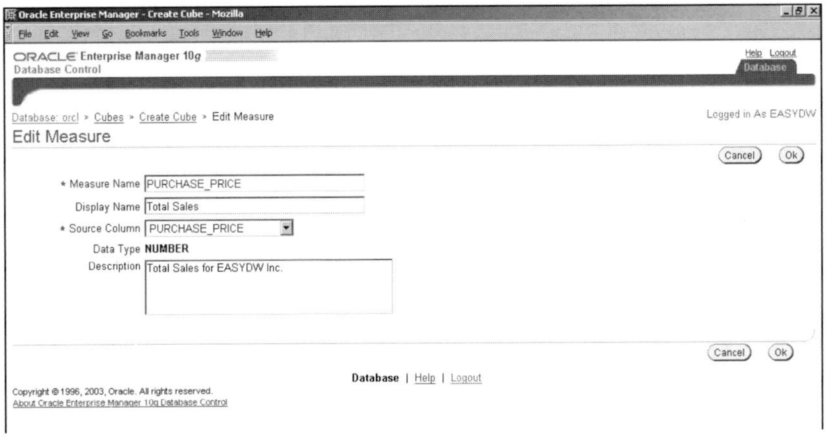

Click *OK* to return to the *Create Cube* page. The final step is to choose the aggregations you would like to perform in this cube—click the *Aggregation* tab and you will see the page shown in Figure 15.10. Along each dimension, you can pick the aggregation operator from a variety of operators.

Figure 15.10   *Defining Aggregations for the Cube*

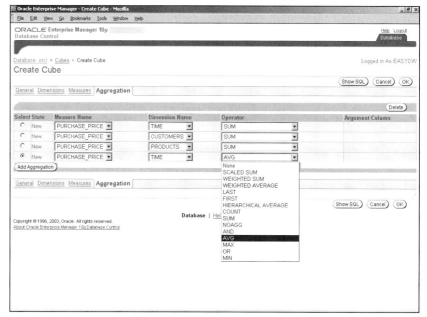

As with the dimensions, the *Show SQL* button allows you to see the CWM APIs to create the cube. Once you have filled in all the information, press *OK* to create the cube.

Note that none of these operations populates data in the cube. They only define which aggregates are available to an application.

15.4.2   OLAP Metadata Views and Validation

The OLAP metadata can be viewed in several views, such as ALL_OLAP2_CUBES, ALL_OLAP2_DIMENSIONS, and so on.

Once you have defined OLAP metadata created using either Enterprise Manager or CWM2 APIs, it is advisable to validate it and verify access to it. This ensures that the metadata definition is consistent with the underlying schema (i.e., all the tables and columns that the cube refers to exist and the user who created the metadata has access to the data in these tables).

You can check whether a cube or dimension is valid or not in the catalog view, ALL_OLAP2_CUBES, as follows. The INVALID column can have a value Y, N, or O. The value N means that the all the tables, columns, dimension levels, and so on referenced by the cube are present. The value O means that the cube is valid for use by the OLAP API, which means that all additional metadata required by the OLAP API is present. Otherwise, the cube is invalid, which is indicated by the value Y.

```
SELECT  CUBE_NAME,  INVALID FROM  ALL_OLAP2_CUBES;

OWNER    CUBE_NAME      INVALID
-----    ------------   -------
EASYDW   EASYDW_SALES   O
```

To validate a cube you must call the CWM2 APIs, as follows, which will validate all underlying dimensions and measures as well. Note that the CWM2_OLAP_MANAGER.SET_ECHO_ON procedure is necessary in order to see the detailed output.

```
set serveroutput on size 99999
EXECUTE cwm2_olap_manager.set_echo_on;
EXECUTE cwm2_olap_validate.validate_cube
        ('EASYDW','EASYDW_SALES','default','yes');
```

The output will indicate if any of the elements of the cube are invalid and the reason will be reported in the COMMENT column (not shown here for lack of space). The third parameter can be default or OLAP API, which will do the basic checks for table and columns or perform additional checks required for using OLAP API. The last parameter indicates whether or not to generate a verbose report.

```
Validate Cube: EASYDW.EASYDW_SALES
Type of Validation: DEFAULT    Verbose Report: YES
Validating Cube Metadata in OLAP Catalog 1
Date: 2004 MAY 21  Time: 22:46:55  User: EASYDW  030922

ENTITY TYPE              ENTITY NAME             STATUS   COMMENT
Cube                     EASYDW.EASYDW_SALES     VALID    ...
  Dimension              EASYDW.CUSTOMER_DIM     VALID
    Hierarchy            CUSTOMER_ZONE           VALID
      Level              CUSTOMER                VALID
        LevelMap                                 VALID
        LevelParentMap                           VALID
```

```
...
  FactTable              EASYDW.PURCHASES         VALID
    FactLevel            (EASYDW.CUSTOMER_DIM)    VALID
    FactLevel            (EASYDW.PRODUCT_DIM)     VALID
    FactLevel            (EASYDW.TIME)            VALID
    FactMeasure          PURCHASE_PRICE           VALID
      FactMeasureMap                              VALID
...
```

If you plan to use OLAP API or BI Beans directly against the relational schema, you must call the following procedure as the final step after defining the OLAP metadata.

```
EXECUTE CWM2_OLAP_METADATA_REFRESH.MR_REFRESH;
```

If you use analytical workspaces, you must instead call the following procedure.

```
EXECUTE CWM2_OLAP_METADATA_REFRESH.MR_AC_REFRESH;
```

These procedures are required to populate some underlying cached metadata tables, which are optimized for queries used by the OLAP API.

Finally, you need to verify that the user who created the cube actually has the privileges required to access the underlying tables by using the procedure CWM2_OLAP_VERIFY_ACCESS.VERIFY_CUBE_ACCESS. The parameters of this procedure are the same as those of the VALIDATE_ CUBE procedure.

```
set serveroutput on size 99999
EXECUTE cwm2_olap_manager.set_echo_on;
EXECUTE CWM2_OLAP_VERIFY_ACCESS.VERIFY_CUBE_ACCESS
        ('EASYDW', 'EASYDW_SALES', 'DEFAULT', 'NO');
```

The output of this procedure will appear as follows. Any problems with access are reported in the COMMENT column.

```
Verify_Cube_Access v_Select_Any_Table:1

***** Verifying User EASYDW access to cube "EASYDW.EASYDW_SALES"
030922.
***** STEP 1:  Validate the Cube Metadata.

Validate Cube: EASYDW.EASYDW_SALES    Type of Validation: DEFAULT
Verbose Report: NO
```

```
Validating Cube Metadata in OLAP Catalog 1
Date: 2004 JULY 02  Time: 01:09:19  User: EASYDW  030922


ENTITY TYPEENTITY NAME  STATUS    COMMENT
Cube         EASYDW.EASYDW_SALES    VALID


...


***** STEP 2:  Verify the Cached Metadata.
***** STEP 3:  Verify Owner.Table.Column access.

***** Validate_Access version 030922 has not found any condition
that would prevent
***** User EASYDW from accessing Cube "EASYDW.EASYDW_SALES".
```

Note that the procedure will also verify access to the cached metadata created for the OLAP API.

Hint: Always validate the OLAP metadata and refresh the metadata tables after creating or making any changes to it. If it is invalid, the OLAP API and tools may not be able to access the metadata.

Now that we have created the logical model, you can use the Analytic Workspace Manager tool, described next, to create an analytic workspace for this cube.

15.5 The Analytic Workspace Manager

The Analytic Workspace Manager is a standalone Java application to create, manage, and refresh analytic workspaces. The analytic workspace created by this tool is in a standard form, as required by the Oracle tools. You can also use this tool to enable the analytic workspace for use by OLAP API, BI Beans, and Discoverer.

Hint: The Analytic Workspace Manager application is available on the Oracle Database 10*g* Client CD. It is not part of Enterprise Manager.

The Analytic Workspace Manager application has two views of the analytic workspaces: the OLAP Catalog View and the Object View. You can switch between the two from the *View* menu. The *OLAP Catalog View* shown in Figure 15.11, shows you the OLAP metadata—namely, the

Figure 15.11   *Analytic Workspace Manager—OLAP Catalog View*

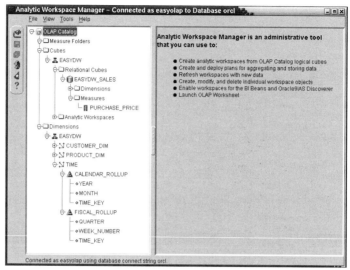

dimensions, cubes, and measures that were created using either the CWM1 or CWM2 APIs (or Oracle Enterprise Manager). For instance, in Figure 15.11, we have expanded the view to show the EASYDW_SALES cube and the various dimensions we created earlier.

Figure 15.12   *Analytic Workspace Manager—Object View*

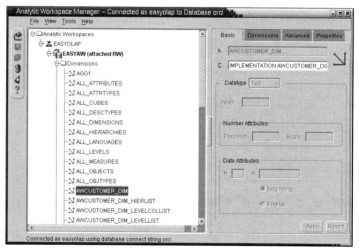

The *Object View*, illustrated in Figure 15.12, allows you to browse through various entities in the analytic workspace—namely, dimensions, variables, relations, and so on which we discussed previously.

This is a very nifty tool, because the standard form workspace, which we will create shortly, consists of a large number of these entities and it can be very difficult to remember their names.

15.5.1 The Create Analytic Workspace Wizard

The Analytic Workspace Manager provides a wizard to create an analytic workspace from a relational cube. You can launch the wizard from the *Tools* menu, shown in Figure 15.11. We will now use this wizard to create an analytic workspace for the EASYDW_SALES cube.

When you launch the wizard, after an introductory page (not shown here), you will see the screen shown in Figure 15.13, where you will be asked to name the analytic workspace, provide a schema where the workspace should be placed, and the tablespace used for storage. It is recommended that you use a different schema to store the analytic workspaces than that used for your relational tables to avoid confusion and potential naming conflicts. The schema owning the analytic workspace must have been granted the OLAP_USER privilege and must have access to the relational tables underlying the cube. Let us assume we have created a new schema, EASYOLAP, and a tablespace, EASYOLAP_AW_DEFAULT, which we will provide here.

Figure 15.13 *Create Analytic Workspace Wizard—Naming the Analytic Workspace*

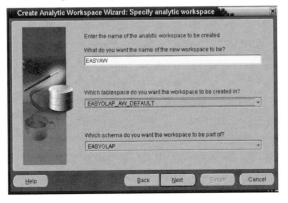

When you click the *Next* button, you will be asked to choose the Cube used to build the analytic workspace, as shown in Figure 15.14.

The next step, shown in Figure 15.15, is to decide whether you would like to load data into the analytic workspace right away or later. Note that

Figure 15.14   *Choosing a Cube for the Analytic Workspace*

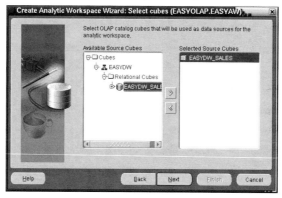

the data population stage can take significant time, and in a production system you may want to schedule this at a later time, such as in load window. The Analytic Workspace Manager also includes a wizard to refresh the analytic workspace, discussed in section 15.5.2.

Figure 15.15   *Choosing Build Options for the Analytic Workspace*

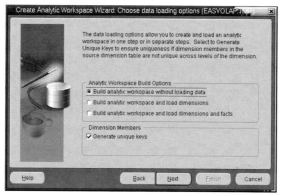

The other option in Figure 15.15 is to generate unique keys for dimension members. Recall that in the multidimensional model, a dimension is just a list of values. So the same value can appear at different levels of the relational dimension table—for example, the name New York could signify either the city or the state. In this case, you may need to qualify the dimension value to distinguish the two levels. If you check the box, the wizard will automatically do this for you.

The next step, shown in Figure 15.16, is to choose an optional naming prefix for the generated objects. In our example, the dimension object PRODUCT_DIM will translate into the dimension AWPRODUCT_DIM in the analytic workspace. It is useful to follow such a naming convention to avoid confusion between relational and multidimensional entities.

Figure 15.16   *Advanced Storage and Naming Options*

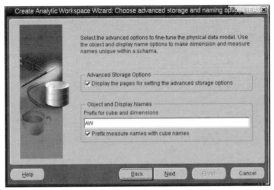

The other option in Figure 15.16 is to decide if you need to change the default storage settings. We will come back to this option in a bit, but for now we will leave it unchecked and accept the d efaults.

Figure 15.17   *Save Analytic Workspace Creation Script to a File*

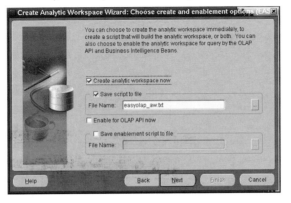

Next, as shown in Figure 15.17, you can decide if you would like to create the analytic workspace immediately or save the script for future use into a file. The script consists of various DBMS_AWM PL/SQL package calls. It can be edited if necessary and executed later in SQL*Plus. You can also choose to enable the analytic workspace for use by OLAP API. This will create several relational views on top of the analytic workspace elements. You can also do this later from the menu.

Figure 15.18   *Analytic Workspace Creation in Progress*

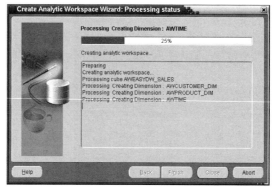

The next screen (not shown here) will give you a chance to review all the options you have chosen. You can then click the *Finish* button and the wizard will start creating the analytic workspace elements, as shown in Figure 15.18.

Figure 15.19   *Analytic Workspace in OLAP Catalog View*

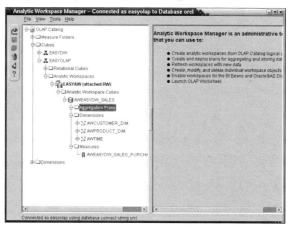

This analytic workspace is now visible under the EASYOLAP schema in the OLAP Catalog View, as shown in Figure 15.19.

Setting Storage Options for the Analytic Workspace

Recall that in Figure 15.16, we saw an option to set advanced storage options for the analytic workspace. By default, in an analytic workspace, a variable stores values for every combination of its dimension values. To understand this, recall the conceptual version of a variable that we saw in Figure 15.3. Every *cell* corresponds to one combination of dimension values. Now, typically, your data may not have entries for every combination—for instance, not every customer buys every product every single day! So we will have a lot of cells with no values, which is a huge waste of space. This problem is addressed by creating a **composite** dimension. A variable that is dimensioned by a composite dimension will only store values for those combinations of dimension values where data actually exists. This can significantly reduce the space requirements for your analytic workspace.

If there exists data for most values of a dimension, the dimension is said to be **dense**—otherwise, it is called **sparse**. By default, the analytic workspace creation wizard assumes that the time dimension is dense and the data across the remaining dimensions is somewhat sparse, specifically that around 30 percent of the dimension combinations have values. Therefore, by default, the wizard creates a composite dimension, which includes all dimensions except the time dimension. If your data does not satisfy these default sparseness assumptions, you can change the default composite dimension or create your own custom composite dimensions.

Hint: For the wizard to detect that a dimension is the time dimension, you would have had to mark it as a time dimension when you created the dimension in the OLAP Catalog.

If you check the box in Figure 15.16, you will get the screen shown in Figure 15.20. Note that composites do add some overhead in processing the queries against the data and hence should not be created unless the data is indeed sparse.

Figure 15.20   *Creating a Composite Dimension*

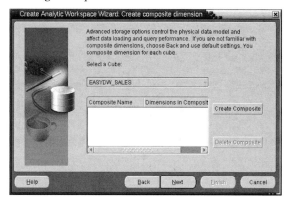

If you press the *Create Composite* button, you will be taken to the screen shown in Figure 15.21. Now you must give a name to the composite dimension and choose which base dimensions to add to the composite. Typically, you should exclude dense dimensions such as TIME, from the composite.

Figure 15.21   *Adding Dimensions to a Composite*

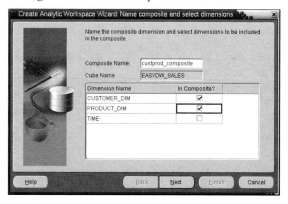

The advanced settings pages also allow you to specify the order of the dimensions for the variable. The order is important, because it affects how data is stored on disk—correctly ordering dimensions within a composite ensures that all data for one value of the composite is clustered together and hence will improve data access performance. Usually, you would want the denser dimensions ahead of the composite and sparser dimensions. For example, if you have transactions for every single day, then the TIME dimension is a dense dimension and should be placed first. Further, on any given day, you would probably have transactions involving most of your products; however, it is less likely you would have transactions involving all your customers. So in this case the product dimension is *denser* than the customer dimension and should be placed before customers within the composite. The next screen, shown in Figure 15.22, allows you to order the dimensions within the composite.

Figure 15.22   *Specifying Order of Dimensions in a Composite*

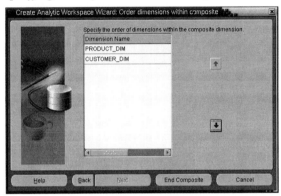

When you press the *End Composite* button, your composite will show up in the list in Figure 15.20.

You can choose to group your base dimensions into as many composite dimensions as required by the characteristics of your data. For example, suppose you had five dimensions TIME, PRODUCT, CUSTOMER, GEOGRAPHY, and PROMOTIONS. You may decide to group the CUSTOMER and GEOGRAPHY dimensions together into one composite; since you don't have all combinations of customers and geographies, the composite will be smaller because it only stores the relevant combinations. Similarly, you can group PRODUCT and PROMOTIONS together into another composite. On the other hand, suppose you wanted to group PRODUCT and GEOGRAPHY into one composite—if you find that you do indeed have transactions for every combination of the two, it would not be advisable to group them into a composite dimension.

Once you have defined all the composites, when you press the *Next* button you can now choose the order between various composites and remaining base dimensions, as shown in Figure 15.23. Recall that you must decide the order based on which dimension or composite is denser. In this example, we have placed the denser TIME dimension before the composite. You can also set segment sizes for their storage. In this example, we have specified a segment size of 5KB for the TIME dimension and 10MB for the larger composite dimension.

Figure 15.23   *Specifying Segment Sizes and Dimension Order*

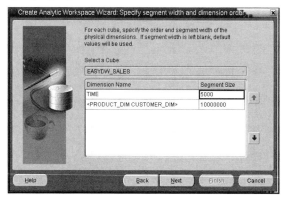

Once you have done this, you will be back into the normal flow of the wizard, starting in Figure 15.17.

Coming back to the OLAP Catalog View in Figure 15.19, if you right-click on the analytic workspace EASYAW, you will get a menu with several options, as shown in Figure 15.24. From this menu, you can populate the analytic workspace with data from the source tables, which we will discuss next. You can also enable the analytic workspace for Discoverer, OLAP API, and BI Beans, which will be discussed in section 15.5.4.

15.5.2   Refreshing the Analytic Workspace

The Analytic Workspace Manager has a wizard to refresh the analytic workspace from its relational source tables. You must refresh the cubes and dimensions every time there is a change to the source tables that you would like to be visible to the analytic workspace. Note, however, that the refresh process is not incremental and so can take a significant amount of time.

To bring up the refresh wizard, in Figure 15.24, select the *Refresh Analytic Workspace Using Wizard* option. After the introductory page, you will get the screen shown in Figure 15.25, where you must choose the cube (or cubes) you would like to refresh.

Figure 15.24   *Analytic Workspace—Right-Click Menu*

The next step is to choose which dimensions you would like refreshed. In Figure 15.26, we are refreshing all three dimensions. However, note that after initially populating the analytic workspace, you do not need to refresh

Figure 15.25   *Refreshing an Analytic Workspace—Choosing Cubes*

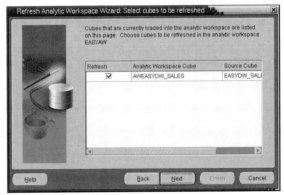

Figure 15.26   *Refreshing an Analytic Workspace—Choosing Dimensions*

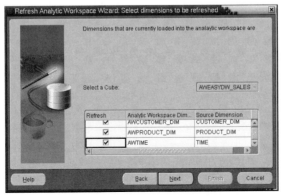

dimensions unless the underlying dimension tables have changed, which, depending on your business, may be infrequent.

The next button will bring you to a screen (not shown here) similar to Figure 15.17, where you can choose a file to save the script to, if you want to make any customizations to it or execute it later. If you would like the tool to refresh immediately, click the *Next* button and you will get the screen shown in Figure 15.27, where you can see the refresh of the analytic workspace in progress.

Figure 15.27   *Refresh of Analytic Workspace in Progress*

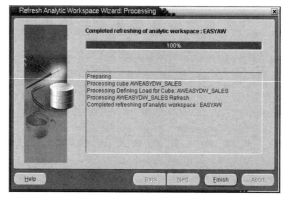

The refresh populates the base-level data into the analytic workspace.

15.5.3   Creating an Aggregation Plan

Once you have populated the analytic workspace, you need to create an aggregation plan for this analytic workspace. An **aggregation plan** or **aggregation map** determines which levels of the dimension hierarchies you would like to store preaggregated in the analytic workspace. Data at all other levels will be computed on the fly when queries request it. Preaggregated data is analogous to materialized views in the relational world and speeds up queries at the cost of storage space. By striking a good balance between which levels you keep aggregated and which ones you compute on the fly, you can obtain optimal performance within the available storage. One common technique is called **skip-level** aggregation, where every other level of the cube is preaggregated. We will illustrate this using the wizard in the Analytic Workspace Manager.

If you right-click on the *Aggregation Plans* node highlighted in Figure 15.19, you will see a popup menu—with one of the options being the wizard to create an aggregation plan. After the customary introduction page, you will be asked to name the aggregation plan (not shown here but assume we have named it AGG1), and then you will see the screen shown in Figure 15.28, where you pick the measures being aggregated.

Figure 15.28 *Aggregation Plan Wizard—Choose the Measures to Aggregate*

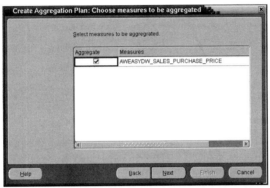

Note that the aggregation operator used by the wizard is the one you pick when you create the measures in the OLAP Catalog metadata for the source data (see Figure 15.10). The default operator is SUM. To change the aggregation operator after creating the aggregation map, you must issue the following PL/SQL API from SQL*Plus. For example, the following procedure shows how you would change the operator for the purchase price measure to average, along the customer dimension.

```
EXECUTE DBMS_AWM.SET_AWCUBEAGG_SPEC_AGGOP('AGG1', 'EASYOLAP',
'EASYAW', 'AWEASYDW_SALES', 'AW_EASYDW_SALES_PURCHASE_PRICE',
'AWCUSTOMER_DIM', 'AVERAGE');
```

The next step, shown in Figure 15.29, allows you to choose which levels should be aggregated for each dimension. In this example, we are doing a skip-level aggregation by aggregating every other level in each hierarchy (i.e., in the fiscal rollup hierarchy we are aggregating at the WEEK_NUMBER level and in the calendar rollup, we are aggregating at the MONTH level).

Once you click the *Next* button, you get to review the choices you have made, as shown in Figure 15.30. Clicking the *Finish* button creates the

Chapter 15

Figure 15.29   *Choosing Which Levels to Aggregate*

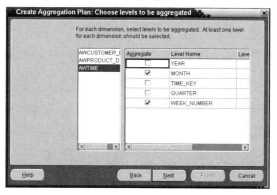

aggregation plan. Note that the aggregates are **not** actually built until you deploy the aggregation plan.

Figure 15.30   *Reviewing the Aggregation Plan*

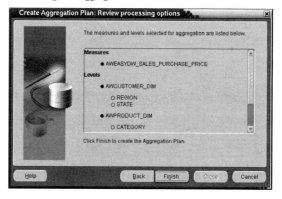

To deploy the aggregation plan, right-click on the desired aggregation plan node in the *OLAP Catalog View* (Figure 15.11) and choose menu item *Deploy aggregation plan using wizard*. This is a simple one-page wizard, which will ask for confirmation and then start the aggregation process to compute the levels specified by the plan.

15.5.4   Analytic Workspace Enablers

The Analytic Workspace Manager provides enablers to adapt the analytic workspace for Discoverer and OLAP API. The enablers are simple wizards and can be launched from the menu shown in Figure 15.24.

Enabling Analytic Workspace for OLAP API and BI Beans

The enabler for OLAP API and BI Beans is very simple (looks like Figure 15.17) and simply produces the required relational views that allow the API to access the multidimensional data. You can also save the script to a file to be executed later.

Enabling Analytic Workspace for Discoverer

In Chapter 13, we saw how to use Discoverer for adhoc querying and reporting for endusers who may not know SQL. You can use Discoverer to query your multi-dimensional data as well. The Analytic Workspace Manager provides a wizard that will adapt the analytic workspace to work with Discoverer.

The wizard produces two items:

■ A SQL script, which contains the relational views that Discoverer needs to access the data in the analytic workspace. This must be run from SQL*Plus.

■ An EEX file, which has an XML script to build an EUL layer. This should be imported into Discoverer using the Administrator, discussed in Chapter 13.

Once you have done this, you can start using Discoverer to access the data.

Hint: If you make any metadata changes to the analytic workspace or the OLAP Catalog, such as adding a new dimension, cube, or measure, you must rerun the enablers.

Now that we have built an analytic workspace in standard form, we will illustrate how analysis can be done on this workspace.

15.6   Querying Analytic Workspaces

Oracle OLAP provides several ways by which an application can access multidimensional data in an analytic workspace. These are shown in Figure 15.31.

The primary language to access analytic workspaces is OLAP DML. OLAP DML is a very simple but powerful language that allows you to

Figure 15.31   *Accessing the Analytic Workspace*

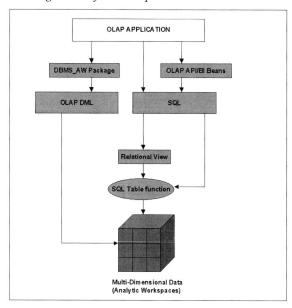

express a variety of calculations and do spreadsheet-like reporting on data stored in an analytic workspace. It provides functions for forecasting, allocation, aggregation, statistical analysis, and financial calculations. You can execute OLAP DML using the OLAP Worksheet application (described in section 15.6.1) or in the Analytic Workspace Manager.

Java programs can access analytic workspaces using the OLAP API, provided that appropriate OLAP Catalog metadata has been defined. SQL applications can access the data by defining Table Functions that convert the data into rows. Relational views may be defined on top of the Table functions, so that the application does not know whether the underlying data is stored in analytic workspaces or tables.

We will now discuss each of these mechanisms in some detail.

15.6.1   OLAP DML

Figure 15.32 shows the OLAP Worksheet application, which is a simple application (like SQL*Plus) that allows you to execute OLAP DML commands. You can launch the OLAP Worksheet from the command line using the standalone executable called wrksht on UNIX or wrksht.bat on Windows. You can also launch it from the *Tools* menu in the Analytic Workspace

Figure 15.32 *OLAP Worksheet in Oracle Enterprise Manager*

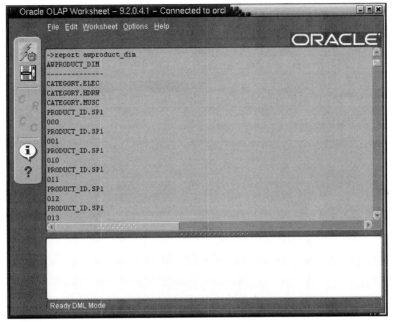

Manager application. You issue the OLAP DML commands in the lower portion of the window and the results appear in the upper portion.

Hint: OLAP DML is very different and completely separate from SQL. However, there is a SQL mode in the OLAP Worksheet, where you can issue regular SQL statements as in SQL*Plus. Conversely, you can issue OLAP DML commands in SQL*Plus using the DBMS_AW package, described in section 15.6.2.

One thing to bear in mind is that OLAP Worksheet is not a graphical user interface to query the analytic workspace. It only allows you to enter OLAP DML commands. In other words, you must know OLAP DML to use this tool. However, the OLAP Worksheet has an excellent help system, which describes all OLAP DML commands with examples. In the next few sections, we will show some examples of using OLAP DML to illustrate the types of calculations that can be done with analytic workspaces. Note that this is not a tutorial on OLAP DML and we will not go into details of OLAP DML syntax.

Attaching to an Analytic Workspace

Before you can access the analytic workspace, you must first attach to an analytic workspace using the AW ATTACH OLAP DML command. The examples in the following sections will use the analytic workspace, named EASYAW, that we created earlier using the Analytic Workspace Manager tool.

Hint: In the following examples, the OLAP DML command is prefixed with the prompt -> and followed by its output.

To attach to the EASYAW analytic workspace, issue the following OLAP DML command in the OLAP Worksheet tool. The **readwrite** keyword allows you to save changes to the workspace:

```
-> aw attach easyaw readwrite
```

Once this command returns successfully, you can then issue other OLAP DML commands to access the analytic workspace—for instance, in Figure 15.32, we are querying a dimension named AWPRODUCT_DIM.

Standard Form Entities

The analytic workspace EASYAW, created using the Analytic Workspace Manager, is in a special format called the database standard form, which consists of several dimensions and relations that describe the structure of the analytic workspace. You can browse through all of these in the *Object View* in the Analytic Workspace Manager, shown earlier in Figure 15.12. To see the definition of any entity in OLAP DML, right-click on it to bring up a popup menu and choose the *View Details* option.

Alternatively, you can issue the FULLDSC command from the OLAP Worksheet. For instance, the AWTIME dimension will appear as follows:

```
-> FULLDSC AWTIME

DEFINE AWTIME DIMENSION TEXT
LD IMPLEMENTATION AWTIME Dimension
PROPERTY 'AW$CLASS' - 'IMPLEMENTATION'
PROPERTY 'AW$CREATEDBY' - 'AW$CREATE'
PROPERTY 'AW$LASTMODIFIED' -'20MAY04_16:23:32'
PROPERTY 'AW$LOGICAL_NAME' - 'AWTIME'
...
```

The various properties are part of the standard form definition and you would not ordinarily need to know the details of these.

Another example of a standard form entity is the variable AWEASYDW_PURCHASE_PRICE_VARIABLE, which was derived from the measure PURCHASE_PRICE in the OLAP Catalog. Its definition is as follows:

```
-> FULLDSC AWEASYDW_SALES_PURCHASE_PRICE_VARIABLE

DEFINE AWEASYDW_SALES_PURCHASE_PRICE_VARIABLE
VARIABLE DECIMAL
<AWEASYDW_SALES_COMPOSITE <AWCUSTOMER_DIM AWPRODUCT_DIM AWTIME>>
```

The items in the angle brackets are the dimensions along which the variable is defined. Notice that a composite dimension has been defined to include all the base dimensions.

We will see more standard form entities in the next section.

Reporting and Aggregating Data with OLAP DML

Previously, we described various entities in an analytic workspace, such as dimensions, relations, and variables. The **REPORT** command can be used to query data in these entities. When reporting data in a dimension, the report command produces the list of values in the dimension. When reporting data in a variable, the report command returns the answer like a spreadsheet, typically with one dimension along the rows and another along the columns.

For example, one of the entities in the EASYAW analytic workspace is the AWTIME dimension. The following command reports the values of the AWTIME dimension. Notice how values at different levels in a hierarchy are all part of the same dimension.

```
-> report awtime

AWTIME
--------------
MONTH.200301
MONTH.200302
...
TIME_KEY.01-JAN-03
TIME_KEY.02-JAN-03
...
YEAR.2003
YEAR.2004
...
```

In the next example, we are querying the AWTIME_LEVELREL relation. This is a standard form relation, which maintains the relationship between each value in a dimension and the level it corresponds to. For example, the value MONTH.200301 corresponds to the MONTH level and the value YEAR.2003 corresponds to the YEAR level.

```
-> report down awtime awtime_levelrel

AWTIME                              AWTIME_LEVELREL
----------------------------        --------------------
MONTH.200301                        MONTH
MONTH.200302                        MONTH
...
TIME_KEY.23-DEC-04                  TIME_KEY
TIME_KEY.24-DEC-04                  TIME_KEY
...
YEAR.2003                           YEAR
YEAR.2004                           YEAR
...
```

At this point, you may find it to be a worthwhile exercise to try similar report commands on some of the other dimensions and relations in the EASYAW analytic workspace. Remember that you can browse the various entities in the Object View of the Analytic Workspace Manager in Figure 15.12.

You can restrict the data you are querying to a specific value or list of values using the **LIMIT** command. This is similar to a selection specified by a WHERE clause in SQL. However, unlike SQL, where the selection is specified on a per query basis, the limit commands in an OLAP DML persist as long as you are attached to the analytic workspace. The next example limits the AWTIME dimension to only those values that have the AWTIME_LEVELREL value of MONTH.

```
-> LIMIT awtime to awtime_levelrel EQ 'MONTH'
-> REPORT awtime

AWTIME
------------------------------
MONTH.200301
MONTH.200302
MONTH.200303
...
```

Now we get to the more interesting part about reporting data from a variable. The OLAP analysis engine automatically figures out the dimensions involved, using the definition of the variable. The keyword **ACROSS** indicates that the AWTIME dimension values will be reported along the row. The engine then automatically places the other dimensions in the report. In the following example, we are reporting sales by state for January through June 2003 for the HDRW product category.

```
-> LIMIT awcustomer_dim TO awcustomer_dim_levelrel EQ 'STATE'
-> LIMIT awtime TO 'MONTH.200301' TO 'MONTH.200303'
-> LIMIT awproduct_dim TO 'CATEGORY.HDRW'
-> REPORT across awtime : aweasydw_sales_purchase_price_variable


AWPRODUCT_DIM: CATEGORY.HDRW
                              AWEASYDW_SALES_PURCHASE_PRICE_VA
                              -------------RIABLE-------------
                              -------------AWTIME-------------
                              MONTH.2003 MONTH.2003 MONTH.2003
AWCUSTOMER_DIM                    01         02         03
---------------------------   ---------- ---------- ----------
STATE.AZ                         501.44     391.75     376.08
STATE.CA                         407.42     391.75     297.73
STATE.CT                         501.44     329.07     407.42
STATE.IL                         454.43     376.08     360.41
...
STATE.OH                         376.08     329.07     329.07
STATE.TX                         376.08     282.06     297.73
STATE.WA                         391.75     360.41     282.06
```

You may be wondering how we were automatically able to generate sales data at a MONTH level without specifying any aggregation functions like SUM, to rollup from the detail data. Recall that in section 15.5.3, after populating the analytic workspace, we created an aggregation plan, which indicated the levels for which to pre-aggregate data in the variable. When creating this plan, we had specified that the MONTH and STATE levels be pre-aggregated and hence we could report along these levels automatically. This is in fact one of the most powerful features of the multi-dimensional model, which differentiates it from SQL.

For levels that were not preaggregated, the aggregation can be performed on the fly by using the **AGGREGATE** function and specifying the aggregation map. In the following example, we are limiting the customer dimension to the REGION level (which was not precomputed), the product dimension to the HDRW category, and the months to January–March 2003; we are using the aggregation plan AWEASYDW_SALES_AGGMAP_AGG1 to compute the total sales.

```
-> LIMIT AWCUSTOMER_DIM TO AWCUSTOMER_DIM_LEVELREL EQ 'REGION'
-> LIMIT AWPRODUCT_DIM TO 'CATEGORY.HDRW'
-> LIMIT AWTIME TO 'MONTH.200301' TO 'MONTH.200303'

-> REPORT across AWTIME:
   AGGREGATE(aweasydw_sales_purchase_price_variable USING
            aweasydw_sales_aggmap_agg1)

AWPRODUCT_DIM: CATEGORY.HDRW
                          AGGREGATE(AWEASYDW_SALES_PURCHAS
                          -----E_PRICE_VARIABLE USING-----
                          --AWEASYDW_SALES_AGGMAP_AGG1)---
                          ------------AWTIME------------
                          MONTH.2003 MONTH.2003 MONTH.2003
AWCUSTOMER_DIM               01         02         03
-------------------------- ---------- ---------- ----------
REGION.AmerMidWest            830.51     705.15     689.48
REGION.AmerNorthEast        1,817.72   1,378.96   1,629.68
REGION.AmerNorthWest          391.75     360.41     282.06
REGION.AmerSouth              376.08     282.06     297.73
REGION.AmerWest               908.86     783.50     673.81
REGION.EuroWest             2,146.79   1,755.04   1,786.38
```

Instead of having end users specifying the aggregation function every time they query, the DBA can set the aggregation plan as a default for a variable, as follows:

```
-> AGGMAP SET aweasydw_sales_aggmap_agg1 AS DEFAULT FOR
            aweasydw_sales_ship_charge_variable
```

Now, every time the end users do a report command, the aggregation will be automatically returned, either by computing it on the fly or by using the precomputed values. This is illustrated in the following example, where we report on the AWEASYDW_SALES_SHIP_CHARGE_VARIABLE.

```
-> REPORT ACROSS awtime: aweasydw_sales_ship_charge_variable

                          AWEASYDW_SALES_SHIP_CHARGE_VARIA
                          --------------BLE---------------
                          ------------AWTIME------------
                          MONTH.2003 MONTH.2003 MONTH.2003
```

AWCUSTOMER_DIM	01	02	03
REGION.AmerMidWest	238.50	202.50	198.00
REGION.AmerNorthEast	522.00	396.00	468.00
REGION.AmerNorthWest	112.50	103.50	81.00
REGION.AmerSouth	108.00	81.00	85.50
REGION.AmerWest	261.00	225.00	193.50
REGION.EuroWest	616.50	504.00	513.00

Here you can see simplicity and the power of the multidimensional model—we do not need to specify the join, aggregation, or repeat the clauses as in SQL!

Defining Formulas and Custom Measures

You can also compute other variables using the variables defined earlier. For instance, the following example defines a variable named AWEASYDW_TOTAL_SALES_VARIABLE and computes it using the sum of two other variables.

```
-> DEFINE AWEASYDW_TOTAL_SALES_VARIABLE
-> VARIABLE DECIMAL
   <AWEASYDW_SALES_COMPOSITE
          <AWCUSTOMER_DIM AWPRODUCT_DIM AWTIME>>

-> LIMIT awtime TO awtime_levelrel EQ 'QUARTER'
-> LIMIT awcustomer_dim TO awcustomer_dim_levelrel EQ 'STATE'
-> LIMIT awproduct_dim TO awproduct_dim_levelrel EQ 'CATEGORY'

-> ACROSS awtime awcustomer_dim awproduct_dim
   DO 'aweasydw_total_sales_variable =
       aweasydw_sales_purchase_price_variable +
       aweasydw_sales_ship_charge_variable'
```

The **ACROSS DO** construct in the preceding example loops over the values in each of the dimensions, as specified by the limit clauses, and performs the computation for each value combination. We can now use it to report the variable, as in the following example. Here, we also illustrate another standard form construct, the PARENTREL relation. This relation maintains the relationship between a value and its parent value in a given dimension hierarchy. We limit the AWCUSTOMER_DIM dimension to those values (states) whose parent (region) is the AmerNorthEast region.

```
-> LIMIT awtime TO awtime_levelrel EQ 'QUARTER'
-> LIMIT AWCUSTOMER_DIM TO AWCUSTOMER_DIM_PARENTREL EQ
                    'REGION.AmerNorthEast'
```

```
-> LIMIT AWPRODUCT_DIM TO 'CATEGOR.HDRW'

-> REPORT DOWN awtime ACROSS awcustomer_dim:
                            aweasydw_total_sales_variable

AWPRODUCT_DIM: CATEGORY.HDRW
               -------AWEASYDW_TOTAL_SALES_VARIABLE-------
               --------------AWCUSTOMER_DIM--------------
AWTIME           STATE.CT    STATE.MA    STATE.NH    STATE.NY
--------------  ----------  ----------  ----------  ----------
QUARTER.200301   1,593.43    1,593.43    1,311.05    1,573.26
QUARTER.200302   1,694.28    1,835.47    1,532.92    1,754.79
QUARTER.200303   1,714.45    1,734.62    1,311.05    1,593.43
QUARTER.200304   1,734.62    1,875.81    1,391.73    1,633.77
...
```

With OLAP DML you can also define formulas to perform calculations using simple arithmetic or analytic functions. Once defined, users can then reference these calculations in reports like any other variables defined earlier. We should emphasize that the end user does not need to know how the calculation was done or which analytic function it used.

The next example creates a formula to determine difference in sales between the current month and the previous month using the LAGDIF function. This function is similar to the LAG SQL analytic function we saw in Chapter 6, except that it returns the difference between the current value and the value at the specified LAG offset. The LAGDIF function in OLAP DML takes as arguments a variable name, the LAG offset, a dimension along which to compute the LAG, and an optional LIMIT command, which can be used to restrict the values of the dimension. In this example, we are using the AWEASYDW_SALES_PURCHASE_PRICE_VARIABLE, along the AWTIME dimension. The LIMIT command restricts the computation to only the month level and the LAG offset is 1—in other words, the previous month.

```
-> DEFINE AWEASYDW_SALES_PREV_MONTH
   FORMULA
   DECIMAL <AWCUSTOMER_DIM AWPRODUCT_DIM AWTIME>
   EQ LAGDIF (AWEASYDW_SALES_PURCHASE_PRICE_VARIABLE,1,
            AWTIME, AWTIME_LEVELREL EQ 'MONTH')

-> LIMIT awproduct_dim TO 'CATEGORY.HDRW'
-> LIMIT awcustomer_dim TO 'REGION.AmerNorthEast'
-> LIMIT awtime TO awtime_levelrel EQ 'MONTH'
```

We can now use this formula to report the sales for the current month and the difference between the sales for the current and the previous month.

```
-> REPORT down awtime across awproduct_dim:
   <AWEASYDW_SALES_PURCHASE_PRICE_VARIABLE,
    AWEASYDW_SALES_PREV_MONTH>

AWCUSTOMER_DIM: REGION.AmerNorthEast

                         ----AWPRODUCT_DIM----
                         ----CATEGORY.HDRW----
                         AWEASYDW_S
                         ALES_PURCH AWEASYDW_S
                         ASE_PRICE_ ALES_PREV_

AWTIME                   VARIABLE    MONTH
-------------------      ----------  ----------
MONTH.200301             1,817.72           NA
MONTH.200302             1,378.96      -438.76
MONTH.200303             1,629.68       250.72
MONTH.200304             1,817.72       188.04
MONTH.200305             1,896.07        78.35
...
```

So far all the examples we have seen could also have been performed with SQL. The following section illustrates one of the advanced features of the OLAP Engine that is currently not available in SQL: forecasting.

Forecasting Using OLAP DML

One of the common operations performed using OLAP DML is forecasting. To forecast a quantity such as sales we must perform the following steps:

- Define variables to store the forecast results.
- Specify the parameters of the forecast.
- Execute the forecast.

We will show a very simple example of forecasting future sales based on historical sales.

The first step is to define a variable called AWEASYDW_SALES_ FORECAST_VARIABLE, which stores the result of the forecast. Note again that we have dimensioned this variable just like the AWEASYDW_ SALES_ PURCHASE_PRICE_VARIABLE.

```
-> DEFINE AWEASYDW_SALES_FORECAST_VARIABLE VARIABLE DECIMAL
   <AWEASYDW_SALES_COMPOSITE
           <AWCUSTOMER_DIM AWPRODUCT_DIM AWTIME>>
```

Next, we constrain the AWTIME dimension to the month level and customers to customer id level. This means that the forecast will be computed using the months in the AWTIME dimension for each customer id value in the AWCUSTOMER_DIM dimension.

```
-> LIMIT AWTIME TO AWTIME_LEVELREL EQ 'MONTH'
-> LIMIT AWCUSTOMER_DIM TO AWCUSTOMER_DIM_LEVELREL EQ 'CUSTOMER'
-> LIMIT AWPRODUCT_DIM TO 'CATEGORY.HDRW'
```

To specify parameters and run the forecast, we must create a handle, which will be used by subsequent commands. The handle, called sf_handle, is obtained by calling the **FCOPEN** command to which you specify a name.

```
-> DEFINE sf_handle VARIABLE INTEGER;

-> sf_handle = FCOPEN('EasyDWSalesForecast')
```

Next, we will set the forecast parameters using the **FCSET** command. We are using the automatic method for forecasting. We will consider three time periods (months) as historical data and forecast using a periodicity parameter of 6, which indicates the interval over which the sales repeat.

```
-> FCSET sf_handle method 'automatic' histperiods 3 periodicity 6
```

Finally, we execute the forecast using the **FCEXEC** command. We must specify the name of the time dimension and also the variable containing the data to be used for the forecast—in our case, AWEASYDW_SALES_PURCHASE_PRICE_VARIABLE. The results are placed into the AWEASYDW_SALES_SALES_ FORECAST_VARIABLE we defined earlier.

```
-> FCEXEC sf_handle TIME AWTIME
   INTO AWEASYDW_SALES_FORECAST_VARIABLE
   AWEASYDW_SALES_PURCHASE_PRICE_VARIABLE
```

Finally, we close the handle as follows:

```
-> FCCLOSE sf_handle
```

You can now query this variable to forecast the sales. You can also use an aggregation map to aggregate the forecast to higher levels. In the following example, we are forecasting sales for January 2005 for customers in Massachusetts (STATE.MA).

```
-> LIMIT awtime to 'MONTH.200501'
-> LIMIT awcustomer_dim to awcustomer_dim_parentrel eq 'STATE.MA'
-> LIMIT AWPRODUCT_DIM TO 'CATEGORY.HDRW'

-> REPORT down awcustomer_dim across awtime:
            AWEASYDW_SALES_FORECAST_VARIABLE

AWPRODUCT_DIM: CATEGORY.HDRW
                                   AWEASYDW_S
                                   ALES_FOREC
                                   AST_VARIAB
                                   ----LE----
                                   --AWTIME--
                                   MONTH.2005
AWCUSTOMER_DIM                         01
------------------------------   ----------
CUSTOMER.AB123410                    31.34
CUSTOMER.AB123420                    15.67
CUSTOMER.AB123440                     0.00
CUSTOMER.AB123450                     0.00
...
CUSTOMER.AB123500                     9.25
CUSTOMER.AB123510                    13.93
CUSTOMER.AB123530                    22.63
CUSTOMER.AB123540                    24.38
...
```

In this section, we have given you a quick but broad overview of OLAP DML and analytic workspaces. We saw how data is stored, aggregated, calculated, and reported in the multidimensional format. We have only scratched the surface of what can be done with OLAP DML, but hopefully you have gotten some idea of the simplicity and power of this language.

Besides interactively issuing OLAP DML using the OLAP Worksheet, you can also use it within an application, as discussed in the next section.

15.6.2   DBMS_AW package

The DBMS_AW package provides functions that allow you to execute OLAP DML commands and programs using PL/SQL programs or SQL*Plus.

The **EXECUTE** procedure can be used to execute one or more OLAP DML commands and print the output to the screen using the DBMS_OUTPUT package. The following example attaches to the EASYAW analytic workspace and reports the dimension AWTIME.

```
SET SERVEROUTPUT ON;
BEGIN
  DBMS_AW.EXECUTE(q'[
  AW ATTACH easyaw
  LIMIT awtime to awtime_levelrel EQ 'MONTH'
  REPORT awtime
  AW DETACH easyaw
]');
END;
/

AWTIME
--------------
MONTH.200301
MONTH.200302
MONTH.200303
MONTH.200304
MONTH.200305
MONTH.200306
MONTH.200307
...
PL/SQL procedure successfully completed.
```

Hint: Use the handy new PL/SQL construct q'[ ]' to enclose the OLAP DML commands, especially if they have quotes in them. This eliminates the need to escape the quotes. For more information refer to the Oracle PL/SQL documentation.

15.6.3   SQL Access to Analytic Workspaces

Applications can access multidimensional data stored in analytic workspaces with SQL by using SQL Table functions. Oracle provides a table function called OLAP_TABLE to do this, but you can also write your own custom table functions.

The OLAP_TABLE function takes four parameters:

1.   The analytic workspace to attach to. You can specify whether to attach the workspace for a query or for a session.

2.   An optional type for the result of the OLAP_TABLE function. Recall from Chapter 5 that a table function is similar to a table and returns rows as its result. So you must first define a type for the rows being returned and a type for the table. This parameter is useful if you would like to control the data types returned. If not specified, the results are converted to SQL data types.

3.   This parameter allows you to specify any OLAP command. A common use of this parameter involves specifying OLAP DML FETCH commands, which indicate how to fetch data from the analytic workspace. It is usually omitted and the next parameter, called the limit map is used instead. If specified, this command is executed prior to the limit map.

4.   The last parameter is called the LIMIT MAP and specifies how data in the analytic workspace maps to columns in the table returned by the OLAP_TABLE function. The limit map defines measures, dimensions, and their hierarchies. When the OLAP_TABLE function is used in a SQL query, the limit map, in combination with the SQL WHERE clause, will issue OLAP DML LIMIT commands to the analytic workspace to restrict data returned.

We will explain these with the following example, which retrieves the data from the variable AWEASYDW_PURCHASE_PRICE_VARIABLE in the EASYAW analytic workspace. We will define a TYPE, named PURCHASES_TYPE, which describes the rows being returned, and a TYPE, named PURCHASE_TABLE, which describes the table of these rows. For each dimension, we will return the value and the GROUPING_ID function, which indicates the level the value corresponds to (see Chapter 6 for a description of the GROUPING_ID SQL function).

```
CREATE TYPE purchases_type AS OBJECT
(cust VARCHAR2(80),
 cust_gid NUMBER,
 time VARCHAR2(30),
 time_gid NUMBER,
 prod VARCHAR2(30),
 prod_gid NUMBER,
 purchase_price NUMBER);
/
```

Next, we define a type, PURCHASE_PRICE_TYPE, which describes a table whose rows are of the PURCHASE_TYPE:

```
CREATE TYPE purchases_table AS TABLE OF purchases_type;
/
```

We will define a relational view on the table function as follows, so that applications can access this data without really needing to know about table functions and OLAP DML.

```
CREATE VIEW purchase_price_view
as
SELECT * FROM TABLE(OLAP_TABLE(
'easyaw duration session', 'purchases_table', '',
'dimension cust from awcustomer_dim
  with hierarchy awcustomer_dim_parentrel
  gid cust_gid from awcustomer_dim_gid
 dimension time from awtime
  with hierarchy awtime_parentrel
  gid time_gid from awtime_gid
 dimension prod from awproduct_dim
  with hierarchy awproduct_dim_parentrel
  gid prod_gid from awproduct_dim_gid
 measure purchase_price
  from aweasydw_sales_purchase_price_variable
'));
```

This view is now queried like any other relational table. For instance, in the following example, we are querying hardware sales in Massachusetts.

```
SELECT time, sum(purchase_price)
FROM purchase_price_view
WHERE prod = 'CATEGORY.HDRW' and cust = 'STATE.MA'
GROUP BY time

TIME                            SUM(PURCHASE_PRICE)
----------------------------    -------------------
MONTH.200301                                  470.1
MONTH.200302                                 360.41
...
QUARTER.200402                              1284.94
QUARTER.200403                              1300.61
...
YEAR.2003                                   5468.83
...
```

Note that when you enable the analytic workspace for OLAP API using the analytic workspace manager, the relational views created by the tool use the OLAP_TABLE function.

Thus, using table functions and relational views, the OLAP DML commands can be completely hidden away, and the SQL application can now be completely unaware of whether the data being accessed is stored in a relational or a multidimensional format.

15.6.4 OLAP API and BI Beans

The OLAP API is a set of Java classes that can be used to develop OLAP applications. It is very well suited to developing thin-client applications that can be accessed with a Web-browser. The OLAP API uses a multidimensional model for querying data; however, it internally translates these queries into SQL. To access objects using this API, you need to have defined the objects in the OLAP Catalog. The underlying data may be stored either in relational tables or in analytic workspaces encapsulated within relational views.

Business Intelligence Beans (BI Beans) is a set of reusable components that allows you to rapidly develop OLAP applications. They are integrated into Oracle's JDeveloper product, where they can be created and customized using simple wizards. BI Beans can perform a wide range of tasks, such as connecting to a database, building queries to perform analytical calculations, and displaying the results in extremely powerful reports, tables, or graphs. These components can then be easily deployed as part of a Java or JSP application.

A novel aspect of BI Beans is that you have full access to the data as the component is being designed, so you can immediately see how the resulting graph or presentation will look. Before you start to build business intelligence components, you must set up a database connection using the Designer bean. Then you can use the Query Builder to define queries, Presentation Wizard to create a report or graph, and Calculation Builder to define calculations.

A detailed discussion of the OLAP APIs and BI Beans is beyond the scope of this book.

15.7   Summary

In this chapter, we have seen how Oracle can be used to perform multidimensional analysis using the Oracle OLAP option. The multidimensional model is an intuitive model for analysis, because the application does not need to know how to join fact tables with dimension tables or to express analytic functions using SQL. Analytic workspaces provide a way to store and preaggregate data in a multidimensional format. The OLAP calculation engine provides several advanced features, such as forecasting and allocation, that are not available in SQL. You can map the analytic workspace back to a relational model for use by OLAP API and BI Beans applications by defining relational views on top of it. The Analytic Workspace Manager tool simplifies creation and maintenance of analytic workspaces from a relational star or snowflake schema and also provides wizards to automatically create the views required for the analytic workspace to be used by applications such as Discoverer or BI Beans.

Thus, regardless of whether you store your data in relational or multidimensional format, the Oracle database provides all the tools and techniques required for advanced business analysis applications.

In the next chapter, we will discuss another technique for business analysis—data mining, which can be used to determine hidden trends and patterns in your data.

16

Oracle Data Mining

Data mining is a process that finds hidden patterns and relationships in data to help make better business decisions.

In the course of running a business, you may encounter data in different forms. Operational data tells you day-to-day information about your customers—what did John Doe buy on August 5, 2002? In the data warehouse, data is organized according to predefined relationships using fact and dimension tables. You can then use OLAP tools to find out various facts about your business: How many people bought electronic products from your store and what was the average amount they spent? How many customers who bought electronic products were engineers? These are all questions based on existing data.

However, you may also like to answer questions such as:

- Which of your customers are likely to buy a personal video recorder?
- What could be a good city from which to launch a new product?
- What might be a good promotion to offer for Christmas?
- If a customer buys a digital camera, what other items is this customer likely to buy?

This is where you need some predictive insight into your data. Data mining uses various statistical and machine learning techniques to discover trends and patterns of behavior. In other cases, you may know what you are looking for. In some cases, there is no clear definition of what the mining process may find. You are saying: Here's my data—find me something interesting to look at. This is indeed the challenge of data mining—it is like looking for a needle in a haystack, only you may not know what the needle looks like! One of the biggest advantages of building a data warehouse is that data has been cleansed and consolidated and is now more amenable to data mining.

Data mining can be used in many applications, such as improving store layouts, fraud detection, mail-order promotions, reducing customer churn, and Web site personalization. It can also be used in life-sciences applications, such as finding patients at high risk for certain diseases.

16.1 Oracle Database 10g Data Mining Option

Oracle Data Mining is an option to Oracle Database 10g Enterprise Edition that embeds data mining functionality in the database server. This allows you to integrate data mining directly into your application logic and workflow, rather than extracting data from your applications for analysis. Data mining involves processing large amounts of data, which often needs to be preprocessed and put into a format suitable for the mining algorithms. By incorporating data mining functionality into the database, the mining algorithms can take advantage of the scalability and performance of the database engine and make use of features such as, partitioning, compression and parallel execution to speed up the analysis.

Oracle Data Mining supports various data mining techniques, such as classification, regression, association rules, clustering, determination of attribute importance, and feature extraction. Oracle Data Mining also supports text mining. The functionality is available through a PL/SQL package and a Java API.

Unlike much of the other material in this book, data mining algorithms need some mathematical background, such as statistics and probability. In this chapter, we will provide you with a broad overview of the data mining process and techniques while avoiding the technical details of each algorithm. We will describe the tasks and briefly illustrate the use of Oracle Data Mining Java and PL/SQL APIs. To read the examples at the end of this chapter you must have a basic knowledge of the Java and PL/SQL programming languages. However, if you are only looking for a conceptual overview, you may safely skip these examples.

16.2 Oracle Data Mining Techniques

Data mining problems can be classified into two categories. In some situations you have some idea of what you are looking for—for example, you are interested in customers who are likely to buy a digital camera. This is known as **directed** or **supervised** learning. In other cases, you leave it to the mining process to find you something interesting—for example, a high incidence of accidents at a certain intersection. This is called **undirected** or **unsupervised** learning. In unsupervised learning, the data mining algorithms describe some intrinsic property or structure of data and hence are sometimes called **descriptive** models. On the other hand, supervised learning techniques typically use a model to predict the value or behavior of some quantity and are hence called **predictive** models.

Oracle Data Mining supports various techniques for mining data, each of which falls into one of these two categories.

1. Descriptive Models/Unsupervised Learning:

   - Association rules or market-basket analysis

   - Clustering

   - Feature extraction

2. Predictive Models/Supervised Learning:

   - Classification

   - Regression

   - Attribute importance

We will look at each of these in some detail. Oracle Data Mining also provides special algorithms for mining of text and for life-sciences applications, which we will not discuss in this book.

16.2.1 Association Rules

We are all familiar with Amazon.com's feature—"Hello, Jane! We have some new recommendations for you." This type of Web-site personalization uses a data mining technique known as association rules. Mining with association rules finds items that occur together frequently. For instance, association ruls may find that a large percentage of users who bought the book *The Lord of the Rings* also bought the book *The Hobbit*. So if you buy *The Lord of the Rings*, it may recommend you also read *The Hobbit*.

Data mining using association rules is also known as "market-basket analysis." When you visit your local grocery store, you may find that the seafood department has lemons or tartar sauce next to the fish. This is because, it has found that 80 percent of people who buy fish also buy lemons to go with it. Most of these stores offer some kind of frequent shopper cards—by keeping a count of what combinations of items have been bought by the same person, they can organize their shelves more appropriately and even send you coupons for the same or similar items for your next visit.

Mining with association rules involves counting how many times a certain group of items occur together. In this case, you do not necessarily know which combination to look for beforehand—hence, this comes under the unsupervised or undirected learning category. The association algorithm comes up with rules of the type "A implies B." There are two quantities of interest to the user of this algorithm: support and confidence.

- **Support** tells us the percentage of the transactions where the combination of items A and B occur together. It helps identify combinations that are sufficiently frequent to be of interest (e.g., purchasing fish alone or purchasing fish and lemons together).

- **Confidence** tells us which percent of transactions that have an item A also have an item B (e.g., how many transactions that have fish also have lemons).

To use association rules, a user must provide the desired level of support and confidence for a rule to be considered interesting. For instance, suppose we specify that for a rule to be interesting, it must have a support of 20 percent and a confidence of 70 percent. If found that in fact 40 percent of all transactions involved the combination fish and lemons, then the combination "fish, lemons" exceeds the minimum support of 20 percent. Now, if we found that 50 percent of all transactions involve fish then the combination "fish, lemons" has confidence (40 / 50) * 100 = 80 percent, so it also meets the minimum confidence criterion. Hence, "fish implies lemons" will be reported as an association rule.

To make meaningful business decisions, both support and confidence are important. Consider this alternate example of an area where fish is not very popular due to high levels of mercury. Maybe only 5 percent of the transactions involve fish. The item "fish" does not have enough support and hence the rule "fish implies lemons" will not make any significant difference to our sales.

Figure 16.1 shows a typical output of mining analysis using association rules, as analyzed using a tool such as Oracle Discoverer. The first two rules say people often buy WINE or LEMONS to go with FISH.

Figure 16.1 *Association Rules*

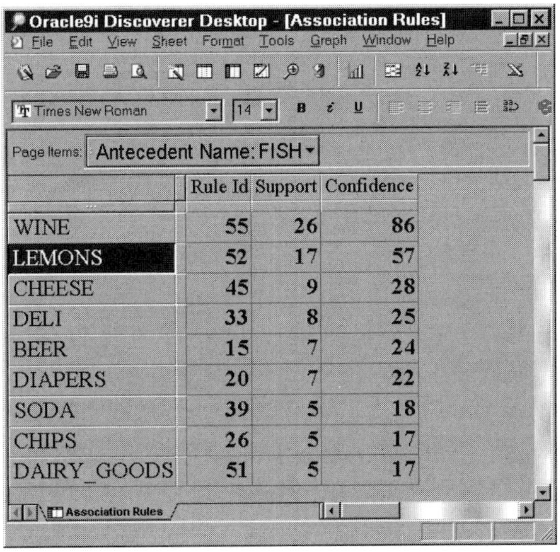

	Rule Id	Support	Confidence
WINE	55	26	86
LEMONS	52	17	57
CHEESE	45	9	28
DELI	33	8	25
BEER	15	7	24
DIAPERS	20	7	22
SODA	39	5	18
CHIPS	26	5	17
DAIRY_GOODS	51	5	17

The algorithm used by Oracle Data Mining for association rules is called **apriori**. The user provides the minimum support and confidence desired. The algorithm first finds single items that occur frequently and have the minimum support—for example, fish. It then finds pairs of items that have the minimum support, such that at least one item in the pair was frequently occurring—for example, fish and lemons. It repeats the process to come up with increasingly larger combinations of items until it can find no more. Once it has found all "frequent item-sets," it then finds those that satisfy the minimum confidence requirement from the user. These are reported as association rules. Oracle Database 10*g* has a SQL-based implementation of this algorithm.

16.2.2 Clustering

Clustering is a technique used to divide a large data set with many attributes into a small number of "closely packed" groups. Such groups are not easily apparent to a human eye due to the large number of attributes involved. For example, suppose you had census data for a population, including several attributes, such as age, occupation, occurrence of diseases, and so on. By clustering this data, may find that there are several pockets where a certain disease is prevalent, possibly pointing to a polluted water supply in those regions. Since we have no definite idea of what we may find, this is another example of unsupervised learning.

The groups generated by a good clustering algorithm are such that all items in one group are quite like each other in some respects and very much unlike items in other groups.

Figure 16.2 illustrates the concept of clusters in data. In this figure, two attributes of the data have been plotted using a scatter plot to highlight the clusters. For all items in each cluster, the values of the two attributes have greater similarity compared with items in different clusters. This is an example where the clusters in the data were apparent by simply plotting a graph. In practice, it is not often possible to visualize clusters in this way, since we may have more than two or three dimensions! For instance, in bio-informatics applications, you can have thousands of dimensions! In these situations, we use mathematical clustering algorithms to identify clusters.

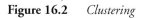

Figure 16.2   *Clustering*

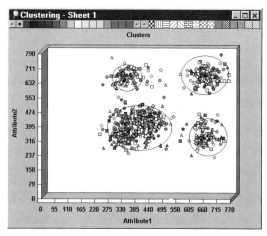

One of the applications where clustering is used is market segmentation. Suppose you were a large retailer selling a wide range of products from soaps to jukeboxes. With clustering, you can segment your customer base into groups based on demographics or past buying habits. This allows you to customize your advertising strategy for each segment and to better serve the more profitable segments.

Clustering is performed by first analyzing a small section of the data to determine clusters. Once the clusters have been determined, the remaining data is then analyzed to assign each individual item to a cluster, with a certain probability.

Clustering Algorithms

Oracle data mining supports two algorithms for clustering:

- Enhanced k-means
- O-Cluster

The k-means algorithm is a clustering algorithm that groups data into a specified number of k clusters. It groups items into clusters based on their relative "distance" from each other. So, all points in one cluster are "closer" to each other than to points in other clusters. The Enhanced k-means algorithm is a variation on the k-means algorithm that forms clusters in a hierarchical fashion. It starts with all the data being in one cluster and then successively splits it into smaller clusters until the desired number of clusters is obtained. It is very efficient compared with traditional k-means, since it only requires one pass through the data and hence can handle large data sets. It works well even for data sets with less than 10 attributes. The metric "distance" used by k-means can only be defined for numerical attributes; hence, if you have discrete values (e.g., color = red, black, blue), then k-means cannot be used.

The O-Cluster algorithm defines clusters using ranges of attribute values. The user does not need to provide the number of clusters to generate. This algorithm can be used for nonnumeric attributes that have a discrete set of values.

16.2.3 Feature Extraction

Feature extraction is a process that identifies important features or attributes of the data. Some examples of this technique are pattern recognition and identifying common themes among a large collection of documents. If the data has a lot of dimensions (such as keywords in a document), then feature extraction can be used to produce a more concise description of the data.

One example of feature extraction that all of us can relate to is spam-detection software. If we had a large collection of emails and the keywords contained in these emails, then a feature extraction process could find correlations among the various keywords. For example, the words Bush and election may appear to be correlated. Thus, the set of emails can now be described using a far smaller number of word phrases than what we started out with. For example, you can tell whether the email is a current news item about the U.S. presidential election or is selling you an unsolicited mortgage product or a new diet solution. Once we have done this, we can then associate certain combinations of words or phrases as spam and automatically out filter these emails. Of course, this is a very oversimplified description of any actual algorithm, but hopefully it has helped you understand the concept of feature extraction.

Feature extraction can be useful to reduce the number of attributes that describe the data. This can speed up data mining using supervised learning techniques such as classification, which we will discuss shortly.

Oracle Data Mining uses various techniques for feature extraction, such as Nonnegative Matrix Factorization (NMF). The details of this technique are beyond the scope of this book.

16.2.4 Classification

Suppose you wanted to target a promotion for a new digital camera and would like to know which of your customers are likely to buy the camera. Classification is a data mining technique that is useful for this application. Classification divides data into two or more well-defined classes. Unlike clustering, where you do not know which groups will be generated, in classification you know exactly what each group represents. In the previous example, the two groups are: customers who are likely to buy a camera and customers who are *not* likely to buy a camera. This is an example of supervised learning.

In classification, you first analyze a small part of your data to build a **model.** For instance, you would analyze real data for people who have bought digital cameras and people who have not bought digital cameras, over a given time period. The data used to build a model is known as **build data**. The model will be built taking into account various factors, such as age, income, and occupation, that are known to influence people's buying habits. These factors are known as **predictor attributes**. The output that is predicted is called the **target attribute** and its values (whether the person will buy the camera or not) are known as **categories** or **classes**. Once the model has been generated, it can be applied to other data to come up with a prediction. This is known as **model apply**, or **scoring**. In our example, you would use the model to predict whether a certain customer is likely to buy a digital camera.

In the previous example, the target attribute has two values: will buy a digital camera and will not buy a digital camera. You can also use classification to predict attributes with more than two values—for example, whether the risk of a person defaulting on a payment is low, medium or high.

Classification is often used to create customer profiles. For instance, once you have determined which of your customers are likely to buy a digital camera, you can then profile them by occupation, as shown in Figure 16.3. From this graph, you now know that most likely buyers are either engineers or executives. So you can now target your promotions more accurately toward these customers and reduce your costs.

Figure 16.3 *Classification*

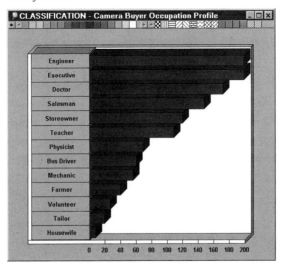

In order for classification to work well, the build data must contain enough samples for each target category; otherwise, it may not be accurate. In other words, your build data must include enough people who have bought digital cameras in the past and enough who have not.

Testing a Classification Model

Data mining using classification usually involves a testing phase to check how good the model is. For this, data where the outcome is known is tested to see how well the model's predictions match it. For instance, you would take data for customers who have bought a digital camera in the past and check it against the predictions given by the model.

Testing a model involves computation of a structure known as the **confusion matrix**. A confusion matrix tells you how many times the model's prediction matched the actual data and how many times it did not. The columns correspond to the predicted values and the rows to the actual values. For instance, in Figure 16.4, the model was correct 555 + 45 = 600 times and wrong 12 + 8 = 20 times. This shows that this model is a pretty good one.

Figure 16.4 *Confusion Matrix*

Actual \ Predicted	Camera Buyer	Non Camera Buyer
Camera Buyer	555	8
Non Camera Buyer	12	45

■ Model predicts correctly

▨ Model predicts incorrectly

Computing Lift

Another metric used to determine the effectiveness of a model is its **lift**. To understand what lift means, consider the following example. Suppose we have a customer base of 100,000 households and on an average about 2.5 percent (2,500 customers) respond to any given promotion. We would like to get smarter and only target those customers who are most likely to respond. With a good classification model, we should be able to identify most of the likely 2,500 respondents by targeting much fewer than the 100,000 households. Given a certain percentage of target customers, lift is the ratio of the number of respondents obtained with the model against the number obtained without the model.

Lift is computed as follows. The classification model is applied to an actual customer data set, where we know who responded to a past promotion and who did not. The customers are then sorted by their likelihood to respond as predicted by the model, with the most likely respondents first. This sorted list is then divided into 10 equal groups known as **deciles**. For each decile, the number of customers in the data set who had actually responded to the promotion is counted. If the model is any good, then most of the respondents should come from the top few deciles, since they were predicted to be the most likely respondents.

If you draw a graph with deciles 1 through 10 on the X-axis and the number of actual respondents on the Y-axis, you will typically get the curve shown in Figure 16.5. This curve tells you that you only need to target the customers in the first three deciles (30 percent households), to get 70 percent of those likely to respond. On the other hand, the straight line in this figure corresponds to a random promotion where everyone is predicted to be equally likely to respond. Without the model to guide you, if you target 30 percent households, you will only get 30 percent of the likely respondents. To get 70 percent of the likely respondents, you will have to target 70 percent of the households!! The higher the curved line is from the straight line for the first one or two deciles, the better the model's lift.

Figure 16.5   *Using lift analysis for targeted promotions*

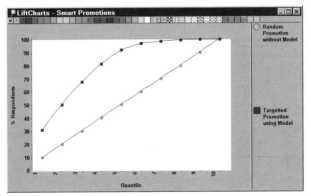

Confusion matrix and lift are both widely employed techniques to determine the accuracy of classification models. Oracle Data Mining provides APIs that will allow you compute these quantities.

Classification Algorithms

Oracle offers three algorithms for classification:

- Naive Bayes Algorithm
- Adaptive Bayes Network Algorithm
- Support Vector Machines

The Naive Bayes (NB) Algorithm is based on the probability theorem known as Bayes theorem and assumes that each attribute is independent from the other. An interesting property of the NB algorithm is that you can build and cross-validate the model using the same data. This algorithm works best with a small number of predictor attributes (less than 200).

The Adaptive Bayes Network (ABN) Algorithm in its most intuitive form (known as single feature build) produces a model in the form of a decision tree, shown in Figure 16.6. From this decision tree you can see that men between the ages of 15 and 35 and women over 26 are likely to buy a camera. Since the model produced by ABN is in a human-readable form, a business analyst or executive would be more comfortable when using it to make a business decision. The ABN algorithm is usually more accurate than NB, but it takes longer to build the model.

Figure 16.6   *Adaptive Bayes Network Decision Tree*

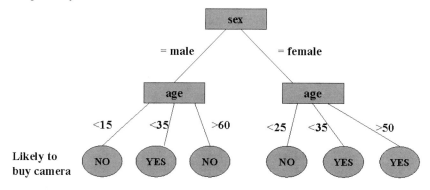

Oracle also provides two other modes for the Adaptive Bayes Network model called Pruned Naive Bayes and Boosted, which *conceptually* allow you to describe the data using multiple decision trees; however, these modes do not provide human-readable rules.

Support Vector Machines (SVM) are a technique for classification based on machine-learning (artificial intelligence) theory. In this technique, mathematical functions called **kernels** are used to transform data, which makes it possible for the data to be more clearly differentiated into different categories. This is a predictive technique, because the machine (algorithm) is first trained using some initial training data and then learns to correctly classify new data. SVM is used in many real-world applications, such as handwriting recognition and classifying images.

16.2.5 Regression

Regression is a predictive modeling technique, which allows you to describe the relationship between two variables using a line or curve. If the value of one variable (called the **independent** variable) is known, the line or curve can then be used to predict the value of the other variable (called the **dependent** variable). The most common technique is **linear** regression, where you find a straight line that fits the data. In Chapter 6, we saw some built-in SQL functions for linear regression analysis. For example, linear regression may be used to determine if the price of a quantity has any relationship to its total sales.

It is important to note the difference between classification and regression: Classification allows you to classify data when the target attribute is discrete, whereas regression allows you to classify data where the target attribute is continuous or numerical.

The Support Vector Machine technique used for classification can also be used to create regression models for the data.

16.2.6 The PMML Standard

The Predictive Modeling Markup Language (PMML) is an emerging XML-based standard to define data mining models. PMML provides a vendor-independent method of defining models so that the models can be exchanged between different applications. Thus, one application may produce a model and another may apply the model to a data set. Oracle Data Mining supports import and export of Association Rules and Naive Bayes models.

16.3   Preparing Data for Oracle Data Mining

In order to use data mining algorithms, the data may need to be in a certain format and you may need to preprocess the data to reduce its size or complexity. In this section, we will describe the requirements for the data format and also the various techniques to prepare data for the mining algorithms.

16.3.1   Data Format

The data to be mined must be accessible using either a single table or a view that encapsulates the access to the underlying tables. Each fact in the data being analyzed is known as a **case**. For example, "customer #3, male, aged 35, a teacher by profession, bought a digital camera" is one case. In the table, a case can be represented using either a single record or multiple records (one for each attribute) as illustrated in Figure 16.7.

Figure 16.7   *Table Formats for Data Mining*

Non-Transactional Format

ID	Age	Sex	Occupation	Buyer
1	15	M	Engineer	YES
2	27	F	Doctor	NO
3	35	M	Teacher	YES
		...		

Transactional Format

ID	Attribute	Value
1	Age	15
1	Sex	M
1	Occupation	Engineer
1	Buyer	YES
2	Age	27
2	Sex	F
2	Occupation	Doctor
2	Buyer	NO
	...	

If all attributes for a case are placed in the same row, the table is said to be in a **single-record** or **nontransactional** format. Alternatively, the table could store each case using multiple records, with the format customer#, attribute_name, attribute_value. This is known as a **multirecord** or **transactional** format.

The transactional format is useful when the table needs to have more than 1,000 columns, which is the maximum number of columns allowed in a table in Oracle. Some algorithms in the Oracle Data Mining Java interfaces will automatically convert the data into a transactional format prior to analysis. When using the PL/SQL interfaces, it is possible to represent the data in a transactional format with nested tables using built-in collection types.

Oracle Data Mining supports all Oracle character and numeric data types. However, any date columns must be converted into either a numeric or a character data type, depending on their meaning.

16.3.2   Data Preparation

Some data mining algorithms require data to be transformed in certain ways—in this case the data is said to be **prepared**. The Java interfaces for Oracle Data Mining assume the data is **unprepared** and will do the required preprocessing. On the other hand, the PL/SQL interfaces require that the data be prepared by the user. There are two important techniques for data preparation—binning and normalization. You can also use attribute importance to reduce the number of attributes as a data preparation step.

Binning or Discretization

Data mining algorithms may require that the data be categorized into a discrete set of bins or buckets for analysis. Binning will group related values together and so will reduce the number of distinct values of a data attribute that need to be considered by the data mining algorithms. This will usually speed up the building of data mining models. Algorithms such as association rules, Naive Bayes, Adaptive Bayes Network, and clustering may benefit from binning.

Oracle provides the capability to automatically perform binning or allow a user to manually bin the data by specifying the boundary values for the buckets. There are several ways to bin data:

- **Using Top N frequently used values (for categorical data)**: The Top N frequently used values each get one category and all other values are clubbed into one bin called "Other."

- **Equiwidth Binning (for numerical data)**: This technique divides the allowable range of a numeric attribute into equi-sized buckets and assigns a number to each bucket. This is similar to the WIDTH_BUCKET function discussed in Chapter 6.

- **Quantile Binning (for numerical data):** This technique divides the range of the numeric attribute into N bins containing approximately equal numbers of records.

- **Equiwidth Binning with Winsorizing (for numerical data)**: A common problem with data is the presence of **outliers**, which are exceptional values that lie outside the normal expected range of values. For example, if you expect the normal daily sales for a product to be between $5,000 and $10,000 but on one specific day, due to extenuating circumstances, the sales were only $50, then any mining model should exclude the outlier case of $50. The quality of models generated by the data mining algorithms can be severely diminished due to the presence of outliers. Winsorizing is a technique that excludes values that fall outside of an accepted range, determined statistically. Equiwidth binning is then performed on the remaining data.

Normalizing

Normalizing of data converts data values so they fit into a specific range, such as between 0 and 1 or between –1 and +1. For example, if you have values between 0 and 100, normalizing the data to between 0 and 1 will convert these values to a value between 0 and 1. Thus, the original value of 50 will become 0.5 and a value of 100 will become 1. Normalizing of data is useful for algorithms such as Support Vector Machines and Nonnegative Matrix Factorization.

Attribute Importance

This technique is useful when building a classification model by narrowing down the relevant predictor attributes. If your data has a large number of predictor attributes, it can be a challenge to determine which ones influence your required target attribute and which ones do not. For instance, age may determine a customer's preference in music; however, the customer's name, height, or eye color will have little impact. Depending on the number of predictor attributes, the classification process can be quite time consuming to compute. Attribute importance automatically ranks attributes by how likely they are to influence the target attribute. You can then choose to pick only a few of the top ranking attributes to build the model.

In the next section, we will look at how to use the Oracle Data Mining interfaces and a few examples. If you are only interested in a conceptual overview of data mining, you can skip over this section and continue on to section 16.5.

16.4 Using Oracle Data Mining Interfaces

Oracle Data Mining is an option in the Enterprise Edition of Oracle Database 10*g*. The data mining algorithms are available to application developers using either a Java or PL/SQL programming interface.

We will start by describing how to install and configure the data mining option and its various components.

16.4.1 Installation and Configuration

Oracle Data Mining (ODM) is available as part of the Oracle Database 10*g* installation using the Oracle Universal Installer. During the installation, if you choose to create a preconfigured database (see Chapter 2), ODM is automatically installed for you. If you choose to build a custom database, then you must use the Database Configuration Assistant (DBCA) to install the ODM option and follow its instructions.

Once the ODM option is installed, you will find that there is a built-in schema, called DMSYS, which stores the repository containing database system tables used by the data mining option. You can unlock the DMSYS account and set new passwords, as follows:

```
alter user dmsys identified by <password_here> account unlock;
```

To run data mining tasks, you must have a user account with certain database privileges. The easiest way to create this user is to run the script $ORACLE_HOME/dm/odmuser.sql. It will prompt you for the user name, password, and the default tablespace for the user. The data mining algorithms produce many internal tables in the user schema, so it is recommended that you use a schema different from the one used for your normal data warehouse tables (EASYDW in our case). Further, it is recommended that you create a separate tablespace, which can be allocated to data mining users to store the mining data and the mining results. The examples in this chapter assume that we have created a user, EASYDM, and a tablespace EASYDM_DEFAULT.

It is also recommended that you use partitioning (see Chapter 4) and parallel execution (see Chapter 6) for data mining tasks, especially for large data sets, since they can achieve significant performance gains.

Now you are ready to start using the data mining APIs.

16.4.2   Data Mining Analysis Flow

The Java and PL/SQL interfaces largely follow the same flow, though the details may be slightly different and will become clear when we look at actual examples.

1. *Preprocessing the input data for analysis*: The raw data may need to be preprocessed before analysis. Some algorithms require that the data be binned. The user can preprocess the data and specify how it is to be binned. This is optional with the Java interfaces, since Oracle can automatically perform binning, if the user has not done so. However, it is mandatory with the PL/SQL interfaces.

2. *Setting up parameters for the analysis*: Next, you must indicate which function you would like to use (association, clustering, classification, attribute importance, or feature extraction). You can also optionally specify the actual algorithm you want to use for that technique. If you do not specify the algorithm setting, Oracle will use a default algorithm.

3. *Building a model*: The next step is to build the model. When using the Java interfaces, the model is executed asynchronously. However, when using the PL/SQL procedures, the model building is synchronous. In both cases the model is stored persistently in the database. Note, however, that models generated using the two interfaces are not compatible with each other.

4. *Testing a model and computing lift*: As described previously, when using classification you may also want to test the model and compute its lift. The test data must have the same format as the build data.

5. *Applying the model to new data*: Once you have built a model, you can apply it to new data to make predictions. You can apply a model on new cases stored in a table or to a single case. To apply the model, you must specify an input table containing the new data, which must be preprocessed (if needed). The input table must be compatible with the one used to build the model. You must also specify an output table, where the results or predictions will be placed, and identify which subset of attributes should be placed in the output table.

Now, we will illustrate the general flow of the data mining analysis using the Oracle Data Mining Java and PL/SQL interfaces. We will present an example using one technique: classification. The detailed description of all the classes and procedures is beyond the scope of this book.

Hint: The Oracle Database 10*g* companion CD contains several sample programs using the Oracle Data Mining APIs. After reading this chapter, you may find it useful to install and try these additional examples to learn how to use the different APIs.

16.4.3   An Example Using the Java API

In this example, we will build a model for classification to predict if a person is likely to buy a digital camera. We will first illustrate how to build a model and then apply the model on some test data. In real-life data mining projects, the model is usually tested before it is applied to new data. Typically, many models are built and evaluated before the "best" model is discovered. In these examples, we will skip the testing phase.

Hint: The examples in this section are in the form of Java code fragments. Please refer to the Appendix for instructions to obtain the complete examples and instructions to compile and execute them.

Building a Model

In this example, we assume that the input data set used to build the model is stored in a table, EASYDM.TEST_BUILD_DATA. The data is stored in a nontransactional format, meaning that all attributes for a case are stored in the same row of the table. The table definition is as follows:

```
DESCRIBE test_build_data;

Name                                          Null?     Type
--------------------------------------------  --------  -------------
CUSTOMERID                                              VARCHAR2(15)
AGE                                                     NUMBER
GENDER                                                 VARCHAR2(8)
OCCUPATION                                             VARCHAR2(10)
CAMERABUYER                                            NUMBER(1)
```

The target attribute, CAMERABUYER, indicates whether the person has bought a digital camera or not. It has the value 1 if the person has bought a digital camera and 0 if not.

Building the model involves the following steps:

1. *Preprocessing the input data for analysis*: With the Java interfaces, it is not necessary to preprocess the data. In this case we will not preprocess the data and will let Oracle automatically perform binning.

2. *Specifying the mining server to use*: First, we need to create an instance of a *DataMiningServer* object, specifying the database to connect to using a standard JDBC URL and the user to login as. On successful login, we get a connection handle (dmConn), which will be used in the subsequent APIs. We are connecting using the EASYDM user.

```
DataMiningServer dms = new
  DataMiningServer("jdbc:oracle:thin:@mypc:1521:orcl",
                   "EASYDM", "EASYDM");
oracle.dmt.odm.Connection dmsConn = dms.login();
```

3. *Specifying the structure of data*: To specify the input data, we must first create a *LocationAccessData* object, which indicates the schema and table name of the input data. Then we create a *PhysicalDataSpecification* object of the *NonTransactionalDataSpecification* kind. (If the table were in transactional format, you would use *TransactionalDataSpecification* instead.)

```
LocationAccessData lad
  = new LocationAccessData("TEST_BUILD_DATA", "EASYDM");
PhysicalDataSpecification pds
  = new NonTransactionalDataSpecification(lad);
```

4. *Setting up parameters for the analysis*: The function settings for analysis are stored in a *Mining Function Settings* (MFS) Java object. The actual API to use to create the MFS depends on the mining technique you are using. An important part of MFS settings is the *Logical Data Specification*, which allows you to specify how each mining attribute has to be treated by the mining algorithm. This will include the attribute type—as in whether the attribute is categorical or numerical; the usage, as in whether it is

a target attribute or a predictor; and its preparation status, as in whether the attribute is prepared or unprepared.

In this example, we will specify parameters to do classification using the *ClassificationFunctionSettings* class. We will not specify any algorithm and will let Oracle determine the algorithm to use. Because we have not preprocessed the data, we will indicate the *DataPreparationStatus* of "unprepared" to indicate that Oracle should apply automatic binning. The target attribute is specified as CAMERABUYER and is of type categorical, because it has discrete values.

```
ClassificationFunctionSettings cfs
    = ClassificationFunctionSettings.create
            (dmsConn, null, pds,
            "camerabuyer",
            AttributeType.categorical,
    DataPreparationStatus.getInstance("unprepared"));
```

If we want to use the Naive Bayes Algorithm, then we must also define the algorithm level settings and pass it into the function level settings. The code would then look something like the following. Notice that we have passed the Naive Bayes settings variable nbs into the *ClassificationFunctionSettings* class.

```
NaiveBayesSettings nbs
    = new NaiveBayesSettings(0.01f, 0.01f);

ClassificationFunctionSettings cfs
    = ClassificationFunctionSettings.create
        (dmsConn, nbs, pds, "camerabuyer",
        AttributeType.categorical,
        DataPreparationStatus.getInstance("unprepared"));
```

After the mining function settings object is created, it is a good idea to validate it to ensure it is correct. You can also persist the settings in the database by specifying a name. This allows you to reuse the same settings in different programs. Therefore, we will verify the settings and store them in the database under the name TEST_DATA_CFS.

```
cfs.validate();
cfs.store(dmsConn, "TEST_DATA_CFS");
```

5.   *Building a model*: To build a model, you create a *MiningBuildTask* object and store it persistently in the database under some name. Then you must execute the task and wait for it to complete. In our example, we create a task named TEST_DATA_CFS_MODEL, store it in the database, and then execute it. You can query the status of the task during execution. When execution is complete, the model will be stored in the database.

```
MiningBuildTask task
    = new MiningBuildTask(pds, "TEST_DATA_CFS",
                               "TEST_DATA_CFS_MODEL");

task.store(dmsConn, "TEST_DATA_CFS_TASK");
task.execute(dmsConn);
MiningBuildStatus = task.waitForCompletion(dmsConn);
```

Once the model is built, you will notice several new tables and views created in the EASYDM schema. These are all internal tables and views, which store the information about the model, and should not be tampered with.

The next example shows how this model is applied to new data.

Applying a Model

Now, we will apply the model we built in the previous example to a test set of customers to predict which of the customers are likely to buy a digital camera.

Applying a model involves the following steps:

1.   *Specifying the mining server to use*: This step is the same as in the previous example of building the model.

2.   *Specifying the logical structure of data*: Next, we specify the location of the data to apply the model to. This is also similar to specifying the input table when building a model. The data used to apply the model must have a format compatible with the build data. In our example, we will use the table EASYDM.TEST_APPLY_DATA.

```
LocationAccessData lad
    = new LocationAccessData("TEST_APPLY_DATA", "EASYDM");
PhysicalDataSpecification pds
    = new NonTransactionalDataSpecification(lad);
```

3. *Specifying the location of the output*: On applying the model, the resulting predictions will be placed in a table. In our example, we will use the table EASYDM.TEST_APPLY_OUT.

```
LocationAccessData ladOut
    = new LocationAccessData("TEST_APPLY_OUT","EASYDM");
```

We must also specify a *MiningApplyOutput* object describing which columns we would like in it.

```
MiningApplyOutput mao = new MiningApplyOutput();
```

Each row of the output table contains a prediction for the target attribute, in our case whether the customer is likely to buy a camera or not. The target attribute is represented by a prediction (1 or 0), a probability for the prediction, and a rank. We define the target attribute using an *ApplyTargetProbabilityItem* object, as follows:

```
ApplyTargetProbabilityItem camerabuyerAttr
  = new ApplyTargetProbabilityItem
        (new Attribute("CameraBuyer",
                       DataType.stringType),
         new Attribute("Probability",
                       DataType.stringType),
         new Attribute("Rank",
                       DataType.stringType));
```

The camerabuyer attribute has two values: **1** meaning the customer is a camera buyer, and **0**, meaning the customer is not. We must define these values as follows:

```
camerabuyerAttr.addTarget
    (new Category("CameraBuyer", "1",
                  DataType.getInstance("int")));
camerabuyerAttr.addTarget
    (new Category("NotCameraBuyer", "0",
                  DataType.getInstance("int")));
```

In addition, we would like to store in the output table the CUSTOMERID for whom this prediction was made. This is copied from the source table EASYDM.TEST_APPLY_DATA to which the model is being mined, and hence we define it using an ApplySourceAttributeItem object, as follows. The first parameter specifies the name and properties of the column in the source table and the second parameter specifies the name of this column in the output table.

```
ApplySourceAttributeItem customerIDAttr
   = new ApplySourceAttributeItem(
         new MiningAttribute("CUSTOMERID",
                             DataType.intType,
                             AttributeType.notApplicable),
         new Attribute("CUSTOMER_ID",
                     DataType.intType));
```

Finally, we add these to the *MiningApplyOutput* object we created previously.

```
mao.addItem(camerabuyerAttr);
mao.addItem(customerIDAttr);
```

4. *Creating and executing a MiningApplyTask*: Now we are ready to apply the model. This is nearly identical to building a model. We create a *MiningApplyTask* and supply it the location of the input data, the name of the model (one we created in the previous example), the location of the output table, and the *MiningApplyOutput* specification. We then store this in the database under the name TEST_DATA_CFS_APPLYTASK and execute it.

```
MiningApplyTask task
     = new MiningApplyTask(pds,
                          "TEST_DATA_CFS_MODEL",
                          mao, ladOut,
                          "TEST_DATA_CFS_OUTPUT");
task.store(dmsConn, "TEST_DATA_CFS_APPLYTASK");
task.execute(dmsConn);
```

Once the task finishes, the predictions are stored in the EASYDM.TEST_APPLY_OUT table. Notice that the columns correspond to the attributes we defined in step 3. Each customerid had two rows: one with the probability of being a camerabuyer (prediction=1) and the other with the probability of not being a camerabuyer (prediction=0). The predictions are ranked according to which is the more likely case. Thus, customer with id AB70466 is unlikely to buy a camera (rank = 1 => camerabuyer = 0), while customer with id AB70481 is more likely to buy one (rank = 1 => camerabuyer = 1).

```
SELECT prediction CAMERABUYER, probability, rank, customerid
FROM EASYDM.TEST_APPLY_OUT;

CAMERABUYER PROBABILITY        RANK CUSTOMERID
----------- ----------- ---------- ----------
    ...
          0 .837545455           1    AB70466   <- unlikely
          1 .162454545           2    AB70466
          0 .756452858           1    AB70472
          1 .243547171           2    AB70472
          1 .687442183           1    AB70481   <- likely
          0 .312557846           2    AB70481
    ...
```

You can also use any of the analysis tools provided by Oracle, such as Discoverer or Reports to analyze this result graphically.

16.4.4   An Example Using the PL/SQL Procedures

In this section, we will build the same model as in the previous section, however, we will use the PL/SQL interfaces. The data mining interfaces are in the PL/SQL package DBMS_DATA_MINING.

We will use the same input data, stored in the table EASYDM.TEST_BUILD_DATA to build the model. We will then apply the generated model to the data in EASYDM.TEST_APPLY_DATA and finally get predictions for which customers would be likely to purchase a camera.

Hint: To run these examples from SQL*Plus connect as the EASYDM user.

We will use the classification data mining technique, which requires that the data be prepared by binning the attributes, as described. Unlike the Java interfaces, where data preparation is automatically performed, the PL/SQL interfaces require the data to be prepared using the DBMS_DATA_MINING_TRANSFORM package (or your own or third-party programs). We will start by briefly describing how we prepare the data for data mining. Note that this step must be performed for both the build data and the apply data.

Data Preparation

The data being used for our model has one numeric attribute, AGE, and two categorical (nonnumeric) attributes, OCCUPATION and GENDER.

The DBMS_DATA_MINING_TRANSFORM.CREATE_BIN_NUM procedure can be used to create a bin boundary table, which holds the bins for the numeric attributes. The DBMS_DATA_MINING_TRANSFORM. INSERT_BIN_EQWIDTH procedure is then used to bin numeric attributes into the specified number of equal sized buckets (specified by the *bin_num* parameter). The procedure will perform the binning on all numeric columns of the input table specified by the parameter *data_table_name* that are not in the *exclude_list*. The resulting bounds are placed in the table specified by the *bin_table_name* parameter.

In the following code, we first create a table, TEST_DATA_ NUM_BOUNDARY, to hold the results of binning. We then perform binning on the AGE attribute of TEST_BUILD_DATA into 10 buckets and place the resulting boundaries into the bin table. Note that the table has two numeric columns, AGE and CAMERABUYER; because we want to bin only the AGE attribute, we specify CAMERABUYER in the *exclude_list*.

```
BEGIN
-- create a bin boundary table
dbms_data_mining_transform.create_bin_num
    (bin_table_name => 'test_data_num_boundary');
-- Create boundaries for age and occupation (10 bins)
  dbms_data_mining_transform.insert_bin_num_eqwidth (
    bin_table_name     => 'test_data_num_boundary',
    data_table_name    => 'test_build_data',
    bin_num            => 10,
    exclude_list       => dbms_data_mining_transform.column_list
                          ('CAMERABUYER'),
    round_num          => 0
  );
END;
/
```

The TEST_DATA_NUM_BOUNDARY table is a simple table, described as follows with three columns: COL column contains the attribute name, VAL has the lower bound for the bin, and BIN has the bin number.

```
describe test_data_num_boundary;

Name                      Null?   Type
--------------            -------  --------------
COL                               VARCHAR2(30)
VAL                               NUMBER
BIN                               VARCHAR2(4000)
```

The contents of TEST_DATA_NUM_BOUNDARY table for the AGE attribute are as follows.

```
SELECT * FROM test_data_num_boundary;

COL      VAL     BIN
-------  ----    ---
AGE      10.6    1
AGE      18.2    2
AGE      25.8    3
...
```

Similarly, we can bin the categorical (nonnumeric) attributes using the DBMS_DATA_MINING_TRANSFORM.INSERT_BIN_CAT_FREQ procedure. The parameters are identical to the previous example. We will use 2 bins for the GENDER attribute and 10 bins for OCCUPATION. The resulting bin boundary values are placed in the TEST_DATA_CAT_BOUNDARY table, created using the DBMS_DATA_MINING_TRANSFORM.CREATE_BIN_CAT procedure.

```
BEGIN
  -- create categorical bin boundary table
  dbms_data_mining_transform.create_bin_cat (
    bin_table_name => 'test_data_cat_boundary');

  -- Categorical Bin for AGE
  dbms_data_mining_transform.insert_bin_cat_freq (
    bin_table_name    => 'test_data_cat_boundary',
    data_table_name   => 'test_build_data',
    bin_num           => 2,
    exclude_list      => dbms_data_mining_transform.column_list
                         ('CUSTOMERID', 'OCCUPATION'),
    default_num       => 0);
  -- Categorical bin for OCCUPATION
  dbms_data_mining_transform.insert_bin_cat_freq (
    bin_table_name    => 'test_data_cat_boundary',
    data_table_name   => 'test_build_data',
    bin_num           => 10,
```

```
        exclude_list       => dbms_data_mining_transform.column_list
                              ('CUSTOMERID', 'AGE'),
        default_num        => 0);
END;
/
```

Now, we use these bin boundary tables to generate views, which will be used as input to the data mining algorithms. We will first transform the input table, TEST_BUILD_DATA, by applying the categorical binning table into a view named TEST_DATA_BUILD_CAT. This will then be further transformed by using the numeric bin table into the final view, TEST_DATA_BUILD_PREPARED, which contains the prepared data.

```
BEGIN
-- Create the transformed view
  dbms_data_mining_transform.xform_bin_cat (
    bin_table_name  => 'test_data_cat_boundary',
    data_table_name => 'test_build_data',
    xform_view_name => 'test_data_build_cat');
  dbms_data_mining_transform.xform_bin_num (
    bin_table_name  => 'test_data_num_boundary',
    data_table_name => 'test_data_build_cat',
    xform_view_name => 'test_data_build_prepared');
END;
/
```

We will not use the TEST_DATA_BUILD_PREPARED view to build our classification model.

Building a Model

As with in the Java interfaces, to build a model you must specify the mining technique to use. In our example, we will be using classification. Further, you can optionally specify the algorithm and its settings to use. In the PL/SQL interfaces, the settings are specified using a table called a settings table, which is a simple table, described as follows:

```
CREATE TABLE test_data_settings (setting_name  VARCHAR2(30),
                                 setting_value VARCHAR2(30));
```

You can then insert into this table the specific settings for your algorithm. For example, we will be using the Naive Bayes algorithm with settings of 0.01 and 0.01, as follows:

```
BEGIN
-- Populate settings table
 INSERT INTO test_data_settings
        VALUES (dbms_data_mining.algo_name,
               dbms_data_mining.algo_naïve_bayes);
 INSERT INTO test_data_settings
        VALUES (dbms_data_mining.nabs_pairwise_threshold,'.01');
 INSERT INTO test_data_settings
        VALUES (dbms_data_mining.nabs_singleton_threshold,'.01');
 COMMIT;
END;
/
```

The model is created by invoking the procedure DBMS_DATA_MINING.CREATE_MODEL, giving the name of the model, the algorithm to use the input data table, the column that identifies each "case," the settings table, and the target attribute on which the prediction will be made. In this following example, we are building a classification model named TEST_DATA_PLSQL_MODEL using the TEST_DATA_BUILD_PREPARED view and the TEST_DATA_SETTINGS settings table. Our cases are specified by CUSTOMERID and the target attribute is CAMERABUYER.

```
BEGIN
 dbms_data_mining.create_model(
    model_name => 'TEST_DATA_PLSQL_MODEL',
    mining_function => dbms_data_mining.classification,
    data_table_name => 'test_data_build_prepared',
    settings_table_name => 'test_data_settings',
    case_id_column_name => 'customerid',
    target_column_name => 'camerabuyer');
END;
/
```

Once the model build has finished, the model will be saved in the database. You can query various aspects of the model, such as the settings, using built-in TABLE functions. The model can then be applied to new data as discussed in the next section.

Applying a Model

The data used to apply the model is stored in TEST_APPLY_DATA and must also be prepared by binning, as done with the build data. The following code uses the same bin boundary tables created for the build data and creates views for the apply data. The final view, which gives the prepared data, is named TEST_DATA_APPLY_PREPARED.

```
-- prepare apply data
BEGIN
  dbms_data_mining_transform.xform_bin_cat (
    bin_table_name  => 'test_data_cat_boundary',
    data_table_name => 'test_apply_data',
    xform_view_name => 'test_data_apply_cat');
  dbms_data_mining_transform.xform_bin_num (
    bin_table_name  => 'test_data_num_boundary',
    data_table_name => 'test_data_apply_cat',
    xform_view_name => 'test_data_apply_prepared');
END;
/
```

The model is applied by calling the procedure DBMS_
DATA_MINING.APPLY. The parameters are the name of the model to
use, the view containing the input data, the column identifying each case
and the table where the results must be stored. In this example, we are
applying the TEST_DATA_PLSQL_MODEL model on the input view
TEST_DATA_APPLY_PREPARED and the results are stored in
TEST_APPLY_OUT_PLSQL.

```
BEGIN
  dbms_output.put_line('Apply on apply data');
  dbms_data_mining.apply(
    model_name => 'TEST_DATA_PLSQL_MODEL',
    data_table_name => 'test_data_apply_prepared',
    case_id_column_name => 'customerid',
    result_table_name => 'test_apply_out_plsql');
  dbms_output.put_line('Completed apply');
END;
/
```

You can then view the predictions by selecting from the
TEST_APPLY_OUT_PLSQL table. Note that the predictions are not
automatically ranked, as in the Java model. You must explicitly issue the
DBMS_DATA_MINING.RANK_APPLY procedure to do the ranking.
This is left as an exercise to the reader.

Hint: Please note that the models generated by the PL/SQL and the Java
interfaces are not compatible. So it is not possible to generate a model using
Java and then apply it using the PL/SQL interfaces.

16.5 Summary

Data mining is a process that finds hidden trends and patterns in your data. Oracle Data Mining embeds data mining functionality in the database server, thereby improving the mining performance and allowing it to scale to large amounts of data. In this chapter, we discussed various applications of data mining and how they can be done using Oracle data mining Java and PL/SQL interfaces.

The next and final chapter discusses how to make your data warehouse highly available and how to protect your critical data in the event of disasters.

17

High Availability and a Data Warehouse

17.1   Introduction

When data warehouses were first built, they were considered as a repository for historical data to be used for business analysis by a chosen few. However, as technology and business practices have evolved, businesses now need to use daily business intelligence at all levels of the organization to stay competitive. The data warehouse, being the central repository of information about the business, thus plays a key role in the day-to-day operation of the business. This means that, as with OLTP systems, the data warehouse system must also be extremely reliable and nearly always available. Depending on how the data warehouse is used in the business, a short downtime could severely hamper the functioning of the business and an extended downtime could mean serious financial consequences. Therefore, when building a data warehouse, it is crucial to have a plan in place to ensure that the data warehouse is always available if needed.

Due to its key role in the business, the data stored in the data warehouse is an important corporate asset and hence must be protected from damage due to system failures and from disasters such as fire or an earthquake. September 11, 2001, highlighted the need to have a business continuity plan in place. It can take months to create a data warehouse, but only a few minutes to lose it! Thus, in addition to normal backup and recovery procedures, you may also need a disaster recovery plan for critical data stored in the data warehouse.

In this chapter, we will discuss how to build a highly available data warehouse based on features in Oracle Database 10*g*, such as Real-Application Clusters (RAC), Automatic Storage Management (ASM), Recovery Manager (RMAN), and Data Guard. Once the data warehouse has been built, it cannot remain a static entity and must constantly evolve to meet the changing needs of the business. You may need planned downtime because the data is being reorganized or the system hardware or software is being upgraded. This chapter will also discuss mechanisms in Oracle Database 10*g*, such as Rolling Patch Upgrades and Online Reorganization, which can reduce the planned downtime for the warehouse.

The right architecture for your data warehouse will be determined not only by the role the data plays in your business and the desired level of availability of the data warehouse, but also by the costs associated with that architecture. We will discuss techniques that can help maintain a balance between the costs and the availability and protection of the data.

We will begin this chapter by exploring the key features of a highly available system.

17.2   What Is a Highly Available System?

In simple terms, a highly available system is one where there is very little downtime. In reality, however, availability is measured by its impact on the users of the system. In other words, if the system were to go down, would it make a significant difference in the *perceived* user experience? In an online store, a 30-second delay may be tolerable; however, in a stock trading system, this could be disastrous.

17.2.1   Characteristics of a highly available system

To achieve high availability, a system must have the three key features: reliability, recoverability, and continuous operation.

Reliability

A reliable system is resilient to failures due to hardware or software problems. In order to be so, it is critical that the all hardware components used are reliable, including disks, CPUs, memory, interconnects, network, and so on. A system with built-in redundancy can be useful to protect against individual component failure. Software reliability encompasses the database, application, and Web servers, as well as the applications themselves.

Recoverability

Recoverability means that the system is capable of recovering from any type of failure. Despite the best design, hardware and software components can fail. No matter how reliable, disks will crash and so it is important to have regular backups and a recovery procedure for data. Failures can also be due to human error, where someone accidentally deletes some critical files or tables. Finally, failures can be due to manmade or natural disasters, such as fire, earthquake, flood, electrical shutdown, or a terrorist attack. It is not only important for the system to be recoverable but also that the recovery occurs within a reasonable period of time. In order to do so, the system must be able to quickly identify failures and possibly automate the recovery process. Thus, monitoring and error detection form important components of a highly available system.

Continuous Operation

Continuous operation is the most obvious characteristic definition of a highly available system: the system downtime should be minimal or within the acceptable limits. The ability of the system to recover from unplanned failures in a timely manner is crucial for continuous operation. Another aspect is to be able to handle planned expansions, such as adding new hardware, upgrading software, or reorganizing the data without interruption in service to the users.

17.2.2 Role of Operational Best Practices

In order to provide these three characteristics, a highly available system not only requires technology infrastructure but also operational best practices. No amount of technology will help if you end up scrambling to find the DBA when the database goes down, because it will take longer than you think to restore the operation back to normal. And you will end up with lost business and unhappy users.

It is therefore important to put in place procedures and plans that dictate how to react when an unplanned failure occurs. Who will respond to the failure? How will they be notified? How long will the expected recovery time be? Is there an alternative system that users can access during the outage? How often can failure be tolerated? How much data can you afford to lose? Finally, it is extremely important to track and document the unplanned outages in the past to identify any recurring problems and to take steps to prevent failures in the first place!

No system, once designed, is ever static, and therefore you should also be thinking about procedures to handle planned downtime. Does the system have enough capacity to handle the user workload? How long can the system operate before you will need to expand the hardware? What is the anticipated growth of data volumes? How will you handle minor software patches and major software upgrades? How often does data need to be reorganized? Can the users query the data while it is being reorganized? What time of year or day is (not) a good time for planned downtime?

To summarize, before you settle on the technology for your highly available system, it is important to have clear answers to these operational questions.

In the following section, we will provide an overview of the Oracle Database 10g for building a highly available system.

17.3 Overview of Oracle Database 10g High Availability Features

Oracle Database 10g provides features that can be used to build an effective high-availability solution for any database system, including a data warehouse.

Some of these features include:

- Real-Application Clusters (RAC)
- Automatic Storage Management (ASM)
- Flashback Table, Database, and Query
- Oracle Data Guard
- Online Reorganization of Data
- Dynamic Reconfiguration of the Oracle Instance

Figure 17.1 shows where each of these features fit in supporting the three characteristics a highly available system.

In any system, there are two causes for downtime—planned and unplanned. Unplanned downtime includes hardware, software, and disk failures. Oracle features such as Real Application Clusters and Data Guard provide protection against unplanned downtimes. Human error is also another possible cause of downtime, and Oracle provides a feature called flashback to help correct problems caused by human errors. Planned downtime includes system maintenance and data reorganization and can be minimized by using features such as Rolling Patch Upgrades and Online Redefinition in Oracle Database 10g. The Oracle Enterprise Manager Grid Control framework provides a centralized management and monitoring

Figure 17.1   *Oracle Database 10g High-Availability Features*

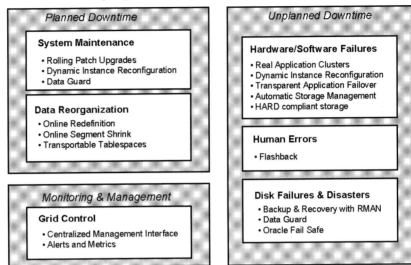

interface, which makes it possible to anticipate failure conditions in advance, detect failures, and recover from them in a timely fashion.

In the next few sections, we will discuss each aspect of high availability, shown by the boxes in Figure 17.1, in the context of a data warehouse and how to use the relevant features in Oracle Database 10*g* for this purpose.

17.4   Protecting against Hardware/Software Failures

If you are designing a highly available data warehouse, the first question that must be answered is: What is the impact to the business if the data warehouse system is down? This will ultimately determine how many minutes or hours of downtime you can tolerate and how frequent your outages can be. If you cannot tolerate unplanned outages, then you must ensure that all hardware and software components are fault tolerant. If you use a three-tier architecture, then your application, Web-servers, and the network infrastructure must be fault tolerant as well. And, finally, the end-user applications that access the data warehouse must be robust. Most importantly, the database server used for the data warehouse must be protected against hardware and software failures.

Let us look at the various features in Oracle Database 10*g* that can be of use in ensuring continuous operation of the warehouse database.

17.4.1   Real-Application Clusters (RAC)

The Real-Application Clusters (RAC) technology is at the core of most high-availability solutions using Oracle Database 10*g*. Chapter 3 discussed the concepts involved in clustering a database and the technology behind RAC. In a data warehouse, RAC provides the dual benefits of improving the scalability and performance of the system and making it highly available in the event of failure.

In an architecture using RAC, if there is a hardware failure in a node of the cluster or if the Oracle instance running on a node dies, the entire system does not become unavailable. The surviving nodes (or instances) will automatically take over the work of the failed node (or instance) within a matter of seconds. This means that while the system will not perform at its full capacity, at the least, the data is still available and user operation is not interrupted.

17.4.2   Reliable Storage

A key part of a fault-tolerant system is the storage architecture. For uninterrupted operation it is important to ensure that the storage components provide redundancy and fault tolerance or that an architecture incorporating redundancy is utilized—for example, mirrored disks. In Chapter 3, we discussed in detail architectures using RAID systems, which could be used to provide redundancy for storage. We also discussed the SAME (Stripe and Mirror Everything) methodology to ensure high availability for storage.

Automatic Storage Management

The Automatic Storage Management (ASM) feature in Oracle Database 10*g*, which was described in Chapter 3, provides data mirroring and striping capability, thereby providing protection against disk crashes. Further, ASM has a concept of failure groups, which allows disks to be classified according to their common points of failure. ASM will mirror data such that the mirrored copies will be in different failure groups, thereby providing storage redundancy. This ensures that no single failure can cause complete unavailability or loss of data. For example, if two disks that share a single SCSI controller are used to store the primary data and its mirrored copy, then failure of the controller could cause the data on the disk to be unavailable. In this case, the two disks are said to be in the same failure group. If these disks are managed by ASM, it will automatically ensure that the data and its mirrored copy will not be stored on these two disks in the same failure group.

Integration with HARD-Compliant Storage

Occasionally, a problem with the storage hardware can cause data corruption, which could be disastrous for a database. There are many ways to recover from such data corruptions, including RMAN's Block-Level Media Recovery, restoring the data from a backup, and so on. However, the ideal situation is when the storage subsystem can be smart enough to identify that a block is corrupt and return an error instead of writing it to disk. Oracle has started an initiative known as Hardware-Assisted Resilient Data (HARD) in association with several leading storage vendors to integrate special checking for Oracle data block corruptions into the storage subsystem. In order to use HARD validation, the datafiles and log files need to be placed on special HARD-compliant storage devices. This technique can also detect corrupted writes due to errors made by the operating system or third-party backup products.

Hint: It is currently not possible to use the ASM to automatically balance files, when HARD storage checking is in place.

17.4.3   Failure Detection and Monitoring

One of the important features of any highly available system is to quickly identify where the failure is. Oracle Enterprise Manager Grid Control provides a complete monitoring framework for monitoring the health of all components of the system. This can be used to monitor hosts, clusters, ASM storage, and databases and has a comprehensive system of alerts to notify the administrator in case of a failure.

Automatic Proactive Notifications

By proactively monitoring your system, it is possible to become aware of a potential problem before it occurs. For example, an alert that a certain tablespace is running out of space can avoid a failed load job in the future. As described in Chapter 11, Enterprise Manager provides a mechanism for a DBA to define alerts; however, in addition, it has a built-in set of best-practice policies, and any violations get reported on the *Targets* page.

17.4.4   Resource Management

As the data warehouse is made accessible to more and more users in a corporation, the load on the system rises. If the system goes down because the load is too much, a user may perceive it no differently than an unplanned outage due to a disk failure. Therefore, it is important to plan for the peak load capacity. The Oracle Database 10*g* Resource Manager is a valuable tool to manage allocation of resources between different tiers of users of the system.

It is also important to ensure that the system has sufficient expansion capabilities so that you don't need a wholesale redesign to accommodate an increase in users or data. In the future, the emerging Oracle Database 10*g* Grid Control framework may allow multiple systems to virtually share resources and provision additional resources as needed.

17.5   Protecting against Data Loss

Building a data warehouse can take a significant amount of time, and it could only take a few failures to lose it all, so it is important to consider the impact of data loss. There are several ways in which data can be lost: media failure, such as disk crash; a human error, such as an operator inadvertently dropping a table; and a disaster, such as a fire, flood, or earthquake. We will discuss each of these aspects.

17.5.1   Recovering from Media Failure

One very important consideration in the case of a data warehouse is to identify how much data loss can be tolerated in the case of a media failure such as a disk crash. An interesting point to note is that before getting to the data warehouse, the data usually goes through a staging process, and so there is already some built-in redundancy in the data. Perhaps it would be possible to retrieve some of the lost data from the staging areas, using the datafiles used for loading the warehouse, or from the operational data store, if you have one. However, if you are going to rely on any of these techniques, you need to test the process, and document how this will be done. On the other hand, it may be acceptable if the last few minutes of data were lost, because it did not make much difference to the analyses performed using the data warehouse.

The amount of data loss you can tolerate will ultimately determine the strategy for recovery from media failure. There are several options to consider:

- Using archived redo logs allows you to recover the database after media failures. The Flash Recovery Area, described in Chapter 12, should be used to simplify the management of backup- and recovery-related files. The Recovery Manager (RMAN), which was also discussed in Chapter 12, provides sophisticated backup and recovery capabilities.

- Techniques such as striping and mirroring, discussed in Chapter 3, can be used to provide data redundancy.

- Physical design techniques such as partitioning, discussed in Chapter 4 can also be useful to protect against complete data loss: by splitting partitions across multiple disks, you may only lose one or more partitions and not the entire table.

17.5.2   Recovery from Human Errors with Flashback

Although most data loss is due to hardware failures, occasionally it may be due to a human error. In a data warehouse, individual changes to the tables are not very common except during the ETL process, and hence you may think that there is not much need for error correction. It is true that you may rarely have to retrieve an individual deleted record; however, accidents happen—for example, someone may inadvertently drop a table or a partition. More commonly, a batch job may get run twice, causing duplicate data to get loaded into the data warehouse. It can be very time consuming to recover from these simple mistakes. In these cases, the flashback features in Oracle can be used to restore the data, often significantly faster than restoring from backup or repeating the ETL process.

The flashback features work by allowing data to be viewed as of a time in the past. It is possible to recover past data at the level of a row, transaction, table, or the entire database. Thus, if you knew that the error occurred roughly at 3:15 P.M. today, you can look at the data as of a few minutes earlier and identify the changes done during this period.

Oracle Database10*g* provides several flashback features:

- Flashback Table
- Flashback Drop
- Flashback Query
- Flashback Database

The *point in time* to flashback is specified using either a TIMESTAMP or an SCN. The TIMESTAMP is just a date and time expression and you are most likely to use this form. However, Oracle actually internally uses a number called the SCN to mark a "timestamp" for committed transactions. You can flashback up to a specific transaction, provided you know the SCN for that transaction. The SCN can be mapped to a timestamp to within a three second margin, so unless you need this level of accuracy, a time stamp is usually sufficient.

Flashback Table

Flashback table allows you to restore a table as of a certain point in time, along with all its indexes, triggers, and constraints, without shutting down the database. This is done by issuing a FLASHBACK TABLE command from SQL*Plus. For minor error correction, this is a much faster method than restoring from a backup. For example, suppose we had incorrectly deleted a new special offer for product SP1300 to the TODAYS_SPECIAL_OFFER table, around July 7, 2004, 1:01 P.M. Querying the table indicates the row is not present.

```
SELECT * FROM todays_special_offers WHERE PRODUCT_ID = 'SP1300';

no rows selected
```

To recover the data before this time, say to 1:00 P.M., the following statement can be issued:

```
FLASHBACK TABLE todays_special_offers TO TIMESTAMP
        TO_TIMESTAMP('2004-JUL-07 13:00:00',
                     'YYYY-MON-DD HH24:MI:SS');

Flashback complete.
```

The flashback table command rolls back the entire table to the time or SCN specified. Now, if we issue the same query again, we will see that the row is restored.

```
SELECT * FROM todays_special_offers WHERE PRODUCT_ID = 'SP1300';

PRODUCT_ID   OFFER_DAT   SPECIAL_PRICE OFFER_PRICE
--------     ---------   ------------- -----------
SP1300       07-JUL-04             200           0
```

Note that in order to perform a flashback table operation, the table must have ROW MOVEMENT ENABLED, because the physical location of any row may need to change—during the flashback. To enable row movement, for example in the TODAYS_SPECIAL_OFFERS table, we had to issue the following SQL:

```
ALTER TABLE todays_special_offers ENABLE ROW MOVEMENT;
```

At the time of writing, flashback table is not supported if the table has any materialized views defined on it.

Flashback Drop

Flashback drop can be used to quickly recover from an accidental drop of a table. In Oracle Database 10*g*, when you issue a DROP command to drop a table, index, materialized view, and so on, the object does not get dropped altogether but is placed in a **recycle bin**. The object can then be recovered back from the recycle bin.

Hint: Note that objects in the recycle bin appear under names such as BIN$, and you can find its original name in the RECYCLEBIN view.

Suppose we had accidentally dropped the YEAR table from the data warehouse. The table will appear in the recycle bin and can be seen by querying the RECYCLEBIN view, as follows:

```
SELECT object_name as recycle_name
FROM recyclebin
WHERE original_name = 'YEAR' AND type = 'TABLE';

RECYCLE_NAME
-----------------------------
BIN$3yV4u7YNbG7gNAgAIOXDhA==$0
```

Now, you can use the FLASHBACK TABLE statement to restore the table, along with any indexes or other items. You can use either the original name or the recycle bin name to restore the object.

```
FLASHBACK TABLE easydw.year TO BEFORE DROP;
```

If you do not want objects to go into the recycle bin, you must use the PURGE option when issuing the DROP—for example, if you truly wanted to purge the YEAR table, you would issue the following statement:

```
DROP TABLE easydw.year PURGE;
```

Once the object is placed in the recycle bin, it is only purged automatically if the tablespace is getting close to full and Oracle needs the space for other purposes. However, if you would like to reclaim the space earlier—for example, if you wanted to purge the YEAR table—you could issue the following statement:

```
PURGE TABLE easydw.year;
```

Thus, using Flashback Drop you can easily recover from an accidental drop of a table without having to go to a backup

Flashback Query

Flashback query is an extension of flashback table, which provides the ability to query the database as of a certain point in time by using a SELECT statement. With flashback query it is possible look at the data as it existed yesterday, a week ago, and so on. This allows you to have a historical perspective on the data. You can also use flashback query to recover and re-insert old data into the table using an INSERT SELECT statement.

To use flashback query, you must use an AS OF TIMESTAMP or AS OF SCN clause for a table in the FROM clause.

Suppose we have the following simple query, which shows the current value of total sales (on July 7, 9:00 A.M.) from the PURCHASES table:

```
SELECT SUM(ps.purchase_price)
FROM purchases ps;

SUM(PS.PURCHASE_PRICE)
----------------------
          19319852.7
```

Now, suppose we deleted records worth $1,000 from the PURCHASES table, at around 10:00 A.M., with the result of the query as follows:

```
SELECT SUM(ps.purchase_price)
FROM purchases ps;
```

```
SUM(PS.PURCHASE_PRICE)
----------------------
            19318852.7
```

If we wanted to see the data as of, say, this morning, around 9:30 A.M., we could issue the following query. The result shows that the deletion of $1,000 is not included in the result of this query and so we are looking at a historical view of this table.

```
SELECT SUM(ps.purchase_price)
FROM purchases AS OF TIMESTAMP ('2004-JUL-07 9:30:00',
                                'YYYY-MM-DD HH24:MI:SS') ps;


SUM(PS.PURCHASE_PRICE)
----------------------
            19319852.7
```

You can also use the DBMS_FLASHBACK package to set a flashback time and then perform a whole sequence of queries as of that time, without using any special AS OF syntax. This is shown in the following example. First we use the DBMS_FLASHBACK.ENABLE_AT_TIME procedure to set flashback to 12:00pm July 7, 2004, then issue our query (in fact you could issue several) and finally issue DBMS_FLASHBACK.DISABLE procedure to turn off flashback.

```
--Step 1. enable flashback
execute  DBMS_FLASHBACK.ENABLE_AT_TIME( -
  TO_TIMESTAMP('2004-JUL-07 9:30:00', 'YYYY-MM-DD HH24:MI:SS'));

--Step 2. issue the query
SELECT SUM(ps.purchase_price)
FROM purchases;

SUM(PS.PURCHASE_PRICE)
----------------------
            19319852.7

--Step 3. disable flashback
execute DBMS_FLASHBACK.DISABLE;
```

Note that it is only possible to do a flashback query up to the point where no DDL has been done to the table. Thus, in the preceding example, if you had added a new column to the table, at 9:45 A.M. before doing the deletion, then you will not be able to flashback to the data as of 9:30 A.M.

Hint: The flashback query and flashback table features requires the Automatic Undo Management feature of Oracle Database 10*g*, to be enabled by setting the initialization parameter UNDO_MANAGEMENT to AUTO. Further, the UNDO_RETENTION parameter must be set to a value (in seconds) large enough to include the oldest data you may need to flashback to. For example, if you expect you may need to see 30-minutes old data, set UNDO_RETENTION to 1800.

Flashback Database

Flashback database quickly rewinds an Oracle database to a previous point in time to correct any problems caused by logical data corruptions or user errors. Flashback database provides granular database recovery, down to a SCN.

To enable flashback database, follow these steps:

1. Make sure that your database has media recovery enabled by archiving the redo logs. To do this, you need to issue the following SQL command.

   ```
   ALTER DATABASE ARCHIVELOG;
   ```

2. Ensure that you have set up a Flash Recovery Area, as discussed in Chapter 12.

3. Set the initialization parameter, DB_FLASHBACK_RETENTION_TARGET, to indicate how far back into the past in minutes you want to be able to restore your database.

4. Execute the ALTER DATABASE FLASHBACK ON statement to enable flashback, as follows:

   ```
   STARTUP MOUNT EXCLUSIVE;
   ALTER DATABASE FLASHBACK ON;
   ```

When the flashback database feature is enabled, Oracle will periodically write the current versions of data blocks to a **flashback log**. These logs are saved in the flash recovery area and are used to flashback the database.

To flashback a database to any point in time, say 12:00 P.M., July 7, 2004, issue a FLASHBACK DATABASE command from SQL*Plus.

```
FLASHBACK DATABASE TO TIMESTAMP
TO_TIMESTAMP('2004-JUL-07 12:00:00','YYYY-MON-DD HH24:MI:SS');
```

Once a flashback database operation has been completed, the database is not yet open for data access. At this point, the database can be opened in read-only mode. You can verify if this is the point in time that is desired and, if not, you can simply roll further back or forward in time. Once you have determined it is the correct point in time to flashback to, open the database with the RESETLOGS option, as follows:

```
ALTER DATABASE OPEN RESETLOGS;
```

To disable the flashback database feature, issue ALTER DATABASE FLASHBACK OFF, which will disable creation of the flashback logs.

Hint: The flash recovery area should be large enough to hold all required files, such as archived redo logs and backups; otherwise, you may not be able to do flashback to the desired point in time.

In a data warehouse, depending on your change volume, the space requirements for flashback logs may become prohibitive, so you may not be able to use this to recover from errors. However, one use for this feature is in a test system when trying out potential schema changes. Rather than writing lengthy undo scripts to undo the schema changes, you can simply flashback the database.

17.5.3 Disaster Recovery Using Data Guard

The importance of your data warehouse to the business will determine whether you need a disaster recovery plan, such as in case of a fire, flood, or earthquake. It may be that you decide that the business can do without the warehouse for a while. However, great care should be taken if you make this decision, because it may take much longer than you think to return to normal working conditions. Chances are that if you have a major failure, especially something that relates to a building, it could be many months before the site is back in operation. Another aspect of disaster recovery is recovering the data itself in the case of a disaster. One technique may be to keep a recent set of backup tapes off-site in a fireproof safe, and then use these to restore the database. A major issue with the data warehouse is its sheer size. Your recovery procedures should take into account the size of the database and the hardware required to rebuild it. Depending on how often the backups are synchronized, you must be prepared to lose data in this process.

If the data warehouse is indeed very critical to the business, you may want to consider having a standby database at a different location, using Oracle Data Guard.

Data Guard Concepts

Oracle Data Guard creates and maintains a copy of a database as a standby database at another site. If the primary database becomes unavailable, applications can be restarted and run on the standby. The standby is initially created from a backup of the primary database. As changes are made on the primary database, the redo that is generated is transmitted to the standby, where it is applied, keeping the databases synchronized. Data Guard can be configured to ensure that no data is lost in the event of a failure. It can also be used to support planned maintenance operations, such as hardware or operating system upgrades. Both the primary and standby systems can use Real Application Clusters.

There are two types of standby databases for use with Data Guard:

- Physical Standby
- Logical Standby

Physical Standby

A physical standby database is an identical copy, block for block, of the primary database. It is kept synchronized with the primary database by recovering the redo data from the primary database (called **Redo Apply**) using the same process that is used for media recovery. When the standby is not performing recovery, it can be open for read-only queries. However, while the standby is open for queries, the redo cannot be applied.

A physical standby database can also be used to offload backup processing from the primary database. RMAN can back up the physical standby database while redo is being applied. Since the primary and the standby databases are block for block copies of each other, a standby backup can be used to recover the primary database in case of a failure

Physical standby databases have been available for several releases of the Oracle database and are currently used to protect many OLTP systems, data warehouses, and operational data stores.

Logical Standby

A logical standby database contains the same *logical* data as the primary database, but its physical structure may be different. It is kept synchronized with the primary database by converting the redo data to SQL and then executing the SQL statements against the standby database (called **SQL Apply**). Data can be queried at the same time SQL apply is applying changes; however, it cannot be updated. Unlike in a physical standby, it is possible to create additional tables on logical standby databases and these tables may be updated at any time. Logical standby databases can be effectively used for reporting or testing purposes, thereby offloading some of the work from the primary database. Additional indexes and materialized views can be added to improve query performance. At the time of writing, there are a number of restrictions on the data types, types of tables, and operations supported on a logical standby.

Logical Standby Databases and Data Warehouse

Apart from disaster recovery, there are a number of ways in which logical standby database could be used to support the overall data warehouse architecture.

- The logical standby database could be used as a source of data for the warehouse. Since it contains a copy of the data from the production system, it could be used as the source for the ETL process, thereby offloading the operational systems.

- The logical standby database could be used to offload reporting tasks from the primary database. It could also be used as the operational data store. Data could then be moved into a staging area on a different system, where it is transformed into a star schema and is ready for warehouse queries.

- The logical standby database could contain the warehouse tables. The tables maintained by logical standby must have the same logical structure as the tables on the primary database; however, additional tables could be created in the logical standby database to create a star schema for the warehouse. It is possible to update these tables as with any normal database tables.

While these techniques do not serve to protect the data warehouse against disasters, they allow a data warehouse to be incorporated into the larger enterprise disaster recovery plan, thereby reducing the overall costs.

Let us now look at the details of using Data Guard and how to set up standby databases.

Data Guard Configuration

A data guard configuration can be made up of one primary database and up to nine logical or physical standby databases. A typical configuration is shown in Figure 17.2. The primary database transmits the redo to both a

Figure 17.2   *A Data Guard Configuration*

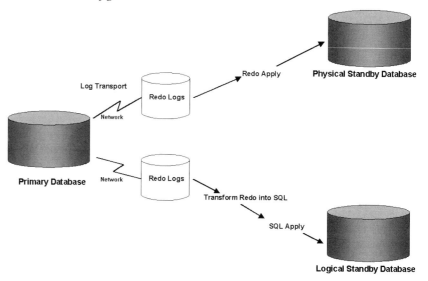

physical and logical standby database, located at a site different from the primary database. The physical standby is used for disaster recovery, and the logical is used primarily for reporting but can also be used for disaster recovery.

There are a number of components that actually make up Data Guard, which are listed as follows:

Redo Transport Services: This component is responsible for shipping the redo data from the primary site to the standby site(s). These services also detect and resolve problems with missing archived logs (also referred to as **gaps** in the redo). Note that redo transport services are also used in the

Auto Log mode of Asynchronous Change Data Capture, which was discussed in Chapter 5.

Redo Apply Services: This component is responsible for maintaining the standby database to keep it consistent with the primary database. In case of physical standby, the redo apply services use the normal database recovery mechanisms to apply the redo logs to the standby database. In case of logical standby, the redo information is first transformed into equivalent SQL statements, which are then executed on the standby database. This is illustrated in Figure 17.2. In Oracle Database 10*g*, the redo apply can either be done from archived redo logs on the standby database as they become available or in a **real-time apply** mode directly from the standby redo logs.

Role Management Services: Typically, in order to perform maintenance on the primary database, you may temporarily transform the standby database to be the primary database, and transform the old primary database to be the standby database. This operation can be done as a planned operation and is called a **switchover**. On the other hand, in the event of a catastrophic failure of the primary database, you may transform the standby to be the primary database. This is called a **fail-over** operation. Role Management Services provide switchover and fail-over capabilities in a Data Guard configuration.

Data Guard Broker

Data Guard Broker is a distributed management framework that automates and centralizes the creation, maintenance, and monitoring of Data Guard configurations. While a Data Guard configuration can be managed using SQL*Plus, management operations are considerably simplified if they are performed using the Data Guard Broker, with the graphical user interface in Oracle Enterprise Manager. The Data Guard Broker also has a specialized command-line interface available as a standalone executable called DGMGRL.

The Data Guard Broker is integrated with Oracle Database 10*g* and uses a special process, known as the Data Guard Monitor (DMON), to perform its various tasks. The graphical user interface to Data Guard Broker in Oracle Enterprise Manager can be used to create new logical and physical standby databases from backups of the primary database, establish communication between the primary and standby databases, perform role transitions between the primary and standby, and so on. The command-line interface cannot be used to create a standby; however, it can be used to configure standby databases, perform role transitions, and various other maintenance and management tasks.

Hint: Please note that to use the Data Guard GUI you must use the Grid Control version of Oracle Enterprise Manager and not the Database Control version.

In the following section, we will discuss how to set up a Data Guard configuration using the Grid Control interface and, along the way, explain some more concepts and requirements for using this feature.

Using Oracle Enterprise Manager to Configure Data Guard

The Data Guard graphical user interface can be reached from the *Administration* page in Grid Control (shown in Figure 17.3) under the *High Availability* section.

Figure 17.3   *Grid Control Administration Page*

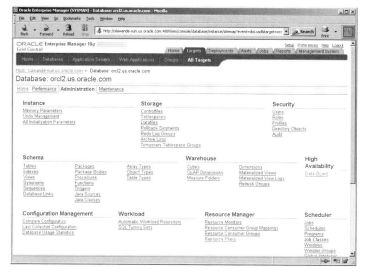

Assuming no Data Guard configuration exists, clicking on the *Data Guard* link will bring up the page shown in Figure 17.4.

At this point, there are no physical or logical standby databases present; clicking on the *Add Standby Database* link will start the wizard to create a standby database, as shown in Figure 17.5.

In this example, we are creating a physical standby database; however, the steps to create a logical standby are mostly identical. Before continuing

Figure 17.4   *Setting up a Data Guard Configuration*

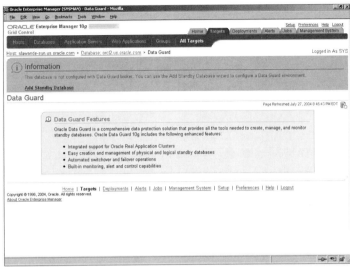

on, you must be aware of some requirements that the primary database must satisfy in order to use Data Guard. In fact, if these requirements are not met, you will be prompted to fix them, when using the wizard.

Figure 17.5   *Adding a Standby Database*

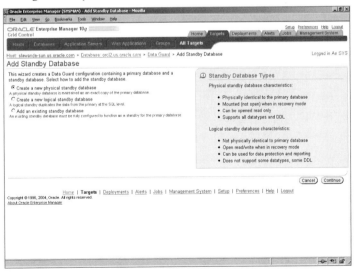

- **SPFILE**: The SPFILE (Server Parameter File) is a mechanism to manage initialization parameters, first introduced in Oracle 9*i*. When the initialization parameters are changed, unlike with a regular init.ora file, the SPFILE is updated automatically by the database server. In order to use Data Guard Broker, the primary database must use an SPFILE because it automatically configures some initialization parameters. Note that if you used the default database installed in Oracle Database 10*g*, SPFILE would already be enabled for you.

- **ARCHIVELOG** mode: In order to use Data Guard, the primary database must be in the archive log mode, which means that before the redo log is overwritten, a copy of it is automatically archived. Recall that the standby database is maintained using the redo logs of the primary, and hence this is very crucial.

- **FORCE LOGGING** mode: Some operations, such as Direct Path inserts (or loads using SQL*Loader), may optionally be instructed to not log redo data, using the NOLOGGING clause. This could be detrimental to the correct operation of a standby database, especially in the case of a failure. To protect against the use of the NOLOG-GING mode, it is recommended that the primary database be set in the FORCE LOGGING mode. Note that this is not mandatory and you will get a warning when using the GUI, but the standby can still be created.

Hint: If you fail to satisfy any key requirements for Data Guard, such as ARCHIVELOG mode, you will not be able to proceed beyond this point.

Recall that the standby is initially created using a backup of the primary database. Pressing the *Continue* button in Figure 17.5 will bring you to the screen shown in Figure 17.6, where you must specify which type of backup to use—a new backup or one that had been previously created by Data Guard. Since this is the first standby database, we will create a live backup of the primary database.

If you are creating a logical standby and the primary database has any tables not currently supported, the offending tables will be indicated to you at this time. Also, in our example, the primary database is not in FORCE LOGGING mode, which is indicated as a warning on this screen (we can still proceed, since this is not mandatory).

The *Next* button brings up the page shown in Figure 17.7, where you must specify the directory where the backup files are stored. The backup

Figure 17.6   *Choosing a Backup Type*

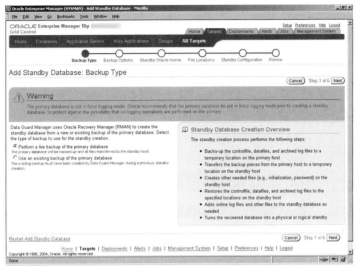

can be retained and used to populate additional standby databases later. Note that in this step, you must specify appropriate operating system user credentials to create the backup directory.

Figure 17.7   *Specifying Backup Options*

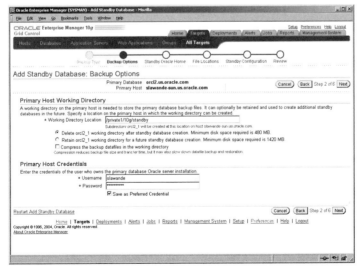

The next step, shown in Figure 17.8, is to specify the Oracle Home where the standby database must be created. The Oracle Home must be one managed as a Grid Control target. In our example, we have the standby database on the same host machine as the primary, but, typically, the standby will reside on a different machine and likely at a different location. Here you can appreciate the huge benefits of using Grid Control, in that it provides a single centralized mechanism to monitor databases and hosts at widely dispersed locations. You must also specify the instance name to use (in our example dg2).

Figure 17.8   *Specifying Oracle Home for the Standby*

Pressing the *Next* button will bring up the screen shown in Figure 17.9, where you specify the location for various files for the standby, such as data files, control files, redo log files, and so on.

Note that if the primary and standby are on different host machines, you should use an identical file system structure on both the standby and primary databases. However, in our example, they are both on the same machine and hence we must have a different structure. Fortunately, the wizard automatically figures this out, so you do not need to worry about the details. If you are curious, you could press the *Customize* button to see the various file locations. Also, in Figure 17.9, you must specify the location of the listener.ora and tnsnames.ora, where entries will be added to allow SQL*Net connections to the standby database.

Figure 17.9 *Specifying Standby File Locations*

The *Next* button brings up the penultimate screen of the wizard, shown in Figure 17.10, where, first, you must specify the *Database Unique Name* for the standby database and the *Target Name*, which is used by Grid Control to list the database under its targets listing. Second, you must specify

Figure 17.10 *Specifying Standby Configuration*

the location (on the standby site) where the archived redo logs from the primary are placed. It is recommended that you use the Flash Recovery Area, described in Chapter 12, for this purpose, because this allows Oracle to automatically manage the space used by these logs and delete them when no longer necessary.

Hint: Set DB_FLASHBACK_RETENTION_TARGET for the Flash Recovery Area to be the same for both primary and standby databases.

The *Next* button will bring up a review screen (not shown here), where you can review your choices. The *Back* button can be used to change the options on any screen. Once you are satisfied with the settings, press the *Finish* button to start the creation of the standby database, which will bring up the screen shown in Figure 17.11.

Figure 17.11   *Processing Standby Creation*

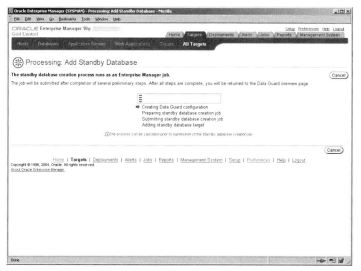

The standby creation will be issued as an Oracle Enterprise Manager job, and once the job has been submitted, you will be presented with a screen similar to that shown in Figure 17.12, which is the central page to manage a Data Guard Configuration. While the standby database is in progress, the *Status* column will show *Creation in progress*, and, once it has finished, the status will appear as *Normal*. On this page, you will see all existing standby databases in the Data Guard Configuration and also the progress of the Redo Apply. The standby we just created, site1, is shown on this page. Press the *Add Standby Database* button to add additional standby databases.

Figure 17.12   *Data Guard Configuration*

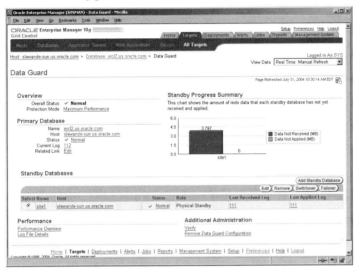

Data Guard Protection Modes

One of the items of interest in Figure 17.12 is the *Protection Mode*. Data Guard provides three operating modes, which give different levels of performance, availability, and data protection. These modes are:

- Maximum Protection Mode
- Maximum Performance Mode (default)
- Maximum Availability Mode

Maximum Protection Mode

This mode guarantees that there will be no data loss in the event of failure of the primary database. In this mode a transaction cannot be committed until its redo information is written both to the redo logs on the primary and at least one standby site. If a failure prevents the redo from being written to the last standby site available in this protection mode, the primary database will be shut down. This level of protection is recommended to protect only the most critical data. It is also recommended that when using the maximum protection mode, you should have at least two standby databases so that hopefully one of them will be reachable at any given time, thereby avoiding a shutdown of the primary database.

Maximum Performance Mode

This mode will provide data protection without impacting the performance of the transactions on the primary database. In this mode, the writing of redo to the standby site is done **asynchronously** with the transaction commit. Thus, the redo logs on the standby will lag the primary database. If the primary database fails, you may lose the data corresponding to this missing redo portion. Depending on the network bandwidth, the missing redo may be minimal.

Maximum Availability Mode

This mode is a compromise between the other two modes. Similar to the maximum protection mode, this mode also requires that the redo be written to at least one standby site prior to transaction commit. However, if the redo could not be written to the standby site, the primary database will not shutdown but will instead operate in the maximum performance mode. This means that there may be temporary durations where the standby site does not have all the redo from the primary. This mode operates on the premise that eventually the missing redo will get written to the standby site, after which the database will resume operation in the maximum availability mode. As long as there were no gaps in the redo, this mode ensures no data loss if the primary database fails. However, in the event of a failure, if some redo was not yet written to the standby site, then you will lose this data, just as in the maximum performance mode.

Note that it is important to understand the difference between redo shipping and redo apply in the context of the protection mode. In the maximum protection and availability mode, the redo shipping is synchronous with the transaction commit; however, the standby may still take some time before the redo is applied. This guarantees no data loss, because as long as the redo is available at the standby site, it can be applied at any time to synchronize the standby to the primary. On the other hand, in the maximum performance mode, the redo shipping may lag behind the actual generation of the redo on the primary. To appreciate this, click the *Performance Overview* link in Figure 17.12, which will bring up the screen shown in Figure 17.13. Here you can see the details regarding the redo data generated by the primary and the progress of the redo shipping services and the redo apply on the standby database. In the graph on the upper-right corner, the dark bar shows the volume of data not yet received by the standby and the light bar shows the volume of data not yet applied.

It is possible to switch between the modes of protection by clicking on the *Protection Mode* link in Figure 17.12. Note that when switching the mode to a higher level of protection, the primary database must be restarted, so you should carefully consider your availability and data protection requirements before deciding on the mode.

Figure 17.13 *Data Guard Performance Overview*

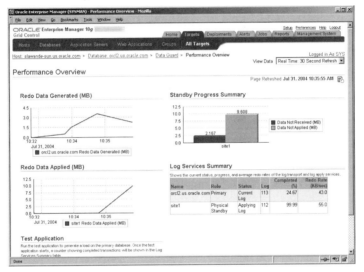

Switching Roles From Primary to Standby Database

One of the major reasons to have a standby is so that it can be used in lieu of the primary database either when performing a scheduled maintenance or during an unplanned failure of the primary. The *Switchover* and *Fail-over* buttons in Figure 17.12 allow you to perform these two functions. In this section, we will illustrate the switchover operation; however, the steps for a fail-over are the same.

Suppose we needed to perform a hardware upgrade on the primary database but would like to have minimal interruption in data access for the application users. In this case, we would like to perform a switchover operation. Selecting a target standby and pressing the *Switchover* button will bring up the screen shown in Figure 17.14, where you must confirm that you would like to switchover. When a switchover occurs, the current pri-

Figure 17.14   *Switchover Operation*

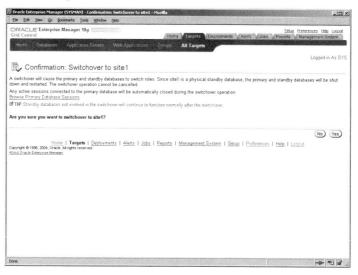

mary database will be shut down and any connected user sessions will be disconnected.

Figure 17.15   *Switchover Complete*

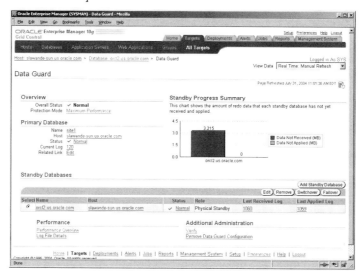

Once the *Yes* button is pressed, you will see a progress screen (not shown here). Once the switchover is complete, you can now see (as shown in Figure 17.15) that the original primary database, orcl2.us.oracle.com, is now the standby, and site1 is now the primary database.

17.5.4 Oracle Maximum Availability Architecture

We can see how easy it is to set up a disaster recovery solution, if you need one, using Data Guard and Grid Control. In a Data Guard configuration the primary and standby databases can either be single-instance databases or they can use RAC. Oracle recommends that the primary and standby databases have identical hardware and software configuration.

In order to assist the design of highly available systems, Oracle provides a detailed blueprint, called the **Maximum Availability Architecture (MAA)**, which gives guidelines for technology and best practices to set up a highly available architecture. This architecture, illustrated in Figure 17.16, is designed to provide maximum protection against both unplanned failures

Figure 17.16 *Maximum Availability Architecture*

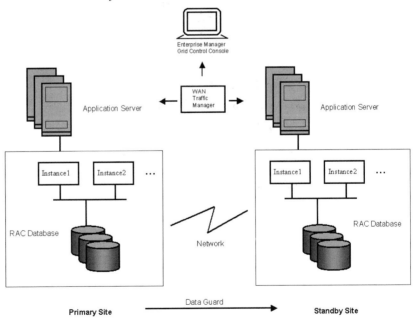

and disasters. In this architecture, redundancy is included at every level, including the network components, application server, database server, and storage. Due to limitations of space, we have only discussed Oracle Database 10*g* in this chapter; however, a key component of MAA is an application server farm running Oracle Database 10*g* Application Server, with a load-balancer providing fail-over capabilities. RAC and Data Guard are integral parts of this architecture, with an RAC database used for both the primary and standby. A WAN traffic manager is used to direct network traffic from the primary to the standby site in the event of a disaster. The entire configuration is centrally managed using the Oracle Enterprise Manager Grid Control console.

Along with the technical details, MAA also suggests best practices that can be followed to ensure continuous operation and quick recovery from failures. Detailed information on MAA is available in the Oracle documentation and at OTN (http://otn.oracle.com/deploy/availability/htdocs/ maa.htm), and we would encourage you to consult this when designing your data warehouse for high availability.

17.5.5 Protecting Metadata

In designing the warehouse, in addition to the data, you may have collected a lot of metadata in the form of schema design, DDL scripts, loading scripts, and so on. Loss of a crucial script can be as disruptive to a data warehouse operation as loss of a critical table. Thus, care must be taken to also include metadata in your high-availability solution. This means all critical files and scripts must be backed up on a regular basis or, alternatively, stored in the database itself. The Oracle Database 10*g* is capable of storing data in all formats, and so, by using the database, you can ensure protection for all critical files just as if they were data. Further, as your business processes evolve, so will your processes for loading and managing your data warehouse. Hence, it is also important to put a change management infrastructure in place to track all changes to the schema and loading procedures over time. Thus, in case there is a problem, you can quickly identify the source and revert back to an older version if necessary.

17.6 Managing Planned Downtime

As with any computer system, the data warehouse typically needs to be periodically upgraded with new hardware and software. When choosing hardware for a data warehouse, it is important to choose hardware that can be expanded online. You should be able to add disks, memory, and CPUs without needing to bring down the entire data warehouse. Similarly, it is important to consider the impact of software upgrades on the system. The upgrade may be as simple as applying a patch or as major as changing the database version. In all cases, you must have adequate testing done before unleashing the new software on users.

Oracle Database 10*g* provides several features to help in this area, which we will discuss now.

17.6.1 Dynamic Instance Reconfiguration

Prior to Oracle Database 10*g*, if you were experiencing an increased user workload and needed to increase the size of the SGA, you had to shut down the database. This can be an annoying interruption to users and can be a significant financial hit to the business. In Oracle Database 10*g*, many of the initialization parameters for the Oracle instance, including SGA and PGA memory settings, can be dynamically altered, using the ALTER SYS-TEM SET command, without shutting down the database.

The initialization parameters can be easily reconfigured using Oracle Enterprise Manager. Further, Oracle will also automatically adjust values of other internal derived parameters whose values are based on the settings of the modified initialization parameter.

17.6.2 Online Maintenance

Usually, data warehouses have a regular maintenance window where data is loaded and all auxiliary structures refreshed. This could happen weekly, daily, or even multiple times in a day. By partitioning data you can perform maintenance on part of the data, while the remaining data is still available for use. Many other operations in Oracle Database 10*g* can be performed in an online fashion, such as rebuilding indexes, reclaiming space for objects (Online Segment Shrink), and allocating additional space (Resumable Space Allocation). Thus, the data warehouse can be made fully or partially available during normal maintenance operations.

17.6.3 Online Redefinition

No database design is ever static, and, as business requirements or perform-ance goals change, the data warehouse schema must evolve to meet these requirements. For instance, you may decide to split a large dimension table into a snowflake for improved load performance, or add a new measure col-umn to the fact table. Also, occasionally you may need to physically reorga-nize the data—for example, to change the partitioning structure or to move it to a different tablespace on a different disk. Traditionally, these types of changes would require a significant scheduled downtime for the entire database. Oracle Database 10*g* provides Online Data Redefinition capabilities to physically or logically reorganize data. This makes it possible to change the data warehouse schema, or reorganize data, while users may still be accessing and even modifying it.

Oracle Enterprise Manager Redefinition wizard and the DBMS_ REDEFINITION package, which were discussed in Chapter 11, can be used to reorganize tables.

17.6.4 Rolling Upgrades

One of the common maintenance activities on any software system is that you periodically need to apply a patch to fix outstanding issues, especially security issues, or to upgrade the database version. The Oracle Database provides two mechanisms to do this without downtime—using RAC and using Data Guard.

Using RAC

In addition to transparent fail-over after an unplanned outage, Oracle RAC also provides the ability for *planned* shutdown of one or more nodes. This is used by the Rolling Patch Upgrade feature, which allows you to apply an Oracle database or operating system patch to one of the nodes in a RAC cluster, without affecting the other nodes. Thus, you can patch all nodes one, by one shutting down the entire cluster, which means that users can continue to use the database while the software is being patched.

There are two steps to perform a Rolling Patch Upgrade:

1.   The node where the patch is to be applied is quiesced, which will mean that all users are automatically directed to one of the other nodes.

2.   The patch is applied to this node, the node is reactivated, and joins the cluster.

Thus, the RAC system now has different nodes operating at different software levels. You can also use this as an effective way to test the patch, because if there is a problem, you can roll back the patch. Thus, you can apply a patch to the entire cluster in a phased manner without any downtime.

Oracle Enterprise Manager can be used to monitor availability of new software patches for the database by configuring access to the MetaLink Web site and can be used to apply the patches on an ongoing basis. However, not all patches can be upgraded in a rolling fashion, and hence the alternative technique using Data Guard can prove beneficial.

Using Data Guard

With Data Guard, you can either apply patches or perform database software upgrades (from Oracle Database 10*g*, Release 1, Patch Set 1 onward) with near-zero downtime by using a logical standby database. Unlike the RAC Rolling Patch Upgrade, which can only be used for select patches, the logical standby database can be used for any Oracle patch set or major release.

This is done using the following steps:

1. The logical standby database is upgraded to the next release. At this point, the Data Guard configuration is running in a mixed mode. In this mode, the upgrade can be aborted and the software downgraded, without any data loss. Also, additional standby databases may be used to protect against unplanned failures at this time.

2. Once the new software version is tested and validated, a switchover operation is done now to make the logical standby the primary database, and all applications must now use the new primary database.

3. The old primary database can then be upgraded to the newer version as well.

Thus, with Data Guard, it is possible to perform database software upgrades and tests with minimal disruption in service for the end users.

17.7 Information Lifecycle Management

Throughout this chapter, we have illustrated the technology Oracle Database 10*g* provides to build a highly available warehouse. Ideally, you would like to keep as much data online and available at all times. However, despite the availability of technology, the sheer size of data involved in a data warehouse could throw any high-availability solution out the window because the costs could be prohibitive! The answer to this dilemma lies in understanding which data is hot and which is not—only the data that is critical and constantly in use needs to be kept in a highly protected and available system. As data gets old or obsolete, it could be moved to cheaper disks or compressed and/or archived to a slower medium such as tape. Thus, it is still available if you need it for some long-term analysis or regulatory purposes; however, it does not cost as much to keep it accessible and protected, if it is not in active use. This is known as **Information Lifecycle Management** and can be the critical success factor in balancing the cost and availability of data in a growing data warehouse.

In order to manage resources effectively, you need to classify data into different categories, based on the age, access frequency, or importance to the business. Typically, the age of the data is the most common criterion for how frequently it is accessed. For example, if the data warehouse stores five years of data, only the last two years of data may be used in daily operations of the business. An effective mechanism to place data in different categories by age is to use range partitioning. However, you could also perform the classification based on some application-specific data value, such as a frequent customer tag, which could then be used as a partition key with list partitioning.

Therefore, data may be classified into active current data, less active, historical, and archival data. Different policies regarding type of storage and protection levels may be used for each class of data. Thus, the cost of storing that data can be controlled based on which category the data falls into. This is illustrated in Figure 17.17. For example, the most current active

Figure 17.17   *Managing Storage Policies According to Class of Data*

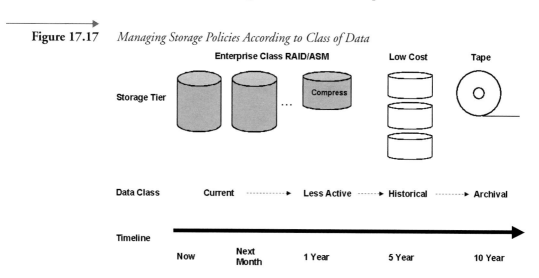

data could be placed in a highly redundant, enterprise-class storage system. At this stage, the data can be kept in a maximum protection RAID system and backed up nightly. As updates to the data become infrequent, the partitions could be compressed. Later, as the activity on the data decreases, it could be moved on to a lower-cost storage tier consisting of off-the-shelf cheap (and potentially slower) disks. Eventually, the data may be obsolete from the business point of view but may need to be kept for regulatory purposes—such archived data could be kept off-line on tape. As time passes and current data becomes older, the data is continuously reclassified, and Oracle Database 10g features such as Data Pump and transportable tablespaces can be used to rapidly move the older data into the next, cheaper tier of storage.

We have barely touched on this topic, but hopefully you can appreciate how effective life-cycle management makes it possible to provide adequate protection to critical data, while at the same time keeping the cost of storage and data protection under control.

17.8 Summary

In this chapter, we have discussed various aspects of improving the availability of the data warehouse. Oracle Database 10g provides features such as RAC to provide fault-tolerant operation in the face of hardware and software failures and allows logical and physical reorganization of data without requiring downtime. We discussed the role of disaster recovery in a data warehouse and also how the data warehouse fits into an enterprise disaster recovery strategy using Data Guard. Finally, we also touched upon the subject of information life-cycle management, which ensures that the data warehouse will continue to be cost effective even as data sizes grow.

A

The Schema for Easy Shopping Inc.

We saw in Chapter 2 how to create our database using the GUI tools, but many readers may prefer to create the database directly from SQL. The SQL to achieve this is shown below, but it assumes that the database has already been created.

The example shown here has been created for a Windows system, a simple edit of the file specs is all that is required for a different platform. Also note that the file sizes here are very small compared to what you would use in a production environment.

A.1   Creating the Tablespaces and Data Files

The first step is to connect to the database using a powerful user name.

```
connect system/manager
```

The next step is to create the tablespaces where the data will reside and their associated data files.

```
-- Temporary Tablespace
CREATE TEMPORARY TABLESPACE easy_temp
  TEMPFILE 'D:\ORACLE\PRODUCT\10.1.0\ORADATA\EASYDW\easy_temp.f'
  SIZE 10m REUSE AUTOEXTEND ON NEXT 16k ;

-- Tablespace to store Materialized Views
CREATE TABLESPACE mview
  DATAFILE 'D:\ORACLE\PRODUCT\10.1.0\ORADATA\EASYDW\easy_mview.f'
 SIZE 6m REUSE AUTOEXTEND ON
  DEFAULT STORAGE
    (INITIAL 16k NEXT 16k PCTINCREASE 0 MAXEXTENTS UNLIMITED);
```

```
-- Tablespace for Dimensions
CREATE TABLESPACE easy_dim
 DATAFILE 'D:\ORACLE\PRODUCT\10.1.0\ORADATA\EASYDW\dimensions.f'
SIZE 5m REUSE AUTOEXTEND ON
 DEFAULT STORAGE
   (INITIAL 16k NEXT 16k PCTINCREASE 0 MAXEXTENTS UNLIMITED);

-- Tablespace for the INDEXES
CREATE TABLESPACE easy_idx
 DATAFILE 'D:\ORACLE\PRODUCT\10.1.0\ORADATA\EASYDW\index.f'
SIZE 5m REUSE AUTOEXTEND ON
 DEFAULT STORAGE
   (INITIAL 16k NEXT 16k PCTINCREASE 0 MAXEXTENTS UNLIMITED);

-- Default Tablespace
CREATE TABLESPACE easydw_default
 DATAFILE 'D:\ORACLE\PRODUCT\10.1.0\ORADATA\EASYDW\
easydw_default.f'
SIZE 5m REUSE AUTOEXTEND ON
 DEFAULT STORAGE
   (INITIAL 16k NEXT 16k PCTINCREASE 0 MAXEXTENTS UNLIMITED);
```

Once the tablespaces have been created for the dimensions, we can now create the tablespaces for the fact table, PURCHASES. Since we will be partitioning the data, we must now create the tablespace for each partition. There will be one partition per month for the data and another partition for the indexes. Here we will create only the January partition for the data and index; simply repeat this process for the other partitions.

```
-- create the 3 month tablespaces for the fact partitions
CREATE TABLESPACE purchases_jan2003
 DATAFILE 'D:\ORACLE\PRODUCT\10.1.0\ORADATA\EASYDW\
PURCHASESJAN2003.f'
 SIZE 5m REUSE AUTOEXTEND ON
 DEFAULT STORAGE
   (INITIAL 16k NEXT 16k PCTINCREASE 0 MAXEXTENTS UNLIMITED);

-- create the 3 month tablespaces for the fact indexes
CREATE TABLESPACE purchases_jan2003_idx
 datafile 'D:\ORACLE\PRODUCT\10.1.0\ORADATA\EASYDW\
PURCHASESJAN2003_IDX.f'
SIZE 3m REUSE AUTOEXTEND ON
 DEFAULT STORAGE
   (INITIAL 16k NEXT 16k PCTINCREASE 0 MAXEXTENTS UNLIMITED);
```

A.2   Creating the Tables, Constraints, and Indexes

Once the tablespaces have been defined, the EASYDW user can be created, which will create that schema where the data will be stored.

```
-- create a user called EASYDW
--  this will be the schema where the objects will reside

connect system/manager

CREATE USER easydw IDENTIFIED BY easydw
 DEFAULT TABLESPACE easydw_default
 TEMPORARY TABLESPACE temp
 PROFILE DEFAULT ACCOUNT UNLOCK;

GRANT unlimited tablespace TO easydw ;
GRANT dba TO easydw ;
GRANT create session TO easydw;
```

The DBA privilege has been granted to the user so they can create and manage the tables and indexes.

Hint: Don't forget to connect as user EASYDW before creating the tables and indexes, or the tables and indexes will be defined in the wrong schema.

```
-- now create the tables
CONNECT easydw/easydw

-- CUSTOMER Dimension
CREATE TABLE easydw.customer
(customer_id            varchar2(10),
 city                   varchar2(15),
 state                  varchar2(10),
 postal_code            varchar2(10),
 gender                 varchar2(1),
 region                 varchar2(15),
 country                varchar2(20),
 tax_rate               number,
 occupation             varchar2(15))
PCTFREE 0 PCTUSED 99
TABLESPACE easy_dim
STORAGE (INITIAL 16k NEXT 16k PCTINCREASE 0) ;
```

```
ALTER TABLE customer
  ADD CONSTRAINT pk_customer PRIMARY KEY (customer_id)
  USING INDEX
  PCTFREE 5
  TABLESPACE indx
  STORAGE (INITIAL 16k NEXT 16k PCTINCREASE 0) ;
```

We have defined the constraint here by adding it via the ALTER TABLE command. The constraint will use an index with the parameters that we have specified and the index will inherit the constraint name, PK_CUSTOMER.

```
-- PRODUCT Dimension
CREATE TABLE easydw.product
(product_id            varchar2(8),
 product_name          varchar2(30),
 category              varchar2(4),
 cost_price            number (6,2)
  constraint cost_price_not_null NOT NULL,
 sell_price            number (6,2)
  constraint sell_price_not_null NOT NULL,
 weight                number (6,2),
 shipping_charge       number (5,2)
  constraint shipping_charge_not_null NOT NULL,
 manufacturer          varchar2(20),
 supplier              varchar2(10))
PCTFREE 0 PCTUSED 99
TABLESPACE easy_dim
STORAGE (INITIAL 16k NEXT 16k PCTINCREASE 0) ;
ALTER TABLE product
 ADD CONSTRAINT pk_product PRIMARY KEY (product_id)
 USING INDEX
 PCTFREE 5 TABLESPACE easy_idx
 STORAGE (INITIAL 16k NEXT 16k PCTINCREASE 0) ;

-- TIME Dimension
CREATE TABLE easydw.time
(time_key              date,
 month                 number (6,0),
 month_name            varchar2(10),
 quarter               number (6,0),
 year                  number (4,0),
 day_number            number (3,0),
 day_of_the_week       varchar2(9),
 week_number           number (2,0)   )
PCTFREE 0 PCTUSED 99
TABLESPACE easy_dim
STORAGE (INITIAL 16k NEXT 16k PCTINCREASE 0) ;
```

```
ALTER TABLE time
 ADD CONSTRAINT pk_time PRIMARY KEY (time_key)
 USING INDEX
 PCTFREE 5 TABLESPACE easy_idx
 STORAGE (INITIAL 16k NEXT 16k PCTINCREASE 0) ;


-- TODAYS_SPECIAL_OFFERS Dimension
CREATE TABLE easydw.todays_special_offers
(product_id              varchar2(8),
 offer_date              date,
 special_price           number (6,2),
 offer_price             number (6,2))
PCTFREE 0 PCTUSED 99
TABLESPACE easy_dim
STORAGE (INITIAL 16k NEXT 16k PCTINCREASE 0) ;
```

For the TODAYS_SPECIAL_OFFERS table, we have defined the primary key to include two columns rather than a single column.

```
ALTER TABLE todays_special_offers
 ADD CONSTRAINT pk_specials PRIMARY KEY
         (offer_date,product_id )
 USING INDEX
 PCTFREE 5 TABLESPACE easy_idx
 STORAGE (INITIAL 16k NEXT 16k PCTINCREASE 0) ;
```

Now we come to creating the all-important fact table, which is called PURCHASES. This table definition is quite complex because it includes FOREIGN KEYS to several tables that are identified by the REFERENCES clause. For the column product_id, two constraints have been defined on the table, a NOT NULL and a Foreign key constraint. Provided each constraint is given a unique name, then is allowed on a column in a table.

Here we have also illustrated how to partition the table, which was discussed in detail in Chapter 4. In this SQL statement example, we are only creating the table with three partitions though the table will actually have 24 partitions for the two years of data that it contains.

```
-- Fact Table PURCHASES
CREATE TABLE easydw.purchases
(product_id                          varchar2(8)
   CONSTRAINT not_null_product_id  NOT NULL
   CONSTRAINT fk_product_id
REFERENCES  product(product_id),
 time_key                            date
   CONSTRAINT not_null_time  NOT NULL
   CONSTRAINT fk_time
REFERENCES time(time_key),
 customer_id                         varchar2(10)
   CONSTRAINT not_null_customer_id  NOT NULL
   CONSTRAINT fk_customer_id
REFERENCES  customer(customer_id),
 ship_date                           date,
 purchase_price                      number(6,2),
 shipping_charge                     number(5,2),
 today_special_offer                 varchar2(1)
  CONSTRAINT special_offer
  CHECK (today_special_offer IN ('Y','N'))  )
PARTITION BY RANGE (time_key )
 (
    PARTITION purchases_jan2002
       VALUES LESS THAN (TO_DATE('01-02-2002', 'DD-MM-YYYY'))
       PCTFREE 0 PCTUSED 99
       STORAGE (INITIAL 64k NEXT 16k PCTINCREASE 0)
       TABLESPACE purchases_jan2002 ,
    PARTITION purchases_feb2002
       VALUES LESS THAN (TO_DATE('01-03-2002', 'DD-MM-YYYY'))
       PCTFREE 0 PCTUSED 99
       STORAGE (INITIAL 64k NEXT 16k PCTINCREASE 0)
       TABLESPACE purchases_feb2002 ,
    PARTITION purchases_mar2002
       VALUES LESS THAN (TO_DATE('01-04-2002', 'DD-MM-YYYY'))
       PCTFREE 0 PCTUSED 99
       STORAGE (INITIAL 64k NEXT 16k PCTINCREASE 0)
       TABLESPACE purchases_mar2002 );
```

In this example, we have created the indexes immediately after the table definition. In a real data warehouse, the number of indexes created prior to loading the data is kept to an absolute minimum to ensure that the loading time is as fast as possible. Therefore, indexes exist prior to loading usually only to enable constraints to be executed as efficiently as possible.

```
-- Now create the indexes
-- Partition on the Time Key  Local prefixed index
CREATE BITMAP INDEX easydw.purchase_time_index
  ON purchases  (time_key ) LOCAL
  PCTFREE 5 TABLESPACE indx
  STORAGE (INITIAL 64k NEXT 64k PCTINCREASE 0);

CREATE BITMAP INDEX easydw.purchase_product_index
  ON purchases (product_id )
  LOCAL
  PCTFREE 5  TABLESPACE indx
  STORAGE (INITIAL 64k NEXT 64k PCTINCREASE 0) ;

CREATE INDEX easydw.purchase_customer_index
  ON purchases (customer_id )
  LOCAL
  PCTFREE 5  TABLESPACE indx
  STORAGE (INITIAL 64k NEXT 64k PCTINCREASE 0) ;

CREATE BITMAP INDEX easydw.purchase_special_index
  ON purchases (today_special_offer )
  LOCAL
  PCTFREE 5  TABLESPACE indx
  STORAGE (INITIAL 64k NEXT 64k PCTINCREASE 0) ;
```

A.3   Defining Security

The next step is to grant some privileges to our user, EASYDW. We will start with the following ones, which will allow us to use summary management, and, as we progress through this book, we will discuss other privileges that should be granted to users.

```
connect system/manager

-- Add privileges
GRANT SELECT ANY TABLE TO easydw;
GRANT EXECUTE ANY PROCEDURE TO easydw;

-- Add privileges for summary management
GRANT CREATE ANY DIMENSION TO easydw;
GRANT ALTER ANY DIMENSION TO easydw;
GRANT DROP  ANY DIMENSION TO easydw;
GRANT CREATE ANY MATERIALIZED VIEW TO easydw;
GRANT ALTER ANY MATERIALIZED VIEW TO easydw;
GRANT DROP  ANY MATERIALIZED VIEW TO easydw;
GRANT QUERY REWRITE TO easydw;
GRANT GLOBAL QUERY REWRITE TO easydw;
```

You will have to repeat these steps for every user that has been created and the privileges granted will, of course, vary by user.

A.4   Final Steps

The final step is actually not completed now, but after the data is loaded. However, it is included here to remind you not to forget this important step, which is to analyze the table and indexes. These statistics are gathered using the package DBMS_STATS and are used by the optimizer. Without these statistics, features like Summary Management will not operate to provide the most efficient access so query performance will suffer. The DBMS_STATS command was explained in Chapters 10 and 12.

```
-- Now Analyze the Tables and Indexes

EXECUTE dbms_stats.gather_table_stats
          ('EASYDW','CUSTOMER');
EXECUTE dbms_stats.gather_table_stats
          ('EASYDW','TODAYS_SPECIAL_OFFERS');
EXECUTE dbms_stats.gather_table_stats
          ('EASYDW','PRODUCT');
EXECUTE dbms_stats.gather_index_stats
          ('EASYDW','PURCHASE_CUSTOMER_INDEX');
```

B

Product Information

This book describes how to use a wide range of Oracle products. To use the software as described in this book, you will need the following products. The version mentioned below is the minimum software version of the product that supports the described features, at the time of writing. It is recommended that you use the latest version of the product available to you.

- Oracle Database 10*g* Enterprise Edition, Version 10.1.0.2
  - Options:
    - Oracle Partitioning Option
    - Oracle Data Mining Option
    - Oracle OLAP Option
    - Tuning Pack to use the Advisor functionality from Oracle Enterprise Manager
  - Oracle Enterprise Manager, Version 10.1.0.2
    - Database Control
    - Grid Control
  - Software available on Client CD:
    - Analytic Workspace Manager for the OLAP Option
- Oracle Application Server 10*g*, Enterprise Edition
  - Portal
- Oracle Warehouse Builder
- Oracle Developer Suite
  - Discoverer
  - Reports

All software can be downloaded at http://otn.oracle.com.

A listing of the EASYDW schema, sample data and all examples used in the book will be made available on the website:

http://www.lilianhobbs.com.

If you have any questions, comments or corrections to report, the authors would be happy to hear from you. You may contact the authors by email as follows:

Shilpa Lawande slawande@gmail.com

Pete Smith   pete.smith@conchango.com

Susan Hillson   susan@thehillsongroup.com

Lilian Hobbs   lilian.hobbs@oracle.com

Index